THE JUDICIAL PROCESS AMONG THE BAROTSE
OF NORTHERN RHODESIA (ZAMBIA)

Frontispiece

NGAMBELA Wina captains the royal barge with the national drums on its
voyage from the Margin to the Plain capital.

Michael Mandle

THE JUDICIAL PROCESS

AMONG

THE BAROTSE

OF NORTHERN RHODESIA

(ZAMBIA)

by

MAX GLUCKMAN

MAKAPWEKA

Professor of Social Anthropology in the
University of Manchester; formerly Director
of the Rhodes-Livingstone Institute

PUBLISHED FOR
THE INSTITUTE FOR AFRICAN STUDIES
UNIVERSITY OF ZAMBIA
BY
MANCHESTER UNIVERSITY PRESS

© 1955, UNIVERSITY OF ZAMBIA
Published by the University of Manchester at
THE UNIVERSITY PRESS
316–324 Oxford Road, Manchester M13 9NR

ISBN 0 7190 1040 3

First published 1955
2nd edition, with corrections and two additional chapters, 1967
Reprinted with minor amendments, 1973

Distributed in the USA by
HUMANITIES PRESS INC.
450 Park Avenue South, New York, N.Y. 10016

Printed in Great Britain by Butler & Tanner Ltd., Frome and London

To
EMANUEL AND KATE GLUCKMAN

CONTENTS

Contents

DIAGRAMS

LIST OF PLATES

TABLE OF BAROTSE CASES CITED

FOREWORD

IT is strange that jurists have not shown more interest in primitive law for in the other social sciences great emphasis has been placed on the origin of the various concepts with which they are concerned. Even so universal a legal scholar as Professor Roscoe Pound refers to primitive law in only a single paragraph in his *Interpretations of Legal History*. It is true that a century ago Sir Henry Maine in his books *Ancient Law* and *Early Law and Custom* discussed this subject at some length, but he regarded it as essentially religious in nature, being ' entangled with religious ritual and observance '. He had little first-hand knowledge on which to base his generalizations so that it is hardly surprising that many of his views, especially in their extreme form, are no longer accepted by scholars today. This lack of interest in the subject on the part of English jurists is all the more remarkable in view of the fact that the British have played a leading rôle in Africa and in Asia.

Perhaps the refusal to recognize the importance and interest of early law may be ascribed to two causes. The first is that early law did not fit into the Austinian definition of law as a command, because it is clear that before the state has fully developed there is no person or group of persons who can issue such commands. This fact could not be questioned, so the Austinians and the neo-Austinians, instead of altering their definitions, preferred to adopt the remarkable view that early law was not law at all. This has been clearly stated by Sir John Salmond in his *Jurisprudence* (10th ed., 1947, p. 54) :

> If there are any rules prior to, and independent of the state, they may greatly resemble law ; they may be the primeval substitutes for law ; they may be the historical source from which law is developed and proceeds ; but they are not themselves law. There may have been a time in the far past when a man was not distinguishable from the anthropoid ape, but that is no reason for now defining a man in such manner as to include an ape.

It is doubtful whether there are many jurists today who are prepared to subscribe to this view. It is now realized that no clear line can be drawn between early law and the fully developed legal system of a modern state, and that the latter has not only sprung from the former but is identical in nature with it.

The second explanation of the jurist's cavalier treatment of early law may be ascribed to the limited amount of material available to him. References to primitive law can be found in many books on anthropology, but they have been, in most instances, only incidental. The enthusiasm with which Professor Malinowski's _Crime and Custom in Savage Society_ (1926) was welcomed by legal philosophers is evidence of the need which they had long felt for some authoritative statement on this subject. His view that some form of civil and criminal law, not religious in origin, exists in primitive societies has been quoted again and again. The jurist had to be content, however, in large part with the conclusions reached by Malinowski because his book did not purport to give in any detail the material on which his views were based. It may perhaps be said that the picture of primitive law was drawn by him only in outline.

That outline has been both amended and filled in by Professor Gluckman in the present book. He has given us here not only his own important conclusions, but he has also furnished a detailed analysis of the facts on which he has worked. Here, for the first time, we have a case book of early law, giving us in detail the evidence produced at the trials and the judgments of the court. We can therefore watch a primitive legal system in action, and we can follow the mental processes of the various judges. The author has applied to the work of an African tribal court the method which Judge Cardozo used so effectively in his _Nature of the Judicial Process_. It is interesting to find that there is a fundamental similarity between the administration of justice in Loziland and in Great Britain or the United States. The sources to which the judges turn to find the law are in almost all respects the same : viz. custom, judicial precedent, legislation, equity, morality, public policy, and the laws of physical nature. The chief distinction is found in the fact that the Lozi precedents have not been recorded in writing. Again the subject-matters of litigation, in spite of great social and economic differences between the two civilizations, are not dissimilar although the Lozi regard the marital relationship as ephemeral and frail, and frequently are compelled to place a monetary value on marital rights.

It is impossible to discuss in a brief preface the large number
of novel ideas to be found in this book, but emphasis may be
placed on one or two points of special interest.

Of primary importance is Professor Gluckman's analysis of
the nature and definition of law. He shows that the Lozi use
their word for *law* (*mulao*), as we do, with many different meanings—it covers a body of rules of right-doing, regularities of
nature, particular judgments, statutes. But the other meanings
derive their significance from the order which ought to exist
in nature and society. Thus the Lozi have a clear conception
of law, and they 'constantly assess the judgments of their *kutas*
[courts] against law as a body of rules'. Hence he suggests
that it is best to use *law* with this primary meaning, and to
specialize other words, such as adjudication, legal ruling, statute,
for the other meanings. The *law* [*mulao*] is defined by the Lozi
themselves as 'the things which ought to be done'. In more
precise and technical language Professor Gluckman defines law
as 'a set of rules accepted by all normal members of the society
as defining right and reasonable ways in which persons ought
to behave in relation to each other and things, including ways
of obtaining protection for one's rights'. As he points out, there
may be no sanction for a particular rule or the courts may not
be able to enforce it, but nevertheless the obligation is recognized
as law : 'sanctions or enforcement are not essential to define
law in this sense, as a *corpus juris* : all societies have it '. And he
adds, in contrasting law with morality, that ' law defines right
and reasonable ways of acting : the ways of morality are right
and generous '.

The Lozi rules tend to be expressed in terms of general standards which, although flexible, are nevertheless legal in character. This flexibility has enabled the Lozi law to adjust itself
to changing conditions. On this point the author has said :

' Reasonable ' and ' customary ', like other legal concepts, are highly
flexible, and they become permeated with changing social presumptions, values, and conditions of life, and can absorb a variety of actual
situations. Their flexibility has enabled Lozi judges to adjust rules of
law to cope with Christianity, schools, work for money in Loziland
and at distant towns, etc.

Professor Gluckman therefore reaches the conclusion that the so-called ambiguity of legal concepts constitutes the strength, rather than the weakness, of a legal system. It is essential, as he points out, to distinguish between the general standards and their specific application. In this connection it is interesting to find that ' the reasonable man ' plays as important a rôle in the Lozi legal system as he does in the common law. The modern attempt to displace him in the English law of negligence by the provision of more specific and detailed rules has not always proved successful. Thus the law concerning the duty of care which must be exercised by an occupier of land has become more and more difficult as new refinements have been introduced, and it is not surprising to find that there has been a strong demand for a return to general principles.

From law as a body of rules we can turn to the administration of justice. It is remarkable to find that the Lozi kuta has the same conception of natural justice as has an English court, and that it insists that both parties must always be given a full opportunity to be heard. The distinction between direct and circumstantial evidence, and between direct evidence and hearsay is also recognized. As there are no counsel at a Lozi trial it is necessary for the judges themselves to conduct the examination of the witnesses. In discussing this practice Professor Gluckman makes the interesting suggestion that the effect of such an examination in a criminal trial is to give the erroneous impression that the prisoner is presumed by the court to be guilty. The cross-examining judge, he says, must frame his questions as if he believed that the examinee were lying, i.e. was guilty, even though he holds no such belief. It follows that a legal system which places the duty of cross-examination on the judge will seem to be less favourable to the prisoner than does one which places this function on counsel. Perhaps this may explain why so many English lawyers repeat the fallacy that under French law a prisoner is regarded as guilty until he has been proved innocent.

From the standpoint of constitutional law it is interesting to find that under the Lozi constitution the king and his councillors are bound by the law and must act by regular procedures. The king can be sued by his subjects in court ; to avoid embarrassment he should act only through his councillors who then become personally liable and may not plead his orders in defence. In making their rulers subject to the law the Lozi have accepted a higher ideal in government than has been recognized in some modern states. The distinction between judicial, legislative, and administrative powers, which has given rise to so much recent literature in the field of political science, is also recognized by the Lozi even though all three powers are exercised by the same body—the kuta.

It is hardly surprising to find that throughout this book Professor Gluckman rejects the tendency to regard primitive law as something quite different from that to be found in a modern legal system. On the contrary, he has made a major contribution to legal philosophy by showing through concrete illustrations how basic is the identity between the two. No legal philosophy, however pure or abstract, will in the future be able to disregard the facts which he has presented in so clear and convincing a manner. It will be many years before a more interesting and a more path-breaking book is published in this field of political science.

A. L. GOODHART.

PREFACE TO THE FIRST EDITION

IN analysing legal problems in an African society one has to use terms and concepts which have been employed by jurists through two millennia, and therefore one ought to be well aware of what these jurists have written. This is an ideal to which no anthropologist can hope to attain, as I realized when I conned the lists of books and cases recommended to me by lawyers with whom I discussed my problems. Had I attempted to follow their excellent advice, I should have been essaying, belatedly, to become a comparative jurist—and I should never have written my report on Lozi law. This is, therefore, primarily a social anthropologist's book for social anthropologists. I comfort myself that insofar as the book might also be a contribution to the comparative study of law, my first duty was to describe Lozi legal institutions clearly.

But I hope that my book will be useful to students of comparative law. I did not come to its writing in entire ignorance of jurisprudence. Besides my recent legal reading for this study, I have had some formal training in law at the University of the Witwatersrand. This means that my knowledge of developed law is not confined to a few textbooks of jurisprudence, but includes the detailed historical and practical study of particular systems of law and of many judicial decisions. I must point out that these studies were in Roman-Dutch and Roman law ; and English lawyers will find that my implicit comparative background for Lozi law is South African law.

I had too some experience in my father's law office in Johannesburg, and through my early life constantly heard lawsuits and legal problems discussed in my parents' home, the centre of a family of lawyers with many lawyers as friends. My dedication of this book to my parents arises not only from general affection and particular thanks for support in a profession as meagre in its resources as it is rich in its delights ; but the dedication also acknowledges a relevant intellectual debt of insight gained in their home. My father before his recent death increased my indebtedness by criticizing my manuscript.

With this background, I am aware that many of the problems

I discuss as if *de novo*, have learnedly concerned the jurists of many countries and centuries. However, to maintain the clarity of my own analysis I have on the whole eschewed any references to their writings. I have not become involved in complex discussions of the meaning of terms, nor considered whether my definitions for this particular analysis will cover the facts of law in other systems. I have tried to use terms with due regard for their instituted use in comparative jurisprudence ; but in general analysis I have found it best to use the most common terms (law, right, duty, etc.) with the connotations given in the *Concise Oxford Dictionary* of 1951. Thus *custom* is ' usual practice ' (p. 205). *Equity* has the connotation of ' fairness ; recourse to principles of justice to correct or supplement law ', rather than the more specialized English legal connotation of ' system of law co-existing with and superseding common and statute law ' (p. 402). *Natural law* or *natural justice* is ' based on the innate moral sense ', interpreting innate moral sense as the socialized conscience, in accord with modern knowledge. One technical term which is not in the concise dictionary is *referent*, the thing or idea referred to by a word. This is to some extent the course of a coward, who frankly has shirked involvement in the highly specialized learning and disputation of jurists. Nevertheless, I hope that my analysis will bear witness that I have not written about African law in entire ignorance of that vast learning and disputation, nor neglected the study of case records and historical jurisprudence.

Therefore I hope that students of comparative law will understand that when I make categorical statements, as for example on the relation of law and custom, or law and equity, these are made by an anthropologist about the Lozi system alone. They are not intended as ignorant impertinences to dismiss as useless the wealth of problems which lie in the terms used, to whose solution so much developed learning and logic have been devoted. If the evidence I adduce on the structure of the Lozi legal system is clear enough for lawyers to use, though it be for them unlearned, this book will be an indirect contribution to the comparative study of law.

A number of lawyers have read my manuscript. Chief among these, at Manchester University, were Dr. T. O. Elias (Simon Research Fellow) and Mr. A. L. Epstein. Dr. Elias is making a lawyer's comparative study of African law. Mr. Epstein has studied the working of the newly formed African Urban Courts in Northern Rhodesia : I gained much from his own penetrating analysis of developments in these courts. A thesis by Mr. J. van Velsen on *Delict in Primitive Law*, written at Oxford under my supervision, helped to clarify my view of the function of flexible legal concepts. Finally, when the book was nearly completed, I had the good fortune to meet and interest Professor A. L. Goodhart in my work. He kindly read and commented on my manuscript before I sent it to press and agreed to write a foreword to introduce the book to jurists.

My discussion of Lozi legal concepts finally involved me in philosophical and semantic problems, through which I was guided by Professor Dorothy Emmet and Mrs. Marjorie Grene.

I need say little in this preface about my book as a thesis in social anthropology, though I must note at the outset that most anthropological studies of law seem to me to have overlooked basic jurisprudential points : therefore I have had to stress these again and again at the risk of appearing banal to lawyers.

I owe thanks for direct and indirect help to many teachers. First among these are the late Professor R. F. A. Hoernlé and Mrs. A. W. Hoernlé, under whom I studied at Johannesburg. I hope Mrs. Hoernlé will feel that what I have written justifies to a small extent all that her husband and she did for me. The late Dr. R. R. Marett, Rector of Exeter College, was my second great teacher. Professor A. R. Radcliffe-Brown, when he was Simon Visiting Professor at Manchester, bore with my incipient formulation of ideas and carefully worked over much of my manuscript. Professors E. E. Evans-Pritchard, M. Fortes, and I. Schapera have helped me immeasurably to clearer sociological thinking. To my colleagues of the Rhodes-Livingstone Institute (particularly Dr. J. A. Barnes, Dr. E. Colson, Dr. I. Cunnison, and Dr. J. C. Mitchell) I am grateful for that companionable stimulus and criticism which slightly younger colleagues, who become contemporaries, can give. It has been an honour as well as a pleasure to work with them. Dr. Colson has read my manuscript in several stages of its development.

The fieldwork on which this book is based was carried out when I was an officer of the Rhodes-Livingstone Institute, in Barotseland during altogether twenty-seven months, in 1940,

1942, 1944, and 1947. The Trustees of the Institute did all they could to help me, and allow me to pursue my studies in freedom. They have generously published this book. To the late Mr. Godfrey Wilson, first Director of the Institute, I am indebted for material and intellectual aid.

I hope that this study will be of use, in the third place, to British officers in the region. The Northern Rhodesia Government and its officers naturally hoped that the Rhodes-Livingstone Institute's researches would have practical value ; but they stressed also the importance of the researches themselves, and encouraged the Institute's academic freedom. Many officers helped me in the field itself, and my wife and I are grateful to them and their wives for hospitality. Mr. J. Gordon Read, C.M.G., Provincial Commissioner in 1940 and 1942, was always generous with his help and encouragement. Commander T. S. L. Fox-Pitt, O.B.E., R.N., Acting Provincial Commissioner in 1947, gave me not only a valued friendship, but added to help in the field the reading of the whole study of which this book is the first part. He corrected and amplified many points. Among other District Officers I mention especially Messrs. M. Billing, F. J. Passmore, C. G. Stevens, H. Vaux, and O. Wallace, because I trespassed on their kindness more than I did on that of other officers equally willing and interested. Mr. J. Ritchie and Dr. J. Winterbottom of the African Education Department were particularly helpful.

Many other Europeans, Government officers and others, were friendly and hospitable to my wife and myself. Again I must limit specific acknowledgments to those we troubled most : Mr. F. and the late Mrs. M. Balme, Mr. J. W. W. and the late Mrs. A. Betts, Mr. and Mrs. R. Coisson of the Paris Evangelical Mission, and Mr. and Mrs. V. Forrester of Lialui Store.

I move last to thank the Lozi and other Barotse peoples as foremost in importance. Clearly without their co-operation I could not have made this study. The late Paramount Chiefs Yeta III, C.B.E., K.M., and Imwiko, K.M., and the Mulena Mukwae Mulima, C.B.E., K.M., gave me permission to work in their country, and indeed welcomed us, treated us as friends, and helped me in my work. The NGAMBELAS Munalula, Wina, and Walubita also did all they could to assist me with friendly help, as did many other councillors, whom I can thank only

in the names of their leaders. To the NGAMBELAS I add therefore
the Ishee Kwandu, the SAMBIS, SOLAMI Inete, MUNONO Mbangweta
and the NAWALAS Muimanenwa and Mutondo. Through these
authorities I can thank all Barotse who made our stay among
them so happy, but I must remember especially the people of
Katongo. Many of our friends there are now, alas! dead. We
recall them and think of the living affectionately : the Mukwae
Mbuywana and Ishee Kambayi, NAWALA Mutondo, NAWALA
Muimanenwa, Sikwela Mwanangombe, Akawi, Batuke and his
brother Mooka, Benson Masani, Musole Sindambwila, Musole
Lufwendo, Salufu, Nameto, Lukonga, Nyakayoya Cipoya, with
their kin, their wives, and their children. They were our
neighbours and adopted people for many months : we could
not ask for better friends.

I trust this record will preserve not only for them, but also
for their descendants, a way of life which, despite its material
hardships and its evils, was on the whole good. It may help
others to understand them, and them to understand themselves.

Finally, I thank a number of devoted people to whom this
study belongs as much as it does to me. My wife has given
me immeasurable support, both in the field and in the writing
of this book. NAWALA Mutondo and the late Sikwela Mwanangombe, and Muyongo, were my constant older advisers and
confidants. My Research Assistant, Mr. Davidson Silumesii
Sianga, guided me in my studies and did much of the basic
work for them, as only in lesser degree did Mwanamulena
Mwendawelie Lewanika. Messrs. Albert Kafunya, David Kali-
mosho, the late INYAMAWINA Mubukwana Mataa, and the late
Mwanamulena Mboo Sipopa, all voluntarily enrolled themselves
to assist me. Miss Barbara Pole grappled nobly with the
secretarial and bibliographical work. Professor Schapera corrected the proofs and made invaluable suggestions on a number
of important points.

M. G.

UNIVERSITY OF MANCHESTER,
  30th May, 1954

PREFACE TO THE SECOND EDITION

WHEN this book first appeared its arguments were considered at some length in a number of reviews, and in addition, both on its own and with other studies of African law which were published at about the same time, it was made the subject of eight articles by anthropologists, sociologists, and jurists. An abstract of the whole book, a long review of it, and a long article on it and another book on the law of an African tribe, have been republished, with editorial comments, by G. Schubert in *Judicial Behaviour: A Reader in Theory and Research* (1964). Its arguments have also been discussed in books and articles. The criticisms of the book, no less than the commendations, for both of which I am grateful, warrant re-publication. But it would be churlish of me to allow this without taking account of the reaction of the scholars who have rewarded my efforts with their careful attention. I would, of course, prefer to rewrite parts of the book, and to make certain general alterations, to meet those criticisms I find to be valid, and to discuss in the text those I cannot accept wholly or partially. But the high cost of re-setting the type, as against photographing the present text, makes this impossible. I have therefore followed the practice of other colleagues, similarly placed, and added additional chapters. Chapter IX is a 'Reappraisal' of parts of my analysis in the light of criticisms, and in it I discuss suggestions for a clarification of my own terminology and of terminology in general for the analysis of comparative law. Chapter X first reports major changes in Barotseland and specific changes in the organization of its courts and in its law, between 1947 and 1965, when I was able to return to Barotseland. It also includes reports on what has happened, in the eighteen to twenty-five years that have passed, to the protagonists in the principal cases reported in this book.

I planned to follow this book with two others on Barotse Law. This study of the Barotse judicial process gained me an invitation to deliver a series of Storrs Lectures in the Yale School of Law in 1963, and these have now been published as *The Ideas in Barotse Jurisprudence* (1965). I discuss in Chapter IX developments in the methods of social anthropology which have delayed my completing the third book, on *The Role of Courts in Barotse Social Life*.

THANKS

I record with pleasure my thanks for help and hospitality on my visit in 1965 to : Paramount Chief Litunga Sir Mwanawina III Lewanika, K.B.E ; Chief Mwendawelie Lewanika ; Ngambela Noyoo ; Mwenekandala Kasindi ; Mwanamulena Mubukwanu Mataa ; Mr. Clement Zaza ; Mr. Francis L. Suu ; Mr. Musole Sindambwila ; Lilume Nawala Sitali ; Lilume Mbasiwana Bwendo ; Headman Mulyachi Muteto ; Nyakayoya Cipoya ; Mwiya ; Sikwela Cakula ; Mundia ; Sinonge ; and other Barotse. I enjoyed renewed acquaintance with Mr. and Mrs. E. Berger and Miss Borle of the Paris Evangelical Mission, who alone of Europeans still in Barotseland, arrived there before I first did so. I am grateful to Mr. Edward Robinson, Principal of the Mongu Boys Secondary School, and his wife, Wendy, and to Professor Alastair Heron, Professor of Psychology and Director of the Institute for Social Studies in the University of Zambia, and his wife, Margaret, for generous hospitality in Mongu and Lusaka respectively. My journey to Barotseland was only possible because of the generous help given me by Professor Heron and the staff of the Institute. Dr. A. L. Epstein and Professor J. C. Mitchell criticized drafts of the new chapters most helpfully. Miss Sheila Perrin, Miss Catriona Miller, and Miss S. M. Davies helped in many ways.

MAX GLUCKMAN

University of Manchester
March, 1966

PREFACE TO THE REPRINT OF THE SECOND EDITION

IN this book I reported trials I observed in Barotse courts in 1942–7, and attempted to analyse the Barotse judicial process in relation to the social life and culture of the Barotse. It was written a score of years ago, but I can claim that at least in its detailed reporting of trials it was a pioneer work in its field (see Fallers 1969 : 326 ; Moore 1969).[1] Since it was published, there have been a number of other studies in the same field, some taking up arguments I presented in this book, both critically and appreciatively, and some proposing comparative contrasts from trials in other pre-industrial societies to set against the Barotse material. In the second edition (1967), in an added Chapter IX entitled 'Reappraisal (1966)', I considered most of the criticism of my analysis. I accepted some criticism and in its light tried to clarify and amend my analysis, while pointing out where I considered other criticisms to be ill-founded. With the selling out of the second edition, I considered rewriting the book entirely, so as to absorb my present view of the problems, taking account of later research. But colleagues whose opinion I value judged that if I did so, the book would lose the original vigour with which both the account of Barotse trials, and the analysis proposed, were put forward ; and I agree with them that it would be a pity if I swamped the Barotse material under a flood of comparative discussion. The book is not only cited often in discussions of new research and legal theory, but it is also used as a textbook in departments of anthropology and schools of law ; and here its value must largely remain in the report of, and comments on, Barotse trials. Hence the book is reproduced here in the form of its second edition ; and I leave a discussion of the implications of the analysis, in the light of more recent research and theorising, until I write an assessment of studies of the law of societies akin to the Barotse in techno-economic development.

Since I wrote my 'Reappraisal' in 1966, the controversy discussed there over how far one can use Western jurisprudential theory and concepts in analysing law in pre-industrial societies

---

[1] Bibliographical references in this preface are given in the form—author date: page(s). Titles are in the bibliography at the end of the preface.

has continued. I argue in my 'Reappraisal', and I still maintain, that most of the criticisms which allege that those of us who have used Western jurisprudence have distorted the systems we studied, were based on inadequate reading, and none of the critics has ever attempted to re-analyse the trials we presented in order to demonstrate the validity of their objections. But I feel now that I understand better whence the confusion, and hence the controversy, arise. I owe this insight to studies by Professor Sally F. Moore (1969) and Professor L. Pospisil (1971), and also to a discussion of the criticism with Professor J. F. Holleman of Leiden. This led me to yet another reading of *Justice and Judgment among the Tiv* (1957), by Professor P. J. Bohannan, the main protagonist of the argument that each 'folk-system' of law has its central dominant conceptions, and that study of these should correspondingly dominate the analyst's study. He argued further that a decision in a Tiv court 'seldom *overtly* [italics added] involves a point of law, in the sense in which we think of a rule or a law. I [Bohannan] have often heard Tiv express rules of action that might be considered laws, but seldom in a *Jir* [court or trial—M. G.] . . . The purpose of most *jir* is, thus, to determine a *modus vivendi* ; not to apply laws, but to decide what is right in a particular case. They usually do so without *overt* [italics added] reference to rules or "laws"' (at p. 19). Later in the book, in discussing the Tiv classification of wrongs, he affirms that Tiv 'also have trouble in making *overt* [italics added] the distinctions of a jural nature which their vocabulary and their very actions contain . . .'

Bohannan incidentally makes references to many problems, but now, after many readings and connings of his arguments, and re-analyses of the cases he reports, I understand that his concentration on the problem of how Tiv categorise in terms of concepts, has prevented him from following up, in his analyses and possibly in the field, the reasoning of Tiv judges. I propose to illustrate this from one case, which I have analysed more fully in a Wilson Memorial Lecture in the School of Scots Law at the University of Edinburgh.[1] Sheriff John Wilson was a judge, and Dr. Nan Wilson studied the Scottish Faculty of Advocates, so I was asked to speak on the legal profession in traditional Africa. I took as

---

[1] To be published shortly in *The Scottish Juridical Review* and then printed, together with the other seven memorial lectures, in a book.

my theme the fact that in traditional Africa, the substantive law was often secreted in the interstices of examination and cross-examination : thus I amend Maine's statement, for early European law, that the substantive law was largely secreted in the interstices of procedure.   Maine's statement was largely correct for early European law ; but procedure was too simple for it to be applicable in traditional Africa (see p. 160 below).   The problem then is, if the substantive law, and its conceptions, are thus secreted, can they be said to be part of the ' folk-law '?   Bohannan says they are not because they are not (to quote him from the passages cited above) ' overt '.   By looking at one of his cases, I shall show that he has confused awareness by the judge of what he is doing, with apparent failure to work out explicitly and abstractly the conceptions involved : which when it occurs is not surprising in a society that lacked writing.

The case I am going to re-analyse was briefly reported by Bohannan (1957 : 103-4) from a hearing in a subordinate court established among the Tiv by the British :

> The plaintiff, a woman, told the court that three or four years before she had been driving a billy goat and a nanny goat to sell at market.   She said that when she was halfway there, the goats became more and more difficult to lead : '. . . since the goats were giving me trouble, and since I am only a woman, and therefore did not quite know what to do, I turned into the courtyard compound of Gbilin's [the defendant's] father because I knew him and his wife.'   She said that the defendant offered to bring the goats the rest of the way to market the next day.   She went to market and spent the night with her kinswoman.   Next day, the defendant arrived at the market with only the billy goat, and made excuses about the nanny.   She sold the billy goat.   Several months later, she alleged, the defendant sold the nanny.   She asked the court for the nanny and the two goats it should meantime have borne.   The defendant replied that she had told him that only the billy was to be sold and that she wanted to leave the nanny with him as care-taker—a standard Tiv transaction known as ' releasing stock.'   But it was sickly : it had no kids, and had perished shortly after he had accepted it.   He claimed that therefore he owed nothing.

The judge asked him : ' Did you go to Wan Igarwa [the plaintiff] when her goat died and tell her it had died, and settle the matter then and there?' The defendant said he had not. The judge continued : ' Did you let the matter drag on, with Wan Igarwa [the plaintiff] not knowing that her goat was dead?' The defendant repeated that he had not told her when the goat died. The judge told him to stop lying, and, said the judge ' you must give her a goat and a kid—it is a debt '. He continued that the goat would have borne two kids in this period ; therefore the defendant must pay for the young male [which had not come into existence], but would be allowed to keep [the equally hypothetical] young female [i.e. he assumed there would have been two kids, one male and one female—M. G.].

The defendant's story was destroyed by the judge's cross-examination which contrasted his actions, as he by implication reported them, with what a reasonable man would do if he were looking after stock for another. He himself claimed the nanny was left with him as caretaker : under this Tiv arrangement, the caretaker gets one kid out of three (Bohannan 1957 : 21 f. including report on case). We are told in a book on *Tiv Economy* (1968: 121, in collaboration with L. Bohannan) that if a goat dies, the caretaker should report this at once to the owner, and if the circumstances of death were mysterious, a replacement may be demanded. That is, though the judge does not *overtly* (as Bohannan stresses is general among the Tiv) set up the standard of how a reasonable caretaker would have acted, this is implicit in his cross-examination, and his conclusion that the defendant was lying (cf. below my general discussion of this technique in cross-examination as used by Barotse judges, Chapter III). Yet clearly we cannot understand how the Tiv judge in this case assessed the evidence unless we see that this was the technique used. When I pointed this out at a seminar in Northwestern University, with reference to this and other cases, Bohannan authorized me to state when the paper was published that 'he accepts all but the final part of my argument. He says that the Tiv clearly work, in cross-examination and coming to judgment, with a general conception of a reasonable man, but it is not explicitly formulated. Hence he does not regard it as a Tiv " folk concept " ' (Gluckman

1966 : 142–3). I consider that this confuses two distinct problems. First, there is the problem of whether the Tiv judge, and the parties and audience, knew what he was doing, and could have explained it if questioned by the defendant, or by the anthropologist. If Bohannan contends that the judge and his hearers were not aware how he arrived at the conclusion that the defendant was lying, then that is unacceptable to me ; and I am sure that Bohannan would not argue so, since in several parts of his studies he has shown that the Tiv are as intelligent as we are. I I cannot then see how, if the judge was aware of what he was doing, we can deny that what he did is explicitly part of Tiv folk-law. The fact that the steps in the argument are not clearly set out, as they would be in our or Barotse courts in most cases, is a second problem. In our courts a judge gives a judgment, or advises the jury, in terms which may in the very form of their words constitute grounds for appeal or establish precedents : hence everything must be explicit. In Barotse courts (see below), in all courts there are several judges giving judgment in order from junior to senior (see below Chapter II), and each judge therefore addresses not only the litigants, but also his seniors and juniors. I consider that the argument why much is left implicit in Tiv examination and judgment is to be understood in the light of their court constitution. Probably also significant is the fact that the customary behaviour expected of a caretaker, and the rules of the transaction, are known to all, so they can seize on the implications.

More interesting is the final decision. Though the judge seems to have accepted the plaintiff's story and said that the defendant was lying, he in fact held (again quite clearly though not overtly stated in Bohannan's record) that the arrangement between plaintiff and defendant was one of placing stock with a caretaker, as the defendant claimed, and not merely, as the plaintiff said, that she left the nanny with him to be looked after for one night and then brought to market. Because the judge used the phrase 'it is a debt' (quaere : could the translation be ' an obligation '?—M. G.), Bohannan goes on to argue, starting with this case, that to grasp Tiv law we must understand that they classify in terms of ' debt ' and not of ' contract ' and ' tort '[1]

---

[1] For a discussion of this problem see Gluckman 1965: Chapter VII, and 1972: xxxv f.; Allott *et al.* 1969: 71 f.; Ghai 1969.

(Bohannan 1957 : 104–5, 111–12, 212 f.). This is an interesting argument, but it distracts all his attention from what the judge actually did. Bohannan says elsewhere (1957 : 112) that Tiv can, and often do, attempt to defend themselves by maintaining that some action was not a breach of norm but ' that it was an act in accordance with some norm or another. It is therefore up to the judges to decide which norm has been broken as well as whether or not the action was actually a breach of norm.' Here it seems to me that one of two reasons, or both, might have been elicited from the judge had he been asked why he selected a breach of the norm of caretaking, since the plaintiff claimed that her arrangement with the defendant was quite different :

(1) The alternative on the information available to us was to convict him of theft. Bohannan (1957 : 121 f.) shows that thieves among the Tiv were beaten and publicly exhibited to contumely, etc. The judge may have wished to avoid this because originally the defendant had agreed to take the goat to help the plaintiff, and because she was a friend (from her statement) of his parents. And it is a cardinal hope of Tiv that they should be able to avoid disturbing social relationships (see Bohannan 1957 : 47–51).

(2) From Bohannan's cases on theft (at his pp. 121 f.) it seems that had the finding been theft, the owner would be entitled only to the goods stolen. Hence, had the judge found theft, it may be that he could have awarded the plaintiff only the value of a nanny goat. It is noteworthy that there is no record that the judge cross-examined the plaintiff on why, if, as she alleged, the defendant sold the goat a few months after she left it with him, she did not complain at once to him, or his parents, and then, if refused redress, go to the court. [I am sure Barotse judges would have seized on this and denied her any offspring because of this unreasonable delay.] By seizing on the chance offered by the defendant's lying story, and holding that there had been a transaction of caretaking, the judge brought it under standard rules : the male kid to the owner, the female to the caretaker to breed for him at the ending of the transaction (this is standard practice in many African tribes). Moreover, as this was what the defendant claimed had happened he could not protest : by his own admission he had broken the rules of caretaking, and could be penalised therefor (see below on Barotse, p. 91).

Clearly the Tiv do not have a general theory of contract—not surprisingly since late Roman law had not developed such a theory. Hence it would be misleading to treat this case as the application of a general theory of contract, and the finding of some form of contract as implied. It would be equally wrong to bring it under the English ' bailee ' since there is no evidence that the Tiv generalize thus about rights and obligations across varied single transactions, though comparison with a bailee would be interesting. But again the judge knew what he was doing, and so did his hearers : to say he found there was ' a debt ' because Tiv law categorizes in terms of ' debt ' is much too simple. Unfortunately, too, this distracted Bohannan's attention from problems in the field (I say this while very conscious of gaps in my own field research—see below). The concentration on how the Tiv categorize at some abstract level, also distracted him from dealing at all adequately with the reasoning, as against the ' distinctions, of a jural nature which their vocabulary and their very actions contain ' (1957 : 117, cited above). There is more than a finding of ' debt ' in this case : we see a judge selecting from possible remedies and providing one by bringing an unspecified arrangement on which the parties disagree, under the rubric of a standardized Tiv transaction, or type of contract. We are forced to speculate on why he selected this remedy and not another.

I touch on three other points :

(a) In his *Law without Precedent* (on Soga law, 1969 : 331–2), Fallers says that he suspected that the Barotse word for *mulao* was derived from the English *law*. He says he has been satisfied by me that this is not so. The root of the word *mulao* is *kulaela*, to order or command. Unfortunately I carelessly omitted to state this in the original text (p. 164 below).

(b) At p. 376 in my ' Reappraisal ', I protested against Nader's citing an unnamed person who characterized my work ' as analogous to that of a linguist who attempts comparison by jamming Barotse grammar into Roman Dutch categories'. Professor Pospisil has told me that the statement occurs in an unpublished doctoral dissertation on ' Approaches to the Study of Legal Systems in Non-literate Societies ' by S. J. L. Zake, Northwestern University, 1962—presumably a pupil of Bohannan. Pospisil (1971 : 16 f.) has read the dissertation and dealt with it as it deserves, if the statement quoted by Nader is typical.

(c) I have inserted my Barotse name, ' Makapweka', under my name on the title-page, since young Barotse I have met know me by that name, a name misappropriated by a British District Officer who was unconsciously instrumental in stirring up an outbreak of accusations of witchcraft in Barotseland in 1957 (see Reynolds 1963). In addition, Mr. Philip Silverman of Cornell University wrote to me that when he asked questions about law at the Barotse southern capital, Nalolo, the SAMBI asked him why he was wasting their time asking questions about their law when they had written a book about it.   And SAMBI produced this book. He was right too : the best part of this book belongs to the Barotse, for the reasoning I have tried to expound was in their words and actions, clear for all to see given a guide who spoke their language.

MAX GLUCKMAN

Victoria University of Manchester,
  May, 1973

REFERENCES

ALLOTT, A. N., EPSTEIN, A. L. and GLUCKMAN, M. 'Introduction' to M. Gluckman (ed.), *Ideas and Procedures in African Customary Law*, London : Oxford University Press for the International African Institute (1969).

BOHANNAN, L. and P. *Tiv Economy*, Evanston : Northwestern University Press (1968).

BOHANNAN, P. J. *Justice and Judgment among the Tiv*, London : Oxford University Press for the International African Institute (1957).

FALLERS, L. F. *Law without Precedent : Legal Ideas in Action in the Courts of Colonial Busoga*, Chicago : University of Chicago Press (1969).

GHAI, Y. P. 'Customary Contracts and Transactions in Kenya' in M. Gluckman (ed.), *Ideas and Procedures in African Customary Law*, London : Oxford University Press for the International African Institute (1969).

GLUCKMAN, M. *The Ideas in Barotse Jurisprudence*, New Haven : Yale University Press (1965).

——'Reasonableness and Responsibility in the Law of Segmentary Societies' in L. and H. Kuper, eds., *African Law : Adaptation and Development*, Berkeley and Los Angeles : University of California Press (1966).

——*The Ideas in Barotse Jurisprudence*, 2nd edition, with extended new preface, Manchester University Press for the Institute for African Studies, University of Zambia (1972).

MOORE, S. F. 'Law and Anthropology' in B. J. Siegel, ed., *Biennial Review of Anthropology*, Stanford : Stanford University Press (1969).

POSPISIL, L. *Anthropology of Law : A Comparative Theory*, New York : Harper and Row (1971).

REYNOLDS, B. *Magic, Divination and Witchcraft among the Barotse of Northern Rhodesia*, London : Chatto and Windus for the Rhodes-Livingstone Museum (1963).

CHAPTER I

INTRODUCTION: LOZI COURTS AND THE SOCIAL BACKGROUND OF LITIGATION

I

THE Lozi are the ruling people of Barotseland. According to Lozi legends, some time after God *Nyambe* first created Man, one of His sons by His own daughter founded a kingdom in the Upper Zambezi Valley. The Lozi believe that with this king there came into existence Lozi Law (*mulao waMalozi*) as a whole body of rules defining rights and duties and of procedures for seeking justice from the king. The Lozi recite many instances of later kings amending laws, of the institution of new customs and laws, and of the adoption of customs and laws from other tribes. Nevertheless they consider that their Law as an embracing body of rights (*liswanelo*) and justice (*tukelo* or *niti* = truth) has existed from time immemorial. They have partially absorbed into it all the requirements and social changes which have flowed from British overlordship.

According to the royal genealogy, the Lozi kingdom was created around A.D. 1600 : but as African genealogies are often telescoped, this date is probably too recent. However, this question is irrelevant for our present purpose. We have to accept that kingship and the law associated with it are sanctified for the Lozi by their divine origin soon after Creation. I shall therefore fix events on their time-scale by numbering reigns from the first reign, and only where there is some historical check will I also place these in Anno Domini.

European historical records, as well as Lozi legends, enable us to affirm with certainty that this Lozi kingdom was well established by the middle of the eighteenth century. It had extended dominion over many surrounding tribes, to whom collectively I shall refer as the *Barotse*, since they are thus marked on general maps. This will enable me to keep references to the conglomerate nation distinct from references to the dominant *Lozi* tribe, with whom this study principally deals, though subjects of all tribes under the Lozi king are, in native parlance,

Lozi. The Barotse nation has had for at least two centuries a governmental political organization including a hierarchy of courts which had power to enforce their decisions. Since the establishment of the British Protectorate by treaty with the British South Africa Company in 1900, the organization of this hierarchy of courts has been altered, and their powers and jurisdiction, especially in dealing with crimes and delicts, have been radically curtailed. In the past—a phrase I use throughout to refer to the period before British overlordship was established—ultimate rightful power to enforce law and maintain order *vi et armis* lay with the Lozi king and his council. Since 1900 this power has resided in the Northern Rhodesia Government, as the British South Africa Company from 1900 until 1924, and subsequently as the Colonial Office. But under the 1900 Treaty, the fourteenth Lozi king, Lewanika (d. 1916), retained most of his juridical and administrative powers. The only rights in these respects granted to the British South Africa Company were to ' adjudicate on all cases between white men and natives '. The king undertook to use his best endeavours to put down slavery and witchcraft. Thus the Government has always ruled Barotseland ' indirectly ', by carrying out certain of its policies through negotiation with the Barotse authorities. Until ' Indirect Rule ' was introduced in 1929 other parts of Northern Rhodesia were under ' Direct Rule ' : Barotseland never has been. However, ' Indirect Rule ' in the modern restricted sense, with the Government's formal recognition of Native Authorities and Courts and establishment of Treasuries, only came to Barotseland when the Barotse King-in-Council agreed to the Barotse Native Authorities and Native Courts Ordinances (Nos. 25, 26, and 27 of 1936, as amended by Nos. 17 of 1940, 12 of 1944, 19 and 23 of 1946—Chapters 159 and 160 of *The Laws of Northern Rhodesia*, 1951). These Ordinances ended a long period of uncertainty about the scope of British Magistrates' powers, since a law of 1905 limited their jurisdiction to cases in which a non-native was involved and ' the more serious class ' of native cases. It was not certain whether the Northern Rhodesia High Court had full jurisdiction in Barotseland. The Government had no power to assist the Barotse authorities to enforce their orders or judgments. I shall in appropriate places consider particular developments of the above legislation and of the powers, jurisdiction, and procedures, established for Barotse courts by it. I need not give initial summaries as these are conveniently available,[1] but note here only the limitations of powers and relations with British courts.

In brief, Barotse courts have lost their power to try :

(a) Cases ' in which a person is charged with an offence in consequence of which death is alleged to have occurred and which is punishable under any law with death or imprisonment for life ' ;

(b) ' Cases relating to witchcraft ', except with special permission ;

(c) ' any case in which a non-native is a witness ' [or, as stated above, a litigant][2] (Section 11 of No. 26 of 1936).

In practice I have seen Barotse courts accept evidence from Whites given in writing, though there could not be cross-examination on these statements, while they tend to reject ' affidavits ' by Africans since these do not allow for cross-examination.

Secondly, the courts have lost the power to inflict certain punishments and remedies, including the death penalty, throttling, and unlimited flogging ; and they have acquired the power to imprison, an unknown practice in the past (Sections 14 and 16 of No. 26 of 1936).

Finally, appeals now lie from the highest Barotse court to the High Court of Northern Rhodesia in civil matters, and to the Provincial Commissioner of Barotse Province in criminal matters, from whom there is further appeal to the High Court (Section 33 of No. 26 of 1936). In addition, under Section 22, reports of all criminal cases must be submitted to Government officers, and under Section 25 a District Officer, subject to the directions of the Provincial Commissioner, may sit as adviser in a native court. Obviously, many offences, and all cases in which non-natives are involved as parties or witnesses, come directly under British courts.

---

[1] Pim, Sir Alan, and Milligan, S., *Financial and Economic Conditions in Northern Rhodesia, 1938*, London : H.M.S.O. ; Lord Hailey, *An African Survey*, London : Oxford University Press, 1946, pp. 456 ff., and *Native Administration in the British African Territories*, London : H.M.S.O., Part II (1951), pp. 88 ff.

[2] There are records of cases involving Whites before the establishment of the Protectorate.

II

The Lozi dwell in the great flood-plain which runs for 120 miles from north to south along the Zambezi River between 14½° and 16° South latitude. The Plain is some 25 miles across at its widest. Rains begin to fall at the headwaters of the Zambezi and its tributaries in September, and in Loziland itself in October. The river overflows its banks in a normal year in December, and by February to March the Plain is a vast lake. In May, when the rains stop till the next year's cycle begins, the floods slowly recede.

Men, animals, fish, insects, reptiles, and vegetation move with the flood. The Lozi themselves build their Plain-villages on higher parts of the Plain to be above the flood-waters, though in years of deep flood their huts may be badly damaged. Most Lozi move out of the flood to dwell for some months in other villages or camps at the margins of the Plain. Some Lozi dwell permanently in margin-villages. Their cattle too move with the flood-waters to different pastures. Their gardens are watered and fertilized by the flood, so that they are able to cultivate several different kinds of gardens in different months to provide a varied and fairly continual food supply. They drain some garden-land, and raise gardens above the flood-level. They catch fish as these spread out with the flood or are trapped in confined waters when it falls, with spears, many types of nets, fences, mazes, and traps. Game, wildfowl, and edible reptiles were also pursued according to the state of the flood, before firearms were introduced.

The Lozi thus have a complex economy which requires that many people co-operate if various productive activities, widely dispersed at the same season, are to be performed successfully. Further, since the flood-plain is unique in the region, they have trading relations with tribes which dwell in the surrounding woodlands, so that they exchange products of the Plain for products of the bush. Most trade lies between the Plain and the woodlands, and not between different areas of woodlands. Thus Loziland, with the rivers flowing into it from the woodlands, is the ecological heart of the region ; and this probably explains why the Lozi have come to be the dominant people. At the height of their power they ruled some 25 tribes, of

300,000 to 400,000 people, spread over 80,000 square miles·
Their domain has been much reduced by their Treaty with
the British : formally they rule the Barotse Province of
Northern Rhodesia, with a population of 260,000 to 300,000
people. The Lozi themselves number 70,000 to 80,000
people.[3]

The complex ecology of Loziland, with its opportunities for
agriculture, animal husbandry, and fishing, has led the Lozi to
develop a complex economy. It is on the whole based on the
simple tools which are typical of all Bantu, in less complex
environments. The basic tools were the hoe ; the axe ; hunting-,
war-, and fishing-spears ; and the knife. Some of these indigenous tools—like other goods—are now imported by White
stores and African hawkers. Formerly these were made by
smiths of the Kwangwa, Totela, and other subject tribes, from
ores which they smelted themselves. With these metal tools
the Lozi and their subject tribes cultivated or killed their food,
shaped their dugouts and paddles, carved pestles and mortars
for pounding grain and wooden tools. They dug and cleared
canals and drained land, and they piled up soil on the higher
parts of the Plain. They dug clay to make pots. They cut
reeds and grasses, and used bark and tree-roots, to make baskets,
mats, fences, traps, and string. The string was netted into
bags, and used to make their most complicated instruments :
great purse-seine nets and gill-nets for fishing.

Originally the Lozi made several types of grass and reed
houses, but under the influence of the Paris Evangelical Mission
they began to build houses with wattle-and-daub walls and
raftered, thatched roofs. Sun-dried bricks were later used for
public buildings. Some of these houses at the capitals are large
and imposing structures.

Lozi clothing was formerly antelope- and cattle-skins, though
some tribes made bark-cloth and others grew and spun kidney-
cotton which they wove on simple looms. These, with the
bellows of the smiths' forges, constituted their only true machines.

---

[3] For full descriptions see my ' The Lozi of Barotseland in North-Western
Rhodesia' in *Seven Tribes of British Central Africa* (ed. by E. Colson and
M. Gluckman), London : Oxford University Press (1951) and *Economy of
the Central Barotse Plain, Rhodes-Livingstone Paper No. 7*, Livingstone : Rhodes-
Livingstone Institute (1941).

But for many years now they have depended entirely on European cloth, and largely on European utensils.

Many of the indigenous products were imported into Loziland from other tribes, such as dugouts from the Lunda and Nkoya. The Lozi used to combine several dugouts into large state barges : now they use European-built barges. Their other artistic products were baskets, with dyed patterns, among the most beautiful in the world ; mats with patterns of home-spun string dyed in several colours ; carved wooden figurines and meat-platters ; and carved ebony and ivory fly-switches and sticks. They themselves say that they were surpassed in most of these arts by other peoples, and they consider that their genius lies in the arts of government and law. We shall be seeing in this book whether their claim is true.[4] It is certainly true that they lack elaborate rituals and dances, and have only a simple ancestor-cult and a general belief in a God. This has enabled them to absorb the beliefs and ideology of Christianity, though comparatively few of them are practising members of the several mission sects. The work of the Paris Evangelical Mission since 1885 has turned the Lozi into a nation of pagan-Christians.

Their mythology is undistinguished, though they have ironic folk-tales, scores of penetrating maxims, and many praise-songs for persons, objects, and places, which are rich in historical allusion and proverbial wisdom. They are keen historians, and I found them to be wise philosophers. But I agree with them that they have a true genius in law, and the elaboration of their political constitution, which we shall shortly consider, would have gratified Dicey. Under that constitution the king and his councillors were bound by the law (*mulao*) and had to act by regular procedures. Lozi law held that the king can do wrong—they were amazed when I cited the English maxim that ' the king can do no wrong '—and can be sued by his subjects in court. To avoid this embarrassment, the king should only act through his councillors and attendants, who then become liable and may not plead his orders in defence.

One of the basic units in the structure of their economic, political, and domestic systems is the village. It is the centre

---

[4] I would add that their adjustment to the flood-plain home shows great genius.

from which they exploit gardens, pasturage, and fishing-sites, and parcels of land are attached to the village-headman's title and theoretically can only be used by his villagers. Everyone must reside in some village, and co-operates chiefly with fellow-villagers. Because their bases are the 'islands' in the flood-plain, which provide the only dwelling-sites, most Lozi villages have a permanent continuity dating far back into their history, and associated with the headman. The village is a critically important political unit under a headman who has a title which devolves on his successor. The headman is responsible for his village to the king in council (hereafter called the *kuta*), and represents the villagers to the kuta.

The old political and juridical organization into which these villages were tied can only be described if we begin at the capitals. Before 1890, there were two capitals only, both situated in the Plain. The king (*Mbumu-wa-Litunga* = great-one-of-the-earth) ruled the main capital, north of the middle of the Plain ; another ruler (*Litunga-la-Mboela* = earth [chief] -of-the-south), held a capital which has never been more than thirty miles farther south. Since the Lozi reconquered their homeland from a band of Sotho invaders, the Kololo, who subjugated it from 1838 to 1864, the southern ruler has been a princess (referred to henceforth as the princess chief). The southern ruler has always been subordinate to the king, though she has a capital which duplicates his faithfully. These capitals in the period with which we are concerned have been built at Lialui in the north, moving at flood to Limulunga, and in the south at Nalolo, from where the court moves a short distance at flood. All villages through-out the Barotse kingdom were attached to one of these two capitals. In the 1890's the Lozi began to establish subordinate capitals in their outer provinces to cope with invasions of other Bantu and with the incoming Whites. The British South Africa Company divided Barotseland into Districts for various purposes. Each District had a District Office at its head. Over the years it has become necessary to have one Barotse capital dealing with each District Office : this has led to the foundation of two new provincial capitals,[1] and the abolition of two old provincial

---

[1] The establishment of a Lozi capital in Balovale District provoked the local people successfully to protest their independence to the Government in 1941.

THE GENEALOGY OF THE LOZI KINGS

K 1, 2, 3, . . . indicates order of reigns

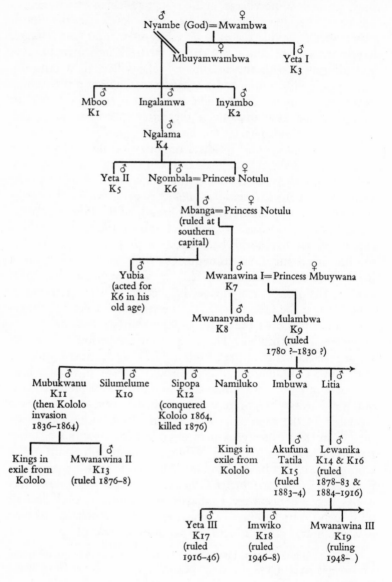

capitals as redundant. Since 1946, Lialui, the capital of the king, has ruled Barotse Province and the Mongu-Lialui District. Nalolo, the seat of the princess chief, is the centre for Senanga District; Libonda for Kalabo District; Mwandi for Sesheke District; and Naliele for Mankoya District.

Every capital has at its heart a central cleared space (called *Namoo* at the two main capitals) on one side of which is the palace and on the other the council-house. The ruler resides in the palace, the full council meets in the council-house to deliberate or try cases. Since the council is not only a court, I use the native term *kuta* throughout, save in general analytic passages. The court-houses, particularly the one at Lialui, are imposing buildings. In the centre at the back is a dais on which the king or ruling member of the royal family sits if he (or she) is present. Usually the ruler does not attend the hearings of cases, though the kuta's judgment is referred to him for confirmation. Even if the ruler chooses to sit in the kuta while a case is being tried, it proceeds as if he were not there. He takes no part in the hearing, and the facts and judgments in the case are referred to him as if he had not heard them.

All Lozi kutas are divided into three sets of councillors, each of which may be called a ' mat', as the Lozi name them, since the councillors by virtue of their titled offices are entitled to sit on mats. The positions of the titles on each mat are fixed, and if a title-holder is discharged, is promoted, or dies, his successor (who is appointed by the ruler-in-kuta) takes his position on the mat. These offices, as distinct from their incumbents, are so important that throughout the book I print them in small capitals, stating their positions by R for right, L for left, and F for royal, according to their status as described in the succeeding paragraphs, and as shown on the accompanying diagrams.[1]

The most powerful group of councillors are those who sit on mats to the right of the king. Their senior member, the NGAMBELA, is head of the kuta: he is so powerful that he is described, in relation to the king, as ' another kind of king '.

---

[1] I have given a general account of Lozi government in *Seven Tribes of British Central Africa*, op. cit., and a detailed analysis of three kutas in *Administrative Organization of the Barotse Native Authorities*, Livingstone, Rhodes-Livingstone Institute Communications No. 1 (1943).

He cannot be a prince who has a right to succeed to the king-ship. I shall call these councillors-of-the-right *indunas*, the general Southern African word for 'councillor' (in Lozi *nduna*, pl. *manduna*), since it has passed into English from Zulu,[1] and we need to standardize a term for African political authorities with varied duties. The Lozi use this term to distinguish councillors-of-the-right from the other 'mats', but there are two words to distinguish two groups among these indunas. The senior indunas are called *makwambuyu* ; *malume* are the group of junior indunas who sit in a row behind them. On mats to the left of the royal dais sit councillors called *likombwa*, which in Barotseland has been translated as 'stewards'. This is an appropriate word, because while they are powerful councillors in national affairs, they are also more specifically responsible for the royal household. The stewards are also divided into seniors and *malume* juniors. At right angles to the stewards, or at the front of the kuta, is the royal mat for princes and for the con-sorts (*bo-ishee*, sing. *ishee*) of princesses, who exercise power for their wives. Opposite the indunas' mat sit clerks, police, and royal bandsmen, leaving a space in the middle for suppliants and litigants.

The senior indunas and stewards, with some senior members of the royal mat, formed a council called *Saa*. The chief *induna*, the NGAMBELA (R1), was not a member of this, nor was the NATAMOYO (R2), a prince who was a sanctuary in that a con-victed man who seized his leg could claim a re-trial. The *malume*, junior indunas, and stewards, with junior members of the royal mat, formed a council called *Katengo*. A third council, the *Sikalo*, was composed of the NGAMBELA (R1), the NATAMOYO (R2), and an indefinite number of other councillors, members of the royal family, and others. These three councils did not meet as courts of law, but to deliberate on legislation and national matters. The Sikalo met with the king at night, the Saa and Katengo separately in the day, and discussion passed backwards and forwards between them in an attempt to reach agreement.

The councillors at Lialui were also grouped under about nine councillors, including the NGAMBELA (R1), who were heads of what I call *sectors* (Lozi : *makolo*, *likuta*). These sectors were

---

[1] *The Concise Oxford Dictionary*, 1949, p. 609.

STEWARDS

- L1 INGANGWANA
- L2 IMASIKWANA
- L3 IMUWANA
- L4 MUBONDA

PRINCES

- F1 DANIEL KUFUNA
- F3 MBOO SIPOPA
- F4 MUIMUI
- F7 ISTEKETO LEWANIKA
- F8 SIKOTA-IMATIWA
- F9 MUBUKWANU MATAA
- F10 MWENDAWELI LEWANIKA
- F12 MWENEKANDALA

[TABLE]

R1 NGAMBELA

INDUNAS

- R2 NATAMOYO
- R4 MUKULWAKASHIKO
- R5 NALUBUTU
- R7 INYAMAWINA
- R10 KATEMA
- R13 NOYOO
- R14 vacant (SIMUNJA-MULASU)

SUU R17 (Administrative secretary)

see F3 R18

LONG'ONG'O R25

CLERK

WITNESSES

LITIGANTS

THE JUDGES' SEATING IN THE LIALUI SIKALO APPEAL COUNCIL (1942)

NOTES : (1) As the King came into public in the large open Kuta building where the Saa-Katengo met, the NGAMBELA (R1) presided here in a smaller office building, and there was no royal dais.

(2) This Council interlocks with the Saa-Katengo Council.

(3) This Council was also considerably altered by the 1946 Reforms which made it the Barotse Appeal Court. Tribal representatives sat below R25, on the right; representatives of District Councils sat according to their positions on the full National Council. Some titles here and in the Saa-Katengo Council were altered and moved.

(4) Generally, the public were not admitted or did not come into this court.

PUBLIC

PRINCES AND
PRINCE CONSORTS

F1 LUBASI WAMUNGUNGO

F2 LITIA LEWANIKA

F3 ISHEE NAMABANDA

and others

KATENGO
STEWARDS

L1 KAKWISANUNGU
L2 ANABA
L3 ILINGUNGA
L4 IKAKENA
and others

STEWARDS

PRINCESS
CHIEF'S
DAIS

AND OTHERS

KATENGO

R22 KAYAMA

R ISHEE KWANDU (chief's husband)
R1 SAMBI
R2 NATAMOYO
R3 MUKWAKWA
R4 BIUNDANG'ONO
R5 SAYWA
R6 IMANGA
R7 MBINDAWINA
R8 MUSHEMI

SIKALO AND SAA

INDUNAS

Bandsmen
Attendants

Police

SUUNGA	R9
SAMBIANA	R10
MOOTO	R11
AKAWI	R12
LIASHIMBA	R13
NALOPU	R14
MUKATA	R15
NAMUNDA	R16
SAKUYA	R17
KAKENE	R18
SIKOBELA	R19
MUNDALE	R20
MUKWALA	R21

PUBLIC

THE JUDGES' SEATING IN THE NALOLO COUNCIL—COMBINED SIKALO AND SAA-KATENGO COURTS (1942)

NOTES : (1) Nalolo Council, considerably reduced in numbers, formed a single court under the 1946 Reforms.
(2) Lialui and Nalolo councillors, with the councillors of subordinate provincial capitals, formed a single National Council, the members interlocking thus : R1. NGAMBELA (Lialui), R2. ISHEE KWANDU (Nalolo—husband of Princess Chief), R3. NATAMOYO of Lialui, R4. SAMBI (Nalolo), R5. SOLAMI (Lialui), R6. NATAMOYO of Nalolo. . . . Thereafter Lialui councillors are generally far superior to interspersed Nalolo members. The heads of provincial capitals entered at 24 and 54–58. Late in 1942 they were moved to R24–28. Other mats are similarly arranged, with Lialui superior.

the military, jurisdictional, administrative, and labour units of the kingdom. All villages were placed in one or other of the sectors ; in some villages different people were placed in different sectors. In Loziland particularly, but not so much in the outer provinces of the kingdom, neighbouring villages often belonged to different sectors. When a dispute between members of the same sector could not be settled at home, or by local arbitration, the case went to the court of the councillors of the sector sitting at the capital in the courtyard of the senior councillor ; if members of two sectors were disputing, councillors of both sectors assembled in the courtyard of the senior councillor to try the issue. Accepted judgments were referred to the NGAMBELA (R1) and the king, and appeal lay to the full kuta. There were fewer sectors at other capitals.

Appeals in the recent past also went from any provincial capital to the main capital, Lialui or Nalolo, to which it was attached. There was no judicial appeal from Nalolo to Lialui, since both were ruled by kings : ' You cannot appeal from one king to another.' However, each was in the past a sanctuary to which people could flee from the other. Appeal from Nalolo to Lialui was instituted under the 1936 Barotse Native Courts Ordinance.

The Lozi were also allotted, in a different manner, to the set of councillors I have called stewards, for other purposes : this arrangement need not concern us here, though we must note it because it is relevant to the manner in which Lozi took their complaints to the capital.

The essence of both these arrangements was that the units of administration and jurisdiction were not territorial units. Loziland, nevertheless, was roughly divided into a large number of named districts (*lilalo*), with vaguely demarcated boundaries. People in a district (note a small ' d ' as against modern Magisterial Districts, capital ' D ') might take cases to a prince or prince consort, or to a locally resident member of the kuta, or to any prominent man, for arbitration. But these were not instituted courts : they could not enforce their decisions.

These districts have become the basic units of jurisdiction within the Magisterial Districts, and in the modern system are therefore sub-districts. The British administrators never understood the sector system, and some territorial arrangement is necessary for modern administration. The *lilalo* sub-districts first were used for registration of residents and tax-collection : since 1936 sub-districts, many of which were amalgamated, have had their own local kutas which try cases in the first instance and which act as the administrative bodies for their area.

Under the 1936 Ordinances the councils at various capitals were reorganized. A council called the Sikalo at Lialui, and generally *ofis* (= office) by the Lozi, consisting of selected members of the old Saa under the NGAMBELA (R1), became the administering body for the Province and the final court of appeal before the Provincial Commissioner or High Court. Other members of the Saa, and members of the Katengo, formed a council called the Saa-Katengo, under induna SOLAMI (R3), which administered Mongu-Lialui District and heard appeals from its sub-district kutas. Senanga District, under the Princess Chief at Nalolo, also had a Sikalo to hear appeals from its Saa-Katengo which heard appeals from sub-district kutas. The other District capitals had never had the arrangement of Sikalo, Saa and Katengo, councils, and under the 1936 Ordinances they had only one kuta each, hearing appeals from sub-district courts. At that time Sesheke District had two capitals, Mwandi under Lialui and Sesheke under Nalolo, built alongside each other and ruling intermingled villages.

In 1946 the Government persuaded the Lozi kuta to accept reforms substantially reducing the membership of kutas and re-organizing the kutas themselves. The Saa-Katengo at Lialui was renamed the Mongu-Lialui District Court ; the Sikalo and Saa-Katengo at Nalolo were combined into a Nalolo District Court ; and the Sesheke capital was abolished leaving Mwandi as sole court of appeal for Sesheke District. Libonda and Naliele capital kutas remain in charge of Kalabo and Mankoya Districts respectively. In place of the old Sikalo, a Provincial Council now sits in Lialui to run provincial affairs and hear appeals from each District kuta, which hears appeals from its sub-district courts. A new council, called Katengo, consisting, first of nominated, and then of elected, representatives of each District and older Katengo incumbents, was formed for the Province in 1947 to debate national affairs : it was to work with the National Council which is composed of certain title-holders from all capital kutas. The new Katengo had no judicial duties.

This bare account of the framework of juridical organization is necessary if readers are to place the kutas whose hearings I shall describe in their political background. The organization itself will come to life in that description. It remains for me in this part of the introduction briefly to summarize procedure in the kutas.

The litigants, supported by their witnesses and kinsmen, sit before the judges against the posts which hold up the roof. The plaintiff, without interruption, states his case with full and seemingly irrelevant detail. The defendant replies similarly. Their witnesses, who have heard their statements, then speak. There are no lawyers to represent the parties. The kuta, assisted by anyone present, proceeds to cross-examine and to pit the parties and witnesses against one another. When all the evidence has been heard, the lowest induna on the right gives the first judgment. He is then followed by councillors on the three mats (indunas, princes, and stewards) in ascending order of seniority across from one mat to the other, until the senior councillor-of-the-right gives the final judgment. This is then referred to the ruler of the capital, who confirms, rejects, or alters it, or refers it back to the kuta for further investigation and discussion. It is this final judgment by the last induna to speak which, subject to the ruler's approval, is binding.

III

Court hearings, as will appear in the cases cited below, are marked by an elaborate etiquette in which rank is strongly stressed. Today, as one sits in a court, one can observe the obvious marks of differences in wealth between councillors and most other Barotse in their clothes alone, though some ordinary people are far wealthier than even senior councillors. Nevertheless, Barotse society is only beginning to differentiate into classes with different standards of living, which barely varied in the past. Chiefs, members of the royal family, councillors, and headmen possessed and handled far more property than commoners, and this was an important part of their power. But the economy remained basically egalitarian. Though the economy was fairly complex, it had certain limiting characteristics. Technological equipment in general was (and still is)

D

restricted to tools which enable a man to produce little beyond what he could himself consume. Goods were all primary— simple food, simple clothes, simple dwellings, etc.—for the Lozi had few luxuries, so that no man, not even the king, could live markedly above the standard of his fellows. There was considerable internal trade for a Southern African society, and in the nineteenth century trade developed with the outside world, but the exchanges of these goods continued to take place within the limiting framework of the economy. Thus though Barotse society was ranked in chiefs and councillors and subjects, aristocrats and commoners, freemen and serfs, this ranking was not accompanied by any radical differences in standards of living. The king had greater security than his subjects, but lived at the same general level as they did. Tribute poured into his capital from the nation of 350,000 people of 25 tribes, but this tribute was given out again to the people. In this type of economy the wealthy man could not use his surplus land, cattle, or food in any enterprise which would produce a considerably higher standard of living for himself : all he could do with it was to use it to attract to himself many dependants, or to outface his rivals.

The nation as a whole was almost self-sufficient. The European goods introduced by traders in the nineteenth century were relatively few and were absorbed into the economy within old relationships. Today the nation exports labour, cattle, and fish : it imports food and large quantities of trade-goods.

Within the nation, the people all lived in villages, each of which, with the kith and kin of its members, was largely self-sufficient. It co-operated in producing most of what its members consumed, and they shared their products. Therefore most of a Lozi's dealings in goods and services involved persons already related to him by kinship or political bonds. The Lozi who cultivated, fished, collected, and herded with his kin on his own and public land, and who shared with them the produce of his and their labour, entered into relations with outsiders to solve a few additional labour problems and to meet a few deficiencies, or to dispose of a limited surplus or skill. There were few specialists, and all of them derived their main subsistence directly from the land. A Lozi used part of his surplus for tribute and gifts to his overlords, and from them he obtained some goods to meet his additional wants. The remainder of his surplus he used to attract dependants and to feast his equals and subordinates. He would even deprive himself of food for these purposes. All these kinship, neighbourly, friendship, and political bonds were permanent, enduring through many years and indeed through generations. Even when Lozi entered into ephemeral transactions with strangers they tended to expand these to more permanent bonds of mutual help. A barter relationship became one of 'friendship' and then perhaps 'blood-brotherhood'—an unlimited exchange of goods and help between set partners. If a man deposited cattle to be herded by another, he ranked as a superior kinsman of the herder. A patient was mystically bound to the doctor who cured him of a serious disease.

Thus in the past, before the coming of the White man, practically all goods and services were held and disposed of in face-to-face relationships established by relative social position. A man was thrust into one set of these relationships, that of the kinship system, by birth : as he matured, these relationships were extended by his and his kinsfolk's marriages. The other set of relationships was defined by the political structure and his links in it were dictated by its authorities. He could satisfy almost all his wants in these two sets of relationships.

The implications of this situation affect both the procedure and purpose of courts, and every doctrine of Lozi jurisprudence. In general terms, their courts aim at the same ends as courts in highly developed societies : the regulation of established and the creation of new relationships, the protection and maintenance of certain norms of behaviour, the readjustment of disturbed social relationships, and the punishing of offenders against certain rules. Their jurisprudence shares with other legal systems many basic doctrines : right and duty and injury ; the concept of the reasonable man ; the distinctions between statute and custom and between statute and equity or justice ; responsibility, negligence, and guilt ; ownership and trespass ; etc. I shall establish the existence of these doctrines and examine how their particular character in Barotseland is determined by their setting within a social system in which most of the relationships between groups and individuals, and between these and land and chattels, are defined by position in the nation, in a village, and in kinship groupings. Since one of my main theses will be to demonstrate this, I emphasize its implications at the very beginning of my analysis.

In all societies men and women co-operate or struggle with one another in activities, organized or informal, which are directed to various ends. Sociologists classify these purposes as sexual, procreative, economic, educational, recreational, religious, political, and so on. The interactions between persons to serve each of these purposes constitute systems of social ties which are contained within the total social system and mutually influence one another. In more differentiated societies a person is linked to a variety of different persons, with many of whom his relationship is formally confined to a single interest, as, for example, that of a labourer with his employer, a bus traveller with the conductor, a housewife with a shopkeeper, even an invalid with a doctor or a churchgoer with a priest. It is chiefly in our simple family that we find the mixed ties that are typical of Barotse society. There nearly every social relationship serves many interests. Men live in villages with their kinsmen or quasi-kinsmen, and by virtue of kinship ties they acquire their rights and obligations. With his kin a man holds land and chattels ; he produces goods in co-operation with them and shares with them in consuming these ; he depends on them for insurance against famine, illness, and old age ; he forms with them religious communites tending the same ancestors ; they are responsible for the main part of his education ; he seeks his recreation with them. He even ascribes the misfortunes which befall him to punishment inflicted on him by his ancestors for quarrelling with his kin, or to his kin's sorcery directed against him. He will be dominantly associated with the kin in whose village he resides. The family village is a group of kin which is defined by allegiance to a headman, a senior kinsman ; the members of such a village are associated together by more important legal ties than those which link them to kin in other villages. Some Lozi live in royal villages, whose headmen are queens, princes, princesses, or councillors, with people of other kin-groups and even tribes. Then their bonds with their fellow-villagers are quasi-kinship bonds. This total set of relationships constitutes the village-kinship system. Its importance is shown in the widely extended system of classificatory kinship nomen-

clature, which groups distant kin with a few categories of close
relatives—a system which all simple societies have.

But the village is also a basic political unit. The headman
is related to his villagers by political as well as kinship bonds.
By birth and by residence in a village a man acquires his civic
status and is linked to a number of overlords. These political
relationships also subsume a variety of ties. The state is not
merely a political organization to maintain internal law and order
and to wage defensive or aggressive war. As a subject, a man
has the right to ask land from his king, and he works for and
may beg help from his king. The nation is a religious community dependent on the king's ancestors for good fortune.

The network of links by which a man is attached to the king
through councillors and stewards is intricate, but it usually
originates in his headman, who occupies a crucial position in
interlocking the political and kinship systems.

Political relationships are single-interest linkages far more than
kinship relationships are, but the two sets of bonds are closely
identified in their simplicity and common values. A chief is
regarded as the parent of his people : he is called ' father and
mother '. Every lord is a father to his underlings, and every
father is a lord over his dependants. Therefore Lozi constantly
use political terms like chief and councillor, as well as specific
titles of councillors, in kinship relations, and use kinship terms
like father, mother, child, brother, in political relations. This
identification expresses the manner in which face-to-face personal
relations dominate Lozi life.

As we shall have constantly to refer to the consistency of
Lozi law with these relationships which serve many interests,
I propose, for brevity, to call them *multiplex* relationships. I
require also a term to cover the structure of relationships in
which a person tends to occupy the same position relative to
the same set of other persons in all networks of purposive ties—
economic, political, procreative, religious, educational. Professor
Radcliffe-Brown has suggested I call this an *uncomplicated*
structure, in contrast to Bouglé's defining our own social structure as *complicated*, since it links us with many different persons
in various systems of ties. ' Complicated ' and ' uncomplicated ' are relative in their connotation. Lozi social structure is
uncomplicated when compared with our own ; but it is

complicated when compared with, say, Andamanese or Bushman structure. Degree of complication therefore defines relatively the degree of congruence in the links between the positions of persons in various systems of ties which make up the total social system.

But it is of fundamental importance to know that each Lozi man or woman is involved in more than one of these sets of multiplex ties. He or she belongs to several sets. Some of these sets of ties are of the same kind : a Lozi has rights in several different villages and several different kinship groupings. Villages and kinship groupings overlap but are distinctive and thus are examples of the different types of groupings of which a Lozi is a member. He is also linked in established relationships with neighbours and blood-brothers and friends, and in several different sets of political relationships and groups through stewards, councillors, and members of the royal family, and with fellow-tribesmen. This multiple membership of diverse groups and in diverse relationships is an important source of quarrels and conflict ; but it is equally the basis of internal cohesion in any society.[1]

IV

With this brief survey of the structure of Lozi society, we may glance in a summary way at the problems we shall be considering. Most Lozi relationships are multiplex, enduring through the lives of individuals and even generations. Each of these relationships is part of an intricate network of similar relationships. Inevitably, therefore, many of the disputes which are investigated by Lozi kutas arise not in ephemeral relationships involving single interests, but in relationships which embrace many interests, which depend on similar related relationships, and which may endure into the future. This, at least, is usually the desire of the parties and the hope and desire of the judges and unbiassed onlookers. The Lozi disapprove of any irremediable breaking of relationships. For them it is a supreme

---

[1] See my article on ' Political Institutions ' in *The Institutions of Primitive Society*, Oxford : Blackwell (1954) ; and especially Colson, E., ' Social Control and Vengeance in Plateau Tonga Society ', *Africa*, xxiii. 3 (July, 1953).

value that villages should remain united, kinsfolk and families and kinship groups should not separate, lord and underling should remain associated. Throughout a court hearing of this kind the judges try to prevent the breaking of relationships, and to make it possible for the parties to live together amicably in the future. Obviously this does not apply in every case, but it is true of a large number, and it is present in some degree in almost all cases. Therefore the court tends to be conciliating ; it strives to effect a compromise acceptable to, and accepted by, all the parties. This is the main task of the judges, which I shall describe in the next chapter of the book. This task of the judges is related to the nature of the social relationships out of which spring the disputes that come before them. In order to fulfil their task the judges constantly have to broaden the field of their enquiries, and consider the total history of relations between the litigants, not only the narrow legal issue raised by one of them. Since the kuta is an administrative body, as well as a law-court, it may take varied action to achieve its aim, or convert a ' civil suit ' into a ' criminal hearing ' in the public interest. The result is that in cases of this sort the court's conception of ' relevance ' is very wide, for many facts affect the settlement of the dispute. This applies particularly to cases between blood-kin and between fellow-villagers. The relationship of husband and wife is more ephemeral, and in disputes between them the court concentrates more on the immediately relevant facts. When a contract between strangers, or an injury by a man on a stranger, is involved, the court narrows its range of relevance yet further.

Lozi, like all Africans, appear to be very litigious. Almost every Lozi of middle age can recount dispute after dispute in which he has been involved : most of these have been debated in family and village ' courts ' but many have also gone to political courts. Many Lozi are ever ready to rush to court where they dispute with great bitterness and determination. In cases where they clearly cannot win, they will proceed from court to court. Their bitterness must be understood from the way in which a dispute provoking a lawsuit precipitates ill-feeling about many trifling incidents in the past both between the parties and among their kin, incidents which may go back over many years. Men may sue knowing they will lose, but that they thus bring to the kuta a kinsman who has slighted them and who will be rebuked. Or a man will commit an offence to induce another to sue him, with the same end in view.

The kuta should not achieve a reconciliation without blaming those who have done wrong. The litigants in coming to court have appealed for a public hearing of their grievances, and these are examined against the norms of behaviour expected of people. The judges therefore upbraid all the parties where they have departed from these norms : judgments are sermons on filial, parental, and brotherly love. This is not inappropriate since the kuta is the central administrative chapter for national religious affairs. People involved indirectly, as well as the litigants themselves, are admonished on how to behave.

When we assemble the norms which are stated in this exemplary way, we shall see that they form that figure which is so prominent in all legal systems—the reasonable man. This figure is also used by the judges as the basis of their cross-examination to arrive at the truth : therefore I pause in my argument to consider the problem of evidence (the significance of direct, circumstantial, and hearsay evidence ; the use of oath and ordeal, etc.), before investigating the nature of the reasonable man in Lozi society. Here we shall find that he is highly specified, in accordance with the specific social positions which the parties occupy. Following up this point we shall find that many disputes, apparently over gardens or chattels, are in fact suits by the plaintiff to have the kuta state that the defendant has not behaved reasonably in accordance with the norms of their relationship.

It will have already emerged from this summary account, that in assessing whether behaviour is reasonable the judges lay blame on those who have erred. Implicit in the reasonable man is the upright man, and moral issues in these relationships are barely differentiated from legal issues. This is so even though the Lozi distinguish ' legal ' rules which the kuta has power to enforce or protect, from ' moral ' rules it has not power to enforce or protect. But the judges are reluctant to support the person who is right in law, but wrong in justice, and may seek to achieve justice by indirect, and perhaps administrative, action.

In the course of this account of Lozi trials we shall also cover a number of other problems. I indicate a few here. First, since almost all a man's relationships exist in his positions in the political and kinship systems, a litigant in many cases arising from these multiplex relationships comes to court not as a right-and-duty bearing *persona*, but in terms of his total social personality. That is, in most disputes a person is not involved merely as buyer, seller, lessor, lessee, landowner, the injured party and the wrongdoer—briefly, the plaintiff and the defendant, the complainant and the accused—but he is involved as an individual in specific relationships with a whole set of other people. In administering the law the judges consider these total relation ships, not only the relations between right-and-duty bearing units. But concepts of these units exist as nuclei for the substantive law.

I conclude this section of the analysis by surveying the relation of the judicial process to 'law' as a whole among the Lozi, and find that it is in essence similar to that process in Western law. The judges have to apply certain normative rules to a particular set of circumstances in dispute. These rules, known somewhat vaguely as 'the law', are contained in customary usages; in statutes; in institutions common to all tribes of the region and in some institutions which they believe are common to all humanity and derive from God; in general equity and justice; in judicial precedent; and in the regular processes of the natural world (in our sense). Customary usage—ritual and secular—is one of the sources of Lozi law, as it has been in all systems; and the Lozi have the same other sources as those other systems.

Theoretically, this total body of law is known and certain and the judges are supposed only to pronounce it, abide by it, and apply it. However, since the law has only recently and barely begun to be recorded, the judges do not make a systematic survey of all the sources and decide what rules are applicable. Generally they tend to form a moral and equitable judgment on the case and then state—and amend—the law to accord with this judgment. Often they cannot do this, and must abide by some well-known statutory law or customary rule. But especially in cases between kinsmen, they are generally able to satisfy their ethical view of the facts. This process emerges notably in the fact that judges refer less often to judicial precedents in previous disputes, than to precedents of people behaving morally in circumstances similar to those of the case they are trying.

This process of judicial reasoning begins with the pleadings of the parties and the judges' examination of the evidence, which at every point is evaluated against moral norms. Nevertheless, the process is controlled by logical reasoning, which proceeds from premisses of fact and premisses of law ('reasons' as the Lozi call them) to certain conclusions, and the Lozi have a developed vocabulary to evaluate the skill or clumsiness of judicial analysis. Judges also try to develop the law by reasoning by analogy and logical development to meet new situations. Thus they employ Cardozo's methods of philosophy, evolution, and tradition. They also employ his so-called 'method of sociology', by which they import equity, social welfare and public policy, into their applications of the law. They are able to do so because the main certainty of the law consists in certain general principles whose constituent concepts are 'flexible'—as law itself, right and duty, good evidence, negligence, reasonableness. The judges' task is to define these concepts for a particular set of circumstances, and in this process of specification they introduce into judgment through the flexible concepts all sorts of social values and prejudices, and indeed personal prejudices and values.

Finally, I conclude by making bold to submit that Western jurists, in maintaining or attacking the myth of law's certainty, have not fully explored the flexible 'uncertainty' of legal concepts; and have particularly failed to arrange these concepts in order either of flexibility or of moral implication. I suggest that this ordering is necessary if we are to understand the relation between law and ethics; for I see the judicial process as the attempt to specify legal concepts with ethical implications according to the structure of society, in application to the great variety of circumstance of life itself. In this process the judges are able to develop the law to cope with social changes.

V

I have indicated summarily the ground which I cover in this analysis of the judicial process among the Lozi. Naturally the analysis does not exhaust the problems involved in a study of law and ethics in Lozi social structure, and I have constantly to skirt over a series of these problems. Some of these are to be dealt with in two further books on *The Rôle of Courts in Barotse Social Life* and *The Ideas of Barotse Jurisprudence*. In a limited study in Western jurisprudence the author can refer his readers to published judicial decisions, and to textbooks and other analyses : I cannot do this because Lozi law and ethics are barely recorded outside my own notebooks. Therefore I here indicate the contents of these forthcoming books.

The kuta is well aware, in dealing with cases between kinsmen, that it cannot by its orders secure that people live together harmoniously. It sees itself as one of many agencies operating to this end and it tries to work in accord with these others. Sanctions maintaining Lozi relationships are general and diffuse, and breaches of their rules lead to far more than a lawsuit in court. General economic penalties attach to the erring kinsman : he may lose not only rights to cattle and land, but also the support of his fellows in many of his activities. The ancestral spirits may intervene, or fears of sorcery are likely to arise and accusations of sorcery to be hurled. Sentiments and conscience operate to bring the wrongdoer to conform or make redress. It will emerge in the present book that this complex process of social control can be understood only in an analysis of the social relationships which are controlled. But it is possible to isolate the specific rôle of law-courts, as sanctioning agencies, in relation to other agencies of control, and study *The Rôle of Courts in Barotse Social Life*. Here I consider first the circumstances in which a family quarrel flares up, and the pressures which are exerted to bring about a reconciliation between the parties. One party to the quarrel often uses the threat to sue in court in order to exert pressure on the other party, though actual resort to the kuta is frequent enough. Political authorities constantly take the initiative to intervene in family disputes. These disputes tend to come before political courts for four groups of reasons :

    (1) the high value attached in a subsistence economy to material goods and the ethical evaluation placed on the way in which people handle these ;

    (2) the manner in which the interests of a number of independent kinship groups meet in an individual ;

(3) the necessity for adjudication in multiplex relationships involving most of the interests of the parties, and many direct interests of others ;

(4) the presence of many authorities among the people and the cheapness of litigation.

The other side of this situation is an analysis of the right and duty of political authorities to intervene in conflicts. They are bound to do so when crimes are committed, and appear to discharge their duty efficiently except in sorcery cases. They may also intervene in other affairs to maintain good order and to secure justice.

I then consider the problem of relations between politically instituted courts and informal courts of princes or councillors, or of villages or kinship groupings. The Lozi distinguish the powers of these different courts : only those appointed by the king can enforce their judgments. But all these courts judge and apply law, and have to be reckoned as part of the juridical system. Lozi both have immediate citizenship in the nation as subjects of the king, and also must have mediate citizenship through membership of a village and other groups. At each stage this involves submission to, and correlative exertion of, authority, including judicial authority. Therefore though the political courts will not directly enforce a judgment of an informal court, but always try disputes coming to them, these informal courts are effectively recognized as parts of the juridical machinery. This has continued to be the case despite the restricted gazetting of courts under the 1936 Ordinances. Nevertheless only courts whose judgments are acknowledged by the royal salute are legally effective courts.

Every person in authority—such as a father, or a husband—constantly adjudicates and makes rulings. This is most marked in the case of the royal rulers. They give judicial decisions in their own affairs and for their own entourage, but where they mulct or punish a man they should do so only after trial in court. This rule is commonly obeyed nowadays, but was less observed in the past. Rulers should be bound by the law, and under Lozi law can do wrong and be tried by the courts. But the heads of courts should not be tried by their own courts, for no man should be a judge in his own cause and therefore the 'owner' of the court cannot be tried in it.

Rulers act judicially also in considering the verdicts of their courts. They should normally abide by the court's decision unless it is patently unjust, but they may pardon persons convicted of offences. This final reference of suits to the rulers is based on the idea that ultimately justice resides in the king and other chiefs. They symbolize the certainty of law which makes ordered life possible for the Lozi as a nation. I suggest that this is why so many persons, places, and things connected with royalty are sanctuaries, and that sanctuaries are not only institutions deliberately created to prevent injustice.

The final chapter in this section of the analysis considers the relation of judicial activity to other types of governmental activity. The kuta has judicial, legislative, executive, economic, military, and ecclesiastical functions. All these duties are performed by the same councillors. But the Lozi clearly distinguish a number of these functions, and to some extent the kuta exercises its various rôles by different procedures. But, since the same persons exercise these functions, their actions in one sphere influence their actions in others.

Judicial authority is an essential attribute of all authority : as the Lozi put it, ' government is ruling people ', and ruling people involves settling their quarrels. Therefore in the hierarchical Lozi structure, submission to the jurisdiction of even informal courts is enforced, since these courts attend on village headmen and leaders of other groups. This basic rule also explains why there must be a system of appeal courts in a nation organized hierarchically like the Lozi. The Lozi themselves rationalize this system by saying that it prevents injustice due to the lack of wisdom or the bias of subordinate courts, and that it ensures that one system of law is applied throughout the nation. Beyond this, since the power to adjudicate is an essential attribute of authority, every authority must exert this power over its subordinates : hence there is appeal from the judgment of subordinate authorities to that of superiors. I suggest that this is one reason why the British have imposed, in the 1936 Ordinances, appeals to British courts, and why this is deeply resented by the Lozi. The work of these British courts therefore has to be investigated, as well as the work of new specialized judicial bodies, such as those of churches.

Since the lower Lozi courts consist of judges who are

intimately involved in personal relationships with the litigants, on appeal allegations of bias are frequently made. This personal involvement obtains to some extent even in higher Lozi courts. But it does not alone explain the way litigants on appeal to British courts may exaggerate the partiality of the kuta : here appeal is from a homogeneous system of judicature to an alien-imposed system, and, despite co-operation, a hostile system. Since British judges have to depend on Lozi assessors for advice on Lozi law, this advice is coloured by the political dichotomy : and it may lead British judges to act as if they believed in the allegations that the kuta is corrupt. This position has introduced a considerable new degree of ultimate uncertainty into Lozi law. That law no longer is what the kuta should rule, but what a High Court on the advice of two assessors may rule.

VI

The last part of my whole study deals with the structure of Lozi substantive law, under the title *The Ideas of Barotse Jurisprudence*. Lozi hold rights in land and chattels in virtue of their positions as members of political and kinship groupings and most of their work and exchanges are performed with others standing in specific relationships. Free ' contractual ' relations between persons not already united by social position existed, but were proportionately few and unimportant in Lozi life. In this respect a study of Lozi law, as of law in most simple societies, validates Maine's most widely accepted generalization, ' that the movement of progressive societies has hitherto been a movement *from Status to Contract* ' : i.e. that early law is dominantly the law of status. Lozi law is the law of status, and as Maine puts it elsewhere, ' the separation of the Law of Persons and the Law of Things has no meaning in the infancy of law, . . . the rules belonging to the two departments are inextricably mixed together, and . . . the distinctions of the later jurists are appropriate only to the later jurisprudence '.[1] We may add that the major part of Law of Obligations is also ' inextricably mixed together ' with the Law of Persons and the Law of Things. Barotse society is comparatively undifferentiated, and its structure is uncomplicated. Courts of law have differentiated out of the kuta but

---

[1] *Ancient Law*, London : John Murray (1909, 10th ed.), p. 271.

their personnel is not different from that of other types of governmental councils. They administer a relatively undifferentiated law. This means that the Law of Persons is basic in Lozi jurisprudence. *The Ideas of Barotse Jurisprudence* involve largely constitutional and domestic law.

Nevertheless, it is possible to examine the elements of property and obligation involved in the Law of Persons. Lozi law, like most systems of law, distinguishes immovable from movable property, and therefore it is important to examine the varying significance of these kinds of property in the social structure. Generally, immovable property, associated with titles and privileges, is important in maintaining the enduring framework of Lozi society, as a structure of social positions which persist through generations, while chattels set up cross-linkages between the incumbents of these and other positions. Generally property in Lozi law does not consist of rights over things themselves for use, but of claims on persons in respect of things ; and things are links in institutionalized relationships between persons. There are therefore very few general terms for rights over property, while Lozi jurisprudence is developed in the refining of terms for social positions and kinds of property.

Similarly, as most important obligations reside in relationships established by birth or marriage, or by political position, the nature of these obligations is defined by the status of the parties involved. All these relationships are marked, in the widest sense, by a stress on generous helpfulness and love and mutual give-and-take. No multiplex relationship can survive if the parties insist on their rights only and try to live by the letter of the law. Husband and wife who guide their conduct by legally enforceable rules do not form a harmonious household. Lozi law in treating the code of kinship therefore stresses duty and obligation rather than right. Generosity and forbearance are the main obligations ; and these are extended to neighbours and fellow-citizens. Different relationships have specific incidents only within this general demand. But these specific incidents, and specific rules of etiquette, are essential parts of each relationship. Finally, things are nuclei for all kinship and political relationships, since the measure of fulfilment of obligatory feelings is inevitably made in material goods. Rights between persons are always defined in terms of property.

These attributes of multiplex relationships all influence, in some respects contradictorily, the Lozi ' law of contract '. Despite the dominance of multiplex relationships in Lozi life, the Lozi have always had a number of ' contracts ' in the sense that they established voluntary agreements with previously un-related persons for specific limited purposes. These agreements were barter of goods, loan of goods and land, employment of services, placing cattle to be herded, and partnership of a share-cropping kind in certain forms of fishing. The law stresses obligation in these agreements, and Lozi courts implicitly have as their rule, ' let the seller beware ', with implied warranty of title, sound goods, and fair return. As part of this incipient multiplexity of obligations, we have already noted the tendency to expand these specific agreements to the pattern of kinship obligations. Despite this general tendency, each form of ' contract ' is specific with its own peculiar incidents : the parties do not devise special conditions within the general framework of each transaction, and there are no general principles of ' contract '.

Finally, some transfer of property or actual performance is necessary to create rights and obligations under an agreement. As rights over each other's property are significant in kinship relationships, so property in the form of gifts is transferred when entering on any new kinship relationship, or altering existing relationships. Similarly, transfers of property create obligations between strangers : a man cannot sue on a bare promise. Executory contracts were only made enforceable in 1946.

When I come to consider the Law of Wrongs, I find it more difficult to present an analysis of the indigenous Lozi legal system. The establishment of British overlordship has altered this sphere of law most, particularly with regard to offences against the State and against strangers. Nevertheless, we shall see that in Lozi law certain actions in tort and suits on failures to fulfil obligations are not clearly differentiated, because any failure to render the dues of a multiplex relationship necessarily has a strong element of wrongdoing. Moreover any misfortune —illness, crop failure, etc.—may be ascribed either to the sorcery of one's kin, or to punishment from the ancestors for failing to observe kinship dues. This situation affects Lozi concepts of crime, guilt, negligence, culpability, etc.

Since the present book sets out to examine only the judicial process itself, in its social background, I plead, where Israel Zangwill jested in his introductory ' Caution ' to *The Bachelor's Club* : ' I have . . . to apologise to my critics for this book not being some other book, though it shall not occur again, as my next book will be.'

VII

The reader will have noticed that I began to describe the uncomplicated structure of Lozi society, and its legal system, in the past tense, and slipped into the present tense. I did so unwittingly, for on the whole, despite recent developments, this is a fair description of Lozi life. But the sphere of relations with strangers has expanded greatly. First, the Lozi work for long periods for Whites both in Loziland and abroad, and sell to and buy from them. These Lozi transactions with Whites, like wrongs committed by Whites against Lozi or Lozi against Whites, have been controlled by British authorities and courts. The analysis of these actions is only partially relevant to my present study, and we shall examine only their influence on the Lozi legal system. But relations with Whites, and the money and goods derived from these relations, have both disturbed kinship and political relationships, and also facilitated and in- creased direct transactions with strangers. The abolition of serfdom in 1906 and the long-period absences of men working for Whites, have compelled Lozi to make more use of ephemeral employer–employee relationships with unrelated persons of their own and other tribes. Tribute was abolished in 1925. Hence- forth the Lozi paid only taxes (introduced in 1904) and in return received impersonal social services, in which British and Barotse Governments employ men for wages. The system by which all men personally served the king and obtained gifts from him was weakened, for Lozi began to make labour and other con- tracts even with the king.

Transactions with strangers become continuously more im- portant in Lozi life. Relationships involved in social positions, both kinship and political, are still of great importance. To live as a Lozi a man must have rights to land, and these he obtains as a subject of the king and a member of a village. The system of land-holding remains unbroken, as part of the political

E

structure which still operates. Only a few foreign clerks are
without some land held in this structure. In holding his land
a man must belong to a village by kinship or quasi-kinship ties,
as well as by political affiliation, and here he co-operates with
his fellow-villagers who are often his blood-kin. From his
kin he inherits position and goods. He is bound to them by
sentiment and ritual bonds. When he marries, he accepts other
kinship obligations. The money and goods he obtains from
his labour or sale of produce in dealings with Whites or stranger
Africans flow into these established political and kinship relationships. Lozi society on the whole is still a society dominated
internally by status rather than contract. This is demonstrated
by the few cases in contract I heard—for data on the law of
contract I depended largely on discussion. It is notable too
that in Professor Schapera's *Handbook of Tswana Law and Custom* [1]
only eighteen pages are devoted to the ' Law of Contract ' and
these include donation and permissive loan which are part of the
Law of Persons. However, we shall be observing the developing
importance of contracts as affecting, and being affected by, the
juristic concepts of a legal system rooted in relationships of
status.

VIII

My study of the judicial process in Loziland is based primarily
on the analysis of cases tried in 1940-7. I have in parts referred
to judgments and matters found in archival material or reported
by informants from the past, and have sought for information
from books by early visitors to Loziland. Strictly my conclusions
state that Lozi judges worked and thought thus in the 1940's.
At that time Loziland had been under the British protectorate for
forty years. The powers of Lozi courts to punish and modes of
punishment had been curtailed by a British overlordship which
is partially hostile to the Lozi authorities, and this overlordship
had reduced the possibility of arbitrary action by king and
kuta. But I believe that my observations not only yield a
valid analysis of judicial practice in Lozi courts at present, but
also that this analysis gives, with reservations for the past made
clear in the text, a true view of their judicial *process* in that past.

---

[1] London : Oxford University Press (1938).

It may not do so for judicial *practice*, since this may have been influenced by political and economic factors in ways which we cannot now assess. But I observed Lozi kutas trying disputes and offences affecting land, cattle, and other property ; social position, marriage, and succession ; theft, assault, and slander ; etc. From these trials, checked against earlier records and informants' texts, I have in this volume extracted the way in which judges approach their task, how they assess evidence, what sources they draw on for judicial decision, the logic of their arguments, and how they apply legal rules to the varied and changing circumstances of life. The modes of reasoning involved in this complex process are so deeply imbedded in Lozi institutions and thought, that I consider my whole analysis emphasizes their indigenous existence. There is no evidence that in these respects the Lozi have been influenced by the work of British courts, whose procedures are alien and often incomprehensible to them. Hence I assert that my study of the Lozi judicial process, which is akin to our own judicial process, faithfully depicts modes of reasoning which are probably found wherever men apply norms to varied disputes. I consider that more specific aspects of this study record processes which are likely to be found in other African states, and indeed in the arbitral processes of societies without governmental institutions. Since the study has by implication wider reference than to the Lozi alone, I argue here that some of its conclusions require that certain current ideas about ' primitive law ' be abandoned and others be reformulated.

Further, the study is of *Lozi* judicial process, and not of all judicial processes in Loziland, for Lozi kutas are not the only courts before which Lozi seek justice or are brought to trial. Major conflicts and difficulties involving Lozi arise from their relations with Whites, and disputes about these come before British courts both in Barotseland and beyond its borders,[1] as well as charges involving the death sentence and charges of witchcraft [sorcery] between Lozi. Had I been concerned with all modes of adjudication affecting Lozi, I should have had to study the judicial process in these British courts. This lies outside my present field and in terms of its problems would require

---

[1] The king has power to terminate the licences of traders and recruiters and expel them. This power has very rarely been exercised. The king would consult the British authorities administratively over such a matter.

another book ; but I confess that my data on British courts are inadequate.   I shall consider these data when I discuss *The Rôle of Courts in Barotse Social Life* : here I say in my defence that most disputes between Whites and Lozi occur outside Barotseland itself, in White-controlled mines, industries, farms, and houses. The Lozi's land has been protected by Treaty and as few Whites are settled in Barotseland there is comparatively little internal employment of Barotse by Whites, save by the Northern Rhodesia Government.   Lozi courts themselves are concerned with matters of deep interest to their subjects, but as they do not deal with some of the major conflicts arising from the absorption of Loziland in world polity and economy, their process, and indeed practice, may seem Arcadian.   It is in courts at White labour-centres to which Lozi migrate to work, that cases involving the present great inequalities of Central and Southern Africa are tried.   There justice, constrained by marked economic differences and by colour conflict, is likely to appear far from Arcadian.   Here we are concerned with Lozi courts at work in the still uncomplicated polity and economy of their homeland.

CHAPTER II

THE TASK OF THE JUDGES

I

THE way in which the judges try to reconcile the disputing parties, or in which they convert a ' civil suit ' into a ' criminal hearing ' in the public interest, is best illustrated, without further introduction, by records of cases. The main part of my analysis is based on detailed anthropological enquiries over a period of thirty months between 1940 and 1947, and especially on cases I heard being settled in various kutas, in which I sat for several months. I do not mean here records of the bare bones of judgments : it will soon be apparent that these do not by any means reflect either the judicial process or the substantive law. The record of a case involves the pleas of the parties, the evidence of witnesses, and cross-examination, as well as the judges' decisions. It is of course impossible for me to reproduce any verbatim record of a whole case. The cases proceeded at high speed in Lozi, which I understood very well but not perfectly. I took down notes in a longhand mixture of Lozi and English. During the hearings I got lost over some details. It was particularly difficult for me to follow the references by parties and witnesses to others by various kinship terms. Where I got confused I asked the head of the kuta, next to whom I was invariably seated, to clear things up for me. Secondly, while the kuta is trying a case some councillors may also at the same time be transacting administrative business, and in trying to follow this I missed some passages in cases. Nevertheless, I am certain that the records I present are fair.

I have naturally selected for presentation here those cases which best illustrate as many points in my argument as possible. I might have taken other cases to illustrate each separate point ; but it has seemed better to me to give full records of a few cases, rather than summaries of many. When readers have worked through the first few, I am sure they will agree with my decision. It may appear, indeed, that the records I present are too full, and that I might have eliminated some of the repetitive judgments.

I ask for forbearance here, because in later analyses I shall refer to the phrasings of various judgments. These records are also the main check on the validity of my analysis, and in describing the Lozi system of law I am handicapped for brevity because there are no published records of cases.

In attempting to base this analysis of Lozi law on case-law, I am of course further handicapped because on many points I did not hear cases. Though I worked through many kuta records and sat in at cases for several months, my reports cover limited themes : four in five cases in Lozi courts are matrimonial disputes.[1] To an important extent, therefore, the lines of my analysis have been shaped by the cases I happened to hear in court.

Other cases are taken from kuta records. Yet others were summarized for me by Lozi, especially my Research Assistant, Mr. Davidson Silumesii Sianga, to whom I register again my deep indebtedness for friendly help. He has also helped me in taking *texts*[2] on cases and disputes which occurred in the past ; most of these were checked by being recorded several times, from the same and different informants over a period of seven years.

I have translated the cases myself freely, since literal translations would be awkward. Occasionally I do make literal renderings where I consider the native phrasing is itself significant. Anyone who knows Africa will agree, I hope, that my renderings are true to the original. I have reduced to the necessary minimum footnotes and parentheses to explain laws and customs mentioned in the records. I have also given those cases to which I frequently refer distinctive titles, in order that readers may fix the cases in their minds and catch later allusions quickly and easily. Furthermore, because these cases are accessible only in my own records, I have, in referring to them on several occasions, thought it expedient to state summarily their main points. This has involved some repetition.

---

[1] Hailey, *Native Administration in the British African Territories*, op. cit., ii, pp. 88 ff.
[2] Note this anthropological technical term for its later use.

CASE 1 : THE CASE OF THE BIASSED FATHER

This was a land dispute between Kwangwa [1] kinsmen and fellow-villagers, heard at the Saa-Katengo Kuta of Lialui on 27th August, 1942, on appeal from sub-district induna SIKWA.

$\triangle$ = male $\bigcirc$ = female
Blacked in when dead

Respondents : Y, Z, V.
Defendants in original
suit.

Appellants : A, B, C (C not present in court).
Plaintiffs in original suit.

A, B and C sued their ' father ' (i.e. father's elder brother), Y, who is the headman of their natal village, for certain gardens on the margin of a small plain.   Their own father, K, died when they were infants and Y raised them.   The law in this case seems clear : ' if you leave the village, you lose your gardens in it.'

Nephew A opened the case : ' We are disputing these gardens.   The trouble began when our " brother " Z committed adultery with the wife of C.   C caught him and injured Z till others intervened.   B was away working in White country.   We failed to settle the matter at home, and went to the sub-district induna SIKWA.   C's wife paid the kuta's fine of a beast, and Z was to pay C two beasts but did not do so ' [until 1946 when the damages and fine were increased, an adulterer paid his cuckold 2 beasts or £2 damages, and the adulteress paid the kuta a fine of 1 beast or £1]. ' Z insulted C.   When C complained to our " father " Y, Y drove him out of the village. He built a short distance away.   I remonstrated with Y that C was aggrieved and was not causing the trouble.   Y came to me in the night and told me to get out of the village.   I said goodbye to my female fathers [paternal aunts, R and S], but not to Y ' [elicited under cross-examination by the court].   ' B returned from White country, and that evening left the village to join us.   Then I found that Z was cultivating our old gardens, and eating our sweet-potatoes and

---

[1] A tribe related to the Lozi and living in the woodland near the Plain.

mangoes.   These were manured gardens.   I protested to our " father " Y who said it was done without his agreement—he would put it right.   He did nothing, so I saw that he was supporting his own son, Z, against the children of his younger brother.   We complained to the induna SIKWA who said we could not live together, we must separate [because they would kill each other—see below].   The induna said we had lost our land.   I cannot see how a person without a fault can lose his land, and his mangoes and other crops, so we have appealed.'

The son Z was called on to speak for the defence : ' Before I committed adultery with C's wife, A had cuckolded the son of the sister of our father Y.   I admit I committed adultery.   I admit I took their gardens, but they were not driven away, they fled in the night. Would I, their brother, drive them away,—I who raised them and made them big ?   I did not insult C, C insulted me.'   He then proceeded to complain of a long series of actions of his ' brothers ', alleging that they took back poles and thatching-grass which they had cut and which his father Y had used in his hut, that they stinted Y fish they caught and goods they brought from White country, etc.   He did this in order to show their hardness of heart.   ' After they left, they told me that they had put medicine [magical substances] against thieves on the mangoes, so the children should not enter. Can you do this, get your child bitten by a snake ? '   [i.e. the magic makes a snake bite a thief, and his child is their child].   ' As for their crops, their wives pulled these up.   How can a man who has moved, work gardens that he has left ?   There is the law of the Whitemen, about cleaning the village of weeds : will they be clearing in the village, or my wives ?   Is it fair for them to have gardens there, and live elsewhere ?   My hens and children and calves will enter their gardens.   If they live in the village it balances out, for theirs will enter my gardens.   But it is not the same if they live elsewhere.'

B told more or less the same tale as A, and added : ' When I got back from White country I tried to get Y, our " father ", to call together the people to settle the quarrel.   Y said it was no longer possible.   I saw that Y was deciding with partiality (*sobozi*), supporting his own child.   So I moved out after A and C.'   He turned to A and corrected him : ' We were not driven out, because our father did not burn our huts.'

The kuta called on headman Y, the father.   He began with a diatribe on how wicked and irresponsible the modern youth are. He described how K [his younger brother and father of A, B and C] died when K's children were small and they grew up on each side of him.   ' I raised them.   If I had been childless, they would have cared for me.   Would I drive away the children of my brother, all

of whom are on my foot? But the children of today are bad.
When they stab fish at the battues, they give me none; they killed
an ox, and my wife bought meat with cassava; they brought me
nothing from White country. I sent my sister, their female father
[paternal aunt], to remonstrate with A after he left the village. B
said someone hated him and had planted medicines to burn up his
crops. I said the sun had burnt B's crops; let him dig up the
medicines. B replied that the person who had done it, had dug up
the medicines when the crops were scorched. I took some poles of
A's to make a partition in my hut, and A came and pulled them up,
and took the grass from the roof. I did not drive them away—they
went at night without reason or farewell. I gave the four sons of
K eight cattle with which to marry.' Questioned by the kuta, A
and B admit this.

These are the main statements of the litigants. Y's sisters R and
S and his wife and son V gave evidence. I briefly indicate the points
on which the kuta cross-examined them.

Steward AWAMI (L7) asked Y: 'Is it true that B asked you to
call the people together to discuss the quarrel?'—Y denied it, and
B reaffirmed that he had. The same councillor asked about A's
taking away the poles; A said the partition had not yet been made.
The poles had been taken and leant against Y's hut. A argued: 'It
was after I was driven out—I did not see why if I were driven out,
Y should have my poles.' Y asserted that he had made the partition,
and the two sides divided on this, each side's witnesses supporting
its leader.

Steward ALULEYA (L8) questioned A and B about whether they
gave Y food generally, and clothes when they returned from White
country with their earnings and purchases. They recited a long list,
which Y and Z denied.

Induna INYUNDWANA (R21) asked A: 'What were the words
which drove you out of the village?'—A: 'He told us to get out.'

INYUNDWANA: 'What did you do?'—A: 'We went to the
sub-district induna SIKWA, who said we must move out or there
would be fights.'

INYUNDWANA turned to question Y, but Induna KALONGA, (R15,
sitting as head of the kuta) intervened: 'You have not finished,
INYUNDWANA. A, when you went to SIKWA, why did you not ask
SIKWA to call you together with your father Y so that the kuta could
decide between you?'—A: 'When SIKWA told us to move, we
moved.'

Z denied this, so KALONGA said: 'We need witnesses.'

The king's Nkoya [another tribe] bandleader, sitting in the kuta,
had already volunteered to give evidence and he now came forward.

Bandleader MWIBA : ' I know this family well because I live close to them, and Z abducted my daughter from another man to whom she was married. . . . The family lived together amicably until Z took C's wife. I was there with the late INDALA [leader of the king's Lozi and Simaa bands], getting the royal Nkoya drum. I heard that Y had driven out K's sons. I went to Y and rebuked him, saying, " It is very bad, you must not drive away your children. You must not back your own son, but must settle quarrels." [Here he began to judge, in effect.] ' Children of one womb do not go to court, but do as B suggested to Y—they meet and settle the quarrel. Y has driven away his family by supporting one person. A man's elder brother is his chief : but the trouble came from Z, as it should not, for he as the elder brother is the chief. Y has spoilt the village and will be left alone. You councillors know the land ; it is the land drained by King Lewanika at Simululwa plain that they live on. I told A, B, and C to come to me and take there the land of their fathers whose village had died out.' The councillors pitted Y against the bandleader ; Y again denied that he had driven out his ' children '.

The councillors questioned A and B at some length about their respective gifts to Y, and those of their absent brother C, and about the poles and grass and the allegation by Z that they stinted Y fish. They pressed Y on what he would do if his own son quarrelled with his sons by his younger brother ; he maintained that he would support the one who was in the right.

Then Steward AWAMI (L7) asked Y : ' Do you want your sons back ? '—*Y :* ' Yes, I do, emphatically.'

AWAMI asked A and B : ' Do you want to return ? '—*B :* ' Yes, it is to our father ; if the gardens . . .'

Several councillors interrupted : ' Leave the gardens, that is easy. Do you want to go home ? '—*A :* ' We still pay tax in Y's book . . .' [the list of members of the village in the District tax-register].

The councillors interrupted : ' The tax register is easy. If the kuta decides, we can fix the book.'—*A :* ' We want to return. I don't know if our younger brother, C, driven away at night, and cursed by Y if he returns, will do so ' [A had alleged that Y struck the ground in the lower court saying : ' May I split inside if C returns '].

Steward AWAMI : ' This is the final kuta. Speak your hearts. We know nothing of your brother who is not here.'—*A :* ' How can we refuse to return home, to our father ? '

Z (questioned) : ' I want my brothers to return home.'

(The councillors muttered to each other, condemning the sub-district induna SIKWA for not bringing A and Y together.)

AWAMI to Y, the headman : ' Then do you agree that Z as well as A is in the wrong ? '—*Y:* ' Yes, Z and A are bad, but not B.'

After going again into details about the poles, etc., the kuta entered into judgment :

Induna MBASIWANA (R46) : ' You children return home. As for the gardens, no-one lives elsewhere and cultivates in the home. It is good that you return, and if you refuse to return home, you cannot return to your gardens.'

Two junior stewards gave the same brief judgment. The second added : ' If C were here, I'd see that he agreed. He was afraid of Z so he left home. Return home, A and B, and bring C with you. If you do not return, you cannot cultivate the gardens. They clean the village and you cultivate only !—no, it cannot be done ! As for this story about medicines to kill the maize, you, B, brought a quarrel. Return home.' (B attempted to speak and was silenced : ' Be silent, your lord has judged.')

Induna IMUTUKO (R28) : ' I say you A have seduced the others. It is an astonishing affair—one leaves the village, and the others follow ! If you get out, you get out—you cannot still cultivate the gardens. You, Z, you have heard your father. When A and the others return home they get the gardens. If you still quarrel, we'll try another path.'

A prince consort : ' I rebuke Y. You acted badly, Y, but I think it good that your children return home. They are the children of your younger brother. And if there is a quarrel again, and it is your own son's fault, you must right it. You, A and B, you must return and tell your brother C to return. Live well with your father, and get your soil, and live well with your elder brother Z. If there is another quarrel we must try another path.'

Induna SAYWA (R27) [1] : ' Y, listen carefully to what the Malozi [reference to a chief or the kuta] say. You must finish quarrels among your children. If your own son starts quarrels with the others, do not support him. You must strengthen your children. Perhaps one of them will care for you—they and their sisters. Finish the quarrels and pray together [to your common ancestral spirits]. You, Z, you have heard this. Your father wants A and B. You and they must listen to him and end your quarrels. You, A and B, you return home and go to your soil. This is right. Leave the quarrels.'

Induna INYUNDWANA (R21) : ' A, if you return to the village you

---

[1] Note that in Case No. 14, p. 89, this induna is accused and convicted of the same fault as Y : supporting his own children in a quarrel in his village. It was heard immediately after this case.

get your gardens. The people at home have dogs and children and cattle ; it is not fair that you live elsewhere and have gardens there. Take the gardens even if Z has cultivated there.' (All the parties clapped.[1]) 'If you leave the village you do not have the gardens. You, A, have behaved badly. As for you, Y, on the bandleader's evidence you sent your children away. This is very bad. However, if they don't return, the gardens are yours.'

Steward AWAMI (L7) [2] : ' Y, in my opinion you have not handled the village well. You must see that your children like one another. A man loves all his children and they strengthen him. The country is well-built when a man and his children love one another. If they refuse to live with you, I would see that they refuse to eat the land of their father. Now I've heard from them that they will return. If they do return and you withhold their gardens, I shall see that you agreed only in the kuta. A child has no soil but from his parent, and a parent is only worked for by his child. Thus if you refuse them the gardens, we shall see that it was you who drove them away. If you give them the gardens, I shall see that you still love them. I shall thank you greatly.

' Now for you, Z. Y is their father, you must give them their gardens. They have only him as their father. You are only one of the children. The man who is oldest in the family, it is just that he is born first. You are not their lord, but merely the first by birth. Hold your brothers well, and they will care well for you. It is good to love one another. Also, you are the one with power. I heard your father say that he may live only another year, and may not see much more. You will be in difficulties. If they rejoin the village, it is to strengthen you.

' Now you, A and B—do not take this affair by another path. Do not think that the kuta has returned your gardens. They are the gift of your father. Also, for the poles you took back—bring your small gifts and work for your parents. I was born as you were and know. Every day your father fed you, morning and evening, and now he is old the position is reversed : you are the parent. He cannot go to the bush to fell hard trees. Do not take your poles

---

[1] Clapping, *kukandelela*, is the Lozi method of greeting. In any formal discussion a man claps to acknowledge any favourable reference to him, and in a lawsuit the parties and witnesses do this, especially when they agree with one of the judges' statements. The judges similarly acknowledge references to themselves by their fellows.

[2] He is noted for the length of his judgments. When he began to judge it was almost 12 noon, and his fellows said he could not finish by the time the *moondo* slit-drum would be sounded for the midday recess. Judging was therefore suspended till 2 p.m.

from him. He is a parent. We thank you because you said in the
kuta you wish to return to your father. If you live well, you will
hear KALONGA ' [sitting that day as Senior Induna and therefore giving
the final judgment ; many councillors were away making fences for
the palace. AWAMI means that if all agree, they will be approved
by KALONGA].

Steward ALULEYA (L8, but sitting FI as a prince consort) : ' Y, we
heard your affairs. By my judgment, I scold you greatly. You and
the father of A and B, you came from one womb, and the soil you
plant is his soil. If you need a child to enable you to live well, it
may be one of them. You are wrong because in the woman affair
you did not take the fighters and settle it by asking what had happened. You backed your own child. You should have washed Z's
wronging of C [by seducing his wife] by giving a gift of washing
[*mpo yakutapa*, a sacrifice of reconciliation], a beast with four legs
to be eaten together. You are an old man, and you do not know
who will bury you [i.e. be your heir], who will control this soil.
You may choose this one, he says he is Y, and yet the family may
refuse him.¹ So I scold you, an old man who enters a fight [i.e.
who is partisan and takes sides not by finding which is right, but by
favouring one disputant]. All that the bandleader said here was
correct—you should settle things by reasons and argument. You
fail in governing the village when you just say, " Get out of the
home."

' Z, you are the person who spoils the village. Be careful, because
the kuta will tell the man who dirties the family to get out of the
village. You are only a child, they are not serfs of yours. You
are one person ; be careful, take care of your younger brothers.
They are your medicine. About the gardens—who will give them
to you ? They are yours of old.

' You, B, I see you are really a man, because you said, " My
brothers, do not leave home." And you went to your father to
adjust matters. You should have persisted more, but your behaviour
when you returned to Loziland shows you are really a man. You
people are wrong about the fish and the poles and grass you took
from your father. You too have children and they will do the same
to you. There is no child who has soil but from his father. The

---

¹ Among the Lozi when a man (or woman) dies an heir is selected who
' eats the name' of his predecessor. Names thus come down through the
generations. The heir is selected by all cognates from among themselves,
and no-one is indicated by law as the heir. Here, Y may think Z will succeed
him, and Z may begin to call himself Y, but the family may choose A or
B or C to succeed. Y's heir would control the village and its lands.

child's chief is his father. He must respect his father' (and ALULEYA gave a long lecture on this theme). 'Be careful in this affair ; if it returns to the kuta we shall fine you.'

Induna KALONGA (R15 sitting as 'finisher', *mufelelezi*, on the right) : ' Y, I have nothing to say to you beyond what the Malozi said. I am shocked at your children taking the poles and grass. You are their only father, they have not two or three. I feel pain, I am sad at a child who does not respect his father. They can cut trees for themselves and go to White country. A child is like a man who is cured by a person.

' What I do not like about you children are the words reported by induna SIKWA [1]—that you said you cannot still live with your father. The affair that settled the matter for SIKWA was your saying that your crops, burnt by the sun, were burnt by sorcery [i.e. when they made charges of sorcery, SIKWA felt relations were too embittered for them to live together amicably]. You deceived this kuta saying you want to return, swearing by medicines [i.e. you have medicines to protect you from the consequences of false oaths here]. I do not believe you want to care for your father. I think tomorrow induna SIKWA will bring this affair of yesterday. We will wait and see. I do not prevent your going home because your father has asked for you. If the affair comes again, you will not be judged as today, but you will be fined. You trouble your father, taking the grass and poles from him. No child can do this. You, A, this elder brother Z with whom you quarrel, you do not let the quarrel die. It is you who is spoiling the village of your father [i.e. as the eldest of K's sons, A is trying to lead them into a rebellion which will make him independent head of their group]. When your brother B came back from White country, instead of going with him to your father, you seduced him to leave home. Live well with your elder brother Z, so that you may both strengthen your father. So I do not agree that you return home, but your father and elder brother have asked for you. If you make trouble, and the case comes here again, we will fine you.

' Y, strengthen your children, hold them well. If you do not, we will hear from SIKWA. If there is trouble, it will not be you, but their changing.'

This was the final judgment, and all councillors, litigants, and people in kuta clapped it.

---

[1] I have not given all the evidence. The hearing spread over two days and R and S, sisters of Y and K, and Y's wife also gave evidence. KALONGA had stated the kuta needed SIKWA's evidence on what happened before him. He arrived at Lialui on the evening of the first day's hearing on other business, and gave evidence.

B asked : ' What about the huts which we built where we moved, and who will work the gardens, since Z has cultivated them ? '

KALONGA (R15) : ' Z cultivated by the judgment of SIKWA, that you moved out of the village because you said you did not want to return.'

Headman Y : ' They will return to their gardens, which are hoed, and they will plant, and if Z says that they cannot plant because his wives hoed ' (Z shakes his head and says ' No ') ' he cannot do it, or complain about his work.'

KALONGA and the kuta clerk said : ' If you still have affairs, dispute at SIKWA's kuta.'

The clerk told the kuta he entered the dispute in the records as over the gardens.

AWAMI : ' Did you make gardens where you moved ? '

IMUTUKO : ' We do not go into that, it is another affair. We do not enter it, the other gardens are their affair.'

KALONGA : ' Go by your father's words.'

Z replied to a question from the clerk : ' No, I cannot deny my younger brothers their gardens. Their huts are still standing in the village.'

KALONGA : ' AWAMI wakens the dispute again.'

AWAMI : ' No, it is they, the owners of the dispute.'

ING'UNDE (laughing) : ' It is AWAMI, he is quarrelsome.'

SOLAMI (R3), head of this kuta, and other councillors returned from working at the palace fences. After consulting SOLAMI, KALONGA said that SOLAMI entered into the judgment of the kuta. ' If you have told the truth that you want to live with your father, who asks for you, all right ; if your father finds that you were deceiving us, and returns to the kuta, the kuta will see what it will do. You, children, hear this—we do not want to hear again of your taking goods from your father. You will all give the royal salute [with which the successful litigant acknowledges that he has received justice].' KALONGA asked the kuta who should get back his deposited court fees, or should all, since all had won ? [Both sides deposit fees, and the loser's is forfeit.]

ALULEYA : ' Their father won, so he gets his money again.'

Y, Z and V went to give the royal salute. A and B remained sitting in the kuta, and were ordered by the kuta to join Y in saluting the king and kuta.

This case involved more than the question, who had the right to cultivate the disputed gardens ? On that point the law is quite clear and was stated early in cross-examination by several judges : ' If you leave the village you lose your rights in its land.' This was how the clerk recorded the case in his records. Sub-district induna SIKWA, who had heard the case, first gave evidence on a chance visit to the capital next day. He had not initially considered this issue but had ruled that the nephews must dwell apart lest they and their cousin fight each other, and therefore they lost the gardens. The quarrel simmered, and it was only when Z began to cultivate the gardens that his cousins brought the case to the capital. By building new huts nearby the nephews did not commit themselves to leaving the village : it is significant that they did not accept the royal bandleader's suggestions that they return to other ancestral lands near his village at another plain. Unfortunately they hurried away from Lialui before I could interview them, but it seems possible that they were waiting for overtures of reconciliation from the ' father '. During this interim period their wives took fruit from the land, and Z's allegation that they protected the crops with medicine shows that he did not regard their departure as final.

However, when Z began to cultivate the gardens and his father did not forbid him to do so, a legal issue was raised on which his cousins went to court in the capital. They sued not for the land alone, but to be established as in the right in the whole quarrel. This shows in the peroration of A's plea : ' I cannot see how a person without a fault can lose his land, and his mangoes and other crops.' Land is held by virtue of position in the nation and in a village, and maintenance of those positions depends on fulfilment of their multiplex obligations. A argued : we have been wronged, and have done no wrong—we should retain the increments of our position. Thus the garden-dispute as a legal issue raised the quarrels and ill-feeling within the village which came to a head when the headman's son Z seduced his cousin's wife. It is into these quarrels, and the emotional entanglements involved in them, that the judges enquired. The headman had favoured his own son, but argued that he had not ; and he wanted to cover up his lack of strength in not summoning all before him so that he could judge who was in the wrong. His son defended his highly blameworthy seduction of C's wife, by asserting that A, B, and C had no right to feel so strongly about it, since this in a sense avenged A's cuckolding of their [classificatory] father's sister's son. To the kuta it was clear that Z regarded himself as superior to his father's younger brother's sons. Some judges suspected that A, as the eldest of the group of full-brothers, was feeding the quarrel in order that they might follow him to found an independent village of which he might be leader. In court he was more intransigent than B. Meanwhile R and S, the headman's sisters, were so determined not to become involved and side with either their brother and one nephew, or their other nephews, that they gave completely colourless evidence.

Stated in the most general terms, each party was concerned to show as far as possible that throughout he behaved lovingly, justly, and generously to the others, as a father should to all his ' sons ', ' sons ' to their ' father ', and ' brothers ' to each other ; and that his opponents had been niggardly and quarrelsome. The measure of these valued emotional attitudes is the rendering of material gifts and of help to each other. The headman and his son heatedly denounced the others for stinting him ; they as heatedly asserted their generosity. Though in relationships between kin there is no formal system of equal exchanges, people in practice balance what is done to them against what they do. When a major quarrel occurs their sense of being stinted or not recompensed, together with feelings of envy and dislike, comes to the surface. A, B, and C, those who were forced into patent loss by the quarrel, were the ones who showed this in charges of sorcery. The case therefore became a general venting of grievances, into which the judges patiently enquired, ruling out nothing as irrelevant. That is, to achieve their purpose of reconciliation, the judges' concept of relevance had to be very wide. Indeed when it became apparent to the Lialui judges that the parties could be reconciled they complained of sub-district induna SIKWA's failure to bring the parties together to thrash out the matter. SIKWA was in a weaker position than the Lialui judges, not only because he had less power but also because he was related to the parties. He had sought to avoid open charges of sorcery or bloodshed by ruling that it was not safe for A, B, and C to continue to live in the village—they should found an independent village, and this entailed losing their gardens.

The Lialui kuta was deeply concerned to avoid this break-up of the village and the breach of relationship between Y and his nephews. It is the duty of the councillors, who are administrators and legislators as well as judges, to try to maintain public order and national strength ; this includes the unity of existing villages and the maintenance of kinship ties. The kuta therefore enquired into all the quarrels and all the feelings of the parties. It established that the headman had fulfilled his obligations to his nephews by helping them with cattle to obtain brides, but the evidence on the giving of fish and clothes to the old man, and the taking of poles and grass from him, was not as definite. At first the kuta called for more witnesses. Then shortly after the bandleader's evidence, which consisted mainly of his opinions formed on hearsay, Steward AWAMI (L7) cut the knot by asking Y if he wanted his nephews back. Obviously it is very difficult to get clear evidence on all the transactions in a village. The judges therefore decided that once the parties had agreed to reunite, they could praise those who had done well, and rebuke those who had done ill. They had sufficient evidence to make up their minds on the merits of the case. Since on several points there was no clear evidence, different judges allotted blame variously, and here personal circumstances may have influenced the judges. All except KALONGA (R15), the 'finisher', strongly upbraided Y for favouring his own son and not calling his dependants together to settle the quarrel. KALONGA also adjured him to act thus. Even before the matter came to court, the king's bandleader, emboldened by his official position which he had held for many years, had entered the quarrel to scold Y : his statement that he had done so was accepted by one judge as evidence, and another quoted his opinions. SAYWA (R27) and ALULEYA (L8) told Y that after SIKWA found Z had seduced C's wife, he should himself have provided a sacrificial meal of reconciliation to reunite all his 'sons' about him. All the judges rebuked Z roundly for this seduction. They told him that on the one hand he must not assume that as the eldest son of the eldest son he would inherit the village, and on the other hand that as the eldest he was especially obliged not to wrong his younger 'brothers' (cousins). A, B, and C were variously rebuked and praised. KALONGA, an elderly man who had himself had difficulties with his children, was particularly annoyed at the allegation that A and his brothers had stinted Y ; and he and other judges considered that A had encouraged the quarrel for his own ends, to raise his own status. He was rebuked for this, while B was praised for some actions and rebuked for others.

In the end all the councillors gave the same judgment : A, B, and C should return to the village where Y and Z were to receive them, and they were to regain their gardens by Y's favour. This was made clear in Y's final interpolation when KALONGA, who disapproved of the young men, ruled that Z was entitled to the gardens by SIKWA's judgment [i.e., that on this point it was *res judicata*]. If they refused to return to the village, they lost their gardens.

Large parts of the judgments read like sermons, for they all lecture on the theme ' your station and its duties '. The standards publicly stated for the parties are the norms involved in their social positions and relationships : people have rights in land by virtue of birth and membership of a village ; members of a village must be loving and forbearing, accepting mischances in a spirit of give-and-take, since the children and stock of fellow-villagers spoil gardens equally ; the headman must be impartial in settling disputes among his followers ; children must love and help their parents, and brothers one another. These are statements of Lozi law and morals, in which the ultimate values here are that ' children ' should love one another to strengthen their ' father ' and their village that ' the country may be well built '. The essence of the judicial process is to state these norms to the world and to assess against them the behaviour of the parties in a specific series of situations. The aim of the judicial process is that when the parties have had their rightdoings and wrongdoings indicated to them, they will be reconciled and live together harmoniously in the future. Nine years later I heard by letter that these disputants were living in amity.

Litigants and witnesses work with the same legal and moral rules as do the judges. Thus all the parties accepted that the break-up of the village was bad : the nephews felt that they had to justify their departure by alleging that they were ' driven out ' or compelled to leave by the headman's bias against them, while the headman and his son asserted that they left without cause. This son, Z, conscious that he had done wrong in seducing his cousin's wife, tried to defend his wrongdoing by accusing the cousin's brother of the same fault. Similarly A, aware that he should not have taken the poles from his uncle, claimed he did so only after he and his brothers had been wronged. And so on. It is not clear in this case what exactly the truth about all these matters was, but we can note that if the parties lied, or were mistaken, they cast their story in such a form that they appeared to have acted rightly and to have been wronged. This point is of fundamental importance, because it means that the judges, working with these same norms, can cross-examine the parties and can give judgments for and against them in comprehensible and acceptable terms, even if the parties continue to deny that they have done wrong.

These norms are an essential attribute of the social relationships involved, and constantly exert pressure through the sentiments and actions of the parties even before the case comes to the kuta. The kuta itself tries to exploit these pressures. It appreciates its own power : some councillors stated that if the parties failed to agree the kuta would ' try another path ', and senior councillors said they would fine the disputants if the quarrel came before them again. But the judges also recognize the limitations of that power, and laid most stress on the positive gains which come from loving and helping one another, and accepting the mischances arising from living together in a spirit of mutual give-and-take. The ' children ' were told to help their ' father ' as he had raised them because thus they set an example to their own children. Mystical sanctions are also significant : the parties feared each other's curses and use of sorcery, and ALULEYA and SAYWA advised that they offer and pray to their ancestral-spirits together.

We may glance in conclusion at three other sets of general problems arising from this case, which will receive fuller treatment later. The early emphatic statement of the law, ' no-one lives elsewhere and cultivates in the village ', was frequently given to me as a basic maxim of Lozi land-holding. It cannot be accepted that this maxim will be applied without qualification. In the present case the rule is applied to force recalcitrants to return to a village which they have left, and to test the headman's and his own son's good faith. The unity of the village is threatened, its land is part of that unity, and therefore *those who leave the village lose the land*. As we shall see in Case No. 47 at page 187 (The Case of the Headman's Fishdams), the kuta held in effect that a headman cannot prevent other kin working his village's land though *they refuse to move into the village*. Ultimately, in terms of legal concepts, in both these cases the kuta was in effect defining the incidents of *bung'a* (ownership) of land. Since rights of ownership of land inhere in membership of a village and kin-group, the discussion in court proceeds in terms of fulfilling the obligations of this membership : ' I cannot see how a person without fault can lose his land,' appealed Nephew A. The kuta rarely formulates these points explicitly, but they lie at the heart of the judicial argument.

Secondly, in achieving its aims the kuta works not only judicially, but also administratively. Thus it told A that it could, if necessary, itself alter the tax-registers. ALULEYA warned Z that if the kuta found that he was ' dirtying the village ', it could order him to leave. The kuta is fully aware of the difference between these types of action.

Thirdly, because the full family dispute was only brought to a head in the suit over the gardens, the court's standard of relevant evidence is very wide. In fact no evidence about the gardens or who worked them was questioned : all the cross-examination was on other matters. Throughout the court was concerned with all the moral issues involved in the family dispute. Therefore it considered all the circumstances involved over several years. These circumstances were presented from the beginning in the pleas of the parties which were not confined to the claim over the gardens. Other circumstances, some bearing on the character of the litigants, were presented in the evidence, full of hearsay as well as of judgment, given by Bandleader MWIBA, as they might have been by any of the judges. There is no refinement of pleadings in Lozi procedure to whittle a suit down to certain narrow legal claims so as to present the judges with a mere skeleton of the facts relevant to those claims.[1] The judges are immediately made aware of the moral perspective of the suit, and they themselves can take judicial notice of anything that falls in their own knowledge which they consider relevant.

To sum up, the kuta in this case was concerned with a garden-dispute between parties linked in permanent and enduring relationships as kin and fellow-villagers, in which their rights in the same soil were part of many other common interests, specific and diffuse. The legal rule over the disputed gardens was

---

[1] A. L. Epstein's *The Administration of Justice and the Urban African : A Study of Urban Native Courts in Northern Rhodesia*, London : H.M.S.O. (1953), has drawn my attention to the importance of this fact.

quickly and simply stated, but the kuta widened its enquiry into the actions of the parties over many years—note the enquiry into Y's making marriage-payment for his brother's children. The kuta tried to adjust the dispute by pointing out who was right and who was wrong in each instance and advised how the disputants should behave to one another in order that their relationships might endure.

II

It is interesting to see how this case was summarized by an intelligent, trained Lozi, Mr. D. S. Sianga, since many analyses of African law are based on similar summaries.

The Case of Muteto and his Children of Simululwa

Muteto and his children gave the kuta very full evidence. Induna SIKWA and induna MOKANELAMO reported to the kuta their judgment which they had given at Makanda kuta. Muteto complained of his children because they did not give him things—of the two of them, one took from him his poles with which he had built a partition in his hut, the other unfastened his grass with which Muteto's hut had been thatched. Muteto informed the kuta that his own son (Z) had loosened his reeds with which he was building a granary for his father.

When the affairs had been spoken of at length, the kuta was taken by the words which had been spoken by Muteto and sworn by him before SIKWA's kuta, that his children should go out of the home and he no longer wanted them to live with him. AWAMI asked the children whether they no longer wanted to return to the village to live with their father. All of them agreed, and their elder brother (Z) also wanted them to return.

The judgment of the judges was then given, reprimanding Muteto together with his children. Indunas IMUTUKO and INYUNDWANA instructed greatly in their speeches. 'Do you not have quarrels among you again. If this affair happens again we will give you a great fine.' These words were spoken also by the stewards and the members of the Katengo : 'If you deceive the kuta that you will return home and you do not do so, you have no right to work those gardens, not at all ; but if you return, all right, you can cultivate them as before.'

KALONGA finished the judgment of the whole kuta. 'Do not disagree again. You, Muteto, do not love only your own child whom you begat ; all of them are your children and you ought to look after them by fair custom, as you have said in the kuta, so that you will have married new wives.[1]   But it will not be thus if you will not see or hear one of your children to find out he has erred—this is good. When you return do not be a parent who is biassed against the children of your younger brother.'   The judging ended, and all of them were told to give the royal salute.

This summary was written some time after the case had been heard, and Mr. Sianga has not remembered correctly all the facts or which judges said what.   I cite his summary, firstly, because it brings out that for a Lozi the case, as he remembered it, was not a garden-dispute, but a general quarrel involving a father and his ' children '.   Secondly, this summary by a Lozi of a case I recorded fully evidences that the full implications of the judicial process cannot be extracted from texts : a Lozi does not consider that these implications need stating and he concentrates on the legal settlement itself.   This shows that the Lozi have a distinctive body of legal rules, but makes clear my difficulty in using similar texts, on points on which I did not hear cases, for an understanding of how these rules are applied.   Thus the following summary by Mr. Sianga of another garden-dispute suggests that the kuta concentrated on the narrow legal issue :

CASE 2 :   THE CASE OF THE RETURNING GARDEN-CLAIMANT

Muyoba vs. *Siyoto, garden-dispute before Saa-Katengo Kuta at Lialui, 24th September, 1942*

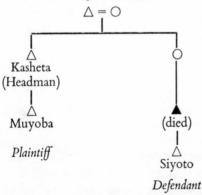

---

[1] i.e. he will have them to care and work for him.

Muyoba complains that Siyoto has taken from him the garden which was cultivated many years ago by Siyoto's father. The father of Siyoto moved out of the village because of the quarrels with his mother's brother, Kasheta. Siyoto's father died when he was still a child, and he went to the north with his mother. When he grew up he returned to the village of Kasheta, his father (he called Kasheta ' my father ' as headman of the village, but he was the child of the child of Kasheta's sister). Siyoto begged Kasheta to give him the same garden as was always cultivated by his father, and Kasheta found that he had given this garden to his child Muyoba who had cultivated it for many years. Muyoba refused Kasheta the garden, and put his cattle in it to fertilize it [by staking them to drop their manure on it]. Siyoto went to the garden and he broke all the cords tying the cattle. When Muyoba heard this he went to S:yoto thinking that he would fight him for breaking the cords. When he was close to Siyoto he changed his mind about fighting but thought he would go to the kuta to sue. The judgment was against [literally, ' felled '] Siyoto because he did not sue for the garden but sought to recover it himself by violence. The kuta told him strongly that were not Muyoba his relative and Kasheta his father he would have paid 5s. for breaking the cords and £5 for committing *muliu* [as fines, probably]. The kuta also pitied him and excused him from paying these fines because he was a child.

The offence of *muliu* was defined by statute of the Lozi kuta in 1928. When the Kololo drove the Lozi out of Loziland in 1836 they took over all Lozi lands. The Lozi reconquered their homeland in 1864 and re-settled it, and Lozi were allowed to make claim for gardens on the basis of ancestral title. In 1928 it was enacted that all these claims must be lodged by midday on a set day ; anyone bringing such a claim after noon on that day would be guilty of *muliu* and fined £5 or five head of cattle. *Muliu* does not apply to claims based on ownership after 1928. In fact, the kuta did not apply *muliu* here because it is a claim between fellow-members of a family, and not based on one family's ancestral title as against another,[1] though it stated the excuse as ' pity '.

In this case Kasheta, the headman, had to deal with conflicting claims. He had, justifiably, given Siyoto's father's garden to his own son who was entitled to refuse to give it up. Kasheta asked his son for the garden because he considered it would give

---

[1] *Obiter dictum* in Nalolo District Court, December, 1942.

a warm welcome to Siyoto's return, but he could not compel its cession. We may be sure that Siyoto got as thorough a lecture on how to live harmoniously in a village as did the young men in Case 1.

III

The need to reconcile the parties is obviously important in cases between people who are linked in permanent relationships as kinsfolk, or as overlords and underlings. But reconciliation is not an ultimate, almost mystical, value of Lozi courts, in the way in which it has been described by writers on some other African tribes.[1] If a dispute arises between two people who are comparative strangers to each other, there is no need for the court to reconcile them, since they are associated only by a single contractual or delictual relationship which can be adjusted by a clear decision. When that has been achieved, the parties go their separate ways as far as the court is concerned. Matters of property-rights, contract or injury in permanent multiplex relationships require reconciliation; the same matters between strangers do not. The differing approach of judges to these two categories of cases will become apparent as we proceed : here I illustrate the varying task of the judges in a case arising out of the contract of loan of gardens, since it contrasts with the previous dispute arising from land-holding within a village and by kinship affiliation. It will be seen that the judges comment on the general implications of the case, for as administrators they are concerned with these. However, they confine themselves to the dispute more narrowly, and the concept of ' relevant evidence ' is also narrower. This case is one example of the judges' approach to cases in contract ; other examples will be given in later parts of this whole study, especially in the volume on *The Ideas of Barotse Jurisprudence*. Similar observations apply to the trial of crimes and delicts committed by men on strangers, as against trials of offences against kinsfolk : cases of this kind will be cited later.

---

[1] For references see below, p. 78n.

CASE 3 : THE CASE OF THE PRINCE'S GARDENS

Prince Mubukwanu Mataa vs. *Mutome, Sikalo Appeal Kuta,*
Lialui, 30th October, 1942

Prince Mubukwanu Mataa was himself a member of the Sikalo
Kuta ; during the hearing he sat at one of the posts, on the ground,
like an ordinary litigant. His father Mataa had been appointed
NGAMBELA in 1921 and deposed in 1929. (They had a princess as
one of their royal ancestresses and therefore were not eligible for
positions as king or as a chief.) Mutome, the defendant, lived in
a village close to Mubukwanu's. Mubukwanu [1] claimed a right to
regain a certain garden from Mutome on the grounds that his father
lent it to Mutome, and said he gave Mutome a year's notice to quit
so that he would have time to seek a new garden. Mutome asserted
he had been given the garden to be his own, and accused the prince
of committing *muliu*.

I found great difficulty in recording the evidence, as the parties,
especially Mutome, were very excited, and shouted at each other and
interrupted the judges. They became so noisy that the NGAMBELA
(R1, chief councillor of the nation) said : ' You leave nothing for
the kuta to ask. But go ahead.' Other judges became annoyed at
the unseemliness and tried to quieten the people, but the NGAMBELA
admonished them : ' Do not prevent a person from speaking.'
Eventually the NGAMBELA cut the argument short and asked : ' Now,
Malozi, do you want to put questions, or get witnesses, or is it
enough ? Will you enter judgment ? '

MUKULWAKASHIKO (R4) : ' No, it is they of Mubukwanu who
want to call witnesses.'

Prince Mwauluka of Mubukwanu's party said he wanted ISHE-
WAMBUTO, induna of the sub-district where the gardens were sited,
to be called.

NOYOO (R13) : ' Do any of you litigants want fresh witnesses ? '
Prince Mwauluka : ' Unless we call the whole nation. . . .'

NGAMBELA : ' The question is do you want fresh witnesses ? You,
Mutome ? '—*Mutome* : ' No.'—*Mubukwanu* : ' No, unless the Malozi
want them or to see the boundaries, the gardens, and the depressions.'

NGAMBELA : ' Then judge, Malozi.'

LONG'ONG'O (R25) : ' All the evidence is for Mubukwanu, and if
I were the NGAMBELA (R1) I would give the garden to Mubukwanu.
You, Mutome, even your own child gave evidence against you. In

---

[1] In the hearing he was called Mataa, as he had inherited his father's name,
and it was the increments of Mataa's position that were in dispute. To keep
the record clearer, I call him Mubukwanu.

the North where we live, we adjoin Prince Isiteketo and suu (R17), and Hamba is there on the gardens of Nandombe. No-one jumps on to the garden of Nandombe ; so Mutome cannot jump on to the gardens of Ngeela village from Kabende village.'

Prince Isiteketo (F7) : 'I speak as LONG'ONG'O. When you, Mutome, went to that land you found Liwalela [the name of an Mbowe hippo-hunter rewarded with the village by King Ngalama (4th Lozi king) ; Mutome succeeded to it]. The evidence is consistent [literally ' one '] : the garden is Mubukwanu's. The garden is on one island, there are four gardens on it. If those gardens are Mubukwanu's, the evidence is that that garden is also Mubukwanu's : for we decide by evidence and indications (*lisupo* = probabilities). How can we give it to you, Mutome ? I scold you because you are no longer trustworthy. You were given the garden [on loan] while you were trustworthy. Also you did not fight over the garden until old Mataa was dead. MUKULWAKASHIKO [R4, in cross-examination] asked whether there is *muliu* [1] in this case : I see there is, because the garden was Mataa's. You cause great trouble ; you have fought in many kutas—at sub-district induna's ISHEWAMBUTO, at MULETA [head of Libonda kuta, Kalabo district capital on appeal], at SOLAMI [head of Lialui Saa-Katengo kuta], now here. You have brought many witnesses [and so on]. Perhaps the NGAMBELA will give you life [reprieve you]—but I say you pay £5 or 5 head of cattle.'

suu (R17) : ' Mutome, I do not believe you were afraid to fight because you were afraid of the NGAMBELA, the finisher [i.e. he believes against the previous judge that Mutome would have claimed the garden even if NGAMBELA Mataa were alive]. You were ready to fight over this garden. I believe Mubukwanu because you belong to a different place, and Mataa, his father, showed you the gardens. About the *muliu*—*muliu* did not prevent the loan of gardens and their reclamation. Loaning of gardens helps people greatly. But you have lied. The judge because of his position seeks evidence, and by the evidence I see that the garden is Mubukwanu's. When two people fight, we do not believe them, we call witnesses. Here it is not my fault—it is the evidence. But by your cleverness in trying to get this garden you have ruined your children who all work gardens they have borrowed from Mubukwanu. You have finished them with your covetousness. Perhaps Mubukwanu will drive them out. I fail to award the *muliu* damages because this garden was borrowed. You say that they *liulula* (claim ancestral land) : but

---

[1] *Muliu* = offence of claiming land on ancestral title before 1928 ; see p. 54 above.

they regained this land long ago. I might have given you a fault for stealing land, but you do not claim a garden which had on it the stalks of Mubukwanu's crops. But I give you a fault of *muluta* [i.e. of going from his own village to Mubukwanu's to fight him], as by our law of 1929. I give you £1 to pay to Mubukwanu, unless your lord the NGAMBELA (R1) saves you.'

NOYOO (R13) : 'Mutome, you have wasted our time.' He gave a long talk on the kuta's not judging corruptly or by bias, and described Mutome's lies, and the way he had disputed with his own witnesses. 'As Ishee Namabanda [SUU] says, you have finished the love of Mubukwanu. On the evidence given [which he cited], what can we judges do ? About what SUU says about *muluta*, I will reprieve you, unless you are killed by your lords above me, because perhaps you did not understand what you were doing. The land is, according to the evidence, Mubukwanu's.'

MUBONDA (L4) : 'The NGAMBELA is the owner of this kuta and he hears. The garden is Mubukwanu's. If you lend a dugout, does the dugout belong to the borrower ? On the question of *muliu*— I agree with NOYOO. Perhaps you did not understand. The lords who finish may find a fault here, but I see there is no reclaiming of ancestral land. You said you were given the garden, they say it was lent only. I do not know what will happen tomorrow, but I see your children are people of Mubukwanu. Perhaps he will be bitter against them in his heart. But everyone disputes—father-in-law and son-in-law ; one does not know.'

INYAMAWINA (R7) : 'You all—I see the affair is hard. MULASU [a deceased councillor] is not here, nor NGAMBELA Mataa, and we know only the words of his children. We do not know what happened. What we do see, is that the witnesses support Mubukwanu. In my heart, I supported Mutome, but I see that the nation [witnesses] backs Mubukwanu. I agree you admit you borrowed one garden ; a garden on the Plain-margin with bushes on it. But because of the evidence, the land in the Plain is also Mubukwanu's. You have no helper.'

PRINCE MBOO SIPOPA (F3 and R18) : 'Mutome, and Mubukwanu, I have heard your case. Mutome, the soil is Mubukwanu's, not this Mubukwanu's, but the old Mubukwanu of long ago. Liwalela was given land because of his hunting ; and this was in the time of King Ngalama [4th king]. It was land of Ngeela village. As for *muliu*, there is no fault, because you borrowed the garden from these princes. So I do not see that there is *muliu*. The garden falls to them, not to Liwalela's name. But I do not see *muliu* because all people borrow gardens. It is we, the royal family, who loan gardens. The borrower then claims the garden, and that is not *muliu*.

I asked one witness how many gardens Liwalela had, and all heard the answer. The garden belongs to Ngeela village, and the big depression is the boundary, since I do not believe a small depression would be the boundary between two villages' gardens. That of Mubukwanu is Ngeela village, of yours is Kabende village. You merely dispute later rights. You do not reclaim ancestral land, so I do not see *muliu*. If you had said the garden had always belonged to the name Liwalela it would have been *muliu*. Tomorrow the gardens of Kabende village will be seen to be those of a prince.'

MUKULWAKASHIKO (R4) : ' Mubukwanu, I have changed my mind (*kukeluha* = to be a renegade) in this affair. I like to know where an affair sits. The land is divided by law. The *muliu* law says, who cultivated the garden ? I do not judge by partiality, and will if it is right kill my kin. Where I fail is over the nation of people [the witnesses]. If Mutome had had four witnesses, I would have changed my mind. I was here, and INGANGWANA (L1), when SAMBI [chief councillor at Nalolo] said that he who did not fight for a garden when the sun was low, and did when the sun was overhead, had a fault of £5. So I would have found that the garden was Mutome's. But [pointing to Mubukwanu's witnesses] that nation which sits behind you, changes my mind. It was not your father [then NGAM-BELA Mataa] who made the law of *muliu*, it was we of the kuta. My thought was that you Mubukwanu had committed *muliu*—I do not hide it. But the evidence is yours, not his. They contradicted his assertion, when they said the garden was loaned. I do not know them at all, they are people of Ndau district and I am of Tungi district. You, Mubukwanu, are a big person and he, Mutome, is a small person, but we are all of Loziland. What I neglected to ask them of Ndau district, was this : all that country given by King Mulambwa [9th king—1780 ?–1830 ?] to his sons the princes, who held it in the time of Ngombala [6th king] ? I should have asked them the names of the holders . . . Mbindawina the Mbowe was moved to the south by King Ngalama [4th king], and Liwalela the Mbowe was brought to Ndau. So I ask : when the law of *muliu* was promulgated in 1928, who was cultivating the garden ? They say not Liwalela, and then it was given [i.e. loaned] to Mutome. So I understand thoroughly, because a case is decided on evidence. So I say, the land is yours, Mubukwanu. Do you hear, Mutome—[as Mutome tries to speak] be silent I am judging— : if you go from here and say the Malozi hate you because they are kin of the other parties, do you hear ?—the evidence decides. We split in our opinions on this case ; but I fail because of those people [pointing to the witnesses]. Your son killed you, he is your *mufubalume* [term used between husband and adulterer, men marrying two sisters, man marrying widow and dead husband's kin, etc. ; that is, his son is the one who worked against him by giving evidence against his father]. I have no partiality. I was not born in this stool of MUKULWAKASHIKO of my father [he became MUKULWAKASHIKO after one other incumbent had succeeded his father] : it belongs to Loziland, it originated long, long ago. It must give good living (*bupilo* = life) to the country. So you fail because you have no evidence on your side. Where is it ? That is why you fail, not because he is a prince. We are each of us a child of the king. And here on the right [the mat of com-moners against that of princes] we have failed. He has witnesses. Will all these [with a gesture at them] hate you ? No one is denied except on evidence. That is how I see the case.'

INGANGWANA (L1) : ' Mutome, I will not say much—I enter where the people have spoken. First, the witnesses support Mubukwanu, and secondly, Mubukwanu showed you the country when you inherited the name of Liwalela. Will he who showed you your land dispute with you about it ? Would I, INGANGWANA, fight the man who gave me living ? About *muliu*, that is another affair. We made the law, I was the one who announced it. That law does not prevent a man from claiming what is in his hand. No, he who says so, just speaks. The law said : " You who have not reclaimed your ancestral garden when the sun is low, when midday arrives, you cannot sue for it." So I say, there is no *muliu*. About the damages spoken of by others, I do not agree because you did not go to claim ancestral land. So I see that Mubukwanu lent you the garden. I see no fault of *muliu*, and none of causing trouble by *muluta* [going to plaintiff's village to fight]. You spoil good fortune, because when people ask for the loan of a garden, those who are asked will remember the case of so-and-so. You stint the people a place, thus, because lenders will fear your case. So I see you have no fault—but the garden is Mubukwanu's. There was not one of the witnesses who was a renegade.'

The NGAMBELA (R1) : ' The kuta has listened long to you litigants. I agree with the Malozi : there is no *muliu* and no causing of trouble by *muluta*, but only the affair of who owns the garden. It is Mubuk-wanu's. In 1926 Mataa, his father, put Liwalela out of the gardens ; in 1928 the *muliu* law was promulgated. Then Mutome borrowed the garden. About the causing of trouble, I see none because you did not get on together well. It was the same at the margin of the Plain, was it not so ? (The councillors : " It was so.") This upset their affairs. So I see no causing of trouble by *muluta*. The witnesses are people of the country, not of Mubukwanu's village. If you were working the garden and they of Mataa came and said it was a garden of princeship, they would have to pay £5 ; for *muliu* prevents king-

PLATE I
Views over the Plain from the Margin, at flood and in the dry season.

PLATE II

Lialui Saa-Katengo-Kuta, 1942, from the stewards' mat, over the backs of
AWAMI and LIOMA. Beyond are litigants and witnesses. On the left is the
royal mat, with, nearest camera, ALULEYA and LITOOMA. The Indunas' mat is
opposite the litigants, off plate, at right.

ship as well. These witnesses all (naming them and their different villages) support Mubukwanu and you know the law of the kuta : a case is decided by evidence. The garden is not yours, it is Mubukwanu's.'

All the kuta clapped this final judgment ; Mubukwanu rushed out, calling his witnesses to give the royal salute to the palace and then to the kuta. Mutome remained sitting at his post and began to speak about the witnesses. He said he begged for permission to appeal to the High Court in Mongu [on Circuit] ; in the meantime, Mubukwanu could cultivate the garden. Mutome did not in fact appeal.

The disputants in this case were neighbours and not kin or members of the same village. Mubukwanu was an important prince in the area, but not a political overlord of Mutome's. The kuta therefore had to disentangle the facts from a complex mass of evidence going back by legend over many reigns, and found these to be : (1) Was either party claiming the garden on the basis of ancestral holding before 1928 ?—to this it answered ' no ' ; then (2) had the land been lent or given by the old Mataa to Mutome—to this it answered that the land was lent, therefore the garden was Mubukwanu's and he could reclaim it ; and (3) had Mutome gone to Mubukwanu's village to start a quarrel—to this the final judges said ' No '.

Some judges paid attention to the background of wider social relationships between the parties, notably two princes and INGANGWANA (L1), whose incumbent ranked as a prince, for it is the royal family above all which has land to give and lend to commoners. Thus Isiteketo (F7) chided Mutome for ceasing to be trustworthy ; Mboo (F3) stressed that it was they, the princes, who gave out land ; and INGANGWANA (L1) pointed out that this sort of case made landholders chary of lending land, lest its return be disputed, though many needed to borrow land. MUKULWAKASHIKO (R4), however, stressed that the commoner indunas agreed with the verdict of the princes. MUBONDA (L4) and SUU (R17) pointed out that Mubukwanu might become angered against all Mutome's family and take back land he had lent them ; and they implied he ought not to do so. Finally, the NGAMBELA (R1) said that Mubukwanu was reclaiming the garden because he and Mutome did not get on well together.

A marked feature in all the judgments is the emphasis that the kuta decides by evidence and reasoning, and without favour.

Judges constantly stress this in cases of all kinds, but especially when the losing party is excitable and obviously feels they are favouring the more important man or their own kinsman. The manner in which some judges commented on the personal relationships between the two disputants, and introduced Mutome's untrustworthiness into their judgment, is referable obviously to the fact that neighbours are in permanent relationship. The court is interested in the preservation of good feelings and friendliness between neighbours, and it may therefore plead with quarrelling neighbours to adjust their differences and may comment on their behaviour even when it is extraneous to the issue. Thus judges pleaded, by implication, with the prince not to oust his opponent's children from land he had loaned to them. Nevertheless the court gives a clear judgment on the issue.

Another process is sometimes also at work in these disputes, which leads to a broadening of the enquiry. This is the tendency for Lozi contractual relations to expand to the pattern of their kinship relationships. If A lends B a garden, or employs B in fishing his traps, or places his cattle with B to herd for him, he ranks as a senior kinsman of B. As soon as people begin to exchange goods regularly, they aim less at a good or standardized bargain, than at keeping up a cycle of exchanges and reciprocal assistance. This tendency is particularly marked in contracts affecting land, for the two parties begin to help each other in many ways extraneous to the loan. Then if a dispute over the garden arises, all these acts of assistance may be brought in pleadings by the litigants before the court, which will enquire into them carefully and try to adjudge them. Thus the borrower of the garden in the following case raised the same general issues as those considered in ' The Case of the Biassed Father '.

CASE 4 : THE CASE OF THE IMMIGRANT LAND-BORROWER

Sinonge vs. Batuke, before Ishee Kambayi at Namalya Kuta,
June, 1947

In 1940 Sinonge immigrated to Namalya and Batuke gave him space to build on and to cultivate on part of one of his mound-gardens in the Plain. Induna MBASIWANA (R46) Mutondo, an old man resident in the area, protested against the loan on the grounds that, when Batuke died, Sinonge and his sons would claim Batuke had given them the land, and would even jump the boundary.

For seven years Batuke and Sinonge lived as close neighbours, helping each other in many ways. In 1947 the (late) king Imwiko, who was related to Batuke through his mother, told Batuke he must tell Sinonge to leave the land as they needed it for their own kin. Sinonge flew into an embittered rage and rushed with his complaints to induna MBASIWANA, promoted to NAWALA as head of the local kuta ; to MUKWAE MBUYWANA and ISHEE KAMBAYI, the local princess and her husband ; and to me, since my main camp had always been in that neighbourhood. For weeks I listened to his bitter accusations of lack of gratitude against Batuke, and to Batuke's counter-recital of all Sinonge's faults. Eventually the matter was argued before the local kuta. Sinonge admitted that the land was loaned to him, but claimed that Batuke had no right to expropriate him since he had done so much for Batuke, that they were as brothers, and he a permanent dependant of Batuke's. He had given Batuke a door, two beasts, a shirt, an overcoat, food, many other things ; he had harvested Batuke's crops and dragged them to Batuke's village when Batuke was ill ; he had used his oxen and sleigh to take Batuke to hospital, and so on. Batuke angrily countered with a series of denials of these favours, and a list of what he had done for Sinonge. They became angrier and angrier, until Sinonge was spluttering with rage, swearing by the name of the late king Lewanika (1883–1916), and smiting the ground, which is a curse forbidden in the kuta. The prince consort, ISHEE KAMBAYI, became angry too, and the men tried to quieten them. But as it became apparent that the kuta considered Batuke was entitled to reclaim his land, Sinonge flew into a rage, alleging they were all against him because he was a stranger. Batuke's younger brother, Mooka, tried to calm Sinonge. Mooka reproved his brother for criticizing Sinonge who had always been a good neighbour : why should they now decry him ? They were asking for their land not because they had anything against him, but because their great kins-man the king said it was wrong that a stranger work their land while their own kin were without gardens. Sinonge settled into quiet grumbling, and when the kuta ruled that the land was Batuke's he said he would sue Batuke for repayment of all his favours. The kuta said he would get nothing, for it was right that he should help a neighbour, especially a neighbour from whose land he had taken his living for several years. Who would accept him now if he claimed repayment ? Indeed, the kuta [at the capital] would fine him for thinking land was something that could be bought and sold, and not land of the king.

That night, when Sinonge brought milk to me, he listened more quietly to induna NAWALA's lecture on this theme : he had lived off the land and in return he had helped the lender ; he had been a good

G

neighbour to others as well as Batuke. If he did not now grudge his help to Batuke, he would still be reckoned an upright man. Therefore, let him yield the land to Batuke with a good grace, and ask the king for a gift of land for himself. Sinonge took this advice, and was placed on royal land in the neighbourhood.

Here the borrower did not assert a full title to the land on the grounds that it had been given, and not lent, to him, as Mutome did against Prince Mubukwanu. The law states that a man may reclaim a loaned garden provided he gives notice at harvest in time for the borrower to get a garden for the next sowing. The claim is barred if the borrower has manured the land, when he is entitled to two seasons' use, or if he has planted cassava, when he may retain it until his cassava roots are grown. Batuke therefore was legally entitled to the land. But Sinonge claimed that their relationship as lender and borrower had expanded into a quasi-kinship relationship. In Mutome's case the councillors felt that Prince Mubukwanu was entitled to reclaim his land, since Mutome had ' ceased to be trustworthy ' ; the Namalya kuta sympathized with Sinonge for he had been a good neighbour to them all, and they knew that misfortune had made him leave his own kin to settle among them. The major part of the hearing was concerned with the parties' assertions and denials of reciprocal favours, till Batuke's brother admitted that Sinonge had done well by them. Induna NAWALA told me that had Batuke of his own accord claimed the land, they would have remonstrated with him, though they could not have denied his legal title to the land. But it was the king's word that Sinonge abandon the land, though the king was acting in his private capacity. Their sympathy with Sinonge led them to excuse Sinonge's ill-behaviour in kuta. But the land was undoubtedly Batuke's, and those who lend land must have their titles to it protected, however hard it be on the borrowers. NAWALA acted to recompense Sinonge as best he could by helping him to obtain other land on a more secure title.

IV

About 80 per cent of cases coming before Lozi kutas are classed by the Administration as ' matrimonial cases '. Some of these are suits for damages by one spouse against another, but the majority are claims by husbands for damages against men who, they allege, have committed adultery with their wives, or have eloped with them, and claims by the wives for divorce from their husbands. I shall cite cases covering all these situations in the next chapter, where I deal with the legal implications of ' reasonable and customary behaviour '. Here I cite summarily the way in which judges conceive their task in adjudicating on these matrimonial disputes.

Suits arising out of an alleged adultery or elopement are almost always treated as straightforward cases in delict. The court has to assess whether adultery has been committed, and if it finds this to be so, orders the adulterer to pay damages to the husband and the wife to pay a fine into court (see ' The Case of the School-boy Adulterer ', pp. 130-3). It will rebuke the wrongdoers and may advise the wife to be faithful to her husband, but otherwise it concentrates on the issue. A man cannot be sued for adultery by his wife, under the system of polygamy, but only by the man who is guardian of his mistress, whether it be her husband or blood-kinsman. Similarly, if a husband alleges that his wife has eloped with another, the court levies damages and fines if it holds the allegation to be true, though incidentally it also divorces the woman (see ' The Case of the Eloping Wife ', pp. 113-19). In this and similar cases, and even in those of adultery, the wife may plead in defence that her husband had treated her in such a way as to divorce her, since in Loziland a husband can of his own will divorce his wife by sending her home ; and he may be held to have driven her home constructively, as by stripping her of her clothes or gardens (see ' The Case of the Contemptuous Husband ', pp. 142-3, and ' The Case of the Prudish Wife ', pp. 145-7). In these circumstances—an eloping wife's plea that she was divorced by her husband, and a wife's suit for divorce —the court naturally has to investigate closely the spouses' reciprocal behaviour over a long period.

Where in adultery or abduction cases the wrongdoer is a relative of the husband's, his misdeed may become one of many subjects in a general enquiry into the relations of the two men, as in ' The Case of the Biassed Father '. Then the dispute is not a straightforward delict—adultery with, or abduction of, a man's wife—but a dispute between kin.

Either spouse may also sue the other for committing an offence against his or her kin.   Here again the court is likely to enquire closely into their reciprocal behaviour, as well as the issue immediately in dispute (see ' The Case of the Insulting Sons-in-Law ', p. 79).   If it is the wife who is offended she may seek a divorce, but she is entitled to bring suit for restitution of her rights or for damages if she wishes to remain with her husband.

CASE 5 : THE CASE OF THE LIBERTINE HUSBAND

In 1942 the two wives of one of my servants complained to me that he spent too many of his nights seeking for women, instead of sleeping with them.   They asked me to reprimand him as they still loved him, but they wished for their rights and they feared that his adulteries would spoil their chances of pregnancy and endanger their lives if they became pregnant.[1]   My attendants upbraided him severely and told him to sleep with his wives.   Induna NAWALA (R46) cited a case in which the two wives of M. complained to the NGAMBELA'S (R1) kuta that he was sleeping ' all over the place ' : the NGAMBELA ordered him to spend six nights a week with his wives.

In this case, NAWALA and the others concentrated on the issue ; in cases where the wife sues for fair treatment or equal treatment with other wives the court holds a general enquiry and gives directions on many matters.

CASE 6 : THE CASE OF THE DEPOSED SENIOR WIVES
(from a text)

An ivory-carver had three wives, the third married being a young girl.   Under Lozi law, wives do not have special rank [such as they have in Southern Bantu law], but are roughly ranked in order of marriage irrespective of age or status.   The incidents of seniority are slight : a man should consult his senior wife first on general matters, he should come to her hut when he returns from a journey, he should bring his guests to her, and he should keep his special working tools in her hut.

One day the ivory-carver went off without putting away his tools. The third wife asked her seniors to clean and put them away, and when they refused she did so.   After this had happened on a couple more occasions, he declared that he would make her his senior wife. The others sued in the local court, which enquired into all their respec-

---

[1] Most Central African tribes believe that if a man commits adultery when his wife is pregnant, she will miscarry, or bear a still-born child, or die in child-birth.   He may have intercourse with his other wives.

tive behaviour, and declared that the third wife was rightly promoted as she alone really cared for and respected their husband.

When disputes of this kind come to court they do so more often as suits by the wife for divorce.   In the next chapter I shall show that the wife then asks the court to declare that her husband has behaved so unreasonably to her, in breach of customary standards, that he has ceased to treat her as a wife.   If it appears that the husband has in fact wronged his wife, the court will grant her a divorce.   Though the court enquires exhaustively into their reciprocal behaviour, it will not attempt to reconcile them. Only if it finds that no divorce is merited, will it urge rightdoing on the spouses and upbraid their ill-deeds (see ' The Case of the Good Son-in-Law ', p. 151, and ' The Case of the Prudish Wife ', pp. 145–7).   In short, the court always broadens its enquiry— i.e. has a wide specification for ' relevance of evidence '—when it has to reconcile, but it may broaden its enquiry without attempting a reconciliation.

The judges approach cases between spouses in this way because marriage among the Lozi is far from being a stable relationship. The divorce rate is very high.[1]   Though the relation between husband and wife is fundamentally important in Lozi social structure, a woman remains, after marriage, primarily related to her own kin-groups and her children acquire legal rights in these through her.   The law does not defend the permanent mainte- nance of any particular marriage if either spouse breaks the rules of marriage.   The transfer of goods, a legal transaction, estab- lishes marriage, and the decision of a court can break it.   Marital ties are not like blood-ties, which are virtually unbreakable. Therefore the judicial process of reconciliation analysed above, though present, is less marked in divorce suits once the woman has shown there are good grounds for her claims to freedom : it comes into play only if the judges refuse a divorce, when they will try to convince the wife that her husband has not wronged her sufficiently to justify her release, and they upbraid both parties for departures from reasonable and customary behaviour. However, while judges act thus in divorce suits, if quarrels

---

[1] For a fuller analysis of this situation see my ' Kinship and Marriage among the Lozi of Northern Rhodesia and the Zulu of Natal ' in *African Systems of Kinship and Marriage*, edited by A. R. Radcliffe-Brown and C. D. Forde, London : Oxford University Press (1950).

between spouses come before a council of their village or of their two groupings of kindred, a reconciliation will probably be attempted (see 'The Case of the Lazy Husband', p. 144, and 'The Case of the Prudish Wife', pp. 145–7).

The Lozi judges' treatment of divorce suits contrasts with the way in which courts approach these suits in African tribes where marriage is important as establishing permanent relations between groups through the spouses. This is marked in tribes where father-right prevails, and I have suggested in the essay referred to above that these father-right tribes have stable marriage, with a low or even negligible divorce-rate. Among them, when a woman complains of her husband's bad treatment, the judges have to attempt a reconciliation, since the relationship has to be preserved.[1] However, the process of reconciling spouses when either sues for divorce is found also among some Central African peoples whose divorce-rate is high.[2] I shall not here attempt an explanation of these variations, but cite them to show that the Lozi are not representative of all Africans when they do not apply to matrimonial suits the process of reconciliation they employ between blood-kin. On the whole the Lozi approach these suits partly as breaches of contract between strangers, and partly as disputes in permanent relationships.

However, the Lozi regard one kind of marriage as unbreakable. If a man and woman who can trace their descent from a common ancestor some four generations away insist on marrying despite the protests of their kin, the kin curse the marriage by saying that only death and not divorce can break it. Unfortunately I have never heard of or recorded a dispute between husband and wife linked in this way ; but it may be that the kuta might then strive more explicitly to reconcile the parties. They would be blood-kin as well as spouses, and the ban on divorce for these

---

[1] My own field-data on the Zulu showed this. It is implied in, e.g., Kuper, H., 'Kinship among the Swazi' in *African Systems of Kinship and Marriage*, op. cit., at pp. 92–3 ; Schapera, I., *Married Life in an African Tribe*, London : Faber & Faber (1940), Chapter I ; Krige, E. J. and J. D., *The Realm of a Rain-Queen*, London : Oxford University Press (1943), Chapter XI.

[2] Epstein, A. L., (i) *The Administration of Justice and the Urban African*, op. cit., pp. 62 ff. ; (ii) *Juridical Techniques and the Judicial Process : A Study in African Customary Law : Rhodes-Livingstone Paper No. 23*, Manchester University Press (1954), pp. 31 f. ; (iii) 'Divorce Law and Stability of Marriage among the Lunda of Kazembe', *Rhodes-Livingstone Journal*, XIV (December, 1952).

marriages is clearly related to this situation. I omitted to enquire into this problem.

As we shall be considering cases of adulterous and absconding wives, I must note in justice to Lozi women that many of them are virtuous and chaste. Their behaviour rarely comes before the courts, though I have recorded cases in which women trapped would-be seducers for their husbands. Moreover, affection and common love for children are characteristic of most wedded couples.

V

The kuta may have before it a different kind of case which compels it to widen the field of its enquiry. The kuta is not only a judicial forum but also a council watching over the public interest in land, in schools, in prices, etc., etc. A dispute may raise a question of public policy : the kuta will then speak as a legislative and administrative council, and enquire into any issue, though as a court it should only punish offences against the law.

CASE 7 : THE CASE OF THE EXORBITANT FISHMONGER

Charge against a youth for selling fish at too high prices.
Saa-Katengo Court, Lialui, 21st August, 1942
(From a summary by MR. D. S. SIANGA)

A youth who was caught by Sergeant Mulele selling fish to people at four small fish for 6d., was sent by the Provincial Commissioner to SOLAMI [R3, head of the kuta]. When the kuta examined his affair, it found that this price of two fish for 3d. was just stealing the people's money—ALULEYA-IFUNGA (L8), LIOMA (L6), KAMAKUNYI (L–), ING'UNDE (R20) and many councillors said the price of fish should return to earlier prices, by which 3d. bought 3 fish and 1s. bought 12 fish.

SOLAMI agreed with all the kuta and said : ' If the kuta wishes to inform the whole country of Barotseland of the price for fish set by the kuta, I have not power at this time to summon the whole nation to the kuta because the NGAMBELA (R1) is not here. When the NGAMBELA arrives I will report this affair to him because we all know very well that reeds, grass and poles are no longer bought at the decent prices agreed to in the past ; and if the prices of fish are increased greatly thus, why is it ? If the owner of the country [the NGAMBELA] agrees in this affair as we have spoken, it is easy for me to gather the country and tell the people the prices set.' SOLAMI went on to scold the kuta, saying : ' All prices are ruined by you of the capital. The year before last you began to sell your sacks at a higher price—a sack of cassava meal we sold for ourselves for £1, of millet for £1 2s. 6d., of maize for 19s. And by this custom the Lunda [trading meal and grain from Balovale District] took these bad prices ; and afterwards when you failed to find food which you could sell, and had yourselves to buy from the Lunda, you complained greatly. The fault was not the Lunda's but yours—they saw it in you of the capital. When you began to complain of the bad prices of the Lunda, you asked me to discuss the matter with the District Commissioner, and indeed I carried out your request. Now a basket such as we set to be the scale of the whole nation has been sent by the District Commissioner—now we have no complaint.' The youth was instructed to go away with his fish.

Here the head of the kuta took it on himself to upbraid his fellow-judges and ruled that general price-control required legislation,[1] which must await the return from a journey of the NGAMBELA, the chief councillor. He dismissed the case under trial since the accused had committed no offence, and added that if the court wished he would raise the matter for legislation.

A kuta judgment may also contain warning of administrative action against a party or parties of whom it disapproves for any reason.

CASE 9 : THE CASE OF THE UNUSED LAND

In 1940 Sikwela and Akawi of Katongo disputed who was holder of certain land on the margin of the Plain. Katongo falls under Tungi sub-district kuta, under Induna MUNONO (R23). Therefore the Saa-Katengo kuta at Lialui ordered MUNONO to investigate the quarrel on the spot with the men of Katongo (Namalya) Kuta and

---

[1] The kuta similarly asserted that legislation could not make an offence of what was lawful before, in :

CASE 8 : THE CASE OF THE HIPPO HUNTER

In 1942 Government accepted a Lozi plea that hippo hides were kingly goods, and not tribute, and that the Lozi Paramount Chief had not lost his rights to half the hide of each hippo killed, under the treaty in which he gave up his claims to tribute (see my *Essays on Lozi Land and Royal Property*, Livingstone : *Rhodes-Livingstone Paper No. 10* (1943), pp. 78 ff. and 87–8). The kuta dismissed a charge against a man who sold the whole hide of a hippo which he had shot before the promulgation of the new edict re-establishing the Paramount Chief's rights.

to draw a boundary between the lands of Akawi and Sikwela. When MUNONO went to the land in question he found that it was not being cultivated and had not been cultivated for many years. He up-braided the litigants harshly, asking them how they could quarrel over unused land, when many people were hungry for land. He warned them that he would report this to the kuta which would take the land from them and give it to landless people. [The kuta in fact has not power to do this ; but the Lozi look so askance at people who hold unused land where land is wanted, that it would have been difficult for the litigants to refuse a request from the king for the land.]

This type of judicial action is carried a step further when the kuta in fact carries out an administrative enquiry and takes administrative action in a dispute brought before it for other reasons. The process is implicit in the kuta's practice of con-verting a ' civil dispute ' between two parties, into a ' criminal charge ' against one or both of them, or even against a witness. The kuta does this because the kuta as a whole is also a political council, and it levies prosecutions for offences either as a body or through one of its own members. It commands a police force, and the police act directly on its orders.

We have seen the kuta threaten to fine for general misconduct in ' The Case of the Biassed Father '. But the case in my records which best illustrates how a kuta may widen its enquiry to investigate the background of a dispute, by virtue of its responsi-bilities as a political council, is one I heard at the Njoko River in Sesheke District at the kuta of sub-district induna SIFUWE, some 100 miles from Mwandi, the capital responsible for the kuta.

CASE 10: THE CASE OF THE QUARRELSOME TEACHER

Munyama, teacher at the Luanja River School vs. Mutepa and other Lubale villagers, 31st January, 1942

Unfortunately I missed most of the litigants' pleas as I was late in getting to the kuta, since I was doctoring my carriers' ills. I arrived to hear the end of the defendants' pleas.

In this case the plaintiff was the teacher at a Catholic school on the Luanja River, two river valleys away from the Njoko River where the kuta stands. He sued a number of Lubale villagers whose homes were near the school, for damage done by their goats to the school gardens. This area is largely inhabited by Totela people as indigenes, but among them are many villages of Lubale and related tribes, immigrants from Angola who are moving steadily eastwards across Barotseland. These people are known by the Lozi and their fellow-indigenes as Mawiko (people-of-the-west). The Wiko now number a considerable part of the Barotse nation, but are in some ways despised by the older tribes. The Lubale defendants admitted that their goats had damaged the gardens but counterclaimed against the teacher on the grounds that he had insulted them, by telling them : ' You wretched Lubale, I'll have you driven out of the country.' The induna of the kuta was an Nkoya, SIFUWE, appointed by the Lialui kuta.

When I entered the kuta, the leader of the defendants was speaking. He was complaining that the teacher had ordered the children to drive the goats out of the garden : ' The children are mine, not the teacher's. The teacher does not own the school. I built the school, and made the things inside it. The school belongs to the country ; if the teacher goes, the school continues. The teacher is not the lord of the school. He works for money. We have lived well with nine teachers ; only with this one are there constant quarrels. The induna is always writing to Sesheke [site of the District capital, Mwandi]. The teacher had no right to scold the children, I the father can do it. The teacher angered me with his bad words, that he would drive me out of the country, the wretched Lubale. Also, if the goats go to the bush they will starve. I did not seize a stick to hit the teacher.'

Teacher : ' Lies, you did.'

Lubale : ' I am not a Totela, or a Lozi, but a Lubale : but even if I am a Lubale, I am of the country.'

Kuta clerk : ' The teacher sent this affair to Sesheke . . .'

Teacher (interrupting) : ' No, I informed the induna. Three men came to the village of the school. I told my White people the missionaries so that they could tell the District Commissioner at Sesheke.'

Lubale : ' I told my brothers-in-law that I did not know if the teacher drinks strong medicine to make him so quarrelsome.'

A long discussion ensued about where the garden was and then the kuta clerk asked : ' Who started the quarrel ? '—*Teacher :* ' The Lubale.'

Clerk : ' I don't know if you drink strong medicines. Listen, teacher, many people come here to complain against you and to ask that you be changed. They are not all Lubale, but also Totela, and women and youths. We have written twice to the LIASHIMBA [the chief councillor of the District capital]. The Totela say that you are their kinsman, but they complain. There is a Totela proverb :

" The crocodile seizes the ox which is a fool," that, is which does not know how to drink, but passes the other oxen to where the crocodile is. We had a case of another teacher, an Nkoya, who was sacked. We don't know about that case, it was an affair of the big missionaries. But perhaps you have anger in your heart. A teacher should not be thus, he should be polite. There are two affairs here—that of the goats, and that of the quarrel.'

The teacher defended himself vehemently.

Clerk : ' Listen, teacher, the things done by you at Luanja are heard here. There is another word of yours : " This is the country of my father." '—*Teacher :* ' The Church is the owner of the country.' The clerk shook his head and a man sitting in the kuta near the induna said : ' No-one can say " It is my country." I cannot and you cannot.'—*Teacher :* ' No, I do not say it is my country.'

Clerk : ' You cannot say it is your country. I can, for my father reported to the Capital [he was related to SIFUWE]. Now at Sama-kala's place [where the teacher's family lived], who is the owner of the country ? '—*Teacher :* ' It is the king.'

Clerk : ' At the moment who rules there ? '—*Teacher :* ' SIFUWE.'

Clerk : ' In the papers of the people, is it signed Samakala [the teacher's senior kinsman] or whom—what chief ? '—*Teacher :* ' SIFUWE . . .' He started to talk vociferously and the clerk inter-rupted : ' You do not listen. A litigant's heart fights. How then can you say you will chase men from the country ? ' He turned to ask all the defendants : ' If you move from Luanja river, whose fault is it ? '—*They chorussed :* ' The teacher's ! '

Teacher : ' This Lubale Mutepa and his people asked money for building the school, for their children working in the school garden, and for many other things [which he listed]. I know only this quarrel with Mutepa, no other. Only once I hit a boy on the head not knowing that he had a sore on the head, and people came and cursed me. I told them : " I did wrong, I did not know of the sore." I know only of these two affairs.'

Clerk : ' There is a third, coming from Totela. We do not know if it is the truth. They complain : " The teacher troubles our children greatly, sending them to pick *manzauli* and *mahuluhulu* wild fruit in the bush and take them to his mother." (The induna interjected : " 5 sacks.") " Our children go to school to learn, not to fetch things for his mother." There is another complaint, also from Totela—because these things come to us—that you took the schoolchildren to the river-bank to carry water to put on a garden like rain. You are ruining the Luanja River community.'—*Teacher :* ' I don't know about the *mahuluhulu* fruit. About the *manzauli* fruit, I did not send the children but asked them to give me of what they got, and they

gave some to me. On the second affair, last year there was no rain,
I heard the boys say they would put water on the maize. This is it :
people talk because they do not understand schools.'

The clerk referred to the teacher's complaint that the Lubale asked
to be paid for work on the school : ' The Catholic Fathers go on
tour asking for complaints. The people have a right to complain
to their chiefs, the District Commissioners and the Missionaries.'

Sankope (headman at Masese stream, sitting in kuta, on the induna's
right) : ' I know this affair for I went to ask the Father at Sicili
Mission for a pass and he told me : " The people of Luanja are
bad." '

The leader of the Lubale spoke about the wild fruits : ' There
were two sacks. On this, teacher, it is your affair. As for payment
for the school, the Missionary said : " If you do not want to give
to collection, it is all right, the children will pay with their millet." '

Teacher : ' The water was not on my own garden at Sizibi stream,
but on the school-garden at the Luanja. This affair is awakened by
hatred [using the English word].'

The clerk quoted : ' The Bible says in the Prophets, " Look at
the mote in your own eye," so you, teacher, must look to your own
faults.'

The induna then rebuked the teacher. He made a long speech on
the theme that the Lubale were people of the king, and so was the
teacher. He concluded : ' This country is that of my father who
cared for it for the king. The case of the goats should have been
brought to us, the rest is very bad.'

Clerk : ' This is my father's place. He took you to the capital
to report you.'

Teacher : ' Mutepa first said he would take me out of the
country . . .'

Clerk : ' This affair of spoiling the Luanja will go to the big kuta
at Mwandi. SIFUWE cannot give people permission to leave the
Luanja to come to the Njoko and leave the school deserted. It is
you who do it—we will get a new person.'—*Teacher* : ' It is they
who make me live badly, and the goats. . . .'

The induna, interrupting : ' Listen, the affair of the goats was a
fault, they admit it. We talk of the big affair of the bad words.
The clerk's and Sibofu's cattle smashed the kuta building. We did
not tell them to get out of the country. They fixed it.'

The teacher tried to speak but was again interrupted by the kuta
policeman (himself a Wiko of the Lucazi tribe) : ' You, teacher,
thought that if you brought a case you would set us against these
people. Not so. You think you cannot be discharged. If the
White District Commissioner wants to pull SIFUWE out of his work,

sifuwe cannot complain and say it was the work of his father. If sifuwe is bad he is sacked and another put in. So if you are bad, you can be taken out of your work. These Lubale are people of the king—you cannot go and say " Get out " to them. No-one can say if he is taken out of his work : " The soil is mine, the water is mine." He goes and another takes his place. The goats are another affair : Mutepa [the Lubale] admits the damage they did and will pay 1s. each.'

Sankope spoke on the theme that the teacher ought to live well with the people. ' The teacher is very full of anger. He must not despise the Lubale, who are people of the country. Do not talk of wretched Lubale—the Lubale have come here to strengthen our king, perhaps tomorrow they will surpass us in strengthening him. (Loud clapping by the Lubale.) It is your angry heart that makes trouble.'

The teacher burst out so furiously that no-one could hear what he was trying to say, and Siloka, another headman, said : ' We want to hear no more of wretched Lubale than of wretched Totela.'

Induna sifuwe : ' Not only words show the truth, but the look in a man's eyes : if he is angry you know he may have done wrong.'

The clerk asked the teacher : ' Where is Samakala's village ? ' [the village of the teacher's family]—*Teacher :* ' At Luanja.'

Clerk : ' No, it is dead, they are at Masese and Sizibi. You are the child of Samakala, now at Sizibi. These Lubale worked the land before you arrived, they planted there always. Remember, no man stops in work forever, if he is bad ; a foreman at the Saw-mills [at Macili, not far away] was sacked because he was bad to the men under him. I have not seen a Lubale complaining before, but Totela, and of your own family, of Samakala. You can be taken out of your job ; that does not mean out of the country.'—*The teacher* burst out : ' I'll leave the work . . . but there is no teacher who will live well at Luanja.'

Siloka : ' Those who complain are not Lubale, but of the country and of your own womb. I agree with the clerk. Who is it that makes the quarrels in the country ? It is you.'—*Teacher :* ' I did not know of all the complaints ; no-one came to me. The sacks were gifts. I know of the complaints of this man Mutepa. I called them politely to drive out the goats.'

There was a pause, then the clerk asked : ' The goats—how many were there ? Let us settle this part.'

The Lubale began to count them, and the teacher said : ' A lot ', to be silenced by the clerk : ' We ask whose goats they were. We'll place the damage.'

When it was worked out that there were four kraals of goats, the induna said : ' These four kraals will pay for the teacher's garden, 1s. for each goat. This affair of the country—soil has no owner ! Soil has one owner ?—it is soil of the king [i.e. people only hold land subject to the king]. This is a bad thing, to say " you have come from far." They are placed by the king. The Lubale will pay.'

Clerk : ' Is the money of the Treasury ? '

Induna : ' The money is of the garden owner ; we do not eat it.'

Policeman : ' Yes, the money is of the owner—the teacher or his lord.'

There was some argument about whether the judgment meant 1s. a goat or 1s. a kraal, and while it was going on SIFUWE muttered to himself : ' Who is he, this teacher, to drive people out of the country ? Just a boy.'

The defendant : ' We'll pay him for the goats, but we'll leave his river.'

Clerk : ' Do not go by a bad custom, to leave because the kuta makes you pay for goats which have eaten crops.'

They then protested that 1s. a goat was too much, and SIFUWE said it should be 6d. or 3d. each ; it was finally fixed at 3d. per goat. The Lubale had lost that part of the case so they paid the kuta fees.

Clerk : ' The teacher has no power here—it is of the kuta. The teacher will teach—a person of the kuta will collect the money of the damages. You people do not meet again in this affair.'

The Lubale defendant said as he paid the fee : ' We must live well with the teacher, as we did in the past. Let him teach.'

Induna SIFUWE : ' You, teacher, these are my people. I am hurt in the Government's service ' [touching an abscess he ascribed to a sorcerer jealous of his position]. ' Direct your own work well. Look at this other school, it is peaceful and the children fill it.' The case ended here, though the Lubale still complained among themselves of the teacher. The teacher later came to me and asked me if he were in the wrong, saying the others did not understand the customs of schools. I told him that if one found all the people were against one, one was usually in the wrong.

This case requires little comment. In effect, the kuta had before it two suits : (1) the teacher claimed damages for the spoiling of the garden by the goats, and the Lubale admitted liability ; (2) the Lubale counter-claimed vaguely because of his threat to drive them out of the country. It was on this issue that the kuta seized its opportunity to cross-examine and upbraid the teacher on his general behaviour. It did this as overseer of the work of all public functionaries in the country. Again, however, we see that the kuta acted thus because in Barotseland relationships are multiplex, and these have to be protected in their entirety. The suit over the goats raised the whole problem of the school's position in the community, and that had to be safeguarded. The ' civil suit ' over the goats included a ' criminal trial ' of the teacher. In criticizing his handling of the school and his relationships with the people, the judges lectured on ' a teacher's station and its duties '. Both the Lubale and the teacher on the whole agreed with the judges' views of these duties ; hence cross-examination and judgment were possible, despite the dispute over the facts.

I must note one other feature of this case, though its full significance falls outside this study.[1] The court clerk here took the most prominent part in cross-examination and judgment, though strictly he is not a judicial member but a servant of the court. This often happens in the inferior kutas, where the clerk may be the only educated man : at the capitals' kutas clerks on the whole take insignificant parts in judicial proceedings. The Lozi still maintain that anyone has a right to take part in the kuta's deliberations ; it is rarer for ordinary men to do so at the capitals where councils have many title-holders.

VI

In short, the task of Lozi judges is the same as the task of judges in all societies. They have to right wrongs, to adjust claims, to defend norms ; and where permanent relationships are con-cerned, they have to strive to prevent these from being broken. In our own society, this last process is not so clearly a part of the judicial function, because lawyers are part of our whole juridical system, and it is they, more than judges, who negotiate recon-ciling settlements in family disputes. Many people in Britain are urging that marriage guidance councils are needed to replace divorce courts, in order to handle matrimonial suits, since the husband-wife relationship at the apex of our isolated small family is so important for us. Similar councils exist to handle employer-employee disputes in another of our basic sets of relationships. There is therefore no special quality about African law and

---

[1] See my article in *Seven Tribes of British Central Africa*, p. 58.

law-courts as such which leads to a stress on reconciliation—
'the restoration of social equilibrium' is the sort of phrase used
to describe an almost mystical process.[1]   Reconciliation of the
parties becomes one of the main aims of the judges when the
parties are in a relationship which it is valuable to preserve ;
and to achieve this aim requires a broadening of enquiry and
hence of the concept of 'relevant evidence'.   But this aim
does not lead to a sacrifice of legal or moral rules, since wrongdoers are upbraided and punished where they have failed to
conform to these.   The search for 'equilibrium' is not to be
explained by saying, as Driberg does, that African 'law is an
organic growth, inherent in the body politic and accepted just
because it is organic, coherent and traditional'.   Social control
in Africa, as elsewhere, operates positively because failure to
maintain norms of a relationship sets up disturbances in the
relationships themselves,[2] but the process of adjudicating on
disputes is highly rational.   This is clear if we consider how in
cases between strangers the judges concentrate on the narrow
issue involved ; it is indeed clear when they are reconciling
litigants who are in permanent relationship.

There is then nothing vague about the judicial process among
the Lozi.   They will not, at any rate nowadays, listen to vague
complaints unless the plaintiff can state what he or she claims,
and unless that claim establishes rights and duties which the kuta
can determine.

CASE 11 : THE CASE OF THE VAGUE COMPLAINT

On 7th August, 1942, a woman appealed to the Saa-Katengo Kuta
at Lialui from Prince MWENEKANDALA about a decision arising from
her husband's divorcing her.   She began a long and rambling story
about the marriage-payment, how they had separated on a journey,
and what her parents and relatives had said.   The judges cut her

---

[1] This is a weakness in an article on a South African Bantu tribe which
otherwise has many excellent points : Krige, J. D., ' Some Aspects of Lovhedu
Judicial Arrangements', *Bantu Studies*, xiii. 2 (June, 1939), pp. 113 ff.   See
also his chapter on ' The Genius of Juridical Arrangements' in *The Realm
of a Rain-Queen*.   The late J. H. Driberg also clearly stated these views in
' The African Conception of Law ', *The Journal of Comparative Legislation
and International Law*, xv (November, 1934), pp. 230 ff.

[2] See Homans, G. C., *The Human Group*, London : Routlege & Kegan
Paul (1951), Chapter 11.

short : ' Come to the point. What are you claiming ? ' (' *Fweka* [land]. *Ubangang'i na* ? ') Again she rambled and again she was told to state her claim : ' We cannot understand your dispute.' They told the clerk to take notes till he found out what she wanted, so that they could have a dispute (*muzeko*) into which to enter.

It happens therefore that in some cases a plaintiff will sue on a claim he knows is unfounded, in order to bring before the kuta some kinsman he considers has wronged him in diffuse ways.

CASE 12 : THE CASE OF THE UNFOUNDED CLAIM

Saa-Katengo Kuta, Lialui, August, 1940

Thus a younger brother sued his elder brother for a beast, knowing he would lose, but hoping the kuta would reprimand his brother for steadily failing to treat him properly. The kuta found for the elder brother, but scolded him roundly for not treating his younger brother properly. Since their father's death he had become the father : he must take care of his younger brother. But [since the hierarchy must be upheld] the younger must respect his senior.

A person may even commit an offence in order to provoke another to hale him to court. In Loziland the relationships of spouses and their in-laws are fraught with difficulties and tension. Husband and wife should be meticulous in respecting and attending on the other's kin. Where a husband fails in his duties to his in-laws, his wife can claim divorce in the kuta. The husband himself can divorce an erring wife but may not wish to do so. Were he just to complain to the kuta, bringing his wife before the judges in order that she might be scolded, he would be a laughing-stock because he was unable to rule her.

CASE 13 : THE CASES OF THE INSULTING SONS-IN-LAW

Therefore two husbands, reliable informants, told me that they insulted their fathers-in-law. One husband snatched food from his father-in-law who was visiting him. Naturally the father-in-law went off in high dudgeon. The husband sent messengers after him with hoes as placatory gifts to explain why he had acted thus. The wife rushed to court and demanded a divorce. She was severely reprimanded and the kuta ordered that the hoes be returned. Thus the husband succeeded in drawing public attention to his wife's behaviour. The other husband acted similarly. In both cases the

H

husband, though entitled to the hoes as being fully in the right, said that he had not taken them back, to emphasize to his father-in-law that he had no quarrel with him.

VII

Cases to be cited in later chapters will illustrate further how disputes arising out of multiplex relationships have to be settled by broadening the scope of enquiry to cover a long history of relations between the parties and their kin and neighbours, and perhaps their forebears. The situation is similar where a man quarrels with one of his overlords or underlings (see ' The Case of the Disrespectful Induna', p. 152). In this volume, I concentrate on presenting the judicial process at work in this category of cases, since they present the judges with their most complex task, and in matrimonial cases. I shall refer to more straightforward cases, of crimes, delicts, and contracts involving strangers, but it eases my task of exposition to cite in detail most of these cases when I analyse *The Ideas of Barotse Jurisprudence*. However, these cases must be borne in mind in a total assessment of the Lozi judicial process.

What has emerged so far is that there should be a ' legal' claim into which the kuta can enter, but the kuta, if there is a multiplex relationship between the disputants, may become concerned with far more than that claim. The concept of ' relevant evidence' may therefore be very wide. The kuta attempts to reconcile parties in permanent relationships. In all these enquiries the judges weigh the behaviour of the parties—the facts in the case, which they arrive at by cross-examination—against accepted customs and accepted standards of law and morals. These customs and standards are commonly accepted by judges, litigants and witnesses : hence even when persons lie they do so in terms of these norms. This enables the judges to cross-examine them, and to give judgments against them which are communicable, even if rejected. The problems involved here will be further considered in the next chapter.

Thus when the judges give judgments, even where they are trying to reconcile the parties, they reprimand the evildoer and praise the good by these norms. For if the parties are to be reconciled, and thereafter to live together harmoniously, they must be shown where they have done wrong, and they and others require guidance to act uprightly and forbearingly. In these cases a litigant comes before the judges not only as a right-and-duty bearing *persona*, but also as an individual involved in a complex of relations with many other persons. Correspondingly, there is no such thing as judicial ignorance, and any judge who knows the parties will volunteer evidence and use his knowledge in judgment. But guilt must be demonstrated in each case and not by previous record. The court takes judicial notice of any relevant matter in its knowledge, as was exhibited in the way in which the judges in 'The Case of the Prince's Gardens' themselves narrated the history of the villages and gardens. This is essential if the judges are to fulfil their task of reconciliation in a particular case. But as they have to maintain the law, they expound in public the rights and duties of headman, villager, father, son, brothers, husband, wife, etc., and these form units which are the nuclei of the substantive law. In other cases, which do not involve persons in permanent formal relationships, the kuta may also widen its enquiry, for all relationships tend to be expanded to the pattern of multiplex kinship bonds. Finally, the kuta, as a body which is judicial, administrative, legislative, ecclesiastical, and military, may also at any point consider any public interests involved; and it may therefore levy a fine in a civil suit, in effect converting it into a criminal trial.

The kuta has a clear conception of relevance in evidence, and of what the law it should enforce is (see 'The Case of the Exorbitant Fishmonger' and 'The Case of the Hippo Hunter', pp. 69–70); but what is relevant varies with the dispute. In cases requiring reconciliation, apparently irrelevant facts may be extremely important. It is clear that were the demands of some British officers, that the kuta should follow English legal procedure, to be successful, the kuta would be prevented from fulfilling one of its main functions—the settlement of disputes arising out of the multiplex relationships which are still basic in tribal life.

CHAPTER III

CROSS-EXAMINATION AND THE ASSESSMENT OF EVIDENCE: THE NORM OF THE REASONABLE MAN

I

OBVIOUSLY the first steps in the judges' work are to listen to the evidence, cross-examine on it, and attempt to establish what in fact occurred. The Lozi have no lawyers, though complainants are presented to the kuta by their over-lord councillors and these may expound their pleas to the kuta : therefore the whole onus of eliciting and analysing the evidence falls on the judges.

The judicial establishment of 'truth' is not always simply finding that 'such-and-such is what happened'. Legal truth involves the assessment of what happened in terms of both legal and moral norms. For the judges have to find out who has conformed with the law, and who has broken it. Indeed, the statements of the parties are usually cast so that they seem to have conformed with these norms, and it is by these norms that the judges examine and attack evidence. They question litigants, and witnesses, wherever their statements seem to show that they have deviated from accepted usage and established be-haviour, and implicitly reprimand any deviations : thus in prac-tice judges begin their task of judgment during cross-examination. This process is most marked in cases in which the judges are attempting to reconcile persons in multiplex relationship.

The Lozi distinguish between different kinds of evidence as hearsay, circumstantial, and direct, and attach different degrees of cogency to these and different degrees of credibility to various witnesses. All these problems will be examined in detail, but I wish first to establish that their chief weapon in attacking evidence is to catch persons in departures from usages and norms. Some of these usages are definite, in the sense that a person either has or has not conformed with them. But many norms of behaviour are of the general pattern : 'respect and help your father'; 'treat the headman of your village properly';

' treat your wife well ' ; ' arbitrate impartially in quarrels among your dependants '. In their daily lives people should attempt to abide by these norms. The norms can be fulfilled in varying degrees, and therefore the judges require a standard by which to assess fulfilment. This standard is ' the reasonable and customary man and what he would have done '.

The reasonable man is recognized as the central figure in all developed systems of law,[1] but his presence in simpler legal systems has not been noticed. My experience with Lozi and Zulu emboldens me to assert that he is equally important in these systems. We have indeed already met the Lozi reasonable man in every case cited, in the guises of the impartial father-headman, the respectful and helpful son, the loving brother, the polite teacher, and the reasonably faithful husband. I shall later expound his full legal significance in these manifold capacities, but here first consider how the judges use him to assess the evidence presented to them. This is brought out clearly in :

CASE 14 : THE CASE OF THE VIOLENT COUNCILLOR

Mutebele vs. SAYWA *(R27), Saa-Katengo Kuta at Lialui, 27th August, 1942*

The defendant was himself a member of the Saa-Katengo Kuta, and the same day had given judgment in ' The Case of the Biassed Father' (at p 41). Since SAYWA was in effect accused of failing to run his village affairs properly, it is interesting to repeat his judgment upbraiding the father : ' Y, listen carefully to what the Malozi say. You must finish quarrels among your children. If your own son starts quarrels with the others, do not support him. You must strengthen your children. . . . Finish the quarrels and pray together.'

This case came on appeal from sub-district induna IKANJIWA (R38). In Loziland there are two types of villages. One type comprises

---

[1] Most textbooks of jurisprudence consider ' reasonable man ' and ' reasonable standards ' under separate heads, such as proof of guilt, responsibility, intention, negligence, etc. ; and the central legal significance of the concept, as the foundation of law, is perhaps best—and wittily—brought out by Sir Alan Herbert in ' The Reasonable Man ', *Uncommon Law*, London : Methuen (1935), pp. 1 ff. He gives a magnificent description of ' the reasonable man ' in a case where the judges hold that ' a reasonable woman ' does not exist in English law.

villages occupied by members of a single grouping of kindred. I call the other type royal villages, because they belong to the king, to a prince or princess or queen, or to one of the kuta titles. A royal village may be occupied by a set of kin, or by a number of men and women of different kinship groupings and often of different tribes. Among these royal villages are the burial villages of kings. Each of these villages is under an induna whose title was established by the king who chose that village for his cenotaph. This induna is supposed to rule the villagers fairly and without partiality in favour of his own kinsfolk. SAYWA was induna of the selected burial village of the then [1942] reigning king.

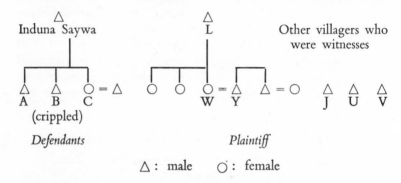

Induna Saywa   L   Other villagers who
                                            were witnesses

A   B   C = △   O   O   O = △   △ = O   J   U   V
(crippled)   W   Y

Defendants   *Plaintiff*

△ : male   ○ : female

The version of the plaintiff and his witnesses was : During the previous year the induna's schoolboy son, A, had made advances to the sisters of the wife of Y, one of the villagers not related to the induna. In 1942 he did so again, and when they remonstrated he said : ' This year is not last year. I have grown up. You cannot make me defaecate.' The reference here is to an old Barotse punishment of throttling a man until he defaecated—hence the boy meant, ' You cannot make me feel small.' Then he insulted the plaintiff's wife. Y, the plaintiff, challenged him. A said Y called him ' bloody fool ', Y said A threatened him : ' You will defaecate ', i.e. ' be choked until you defaecate when we fight,' a common and insulting threat. They fought. L, father-in-law of Y and head of the household in which Y lived, came in and heard the noise. In his evidence L said : ' I reproved Y for unseemly behaviour in his father-in-law's court-yard, saying that in the past a young man would kneel before his father-in-law.' A and Y still fought, with L intervening. They knocked over the gateway of L's courtyard fence into the fire, and upset a pot of water. L had warned Y that he would be responsible for damage, but it was L who put out the fire. L then caught Y by the wrist, saying, ' When you are fighting and your father-in-law seizes you by the wrist, you stop.'[1] Y stopped fighting and L led him to his own hut. L returned, and asked an old woman who had been by the fire whether she had been hurt. She replied : ' I do not feel burnt, but I may be burnt.' L rebuked her : ' If you are burnt it is your own fault, because when people are fighting by a fire, you should get out of the way.' [Note the implication : if you do not behave reasonably you cannot blame others for your injuries.] Y's wife, W, tied up the gate of their courtyard to stop Y going to the induna's courtyard, for she said if he did the induna's children would kill him : ' They are bad ; truly you will have died.' L, who was eating, said he heard his daughter [wife of Y] say this, and then shout that Y was going to the induna's courtyard. Another man, J, followed him. Y entered the induna's courtyard and alleged that he was there attacked by the induna's children.

Y said he fell on the ground, being choked by some of the children and seized around the middle by another. SAYWA then dragged him several yards by the wrist with the youngsters still clinging to him. He screamed : ' SAYWA is breaking me, SAYWA is breaking me.' Y's wife arrived and shouted at SAYWA : ' You are fighting, leave him.' SAYWA did so. He went and got a whip which was taken from him by his son-in-law. He then sent a child for a stamping pole which was also taken from him. The induna's daughter, C, who had Y round the belly, then cried, ' He has defaecated,' and they released him. Y was carried to his courtyard by his wife and another man, U, who came along. U's evidence was that he heard Y screaming ' SAYWA is breaking me ' and the daughter call out ' He has defaecated.' He also gave evidence that Y's arm was swollen. Another man, V, confirmed that he too had heard these shouts.

Y sued the children, joined with their father, at the local sub-district kuta. The case lasted two days : he claimed £1 from the induna and from each of his children. Y said in the appeal kuta, hearing the case anew, that the sub-district kuta head, IKANJIWA (R38), in court had sent a man for hot water to bathe Y's arm. SAYWA (R27) was IKANJIWA's immediate superior in the indigenous political organization, but IKANJIWA sentenced him to pay £1, 10s. to Y, and 10s. to the kuta as a fine. Y asked for a letter of appeal because the kuta was taking his money, and IKANJIWA offered him 15s., with 5s. for the kuta. Y still said he would appeal. His wife claimed that all the members of the sub-district kuta decided that the induna and his children should each pay £1, but the head of the sub-district kuta penalized only the induna.

---

[1] Lozi should treat parents-in-law with great respect.

SAYWA's sons and daughter denied the whole story of the choking and squeezing.

SAYWA's defence was : ' Y came in and insulted my son, saying " A will defaecate today." I went to intercept Y at his courtyard to prevent a fight. Y was at his elder brother's courtyard so I missed him, and when I returned to my own place my children, two sons and my daughter, were on top of Y who was on the ground. I seized Y by the wrist to stand him up. When Y's wife came in I got a whip to scare the fighters. It was taken away from me. I got the stamping pole to put it out of the way so that no-one should use it as a weapon. I did not drag Y along the ground. The trouble in the village is made by the two sisters of Y's wife, who are whores and have been driven out of three villages. I have held my title for fifteen years and there has never been trouble before.'

The kuta suspended the hearing to send for the man, J, who had followed Y to the induna's courtyard. When he arrived next day he confirmed Y's version. He had followed Y to the induna's where the induna's children attacked Y. He, J, took B, the induna's crippled son, off Y's waist. The induna did drag Y. Then the daughter cried out : ' He has defaecated,' and they released him.

The direct evidence here was sufficient to enable the judges to find for Y, but they had to meet a statement by the induna which, I was told, was supported privately by a couple of judges who were related to him, that the people hated their induna and were ' binding him with lies ' ; and in addition they had to expose his ingenious defence of the motivations of his witnessed actions in order to establish his moral guilt of intention. Therefore they proceeded in cross-examination to break down his story. They examined the witnesses at length, stressing the importance of direct as against hearsay evidence. One witness was told : ' What you heard with your ears, what you saw with your eyes, describe to us. Hearing and seeing the quarrel and the fight are good, hearing about them is not.' They also took up the point that witnesses will perjure themselves for a kinsman. Thus they examined Y's arm to confirm for themselves that it was swollen. They told Y's wife that she should have shown Y's faeces to an independent witness before she washed his clothes. They went at some length into the times and places of various incidents and the positions of different witnesses in order to trap them into inconsistencies.

Then Prince Litooma tackled the induna's party on their denials. He cross-examined the induna : ' When Y came into your courtyard, why did you not tell him to sit down, and then summon your children, and the men of the village, so that you could enquire into the dispute between them?'—SAYWA hedged: 'They are binding me with lies.'

SOLAMI (R3), head of the court, pressed him: 'Why did you not make them sit down so that you could judge between them?'—SAYWA: 'I did not do this.'

SOLAMI, who is usually noted for his gentleness, went on angrily: 'You should have sat Y down, called your son A, and then summoned all the men of the village to hear their quarrel.'—SAYWA: 'I did not do this.'

SOLAMI: 'This is indunaship (*bunduna*)—this is ruling.'—SAYWA: 'It was night, I could not.'

SOLAMI: 'If an affair comes here to me in the capital at night I go to the NGAMBELA (R1, chief councillor), I call the senior councillors. If it is a thief, we put him in prison for the District Commissioner. Also, you say you tried to stand Y up, that you did not drag him. What manner of arbitrating in a fight is this, to seize the one who is on the ground, who is being fought, not to seize those who are overwhelming him?'

Here the kuta has set up two standards by which it can break down SAYWA's story. First, he did not behave as a reasonable man would do when arbitrating in a fight; second, his whole behaviour was not that of a reasonable induna, following the customs of a good induna. The kuta was aware that SAYWA was not so much concerned about the £1 damages and fine, but was afraid lest he should be discharged from his post, since it is a heinous offence for any councillor to use violence. This is implicit in another question asked him, though it seems to stem only from the concept of a reasonable man, for the kuta knew SAYWA hoped it would not hear of his case.

Prince Litooma challenged him: 'You deny that you were at fault. Why then when the lower kuta penalized you £1 did you not appeal?'—SAYWA: 'If a man is penalized, what can he do?'

Prince: 'He can appeal.'—SAYWA: 'I would have appealed if Y had not done so.'

Prince: 'But you did not protest in the lower kuta. This boy complained that the kuta was taking 10s. of his money as a fine, you did not protest that you should pay nothing.'—SAYWA: 'I thought we should go by IKANJIWA's judgment. I was being fined for my children's fault, not my own.'

ALULEYA-IFUNGA (L8): 'IKANJIWA would then have given damages against your children and you would have paid for them. But

IKANJIWA left them on one side. Your fault is that you, an induna, entered into the fight.'

With this dictum, the bias of the enquiry shifted openly from the assault to the issue of SAYWA's fitness to be an induna.

IMUTUKO (R28) : ' Why then when the plaintiff's wife cried, " The induna is fighting," did you release Y's wrist if you were trying to raise him ? You knew you were wrong, as an induna, to fight.'

Another prince : ' You say you came with the whip to frighten them. Is it your custom to threaten with a whip ? '—SAYWA, caught in a cleft stick because an induna, who is not a policeman, should not show violence, had perforce to answer ' No.'

Prince : ' Did you shout as you came with the whip, to show that you wanted to beat them, and did not mean to beat them ? ' —SAYWA : ' Yes.'

Prince : ' Then why has not one witness, of all who heard Y cry, said that he heard you shout ? '

The kuta adjourned to give judgment next day. My own servants and attendants, mostly members of SAYWA's political sector, that night canvassed SAYWA's chances of being discharged and stated explicitly for me precedents of the kind that were in everyone's minds : previous cases in which councillors had been punished for themselves using violence.

(1) NAWALA (R42) Muimanenwa, in a case at Namalya Kuta between two Wiko over a duiker, helped to tie up a Wiko. MBASI- WANA (R46) Mutondo (who told the story, which was confirmed by others) was not there. When he arrived he said NAWALA was wrong and must pay the Wiko damages. NAWALA refused and the others present supported him, so the case came before the kuta at the capital. The NGAMBELA (R1) supported MBASIWANA, and said that all present must pay, the king said only NAWALA. This NAWALA had been Head Messenger at the magistracy and was forgiven and reprieved from discharge because he acted by the customs of govern- ment messengers.

(2) KALONGA (R15) Mubita at Namakau Kuta told E to pay four beasts for adultery. E refused. KALONGA said E was mad and helped to tie him up. The kuta at the capital wanted to discharge KALONGA, but King Lewanika said, ' No, fine him.' He paid 10 beasts. At the time the Administration wanted to sack him, but the king said he would not.

(3) King Yeta III, who disapproved strongly of beer-drinking, once found some people with pots of beer in the capital. He himself broke the pots. The kuta, so my people said, summoned him into kuta, sat him on the ground and not in his chair, and wished to discharge him from the kingship. The councillors contended he was

a policeman and not a king, but the Whites intervened and pleaded that he be only reprimanded.

(4) In 1912 the NGAMBELA (R1) Mukamba's cattle went into the garden of a capital policeman, Wamunyima. Wamunyima hit the herder, Mukamba's son, and gave him a stiff neck. Wamunyima also came to the kuta in war-dress, with his shield and spears. King Lewanika declared that Wamunyima was making war and must not enter the kuta. So Mukamba was allowed to divest himself of the NGAMBELAship and fought Wamunyima, who was choked till he defaecated. King Lewanika would not interfere. Mukamba remained NGAMBELA, and of his own accord, but not by order of the kuta, paid Wamunyima a beast for the damage of his crops. [This case is by analogy in reverse : the NGAMBELA was allowed to resist force with force.]

(5) Before the Whites came, five indunas and the people of Ikatulamwa royal village attacked the resident induna, NOYOO (R13). They said he was a sorcerer. Each of the five indunas paid two beasts while each commoner paid one.

My people concluded : ' SAYWA has died, he was killed by IKANJIWA because he divided the money ' ; though MBASIWANA said it was all right for an induna to threaten with a sjambok to frighten people.

One of them reported to us that some important indunas, meeting with SAYWA that evening, contended that SAYWA was being trapped with lies ; not one person had changed his evidence to back SAYWA, which showed that all hated him. The head of my carriers commented dryly : ' It shows they have one tongue because they are telling what actually happened.' These indunas hoped for a fine and not dismissal, since ' a fine does not kill a man, but dismissal kills a man.'

I give a few of the unanimous judgments next day. A couple of the judges who were related to SAYWA did not give judgments, and their silence was reprimanded by the others.

IMUTUKO (R28) : ' SAYWA is in the wrong. He did not arbitrate. Why did he not tell Y to sit down so that he could enquire into the quarrel ? All the people in the village say you fought. You are their parent, and Y is just a person. If they were perjured, they would back you [i.e. this would be reasonable]. I see they tell the truth. The fault comes from your children, reaching to you, the parent. You must pay £1 for your children to Y. The lower kuta should not have taken a man's money for the Treasury.'

Prince Litooma : ' You, induna, we have heard all the evidence. The evidence kills you. All the evidence is good. The reasons which finish you are these : (1) Y came to your courtyard to explain the quarrel. You did not attend on his words. (2) I find that you fought because you were enraged. Why were you enraged?—because your crippled son fought Y. (3) In a fight, he who is arbitrating does not have his name shouted out : " So-and-so is breaking me." £1 is proper for an insult ; I say £2 because it was war, because you are the owner of the village who should arbitrate. You, A [the son], your behaviour was very bad. If you do it again, you will cause your father grievous trouble. Quieten your heart and change your ways. Whosoever comes to your father, do not fight. A child should tell his father of his quarrels. Your father is a big induna, who can call you all to his place so that he can enquire into grievances. You, SAYWA, do not favour your own children.'

INYUNDWANA (R21) : ' A, I agree. Your parent has erred greatly. You, SAYWA, you have erred so that we are astonished. A person entered your courtyard—that you should seize him, you, their parent ! And when his wife got you to stop, you seized a whip ! Nowadays with the White people here a whip is never taken for adults, only for children. Those who were eating heard Y call out " SAYWA is breaking me," and were afraid to enter a quarrel with you. [This was stated in evidence by two witnesses.] You have erred grievously. Today I am only cutting a walking-stick and you should pay £2 ' [i.e. if you repeat the offence the punishment will be far more severe, probably implying discharge].

SOLAMI (R3, head of the court) : ' You, SAYWA, you have erred very gravely. You do not rule the village as an induna should. You will pay £1 to Y, and it is all his. If you do it again, we will discharge you. And you, A, and your younger brother and your sister, you have no right to behave like that. You live in a village of the king, it is not your own village. You spoil that king's village —your behaviour and your father's will drive all the people from the king's village. The title of your father, SAYWA, is not a name that belongs to your family, and you need not think that you will inherit it. You are mere people, like the others in the village. You will bring an accident on your father. IKANJIWA did wrong in the lower court when he divided the money ; he should not cut the money of people, steal the money of people.'

Before I consider the relevance of this case to my present theme, the assessment of evidence, I glance at the way in which it illustrates the points made in the last chapter. I have shortened the case considerably. The facts were simple enough, but the kuta spent a couple of hours driving into the defendant's own story in order to convict him out of his own statement by exposing its ingenious falsity. SAYWA had elaborated an account of his witnessed actions—dragging the defendant, seizing the whip, picking up the stamping pole—to make it appear as if he had tried to stop the fight, and thus behaved as required by his rôles of citizen, headman and councillor. This story was also intended to cover up his, gross failure to summon a village-council to judge on the quarrel. In short, SAYWA accepted the same norms as the judges, and used them in his probably lying statement to make his behaviour appear reasonable. Hence the judges were able to cross-examine and expose him, and give judgment against him, by these same norms.

SAYWA would not admit that he was guilty, when I questioned him even five years later, but the judges undoubtedly demonstrated his wrongdoing to him. He may indeed in the heat of the moment have merely acted unwisely in trying to stop the fight, but this possible unwisdom arose from his failure to follow the appropriate rules of behaviour required of one in his position. Deviation from these rules in itself convicts, independently of the motives of the alleged wrongdoer : this will be further illustrated when I cite cases of adultery.

However, the judges obviously took considerable trouble to bring home to SAYWA the enormity of his offence and their disbelief in his innocence—if he were innocent, why did he not appeal ? Indeed, he did not appeal beyond this court to the higher Sikalo Court. They did so because the suit was not a complaint of assault by one stranger on another, but a complaint against the induna of a royal village and his children by one of his subordinates. They lived in the same village, and—unless the induna and his family were to be expelled from the village—future peace in the village depended on the settlement of the dispute and the guilty parties' recognition of their wrongdoing. The relations of the induna with all the villagers were implicitly involved : the people of the king's village should not be driven away from it. Here again the parties were not before the court as assaulted and assailant. A large part of their social personalities was involved : the assailants were an induna of a royal village and his children who had not stronger rights in the village than the other villagers, and the assaulted was one of these villagers. Should the offence merit the induna's discharge, he and his children might lose land-rights as well. The right-and-duty

bearing units involved were far more complex than those involved in an assault by one stranger on another. Similarly, in
'The Case of the Biassed Father' it emerged that a man cannot
sue for land merely as a landholder. A suit for land involves
his position as headman or villager, and his position in a kinship
grouping, and it may involve questions of how he has fulfilled
the general obligations of those positions.

In that case the garden dispute required, beyond judgment
on the simple rule of who had cultivating rights in the gardens,
an attempt to reconcile an extended family that was breaking
up. The past behaviour of all the parties was investigated and
they were all reprimanded. In the present case the kuta, both
as a court and as a political council, seemingly was so astonished,
and even horrified, by SAYWA's behaviour, that it concentrated
on what he had done without enquiring into the origins of the
quarrel : the plaintiff's behaviour, the allegations against SAYWA's
son, and the charge by SAYWA that the plaintiff's sisters-in-law
were whores. I suggest, too, that the less intimate relations of
unrelated royal-villagers require less emotional adjustment than
the relations of kinsfolk. The civil assault case was therefore
early on converted into a trial of the induna, with his seat on
the kuta and his position in the royal village both in jeopardy.
He might have been discharged, and this was made clear by the
judges even though their final decision was on the issue of
assault brought by the complainant to the kuta. The court
could have levied a fine as well as damages, like IKANJIWA, though
it did not do so. But in his judgment SOLAMI (R3) censured
SAYWA for not ruling as a reasonable induna should, and he and
other judges stated what the norms of indunaship are. They
scolded SAYWA's children for quarrelling in a village of the king,
and reminded them and their father that SAYWA was a national,
and not a family, title, in which their rights were ephemeral.
They could all be expelled from the village if their behaviour
frightened people away from the village. In short, because the
dispute arose in a multiplex enduring set of relationships the
kuta took time to convict SAYWA on his own version of the
facts, in order to fix his guilt firmly and to strengthen its up-
braidings : if he were to remain headman, he had to realize
that he must rule wisely. As a statement of the law, this had
to be affirmed for others.

In assessing the evidence judges asked for direct as against hearsay evidence : ' What you heard with your ears, what you saw with your eyes, describe to us. Hearing and seeing the quarrel and the fight are good, hearing about them is not.' The judges also stressed the importance of having independent witnesses, not related to the disputants, to corroborate their accounts. The complainant's wife was told she should have shown his dirtied trousers to an independent witness, and SAYWA was asked :

' Have you any favourable witnesses ? '—' No. '

' They are all your children ? '—' Yes.'

I shall return to these problems shortly. I stress here that in this case the defendant was convicted because the kuta was able to show that when his actions as he described them were measured against the ways in which a reasonable man would have behaved in the situation in question, they were the actions of an unreasonable man. Conversely, since the law presumes that good people act reasonably, the inference that the judges draw is that his actions could only be reasonably interpreted as those of a guilty person. Again, I note that SAYWA was guilty of wrongful behaviour for an induna, whatever his motives and intentions.

The kuta's main technique in cross-examination is therefore to state the norms of behaviour of a specific position, as the reasonable man would act in a perhaps unique situation. Wherever a party's own account shows deviations from these norms, the judges are able to attack him. Using these standards, they were able to drive wedges into SAYWA's story, break it up, and expose its probable falseness. These norms and standards form a large part of the body of rules which make up the *corpus juris* of Lozi law. In stating them the kuta may quote precedents of past decisions in court : in SAYWA's case, these precedents were implicit, though my own attendants quoted some to me. More often, the judges cite not past court-decisions, but actual instances of upright behaviour, to show how people ought to behave. Thus SOLAMI told SAYWA how he himself handled affairs coming to him at night. Law in this sense is constantly exhibited in the conformity of upright people to norms.

The norms erected by the judges in this process are both general and also specific to particular positions. The general standards were : if SAYWA wished to stop the fight as he claimed, why did he not drag off his assaulting children (as J did), but instead drag the plaintiff by the arm ? and if he were innocent, why did he not appeal against the decision in the lower court ?   [Court fees are low, and are not a consideration.]   The specific standards were :   why did not SAYWA, as a reasonable induna should, sit the plaintiff and his children down and summon the village kuta to investigate the quarrel ? and why, if he were using a whip only to frighten everybody, had he not shouted ?   The standard of the reasonable induna and headman, involved in a situation of relations between induna and underling in a royal village, required that SAYWA act by the customs of indunaship. Note how SOLAMI (at p. 87) pinned SAYWA : ' This is indunaship—this is ruling.'

The norm of the reasonable man is thus differentiated both in cross-examination and in judgment, according to the social positions of the parties.   The case in essence then became, not merely, ' Did SAYWA and his children commit the alleged assault ? ' but also, ' Did SAYWA conform to the norms of his office ? '   Wherever he did not, his departure from institutionalized behaviour counted against him and helped discharge the complainant's burden of proof.   A number of these breaches of custom together constitute circumstantial evidence amounting to probability of guilt.   Customs which are not legal rules, in the sense that the kuta will enforce conformity to them or penalize failure to observe them, become in this way indirectly enforceable at law.   In the process of social control every breach of custom is significant, since it disturbs the flow of social life : in courts of law almost all customs are sanctioned, indirectly if not directly.

This use of ' the reasonable man ',—or rather the reasonable and customary incumbent of a particular social position— obviously involves more than a technique of cross-examination. In Loziland it may pose the real issue of the case—was SAYWA a reasonable induna ? was the Biassed Father a reasonable headman ?   Many Lozi cases are thus converted from their original issue, for reasons examined in the preceding chapter.

We shall enquire into this process again. I have still, in considering SAYWA's case, to comment on the burden of proof, and where it lies.   In the course of an African trial it may seem that the defendant is considered guilty until he can prove that he is innocent. This is certainly not true of the Lozi.[1] The Lozi insist that responsibility and liability must be fixed, and I have heard many cases dismissed ' because the evidence is not strong ' (see LIOMA, L6, in ' The Case of the Schoolboy Adulterer,' below at p. 132). The NGAMBELA (R1) Wina showed me notebooks of cases at Lialui stretching from 1923 to 1930, before Lozi courts came under British supervision, and these are full of the decision : ' Case dismissed for lack of confirming evidence.' It is true that Lozi courts may find for a plaintiff, where a British magistrate would not on the grounds that the burden of proof was insufficiently discharged. But the kuta pounces on all unorthodox behaviour to find against the defendant, and British magistrates rarely have the knowledge to assess whether the litigants' accounts of how they behaved are or are not reasonable in the fullest sense. Though I had made a detailed study of Lozi custom, as I sat in court I occasionally felt myself forced into thinking ' not proven ', or so bewildered that I could not sort out the truth. Almost invariably as the judges expounded their reasons, I found these were sound.[2]

I may remark here that clearly it is difficult for a White to adjudicate in any complicated issue between Lozi, even with the help of assessors. Further, the demand of some law officers that African courts should confine themselves only to issues directly relevant to the subject of dispute is unwise. Were they to do this, they would be robbed of their main method of arriving at the truth. During my short visit to Loziland in 1947 I noted in the senior kutas that, since 1942, the kuta clerks had begun to record statements from the main litigants. In doing so, they bullied the litigants into confining themselves to what the clerks considered directly relevant to the claim in issue. Thereafter the hearing proceeded as before. Relevancy, as defined by the law officers, cannot be applied in a society such as that of the Lozi. We have already seen that it would also prevent the judges from fulfilling their rôle of adjusting the

---

[1] Or the Zulu, in whose courts I have also heard many cases tried.

[2] Professor J. D. Krige's statement that though he had been a practising barrister he would not give judgment when invited to do so by Lovhedu courts, because he felt that he could not achieve their justice, shows that this is a general, and not my personal, reaction. See his article, ' Some Aspects of Lovhedu Judicial Arrangements ', op. cit., pp. 114-15.

I

enduring and multiplex relationships which are still basic in tribal society.

I do not suggest that these difficulties for Whites arise because African law is in its essentials different from our law. Part of the argument of my book is that African law contains the same fundamental conceptions as our law. But sound judicial work in any society is obviously based on the judges' awareness, often subconscious, of customs, standards, and ways of life of the people to whom they have to administer justice.

However, I do not believe that the mistaken idea, that African courts consider the defendant guilty till he is proved innocent, might arise with a European observer only because African judges are taking into account as evidence incorrect and inadequately explained behaviour, whose significance is not apparent to observers without full knowledge of the particular people's way of life. A more important process is at work. Since the parties are not separately represented by lawyers who cross-examine the other side and its witnesses, it is the duty of judges to cross-examine. In order to arrive at the truth by cross-examination a judge or lawyer must assume that the person questioned has been lying : only in this way can he test that person's evidence. He therefore proceeds in cross-examination *as if* he believed and assumed the examinee to be lying ; and this means that where the examinee is the defendant or the accused, the judge acts *as if* he assumes him to be guilty, and requires him to discharge the onus of guilt and establish his innocence. In addition, the work of detectives and police is often done by the judges in court. The ' assumption ' of guilt in Lozi courts is thus an aspect of the judges' cross-examination, and it is accentuated because during the cross-examination the judges give judgments on behaviour in relation to norms. This is made clear by a judge who, during such a cross-examination, relieved the apprehensions of a worried defendant : ' Do not think I am reprimanding—no, I am seeking to understand properly.' [1]

In English courts, where the judge is an impartial umpire, opposing counsel and prosecutor, regarded as partisan, act in this way, while the judge is generally aloof from the process of cross-examination. In French courts the judge is not an

---

[1] ' *Musike mwahupula nanyaza—batili, nibata kuutwisisa.*'

impartial umpire presiding over a duel between counsel : he has himself to see that the truth is established. Hence he may cross-examine more than his English brother. This may explain why English lawyers say of French courts, as of African courts, that these regard a man as guilty till he establishes his innocence.

II

I pause here in my analysis of the Lozi concept of the reasonable man, to dispose of some simpler and more formal problems in the law of evidence. I take first the use of extra-judicial and magico-religious methods of arriving at the truth in disputes. Generally Lozi courts operated by hearing evidence and cross-examining on it, but early books record, and elderly men have described to me, the use of these methods in Lozi kutas in the past in certain classes of cases. Undoubtedly the most important class consisted of charges of sorcery.

Sorcery itself was a mystical technique for harming others, and if it was practised at all must have been practised in secret. Obviously, then, a charge of sorcery could only be proved or disproved by another mystical technique. According to my informants,

the alleged sorcerer was first isolated from a number of suspects by a diviner and then taken to the kuta. On a special mound near Lialui, he was seated on a platform over a fire and given *mwafi* [a plant containing strychnine] to drink. If the *mwafi* stupefied him so that he fell into the fire, he was guilty and killed ; if he vomited the *mwafi* he was innocent. [Coillard and other pioneers of the Paris Evangelical Mission, which entered Loziland in 1884, reported that many people were killed thus, and that the mound of sorcerers, which they were later given for their mission station, was full of bones.] Partly under the missionaries' influence, King Lewanika declared that charges of sorcery were lies fostered by hate and envy. He sent accused sorcerers to colonize the Matebele Plain between the Zambezi and Mashi Rivers and pointed to their prosperity there as proof of their innocence.[1]

Sorcery charges were also investigated by the boiling-pot ordeal, which I describe below. The missionary, F. S. Arnot,

[1] He banned the poison ordeal in 1891, and trials for sorcery and witchcraft in 1892.

who visited Barotseland in 1883, among other writers described its use. He recorded in his diary two such trials, and said they were 'of almost daily occurrence'. The convicted sorcerers were burnt.[1]

Since Lewanika forbade the charges, it has been a punishable offence to accuse anyone of sorcery, and I know of no criminal trials for sorcery at the capitals.

CASE 15 : THE CASE OF MAGIC AGAINST THE KING

Thus even when one of the paralysed king's attendants in 1942 was caught tampering with the king's private possessions to make magic to secure royal favour, he was dismissed without punishment.

However, though King Lewanika's edict, backed by the agreement with the British to ban 'witchcraft', has been observed, most Lozi, including important princes and councillors, still believe in sorcery, and especially in the idea that to attain unusual success a man must kill one of his kin. He has to provide the corpse for the sorcerers' necrophagous feasts in whose staging most Central African peoples believe. Here I note only that though people are not tried and punished by the kuta for practising sorcery, the relations of Lozi with one another are still influenced by these beliefs. I know that divining to detect sorcerers responsible for misfortunes goes on continually in villages, and that occasionally accusations are made against specific persons. Many of these cases come before the District Commissioners every year under the Witchcraft Ordinance. I have been told that

since sorcerers mainly harm their own kin, when members of an [extended] family suspect one of themselves to be a sorcerer, they will secretly give him *mwafi* in his beer. If he vomits it and shows he is innocent, they commiserate with him on the bad beer ; if he dies, they bury him and no-one outside the family knows.

King Lewanika also abolished the use in kuta of ordeals to convict thieves. According to my informants,

A suspected thief, against whom there was some but insufficient evidence, was made either to lick a hot iron or to take a stone out

---

[1] *Garenganze ; or Seven Years' Pioneer Mission Work in Central Africa,* London : Hawkins (? 1889), at pp. 66 and 92.

of boiling water. Fat was then rubbed on tongue or skin, and if a blister formed, the accused was guilty. Where a man was clearly guilty, he was not subjected to the ordeal. King Lewanika said these ordeals were tricks to rob the people and he would have none of them.

No Lozi senior kuta would today use these ordeals, and I have not heard of a junior kuta doing so.[1]

Professor Evans-Pritchard has described how the Azande of the Anglo-Egyptian Sudan used divination to test accusations of adultery. This has never been done among the Lozi.

While divining has not been used to validate charges of adultery, when I was in Barotseland two cases occurred in which sub-district indunas in the distant woodlands had tortured women, by twisting a leather thong about their heads, to extract confessions of adultery from them. The indunas were punished and discharged by the kuta. My informants have told me that this method of turture, and partial throttling and flogging, were in the past used to make criminals confess, but not in other suits.

Overall, it is impossible now to evaluate how far the kutas in the past supplemented their method of trial by evidence and cross-examination with divination, ordeal, and torture. Obviously, as stated, divination and ordeal must have been used in sorcery charges, when sorcery was recognized by the state as a crime and a delict. My data indicate that ordeals were also used in charges of theft where the verdict on the evidence was 'almost certainly guilty but not proven'. Informants deny that divinatory techniques were ever used in civil suits where the evidence was evenly balanced.

No published record on the Lozi mentions combat by arms to decide on the rights and wrongs of disputes, and my informants denied its use in the past. Among the precedents I was given in 'The Case of the Violent Councillor' (p. 89) was the story of how Wamunyima came armed to the kuta to challenge the NGAMBELA (R1) Mukamba, whose cattle had eaten his crops. The NGAMBELA was allowed by the king to shed his

---

[1] No Lozi told me that an accused person against whom evidence was very strong might claim the right to be submitted to an ordeal. Dr. Mitchell tells me that this occurs among the Yao.

title and fight, and he was victorious ; but of his own accord he paid the damages. The Lozi considered that Wamunyima by coming in arms had abandoned his right to sue the NGAMBELA in kuta, so that the kuta would not sit in judgment on his case. This did not mean that the kuta considered the NGAMBELA was not liable, but it meant that the kuta would not protect Wamunyima's rights. Similar observations apply to the following law ascribed to King Mulambwa (9th king : 1780 ?–1830 ?) by M. Adolphe Jalla in his history of the Lozi nation.[1]

> Any person condemned to death must be immediately informed of this judgment by the chief who will give him the name of the induna appointed as his executioner and advise him to summon his relatives to fight for him. If the induna should be killed his slayer would be blameless because it was done in battle and by a brave man.

Here again the duel gave no judgment on the original offence, but merely held that a victorious 'criminal' was not to be blamed for the death of the induna. It is worth recording how Jalla's account proceeds :

> At other times the king would only warn the condemned man to fly. This bad custom was noticed by the indunas and they also took to warning condemned men to fly and to warning anyone condemned to death by the king to free themselves or to flee to the NATAMOYO [R2—a sanctuary] or to the NGAMBELA [R1] or another induna. (This is evidence of the evil of laws which are not made by the king in consultation with his indunas.)

Therefore we may conclude that the duel was never recognized by the Lozi as a means of determining right and wrong.

III

According to my information, the kuta never administered oaths with supernatural sanctions to litigants or their witnesses. I have never heard anyone be required to take an oath. Witnesses often do make oaths to affirm their evidence more vehemently, swearing ' by the king ', or by a specific king's name, especially

---

[1] *Litaba za Sicaba Sa Malozi* [History of the Lozi Nation], Sefula, Barotseland : The Book Depot of the Paris Missionary Society (4th ed., 1939), Chap. XVI.

that of Lewanika, or by one of their parents. The kuta attaches no more credibility to evidence thus affirmed than to evidence given without an oath ; nor does it prosecute a man who has given false evidence after swearing by the king's name. In practice, to swear ' *kamulena* ' (' by the king ') or ' *kaLewanika* ' (' by King Lewanika ') seems to work out as a method of emphasizing one's statements.

An oath of affirmation severely regarded is smiting the ground. This does not strengthen one's credibility, since there are medicines to protect one against false oaths (see KALONGA's judgment in ' The Case of the Biassed Father ', p. 44), but Lozi believe that it may bring down misfortune, through the earth, on the other party. In ' The Case of the Biassed Father ', the recalcitrant nephew alleged that the headman had thus cursed his absent brother before SIKWA (p. 40). The threat to the innocent explains why ' the Immigrant Land-Borrower ' so enraged the prince consort by smiting the ground in his anger (p. 63). This oath is reprobated because it may attack the innocent party, and I have never seen a man use it in a kuta at a capital.

Another oath, which has similar effects, is to say, ' may I split inside '. Again, I have not heard it used in a senior kuta. If falsely sworn by a man with powers of witchcraft it is believed not to kill the perjuring oath-taker, but the other party who is telling the truth ; and even the oath itself is dangerous. Thus if T has stolen O's property and swears he has not, his oath by O's goods may cause O to die.

CASE 16 : THE CASE OF THE PERJURING OATH-TAKER

in Namalya Kuta before Nawala Mutanuka, many years ago but in the time of the Whiteman (from a text).

S was accused by H of committing adultery with his wife. The wife admitted the accusation ; S denied it, swearing : ' May I split inside if I was her lover.' Within a couple of days the woman died : this proved S was guilty, but nothing was ever done about it. Again this same S accused a woman of stealing his crops. She denied she had taken them. S swore the same oath that she had done so : within a couple of days she died. This proved she was innocent.

S is feared as a powerful witch, though I should not have known it merely from my long observation of the neighbourhood. People behave normally to him, but with heightened politeness.

In short, oaths are not only disregarded in assessing evidence, but strong oaths are dangerous to the innocent. Hence they are rarely used in court, and are severely censured by the judges.

IV

It is clear that public trial and examination of litigants and witnesses have always been the most important method by which Lozi have sought to establish the truth in disputes.

The first and basic rule of the kuta is that the kuta should hear both sides before it decides on the rights and wrongs of a dispute.

CASE 17: THE CASE OF THE ONE-SIDED PLEA

before Mongu-Lialui District Kuta, 25th June, 1947

A man asked IMANDI (R5), sitting as head of the kuta, not to pay herders in the employ of the Barotse Native Government, whose cattle had spoilt his crops, but to recompense him with their money. IMANDI said he could not do this. The complainant must arrange matters with the herders ' on the side ', or summon them to dispute in the kuta which would send someone to assess the damages. ' The kuta ', said IMANDI, ' has no power (*mata*) just to take money '. [*Note :* Here damages would not fall on the kuta as the Native Treasury, since under Lozi law a man is not responsible for the negligence of his servants, unless they be also his children.]

The kuta should therefore give judgment only by due process of law (*kanzila ya mulao* = in the path of the law, *kamulao wakuta* = by the law of the kuta). This process involves hearing both litigants, and cross-examining them in one another's presence. Several proverbs and praise-songs of titles rebuke councillors who form an opinion on a dispute after hearing only one side. They should also summon others to assist them, for ' if one man has a fly in his eye, the other man will drive it out ' : [1] i.e. people correct one another. Thus SOLAMI (R3) once in my hearing told a complainant : ' SOLAMI alone cannot finish an affair : tell the kuta '. It was for failing to summon village councils, and for taking sides in a quarrel without hearing evidence, that the Biassed Father and the Violent Councillor were condemned.

---

[1] *Wili ni muwa wambute nombangole* (Luyana, the old language of the Lozi, not the Sotho-ized Lozi).

These rules are generally, but not always, observed. The importance attached to the rule, and the tendency of councillors to deviate from it, appear in the following case :

CASE 18 : THE CASE OF THE EXPROPRIATING STEWARDS

Complaint to the Saa-Katengo Kuta at Lialui, 30th July, 1942

Muwana and five other men complained that their gardens, four big and two small mounds, had been taken from them by INGANGWANA and IMASIKWANA (L1 and L2, members of the Sikalo Appeal Kuta). Questioned, they stated that the stalks of their last year's crop were still in the ground and their cattle were manuring the gardens ; they had been told to take out their cattle. The gardens had been taken for Prince Imbuwa [a Lozi prince from the north who was employed at a Mongu store]. They complained that the gardens were theirs, and their fathers' and grandfathers'.

SOLAMI (R3, head of the kuta) explained that Prince Imbuwa asked the king for gardens, who said he had none. Imbuwa pointed out some : the king replied that they were INGANGWANA's (L1) and he could not take them. INGANGWANA agreed to give them to the king, and INGANGWANA and Imbuwa gave the royal salute.

KALONGA (R15) : ' The gardens are INGANGWANA's *masimu aluu* (gardens-of-the-title) ; he is not giving his own, we should have been consulted.'

SOLAMI left the kuta. Some judges said they could not hear the case when the NGAMBELA (R1), 'the owner of soil', was away. AWAMI (L7), ALULEYA-INFUNGA (L8), and IMUTUKO (R28) maintained that it was not a case of a person asking for soil, which cannot be handled in the absence of ' the owner of soil ', but a complaint by people turned out of their gardens. [Thus they distinguished administrative from judicial work.] Then there was the question whether they could continue to cultivate. To this some said, ' Yes,' but others countered : ' No, that is prejudging, we cannot say that without hearing why INGANGWANA took the gardens. INGANGWANA and IMASIKWANA should come and explain.'

SOLAMI returned and approved this : he sent to tell the NATAMOYO (R2, head of Sikalo kuta in the NGAMBELA's absence) that these two stewards were wanted at 2 p.m.

The feeling of the judges was clearly for the complainant, Muwana. They seemed to know the gardens were his, and expressed astonishment at people being turned out of *six* gardens ! When Muwana told how they refused to take out their cattle, NAMUNDA-KATANEKWA (R11) approved : ' Be strong.'

Muwana said : 'We did not quarrel with INGANGWANA, IMASIK-WANA, and Prince Imbuwa because they were lords. We did not get carried away by anger. Now, a week afterwards, we are bringing our complaint (*pilaelo*) to the Malozi.'

They were told to sit on one side till 2 p.m., but the kuta continued to talk about the gardens, whose history some knew, with Muwana's party clapping from the side. The kuta cited decisions in similar cases, all to the effect that people could not be turned off the soil of their forefathers.

At 2 p.m. INGANGWANA was called from the palace where he was working. Like any other litigant, he sat on the earth by a pole. He said he knew nothing, he only knew the gardens which were pointed out to him as those of the title when he was installed as INGANGWANA. Sicolo and some other men had been sent round with him, to point out the land of the title INGANGWANA. He asked that these men be called as witnesses, and the kuta arranged to do this. INGANGWANA was obviously afraid he had committed *muliu* (claimed old land of a title), and he kept insisting that it was not an affair of *muliu* : he did not know what he was being sued for, since he was not taking the gardens, only giving them on the king's gift. SOLAMI (R3) said the witnesses should be taken to NAMUNDA-KATANEKWA (R11) lest INGANGWANA corrupt (*kushonga*) them. The kuta said a corrupted witness may answer three or four questions, but then breaks down. SOLAMI instructed the kuta not to discuss the case lest the litigants should feel it had been prejudged.

[The case never came up again : the plaintiffs were confirmed in their holding of the gardens.]

In this record we see also that the judges are confident that their questioning will break down any false or bribed witness, or a witness who is afraid to oppose the powerful.

Thus the judges ought to hear both sides, and they ought to make sure that they have heard all the evidence, of all witnesses, which may be necessary for judgment. In 'The Case of the Prudish Wife', to be described later (Case 36, pp. 145-7), the kuta asked principals if they wanted to call any more witnesses. The principals said : 'No.'

LIOMA (L6) : 'Then what are we wasting time for ? Let us decide.'

An induna : 'We cannot always try to find out how many witnesses the complainant brings, but we should listen to what they say, and judge the case. Every man should give a decision according to what he thinks.'

A prince : ' Has he no more witnesses ? Isn't he going to call those who treated his wife ? '

Husband : ' I may. I listen to what the kuta says. I may make an appeal again. If I see you decide against me on facts for which I know there is evidence, can I call the witnesses in case of appeal ? ' [Lozi appeal courts hear cases anew with all the evidence.]

Kuta : ' We do not refuse you that witness.'

A judge : ' He should call all his witnesses now, for if we simply make a decision now and then an appeal is made to another kuta, this kuta will be blamed for lack of judgment in failing to call the other witnesses.'

The judges have then to sort the evidence, so that they can state to litigants—as we have heard them state in cases cited above—that they decide not by *sobozi* (partiality or prejudice), but by *bupaki* (evidence), *lisupo* (indications, probabilities, presumptions), and *libaka* (reasons, reasoning). For judgments frequently include such statements as : ' We are not partial. We decide by reasons, and we decide by what has been witnessed.' ' The evidence kills you.' ' These witnesses made me change my mind.'

V

There are a few rules which state that in certain types of case responsibility should be established by particular kinds of proof. To convict a thief it is preferred that he be found in possession of the goods.

CASE 19 : THE CASE OF CONVICTING A THIEF

Thus on 6th January, 1921, the Paramount Chief wrote to the Native Commissioner, Lialui, who had sent an alleged thief to the kuta, ' According to our custom the kuta cannot punish for a theft a man unless he has been caught with the goods which he had stolen.'

This rule is no longer—if it ever was—applied absolutely, as ' The Case of the Foreign Thief' shows (below, p. 108). Thieves are nowadays convicted on circumstantial evidence. It is possible that the rule was established after King Lewanika in the early 1890's banned the use of ordeals to fix the guilt or innocence of accused thieves against whom a *prima facie* case had been made out. Since the Lozi have no system of fingerprinting, etc., to establish proof of guilt in doubtful cases, the existence of such a rule, though it was rebuttable, is understandable. Unfortunately the letter does not give the circumstances of the particular charge. There is no firm evidence, but on the basis of what my informants told me and of our general knowledge of African systems, it seems possible that there was little true theft in the past. Many actions brought as charges of theft resolved—and still resolve—themselves into cases where men claim or take the property of others by virtue of kinship ties.

CASE 20: THE CASE OF THE THIEVING KINSMAN

In the Saa-Katengo Kuta at Lialui (June, 1947) it was held that there was no case against a man who had killed another's beast, because he was a relative (in this case, a classificatory brother).

If theft were common, it seems difficult to understand another law of King Mulambwa (9th king: 1780 ?–1830 ?), as reported by Jalla (loc. cit.):

As regards theft, the king said: ' A thief is a brave man and must not therefore be put to death but must be brought to the king who will give him a village or cattle and make him his tribute collector. People will then see if he will thieve again or become a good citizen.'

In later times, the punishment for theft was payment of double value to the person robbed, and the hands of confirmed thieves were cut off.

The Lozi had the common Southern Bantu ' spoor law ' under which if a missing beast was tracked to a village, the villagers had to demonstrate that it had passed on or be held responsible for it. I have not heard such a case under trial.

In charges of adultery the husband's case is strengthened if he can seize an article of the defendant's clothing (see ' The Case of the Adulterer's Stockings ', below, p. 329) but this is not essential for conviction, and adulterers are found guilty on circumstantial evidence (below, p. 132). Generally a wife's admission that a man is her lover requires rebutting, but if he denies the allegation other circumstances should convict him. Here the kuta may compare the faces and bodies of an alleged adulterer or seducer with his putative child to determine paternity.

CASE 21 : THE CASE OF DOUBTFUL PATERNITY (*from a text*)

When two lovers of one woman claimed to be the *genitor* of her child, the Saa-Katengo Kuta decided to wait until the child was old enough to show resemblances to its *genitor* before deciding.

VI

Since Lozi technology is comparatively simple, the kuta rarely calls for ' expert evidence '. Most judges—and indeed most Lozi—have some knowledge of all Lozi customs, of technological actions, and of general and specialized activities such as leechcraft. Furthermore, there is no requirement that facts involved indirectly in a case should be proved, nor is there any fiction of judicial ignorance. Various judges know also the customs and practices of other tribes, and inform their fellows of these. Here, however, the kuta may call for someone to tell it what these other tribal rules are. Otherwise, there are only two situations in which I have heard the kuta ask for expert evidence. One situation is where they refer to Government doctors for an opinion on the extent of injuries. The other situation is in adultery or divorce or seduction cases, where it is alleged that one person has infected another with venereal disease—an action on which damages and a fine were imposed in 1946. Here too the parties are referred to the hospital for examination. The doctor's, or even the African Hospital Orderly's, evidence is accepted as final, and there is no questioning on it.

VII

I have already shown that the Lozi distinguish between different kinds of evidence, and regard some kinds of evidence as more cogent than others. Thus they attach much less weight to hearsay than to direct evidence. One judge defined good evidence to a witness thus : ' Good evidence is what you saw with your own eyes or heard with your own ears. Do not tell us everything that you have heard from other people who were there.' Though the judges demand direct, they do not exclude hearsay, evidence, and witnesses frequently give hearsay evidence. The judges may distinguish this in their decisions, though some of them may quote a witness's hearsay evidence and opinions as if these were valid. INYUNDWANA thus quoted Bandleader MWIBA in 'The Case of the Biassed Father' (at p. 42). But the distinction clearly exists and it is important.

The judges also prefer direct to circumstantial evidence, but they have frequently to decide cases on the basis of the latter. This is forced on them in many cases where it is impossible to obtain direct evidence, such as disputes about titles to land in the distant past, since there is no registration of land and there are no written records. In 'The Case of the Prince's Gardens' (p. 57, above), one judge even found against the land-borrower because he had not disputed the land until two important witnesses against him were dead. Furthermore, the Lozi do not have detectives to collect evidence nor, as stated above, any techniques for fixing responsibility by finger-printing, comparison of hairs and blood, etc. They use both clocks and calendars nowadays, but on the whole their activities are still timed by season and sun. Hence judges cannot cross-examine meticulously on the respective timing or dating of reported actions. In 'The Case of the Violent Councillor' checking of times by judges occurred in cross-examination which I did not quote in detail, but the standards were the flexible times of gardening and fishing activities and of meals. The kuta therefore looks at all surrounding circumstances of a situation for proof, as shown in

CASE 22: THE CASE OF THE FOREIGN THIEF

Prince Imbuwa vs. Mulenga of Tanganyika, Saa-Katengo Kuta of Lialui, 6th August, 1942, Mulenga appealing from a sentence of one month for theft by sub-district induna MUNONO (R23)

Imbuwa complained that Mulenga whom he befriended and gave a sleeping-place stole thirty shillings from him. Mulenga called one witness who contradicted his defence, and was attacked by Mulenga until SOLAMI (R3) asked: 'Is he a disputant or a witness?' Mulenga had been seen with money minted in 1940, not previously known in Loziland, and IMUTUKO (R28) asked him: 'Theft is a hard matter. Would you like to call as witnesses the people from whom you claim to have got the money?' Finally, his sentence was confirmed. I quote part of SOLAMI's judgment. He reproached Mulenga for spoiling the friendship of Imbuwa, who gave him a sleeping-place with a blanket and pillow. He reconstructed events, referring to the evidence of different people and the accused, and pointing out the inconsistencies in the accused's behaviour. In short, the following circumstances convicted him :

(1) Mulenga did not buy relish in Imbuwa's village where he was staying but elsewhere, and he only paid his servants after leaving the village and not when he arrived there ;

(2) His witness gave evidence against him on every point on which Mulenga swore he would be for him ;

(3) Mulenga was in the hut from which the money was missed ; the other people of the village were away except for Imbuwa who was asleep ;

(4) The others were searched and nothing was found ;

(5) He suddenly produced money to pay his servants, and it was new money of 1940, not previously seen in Loziland, and only used to pay princes and councillors their money for the last quarter [this quarter had just ended—note that money is not plentiful in Loziland and therefore points 1, 2 and 5 are more damning than they would be in Britain].

SOLAMI concluded : ' We lack only a man who saw you go to the portmanteau and take the money. You will go to prison for one month and pay 30s. to Imbuwa.'

An eye-witness—direct evidence—is clearly recognized to be needed for conclusive proof. But here the mass of surrounding circumstances, such as where a man paid his carriers and bought relish, accumulate to show his behaviour is only understandable (*utwahala*)—reasonable—if he had committed the wrong, even though these circumstances do not bear directly on the deed.

The judges also attach varying degrees of credibility to different kinds of witnesses and evidence. In general the judges favour the evidence of independent witnesses.

CASE 23 : THE CASE OF THE FATHER AND HIS SON'S CATTLE

Provincial Kuta, Lialui, June, 1947

A man was imprisoned for manslaughter and left cattle he had earned himself in his father's care. His father placed the cattle to be herded with a neighbour. After a few years, he went to see these cattle and their calves, and divided them into two herds : one he took home, the other he left with the herder. He said the herder could also have one heifer for himself as reward. Giving this reward-ing heifer before he took away the whole herd was contrary to usual practice, and the herder said the son would reject the gift when he came out of prison. The father said his son would not, but agreed to call in the chief councillor at Nalolo capital (SAMBI) to be witness of the transaction. Both parties died ; and when the son was released from prison he claimed all the cattle and their offspring, save for one heifer to be left with the herder's sons as their reward. SAMBI's evidence was declared to be good, and the kuta commended the dead herder's insistence that he be summoned, but asserted (as SAMBI had at the time) that the son should have been consulted. Even if he were in prison, it was only the local prison at Mongu where he was accessible. The final judges (but not all judges) awarded all the cattle but one heifer to the son. They held that the father could use his son's cattle himself ; but that nowadays when men earn for themselves, the father could not give away the son's cattle to another in variation of the usual terms of this contract, though the contract was in the son's interests. Other judges had sought to support the herder's scrupulous honesty by holding that the father had such property rights in his son's cattle.

Here is the good independent witness, whom a wise and reasonable man summons to listen to important transactions.[1] But note that there is no ceremonial in these transactions.

The Lozi approve of this kind of independent witness—as we have already seen in ' The Case of the Violent Councillor ' (pp. 93 ff.)—who is not related to the parties. They believe that people will distort their evidence, and even commit perjury, to favour their kin, though it is wrong to do so.

In ' The Case of the Prince's Garden ' (pp. 56–61), the defendant stated : ' The evidence of my wife is useless because the judges will say it is biassed. As for my other wife, can I ask her to give evidence against her father, who is a witness for the prince ? '

SUU (R17) : ' Do you refuse their evidence, or is it we ? '—*Defendant :* ' NOYOO (R13) does.'

I give no other examples here, for this favouring of kin will appear frequently in cases cited below.

Conversely, if a man's kin give evidence against him, the judges credit this heavily and may therefore find against him. This is clear in ' The Case of the Prince's Gardens ' (p. 59) when

---

[1] I shall discuss the full implications of this case for the Lozi law of contracts in *The Ideas of Barotse Jurisprudence* ; and discuss its implications for the growth of law below at p. 287.

MUKULWAKASHIKO (R4) said to the defendant: 'Your son killed you, he is your *mufubalume*' (i.e. sexual competitor). It will also emerge in cases to be cited later.

Judges also believe that witnesses are liable to favour the powerful against the weak. They told the Violent Councillor that were his villagers to lie, it was reasonable to suppose that they would lie in support of their overlord, and not of an ordinary young man. Again, in 'The Case of the Expropriating Stewards' (p. 104) where men complained against the two most powerful stewards and a prince for taking their land, we have seen that SOLAMI (R3) feared that the witnesses when summoned would be corrupted by the defendants' power, and therefore they were to be put in charge of an important induna. SOLAMI made this suggestion about his fellows without intending any imputation against them, nor were they offended. In 'The Case of the Foreign Thief' a prince was suing a foreigner. When the witness called by the latter came to the post, SOLAMI adjured him: 'You must speak the truth. Do not perhaps think that Imbuwa is a prince, or that Imbuwa is a Lozi like you, and therefore support him. Tell your lords the truth, so that God will know. We hear your mouth, but He sees in your heart. Let Him see the truth. We want the truth. That is all.'

That is, the judges expect parties and witnesses to lie. It is considered wrong to do so, and perjury is and always has been an offence. Judges frequently threaten to prosecute witnesses if they do not tell the truth, but very rarely do so. Lying when giving evidence is thus treated as normal but reprehensible. I have occasionally heard a judge, in order to show a litigant that the evidence was damning, admit that he himself had been guilty in a similar case in which he had denied liability but been convicted. MBASIWANA (R46) did this in 'The Case of the Schoolboy Adulterer' (below, at p. 131), and provoked only laughter.

I need not cite specific instances of how the kuta values corroboratory evidence.

For all these reasons the kuta, and Lozi generally, attach the greatest importance to cross-examination of the litigants and their witnesses in public as the procedure for arriving at the truth. This is made manifest in their attitude to letters. Letters are frequently treasured by Lozi and submitted in evidence. The kuta gives some credence to them, especially if the witness is ill, or if a woman brings a letter which she claims was written by her husband who is at work for Whites elsewhere, and which divorces her. The kuta itself decides who wrote the letter, though frequently letters are dictated by illiterates to others. But the judges always complain that letters are unsatisfactory because they cannot be cross-examined.

CASE 24 : THE CASE OF THE IMPREGNATED WOMAN'S LETTER

(1942)

A group of Lubale accused sub-district induna SIKWA of impregnating one of their women whom he had imprisoned. The plaintiffs came to the Saa-Katengo Kuta at Lialui to report that the woman was very ill, but they had brought a letter of hers. SOLAMI (R3) and other judges said : ' SIKWA [the defendant] cannot dispute with a letter. You cannot ask a letter questions. The kuta proceeds by asking the man and the woman questions. If you question a letter, who will answer ? You people must return with the woman.'

This statement brings out the importance which the kuta attaches to its cross-examination. In ' The Case of the Prince's Gardens ' (p. 56), the NGAMBELA stated this to be the kuta's duty when he reproved garrulous litigants who argued with each other : ' You leave nothing for the kuta to ask. But go ahead.' Again, in ' The Case of the Prudish Wife ', below, a witness complained that the kuta was trying to trap him with its questions. The judges laughed : ' That is our business.'

The judges thus depend mainly on their own cross-examination to extract the truth from conflicting evidence. Cross-examination is free in that there are no improper or objectionable questions, and no-one who can protest against any question on behalf of the litigants or their witnesses. The only intervention of this kind I noted was when the NGAMBELA (R1) reproved judges for silencing the garrulous litigants in ' The Case of the Prince's Gardens ' : ' Do not prevent a person from speaking.' But the judges cross-examine by traditional procedure and rules which classify evidence as hearsay, direct, or circumstantial, and weight it by credibility, cogency, reasonableness, and corroboration.

VIII

However, it is clear that the judges' chief weapon in cross-examination is 'the reasonable man', for they attack people's statements wherever these show departure from his standards of behaviour. I return now to the problems involved in this process, by considering cases involving persons in various social positions.

The following case involves the relationships between husband and wife, between son-in-law and father-in-law, between a would-be husband (here a man who eloped with the wife) and his mistress and her father, between father and daughter, between subjects of different tribes of the nation, and between citizen and law-courts. It incidentally illustrates that in matrimonial cases the courts strive less for reconciliation than they do in cases between blood-kin. The case involved the breaking of marital ties and this was severely reprobated; but the judges were really horrified by the woman's abuse of her father, with its threat to the filial tie.

CASE 25 : THE CASE OF THE ELOPING WIFE

on appeal to Nalolo District Kuta, 2nd June, 1947

Sub-district induna KAKENE had ordered that a man who had eloped with another's wife should pay £5 to the husband, and that the eloper and the wife should each pay £2 to the kuta. The eloper appealed because he did not see why he should pay, since he did not 'abduct' (*kuyanga*) the wife, but was given her by her parents, whom he paid 30s. Questioned by the court, he said her parents told him she was a divorcee. [Had the parents done this, and had the woman not been divorced, damages to the husband and a fine for the Court would fall on them—see Case 48, p. 198]. Therefore when the clerk recorded the defendant's statement, SAMBI (R1, Nalolo) said : ' You do not quarrel with her husband, but with your father-in-law.' While the husband's statement was being recorded, the eloper interrupted, and a policeman silenced him : ' Calm yourself. Your time will come. Everyone finishes what is in his heart, and lands.'

The cuckolded husband's evidence : ' I came to work where my parents-in-law lived at Senanga [magisterial headquarters]. So did the defendant. That is why our case was heard in KAKENE's court, and not in our home sub-districts.[1] I was working at Senanga, it

---

[1] The forum of a case has always been that of the defendant.

was the dry hot season. I was killing catfish. There was great hunger and I often sent my wife to the labour-recruiting bureau [for the Witwatersrand Gold mines] to buy meal. I noticed that my wife also often went there on her own and remained there a long time, so I asked her why. She replied that she could not be stopped from visiting her friends. Then my wife complained that I was a Wiko [an immigrant of the Lubale tribe from Angola], and I replied : " You knew I was a Wiko, and I knew that you were a Lozi, but we agreed to marry. Have I changed ? It is four years since we married." My wife said she no longer loved me, and we quarrelled. After the quarrel she said she was going home, and I told her to go. She came back, and we quarrelled again. She upbraided me : " Why do you not beat me, are you a man ? " I replied that I did not like that custom.

' Some time afterwards I went to the labour-recruiting bureau and found her in a hut with the defendant. He said her parents gave her to him. He called me a wretched Wiko. I went to my father [i.e. father-in-law] who asked me where my wife was. I told him I had caught her with the defendant. He said : " Go, we have heard ; I will call them tomorrow." The next day, he told me that my wife said I had stripped her of her clothes and insulted her. He had then asked her : " Do you sue on the insults ? If he stripped you, why did you not come to us ? "

' Judgment was given for me at KAKENE's kuta, and the defendant said he would appeal to SAMBI [R1 at Nalolo] at the capital. KAKENE told him : " All right, this kuta is also SAMBI's." '

SAMBI invited Prince Mwendawelie, a son of King Lewanika travelling with me : ' Mwendawelie, here is a dispute, enter it.' Mwendawelie replied, ' I'm a stranger here,' and the court clerk, also a prince, said : ' You a stranger !—don't say that. You own the capital.' SAMBI capped him : ' Yes, no prince is a stranger here.' Mwendawelie therefore asked the woman whom she regarded as her husband, and she broke into her tale. She maintained that her husband, holding a spear and a knife, had chased her away, and then she married the defendant. Her mother and elder sister were there.

SAMBI : ' Where are they ? '—*Woman's father :* ' Her sister is ill, and her mother is nursing her.'

ANABA (L2) : ' The important witnesses are absent.'

Kuta clerk : ' Did you write down their words ? '—*Woman's father :* ' No, I cannot write.'

The woman resumed : ' I asked my husband for a letter saying he had divorced me. He would not give it to me. I ran to the bush ; then I went back to my courtyard to get my goods. My husband gave me nothing, not a blanket or anything. He left me only what I was wearing, and gave me one basket and one pot.'

Under questioning by the court, she said she stayed at home for two days, and on the third day married the defendant. Her husband found her on the third day in the defendant's hut.

Asked if she had finished, she went on : ' I thought I would take my husband to the kuta to get a divorce, then this man came to marry me and I saw it was late so I married him.'

The kuta laughed and exclaimed : ' Late to wait two days ! '

The clerk : ' Who took the matter to court, you or your husband ? ' —*Woman :* ' I did, to get a divorce.'

A judge : ' Then you wanted a divorce because your husband troubled you ? '—*Woman :* ' Yes.'

Judge : ' Then he did not chase you away ? '—*Woman :* ' He did.'

SAMBI : ' In two days, this man came and you agreed with him, and he got you from your parents and you married him ? '—*Woman :* ' Yes, on the first day we agreed and on the second day he brought the money for my parents.'

SAMBI : ' Have you more to tell us ? '—*Woman :* ' Yes '—and she told a long story of what occurred at her father's village.

Clerk to woman's father (who sat beside the deserted husband, in support of him) : ' You've heard the statements of your children, and I will read you the defendant's statement because you did not hear it (does so). What have you to say ? '—*Woman's father :* ' I lived in the Plain in order to fish every day and sell the fish to the District Commissioner. I knew nothing of how the case went to the kuta at Senanga. My wife may know, for I sent her to the margin to cultivate her gardens. The day of the quarrel between these two I came in to the margin from the Plain. This man just took her, on the same day as she left her husband. I've no relationship with this man at all : you judges seek for those who gave my daughter to this man, his parents-in-law whom I do not know. She met her " small mother " [mother's junior fellow-wife] and told her she was married to the defendant. I know nothing about it. . . . Then he came to ask me for her in marriage and I scolded him : " How can you come to ask for a girl in marriage when you come from the mat on which you have slept with her ? You must pay, do you not know the law ? " '

A judge : ' What law (*mulao*) ? '—*Woman's father :* ' The law that comes from Nalolo, which we work here—the law that if a man steals a child he must pay £1. Also, it is a big fault that he took her in the hut of her husband. I know nothing of a divorce. This is the affair as KAKENE saw it.'

The woman denied her father's story, and said he was mad and he ought to pay the damages due to her husband, in place of the defendant.

NATAMOYO (R2) : ' Was it £1 or 30s. he paid ? '—*Woman's father* : ' It was 30s.'

NATAMOYO : ' This 30s. they speak of, was it a fine or marriage-payment ? '—' It was a fine.'

NATAMOYO : ' When was the fine 30s. ? '—' You made the law.'

SAMBI (R1) : ' You teach us the law, but we made it. It was £1.'

Prince Mwendawelie : ' Did you not think of waiting until after the case of the husband had been heard ? '—*Wife's father* : ' No, I did not think of it.'

SAMBI : ' I help the prince. Who has power to fine, you or KAKENE [the sub-district induna] ? '—' KAKENE has.'

SAMBI : ' Why did you not go to KAKENE ? '—' I did not think of it.'

SAMBI (to woman) : ' Who escorted you from your parents' home to the defendant's home ? '—*Woman* : ' No-one.'

SAMBI : ' Do you not know it is our marriage-custom that the bridegroom's people, even if only his friends from the compound where he works, come to the girl's home, and they both bring her to his hut ? '—Woman did not reply.

SAMBI : ' Are you a good person ? '—*Woman* : ' Yes, I am.'

SAMBI (to the defendant) : ' Do you know our laws about marriage and the stealing of a man's wife ? '—*Defendant* : ' You tell me, for you are the owners of the law.'

SAMBI : ' Were you married to this girl the first night you slept with her ? '—' I admit the first night was not marriage, but fornication.'

KAKWISANUNGU (L1) : ' How can you take a woman to *sinawenga* [the marriage feast], and the next day go to her father to ask for her, when the *sinawenga* is over ? '—Defendant did not reply.

SAMBI : ' You, Kashweka [the defendant], are the son of Kashweka of Katongo : you are known to us all. Not so the husband, Jesu. Whom do we know better, you or this Lubale ? '—*Defendant* : ' You know me.'

SAMBI : ' Then if we see you have taken his thing, can we make you return it ? '

NAWALA (R46 at Lialui, travelling with me) cited a case when his daughter was abducted, and he complained to the NGAMBELA (R1 at Lialui) and SAMBI (R1 at Nalolo). The abductor paid a beast as fine, and NAWALA took his daughter and married her elsewhere.—*Defendant* replied : ' But you went to NGAMBELA and SAMBI, and he did not go to KAKENE.'

SAMBI : ' You, NAWALA, this man is your child, and though you no longer have the power (*mata*) to judge here since that lion the [Government] Reform has eaten us, do you show us the way.'

NAWALA (R46 at Lialui) : ' What can I say, my lord ? He must pay. Where will you get it, Kashweka ? Now we have indeed died.'

The Clerk (a prince) (to the woman's father) : ' You, Nyambe, if you'd given your child to the defendant, we would give you a fault. But we do not believe any parent would have agreed to a marriage, when his daughter was already married, and when she made a wedding ceremony on her own without it being known at her home. You, woman, are wicked ; look how you insulted your father by calling him mad. The defendant will pay the husband £5 and £2 to the kuta, and the woman pay £2 to the kuta ; and they must pay before leaving the capital. You, Kashweka, do not insult a man by saying he is a Wiko. A Wiko is a person. If a Wiko steals your wife, he pays you, and if you steal a Wiko's wife, you pay him. If an induna had done what you have done, he would sit there by the post and not on the mat.'

ANABA (L2) : ' Kaskweka [defendant], you have done very wrong. If you want to marry a divorcee, ask where her home is and go to ask for her. I give the same judgment as KAKENE.

' You, Inonge [woman], you are a bad child. Now your father has no child, because you insulted him.

' You, Nyambe [the father], you too have done wrong. You had no right to fine this man when her husband had not got anything. You will give the 30s. to Kashweka to pay for his fault. By what right [literally : " how "] did you eat this money ? She is not unmarried, and the money should be eaten by her husband, not by you.'

NATAMOYO (R2) : ' I do not know, for SAMBI is the finisher. I agree with KAKENE—we believe Nyambe [the father], even if he has a small fault, that he should take £1 and not 30s. I agree on that with the prince—ANABA—there. Kaskweka, you must pay. I approve of Jesu [the husband] for saying that if his wife's father had given his wife to another, he would have sued his wife's father. It is you people who ruin marriages—the marriages of today in Loziland are not strong.'

SAMBI (R1) : ' Nyambe [the father], it is true that the law says if a man takes a father's daughter without his permission, he pays £1. If she is a *namakuka*, a divorcee sent away by her husband, you can fine an abductor £1, and if she is a virgin £3. But if you have given your child to a husband, and he has made the marriage-payment, you cannot fine. For the abductor does not find her in your courtyard. So here Kashweka found your child not in your courtyard, but in the courtyard of Jesu. You had no right to that 30s. Return it to Kashweka to pay Jesu. You gave your daughter to Jesu and you cannot take her away. You no longer have power (*mata*) there.

'Kaskweka, about his being a Lubale. Mbunda, Totela, Lubale —all are people under our one great king (pointing to the north where Lialui is). This girl is Jesu's wife—and she still is. You will pay him £5 and £2 to the kuta, and the woman will pay £2 to the kuta. If you cannot pay, I'll show you. Policeman, if they cannot pay, handcuff them and send them to Senanga [the magistracy jail]. You are the people who ruin marriage. You, Nyambe, do not fine on your own outside the kuta.'

SAMBI instructed ANABA to report the case to the Princess Chief, and the clerk reminded him that there was an appeal possible [to the Provincial Court at Lialui].

SAMBI : 'If you wish to appeal, go forward.'—*Defendant :* 'No, what other kuta is there?'

NATAMOYO (R2) : 'Do you admit you took this woman?'—'No, but what can I do if I am found at fault? I won't go forward to trouble the kuta.'

SAMBI told the father to hurry home to get the £2 to pay his daughter's fine and free her. He refused, saying that she had insulted him and she could go to jail. SAMBI said aside to me : 'Wait till he sees his child handcuffed and hears her weeping. Then he will find the money. A father's heart forgives his child anything.'

ANABA reported to SAMBI the Princess Chief's verdict, after a ten minutes' conversation with her. She and her husband, the Ishee Kwandu, approved of the kuta's judgment. 'It is very very bad to spoil marriage. If you have taken a woman to your hut and then go to her father, what do you ask for? The girl is very bad and must be scolded heavily for her insults to her father. It was also very bad that the father was judge in his own case. Here in Nalolo there had been a hearing, and the facts were examined. It is all right for a father to take damages for a divorcee, but not for a man's wife.' Here the clerk interjected : 'The defendant must still give £1 marriage-payment [to the father] or no-one can commit adultery with her' [i.e. the defendant acquires no rights over the woman till he validates the marriage]. SAMBI explained to me : 'She is the wife of her abductor, for if we return her to live with her husband they will fight.' He added that this was her third divorce.

SAMBI then announced the Chief's judgment : 'Kashweka and Inonge will pay £9—your household has lost £9. You, Nyambe [the father], were bad, you had no right to take the money, since the marriage-payment gives him the right. You should first tell the husband. Return the 30s., they belong to the husband. If your child is a divorcee, take only £1 and do not exceed the law (literally : "jump over the law" = "break the law" in other contexts). You get £1 from Kashweka for the marriage after he has settled with the husband. You, woman, the Chief says you are very wicked ; you insulted your father so that his heart is dead when it was yours —who will pay for you to keep you out of jail?' (Her father loudly agreed with SAMBI.)

SAMBI told the clerk to return the husband's court-fees and went on : 'There is no such thing as a Lubale. We are one thing, with two eyes and two ears, and our children marry them. They and the Mbunda feel hunger like us and ask us for land which we give to them—a Lubale we place in the bush, a Lozi in the Plain.'

Nyambe said he had no money to refund to the defendant and was told to go home to fetch it. The girl started to leave the court but was brought back, struggling, by a policeman. SAMBI ordered him to handcuff her, and she wept, crying that she would earn the money.

SAMBI : 'It is your own fault, for whoring and for insulting your father that you suffer for. Who will pay for you? Find another father.'

The two defendants were handcuffed and removed to huts before being sent to jail at the magisterial centre. Next morning, her father offered to pay for the woman. He had to go home to fetch the money and wished to take his daughter with him. SAMBI consented, but the clerk advised not, and the kuta agreed with him. When the matter was referred to the Princess Chief, she said the girl was not to go. She had seen the girl's struggles in the court : 'She is a very bad woman, who must be punished—did she not insult her father grievously?' The man was sent, still handcuffed, to his relatives to beg for the money. SAMBI explained to me that they used to give people time to pay, but they ran away to White Country. Another man travelling with a policeman had run away, so they now handcuffed wrongdoers. The Princess Chief added : 'We do not jail because we wish to, but because we must.'

The issue in this case rested on the credibility of the woman and her new husband as against her father since there were no independent witnesses. Their dispute was whether the payment which the father admitted receiving from Kashweka had been a fine or marriage-payment. For the kuta soon disposed of the woman's plea that she had been divorced—literally, 'driven away'—by her husband. First, her own story, that she married the defendant two days after leaving her husband because she saw ' it was late ', was clearly unreasonable.   The kuta looks at the time which elapses between different actions to judge whether litigants' or witnesses' statements are reasonable.   Here the time was laughably absurd.   But secondly, had she and her would-be new husband been good citizens, they would have waited until she sued in court for divorce with her father's support.   And thirdly, had they conformed to custom the man would not have approached the father with an offer of marriage-payment the morning after he had slept with the daughter.   These all indicated a hurrying-on of actions which could be ascribed, almost with certainty, to the behaviour of an eloping wife and her seducer.

Nevertheless, had the father connived at this elopement he, and not the seducer, would have been held responsible to the husband.   Here, as between the errant couple and the father, the above listed facts all counted against the couple.   They were linked to the probability that the father had taken the money as a fine by judicial presumption : no father would accept marriage-payment from a man coming to him from a bed of fornication with his daughter, who had ' arranged her own wedding-ceremony '.   This presumption rests in the judges' ' science of psychology '—their idea of the reactions of fathers. Moreover, the woman had abused her father shamefully, and she and her seducer had not sought the court's aid like good citizens, and indeed like bad citizens had abused a fellow-citizen by his foreign tribal origin.   All these deviations from reasonable and upright behaviour destroyed their credibility.   She as wife, as daughter, and as citizen, had behaved wrongfully ; he had behaved wrongfully as citizen and as would-be son-in-law. Altogether they were ' bad lots '.

Hence the judges did not believe them at all.   Their misdeeds, in all of the several social positions each occupied, accumulated the proof against them, and influenced the judges to severity in handcuffing them.

The father had also behaved wrongfully as against his son-in-law, and also as a citizen in fining on his own instead of going to court, and in exceeding the statutory fine of £1.   He had not conformed to appropriate norms either as father-in-law or as citizen.   But the court, for the reasons given above as counting against the couple, believed that he had taken the money as a

(*a*) The kuta building at Nalolo capital.

(*b*) Nalolo's Kuta has been destroyed by fire, and the Sikalo tries a case in the shade of trees.

PLATE III

(*a*) Sikwela's village (see 'The Case of the Unused Land').

(*b*) Batuke's village (see 'The Case of the Immigrant Land-Borrower').

PLATE IV

VILLAGES IN THE PLAIN

fine and not as marriage-payment. This is the significance of NATAMOYO's statement : 'We believe Nyambe, even if he has a small fault, that he should take £1 and not 30s.' The father was therefore ordered to return the money to the seducer to pay the husband. This presumably emphasized that a father has no rights to damages from his married daughter's seducer, as might have appeared to be the case had he handed on the money to his wronged son-in-law. The damages had to pass from seducer directly to the man wronged in his rights. It is worth noting that the overpayment by 10s. over the statutory £1 for a fine for abduction and for marriage-payment of a divorcee was not taken as indicating the nature of the payment : at the time there was rapid inflation in Barotseland and fathers often exceeded their statutory claims.

The kuta could have punished the father for taking damages on his own without reporting to a kuta, since if a wife elopes the kuta is entitled to a £2 fine. It may have excused him (I omitted to enquire) because it pitied his distress under his daughter's abuse.

In the end the daughter did not suffer for this abuse, which so horrified the authorities. Had the father not met SAMBI's expectation that he would pay the fine when he saw his daughter handcuffed and heard her weeping, she would have gone to jail. But it was difficult for the kuta to punish her without mulcting the offended father. Had it insisted on her going to jail, the father would have been hurt in his sentiments. Had it levied an extra fine, as it could, this would have fallen on the father, though he could have insisted that her maternal kin pay. Similarly the kuta could have ordered her maternal kin to pay damages for their child's offence to her father. These last two courses might have caused ill-feeling between the wronged father and his in-laws, which any court would be reluctant to risk. On his own initiative the father could have made such a claim. It is legally valid, but I have never heard of a man bringing such a suit.

The kuta thus checks the evidence for credibility and cogency by several fixed standards, some implicit in the fixed order of the environment and of human action (as in a father's psyche), and some in the recurrent usages of society to which reasonable men conform. In this case we have seen how the kuta uses 'social time', the periods which *ought* to elapse between the performance of certain actions : leaving a husband and marrying again, consulting a father and marrying his daughter. But time-periods also check on evidence in other ways. I heard several cases in which kutas calculated the number of calves which cows, and their own calves, might reasonably be expected to have had over a number of years, allowing for a reasonable number of bull-calves against heifers, for a reasonable number of barren heifers, and for a reasonable number of barren seasons for other heifers. This issue was considered in ' The Case of the Father and his Son's Cattle' (p. 109), where the plaintiff complained that his herd left by his father with the defendants had increased less than the herd derived from the cow his father had (wrongfully) given the defendants. A similar issue was involved in

CASE 26 : THE CASE OF THE ALLEGEDLY PREGNANT BRIDE

Saa-Katengo Kuta, Lialui, June, 1942

A Lubale asked the kuta to declare that his marriage was null and void, on the grounds that his wife was pregnant when she came to him, and that therefore he should be entitled to recover the first £1 paid to his father-in-law, for the right of sexual intercourse, and the additional payments for her untouched ' virginity ' and fertility since she was alleged to be a virgin when they married. At the time of the trial, her child was about fifteen months old. The kuta tried to fix the number of months after the marriage that the child was born, by reference to the Lubale names of months, and the state of weather and rains and flood and various kinds of crops at each event.[1] Eventually it was decided that she produced a complete and healthy child eight months after marriage, and this was reasonable since the period of gestation for a normal child varied from six-and-a-half months to a year.[2] In addition, if she had been pregnant at the time of the wedding, the husband should have noticed signs of pregnancy shortly after marriage, and he should have complained at once to his village headman and to his parents-in-law, who would have got old women to examine her. He had not done so, and indeed had only brought

---

[1] As girls are artificially deflowered by women at puberty ceremonies, the men seem to be ignorant of the existence of the hymen, and virginity cannot be tested by bleeding after intercourse.

[2] Calculations of this kind are necessarily imprecise.

his suit over a year after the birth,[1] when good evidence could not be obtained from his wife's physical condition. Hence his whole plea was unreasonable, and he had brought his suit because he was tired of his wife. He could divorce her if he pleased, but he would recover nothing from her parents, and he must give her half her crops and half of the ' goods of the hut '.

To explain this decision fully, I must interpolate that if a Lozi marries a virgin, he should under the 1917 Marriage Laws of King Yeta III pay two beasts or £2 ; the first is ' the beast of shame ' for his right of sexual intercourse, the second is for her untouched fertility. If there is a divorce and she has not conceived, he can reclaim the second £1 or second beast and its progeny ; he loses this claim even if she conceives and miscarries. No such beast is paid for a bride who is not a virgin. The ' beast of shame ' never returns. The husband here asserted he was deceived into the second payment, since she was pregnant and not a virgin ; and also into the first payment, since a pregnant woman should not go to another man. The court held he was lying, and both payments were fair (see ' The Case of the Barren Widow ', below, pp. 174–5). Secondly, if a man divorces his wife she is entitled to half the crops grown by her in his land allotted to her, and to half the ' goods of the hut ' (clothes, pots, blankets, etc. given her by him). If she sues him for divorce and obtains it, she is entitled to half the crops as above, but not to any ' goods of the hut ' since she rejects them with the marriage (see ' The Case of the Ungenerous Husband ', below, pp. 172–3).[2]

The kuta thus looks at different kinds of time in order to assess the reasonableness of evidence.[3] These are cosmological time—

---

[1] He could not have sued until the child was born, since a suit involving a pregnant woman may cause miscarriage and even death.

[2] Some informants, including several councillors, told me that she is entitled also to half the goods, since she has ' worked ' in the marriage, by growing food for her husband, cooking, cleaning, bringing wood and water, nursing him when ill, and so on. Since I recorded cases showing the opposite judgment, I take it that these other views show a changing public opinion which reflects the increasing tendency to place material value on work even in intimate relationships. The husband of the Princess Chief gave me the orthodox view, but added that a man divorced by his wife would be unwise to refuse to give her anything, since other women would note this and he would not be able to get another wife.

[3] On various kinds of time and space concepts in social life, see Evans-Pritchard, E. E. *The Nuer*, Oxford : Clarendon Press (1940), Chap. III.

e.g. the position of heavenly bodies, night and day ; ecological time—e.g. the state of the weather and the crops ; physiological time—e.g. periods of gestation of cows and women ; social time—e.g. the lapse of time before the plaintiff complained of his wife's pregnancy, as against what a reasonable man would have done. This last kind of time was also illustrated in ' The Case of the Eloping Wife '.

In this case we also saw how deviation from custom and convention can be construed as unreasonable, and constitute grounds for convicting on circumstantial evidence. The kuta seized on the couple's failure to approach the father properly, and to arrange a *sinawenga* (wedding-ceremony). Had the defendant and the woman been honest, she would have returned home. Then, even had they not gone to court for a divorce, her new lover would have paid money to her father to open discussion of the marriage, a joint party of her friends and his friends would have taken her from her parental home to his hut, making other payments on the way, and after the first night of marriage they would have made public payments to one another to express their mutual satisfaction as bed-partners. These ceremonial actions are not all essential to constitute a valid marriage : once when I was travelling a young man among my paddlers arranged through a relative in our party and myself to marry a girl ; he paid the gift to open discussion one evening, the next evening concluded arrangements, and the following morning we went in a party and took the bride on our journey home. Wedding conventions thus are not directly enforceable at law, but observance of the customs and ceremonial is proof of reasonableness, and deviations have to be explained by unusual circumstances. In fact in ' The Case of the Eloping Wife ' a valid marriage could not be instituted by any ceremonial : the woman was still another man's wife. Deviation from custom placed the blame on the couple, and not on her father.

In short, in any case where the issue has to be settled by circumstantial evidence, as against the direct evidence of disinterested witnesses, the court surveys all of the parties' behaviour, and is likely to find against them wherever they have acted unreasonably. Unreasonable actions include deviations both from custom and from commonsense behaviour. The court works with certain stabilized norms to check the evidence :

these norms are present both in the physical and biological world (e.g. cosmological, ecological, and physiological time, and topographical space), in the usual reactions of persons (e.g. a father would not accept marriage-payment from a daughter's abductor), and in the instituted customs and usages of the different social positions which one or more parties and witnesses occupy. Thus in the judicial process, ceremonial and customary usages, like 'laws of nature', are fixed standards by which the flow of varied social action can be measured.

IX

It is perhaps now reasonable time that I gave the Lozi phrase for 'a reasonable man'. It is clear from the texts and from my discussion of the preceding cases that in practice judges do not often use such a phrase explicitly, but that the reasonable man is usually implicitly present when they contrast reported behaviour with the norms of behaviour of particular positions. One *general* phrase in Lozi is *mutu yangana : mutu* = person, and *ngana* = mind, wisdom, intelligence, intellect, reason, sense, commonsense.[1] From the many contexts in which I have heard *mutu yangana* used, I consider it is best translated as 'a man of sense', with the meaning that Jane Austen brought out in *Sense and Sensibility*. Thus it means 'a sensible man', in the way in which she introduces Mr. Knightley in *Emma* immediately as 'a sensible man'.[2] It includes the idea of 'having sound principles'. This is made clearer in the more common general Lozi phrase used in contexts where people are being judged : *mutu yalukile*, of which 'an upright man' is probably the best English rendering. '—*Lukile*' is an adjective from the verbal root *kuluka*, 'to go straight', 'to stand upright'. 'Straightforwardness', 'uprightness', 'decency', 'principle', 'virtue', are therefore the qualities which the Lozi demand of people. This demand includes both sense or reasonableness (*ngana*) and uprightness (*kuluka*). By contrast *butali*, which means wisdom, also means cunning (see below, p. 138).

---

[1] Jalla, A., *Dictionary of the Lozi Language*, London : The United Society for Christian Literature (n.d.), at p. 210.

[2] William Empson (*The Structure of Complex Words*, London : Chatto & Windus, 1951, Chaps. 12–15) appears to me to miss completely this frequent meaning of 'sense' and 'sensible' in Jane Austen's writings.

That *mutu yalukile*, an upright man, embraces both sense and uprightness is apparent if we recall the cross-examinations and judgments in cases cited. In 'The Case of the Biassed Father' the village headman would have behaved sensibly and uprightly if he had been impartial in settling the dispute between his sons and his nephews, as would SAYWA in 'The Case of the Violent Councillor' had he not backed his own children. Reference to any of the praises or reprimands bestowed by judges emphasizes this partial identification. However, the identification is only partial, and *mutu yangana* and *mutu yalukile* are distinguished. For though the judges assess behaviour, in considering evidence, by the standard of the upright man, and urge this standard on litigants, the law only demands 'reasonable' behaviour—the standard of 'the sensible man'. Hence the upright man does not have mistresses, but the law only requires that a man should not neglect his wives while he pursues mistresses, and allows him mistresses if they be not married to others. This distinction and its consequences will be elaborated in the next chapter.

Lozi judges do not make continual explicit use of the general phrase for a reasonable man because in most cases they are giving judgments on the behaviour of persons occupying specific social positions in multiplex relations—they are chiefly concerned with relationships of status. Therefore the judges more often work explicitly with the phrases, 'a good husband', 'a sensible induna', and so on. Indeed, they often use the term for the social position without using the qualificative. This in itself states the norms of customary behaviour and reasonable fulfilment of obligations. The emphatic use of terms defining social position is very common in praising people. For example, Lozi rarely speak of a woman as an industrious gardener without adding, '*Kimusali*' ('she's a wife'), or, '*Kimwana*' ('she's a child'), since gardening is so important a duty of women. Similarly, when it became known how much Nyambe, the son of NAWALA (R46) Mutondo, had brought back from Johannesburg for his kin, people said of him: '*Kimwana, uezize*'—'he's a child, he has done [what he ought to have done]'. This phrase, '*Uezize*', ('he [or she] has done') is often used on its own of a man who has fulfilled his obligations, beyond reasonable demands. Similarly, Lozi say, 'He's a chief—an induna—a headman—a subject,' for political positions ; 'He's a fisherman—a herdsman—

—a servant,' for employees ; 'He's a magician—a smith—a potter—a carver,' for specialists ; and so forth.

Judges also use this common practice of reference, and in doing so they are setting up the differentiated standard of the reasonable and perhaps even upright incumbent of a particular social position. Recall what ALULEYA (L8) said to one nephew in 'The Case of the Biassed Father' : 'You, B, I see you are really a man, because you said, "My brothers, do not leave home." And you went to your father to adjust matters. You should have persisted more, but your behaviour when you returned to Loziland shows you are really a man.' 'A man' here means one who tries to see that a family dispute is argued out and settled.

Again, in 'The Case of the Man who Helped his Mothers-in-Law Cross a Ford' (below, p. 148), a judge praised a girl who said she could not live with her husband after he saw her two maternal uncles' wives naked and slept with one of them. He told her husband : 'I support your wife ; she is a good girl, a true woman [wife].[1] If our children were the same, we would have children.' Here the girl is praised because she recognizes her duties to her maternal uncles, so she is 'a child', and these conflict with her duties as a woman and wife of their wives' seducer, so she is 'a woman'.

This usage is not, of course, peculiar to the Lozi. We have it in phrases such as, 'he's a man—a gentleman—a sportsman—a king', and so on. In both cultures it implies approbation of a person showing the qualities and conforming to the norms demanded of a certain social position ; or in the negative—as 'hasimulena yo', 'he is not a chief',—it states disapprobation of a person who has failed to show these qualities, or has exhibited contrary qualities, and has violated the appropriate norms. Note how in 'The Case of the Eloping Wife' the judges said of her insults to her father : 'Now your father has no child' . . . 'Find another father.' But this sort of phrase, common though it be in everyday usage presumably everywhere, is of great sociological importance because it covers the whole social process of judging people against norms, and it is therefore very significant when it is used in the judicial process, as among the Lozi.

---

[1] *Musali* = 'woman' and 'wife'.

It is their ' reasonable person ' differentiated by sex and in manifold social positions.

In addition to these phrases for the reasonable incumbent of a social position, the Lozi also apply the verb ' *kuutwahala* ', ' to be understandable ', ' to be obvious ', ' to be reasonable ', to the whole of evidence or to particular actions. *Kuutwahala* is a derivative of *kuutwa*, to hear or understand, which is also used frequently by judges. *Kukolwahala*, to be credible, from *kukolwa* (to believe) is similarly used. *-Lukile*, right, is also applied to actions and to evidence ; but I did not record this use of *-ngana*, sensible, without a noun of social position. Again, the Lozi do not always use these phrases explicitly—at least they do not appear often in my necessarily abbreviated records and I do not recall their frequent use. Unfortunately, while I was in the field I was not yet on the look-out for them. But I noted their appearance sufficiently often to be able to cite them as established legal concepts, and to say that they are always implicitly present in the judges' statement of norms against the recapitulation of witnessed or reported actions. These phrases too are commonly used outside the courts.

The judges therefore use in this aspect of their work a process and standards that are common throughout the society. They are setting up minimum standards which people ought to observe, if they are not to be punished, for various social positions. These are not always ideal standards, for Lozi ethics demands fulfilment of obligations beyond the basic reasonable norm, and generous refusal to insist on rights. The concept of ' reasonable ' measures the range of allowed departure from the highest standards of duty and absolute conformity to norm, and the minimum adherence which is insisted on. Professors Llewellyn and Hoebel drew attention to this important problem in their *The Cheyenne Way : Conflict and Case Law in Primitive Jurisprudence*, when they wrote : '. . . one phenomenon of law, as of institutions in general, which has received altogether too little attention save in relation to bills of rights and the due process clause, is the two *ranges of leeway* of man's conduct which are a part of any legal or social system—the range of permissible leeway, and the range of actively protected leeway '.[1] Curiously, though Professor

---

[1] Norman : University of Oklahoma Press (1941), at p. 23.

Llewellyn is a jurist, he did not suggest taking over the legal concept of ' reasonable standards ' to handle this problem, though I hope I have already shown how these standards among the Lozi cover both ' the range of permissible leeway, and the range of actively protected leeway '. Indeed, it seems to me that ' the reasonable man ' should become as important in sociology and social anthropology as are concepts like the ideal type, the average man, and the deviant. If ' the reasonable man ' is more precisely the man who conforms reasonably to the customs and standards of his social position, clearly he corresponds closely with the concept of ' the *rôle* of a particular *status* ', which has become so important in current anthropology and sociology.[1] The rôle of a status—for which I prefer the term (social) position to avoid the plural ' statuses '—is that series of actions which a person ought to perform, and which his fellows are entitled to expect from him. Professors Parsons and Shils thus speak of the expectations of the rôle ; and Mr. A. L. Epstein, in his analysis of how African Urban Courts work in Northern Rhodesia, has qualified these as ' reasonable expectations '.[2] This qualification is important, for it sets those standards of conformity in meeting the demands of one's rôle which courts will enforce for a particular situation. The situations which confront people vary greatly, particularly at times when major social changes are occurring. Many rôles, defined in general terms such as ' a husband must care for his wife ', remain constant ; but in all the variety of actual, and even changing, situations, the concept of ' reasonableness ' enables judgments to be passed on actions in terms of new as well as of established standards. I shall consider at the end of this chapter this operative utility of the concept.

X

I have dealt so far with departures from norms of good conduct and breaches of approved customs. Among the Lozi there are also ' norms of misconduct '—customs which appertain to

---

[1] See, e.g., Linton, R., *The Study of Man*, New York and London : Appleton —Century (1936), pp. 114 ff. and Parsons, T., and Shils, E. (editors), *Towards a General Theory of Action*, Cambridge : Harvard University Press (1951), passim.
[2] *Juridical Techniques and the Judicial Process*, p. 12.

wrongdoers (*mikwa yabafosi*). These are highly significant for the judges when they try charges of adultery, theft, slander, or assault.

CASE 27 : THE CASE OF THE SCHOOLBOY ADULTERER

Husband joins with his wife in charging defendant, a schoolboy, with adultery with the wife, Saa-Katengo Court at Lialui, 27th and 28th August, 1942 (on appeal by defendant from conviction in court of sub-district induna IKANJIWA, R38).

The husband's story was : He was cook to a missionary. He went round touring schools with the missionary and left his wife at the mission station. When he got back in the early afternoon several days later, he found his wife out and their children unfed and late for school. He fed them. When his wife came back she said she had been hoeing. Next day when he came back to his hut after serving lunch at the missionary's house, again she was not there, and the children had not been fed or sent back to school. Again she said she had been hoeing. When he found her away on the third day, he went down to the garden asking in the villages he passed for his wife. He came to the garden and moved her hoe from where she always hid it to another place. He returned by an alternative path to his hut to find she had not returned. When she came home and she said she had been hoeing, he challenged her with his visit to the garden, proving it by his having moved the hoe. She confessed she had been lying in the bush with the defendant.

The defendant denied he had been with her ; she confirmed her husband's story. Hence she was joined with her husband in suing the defendant, and sat beside her husband ; in most adultery cases, when both wife and the man accused deny the charge, they sit together. This woman had already been convicted twice of adultery and her husband had got damages in those two suits.

The defendant denied the charge, though he admitted that the woman had tried to seduce him into becoming her lover. She wrote him a letter inviting him to come to her which he showed to his schoolfellows who gave evidence of this. He asked them what he should do ? Some said take her, others said, no, one maintaining : ' No woman tempts a man, perhaps she has a disease ' [and believes she can get rid of it by passing it on to the man, since this woman was a well-known whore].

Evidence for the wife was given by a woman friend who said that she had been told by the wife that the schoolboy was her lover and had been shown 2s. by the wife which she alleged he had given her.

This friend stated she saw the defendant go to the wife's hut. She and another woman gave evidence that they saw the defendant and another schoolboy sitting on deckchairs at the hut and eating oranges with the wife while her husband was away, and heard her put a riddle to the other schoolboy : ' If someone offered you porridge, would you eat ? ' He replied : ' If she always offered it, I would eat ; if only once, I would not.'

The defendant took his stand on three points : (1) He said the woman was using him to conceal her true lover. (2) He ridiculed the way in which the husband learnt his name : ' I ask you, Malozi, would a woman if her husband failed to find her in the garden, just like that, at once give her lover's name ? ' (3) He was afraid to commit adultery because if caught he would not only be made to pay damages, but would also be dismissed from the teachers' training course.

The lines of cross-examination emerge from the judgments :

Kuta clerk : ' Woman, you are a liar, you are not the mistress of the defendant. You loved him. But why did he not reply to your letter ? You turned against him, to get him into trouble because he refused you. I do not believe that a woman would just tell her husband the name of her true lover because she was late ; and you women learn at the puberty ceremony (*mwalyanjo*) to name someone else if you are trapped. If you have a lover, it is another. You must pay damages to the defendant because you have made trouble for him.'

MBASIWANA (R46) : ' In NGAMBELA Mataa's time [1920–9] I was charged with doing wrong with the wife of X. X sought her in the garden. She said she was with me. We were summoned to the kuta, where the woman confessed. I denied it, but I was convicted. Of course I was with her.' [The kuta laughed—SOLAMI shook his head and said to me, sitting next to him, ' This MBASIWANA ! ', as MBASIWANA was an attendant of mine.] ' So I see that the woman would tell. I see that the boy would not let the woman go—how would he fail to take her ? He must pay cattle. As for you, woman, I know your ways are bad ' [she was related to him as a distant classificatory daughter, and a member of a family near his home]. ' You are a whore and a liar. You must pay the kuta.'[1]

ATANGA, another Katengo induna, refused to judge, as he was related to the defendant ; KALONGA (R15) told him he must, but he did not.

Prince Mwananyanda : ' Girl, your suit is not good. It is your

---

[1] In 1942 an adulterer paid £2 or 2 beasts to the injured husband, and the wife paid a fine of £1 or 1 beast to the kuta.

complaint, not your husband's, for it is you and not he who quarrels with the defendant. If this man was your lover of old, why were you afraid of the man who tried to enter your hut at night ? ' [Neighbours had heard her cry out one night when her husband was away, and she said someone tried to enter her hut.] ' These are your lies to bind this man because he refused you. On that affair of the garden—the story of your delay in the garden was also lies. How can he be your old friend [lover], if you say you had three different days been with him in the bush ; and if he were your lover of old, why did you write him the letter ? You do not know this boy at all. I think you should pay him damages for false accusation.'

IMUTUKO (R28) : ' I think you, boy, and this woman, you know one another. I think the garden affair is true : the woman tried to hide it but failed because her husband had been to the garden. I think you had this woman, were then afraid of the school and your parents, and stopped. Your friends did not tell on you. The other woman was told by this girl that you were her lover. Indeed you were, and you were not children playing together. If you sleep with a woman once, she is your wife . . . I see you knew one another.'

ING'UNDE (R20) : ' Boy, I follow in this judgment because of the tempting seductiveness of women. We know them because we also have our sweethearts.' He recapitulated the story of the husband going to the garden. ' Then the woman failed, and had to tell the truth because her husband was angry. There is also the other woman witness : (1) When they were washing at the canal she saw the 2s. left from the money you gave your sweetheart : and (2) she saw you enter the hut of the woman. What other evidence do we want ? On the letter : there was an affair where Z showed the hospital orderly a letter tempting him, from a woman he did not love. The orderly told him to show the letter to her husband. He did so and was released from any fault ; the woman admitted it.' [The boy had been cross-examined on why he did not show the letter to the woman's kinsmen or to the husband as soon as he returned.] ' There are many other things, which I lack time to expound. Perhaps SOLAMI, your owner, will give you life. I see you have done wrong.'

LIOMA (L6) : ' You, woman, I agree with Prince Mwananyanda. We like a person to be really caught—I say nothing, but that you should pay him damages for false accusation.' He called on NAMAMBA (R12) to judge, but NAMAMBA said : ' It is only NAMUNDA (R11),' meaning that he would not give a judgment, and only NAMUNDA remained on the right save for SOLAMI (R3), the finisher.

ALULEYA-IFUNGA (L8, sitting as F2) : ' Boy, your case is hard.

This case defeats me. There is that riddle of the porridge, and the way you told your friends she was a whore. It was your cunning to show the letter to your friends and say you would not take her. . . . How could she refuse to tell her husband? I agree with those who say "this woman and you know one another". In their evidence your friends tried to help the kuta, but their evidence does not enter [i.e. it is irrelevant]. You, woman, you are a whore, and your parents know it.'

NAMUNDA-KATANEKWA (R11): 'Boy, your case has no doctor, unless the doctor is the finisher. You and this woman are accustomed to one another. She told her friend you were her lover and showed her the 2s. You ate this man's oranges and sat in his chair. You kept the affair of the letter secret. I see that you have done wrong. Our finisher will speak to you.'

SOLAMI (R3): 'Boy and woman—I do not agree with ATANGA who will not enter into judgment in the case of a relative. When a policeman is sworn in, he must agree to arrest his father, his mother, his sister, and so on. So I do not mind whom I try. Your difficulty, boy, was seen by ING'UNDE in his judgment. You say you knew the ways of this woman—that she was a well-known whore. If so, why did you not show her letter to her husband? She is your sweetheart. You should have shown the letter. On the length of rope, I do not judge, because I do not know it.' [The husband went to the place in the bush where the wife said she lay with the defendant, and found tracks and marks on the ground; he measured their distance from the path with a rope.] 'I judge on the letter, and on the woman who saw you at the hut. You pay the husband £2, and, girl, whether or not you have cattle to pay a fine you will go to prison. In future we will not make people pay damages for sleeping with you. For you, my child, I am sorry to say are the biggest whore I have seen in this kuta. You sell yourself to get riches. From now on, you are a wife of the country. If I were you [to her husband] I would divorce her, whatever my heart felt. You, boy, will pay £2 and the woman will remain here in prison.'

The defendant said he was not guilty and would not pay the damages. ALULEYA-IFUNGA reprimanded him: 'No-one can refuse of his own power to pay. You must appeal to the Sikalo Kuta.' The woman was jailed. The defendant appealed to the Sikalo and was upheld on the grounds that the evidence was not conclusive and the woman might have been concealing her true lover. The lower kuta's strictures on the defendant's behaviour over the letter, the oranges, etc., were repeated, and presumably (I did not hear the judgments) the husband was therefore absolved from paying damages for false accusation to the schoolboy who had behaved so foolishly.

In this case, even allowing that the defendant was acquitted on appeal, we see that both judges and parties continually work with norms of reasonable behaviour. There are norms of general reasonableness, such as that raised in the defendant's plea that he would have feared to commit adultery, since he knew that if caught he would be expelled from school. The judges too used such norms. Thus Prince Mwananyanda argued that if the charge were true, why did the woman write the letter and why did she cry out in the night when a man tried to enter her hut? Other norms are more specific to the situation of alleged adultery. NAMUNDA-KATANEKWA held that because the defendant sat on the absent husband's chair and ate the husband's orange, and because he had not reported the letter, as an innocent man might reasonably be expected to do, he was guilty. SOLAMI added that as the woman was a well-known whore, an innocent man would even more probably have shown her letter to her husband on his return. (But note that the fact that she was notoriously a loose woman would not directly have made the judges accept that she was guilty of this particular adultery. In fact she admitted guilt.) Here the judges go on the presumption that the good behave uprightly in all situations. Since Lozi men presume [1] that the high incidence of adultery and divorce is primarily due to the evil nature of woman, they argue that if a woman tries to seduce a man and he does not respond, he will tell her husband. If he does not report her, the probability is that he is guilty For they also have a presumption about men that few will refuse a woman who offers herself (see MBASIWANA's judgment). Again, Lozi law presumes that there is no platonic relationship between unrelated men and women. It is not customary or right for a man to accept food privately from an 'accessible' woman, or give her snuff or other things, unless he is her lover. Who is an 'accessible' woman varies with the tribe.

CASE 28: THE CASE OF CROSS-COUSIN ADULTERY

Thus at Namalya Kuta under NAWALA (R42) an Mbunda accused another Mbunda, one of my servants, of committing adultery with

---

[1] This presumption is discussed below, pp. 215–16.

his wife. His case was that the defendant had given his wife a mat and a basket of meal. The defendant proved that the woman was his mother's brother's daughter, therefore his ' sister ' by Lozi custom, and he was entitled to make gifts to her. NAWALA and the other Lozi held that had he been a Lozi he would have been acquitted. ' For were you a Lozi she would be your sister indeed, though even a Lozi makes gifts to his sister in public. But we know you Mbunda do not call the daughter of your mother's brother " my sister ", and you can marry her. If you can marry her, you can commit adultery with her. If you were making presents to her because she is your relative, you should have given the things through her husband. Then he would have thanked you, for you would have been giving them to him. But you gave them on the side : you gave to her as your mistress. You will pay him £2, and she will give us £1 to send to the kuta.' [Four years later the defendant admitted his guilt to me.]

Other presumptions held by the male judges about women influence their decisions, for men have certain ideas about the customary ways of women. In ' The Case of the Schoolboy Adulterer ', for one judge it was reasonable for a woman to accuse an innocent man of being her lover in order to protect her true lover, and this is what he, with many other men, believes girls are taught during their puberty seclusion. Another judge, who has been caught himself in an analogous situation, has learnt that adulteresses reveal the names of their true lovers ; this then is reasonable behaviour for an adulteress. His personal experience rebuts the above presumption. Men also believe that it is customary for women, especially for a woman and her husband's sister, to tell each other of their affairs. The judges are thus working with a series of presumptions based on social and personal belief, and also personal experience. Here men are arguing in terms of what they believe women do and what women's customs are, and I cannot say whether their presumptions are sound or not.

These last presumptions, like others cited earlier, illustrate that for the kuta there are acts of behaviour which can only be reasonably explained on the assumption that the doer is an adulterer or adulteress. It is a false paradox, but perhaps illuminating, to say that the kuta has a view of the ' reasonable and customary ' adulterer or adulteress. For lovers and their mistresses behave in certain standardized ways, which are not those of the innocent.   These ways are well known, and assemble into social stereotypes.   ING'UNDE began his judgment:

'I follow . . . because of the tempting seductiveness of women. We know them, because we have our sweethearts.'

When the defendant said under cross-examination that he just took the orange because he was offered it, one judge countered:

'Come on, you cannot deceive us ; we all have our mistresses and know how a woman behaves with her lover.'

Indeed, when the accused woman tried to substantiate her allegation that the schoolboy was her lover, by describing how she sent him the letter and entertained him and his friend, she said : 'You, Malozi [judges], you know how lovers behave. . . .' It was this, and the way she boldly looked the judges in the eyes, that made SOLAMI insist on her going to prison ; he said her behaviour showed her to be a whore, and contrasted her mien with that of an admitted adulteress in another case. She had kept her eyes fixed on the ground and obviously had been ashamed : 'She behaved as a woman caught in adultery should behave.' [1]

The Lozi thus have patterns of behaviour, customary usages, which are appropriate for adulterers (*mikwa yabonyatsi*).   Some of those patterns cover modes of sexual intercourse : Lozi men told me they practised sexual actions with their mistresses which they considered would be wrongful with their wives.   These customs of adulterers cover the ways in which the lovers treat each other in public, as well as privately.   This raises the problem of whether the existence of these beliefs and customs in fact influences the behaviour of adulterers so that, in effect, they give themselves away.   A man likes to give his mistress gifts and she expects them, but my servant in 'The Case of the Cross-Cousin Adultery' could have given his kinswoman-sweetheart the presents he wished to publicly before her husband.   Had he done so, he would not have been suspected, let alone convicted.   Was it guilty conscience, or the wish clearly to give as a lover, which prevented him ?   But it is worth noting, though this was not

---

[1] She was travelling on a barge and the clerk of the transport company seduced her with 10s. to one act of adultery.

raised by the judges, that he gave her not money or beer or clothes, which are appropriate gifts to a mistress. The gifts of a sleeping-mat and a basket of meal are more fitting for a wife or a relative. It is possible that the norm under which she was a cross-cousin, and therefore a potential wife, influenced him here.

Again, in 'The Case of the Foreign Thief', there was no reason why the accused should not have paid his servants and bought relish in the village where he slept. He seems to have tried to conceal his theft by concealing that he had money. These two circumstances helped convict him : had he behaved as if he had money rightfully his, like an honest man, he might have escaped conviction. As there are *mikwa yabonyatsi* (customs of adulterers) so there are *mikwa yamasholi* (customs of thieves). Indeed, the Lozi language is very rich in special terms to describe different ways of stealing. Similarly there are *mikwa yabaloyi* (customs of sorcerers), *yababulayi* (of murderers), etc. I did not think of investigating this problem in the field ; and I hope that others will pursue novelists' and autobiographers' hints that social stereotypes of wrongdoers in fact influence the behaviour of actual wrongdoers.

I have suggested that we might speak of the existence of a reasonable adulterer or a reasonable thief because, as I understand the reasoning of Lozi judges in these cases, they argue that when all the accused's acts are considered, these acts assemble into one of these social stereotypes. In our terms, they become guilty 'beyond reasonable doubt'. I have not heard a Lozi judge use any phrase which could be interpreted as 'reasonable doubt', nor can I myself translate it into Lozi. When Lozi judges acquit an accused person they state in general terms, 'the evidence is not strong', or 'there is no evidence', or 'I do not believe (*hanikolwi*) that . . .', or more rarely 'Hakuutwahali that . . . (it is not understandable—reasonable—that . . .)'. More often they affirm particularly, 'You, woman, you do not know this boy at all . . .', etc., and then state the evidential grounds for this conclusion. What they seem to me to do, in the absence of direct convicting or rebutting evidence, is to assess reported behaviour against their social stereotypes of wrongdoers. Unfortunately, I heard very few varied cases of this type under trial.

Wrongdoers for the Lozi thus in a way behave 'reasonably'—

their actions are *utwahala*, which primarily means ' understand-able ', but which also can mean ' reasonable '. But obviously they behave without ' uprightness ' or ' sense '. They have not *ngana*, sense, but *butali*, which describes ' wisdom ' or ' intelligence ' and ' cunning '. Lozi speak of *muatuli yabutali*, a wise judge, but it is in the sense of ' cunning ' that *butali* is ascribed to wrongdoers. There is *butali* (cunning) *bwamasholi* (of thieves), *bwabonyatsi* (of fornicators), *bwabaloyi* (of sorcerers). Women, too, are more often described by men as having *butali*, cunning, rather than *ngana*, sense ; and the Lozi use *butali* to describe the wonderful material achievements of White men as against their lack of human kindness.

XI

The preceding cases have been cited to illustrate that a Barotse *kuta* cross-examines and assesses evidence by the standard of how a reasonable man or woman would have behaved, meticulously according to custom : refusing oranges from another man's wife and making a point of showing him her letters tempting to adultery ; calling in outsiders and arbitrating calmly when his children are involved in a fight ; exhibiting the evidence of faeces to unrelated witnesses before washing clothes ; and so on. Thus in seeking the truth judges are matter-of-fact, probing for inconsistencies and improbabilities in the evidence, demanding direct in preference to hearsay and circumstantial evidence, prying at those significant departures from customary and reasonable behaviour which will indicate that a man has erred. Probably even in the past, magical ordeals and divination were resorted to only when the *kuta* could not arrive at the facts by ' objective ' evidence : in *prima facie* allegations of theft, and above all in accusations of sorcery where there could not be ' objective ' evidence.

The reasonable man is further differentiated, because the *kuta* is usually concerned with a person occupying a specific position and acting in a specific situation. Each of these positions, including positions of wrongdoing, has its own norms and customs. Some of these are publicly exhibited and known to all Lozi. Others are believed to be the practices of particular types of persons, but still constitute presumptions which guide the kuta's cross-examination and judgment. As men the councillors hold certain beliefs about women's customs and rules ; they also have ideas of how wrongdoers behave. They apply these varied standards, as well as general standards, according to the positions of the parties involved. Contrariwise, women, though they are not judges, hold beliefs about how men should behave. Thus the Eloping Wife berated her husband for not beating her, and asked if he was a man.

The kuta may have before it in many cases reports on the behaviour of the disputing parties, and of others, over a number of years. It considers in detail whether they conformed to the norms of a particular type of relationship. The parties in litigation frequently are father and son, or brother and brother, or husband and wife, or fellow-wives of one man, or husband and wife and adulterer, or headman and villager, or lord and underling. The specific relationship of the quarrelling parties is set in the life of a small community where they have other specific relationships with different types of kinsfolk and in-laws or other lords and subjects, who often are witnesses. Behaviour in all these relationships is examined by the kuta. The standards therefore are not simply, did X behave in a particular situation as a reasonable man would have behaved, allowing for age, class, and education : but, did X behave reasonably by the customs of indunaship ; and, did he give reasonably of his catches and earnings to his father to show that he loved and respected him ; and, did he observe the customs of in-lawship, or blood-brotherhood, etc. ? The standards are a reasonable councillor, a reasonable father, a reasonable son-in-law, a reasonable husband, a reasonable wife. And always there is the presumption that *mutu yangana yalukile*, the sensible upright person, conforms to appropriate customs and norms.

But the legal significance of reasonable and customary behaviour extends far beyond its use in cross-examination and in assessing evidence to provide for judgment. The issue before the kuta may turn from a narrow, legally enforceable claim into an examination of whether the parties observed the obligations due to each other. Thus the claim for a garden in ' The Case of the Biassed Father ' became an enquiry into the behaviour of the parties as headman, son and nephews [also ' sons ' in Lozi], brothers [cousins]. The suit was thus reduced to the issues :

had Y been a reasonable substitute father to his nephews and a reasonable headman, ruling impartially ? Had his son Z been a reasonable elder ' brother ' to his cousins ? Had these cousins been reasonable ' sons ' and reasonable subjects of the headman, and reasonable younger ' brothers ' to their cousin ? In short, ' reasonable behaviour ' becomes the central issue in this type of case. The complainant contends that ' so-and-so did not behave reasonably to me ' (*haasikaeza hande*—he did not behave well) ; and the defendant counters in similar terms. What constitutes ' reasonable behaviour ' will obviously again be both general and also specific to the relationship between the parties.

The problem of whether a person has fulfilled his obligations to another may be simple, if there is a clear breach of custom ; or it may be complex in that a norm such as, ' A husband must care for his wife ', has to be applied to varying circumstances. Thus a wife may claim divorce from her husband on the grounds that he has committed an absolute breach of custom which cannot be remedied by damages or apology.

CASE 29 : THE CASE OF THE URINATING HUSBAND
(*from a text*)

A drunken husband, sleeping with one wife, when going out to urinate turned at the wrong door, entered his other wife's room, and urinated on her. Induna ISHEWAMBUTO (Namakau Kuta) granted both wives immediate divorce : a husband must not mix his sexual actions with two wives.

CASE 30 : THE CASE OF THE WIFE'S GRANARY (*from a text*)

A wife was away visiting her parental home. Some of her kin came to her husband's home and he took food from her granary for them. Later people came prepared to pay a good price for grain for a feast : her husband took some of her grain and sold it, and on her return gave her the money. She claimed divorce and was granted it by the Lialui Kuta despite his protests that he was dispensing hospitality to her kin and selling the grain to her advantage, because it is prohibited for a husband to go to his wife's granary.[1]

But a wife usually seeks a divorce by asking the kuta to declare that her husband has behaved so unreasonably that he no longer

---

[1] A rule necessary to protect the wife's rights, whose significance will be dealt with in a later work.

regards or treats her as a wife. This, in Lozi thinking, is why they have passed statutes to divorce women from men who have gone to White country for more than a certain number of years, a number which has steadily been reduced. It is unreasonable for a man to expect his wife to live alone for too long a period.

CASE 31 : THE CASE OF THE MIGRANT HUSBAND
(from a text)

Where one absent husband's kin opposed the divorce claimed after the statutory three years on the grounds that he constantly sent his wife money, clothes, and blankets, the NGAMBELA's (R1) kuta held : ' This woman did not marry a blanket.'

Within a month of the divorce the husband returned home : he had in fact been on his way back from Johannesburg when the suit was brought. He found his wife gone and went to reclaim her. She wished to return to him, but her father said she had been divorced by the kuta [*res judicata—taba iatuzwi*, the case has been judged] and her husband must give a new marriage-payment to remarry her. He was willing to do this, but his guardian, his dead father's elder brother, objected, saying a man could not marry a woman twice and that if the kuta had known the husband was on his way home, it would not have granted divorce. He upbraided the father-in-law for being greedy. The father-in-law insisted on his demand, and the husband, to get his wife back, paid a beast.

The husband's father insisted that this was wrong, and brought suit before the NGAMBELA's kuta. It held that if it had known the husband was on his way home it would not have granted divorce, and ordered the wife's father to return the beast. This decision, to interpret ' return home ' as ' leave place of employment ', overrode the *res judicata* rule. The statute aimed to bring husbands home to contented wives and to maintain marriages : hence it is a decision in the interests of good morals and public policy. Also the kuta was objecting to her father's unjust enrichment, which was what annoyed the man's guardian. At least he did not object strongly to, though he protested against, the husband's leaving the beast with his father-in-law for the sake of friendly relations. I heard this case when I was travelling in a barge with all three men, and the two elders as *bashemi bange* (' other parents ', the parents of spouses) were joking. The husband's guardian and other men scolded the wife's father as a greedy man who sold his daughter, and who had been exposed in the kuta ; he laughed shamefacedly, and said : ' Anyway, I got my beast.'

Husbands can divorce their wives of their own will. In many

divorce suits brought by wives, the kuta has to apply certain general rules, stating how husbands ought to treat their wives, to a husband's conduct in a set of particular circumstances. The circumstances fall into certain patterns and are very rarely unique —I shall cite one case where they were—but it is often not easy for the kuta to judge, on contradictory evidence, whether the husband acted reasonably. I cite first a simple case.

CASE 32 : THE CASE OF THE CONTEMPTUOUS HUSBAND

before Saa-Katengo Kuta at Lialui, on 29th July, 1942 (judgment given in the husband's absence, he being away in White country)

The woman was held to be divorced on the following grounds :

(1) After the husband married again he forced her to pull up newly planted cassava so that he could manure the garden for his new wife. He had already taken two gardens from her. When the old wife refused to obey the new wife, the latter told her to obey their husband, the owner of the garden. This was *kuleleka* (to drive her away).

(2) When the village moved at flood-season, the husband took the hut of his first wife, and gave it to his second wife. This should not be done.

(3) Since the husband had gone to White country, he had sent nothing to his first wife.

(4) The husband counter-claimed in a letter that his wife had committed adultery. This was held to be a separate issue.

(5) The kuta considered that the husband wanted to keep the wife as a trap to get cattle if she married again. ' This cannot be done. No-one shall place the child of a person in slavery, to make her a trap, in order to get cattle from people.'

(6) ' He insults the kuta because in his letter from White country he instructs us what to do. He puffs himself up with pride. Does he think he sits on these our stools ? '

(7) ' We are suspicious of his evidence because he refused to appear before sub-district indunas NAWASILUNDU (R29), or MWENECIENGELE (R32), saying of the latter, " I do not enter the kuta of an Mbunda " : [1] and then before MUNONO (R23) ' [when NAWASILUNDU sent the case to him, as MUNONO's kuta was close to Mongu where the husband worked as a cook]. ' Finally, when he was summoned to the capital he ran away to White country.' NAMUNDA-KATANEKWA (R11) rebuked him for his insult to MWENECIENGELE : ' No-one must call

---

[1] The first MWENECIENGELE was an Mbunda chief who immigrated to Loziland with his people about 1800.

them Mbunda. They came long ago, to our grandfathers. We are the same people, one nation. No-one can cheapen people. And his kuta is a kuta of the king, of the NGAMBELA. When the culprit returns we will fine him severely.'

The first two grounds freed the wife because the husband had broken the rules that require a man to treat all his wives similarly. The third ground freed her because an absentee husband must still care for his wife. The fourth ground freed her because he unreasonably wished to prevent her marrying again after he had ceased to treat her as a wife, unless she could find a lover to elope with her, in which case he could claim three cattle [1] from the lover. The kuta stated that it was against public morals and policy to allow this (' No-one shall place the child of a person in slavery, to make her a trap, in order to get cattle from people '). Grounds six and seven were relevant because they justified the kuta in giving judgment by default, which it is reluctant to do.

CASE 33 : THE CASE OF JUDGMENT BY DEFAULT

Thus the Lialui Kuta told me in July, 1947, that it was unusual for the kuta to give judgment by default. It preferred to fine the defaulting party for contempt and summon him to the case. In one case sub-district induna IKANJIWA appealed to the Lialui Kuta for help when a defendant had three times rejected summons to attend. SOLAMI (R3) commented : ' These sub-district indunas do not know their powers. He should fine the man, then if he does not come to court give judgment against him.' I was told that in the past no-one would have dared to disobey the kuta's summons.

The husband in Case 32, by insulting and avoiding the kutas, had abandoned their protection of his rights. Finally, the counterclaim for adultery was irrelevant. If a man's wife commits adultery, this does not absolve him from his duty to care for her.

CASE 34 : THE CASE OF THE ADULTERESS'S GOOD HUSBAND

(Mongu–Lialui District Kuta, July, 1947)

Thus a man who continued to care for his wife and her parents after he had decided to divorce her for getting a child in adultery,

---

[1] Raised to five cattle in 1946.

was highly commended by the kuta for being a proper upright man.

The way in which the problem, whether the husband behaved reasonably, alters with the circumstances is illustrated by a case which involved a situation resembling in some ways that of Case 32 ('The Contemptuous Husband ').

CASE 35 : THE CASE OF THE LAZY HUSBAND
(from a text)

This case was first heard by the elders of the village of the husband. The wife complained that when her husband took a second wife, he had failed to prepare a hut for the latter. He begged his first wife to move into an old hut, because it was not proper for a newcomer to be received in a shoddy hut, and he would build her a new hut. She agreed. Throughout one year he had made excuses for not building the new hut : now in the second year he had not even collected the posts. The village headman stated he knew her story to be true : he had himself cautioned his younger brother about how badly he was treating a good wife. The latter ought to pay his wife 10s. as a gift and build the hut at once ; this was what the kuta would order. The wife insisted she wanted a divorce. The headman said he could not quarrel with his brother by supporting her in this claim : she must go to the kuta. She went to the kuta of sub-district induna ISHEWAMBUTO (R50) which held that the husband's behaviour in placing his new wife in a good hut was not right ; but that since his first wife had agreed he should have hastened to build her a new hut. To keep her waiting two years was unreasonable, and he should pay her 10s. ; and though she was claiming divorce, she should have half the goods of the marriage, since virtually her husband had divorced her.

Justice is here achieved by a fiction, in holding that the husband's action amounted constructively to divorce, for if a husband divorces his wife, she is entitled to half her crops and half the goods (clothes, pots, blankets, hoes) of her hut. If she seeks and gets divorce, she is entitled only to half the crops, since she has rejected the marriage, and therefore its goods.

Here is a far more complex situation in which a woman claimed a divorce, since her husband had not committed, except incidentally, an absolute breach of custom. This is the commonest type of divorce case.

CASE 36 : THE CASE OF THE PRUDISH WIFE

Mongu-Lialui District Kuta, 23rd June, 1947, on appeal from the sub-district kuta Yuka of Prince Mwenekandala (F12)

The woman's claim for a divorce was refused in the lower court. Her kinsman guardian was SIKOTA-MUTUMWA (L5), then senior steward of Mongu-Lialui District Kuta, but as he did not support her main plea he remained seated in his place on the mat and did not join her at the plaintiff's post.

The woman's claim was based on three grounds. (1) When she was ill her husband delayed divining the cause and treating her, and finally he did not treat her in his home but sent her to her parents for treatment. The husband's defence on this ground was that his father had supplied the medicines as he knew this illness, since he had just been cured of it. The father-in-law stated he supplied the medicine, to be inserted in cuts on the body, but could not treat his daughter-in-law as he could not see her stripped ; nor could her mother-in-law. The husband could not treat her himself as she was ashamed to be seen naked by him [astonishment in court]. Finally, the husband could not have her treated in his village which was inhabited by members of the Watchtower sect who would not allow drumming for illness. So he carried her on his back to her parents' village through the flood. Here the kuta had two unprecedented situations, created by the wife's unique modesty and the refusal of Watchtower members to allow drumming. The judges held that it was quite reasonable for the husband in these circumstances to take his wife to her parents, where she could be drummed for and her mother could apply the medicines. ' Where else should he take you ? ' He demonstrated his care for her by bringing food, water, and wood to her.

(2) She further claimed that her husband had divorced her by snatching from her and taking with him to Senanga some blankets and a pot and using them with a new wife. This is a common sort of allegation, that a man uses one wife's property with another wife. She alleged, supported by her mother, that he had dragged the blankets off her. The husband maintained that she agreed to give him two blankets and a sheet, out of eight blankets and four sheets, for himself. The woman under cross-examination admitted the numbers, and was told that this was riches : ' Do you not know that if you marry some are rich and some are poor ? Your husband could [reasonably] take from this plenty which is more than most women have ! ' On the allegation that the husband had snatched the blankets from her in her mother's presence, the attitude of the

kuta was summed up in the following piece of cross-examination, when the mother had gone home after giving evidence :

A prince (to woman) : ' I'm sorry I did not put this question before your mother went away. You say she saw you being ill-treated, your blanket being pulled away from you when you were ill. Why didn't she at the same time report to some people in the village ? '—*Woman :* ' No, she did not do this, but said, " Wait a bit." ' Moreover, the mother had asked her son-in-law for envelopes and stamps so that they could tell him how his wife was progressing ; and he produced a letter from his wife, saying she was better and acknowledging £1 he sent—which she said she had not spent as it was a trap for her.

The kuta therefore held on grounds of reasonableness that the wife and her mother were lying.

On the allegation that the husband took other of her goods from her, the kuta found that these amounted to one pot with a hole in it which he had taken to be repaired. He had written to her a letter to tell her about this. She was asked : ' If a man takes a pot to be repaired and informs his wife, telling her of the affairs of the house, is this driving her away ? ' The kuta therefore held that the husband had acted reasonably in taking blankets for the journey from his senior wife, out of the many he had given her, and had altogether behaved as a husband who respected his wife.

(3) The soundness of the husband's case was admitted by the woman's guardian, SIKOTA-MUTUMWA (L5), who, leaving his place, sat on the ground and said he thought the man a good husband and son-in-law but went on to say : ' I ask for divorce for a different reason. Malozi, I wish to say something. I told you I am related to the girl ' [he had refused a request by other judges that he cross-examine]. ' They brought the matter to me, my child and my son-in-law. I said, " I cannot do it. You must go to many people,[1] about all this affair of your claiming he chased you away." She returned on my advice to ask many people. They said on two occasions, " Go back to your husband. It is your foolishness." This now is the third time. I said, " I am not only your parent, I also belong to the kuta " [i.e. I must take this affair to the kuta]. But this time she has left him over a fellow-wife. When he was at Senanga he abducted and married my sister—NAMAMBA (R12) over there is owner of the girl with me. He made this woman my child's fellow-wife. So that his two wives are both my children—one is my sister, one is my child. I do not know anything about all this

---

[1] The customary way of stating the affair should be placed before a village, family, or State kuta.

affair of the blankets. What I see that is bad is that two of my children should join in one man's hut. And it is not we who have taken the other there ' [because the husband stole her from her previous husband]. ' What I want to ask the Malozi is this : " Is it right for two children who originate from one man's place to join in the hut of one man ? " The Malozi missed this in her statement.' It appeared indeed that the kuta, weeded of its best judges by the chance of recent ' reforms ', had missed this plea. A policeman from the lower kuta stated that the plea had not been advanced there, and after the judges had stated they knew the law against two kinswomen being married by one man, they held they could not enquire into it and dismissed the claim. To SIKOTA-MUTUMWA's question, they said they had not decided on it and he could raise it as a new suit in the lower kuta.

On this, I comment here that my own people said that in 1942 [before the ' reforms '] the kuta would have at once seized on this point and granted the divorce without enquiring into the other allegations. The law states unequivocally that if a man marries a wife's kinswoman the former is entitled to divorce. Here the kuta is beginning to act according to its views of British procedure.

In this case we see the kuta carrying out one of its most frequent duties : determining whether a wife is or is not entitled to divorce on the grounds that her husband has behaved unreasonably in certain specific circumstances, according to certain very widely stated laws. Thus a husband must not take anything away from his wife, and above all not give it to another wife ; and a husband is responsible for the medical treatment of his wife when she is ill. The plea, which was not entered into, shows that the fulfilment of marital duties is also considered in a setting of other relationships. A man must not marry his wife's kinswoman.[1] This is a specific law, which can be easily applied. There may be some dispute on the facts when the allegation is that the husband committed adultery with his wife's kinswoman, or committed a breach of customary respect for her. Adultery by a man with an unrelated woman does not constitute grounds on which his wife can obtain a divorce, though persistent fornication with sexual neglect of the wife is such a ground (see ' The Case of the Libertine Husband ', p. 66).

---

[1] I have recorded several cases of women who in this situation left their husbands. The husbands did not take them to court. Increasingly, the kuta demands that it should be informed of divorces of this kind.

CASE 37 : THE CASE OF THE MAN WHO HELPED HIS
MOTHERS-IN-LAW CROSS A FORD

*before the Barotse Province Appeal Court, June, 1947, appeal by husband
against judgment of Libonda (Kalabo District Kuta)*

In this case the wife sued for divorce mainly on the grounds that
her husband committed adultery with her mother's brother's wife,
who ranks as her mother. She also brought forward proof that
before this her husband had neglected her and taken goods from her,
and to redress this had paid a pot to her father. Later, when her
father was ill, the husband had not come to visit him, nor had the
husband come to mourn on her father's death. I give some representative judgments :

SILISONGO (representative of Makoma tribe—right-hand mat) :
' The pot shows that you were in the wrong the first time, and later
you were wrong in not going to your wife to mourn the death of
your parent-in-law. Then I would increase your fault with sleeping
in the Mawiko village with your small mother-in-law, and crossing
a ford with your small and your great mothers-in-law. You have
entered the huts of two mothers-in-law. As for the girl, you just
fight her. You drove her out, so you brought a pot to her father.
Above all, no-one marries a girl and then her mother ' [in the previous
case the relationship was of girl to her mother's brother's classificatory
sister, i.e. to ' mother ' also]. ' You, girl, when you look at this
man he is your father. You may be returned to him by your lords :
for me you are free.'

LIASHIMBA [1] (temporary representative of Nalolo—right) : ' The
taboos between parents-in-law and children-in-law are not made by
government, but come from the beginnings of our people. I believe
there was adultery with your wife's mother's brother's wife on the
journey. How can an innocent man go on a journey with the wife
of an absent man, and carry her dress and cross a ford together with
her ? No-one crosses a ford with a woman. If you see a woman
crossing, you turn back and hide till she has gone.[2] This is an old
law made by our government. You know this, that one must not
meet a woman crossing water, and that if you do you can be fined.
You know these laws. Long ago you drove out your wife, and
when you returned to the village you came to your liaison with your
mother-in-law. You did not go to your wife's father's illness—how

---

[1] A different council-title though of the same name as that of the head of
Mwandi Kuta—see ' The Case of the Quarrelsome Teacher '.

[2] Since a woman may strip or draw her skirt above her knees to cross.
In this case the women stripped and their nephew-in-law carried one's dress.

did you love him ? You knew you were wrong and it is shown by the payment of the pot. No-one just pays—it shows you had a fault. On top of that, then you went into the hut of her mother. I do not know you, X, I do not hate you. I am a child here, a pupil with my teachers,[1] and like you will learn from them ; but I see that she is not your wife, she is the child of her father.'

IMENDA (chief of the Mbowe tribe—right) : ' You were a year at Kalabo without going to your wife. You took the goods of your hut to Kalabo. Your wife's father was ill and you did not go there, or to mourn : you freed your wife, and this was shown by your taking your pot there, and you knew it. But the bad thing is your crossing the water with the two women. You said you did it to protect them from the crocodiles. Why then did you not turn back to guard the other woman when she crossed on her return ? You cared for the one and you slept with her. The law of incest is old, and in the past you would have been killed for this. You know that one does not see the wife of another man naked, or even her thighs. I am astonished that you are not ashamed. How can the two maternal uncles of your wife who live in one village receive you in the village ? I cannot marry you there where they are—you will kill one another. Let her marry another who will get on with her. I agree with the others, but I do not know what will happen at the finish, because our law (*mulao*) does not go straight like cattle to water, but here and there to the finisher.'

The other judges all followed these judgments, and I therefore quote without context, some of the statements in judgments, in their order, as they illuminate the themes we are considering. ' Your giving the pot shows that you had done wrong to her and her parents, and you were buying her again ; but before you could take her home there came this new quarrel ' . . . ' I support your wife ; she is a good girl, a true woman. If our children were the same, we would have children. She sees the incest, and asks, " Is it my husband who goes to my mother ? " ' . . . ' You slept with your wife's maternal uncle's wife, or you would have appealed [he had been fined in a separate case for this adultery]. The law does not agree that one enters the hut of another man, or ask his wife for snuff, outside of him ' . . . ' The law of nakedness is inherent, it comes from childhood ; small boys and girls hide their genitals. And as IMENDA, my lord, says, the law of hiding from women crossing water is from King Lewanika [d. 1916]. Also, as IMENDA says, you were not protecting her from crocodiles or you would have worried

---

[1] Under the 1946 reforms, the other capitals send their councillors for short periods to Lialui to ' learn ' how to rule.

about the other woman. If it were I, I would fine you for three
things : (1) crossing the water with naked women, against the law
of Lewanika ; (2) not being afraid of the nakedness of your mother-
in-law which is sleeping with your mother-in-law ; and (3) sleeping
with another man's wife ' . . . ' I do not enter into the affair of
the pot or the other affairs. Your wife is freed by your crossing
the water with her mother. To sleep with your mother-in-law and
to commit shame by seeing her naked are the same thing. You
cannot call your mother-in-law to see you undress, or asleep. I see
your wife is truthful when she says she cannot return to you. I
might have returned your wife on the other affairs because you paid
a pot, but I am stopped by the crossing of water with your mother-
in-law. I do not separate these. Your wife is freed, unless you are
given her by the NGAMBELA (R1) ' . . . ' Man, I speak by the law.
I would have called as witnesses the people of the village where you
and she slept, but in the other kuta you admitted your wrongdoing
—crossing the water with a woman who ought not to be seen
familiarly. You cannot even do that with a sister-in-law [with
whom there is a joking relationship]. It shows you look on her
as a wife. And even if it is an ordinary woman you should fear to
cross. But *bukwenyani* (relationship of parent-in-law and child-in-
law) is a thing brought by God. You are mad. Your wife asks for
a divorce and I free her ' . . . ' You, my kinsman, I cannot be a
renegade. You call your mother-in-law sister-in-law. You know
one must avoid one's wife's maternal uncle's wife in the village. To
cross water with a woman, an ordinary woman, is bad. You did
with your mother-in-law, she was naked and you carried her dress.
This is like sleeping with her. This is a terrible thing by our law :
to have intercourse with a dog, to have intercourse with a cow, to
have intercourse with a tabooed person like your mother-in-law
here. So the girl can come out of your hut.'

In this case we see that the kuta may grant a woman divorce
because her husband does not behave dutifully to his father-in-
law, visiting him when he is ill ; it will do so immediately a
man commits a serious breach of the patterns of behaviour
requiring avoidance of his senior female relatives-in-law. Here
the man puts himself in two incompatible positions in relation
to the woman, as her ' father ' and as her husband. Note, too,
that a man may be fined for offences brought to the kuta's notice
in a civil suit.

Breaches of the patterns of behaviour owing to relatives-in-
law are not always so clearly defined. There are general

obligations to assist and work for in-laws, as for all kin, and to treat them with respect—indeed, the really moral man is judged by how he behaves to in-laws rather than to blood-kin, whom it is natural to help. When a wife asks that she be divorced because of dereliction in these duties the kuta has to use general reasonable standards.

CASE 38 : THE CASE OF THE GOOD SON-IN-LAW

before Saa-Katengo Court, Lialui, 17th August, 1942, on appeal from sub-district induna MUNONO *(R23) who refused the divorce.* The woman's father refused to support her in her plea and sat with the husband's supporters

After the woman had made various allegations about the way her husband treated her and her kin, the kuta accepted his evidence, backed by her kin, that he had behaved more than punctiliously. In his final judgment, rejecting the suit, KALONGA (R15) said : ' You, woman, have astonished us by your suit. You thought you would shame your husband before the country which is us. But you have instead brought honour to him for we have never heard of so good a son-in-law. Your father told us the overcoat he wears is a present from your husband ; see how your husband sits himself in a ragged jacket. He is not a rich man, but when he brought an overcoat for his father, he brought one for your father ; when he brought a dress for his mother, he brought one for your mother. He gave shawls to your unmarried sisters, and he built granaries for them and moved their harvest on the flood, not in the dugout of your village, but in his own dugout. And so on. You have not disgraced your husband here before the Malozi, but you have brought fame to him for none of us is as good a son-in-law as he. You, my son, we admire what you have done, and we thank you. Do not cease to behave thus because your wife has brought you here : continue to look after your in-laws as you have done in the past. We thank you.' KALONGA then instructed his fellows and all in court to join him in saluting the husband.

We have thus seen, in specific cases, how the kuta is concerned to assess whether kinsmen, husbands and wives, and in-laws, have behaved reasonably according to the norms of their relationship. ' The Case of the Violent Councillor ', SAYWA, affords an example of the application of the norms between lords and underlings. I cite a further example of a case which arose in a political relationship :

CASE 39: THE CASE OF THE DISRESPECTFUL INDUNA

The Princess Mbuywana vs. Induna INDIYE *Sampaya, before*
Namalya Kuta, 1943

Sampaya inherited the title INDIYE in his family, though it belongs to the princess. With it he acquired headship of a village and holding of land. The princess complained that he did not help her at all in the work of her gardens and village and that he did not respect her. INDIYE said that he could not work for her as he was overseer of a barge plying between Livingstone and Mongu. The kuta held that this absolved him from working for her, but he did not call on her when he returned to Mongu or bid her farewell when leaving, which he could [reasonably] do, and expelled him from the title, the village, and its lands.

This case had a long background, for the princess had not wanted Sampaya to succeed to the title INDIYE, but had favoured his younger brother. The local men insisted on Sampaya inheriting. The princess gave much of the land-of-the-title to his younger brother, and some time later ordered cassava planted by Sampaya to be uprooted. Local indunas stopped her, and reported her action to MUKULWAKA-SHIKO (R4) at the capital. She was rebuked, and Sampaya could have claimed damages from her, but ' excused ' her and replanted his cassava.

In the later development of this case we see that the rule ' an induna should respect his overlord prince or princess ' is applied by reasonable standards, which involve recognition of the need for indunas nowadays to earn money by working for Whites.

Thus we see that in many cases the issue in dispute is whether the parties behaved reasonably by the customs and standards of a specific position. This was also the issue in a number of cases cited in the previous chapter—as in ' The Cases of the Biassed Father ' and his ' children ', and of ' The Quarrelsome Teacher '. In the present section we were largely concerned with matrimonial disputes, but a garden-dispute, a suit for trespass, a suit for assault, or any other type of case may be converted into a similar enquiry.

Therefore in nearly all cases the judges have first to ascertain the social positions and status of the parties and their witnesses, in order to test whether their behaviour has been reasonable and customary. The judicial process concentrates on the obligations involved in social positions : this is reflected in the way in which my appropriate titles for many cases are formed by an adjective, which usually defines a fall from grace by the incumbent of a social position, which is defined by a noun. As the law of persons is basic in Lozi substantive law, so it dominates the judicial process.

XII

There are a number of important implications in the Lozi use of the standard of reasonable behaviour, both as a measure for evidence and as the central issue in multiplex disputes.

First, it is largely through the concepts of *ngana* (reason, sense) and *kuluka* (uprightness) that the judges import their view of human nature—their psychology—into the law. There are, of course, many other Lozi legal terms which deal with intention and motivation : *kufosa* (to do wrong, to be guilty) and *kusafosi* (to be innocent), provocation (*lishamaeta*), negligence (*buswafa*), and so on. The judges always impute intention and motivation by the test of ' reasonable and customary ' interpretation of actions. This is manifest in ' The Case of the Violent Councillor ' : all SAYWA's departures from custom and other unreasonable actions pointed to his partiality in favouring his own children. In ' The Case of the Biassed Father ' the eldest nephew's attempt to prevent his homecoming brother consulting their uncle was unreasonable and explicable by his desire to found his own village with his brothers as his followers. The judges operate with a whole set of presumptions about how people of different social position act in Lozi life. They introduce these assumptions into judgment, and therefore into their assessment of motivation, when they specify whether certain behaviour was or was not reasonable in a particular situation. There are therefore reasonable and unreasonable judges.[1] The psychology which the judges employ here is in the first place commonsense and somewhat naïve. It is concerned only with the surface nexus between action and motivation. That is, it is a legalistic psychology concerned mainly with action, and beyond that with patent motivation. As we say, a man is presumed to intend the natural consequences of his actions ; and, as it appears in reverse in the judicial process, a man is presumed to have the motives which account

---

[1] See below, pp. 202-3 and 321-2.

naturally and reasonably for his actions. For by casting their statements so as to make their witnessed actions appear rightful, the litigants hold themselves out to be reasonable and moral persons. Indeed, though the judges rebuke parties for their wrongful feelings and intentions, they are not always concerned with these. The Violent Councillor had behaved wrongfully even if he had in fact been trying to stop the fight. A man who behaves familiarly with another's wife is usually found guilty of 'adultery' whether or not he is proved to have slept with her.

CASE 40: THE CASE OF THE INCESTUOUS ACTION
(from a text)

A young man was sitting with his sister in a hut with the door closed. Their kin accused them of committing *sindoye* (incest) and demanded a beast for sacrifice from him. He insisted that he had done no wrong and appealed to SOLAMI, R3 at Lialui. SOLAMI said to him : 'I am sure you did nothing wrong with your sister, but you should not sit alone with her in a closed hut. You must give the beast for sacrifice'.

The Lozi apply this straightforward psychology in legal decision though they are well aware of the complexities, and in a sense of the unconscious pressures, in human motivation. This awareness is exhibited in a song :

> He who kills me, who will it be but my kinsman ;
> He who succours me, who will it be but my kinsman.

Prince Litooma thought the Violent Councillor had been carried away with rage because his *crippled* son was involved in the fight. I have heard an induna rebuke villagers, who accused an old woman of sorcery, with the charge that they said she was killing them, because she was now old and they grudged her the food they had to provide for her. King Lewanika saw that sorcery charges were fostered by 'lies and envy'. In *The Rôle of Courts in Barotse Social Life* I shall describe how Lozi are tolerant with difficult and quarrelsome people from understanding how circumstances have shaped and moved them. The kuta may take accord of these psychical facts in giving sentence, but it neglects them in fixing guilt and innocence.

Secondly, this judicial psychology is an ' ethical psychology '. It is not concerned with an objective assessment of why people act as they do, but with how their actions and presumed motivations appear in comparison with legal and moral norms. The reasonable man (*mutu yangana*) is partially identified with the upright man (*mutu yalukile*). When actions have been considered against reasonable standards and accepted norms, they are judged as ' guilty ' or ' innocent '—the Biassed Father and the Violent Councillor showed lack of judgment and partiality in ruling their dependants, and these emotions are disapproved of.

Thirdly, the core of the concept of the reasonable man is a generally reasonable man with, so to speak, a general psyche. The converse is the psyche of the wrongdoer, who adds to abducting another's wife or neglecting his own, lies, insults, contempt, and the denigration of other peoples (see the Cases of ' the Eloping Wife ' and ' the Contemptuous Husband '). But the general psyche is also, to some extent, influenced by the position of the parties. Women have their typical reactions and customary modes of behaviour which are different from those of men. Fathers tend to be biassed in favour of their own children. Husbands—wives—mothers—strangers : all these act in typical ways.

' Reasonable behaviour ' thus covers different measures of conformity with ideal norms, as envisaged by the kuta. In part, it demands scrupulous observance of important modes of behaviour, and some conformity with unimportant modes. Even observances of etiquette and convention may enter into it. Since Lozi courts are largely concerned with the behaviour of parties occupying positions of status, each party should have conformed to the customary usages, etiquette and conventions which are appropriate to his social position in a specific relationship. Hence the reasonable man of Lozi law might be more accurately described as the reasonable and customary occupier of a specific position.

Most important disputes in Loziland arise between individuals in multiplex enduring relationships, of a highly specific kind ; and the customs institutionalized for those relationships may all become legally significant, and therefore tend to be binding. Lozi society is on the whole homogeneous, and customary modes of behaviour are widespread, constant, and generally known to all, despite tribal and status differences. Many customs of the different tribes are known by others, as we have seen in ' The Case of Cross-Cousin Adultery '. In the next chapter we shall see that only some of these customary modes of behaviour are themselves legally enforceable, in that the kuta will compel their observance or punish breach of them. But failure to observe other customs, which are not themselves subject to legal sanctions, may in practice be penalized, since they are used to assess whether a man is telling the truth.

Almost all Lozi relationships, including relationships of misconduct, are marked by many institutionalized modes of behaviour—I think of them metaphorically as ' full of custom '. Some of these customs are given such weight that mere failure to observe them is reprehensible. In the relations of kindred and of neighbours, of rulers and subjects, one or other frequently commits a breach of custom for which he or she has ' to wash away the fault '. These payments are voluntary indemnifications, made outside the courts and often for faults the courts would not penalize. The performance of other customary actions is essential to establish rights, and in a society without writing may indeed have irrebuttable significance as proof.

CASE 41 : THE CASE OF THE PREGNANT GIRL'S BEADS
(from a text)

Thus where a man had refused to put white beads on a pregnant woman's wrist, it was held that he could not later claim her child (before NAWALA, R46, at Namalya Kuta).

The installation of an heir is similarly fixed when he gives the royal salute at the capital (below, pp. 186–7).

But disputes over the observance of law and custom do not usually arise in these simple forms. Life is lived through a series of highly variable situations, and the judges have to assess whether the parties have abided by customary norms as reasonably applied to each situation. Hence the concept of reasonable behaviour is to some extent variable, and ' reasonable and customary ' are standards applied in combination to establish the truth in cross-examination and to assess substantive rights in judgment. Here ' reasonable ' measures conformity in degree of performance of duty (liabilities) and exercise of rights (privileges and powers). Rules such as that which says a headman must be generous are tested by what he has done, and again custom lays down standards. Correspondingly, since a man's respect for his seniors is partly measured by the gifts he gives them of fish and other necessities, or of help in work, these have to be assessed in relation to his age, strength, skill, wealth, and overall obligations to others (see ' The Case of the Good Son-in-Law '). A man may have different demands on his goods or skill : he must keep a balance between them.

CASE 42 : THE INCIDENT OF THE KING'S IVORY-CARVER

(*June, 1947*)

After a sacrifice at Namalya royal-grave, the men sat talking. NAWALA (R46) began to rebuke a passing ivory-carver of the king for failing in allegiance to the local princess. He resided on her land, but during all the years he had carved flyswitches for the king, he had never given one to the princess or her husband. The carver replied that he had to account to the king for all his switches. NAWALA retorted that the king would thank him for carving for the princess his overlord, and the ' parent' of the reigning branch of the royal family [her title is that of the mother of King Mulambwa, 9th king, ?1780–?1830, progenitor of all later kings]. NAWALA cited a case where King Lewanika approved his taking this line.

In this allocation, as in the fulfilment of marital duties, there are again customary standards.

The norms and customs of most social positions are not only well known, but they are also commonly accepted as right and reasonable, and therefore judges and litigants can meet in argument. Litigious consensus breaks down when judges and litigants have different norms. We shall examine later cases where there were differences of opinion even among judges on what the norm should be : some such difference emerged in ' The Case of the Father and his Son's Cattle ' (p. 109). But nowadays situations could arise in which the judges and litigants would be at such cross-purposes that they could not meet, as where a Catholic husband might deny the kuta's power to divorce his wife, though it undoubtedly holds this power.

The most striking case of this kind which I recorded was one which involved members of the Watchtower sect. Both British and Barotse authorities disapprove of the sect : the Barotse have always banned it.

CASE 43 : THE CASE OF THE WATCHTOWER PACIFISTS

Saa-Katengo Kuta, Lialui, August, 1942

Four men and two women of the Watchtower sect (Jehovah's Witnesses) were charged with refusing to pay a levy of 6*d.* for War funds imposed by the Barotse Government. They asserted that they would not pay for God had ordained against war when he said to Noah, ' Whoso sheddeth man's blood, by man shall his blood be shed, for in the image of God made He man ' (Genesis ix. 6). The judges began, by their usual method, to try to convince the accused that they were unreasonable. They asked : ' What would you do if you saw a lion killing your child ? ' The accused replied that the edict was against the killing of man. Similarly they countered a question about poisonous snakes. They said they would flee from hostile enemies. As the judges failed to establish consensus with the accused, they became heated, and men at the sides of the kuta joined in to an extent I had not seen in any other case. Quotations from the Bible were bandied about by pagans as well as Christians. The irate judges began to attack the Watchtower people with commonly held taunts on their general immorality : they had no church-buildings but worshipped in the bush like animals, they held their women in common, they did not respect authority. The accused calmly denied the first two accusations, and said that God had ordered them in the Third Commandment not to bow down to anyone but Him, and therefore they would not kneel to king or induna or District Commissioner ; and moreover in Hosea viii. 4, He had said, ' They have set up kings, but not by me ; they have made princes, and I knew it not.' After some hours debate the irritated judges, seemingly helpless, fined the accused and sent them to the Provincial Commissioner. He held that they had committed no offence since the Barotse Authority could not impose a tax without the Governor's consent.

Thus in this case where the accused had different norms from the judges, these confessed their helplessness to bring it to a successful conclusion, as this requires that the guilt of the accused should be established for the accused themselves. The kuta could fine them, but not ' convict ' them. They hoped that the British authorities could achieve this ; but these followed the same unsuccessful line of attack, in that they could not convince the accused that their norms were wrong. Cases of this type are still very rare in Lozi kutas. They demonstrate the importance, for a satisfactory judicial process, of the acceptance of one law by judges and litigants. In Loziland the difficulties that arise where this is lacking are most marked when Lozi come into British courts, in cases involving sorcery and other matters on which British and Lozi have quite different judgments.

This is brought out in :

CASE 43*a* : THE CASE OF THE SORCERER'S THREAT

Saa-Katengo Kuta, Lialui, 6th August, 1942

A sister's son of SOLAMI (R3, head of the court) complained that a Wiko leech who had treated him for a sore on the neck demanded payment though the sore did not heal. When the complainant refused to pay, he said the leech threatened him : ' The king, princes, indunas, all pay for treatment—I will cure you with the fat of flies.' The kuta said it would summon the leech, for, if the complainant's statement was true, ' This was very bad.' One very senior induna told a story of how a man forbade his son to exchange wives with this leech, and the leech told him he would ' eat the fat of flies '. The man and his wife shortly afterwards were upset in a dugout by wind and were drowned. When we left the kuta I asked this induna if the threat was sorcery, and he replied : ' No, you teach us it is not sorcery, but it is very bad.' My own people laughed in astonishment when I told them the story, and said it was sorcery. MBASIWANA Mutondo told me that he had once wanted to marry a woman, but when another man said, ' He who marries her will eat a calabash of the fat of flies,' he left her. But a prince laughed : ' He only frightened you ! '

The case did not come before the kuta again. I failed to enquire why.

The threat hinges on the fact that a Lozi patient does not pay his doctor unless he is cured. But this case exhibits, like ' The Case of the Perjuring Oath-Taker ', how helpless the Lozi kuta feels when dealing with what, to its members, are patent criminals protected by British law. Trials in British courts under the Witchcraft Ordinance exhibit a similar conflict.[1]

Finally, customary reasonable standards for specific norms are applied by the judges in assessing the behaviour of persons, but these standards are flexible. Many legal rules are of the type, ' a husband must treat his wife properly and care for her '. The rule has definite meaning but it has to be *specified*, by being

---

[1] To be further dealt with in *The Rôle of Courts in Barotse Social Life*.

N

applied in a variety of specific situations to particular circumstances. Since the standard in any such situation is *munna
yalukile*, ' an upright husband ', the judges are able to specify the
rule in terms of current as well as traditional usage. They may
state norms, and quote precedents or exemplary behaviour of
themselves or of others, but they can also adjust the law to meet
new developments (the emergence of the Watchtower sect, the
introduction of coats and sheets and blankets and metal pots, the
migration of men to work, the establishment of schools, etc.).
The central legal rule, ' a husband must treat his wife properly
and care for her ', has persisted from before British occupation
until today. The specification, or definition, of ' the upright
husband ' (*munna yalukile*), of ' treat properly' (*kuezeza hande*) and
of ' care ' (*kubabalela*), has altered to absorb these changes in
social life. British governmental and Christian' rules flow into
Lozi law through these concepts. Thus the law lives and
develops because its key concepts, ' reasonable' and ' customary ',
define general standards which are applicable to social positions
and actions which are themselves only definable in similarly
general terms. The concepts are, in the usual jurisprudential
terms, *flexible* : more specifically, they are *elastic*, in that they
can be stretched to cover new types of behaviour, new institutions, new customs, new ranges of leeway. This flexibility is
a characteristic of all legal concepts, which I shall analyse in
Chapter VI. Here I emphasize it as an important attribute of
' the reasonable and customary man '. This attribute allows the
judges to take cognisance of changes in mode of life, changes in
morals, and changes in the social structure. In the process of
applying ' reasonable ' and ' customary ' (*mikwa yelukile* = rightful customs) as standards to actual occurrences, the judges work
these changes into the flexible concepts, while the forms of most
legal rules remain unchanged. Though the Lozi distinguish law
(*mulao*) from facts (*litaba*), they have not hardened this into a
distinction which binds the judges, who may therefore accept
these changes as constituting the law and the customs of the nation.
This process is not trammelled by writing or recording of
precedent or procedural device. In practice, the judges may
develop and even alter the law by fitting new facts into the
specifications of ' reasonable ' and ' customary ' behaviour for
the incumbent of a particular social position.

XIII

Descriptions of cases in old records are so poor that they do not show well the working of the judicial process. I think that it emerges from all the cases that the conception of reasonableness is indigenous. Its implications are clearly stated in only one described case. In 1899 Major St. Hill Gibbons was surveying Barotseland with the help of King Lewanika, who gave him two councillors as guides. They refused to continue his march with him and he was compelled to turn back. When he complained to the king, they were tried in the kuta.

The Mokwetunga (son-in-law to the king) . . . opened the proceedings by charging the two prisoners to this effect :
' You, Luombomba, and you, Litsolo, are accused of disobeying the king's orders, inasmuch as you made it impossible for the white man to continue his journey, and complete the work he had undertaken in the interests of the king. . . .   What excuse for your conduct do you make ? '
' Luombomba, speaking with his usual silvery fluency, said he knew it was the king's wish that he should accompany the white man to Lovale, but that he adopted the course he had for two reasons : first, the boys wished to return to their homes, as they were hungry, and food was scarce ; secondly, he feared that when they reached Nyakatoro the people would plunder the white man.'

Here Luombomba tried to defend his conduct by showing that he had acted in the interests of the white man.

Litsolo, in his defence, said, ' I was anxious lest when the boys passed through the villages they would fight with the people, and take their food from them by force, and this would lead to trouble.'

St. Hill Gibbons replied to both these defences by stating that food was plentiful, that he had shown throughout his journey through the countries of many tribes that he could look after himself and his goods, and that in all these tribes his carriers had not given any trouble by fighting or robbing the people : why should their future conduct cause anxiety ?
Gibbons then describes judgments as going in order from the junior to the senior councillors, save that the top three councillors

gave their judgments in the opposite direction.   He quotes only one judgment :

'You say you were tired and hungry,' said one.   'The white man has travelled all the way from England in addition to the journey you have shared with him, yet he never complained of being tired, but wished to finish the journey he had begun.   Are you men that you should talk thus ?   Or are you women and children ? '

Of the other judgments he states generally : ' One would dilate on the case so far as it concerned Luombomba, another would pick Litsolo to pieces, some would couple the two together. . . . Each had his argument in condemnation of the accused.' [1]   This erection of the standard of courage and perseverance for men, as against women and children, surely witnesses that the Lozi have always used the modes of judicial cross-examination—of ' picking to pieces '—and of argument described in this chapter.   The case shows also that defendants have always erected their defences by using the same reasonable norms as their judges.

---

[1] Gibbons, A. St. H., *Africa from South to North through Marotseland*, London : Lane, The Bodley Head (1904), i, pp. 249 ff.

CHAPTER IV

LEGAL RULES, CUSTOMS, AND ETHICS:
THE LAWS OF GOD AND OF NATIONS

I

I HAVE considered how in many disputes Lozi courts have to determine whether some person has acted according to the rules enjoined by his or her social position in relation to another. Some of these rules are rigidly defined—e.g. ' a husband must not go to his wife's granary ' ; but others state wide and diffuse obligations —e.g. ' a man must care for his wife properly '. All these rules have to be applied to the varying, and now altering, reality of life. That is, Lozi courts have to cope with the task that confronts all courts everywhere. They have to determine the facts, and then to determine what are the relevant laws and how these apply to the facts. Here I press my analysis further in order to show how ethical ideas of equity and justice influence the judicial process.

Since the Lozi are, and were in the past, a strongly organized kingdom containing a hierarchy of courts with power to enforce their decisions, they have reached a stage of political development where they possess law as ' the product of organized force '.[1] This definition of *law* is widely accepted, and is perhaps best known in Dean Roscoe Pound's words, by which law is stated to be ' social control through the systematic application of the force of politically organized society '.[2] It is indeed essential to have some word to distinguish forceful processes of social control in societies which have developed courts as against societies which have not reached this stage of political development. Further we

---

[1] Seagle, *The Quest for Law*, New York : Knopf (1941), p. 35.
[2] It has been accepted by that doyen of social anthropology, Professor A. R. Radcliffe-Brown, and is quoted in his ' Preface' to *African Political Systems* (ed. by M. Fortes and E. E. Evans-Pritchard), London : Oxford University Press (1940). See also his article on ' Primitive Law ', *Encyclopædia of the Social Sciences*, New York : Macmillan (1933), ix, pp. 206 ; reprinted in Radcliffe-Brown, *Structure and Function in Primitive Society*, London : Cohen & West (1952), at pp. 212–19.

need a word to distinguish, in a society with courts, those rules which ought to be enforced, or breaches of which ought to be penalized, if the delinquent is brought before the courts, from other rules which are not thus sanctioned.[1]   I shall consider this problem in more detail in the next chapter, when I discuss *Judicial Logic and the Sources of Lozi Law*.   Here I state baldly that I accept the arguments which Vinogradoff and others have raised against restricting *law* in this way.   I shall therefore use *legal* to demarcate the procedures Lozi courts ought to follow, the rules they ought to apply, and the sanctions they ought to enforce.   *Law* I shall employ more loosely with various meanings as the Lozi do their equivalent word.   More specifically I use it to describe the whole reservoir of rules, the *corpus juris*, on which the judges draw for their decisions.

Like the English, the Lozi use more than one word to describe the rules which I have classed as 'legal', and each of these words refers to a number of other kinds of rules.   These words are as *flexible* as Lozi words for 'reasonable', and their chief characteristic is that they refer to a multiplicity of rules, institutions, and processes.   In technical semantics they are 'multi-definitional', but it is simpler to regard them as expressing *multiple concepts*.   The most important of these words is *mulao* (plural, *milao*).   *Mulao* means variously, according to Jalla's *Lozi-English Dictionary*, 'commandment, law, rule, regulation, order'.   The Lozi use it to describe all the rules and the whole procedure by which their society is controlled : thus they say ' even the king is a slave of the law (*mulao*) '.   Standard phrases are : *kubuluka mulao*, to observe the law ; *kuloba mulao* or *kutula mulao*, to break the law ; *sesilumelwa ki mulao*, what is lawful.   It is the word which they invariably employ when they have to distinguish what the kuta should enforce from what it should not ; or when they speak of some rule (statute) passed by a certain king or NGAMBELA (R1), or by the British Government—*kutoma mulao*, to set up a law.   But *mulao* is also used in contexts where we might better translate it as custom, traditional usage, manner, habit, innate propensity, or technical rule of craft.   *Mulao* is also used for rules issued by people for their underlings, even though

---

[1] Professor I. Schapera accepts *law* to define this distinction in his *Handbook of Tswana Law and Custom*, pp. 37–8.

they could not have the rules enforced by the kuta. Thus a man told me : ' It is my rule (*mulao*) that each of my wives in turn cooks for the whole household, instead of each wasting most of every day cooking for her own children.' Here, indeed, the kuta should support the claim of each wife to have her own kitchen and to cook for her own family and her husband, for the general law (*mulao*) emphasizes the distinctiveness of each wife.

The Lozi also describe what we call a scientific law of the natural world as ' a law (*mulao*) of God *Nyambe* '. For example, they are laws (*milao*) of God that crops grow from seed ; that rain falls in the month of *Muimunene* (September) ; that plentiful fish, caught in high-flood years, and plentiful grain, reaped in low-flood years, are not obtained together. The Lozi are inclined to import an ethical significance even into this use of *mulao*, for to keep ' laws ' like the first two instanced in operation, people must fulfil their duties lest God or the ancestors punish them. The third example is an instance of the general moralistic maxim, ' God does not give two things ' (*Mulimu ha'afani lika zepeli*), which restrains greed, and which emphasizes that people are compelled to co-operate because each lacks something the other may have. They similarly evaluate the law of God that their Plain supports many cattle and breeds fish and grows crops of certain kinds to yield products which differ from those of the surrounding woodlands, so that there should be profitable exchange and peaceful complementary interdependence between the different tribes.

Other laws (*milao*) of God, which more patently refer to certain moral premises in Lozi social life, are also called *milao yabutu* (laws of humankind). We met examples of these in ' The Case of the Man who Helped his Mothers-in-Law Cross a Ford ' (p. 149) : people are ashamed of nakedness and people should avoid familiarity with in-laws of different generations, particularly those of the opposite sex. There are also *milao*, such as those of marriage, which lie at the basis of social life everywhere.

Some of the possible translations of *mulao* in various contexts which I have listed above, have apter Lozi equivalents. *Mukwa* (plural, *mikwa*) may be used for a legal rule, as defined above, but this is rarely done. *Mukwa* generally means *a custom* in the sense of a tribal practice distinct from the practices of other tribes, while the plural *mikwa* is used for the habits of men in general. *Mukwa* can also mean the distinguishing idiosyncrasy of an individual, and *twaelo* (plural, *litwaelo*) similarly denotes individual habit or traditional usage. Individual habit is also *njimo*, or *nto yasizwalo*, ' a thing of birth '. *Mukwa* has a further distinctive meaning of ' the method ' of doing something.

Multiplicity of referents and hence ambiguity, and the existence of synonyms, similarly distinguish Lozi concepts for the four basic constituents of legal relations—in English, right and duty, and wrongdoing and injury. *Swanelo* (plural *liswanelo*) means both right and duty or obligation. Thus ' *litunga unani swanelo yakunga manaka atou*, the king has a right to take elephant tusks,' and ' *litunga unani swanelo yakukutiseza muzumi linaka leliling'wi*, the king has an obligation to return one tusk to the hunter '. The root of *swanelo* is *kuswanela* which can be translated as ' it behoves, it ought ', so that *kuswanela* has the same reciprocal meaning as these words in English : ' the king ought to get the tusks ' and ' the king ought to return a tusk '. *Swanelo* is not confined to rights which the kuta ought to enforce : it covers moral as well as legal duties and rights.[1]

Swanelo is the word most commonly employed here. *Litukelo* (singular, *tukelo*) also means the ' rights ' of a particular person, but more commonly the rights of a particular social position, as *litukelo zabatanga*, the rights of serfs. *Tukelo* is a noun derived from the verb *kuluka*, to be straight, which we have already met as the root of the adjective in *mutu yalukile*, the upright man. *Tukelo*, like *swanelo*, means duty as well as right, and refers to general rights and duties, as is evidenced by its wider meanings of ' justice ' and ' equity '.[2]

The principal Lozi words for right and duty are thus identical, and cover general, moral and legal rights and duties. However, they have words to refer to some of the fundamental juridical conceptions which the late Professor Hohfeld analysed in the general ideas of ' rights ' and ' duties ' and which he argued

---

[1] Schapera, *Handbook of Tswana Law and Custom*, op. cit., at pp. 35–6, gives a list of Tswana terms for all these legal concepts. The similarity of the Lozi and Tswana terms is because these words in Lozi come from the Sotho of the Kololo.

[2] Jalla's *Lozi-English Dictionary*, op. cit., p. 347.

should always be kept distinct.[1] He set out two tables of jural opposites and jural correlatives.

JURAL OPPOSITES

| right (*or* claim) | privilege | power | immunity |
| no-right (*or* no-claim) | duty (*or* obligation) | disability | liability |

JURAL CORRELATIVES

| right (*or* claim) | privilege | power | immunity |
| duty (*or* obligation) | no-right (*or* no-claim) | liability | disability |

These eight concepts establish pairs of fundamental legal relations, each of which defines a reciprocal bond between two persons. Hohfeld says that the concepts are *sui generis* and that they cannot be defined but can only be exhibited by their opposites and corre-latives. That is, these concepts of law can be defined only within their context in a system of law composed of many concepts related to each other.[2] Thus :

A *claim* means that X can demand certain things from Y who is under a correlative duty to render them ; and *no-claim*, the opposite, implies that Y cannot prevent X claiming them.

A *privilege* means that X is free to behave in a certain way in respect of Y who has *no-claim* (the correlative) to prevent him, and a *duty* (the opposite) to allow him to act thus.

A *power* means that X may create a legal relation affecting Y whose correlative *liability* is to be bound thus, and whose *disability* is the opposite of X's power.

An *immunity* means that X is not subject to being bound by Y in a new legal relation, so that Y is correlatively under a *disability* from binding X, and, in opposition, has a *liability* in that he cannot do so.

Hohfeld used both judgments in court and jurisprudential analyses to show that the failure to make these distinctions had led to flaws in juridical reasoning. His argument certainly

---

[1] Hohfeld, W. N., *Fundamental Legal Conceptions as Applied in Judicial Reasoning, and Other Legal Essays* (edited by W. W. Cook), New Haven : Yale University Press (1920), especially at pp. 35 ff.

[2] See Hart, H. L. A., *Definition and Theory in Jurisprudence*, Oxford : Clarendon Press (1953).

convinces me, with Professor Hoebel,[1] that the distinctions would assist an anthropologist clearly to record the substantive law of an alien people.   Unhappily I was not aware of these distinctions when I was in the field, and I fear that in taking down judgments in my mixture of Lozi and English I may not always have noted precisely what Lozi word was used.   Nevertheless, I shall be able to show how Lozi judges, constrained in their reasoning by the tools of their language, employ the ambiguity of *liswanelo* and *litukelo*, which mean all the eight conceptions of Hohfeld, to import their ethics into their law.   Occasionally they do use other words to distinguish these different conceptions :

(a) *Mata*, generally ' power ', is used for both ' privilege ' and ' power ' in Hohfeld's scheme ; and *sibaka*, ' place ' or ' permission ' or ' cause ', is also ' privilege ' ;

(b) *Mubango*, a law-suit or claim, is occasionally used for his ' claim ', as is the phrase ' *ukazeka* ', he can sue, i.e. he can claim ;

(c) *Sipululu* and *sikoloti*, debt, are occasionally used for ' obligation ' as the opposite of ' claim '.

The other conceptions are all expressed by the negative use of these terms, or of the more general *swanelo* and *tukelo*.

The other general terms commonly employed by Lozi judges refer to wrongdoing and injury.   Here again they frequently interchange words.   *Kufosa*, ' to do wrong ', is their most general term—it is an infinitive or verbal noun of *-fosa*, with *poso* (plural *liposo*) as another noun.   A large part of the kuta's duty (*mata* = power) is *kulukisa liposo*, to right wrongs.   I generally translate these terms as ' wrongdoing ' in contrast with rightdoing (*kueza* —to do, to fulfil—, *hande*—well).   Again, *kufosa* and *poso* are not restricted to offences that will be punished by the kuta, any more than ' wrong ' or ' wrongdoing ' in English cover offences that will be punished by courts of law.   The Lozi have no specialized terms for this type of offence such as our ' crime ' and ' felony ', and to some extent ' misdemeanour ', though a great wrongdoing is *mubonda*.   *Mulatu* (plural *milatu*) also has this general meaning of ' wrongdoing '.   Thus the judges say to a litigant, ' *ufosize, unani mulatu* ' (' you have done wrong, you have a fault ').   Here *mulatu* carries the double connotation of

---

[1] ' Fundamental Legal Concepts as Applied in the Study of Primitive Law ', *Yale Law Journal*, li (1942), pp. 951 ff.

' wrongdoing ' and ' being required to pay indemnification or fine '. This second connotation is covered also by *tifo*, which means too ' price '.

The kuta in ' righting wrongs ' may be protecting positive injunctions or punishing the performance of forbidden actions. *Mwila* (plural *miila*) defines anything that is forbidden, either generally, or to an individual by his physical constitution or history, such as inability to eat a certain food. This general meaning of being forbidden is also covered by *kuhaniswa*, the passive causative of *kuhana*, to refuse, to forbid. *Kuhaniswa* is less often used to describe a rule the breach of which is sanctioned by the ancestor's wrath or some other spiritual or supernatural sanction, while this is a more specific meaning of *mwila*. *Mbamba* also refers to things or actions which are prohibited because they bring ill consequences by what we consider mystical means.

Finally, the Lozi describe injury or damage generally as *sinyeho* or *sinyehelo*, nouns from the verbal root *kusinya* = to spoil or to injure.

The Lozi have very many different words to describe various kinds of wrongdoing : these will be considered in my volume on *The Ideas of Barotse Jurisprudence*. Here I am concerned to show only that in their basic juridical vocabulary they do not have separate words to distinguish the legal from the natural order, or legal from moral rules, wrongs, rights, and duties. However the multiplicity of referents for words like *mulao* (law) or *mukwa* (custom) or *kufosa* (wrongdoing) or *mulatu* (fault, debt), and the extent to which some words are interchanged, are not peculiar to Lozi. In English, too, adjectives like ' legal ' and ' moral ' have to be used to make distinctions. Hohfeld's critique shows the ambiguity that exists even in our refined jurisprudence. The Lozi can also make distinctions when necessary by qualifying words or phrases, so as to distinguish actions forbidden ' by the kuta ' from those forbidden ' by God ' or by ' good manners (*likute*) '. A right or duty can be defined as ' enforceable by the kuta ' or as ' required by decency ' (*sishemo*). Indeed, some of their separate words do contain the seeds of differentiation. *Mulao* can mean any rule, but it alone properly describes the statute of a king, quite clearly the law, or a rule which the kuta should defend. *Mwila* can be used for all actions which are forbidden, whether by statute, ' common law' and customary practice, sound ethics, good manners, practical techniques, or by religious or magical sanctions, but more specifically it means the last, as does *mbamba*—a *taboo*, as this word is generally accepted into English.

The refinement of a vocabulary of legal and ethical terms has been the work of specialist jurists and philosophers, who had writing to assist them, and has accompanied increasing differentiation and complication of our society.   Nevertheless the basic words in our legal and ethical systems are still those which to a large extent have various and unspecific connotations, like 'right', 'wrong', and 'duty'.   In my analysis of *The Ideas of Barotse Jurisprudence* I shall show that it is not necessary for the Lozi to have, in addition, many specialized terms for types of rights and duties, and wrongs, since in a society dominated by status the determination of the social positions of litigants or the nature of the property over which they are disputing, fixes the rights and obligations involved.   However, the persisting dominance of words like 'right' and 'duty' in judicial analysis even into modern times, indicates that their 'ambiguity', 'vagueness', and 'generality' have judicial value.   I have already suggested that it is these characteristics of fundamental concepts like 'reasonableness' which makes them flexible to cope with the variable, and above all the changing, situations of social life.   The analysis of this problem will conclude my study of the judicial process among the Lozi.   In the present chapter I hope to demonstrate how this flexibility allows the judges to serve justice (the right—*tukelo*) as well as the law (*mulao*).

II

The ambiguity of these basic Lozi legal terms raised some difficulties in collecting data about Lozi law.   Nevertheless I could usually phrase a question to ask what the kuta ought to do in any situation, actual or hypothetical, and get an answer. The kuta is fully aware of what it is entitled to do by law (*kamulao*).   It distinguishes its power (*mata*) here sharply from its refusal ('*lwahana*' = we refuse) to enforce observance of other rules, whether these be what we would call mere customary obligations, or moral obligations.   In 'The Case of the Biassed Father', the kuta 'ordered' (*kulaela*) the young men to return to the village and their father's brother to accept them. In fact, the judges made it quite clear that they were enforcing the law that 'no-one works gardens in the village and lives elsewhere', and that the complainants were returning home because they wished to and their uncle wanted them : 'I do not prevent your going home because your father has asked for you,' said KALONGA (R15). 'If the affair comes again, you will not be judged as today, but you will be fined.' They were to be fined for deceiving the kuta, since the rule that a man should love and treat his 'father' well cannot be directly enforced, and the kuta no longer has power, as it had in the past, to compel residence in a particular village. The law now is : a person may reside where he or she pleases, provided that it be in a recognized village.

CASE 44 : THE CASE OF FREEDOM OF RESIDENCE

Saa-Katengo Kuta at Lialui, 31st July, 1942

A Lubale chief in Balovale District claimed the daughter borne by his sister to a Lozi during her first marriage. [Note : The Lubale are matrilineal.] Questioned by the kuta, the girl said : 'My mother deserted my father and me long ago. I cannot go to Balovale, let my mother come to me.' Pressed three times, she said she wished to remain with her father. SOLAMI (R3) stated : 'All right. It is the law (*mulao*) of our White lords that a person should live where he likes in his heart.'

Thus the kuta in 'The Case of the Biassed Father' could not now compel the youths to return to the village, and it was well aware of this, as it showed in recording that its judgment was on ownership of the gardens. It may only punish people who do not reside in any village. But though the judges knew the limits of their legal powers, in practice they exerted economic and moral pressure on the litigants to return. The judges went further in exhorting them in moral terms to sound behaviour and unity. The kuta may thus concern itself with moral as well as legal problems. I proceed to consider the manner in which it does so.

Let us look first at a case where the kuta felt unable to go beyond its legal powers and order a man to behave morally, since this illustrates that the Lozi recognize a distinction between legal and moral obligations.

CASE 45 : THE CASE OF THE UNGENEROUS HUSBAND

Saa-Katengo Kuta at Lialui, August, 1942, on appeal from MUNONO's
(R23) sub-district kuta

In this case the wife sued for divorce, alleging ill-treatment by her husband, and that he had infected her with syphilis acquired in fornication. The husband counterclaimed for damages on the grounds that his wife had got syphilis in adultery and infected him, and through him her co-wife. The kuta held that the husband was responsible for the infection, and granted a divorce.

KALONGA (R15), giving the concluding judgment, stated : ' The woman is freed, and she will take home with her half of the crops which she planted. There has been so much ill-feeling in this case that we will send an induna to see that it is fairly done. Now what else (to the husband), my kinsman, will you give her of the goods of the marriage to take with her ? ' [As stated above, a woman who sues for divorce loses her rights in all goods of the marriage which she has rejected, save in crops planted by her.]

Husband : ' I will give her nothing ; she has made me diseased and bound me here with lies.'

KALONGA : ' Come, my kinsman, you cannot do this. When you married her, taking her from her parents, you all rejoiced together. You hoped that you would have a strong marriage, with children to bind you together. It has not worked out thus, but you cannot send a woman home to her parents, naked like a dog. We beg you, give her a blanket and a dress and some plates.'

Husband : ' I will give her nothing, not even a shawl.'

KALONGA : ' Very well. We have power (*mata*) to make you divide the crops, for this is our law (*mulao*), and we will send someone to see this is done. But we have not power (*mata*) to make you behave like an upright man. Go.'

This was shortly before the kuta adjourned for its noonday recess. As it was about to adjourn for the day at 4 p.m., the husband returned to the post and asked if he could speak to the kuta. He said that he had been reflecting on KALONGA's words and saw that he was wrong (*nifosize*). He would give his wife a dress, a shawl, a blanket, a hoe, a pot, and a plate.

KALONGA thanked him : ' We thank you, my child. This is behaving like a decent upright man ' : and he and the other judges clapped their acknowledgments.

The lists of goods involved are very poor to our eyes : they are important and hard for Lozi to obtain, for Lozi material poverty is great.

Thus the kuta has clearly in mind a distinction between obligations it can compel people to observe, and obligations it can only urge on them as right. This gives the Lozi a distinctive body of legal rules which does not cover all obligations which are approved as moral.

III

Most mature men participate directly in political and forensic activity, so the law is generally widely known. There is also little difference of opinion about what the law is, with few points on which it is uncertain or obscure. Lozi technology and organization are still comparatively simple and disputes rarely involve complex technical situations, however complex they be in emotional entanglement.

The judges in coming to a decision consider that they are bound by the statutes passed by their own government in its long history, and nowadays by edicts of the Northern Rhodesia Government. They should follow ' the law of long long ago '— the common law—where it is not contrary to these statutes or to treaties with Britain. The common law is not only enshrined in maxims and in judicial precedents, but it is also embedded in living relations.

In the past statutes and precedents could not be recorded. Today judgments are written as very bald statements giving a few of the facts and a general statement, which may be unintentionally misleading, of the final decision. Therefore when judges have to apply these precedents from memory to a disputable issue, they are unable carefully to compare the circumstances of a particular precedent with the circumstances before them. The judges tend to remember the central legal rules involved and the moral judgment which guided their application. The moral judgment is remembered clearly because the nature of disputes involves an enquiry into the specific history and interrelationships of the litigants as individuals. This moral judgment, combined with the judges' view of the merits of the case under trial, guides the application of the precedent. Indeed, the ' precedents ' cited in preceding cases were more often instances of people behaving morally so that no dispute arose, than past decisions of the kuta. Thus Induna SIFUWE chided the Quarrelsome Teacher : ' The clerk's and Sibofu's cattle smashed the kuta.   We did not tell them to get out of the country. They fixed it.'

Presumably in all societies moral judgments on the merits of particular cases may guide judicial decisions, and thus influence the development of the law.   This process is today very important in Loziland, where life is undergoing radical transformation.   Statutes and common law cannot cover every contingency which arises, and people bring suits which previously they would not have brought.   Often when it is faced with one of these cases which is covered by neither established custom nor statute, the kuta is guided in coming to its decision by its conceptions of morality, and it tries to adjust the law to meet these.   Let us see how this process works.

CASE 46 : THE CASE OF THE BARREN WIDOW

In 1946–7 the Lozi of Lialui District were upset by a decision of the High Court of Northern Rhodesia, reversing their own Provincial Court's verdict in the following case.

The agreed facts were that a man married a virgin in 1938, giving three cattle as marriage-payment.   He died in 1944, thus ' dissolving ' the marriage.   The wife had not conceived.   It was further agreed that, under the 1917 Marriage Laws of King Yeta III, on the divorce of a woman who was married as a virgin and did not conceive, the second of the two beasts sent as marriage payment, and its progeny, should be returned to the bridegroom.   The dead husband's father now claimed the return of one beast and its calves ' as is done in all dissolved marriages ', i.e. including those dissolved by death.   The Sikalo Kuta [Provincial Appeal Court] at Lialui held : ' In view of the Native Law and Custom by which bridewealth [1] is not returnable if marriage is dissolved as a result of death, the Sikalo Court upheld the finding of both the Sulu and Saa-Katengo Courts and dismissed the appeal.'   The Chief Justice of Northern Rhodesia, on the basis of statements of the law by two Lozi assessors who were not members of the kuta, held that the law was that one beast should be returned whether the marriage was broken by divorce or death, and reversed the judgment of the lower courts.

This case was being discussed widely when I returned to Lialui District in 1947.   In the Sikalo Kuta it was said that only once before, in 1920, had such a case been brought.   The kuta, or at least the

---

[1] This term was adopted by the kuta from my earlier writings.

concluding judge, then held that the second beast should be returned, but when the decision was referred to King Yeta III he overruled it, saying that no-one was at fault since God had taken the deceased ; therefore let them mourn together and not sue. I could not check this report with King Yeta as he had had a stroke and was unable to speak, but he appeared to confirm this account of it.

In Lialui District the High Court's judgment had stirred other litigants to action and the Sulu sub-district kuta had already followed it. One man said in my hearing that his son-in-law had died within a month of marrying his virginal daughter, and the deceased's father had reclaimed the second beast : ' I returned it because it is now the law (*mulao*), but anyway I felt I ought to return the beast, since a month is not a marriage. But before no-one would have sued, we would have mourned together.' Later I visited the southern capital, Nalolo, where NAWALA (R42) Mutondo, travelling with me, reported the High Court decision to the kuta. The councillors there had heard neither of this nor of King Yeta's decision in 1920. All of them said at once : ' We have never had a case like that. Nothing can be claimed when God kills a person.' After reflecting a while, a few councillors said : ' But if someone lacked the decency to claim, one beast should be paid, because there was no conception.' I put the issue as a case stated to the PRINCESS CHIEF at Nalolo and her husband. The latter immediately replied : ' No-one would sue in those circumstances. It would not be decent. They would be mourning together. I have never heard of it, but perhaps people fix these things themselves in their homes.' The PRINCESS CHIEF said : ' The doctor is not asking what good people do, but what the kuta would order (*laela*) if someone did claim.' She stated she thought a beast was due to be returned, but she had never heard of a case like this ; people would be ashamed to claim.

I consider that the history of Lozi marriage law shows that there was no foundation for the claim in established law. In the past the Lozi gave only small gifts of mats and hoes on marriage, and exchanged beasts which were eaten by the kin of the two spouses separately. In the first decade of this century, during the reign of King Lewanika, they began to give cattle as marriage-payment. In 1917 King Yeta III and the kuta, in a series of promulgated rules on marriage, laid down that two beasts should be given for a virgin, with one returning on a divorce if the wife had not conceived. (One beast was to be given for a woman who was not a virgin.) The edict made no mention of what should happen if one spouse died and the

o

virginal bride had not conceived. Therefore when in 1920 a dead husband's kin sued for one beast, there was neither statute nor precedent to cover the issue. The Southern Bantu (Zulu, Ndebele, Sotho, Venda, Tswana, Tsonga) seem all to have allowed a claim for return of marriage-payment if the *wife* died without children ; if the husband died, his widow remained married to him by the levirate, cohabiting with one of his kinsmen to bear children to his name. Since the levirate has been frowned on by Government and missions, the marriage-payment is returned or claimed from the new husband if the wife remarries, with deductions according to the number of children.[1] Acquaintance with some of these tribes may have stimulated the plaintiffs in 1920 and 1946 to bring their suits. In 1920 some judges, including the concluding judge, seem to have argued that dissolution of marriage by death created a legal situation analogous to that provided for in the 1917 statute covering dissolution by divorce. When this decision was referred to King Yeta III he overruled it on moral grounds, depending on the Lozi idea of decency as against the customary laws of the Southern Bantu near-neighbours of the Lozi. This was the argument of almost all judges in 1946.

King Yeta had an analogous precedent for his decision in a statute of his father, King Lewanika. In the past when either a husband or a wife died, the survivor's kin had to pay a beast (*komu yatoho*, the beast of the head) to the kin of the deceased. In the 1890's Lewanika got his kuta to agree that this payment was immoral and against decency, for when a husband or wife died both sets of kin should unite in mourning and neither should claim goods from the other. Lewanika in taking legislative action, and Yeta in making a new judicial decision, both thus argued from general principles of morality. The Lozi explain these as *milao yabutu*, the laws of humankind, or *milao yaNyambe*, the laws of God.

Before pursuing my argument, I must pause to consider two points raised by ' The Case of the Barren Widow '. First, we see that Nalolo Kuta had not heard of this case, nor of the analogous one in 1920. It is apparent therefore that, though all laws

---

[1] See my ' Kinship and Marriage among the Lozi of Northern Rhodesia and the Zulu of Natal ', pp. 185 ff.

PLATE V

INDUNA SOLAMI INETE

(1942)

PLATE VI
INDUNA FRANCIS L. SUU
(1942)

are supposed to come from the main capital and all kutas should follow its judicial decisions and those of the High Court, subordinate kutas are not always informed of these.

Secondly, we see that though my questions might be designed to get an answer to 'What will the kuta order?', both Lozi rulers and public sometimes replied by giving an immediate moral judgment on the claim itself: the good man would not sue in those circumstances. Thus though the Lozi distinguish legal and moral rules, as is clear from the PRINCESS CHIEF's correction of her husband, I had difficulties in compiling an outline of the law through cases stated. My experience in listening to the kuta at work showed too that answers to cases stated, which I could formulate only in general terms, did not necessarily give an understanding of how the kuta would apply these laws in particular suits, where it might be influenced by moral issues and moral judgments on the litigants' actions.

IV

Inevitably in some cases the law supports the person who has behaved wrongly, and its enforcement conflicts with justice and equity. We have already had an example of this in ' The Case of the Ungenerous Husband ' (p. 172), where the judges held that they could not compel a husband who had wronged his wife to give her other goods besides half the crops she had planted since she had claimed divorce. But the judges are reluctant to take the view that theirs is only a court of law and not a court of justice or morals, and they may try to state and apply legal rules, without apparently altering the law, so that justice is achieved. This happened in ' The Case of the Lazy Husband ' (p. 144) where, as against ' The Case of the Ungenerous Husband ', a sub-district induna ordered the husband to give half the marriage-goods to his wife, to whom it had granted a divorce. The kuta argued that since he had not in two years fulfilled his promise to replace the hut she had yielded to a new wife, he had himself divorced her. (*Quaere* : Would this judgment have been upheld at the capital if the husband had appealed ?)

To illustrate this process, I select a case which involved the law that ' no-one can work land of a village and live elsewhere ', since we saw it applied, in specific reference to gardens, in ' The Case of the Biassed Father. It is important to remember that the Lozi attach the greatest value to maintaining the number of a village's inhabitants, if we are to understand the dog-in-the-manger attitude of the headman in this case.

CASE 47 : THE CASE OF THE ' DOG-IN-THE-MANGER '
HEADMAN (*or*) THE CASE OF THE HEADMAN'S FISHDAMS

(MAHALIHALI'S CASE), *Mongu–Lialui District Kuta, June, 1947, on appeal
from Yuka sub-district kuta of Prince Mwenekandala*

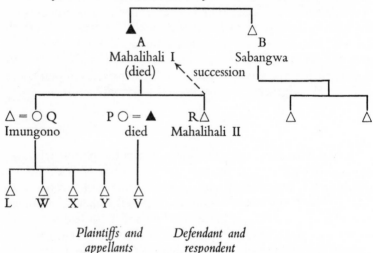

The facts, agreed, were : Mahalihali I (A) was an Ndebele who fled in the 'eighties to Loziland and became important. He was given a big village by King Lewanika. He was a quarrelsome man, and his brother Sabangwa (B) complained of his treatment to the kuta which ordered him to build a new village some fifty yards away, while continuing to use the old village land. This included fishdams which the king owned, receiving the catch on alternate days, since the dams were on the banks of a canal dug by King Lewanika. The suit was over some of these fishdams.

Many years before old Mahalihali had accused his daughter P of killing Mushembei, a member of the family whose relationship I did not determine, by using a zombe-sprite, i.e. by sorcery. She complained in court that he forbade her to get dung from the cattlekraal to mud her hut, dug up her sweet-potatoes and fed them to the cattle, and killed a beast which came from her mother's home. She fled to her mother's village. From there she married and went to her husband's village. She returned to her mother's village with her son after her husband's death, but continued to use the fish-dam which before the quarrel had been allotted to her by her father on his land. He had also given a dam to another daughter, Q, who was living in marriage nearby. Owing to A's ill-nature his village got weak in numbers. He begged a son from his daughter Q's husband, and was given L. L went away to White country and was 'lost'. Q's other sons, living in their father's village, continued to work the fishdams of their mother's father's village. Old A died, and his son R, not much older than his uterine nephews, succeeded him as Mahalihali II. R asked his sister Q's husband for another son to live with him and was refused. Therefore he took away Q's dam, and also P's. P's and Q's sons sued for the fishdams with their mothers as witnesses. Sabangwa (B) joined with his elder brother's son, Mahalihali II, who was defendant.

Prince Mwenekandala (F12) in the lower kuta held that all the dams were Mahalihali's, because no-one works land in the village and lives elsewhere, and the plaintiffs had appealed to Lialui.

P admitted that when her father drove her out, her brother, now Mahalihali II, came to see if she were all right, and some time after he succeeded asked her to return home. She refused. Then her son, V, returned from White country and when he tried to work the dam was prevented from doing so. Her son maintained that when he returned from White country and asked Mahalihali II about how his mother was treated, he did not get a good reception. He asked the kuta : ' Why has not my mother's father's son, the successor, asked his sister and her children to return home ? '

His mother pleaded : ' I did not reject my father, he rejected me.'

IMANDI (R6—sitting as head) : ' This you cannot tell. If you had come to us, or gone to the [British] District Commissioner at Mongu, to say your father accused you of sorcery, we could have enquired. Now we cannot enter this affair. Speak of the dams. Will you go back to your father's people ? '—*She* (P) : ' Does a person live as well at the mother's as at the father's ? At the mother's she finds much trouble.'

A son of Q's : ' We fished at my mother's father's. My young brother L went there and worked with him. He went to White country. I worked the dam for my grandfather Mahalihali—his wives chose fish to cook. My grandfather died. They put R in the position of my grandfather. You know when he inherited [i.e. was formally installed at the capital] we were told to share with the village, but they divided the goods among themselves. It is his own fault that he is alone. I worked the other dam for my mother [i.e.

mother's sister, P] while her son was away ; she got it from her father.'

Q pleaded : ' Malozi, I got my blanket and my dress from my dam. I cannot have the dish of my father taken away. He had four daughters ; one was taken into the palace of the late King Lewanika, the others were married. I go on my knees to you, my lords ; do not take my dish' (laughter).

NAMUNDA-KATANEKWA (R11) : ' Do you live at your mother's too ? '—Q : ' No, I live with my husband. Now we have given a son to Mahalihali, the one who went away, and they cannot take another though he is begged for by Mahalihali's successor. I am prepared to go myself to live with him.'

The kuta asked P if she would go.—P : ' Old people cannot refuse. How can they refuse their relatives ? No-one rejects her relatives.'

Her son, V, objected : ' Will R care well for his sister ?—what about the quarrel ? '—IMANDI (R6) : ' R did not go to your mother because of the quarrel. We are making [moulding—of a pot] peace among you (*lubupa kozo fahali mina*). Mahalihali is the NGAMBELA [i.e. chief] who has inherited everything.'

SIKOTA-MUTUMWA (L5—head of stewards) questioned R on whether he went to greet his sister, P.—R : ' I did.'

Ishee Kamona asked R about the quarrel between his sister and his father, and told him : ' Your elder sister is your mother. You should have straightened it out. You should have become your father.' He pressed R on why he did not go into the quarrel and ask his sister about it.

Here, as in previous cases, we have the question of the holding of dams becoming an enquiry into whether people behaved as proper kinsfolk ; but there is also another moral issue, the rights of the sisters to the use of paternal land, especially when they are old, which catches the judges between moral and legal obligations. This emerges clearly in the judgments :

Prince Litooma : ' Mahalihali—your complaint is good. If you do not build with me I refuse to give you the things for which I gave the royal salute to the NGAMBELA. This is the law (*mulao*)— we know it of old. But there is the word of IMANDI (R6) that they gave you the man who was lost in White country. This you ought not to do, to take from her the fishdam. That is on Q's side ' [i.e. legally the dam is Mahalihali's, morally he should let his sister Q work it, especially as she and her husband gave him a son]. ' As for P and her son, they have no right to the dam unless they return to your village.' (IMANDI threatened to commit Q's sons for contempt when they showed they were dissatisfied.)

Ishee Kamona : ' I give the same judgment as Prince Litooma. I scold Mahalihali for taking the dam from Q's sons. Live well with them and they will make you live ' [i.e. treat them generously and in turn they will help you prosper].

SAYWA (27) : ' Mahalihali, on the side of them of Q—they gave you the lost one. They cannot give you his brother. Do not ask again. Their power is at her husband's. Though she is at her marriage, you have no power to take from them what her father gave her [i.e. in this judgment the moral obligation is made legal].

' As for P and her son—they are of your village. The son should have come from White country when he heard of the quarrel, or sent for his mother to ask for the truth. If he were a good boy, he would have come to you to find why his mother was driven out. They are your people, of one womb. I scold you, Mahalihali, for not going to fetch your sister. What your father left, you must " eat " together. Take your sister P and her child and give them of the things of your father, so that you may be together and when one goes to White country the other is left to hold things. But they of Q, I refuse. For my part I see you are wrong, to take from her what was given by her father.'

Prince Mushamuko : ' R—you are wrong on the side of Q. There is no complaint about her three sons. You get sons from her only by her permission. You cannot take her children from where she has married to bring them here—or say to her children " Leave there." As for you, P, you have no right to eat things at the village of your father and take them to the village of your mother. You have no right (*mata* = power) to pick up a thing to take to your mother's.'

INYUNDWANA (R21) : ' Mahalihali, as for Q, he who went to White country was yours. You cannot get another. Your father had power to give to his grandchildren. As for P, I see that you do not like her. She told her son to come out quickly : and he found it so, and the crops given to the cattle. Why did you not go to try them, whether they would return ?—say to yourself, I am dying for people ? And your elder sister Q says you have not been to her. So you suffer for not going to P and saying, " What is past is lost, come to me, I return to peace." If you will live with peace, or hear the words of the Malozi, I do not know ? ' [Here a judge dodges the issue.]

Prince Namiluko : ' Mahalihali, by the law (*mulao*) of the Lozi one has no power (*mata*) over the sister's son. Among the Lubale it is otherwise. With us, we refuse—the children are my own [as against the mother's kin]. I do not see where you have power to force your sister's sons to come here. Our family law (*mulao*) is of old, if we see we are alone, we have to *beg* for the sister's son. I see your parent [sister] gave you a son long ago. You were unlucky —he was a lost-one. These children do not sue, but their mother. She is the owner of the dam from your father—what took her away is marriage. What took her to Imungono [her husband] is her work —marriage ; her true home is with you (*haenu*). If she had had children who died, she would return to you, what if her garden were gone ? So leave her dam to her.

' P, you sue, not your son. Your children cannot sue in the place of your father. You cannot claim in Likokota [her mother's village]. Really I see that you must return to Mahalihali—it is your home. Mahalihali, these, P and her son, are your people. You must go to her, because she is your mother. We heard from her that when she quarrelled with your father you took her with both hands. She lives badly at her mother's—if she rejects your offer, it is her affair. You have tried. This is my opinion—you will hear from them who can judge.'

NAMAMBA (R12) : ' Mahalihali, your sister Q went long ago when your father was alive to where she married and she took the dam with her. It was like a cow which goes with a woman to provide food and which produces more cattle. I had a similar case in my village at Likapai ' (which he cited).[1] ' The dam has gone and passes to her sons—it was given by the old people, and it comes from long ago ' [i.e. NAMAMBA holds that this dam has passed from the title Mahalihali to the title Imungono. This is a real reversal of the law].

' As for P—I see you are afraid of the zombe—afraid she will bring it back because it killed Mushembei. You love her but you are afraid of her. You drove her away and took her things.

' As for her who went to marry, you cannot take the things. You take P and her son, he goes with his mother, and will work gardens with you. We Malozi hear today for the first time that she killed Mushembei. Take her and care for her and when you are away she will take your place. Greet her and welcome her. Old people are our life—we all have them.'

ALULEYA-IFUNGA (L8 and F2—a prince consort, sitting as head of royal mat) : ' Mahalihali, I see you are unlucky. But why is not your uncle Sabangwa (B) with the defendants ? He has built on his own—why do you not ask him to come back ? He works his gardens yet is not in the home. You have done wrong to P who

---

[1] He says ' my village ' because he is headman. The village belongs to the PRINCESS CHIEF Mulima as a princess, and not as PRINCESS CHIEF.

came out in a quarrel. For Q, I say the same as the other lords—
she went with the dam given her by her father.' [It was not clear
if he meant permanently as in NAMAMBA's judgment, or for her use
as in others.] 'I do not agree with the others—you missed in all
these affairs. You cannot take from Q the dam given to her by your
father long ago. You will have your children and see it—you are
not God. On P's side, your other sister, your mother : I heard all
the things which happened to her—you also saw them. You left
it on purpose (*kabomu*). Why did you not go to call her ? I agree
with NAMAMBA. You should have gone to her. And her son came
back to you—why did you not fix the affair with him ? So you too,
P's son, you go to the village of Mahalihali and you, Sabangwa, (B)
are to join it.'

AWAMI (L7) : 'Sabangwa, I blame you for not advising Mahalihali
well. He is the successor but he is younger than you are. For Q,
—by the law of the Lozi (*kamulao waMalozi*), a man belongs truly
to his father, and yet he does not differ from them of his mother.
Q went out to marry ; she grew old at her husband's. But she still
has a right (*tukelo*) in her parent's home—gardens, dams, cattle. She
is not separated from them. You too, if your mother's brother dies,
can get something, if it is cattle only. Every Lozi builds with his
father but eats at his mother's. So it is with the dam. As for your
loneliness, Mahalihali, Imungono, the father of Q's children, may
refuse to give you a son. If he does, do they not eat over here ?
I wonder at this—I see it for the first time in the kuta. If you quarrel,
it is you yourself who strips yourself. As for your being heir and
getting all, you get all but only to manage it for them. Indeed you
ought if rich to add to theirs, not take from them. They have done
nothing wrong,—if they had, there would be a case. The dam is
theirs ; this is our old law (*mulao wakaale*). You take from her what
her father gave her !—what wrong has she done ? She who carried
you on her back ?[1] There is no such affair in Loziland.

'Here for P—a man can bring a case here. If you saw your sister
had no sorcery, why did you not fetch her ? Did you see what
your father saw ? Her son got angry. If he had found that you
came to his mother and said, "Come home and eat the-things-that-
are-yours (*zahao*)," he would have come to you. He would have
said to his mother, "Look, the heir has turned about (*kwenuhile*),
let us go to him." When he saw that you were silent, he thought
you entered into the mouth of your father. We judge because you
did not see the affair well. So I see that P came out because she

---

[1] As Q was much older than Mahalihali, it was probable that she nursed
him as an infant.

was driven out, not because she wanted to. The successor should fix the affair—so we questioned you. So we say you should speak well with your sister and sister's son and get them home—they have no fault, because they did not come out of the village, but were driven out.'

NAMUNDA-KATANEKWA (R11) : 'Mahalihali, the sons of Q have the right (*mulao*). You should have spoken nicely about it. You got the lost-one—*they* could say : "We cannot leave our father." If you had asked for your sister Q to be your parent, she could have come to you and gone to greet where she married, to greet her husband and her children. Her children would have fished and worked gardens for her, since they are close by. Your father gave the dam to Q. You do not know, perhaps one day their younger brother who is a lost-one may come back and eat her dam. You should not have brought the case, but you should have asked for your sister. Her sons, and their wives, would have come always to greet her. As for that milking cow, the dam given her by her father, you cannot take it from her. She does not move it to her husband's —it remains still in your hand [*lizoho*, here = power]. Her children eat [i.e. inherit] at their father's.

'Sabangwa [Mahalihali I's brother], I know your affair. I have been here long. First, as an attendant on the king, and in the name of NAMUNDA. My father died in the same year as King Lewanika [in 1916 ; he was appointed to the title held by his father]. When you had a quarrel with your elder brother Mahalihali, the Malozi split your village—they refused to let you go elsewhere. When your elder brother's son was taken to be Mahalihali, you should have gone back. You were prevented from doing so because you did not like to lose the village title, Sabangwa. I say with the Malozi go back to your elder brother's son and build with him. He is a young man, you are old. The land is all yours. The name of Mahalihali is very big—make it big : let the name of Sabangwa on the bank of the canal die. You have only two sons—go to your child and build together. Have a strong village.

'As for you, P—no. Q's beast is all right—it is not a beast which is struck ; it is soil [i.e. it cannot be moved like a cow]. They of Imungono, Q's husband, are close to Mahalihali—he cannot take her dam. You, P, came out because of a quarrel with your father. These affairs of sorcery we do not hear—they are of long ago. But you cannot work a dam at Siwito from Likokoto in Salondo. I say with the Malozi go back to your father's from your mother's and eat the things that are yours. To eat from Likokoto, the village of the *Musubia wahesu* [i.e. 'man of the Subia tribe related to us'— the judge]—'I cannot agree. You cannot draw the dam from down here' [putting the law on the basis of distance]. 'Agree amicably with your brother. Q can take—her father let her work the dam when she went with her children.'

SIKOTA-MUTUMWA (L5) : 'Mahalihali, you are the parent. You cannot work on your own. You came here to the kuta to succeed. You, Sabangwa, go back. You, Mahalihali, were here to succeed when the Malozi said you must agree with Sabangwa. So you are wrong to pass him over and go elsewhere to find people. Sabangwa must move his huts back to you.

'For Q—her husband did well. He gave you a son—he is a lost-one. You had no fault in asking for another, it was begging. The woman is a person, and the man is a person ; if you fail with your father you go to your mother. The man who can rule well, will get the children. If the man cannot, they will go to the mother's, to the woman. All is one family. You did no wrong in asking for a successor for the lost-one—you had a right (*swanelo*) to ask for him. Imungono (Q's husband) could give if he wished to. You, V (son of P), you acted wrongly, I scold you for not going to Mahalihali and his father about your mother's being accused of sorcery. You should have returned from White country to see about it. Where is your father's home ?' (V answered : 'At Mabumbu. I grew up with my mother's father Mahalihali, and went with her to my mother's mother's home.') 'You come out of there and go with your mother to Mahalihali. You know the word of sorcery is forbidden. You go to Mahalihali, where you will eat gardens and dams.'

IMANDI (R6, senior induna sitting in court—all clapped hands before he judged ; he spoke loudly and violently) : 'I do not separate the two women. I cannot see how you divide the cases. I fail to.' (He asked where the dams were.) 'We cannot change the law (*mulao*) against Mahalihali. Our law (*mulao*) comes from long ago. These for Q—as for the lost-one, he did not come to the present Mahalihali, but to his father. So Mahalihali has a right (*tukelo*) here. But a woman must live where she marries—she must get things for her living where she stays with her children. And for P it is the same. Mahalihali went at the flood to ask for a person—Imungono refused because he had given the lost-one. They say, how can you even if you are the successor take all ? No—our heir at Liyala Village owns our things but he does not take them. The women have no fault, but their children have. They did not speak well with Mahalihali. Q's sons eat with their mother. And I do not believe that Q and P can live well with Mahalihali. Mahalihali is the owner of the dams—he who says you can take them to Imungono's only deceives you. But I do not like a quarrel in a family. If you, Q, have a dam it is in the power (*lizoho* = hand) of Mahalihali—he gave the royal salute when he was installed as heir—it is he who was given these things. The dams are his.

'Mahalihali, your sisters are brought into the kuta by their children. If they fish, it is by your right (*mata* = power) and permission (*sibaka*). If you, you sons of Q, get fish, it is from your mother, but it is from Mahalihali.

'So for P, it is the same affair. You work the dam in the power (*mata*) of Mahalihali ; if he gets angry he can drive you out.

'But you, Mahalihali, you listen, hold your sisters well, give them food. But if they quarrel with you, you can put them out—you were given the dams. We cannot take them from you unless we change the law (*mulao*). Let them fish, but let them know that they eat from you, their parent. This is my judgment—the dams are Mahalihali's. But we'll see what SOLAMI (R3) says.'

SOLAMI was head of that kuta. During the hearing he was only in court occasionally, and then was continually occupied on administrative business. He was constantly called to the king or to the NGAMBELA'S kuta. Next day the parties appeared before the kuta again for his judgment—he had had the case, and the other judgments, reported to him during the night.

SOLAMI, very gently as was his wont, asked them if they had heard and agreed with the judgment of the kuta. 'It was a bad thing, the sons of Q going to fish outside of their parent Mahalihali. The kuta told you, Mahalihali, to leave your old sister so that she can live on the dam. It was not that L left your village—he went to White country. The kuta scolded Sabangwa because he did not do well. It said live well with your relatives ; if the sons of Q fail at their father's they will come to live with you. No, I've asked all —they say they are satisfied—what can I do ? '—*Mahalihali* : ' No, I agree with the words of IMANDI, take the dams of Mahalihali.' SOLAMI : ' No . . .'

I was then invited to see the king and left the kuta. I was told that SOLAMI followed the judgment of the rest of the court : Mahalihali had no right (*mata* = power) to take the things of his sister— they and their sons could work them if Mahalihali were rich. What will children eat if they have nothing at their mother's home and fail at their father's ? But P and her son must return. If Mahalihali persisted in opposing this, they would get a new Mahalihali. Still, the dams were Mahalihali's. He scolded Sabangwa, who should rejoin Mahalihali. Mahalihali said he would appeal to a higher kuta. The judgment entered was that Mahalihali owned the dams but his nephews should fish them : it was against this that Mahalihali said he would appeal.

When I arrived at the palace, I found the NGAMBELA (R1) and SUU (R17), the administrative secretary, with the king. They asked me what case I had been listening to, and immediately said : ' The law (*mulao*) is that if you leave a village you cannot eat of its land.' When I told them of the kuta's majority judgment, they agreed with this, and said : ' No, the sister can work land at home while she is married, and also her children. They have a right there, to gardens and fishdams. They can move to settle in the village, but even if they do not they cannot be prevented from using its land. But the land remains in the name of the village.' The king referred to an earlier discussion we had had : ' I can work land at my mother's, on my commoner side, without taking it to the kingship.'

First, this case further illustrates theses we have already considered. To settle a matter of land-holding within an extended family the kuta investigates the behaviour of the parties to one another, and to their dead kin, over a long period of years. It assesses their behaviour against the standards it demands, for a series of situations, of the reasonable brother, sister, brother-in-law, nephew, and headman. But we notice again that the upright man is implicit in the reasonable man. We are here concerned with the legal implications of this partial identification. In the case we are now considering, this emerges even more clearly because the law (*mulao*) here appeared to support Mahalihali who had not behaved uprightly. In the beginning of the quarrel he should have sought out and comforted his sister when she was ill-treated by their father, perhaps even have braved their father's wrath to adjust the quarrel. When he became heir he should have sought to draw his uterine kin to him by generosity, not by threats. Therefore, though one of the most important laws in Loziland is that a headman can only be compelled to allow his own villagers to work his village land, most of the judges were reluctant to support him. Three only came out in unhesitating defence of Mahalihali's rights, as these had been upheld in the lower kuta. Prince Litooma opened the judging with an unequivocal affirmation of this fundamental premiss of Lozi land-tenure law : ' Mahalihali, your complaint is good. If you do not build with me I refuse to give you the things for which I gave the royal salute to the NGAMBELA (R1). This is the law—we know it of old.' To take land from the title of a village headman, and move it to one's mother's or father's or husband's village as the case may be, should not be done. I shall argue when I consider the concepts of property in *The Ideas of Barotse Jurisprudence*, that this would undermine the whole structure of Lozi society as it is rooted in the relations between the fixed abodes of king, headmen, and villagers, on the land.[1] Prince Litooma, however, went on to exhort Mahalihali that though these were his legal rights, he ought not to prevent his sister Q, living nearby in marriage, from fishing. He considered that the other sister, living in widowhood at her mother's village, was free to come with her son to live with Mahalihali or lose the dam, and she had said she was prepared to return. As in 'The Case of the Biassed Father' the judge tried to use desire for land to exert pressure on people to bring them back to a village ; and, as in 'The Case of the Ungenerous Husband', the judge exhorted people to behave morally beyond their legal duties.

Except for Ishee Kamona's immediate and brief concurrence, the judges who followed on Prince Litooma were more uneasy about supporting Mahalihali—this uneasiness is epitomized by INYUNDWANA's failure to say anything. Almost all of them agreed with Litooma that the sister accused of sorcery and driven away by her father, should return with her son to Mahalihali. Mostly they distinguished between the two sisters on the grounds that one was still living in marriage, 'her work', with her husband, though some said she too could return to her true home, her birthplace. NAMUNDA-KATANEKWA made the distinction between the two sisters on the basis of the respective distances at which they resided from Mahalihali's village.

It is not clear what legal rights were stated by most judges about the still-married sister's position. Only NAMAMBA said quite definitely that the dam had passed from Mahalihali to her and her sons in her husband's village, that it was like a beast driven there. This amounted to an absolute reversal of the law. SAYWA and ALULEYA-IFUNGA almost said this. However, most of the judges ruled that the dam remained in the holding of the name Mahalihali, but that his sister and nephews, though they did not reside in the village, had a right to use it when in need. These judges did not make clear how firm this right was. Their judgments were exhortations to Mahalihali, as when

---

[1] See also my *Economy of the Central Barotse Plain*, pp. 24 ff.

AWAMI told him that he ' ought if rich to add to theirs, not to take from them '. Others urged him to win them to him by generous treatment. Some stressed that as Mahalihali's brother-in-law had given a son to the village he had a moral right to profit from its wealth. The judges emphasized that these people had done no wrong to Mahalihali : if they had, he would have had a sound case in applying for their expulsion from the dams.

ALULEYA-IFUNGA, followed by his seniors, introduced the uncle Sabangwa into the case. Mahalihali should have invited him back—and Sabangwa should have volunteered to return instead of encouraging Mahalihali's attack on people properly resident with their father. These later judgments ordered Sabangwa to return.

The judgments thus moved in support of justice and against the letter of the law to IMANDI, sitting as head of the kuta. He, however, insisted that both cases were identical : ' I do not separate the two women. I cannot see how you divide the cases. . . . We cannot change the law (*mulao*) against Mahalihali. . . . Mahalihali is the owner of the dams.' But IMANDI, like Prince Litooma and Ishee Kamona, insisted that though the dams were Mahalihali's, he ought to let his sisters and their sons fish them.

The case was given, for the Lozi, its most satisfactory solution by SOLAMI. When his hopes that, ' No, I've asked all—they say they are satisfied—what can I do ? ' were disappointed by Mahalihali's insistence on his legal rights, SOLAMI stated a new sanction : if Mahalihali persisted in his intransigence, the kuta would appoint a new Mahalihali. Thus though the kuta should follow the law, a judge may combine different principles of law so as to create, in effect, new law, and he does so in order to satisfy the requirements of justice. Since clearly Mahalihali's village had more land than the residents required, it was fair for kin elsewhere to claim a share in this land. However, the decision of some judges that those claims should be directly enforced by the kuta was a serious alteration of the law as I had frequently heard it stated. The wise and experienced SOLAMI solved the judicial dilemma by threatening to apply in an unprecedented situation the kuta's power to discharge a headman. This would leave the rights of headmanship in the dams untouched, but would establish as legal the power of the kuta indirectly to enforce claims by kin, resident elsewhere, in village lands. The law was developed to meet the demands of morality and justice.

This cannot always be done. The case of the husband who would not give goods to his wife shows that the kuta cannot enforce decency if this is in too radical conflict with established law, though I have quoted a case [1] where a junior kuta ordered a husband to do this. I myself think, though I omitted to discuss this point with the Lozi, that Mahalihali's case and that of the Ungenerous Husband are distinguishable in Lozi ethics : the ungenerous husband's relationship with his wife had come to an end, while nothing could break Mahalihali's blood-kinship with his sisters and their sons, however much they quarrelled. This kinship was established by common ancestry which was tied to the village and its land—as Prince Namiluko put it of sister Q : 'What took her to Imungono is her work—marriage ; her true home is with you [Mahalihali].' The kuta had to defend the law protecting a headman's title, to achieve justice, and to mould peace and good-feeling in the Mahalihali extended family. SOLAMI saw that if Mahalihali was intractable, all these aims could be achieved by replacing him with another who would allow the inheritance to profit all kin, including the discharged incumbent, reduced to the status of an ordinary villager. In-lawship, on the other hand, as it is entered on by the legal act of marriage, is broken by the legal act of divorce ; and especially where there were not children to relate the divorced spouses, it was not so important if the husband did not behave decently. The kuta could only state for him, and for the public at large, the standards of decency it approved for husbands. I have already shown that in women's suits for divorce the judges do not always try to reconcile the spouses, while they always try to reconcile quarrelling blood-kin.

The threat to discharge Mahalihali from the headmanship was made by SOLAMI in virtue of what we would call the kuta's administrative powers. The kuta confirms the appointment of all heirs to headmanships, and has a direct interest in how they carry out their duties ; therefore it can discharge them. Headmen have been discharged for failing to carry out the duties

---

[1] 'The Case of the Lazy Husband', p. 144.

laid on them by the British or Barotse Governments. I have been told also of discharges of headmen in the past for offending the king or kuta, and have recorded two cases where whole villages had been dispersed because of their headmen's serious offences. My informants stated that if a headman fails to hold a village together amicably and is niggardly to his kin these may sue to have him discharged, but they cited no actual cases where this was done. They added that if when the kin selected him as headman, the kuta warned them that he would be unsatisfactory, it is likely to tell them that they must suffer for their stupidity. Apparently, therefore, Mahalihali's kin might themselves have sued for his discharge : I failed to ask the kuta this. As it was, SOLAMI converted the case into an administrative decision on Mahalihali's fitness for the headmanship.

For here, as in the Cases of 'the Biassed Father', 'the Violent Councillor', and 'the Quarrelsome Teacher', we must bear in mind the manifold functions of the kuta if we are to understand how councillors try to enforce upright conduct as well as legal obligations. Not only as judges, but also as legislators and religious leaders, they are constantly concerned with upholding ethical values. Therefore they are reluctant to enforce rights where these are unjustly sought, even though sometimes they may have to admit that, ' *kitata, kono ki mulao*— it is hard, but it is the law '—, with our implication that ' hard cases make good law '.

CASE 47*a* : THE CASE OF THE ADULTERINE CHILD
(*from a text*)

A man was away at work in White country for some years. When he returned home his father met him, and told him that his wife had had a child by a well-known ne'er-do-well, and begged him not to beat her. The father considered that the son had driven his wife to wrongdoing by his long absence, and that she was nevertheless a good wife. The son accepted these admonishments and agreed to retain his wife unreproved and to accept the adulterine child. The kuta at Lialui upheld his suit for damages against the adulterer, but refused to countenance his plea, against the adulterer's father, that he keep the child. The kuta admitted that the adulterer was too much of a wastrel to pay the damages or to care for the child as well as the offended husband would, but held : ' It is hard, but it is the law : a child must go to its father.'

P

Nevertheless, as in Mahalihali's case, the judges usually try to amend the law, if they can without altering its substance, to meet those hard cases. Only one judge, NAMAMBA, stated un-equivocally that Mahalihali had lost his rights in the dam.

It is doubtful, however, whether even NAMAMBA intended to state the law always to be that a woman marrying out of a village took with her title to gardens or land allotted to her, though he said this title would pass to her sons even if they resided in her husband's village. He seemed to state this, for he said that the dam ' was like a cow which goes with a woman to provide living and which produces more cattle '. Indeed, the analogy makes clear that even NAMAMBA intended to rule that the sister and her sons had rights in the dam as against Mahalihali—i.e. that ultimately the dam remained vested in the title Mahalihali, but that he could not stop his sister or her sons from fishing it. For if a woman takes to her marriage a beast from her parental home to provide sustenance for herself and her children, this beast and its offspring do not pass to her husband and his heirs. If there is a divorce, they return with her to her home. If she dies, they pass to her sons and not her husband, or if she is childless to heirs at her home. Similarly, I do not believe that NAMAMBA would have upheld a claim by her husband to the dam—the husband gave no evidence in the case, and in court sat at the side and not behind his wife in support of her, presumably because he was anxious not to become involved in the affairs of what was, for him, ' another family '. I am certain that NAMAMBA would have upheld a later claim by Mahali-hali had his sister or her sons attempted to transfer the dam to other of her husband's kin, or to give it without Mahalihali's permission to the king for disposal to an outsider, or even to lend it to an outsider without Mahalihali's permission. In an analogous case, had NAMAMBA felt that the sister and her sons had wronged the headman, he might have given a contrary decision. For as judges are not bound by past decisions since these are unrecorded, so in practice they do not bind themselves by a particular decision which also is not recorded, and which they will remember principally for the ethical grounds on which it was made.

Implicit in this analysis of what was contained as *law* in NAMAMBA's judgment, is the substantive issue that was determined in this case. This is, what property rights did Mahalihali, and his sisters and their sons, have in the same dam ? The kuta was specifying the significance of *bung'a*, ownership, in Lozi law in its application to a particular set of circumstances. I have left consideration of this point to the last, because it was not thus explicitly formulated. The judgments do not proceed by defining *ownership* and seeing how it covers the respective rights of the parties. They have indeed to work with one word, *bung'a*, though it covers a range of quite different rights which depend on one another. These rights are summarized by their use of possessive formatives (prefixes in Bantu languages) which I have translated as, e.g. : ' The dam is Mahalihali's.' The judges take the definition of ' ownership ' (*bung'a*) for granted throughout. In Lozi law ' ownership ' of land inheres in social positions and therefore, as stated in my comments on ' The Case of the Biassed Father ' (p. 46), it depends on citizenship, and on membership of a village and/or a kinship grouping. The maintenance of these rights of ownership requires fulfilment of other obligations demanded of incumbents of those social positions. I shall consider this problem and its implications when I discuss the substantive law of land tenure,[1] but note summarily here that a whole series of rights are held by various people in the same piece of land. Ultimately, the king is owner as trustee for his people, but he allots primary holdings in blocks of land to village headmen like Mahalihali. Each headman allots a secondary holding to heads of households in his village, and they allot tertiary holdings to their dependants. Other kin, resident outside the village, have rights to use this land if there is more than sufficient for the villagers. Thus several persons may have rights of ownership at the same time in the same piece of land. The acquisition and maintenance of these rights depends at every stage of the hierarchy on the holder's fulfilling the duties of his station to both his superiors and inferiors. Thus after IMANDI had affirmed that the dams were Mahalihali's he continued : ' If you, you sons of Q, get fish, it is from your mother,

---

[1] I published a preliminary analysis in *Essays on Lozi Land and Royal Property*, *Rhodes-Livingstone Paper No. 10*, Livingstone : Rhodes-Livingstone Institute (1943), the argument of which was summarized in ' African Land Tenure ', *The Rhodes-Livingstone Journal*, III, (June, 1945). See also my essay on the Lozi in *Seven Tribes of British Central Africa*, pp. 61 ff.

but it is from Mahalihali. . . . But you, Mahalihali, you listen, hold your sisters well, give them food. But if they quarrel with you, you can put them out—you were given the dams. Let them fish, but let them know that they eat from you, their parent.'

IMANDI thus stressed the duties of the subordinates to their senior kinsman and village headman. Similarly, AWAMI chided Mahalihali for his treatment of his still-married sister. ' They have done nothing wrong—if they had, there would be a case. The dam is theirs ; this is our old law. You take from her what her father gave her—what wrong has she done ? . . . [and for his other sister] : So we say you should speak well with your sister and sister's son and get them home—they have no fault, because they did not come out of the village, but were driven out.'

Superiors too must fulfil the legal and moral duties of their station : all the judges, even those who supported Mahalihali, advised him thus. SOLAMI, establishing a new sanction, threatened to discharge him for failing to be as generous as a headman should be, the example for which was set by IMANDI : ' Our heir at Liyala Village owns our things but he does not take them.'

This issue of what rights of ownership different people hold in the same parcels of land lies at the heart of every land dispute. But since these rights inhere in social position their maintenance is protected only if the duties of that particular position are reasonably fulfilled. In ' The Case of the Biassed Father ' the court held that the nephews lost those rights if they left the village, since they as well as the headman were in the wrong. However, though the trial of a land-dispute between kin or villagers involves an enquiry into the reasonableness of their respective behaviour, the judges are applying to the facts definitions of the flexible concepts of ' rights and duties of ownership ' as attached to a series of social positions.

This situation emerges even in cases which involve quite different types of rights in land—those held by borrowers and lenders of land. The Immigrant Land-borrower (p. 63) pleaded at length that he had done so much for the lender that he had established a stronger right than mere borrowing of the land : the lender, though he could merely exercise his right to expel the borrower, felt constrained to plead that the borrower had behaved badly. The kuta enquired into similar pleas by lender and borrower that they had returned ill with good in 'The Case of the Prince's Gardens' (p. 56).

In the present case the judges argue by using words like *swanelo* and *tukelo*, which mean both right and duty, and *mata* or *lizoho* which mean power but also responsibility and liability. They contrast *swanelo*, what *ought* to be done as an obligation claimed as a right, with the plaintiffs not having done any wrong, which implies rightdoing (*kueza hande* or *kueza yeswanelwa*). From the rightdoing of the plaintiffs,—doing what ought to be done (*yeswanelwa*)—the judges jump a step in argument to say they have a right—*swanelo*, from the same root—to their land. The judges could do this with the words *yelukile*, to be upright, and *tukelo*, a right. The flexibility of the concepts, their multiplicity of referents, enables the judges to build logical arguments by which rightdoing establishes a legal claim on the land, and to import justice into judgment.

In Mahalihali's case, the king had two different sets of rights in the dams. First, he holds all land of the nation for distribution to his people, to whom he must give land, and he has therefore an interest in how headmen exercise the powers (rights) he has granted them. Though this was not stated explicitly by SOLAMI, it is in virtue of this royal and governmental interest in land that the kuta could discharge a headman for not distributing land fairly to his dependants. Secondly, the king had a special interest in these particular dams because he held them in his own right and was entitled to the catch on alternate days. It is interesting that these royal rights were never mentioned during the hearing. Had the dams been given absolutely to Mahalihali, he may have lacked labour to fish them, and perhaps some readers may therefore suggest that the judges' support of his nephews was to secure the king's fish catches. This point has only occurred to me while I was writing up the case so I did not put it to Lozi. As it did not come to my mind, I feel it was not present in the minds of either judges or litigants. The sisters and their sons did not plead this as a reason that they be allowed to fish the dams : and I therefore consider that we may conclude it was not significant in influencing the judges' decisions.

V

The background of the judges' work in this case is again the type of relationships out of which disputes arise : they are quarrels between people involved in a set of muliplex ties. The judges are not only concerned to define the legal rights and duties of the *personae* involved, which are almost invariably well known, or even with their application in a particular case. IMANDI's reprimand in Mahalihali's case, 'We are moulding peace among you,' sums up the judicial task. To reconcile the parties by getting wrongdoers to see the error of their ways so that in the future all may live together in amity, requires that judges take into account ethical ideals as well as legal rules.

Relationships of this kind involve far more than recognition of legal rights and duties. They are too complex and intimate, too dependent on individual temperament and adjustment, too coloured by emotional involvement and ethical evaluation, for their disputes to be settled on this basis. In the relationships of parents and children, spouses, kinsmen, villagers, overlords and underlings, which constitute the fabric of Lozi society, moral judgments are made on almost every action. The success and diligence with which a man earns his living on the land, and the way he distributes his products among his wives and kin, are evaluated as good or bad. Similar moral judgments attach to the diligence of children in helping their parents, women in cooking and providing water and food, and commoners and stewards in attending on their lords. Moral judgments of this kind are made on almost all the actions of people in any society : they have heightened significance in multiplex enduring relationships, since they are an essential part of these. Therefore when disputes come to the kuta, it constantly puts an ethical evaluation on the facts of the case. The facts are not that so-and-so did this, and so-and-so that, therefore these are the legal rights ; but that so-and-so did this and it was immoral, while so-and-so did that and it was moral—therefore the latter merits the support of the law. Since all facts are scrutinized as ' good ' or ' bad ', and the kuta correspondingly praises and blames people for what they did with fish, grass, poles, money, ethical valuations thus not only influence the kuta's decision, but colour its views of the very facts themselves. Necessarily, therefore, the kuta ends by *trying* to protect the ethical code, even if it is against the application of the letter of the law.

This ethical code in brief demands that the upright man should help and sustain his peers and dependants and overlords as prodigally as he can, and be benevolent in exercising his rights. He should extend these patterns to neighbours and strangers. I shall argue in *The Ideas of Barotse Jurisprudence* that this code of ethics applies to more ephemeral relationships by tending to make all contracts *uberrimae fidei*—of the utmost good faith.

In Mahalihali's case, the code is best illustrated by SIKOTA-MUTUMWA's indication of the path of wisdom :

'The woman is a person, and the man is a person : if you fail with your father you go to your mother. The man who can rule well will get the children. If the man cannot, they will go to the mother's, to the woman.' His sermon advised Mahalihali : if you are generous to your sister's children, in time they will leave their father and join you. Do not try to browbeat them, but win them to you.

Social life ideally should consist of a mutual give-and-take, distinguished by amiability, generosity, and benevolence in reciprocal co-operation. Naturally life does not run thus smoothly and quarrels are frequent. Some quarrels come to court. As we have seen again and again, the court does not confine its enquiry to the single element in the relationship which is the subject of the legal claim, but enters into considerations of justice and morality which arise from the relationship as a whole.

Cases may occur in which a man is caught in a conflict between rules appropriate to different relationships, or different elements of a single relationship—as, for example, between political and kinship obligations. The Lozi always hold that political morality overrules kinship allegiances, in that, e.g. the Violent Councillor and the Biassed Father should have been impartial and not have backed their own children. We have heard councillors upbraid their fellows for refusing to condemn kinsmen who were wrong, and SOLAMI (R3) say he did not care whom he tried, as a policeman must arrest his father, mother or sister. Therefore in 'The Case of the Eloping Wife' (p. 117) SAMBI (R1 at Nalolo) asked the visiting NAWALA to be first to convict his kinsman to show that he was indeed guilty ; and this NAWALA unhesitatingly did. In every situation which came to my notice the Lozi could say what the upright man should do, on their scale of ethical judgments. The highest duty is to law and justice : and justice must give way to law. The higher virtue of political loyalty over kinship and other loyalties theoretically resolves all conflicts, and enables the system to function.

VI

We can now examine with additional insight the Lozi view of the *personae* involved in cases of this kind. The kuta must deal with an individual person occupying specific positions in society, related to a variety of other specific individuals, and having a specific character and history—who has behaved morally or immorally. Anything about him or her may be relevant for the judicial settlement. The judges cannot regard the litigants simply as right-and-duty bearing units, whose respective claims have to be adjusted strictly according to law. In Mahalihali's case, therefore, the law could be applied differently for the two sisters, since one was still married, the other a widow living at her mother's village. The uncle Sabangwa, present as a witness, was converted by the judges into a litigant. The kuta's concern with ethical judgments as well as legal rules and its view of the *personae* involved are interdependent. Note how AWAMI admonished Mahalihali : ' They have done nothing wrong—if they had, there would be a case.' In Case No. 9 (p. 71) we heard litigants reprimanded for disputing over unused land. An ethical judgment may be made even on the subject of the dispute.

Since the kuta views the litigating *personae* in this way it may out-of-hand impose an additional—not a higher—fine on people who have broken the law because they have official standing.

CASE 48 : THE CASE OF THE OFFICIAL WRONGDOERS,

Saa-Katengo Kuta, Lialui, 1942

H_1 sued H_2 for abducting H_1's wife, but H_2 was able to prove that he found her at her natal home, solicited her in marriage from her father and mother's brother, and gave them the marriage-payment. Her father's and uncle's defence was that she returned home and told them that her husband, H_1, had divorced her. The kuta held that H_2 was innocent : H_1's claim must be satisfied by her kin. They were guilty because they knew that a wife sent home by her husband should bring a letter from him or be escorted by one of his kin. They should have summoned her husband or brought them all to the kuta. They would pay H_1 the three cattle due to a husband from the abductor of his wife, her fine of two cattle to the kuta, and an additional two cattle to the kuta ' because you are people of the capital who know the law (*milao* = laws) '.

This judgment may be contrasted with a judgment excusing people who could not know the law.

CASE 49: THE CASE OF THE IGNORANT FOREIGN WRONGDOERS (*from a text*)

Some Lunda traders from the north entered one of the king's reed-beds by the Zambezi and took nestlings to eat. This is against the law, for these nestlings are taken in communal drives on days appointed by the king who takes a share of the catch. NAWASILUNDU (R29), the induna in charge of the reed-bed, bound and fined the Lunda, and took from them the meal they had brought to trade. When he reported his action to the kuta, he was ordered to return their goods, to pay them damages, and to pay a fine : they were foreigners who did not know the law (*mulao*) and hungry travellers who thought they could take wild food.

We have already seen that adultery between a man and another's wife is a wrongdoing by both, but that he pays damages to the husband, and she a fine to court. The Lozi do not regard this as classing his action as a tort or private delict, and hers as a crime : both are wrongs (*liposo*). He pays his cuckold for the wrong, but Lozi say she cannot do so lest it lead to connivance between husbands and wives to turn to prostitution. She can only make recompense for her wrong by paying the court. However, this distinction emphasizes that men and women have quite different social positions, especially since intercourse between a married man and an unmarried woman, though called *kufosa* (to do wrong), does not give the wife a claim against her husband.

As the kuta in judgments distinguishes people by their specific positions, so it may vary its legislation.

The 1917 Marriage Laws ordered a man who fornicated with the wife of a councillor or prince to pay seven and not two cattle, and ten cattle if it were the NGAMBELA'S wife ; and a prince or councillor who committed adultery paid equally high damages to his cuckold, and was liable to be discharged. Heavier penalties similarly attached to the prince or councillor who attended a beerdrink.

That every litigant appears in court in terms of most of his social and individual personality shows in the judges' mode of address. In citing cases I have used letters instead of names, or reported the judges as saying ' man ', ' woman ', ' teacher ', ' headman ', ' induna '. I have done so to spare my readers confusion. The judges do indeed refer to people by their social positions, which determine the legal issues, but generally they use the parties' names. Any judge who knows a party will invariably do so, and in his judgment make use of his own knowledge of the parties, and his own relationship to them, though no evidence has been led on this point. I have mentioned this before, but repeat it, for we can now appreciate better how there is no such thing as judicial ignorance on one side, and on the other side litigants come to a court which may consider anything in their past history and their social connections. But this does not mean that a defendant is convicted on past record ; he must be guilty on the facts disclosed in the case under trial.

Though the judges generally address and refer to litigants by their names, with all this implies, there are terms to distinguish the right-and-duty bearing units involved in disputes. Among these we have met ' councillor ', ' headman ', ' husband ', ' wife ', ' father ', ' son ', etc. The rights vested in these *personae* are frequently referred to as ' ownership ' (*bung'a*—with *mung'a* = owner), and judges fix rights by speaking of, e.g. *mung'a musali*, the owner of a woman, being her husband or guardian kinsman, or *mung'a mubu*, the holder of land. These are right-and-duty bearing *personae* involved in social positions of status. There are others in more ephemeral relationships involving single interests, such as that of the borrower of land (*mukalimi*) against the holder, or of the herdsman of cattle (*mulisana*) as against the owner (*mung'a likomu*), or of the buyer (*muleki*) as against the seller (*mulekisi*). In these ephemeral relationships the judges pay less attention to the ethical implications of cases, as we have seen in ' The Case of the Prince's Gardens ' (p. 61) and ' The Case of the Father and his Son's Cattle ' (p. 110).

The right-and-duty bearing *personae* designated by these terms are always present in judgments ; they lie behind the use of personal names. However much they be submerged in the judicial process, without these conceptions of right-and-duty bearing units the Lozi would not have a system of law at all. There must be patterns, defined both by law and ethics, to which people should have conformed and against which actual situations can be assessed. The cores of these patterns are a few simple rules which are definable as legal. They relate together, outside of contracts, political and kinship positions in reciprocal relationships. Their existence is evident in the practice of praising a person by stating that he or she is a councillor, a woman, a child, a father, etc. (see p. 126 above). But recognition of the legal rights and duties of positions linked by multiplex ties does not enable the relationship between the parties occupying those positions to endure. This can be but the framework of a living relationship in which ethical ideals of generosity animate the parties. A person cannot practise upright conduct unless he acknowledges the moral as well as the legal claims of others. This is less significant in political than in kinship relationships, but in this uncomplicated social system the two types of relationship influence each other.

Since judgments do not concentrate only on the legal rights and duties of *personae*, the legal rules involved appear to be qualified to meet the specific circumstances of a particular individual and his relationships. The law may be applied strictly to one sister, developed to get justice for another. This makes it difficult to draw up a code of Lozi law. We might do so by stating the central rule and giving a series of provisos thus : No-one can work village land and live elsewhere, unless, if the village has a surplus of land, (*a*) he is a kinsman resident nearby, or (*b*) a kinswoman married out of the village, and so on. This formulation does give us the pattern of a set of relationships, but I do not consider that it expresses the attributes of Lozi legal rules or brings out the way judges will apply these rules. A better formulation is : there is a law that no-one can work land in a village and live elsewhere, and the kuta should refuse to allow land to be taken from the title of the village headman ; there is another law that the headman shall administer the goods of the title in the interests of all kinsfolk of the title, who respect his position, and if he does not he can be replaced at the suit of the kin.   Yet another law states that the kuta has the power to discharge a headman of its own initiative if he is unsatisfactory. Other laws are : the true home of a man or woman is at the father's village, but he or she has a right to seek help at the mother's village ; and, a married woman should reside at her husband's but does not lose her natal rights.   Since the laws attach to different kinds of social relationships and activities, they are of quite different character.   The judges have great discretion in applying the laws in varied combination to particular circumstances.   Different laws can be stated separately with certainty.   When they are combined in application to particular situations, various laws are given different weight, in order to achieve justice.   For in the uncomplicated structure of Lozi society, relations between kin and in-laws, relations between villagers and other kin and the village headman, relations between headman and kuta, and rights to particular pieces of land, are intricately intertwined and interdependent.   A just decision in one relationship may be implemented, against the hard letter of its own law, by applying sanctions in allied relationships. Indeed the laws may even be contradictory.   You must reside in the village to hoe its land, and you need not so reside.   To some extent their contradictions are concealed by the very general and flexible terms in which they are formulated : in the widest terms, the law states that rights to land of a village depend on membership of it *or* of its kinship grouping, and that continued membership depends on fulfilling reasonably all duties involved in those memberships.   Since, as shown above, the words for ' right' and ' duty' are themselves ambiguous, the judges manipulate this ambiguity, with the different laws and the contradictions between them, to achieve justice.

VII

This idyllic picture is of Lozi ethics and law, not of Lozi life.   Some men and women, and some lords, do attain these high standards.   Many do not, and mean, greedy, quarrelsome, vindictive, envious, or litigious people are common enough. We have seen that charges of sorcery gave legal cloak to blaming many natural misfortunes on the evil nature of one's fellows. Judicial wisdom and integrity may break down, for the Lozi recognize that there are foolish, cowardly, and even biassed and unjust judges. They recognize also that the kuta may come to a wrong decision, through mistaken appreciation of the facts or even prejudice. Hence Lozi law is what the kuta should enforce, not necessarily what it always does enforce. If all Lozi are aware of these occasional failures of the kuta, then obviously even when public opinion supports the kuta, litigants themselves are likely to consider its decisions unjust. Certainly the Quarrelsome Teacher, Sinonge in ' The Case of the Immigrant Land-Borrower ', and Mahalihali, thought so. Almost all litigants vehemently assert their innocence : perhaps in the nature of these intimate disputes it must be so. But on the whole outsiders can almost always support the kuta.

Generally Lozi consider that their major laws are *milao yabutu*, laws of humankind, or *milao yaNyambe*, laws of God, and that they embody general principles of morality (see above, p. 165). They believe that these laws and principles are of themselves obvious and self-evident to all men, even to Whites. SOLAMI (R3) rebuked the Foreign Thief (p. 108) who protested he was helpless as a foreigner in a Lozi court :

' My kinsman, we are thus far from partiality because we hold the country to rule it, and the Whites find the same right and wrong.'

Since the Lozi consider that this ' same right and wrong ' is inherent in the reason (*ngana*) of Man, that it is obvious to and accepted by all men of all tribes and nations, and that ultimately it derives from God, I feel justified in saying that they recognize *natural justice*—in embryo, the *jus naturale* itself.

We have considered cases in which the judges tried to apply natural justice and equity against the strict letter of the law. Generally they employ natural justice and equity in five different ways. First, as markedly in ' The Case of the Man Who Helped his Mothers-in-Law Cross a Ford ' (p. 148 f.), they support their statements of the statutory or customary legal rules which they are applying, by affirming that these are laws of natural justice, and they affirm all their moral judgments as if these were self-evident. Or the judges explain that the laws in themselves exhibit *general equity*—thus judges explained to the plaintiffs in ' The Case of the Biassed Father ' (p. 41) that it was not fair or equal (*kulikana* = to be equal) that they work the village's gardens and do not live in the village, since they would not have to clean the village and their children and stock would not damage others' gardens to balance damage to their gardens. Secondly, this spirit of equity in general, defined by Sir Carleton Kemp Allen as ' a liberal and humane interpretation of law in general, so far as that is possible without actual antagonism to the law itself', clearly animates the judges in applying the law in particular cases—*see* ' The Case of the Biassed Father ' and ' The Case of the Barren Widow '. Thirdly, the judges may draw on equity in general to achieve a particular equity—' a liberal and humane modification of the law in exceptional cases not coming within the ambit of the general rule ' [1]—*see* ' The Case of the Headman's Fishdams ', and ' The Case of the Lazy Husband ', where, in order that it might give her goods of the hut, the court held that the husband had constructively divorced his wife. Fourthly, the judges for equitable reasons may declare during the hearing of a case that custom has changed, as in ' The Case of the Father and his Son's Cattle '. They argue similarly when they sit in legislative debate that their reasoning is dominated by equity. Fifthly, the court considers natural justice, good morals, and general equity, in deciding whether it will enforce customs of its subject tribes.

In 1947 I discussed this last problem at length with the Princess Chief and her husband. Their statement of old Lozi policy coincided with my observations of what is done today. They said Lozi policy has always been that in ' national matters ' (*litaba zasicaba*) such as theft, murder, beer-drinking, etc., all tribes have to follow national laws, but that in matters of inheritance and other aspects of family law (*litaba zamwahae*—affairs of the home) each tribe can follow its own customs. ' We hope that they will see that our laws are better and follow them,' said the Princess Chief. They compared their policy for their subject tribes with the policy which Britain follows for them ; and they [and other rulers on different occasions] blamed the prince sent to rule Balovale District for provoking the local tribes to protest independence, by trying to impose Lozi law. However, they said that they would not uphold specific tribal laws where these were bad. Thus (to examples supplied by me) they would not admit a suit for adultery committed during the general sexual freedom of Wiko circumcision-feasts, if the husband had permitted his wife to join in the dances, since this would be enriching the husband for something he had connived at. Similarly, if a Wiko sued a man

---

[1] Allen, C. K., *Law in the Making*, Oxford : Clarendon Press, at p. 307.

who had been circumcised with him for adultery with his wife, to whom he had granted the other access as enjoined by the circumcision-lodge rules, the kuta would not allow the suit. Nor would it admit the husband's suit if he then sued the other for refusing him access in return to the other's wife. Indeed, the kuta might fine them all for immorality, as they would be parties to a wife-exchange or -lending agreement such as is known to Ila and Lubale [Wiko] law.[1]

Thus Lozi courts would appear here to have the same equitable legal and moral reasoning as is contained in the maxims of Roman Law : *ex turpi causa non oritur actio* (no action arises from an immoral agreement) and *in pari delicto potior est conditio defendentis* (in equal guilt the position of the defendant is stronger).

I cite these Roman Law maxims to indicate how general are the principles of morality which lie at the basis of Lozi juristic reasoning. For the same reason I now give a motley collection of examples of their moral defences of juridical institutions and rules.

The Lozi hold that it is self-evident that a man must be convicted by strong evidence, or that civil disputes are decided by the weight of the evidence. They hold too that if one man acts negligently or purposefully so as to harm another, he must pay damages to the injured because this is fair (*kwalikana*). Their standard of negligence is indeed so high that it appears as if their law does not recognize moral guilt in assessing damage, as has been frequently stated for all primitive law. Responsibility appears to be absolute. Thus even if a man brings a *prima facie* well-founded charge of adultery or theft which is not sustained, he may be ordered to pay the accused damages for wrongful accusation (*kutanta*). I have seen a plaintiff in the Saa-Katengo Court at Lialui (1942) ordered, and cheerfully agree that he ought, to pay £1 damages to a defendant whom, on good grounds, he had summoned to court as an adulterer in mistake for another (*Case 50 : The Case of the Wrong Defendant*). But Lozi law shows its regard for intention or culpable negligence in its maxim that ' fire and water are other lords '. No suit lies for damage by fire or through the overturning of a dug-out, howeyer negligent the originator of the accident may have been. They argue in defence of this maxim that no-one can control fire in their houses made of grass, or prevent children in their charge from falling into the open cooking

---

[1] I do not know if in fact Ila and Lubale courts would enforce these suits.

fires; and that the dangers which lurk in the waters and the wind are so fearsome that no-one can be blamed for them. They also recognize some actions as purely accidental : thus they have refused to grant damages when men have been stabbed with fish-spears at the communal fishing-battues. Here too they apply their equitable maxim that 'if you are invited to a meal and a fishbone sticks in your throat you cannot sue your host' (cf. *volenti non fit injuria*). Secondly, they hold that a man is not responsible for damages caused by his employee, unless it be his child, since the employer has done nothing wrong.

In thus briefly giving examples of responsibility for negligent action, or vicarious liability for the actions, I am aware that in law this is not a simple case of 'moral guilt or intention'. I repeat, I am here quoting Lozi arguments to illustrate only their view of equity and natural justice.

As this does not pretend to be a handbook of Lozi legal ideas I shall not multiply examples of these general principles of morality which are supported by Lozi law. However, I must note again that not all principles of morality are armed with the kuta's sanctions. The kuta cannot legally compel a husband whose wife has been granted a divorce to give her 'goods of the hut'. The kuta did not enforce executory contracts—bare promises (cf. *ex nuda pacta non oritur actio*)—even though the Lozi have a special pejorative term to describe people who break their promises.

VIII

The Lozi have even explicitly formulated a general concept of natural justice, in so far as they state generally that the kuta must decide what is just (*tukelo*, or *niti* = truth) and equitable (*kwalikana*). But often they do not distinguish moral maxims as such from particular principles contained in their own laws, or in the laws of the peoples of their region, though they explain many of the laws by ethical arguments which they regard as self-evident. From my discussion, just quoted, with the Princess Chief and her husband, it must be apparent that the Lozi have an embryonic concept of a *jus gentium*.

The Princess Chief went on to explain to me that there are certain *milao yamacaba kaufela*, 'laws of all nations'. Every tribe has laws enjoining respect for chiefs and for parents, taboos on sexual relations with certain kin though who these are may vary [cf. ' The Case of Cross-Cousin Adultery,' at p. 134], laws of avoidance of senior in-laws of the other sex, and so on, as well as laws forbidding people to steal, to assault, and to kill. These are ' the laws of all nations '. Then each tribe has its own laws : the Lozi favour agnatic succession, though they allow uterine succession ; the Wiko allow only uterine succession. There is nothing wrong with this uterine succession, so it can be enforced by Lozi kutas. She concluded in answer to my questioning, that when cases arise in which there is conflict of laws, as where a Lozi marries a Wiko, the kuta goes by ' what is right ' ; or if it is in doubt, or no moral issue is raised, the kuta follows Lozi law.[1]

' The Case of Cross-Cousin Adultery ' (p. 135) illustrates the application of this type of reasoning.

Many implications reside in the Princess Chief's description of the law of nations. The Lozi formulate the core of this embryonic *jus gentium* explicitly, as they do the core of the embryonic *jus naturale*. In addition, they regard the two as closely related, for they believe that most tribes and nations share with them these ideas of the laws of humankind (*milao yabutu*) and that these ideas lie at the basis of those institutions and rules of action and prohibition, which are common to African tribes. Some are also found among Whites though these tend to lack human kindness and fairness. All African peoples have institutions of marriage, property, taboos on incestuous marriage, funeral rites, other ritual, and so on ; and most have institutions of chieftain-ship. The customary incidents of these institutions and rules vary considerably, but their core is similar. Once at MUNONO's (R23) Sulu sub-district kuta men began to discuss whether the Bushmen who live in Western Barotseland were human beings. MUNONO held they were not for they neither cultivated nor kept cattle. As soon as I described Bushman marriage and exogamic taboos, and funeral rites, he said : ' They are indeed men, with laws of humankind.' Similarly, when this point was discussed in the Palace at Lialui, King Imwiko said : ' They are men. Once in Liuwa I shot a giraffe. The Bushmen came and hovered on the edge of the bush. We offered them meat : they came

---

[1] I gratefully acknowledge here the stimulus of Dr. I. Cunnison's analysis of *custom* among the peoples of the Luapula valley, in an unpublished thesis.

Q

running, crouched before us as chiefs, cut up the meat and cooked it for us. They know kingship, and so they are of humankind.'

In view of the comparatively undeveloped state of internal Lozi economy, the significant laws of nations with which their kutas become concerned are mainly limited to institutions in the laws of persons—marriage, birth, kinship, succession, in family law ; and rules of allegiance, tribute and rights to land and lawful protection in constitutional law. All tribes have concepts of ownership of property, but these are mainly involved in the law of persons. In addition, even before the coming of the Whites, barter exchange, developing into 'friendship' and bloodbrotherhood exchanges, allowed trade with people beyond the Lozi frontiers. Lozi assure me that though it was dangerous to travel outside these frontiers, they would have protected the rights of abused foreigners who sought relief in their courts, since these agreements were common to all men. But they were unable to cite any cases of foreigners seeking such relief.

Certain common ritual symbols of chieftainship are said to have been recognized and respected throughout the region. Chiefs' bands and bandsmen were regarded as sanctuaries to whom in battle fighters on either side might flee for refuge ; and old warriors have described to me, incidentally in their tales of battles, how men were succoured thus. Hence, say the Lozi, they have allowed most foreign chiefs who came to seek refuge among them, or who were conquered by them, to retain bands and also the eland-tail fly-switch which is the symbol of chieftainship. MWENEKANDALA (F12) lost these rights when he led his Mbalangwe to King Mulambwa (9th king : 1780 ?–1830 ?) because he was adopted into Mulambwa's family and became a prince. MWENECIENGELE (R32) who came with Mbunda followers shortly afterwards was not so adopted, and his successors have retained these chiefly symbols. These symbols represent for the Lozi all those attributes of chieftainship and citizenship which they reckon among the laws of nations. They also stress in their accounts of these laws that emissaries from one chief to another were sacrosanct.

Since the Lozi rule a nation composed of many tribes, they have a set of rules inherent in their idea of kingship which covers all their subjects. The Lozi kings have asserted that all the tribes in the nation are equal—see the judges' statements in the Cases of 'the Quarrelsome Teacher' (p. 75), 'the Eloping Wife' (p. 119), and 'the Contemptuous Husband' (p. 143). All people under the king's sway were entitled to land for their sustenance and to be protected in these rights and others by the king's courts (see the cases just cited). This protection was extended to serfs, prisoners-of-war tied to particular masters. The Lozi had no debt-slavery. The serfs' main disability appears to have been that they could not leave their masters' villages. Serfs could seek redress from the courts for ill-treatment by their masters : I recorded, both from Lozi and from former serfs, several descriptions of how the king freed or took under his own protection the serfs of bad masters.

Matters arising from the laws of nations come before the courts chiefly out of intermarriage between the different tribes, which has led to the establishing of links of in-lawship and ultimately, with the birth of children, to cognatic ties between them. Lozi, and indeed all Barotse, say that they can intermarry thus because all tribes have marriage (see 'The Case of the Eloping Wife', p. 119). The rights and duties of the spouses of different tribes vary, as do the ritual customs they must observe. A Lozi who marries a Wiko woman must expect her to be more familiar with her male cross-cousins than a Lozi woman would be with her cross-cousins who are 'brothers' to her (see 'The Case of Cross-Cousin Adultery', p. 135).[1] Wiko women observe different rules of etiquette and ritual purification, and Wiko have different wedding ceremonials, birth ceremonies, and initiation ceremonies for their children. Conflicts may thus arise out of these intermarriages that do not occur in tribal marriages. Nevertheless they are marriages made possible because all human-kind marries : and the courts will protect them. This was strongly emphasized by several judges in 'The Case of the Eloping Wife' (pp. 119 ff.) where the defendant abductor tried to minimize his wrongdoing by saying that the plaintiff husband was a Lubale (Wiko).

The Foreign Thief in Case No. 22 (p. 108) complained that he was helpless, because he was a foreigner. SOLAMI rebuked him : 'We do not dislike Ngoni or other foreigners. All are one people. Some

---

[1] However, Lozi say they drove out Mwanawina II (13th king : 1876–1878) from the kingship because his foreign relatives-in-law treated the queens, his wives, familiarly. They say queens must be respected.

of your people are here, their girls marry us—and you marry a Lozi girl. To say this man is a foreigner, therefore we decide against him —it does not happen here' (see also below, at pp. 214–15).

But Mr. J. Ritchie, who was for seventeen years Principal of the Barotse National School, told me that the kuta would not convict Lozi men accused of adultery with Lozi wives of Ngoni teachers and clerks, until King Yeta III intervened. All Lozi deny this, and I believe it must have been a canard spread by Ngoni who had failed to substantiate their charges. Hostility between the Lozi and those well-educated Ngoni who hold important teaching and clerical posts has been, and remains, acute.

Thus the Lozi courts have protected and sanctioned these inter-tribal marriages. Since 1917 they have done so under King Yeta's marriage laws, which lay down the conditions for estab-lishing a marriage : the guardians of the woman must accept the marriage-payment established under the edict, and the girl must consent to the marriage. If the marriage-payment is promised, but not transferred, the woman is a ' wife of the country' with whom any man can fornicate or elope, without penalty (Court decision at Lialui, Saa-Katengo Kuta, 1942— *Case 51: The Case of the Improperly Married Wife*). Lialui kuta has held that it would not enforce a claim for restitution of marriage-payment in excess of the statutory amount, if this excess had been paid according to Lubale law, since this would defeat the purpose of the statute. Where the husband claimed £2 10s. in excess of the statutory amount of £2, which he had paid according to Lubale law, the kuta told him : ' That was your wealth' (in ' The Case of the Allegedly Pregnant Wife', p. 122). Thus nowadays a valid marriage is established for all tribes of the Barotse nation by adherence to statutory rules.

Nevertheless the kuta pays attention to many other specific tribal customs. In divorce cases between Lubale and Nyengo spouses, wives have been granted divorce for infringements by their husbands of tribal customs unknown to the Lozi.

Similar problems may arise from the very fact that people of different tribes with different customs reside together in neigh-bourhoods and indeed in royal villages. They are bound to observe to one another the rules incumbent in their social posi-tions. But they must respect one another's customs, for every tribe is entitled to its own customs.

CASE 52: THE CASE OF THE MBUNDA CIRCUMCISION-
LODGE (1940)

Some Kwangwa men, and separately some Kwangwa women,
passed near an Mbunda circumcision-lodge. The Mbunda threatened
the men with axes, and pushed the women away. The Mbunda
complained to SAMBO, the local induna, because the lodges are taboo
to all women and to the uncircumcized Kwangwa men. The
Kwangwa counterclaimed that the Mbunda had been violent, and
a woman said one man had pointed a finger at her and said, ' You
will see '—an indication of future sorcery. SAMBO scolded the
Kwangwa for going near the lodge, since they knew it was secret
for Mbunda : they must not cause fighting. Then he scolded the
Mbunda for threatening and pushing the Kwangwa, instead of asking
them politely to go away and use another path. He said they were
neighbours who must live in peace (*kozo*) and respect (*tompeha*) each
other's customs (*mikwa*). The Mbunda held their lodges with the
king's and the kuta's permission (*sibaka*) and the Kwangwa knew the
lodges were secret. Let them all cease to be foolish.

Lozi, who were with me, approved of all he said, and later when
I told the kuta of the incident, the judges said in these circumstances
they might fine the Kwangwa and order them to pay damages to
the Mbunda for ' causing a fight ' (i.e. breach of the peace).

Thus while the Lozi courts enforce on all Barotse national laws,
laws of general morality, and laws of the nation, groups of
Barotse have also their own particular laws and customs which
the kuta will try to protect. All tribes, as subjects of the king,
have equal rights in court : but to some extent it is true of
Barotse law that individuals carry much of the customary law
to which they are subject with them, according to their tribal
membership.

In ' The Case of the Prudish Wife ' (p. 145) SOLAMI (R3) said:
' There is no path of slavery in the kuta. . . . A foreigner sues
by the customs of the foreigner ; a Lozi sues by the customs of
the Lozi.' [1] Indeed, on occasion this rule may be held to
penalize Lozi. I have been told that in the years before Lozi
cultivated substantially land on the margin of the Plain or in the
woodlands, they were rebuked by King Lewanika (d. 1916) if

---

[1] ' *Nzila yabutanga haiyo mwakuta. . . . Mung'ete uzeka kamikwa* (customs)
yasing'ete, Mulozi uzeka ka mikwa yasilozi.'

they disputed over such land : ' You are a Lozi, not an Mbunda or Kwangwa. Dispute in the Plain ! '

IX

Nowadays the Lozi consider that the demands of natural justice should guide kings and councillors both in debating new legislation and in settling disputes.   That these demands influence practice is apparent if we reflect on how ideas of fairness, general morality, and public interest, guide the judges' application of the law in their reasonings and exhortations.   Beyond this, the Lozi defend most of their customs by reference to these standards.

Thus they say it is just [equitable, to be equal = *kulikana*] that when an army goes to war, or a party to hunt, the booty or kill should be divided also among those who remained at home.   ' They too fought ', for they protected the homeland against unexpected incursions, and cared for the women and children, the cattle, crops and fishing.

Natural justice is present in so many judgments made by the Lozi, when discussing their own customs and comparing them with those of other tribes, when evaluating rulers' and people's conduct, and when assessing the merits of disputes, that I consider we may safely conclude that it is an indigenous conception.   I must admit that though this point is not explicitly discussed in early records of missionaries and travellers, most of these describe the Lozi as immoral liars and their rulers as arbitrary tyrants who were not interested in the welfare of their subjects.   These judg-ments contrast markedly with Livingstone's impressions of the Kololo, and I cannot help feeling that Livingstone would have found the Lozi to be like the Kololo.   Major St. Hill Gibbons went out of his way to praise the justice of the Lozi trial in which he complained to the kuta that two councillors had deserted him. This was in 1899.[1]   My older informants reported many similar examples of this kind of case.

Some Lozi kings and councillors are described by the Lozi themselves as tyrants, and they explain their forefathers' rebellions

---

[1] *Africa from South to North through Marotseland*, op. cit., i, pp. 256 ff. ; see above pp. 161–2. For Livingstone on Kololo trials, see his *Missionary Travels and Researches in South Africa*, London : Murray (1857), pp. 183–4.

against these rulers by reference to these rulers' breaches of justice. Thus they drowned Yeta II (5th king) because he was a cannibal, and drove out Sipopa (12th king : 1864–76) because he used to covet the wives of his subjects and kill men who refused to yield their wives to him. These rebellions themselves warrant the assumption that the Lozi have always had standards of impartiality, morality, and justice by which to judge their kings. Most kings, and many councillors, are approved in memory as just and good, beloved by their people.

The Lozi also rely on natural justice when they explain the motives of ancient kings in passing laws.

For example, they justify as obviously fair a law that when an army marched out to war it must receive from the king provisions and cattle for its journey, and also for its return. Jalla [1] ascribed this law to Mulambwa (9th king ; 1780 ?–1830 ?), and it may have been re-enacted by Lewanika (14th and 16th king ; 1878–84, 1885–1916) who, according to my informants, ruled thus in order to prevent the pillaging of Barotse villages on the army's route. Lozi also justify thus Mulambwa's law that the parents of a man killed in battle must not be in want ; serfs brought in as tribute or plunder must be given to them, one to the father, and one to the mother. I have described above Lewanika's abolition of the payment of compensation\ to the kin of a deceased spouse. Lozi explain similarly his banning of ordeals to detect thieves, and of the divining of sorcerers. Here he argued, partly under the influence of missionaries, that misfortune is the common lot of mankind, coming from God, and that men only blamed it on their fellows whom they hated or envied. This was wrong and unjust. A third example will suffice. Throughout most of the tribes of Central Africa when a man killed an elephant he had to render the ground tusk to his chief. The Kololo chiefs in Barotseland claimed both tusks, holding, according to Livingstone, that they could get better terms in trading ivory for goods from Arabs and others than their subjects, to whom they would give goods. This law was maintained after the Lozi reconquest of their homeland by the Kings Sipopa and Mwananwina II, but King Tatila Akufuna, during his short reign in 1884, held that it was unjust that the hunter who took the risk should not get a tusk from which he could profit himself.

These ideas still dominate in political discussion today, as may be seen by referring to my report of a debate on price-control.[2] Similar

---

[1] *Litaba za Sicaba sa Malozi,* op. cit., Chap. XVI.
[2] *South African Journal of Economics,* xi. 3 (September, 1943).

considerations guided the kuta in its decision in 1946 to protect executory contracts.

In the nature of things new issues requiring legislation or unprecedented judicial decision must have been rare in the past, when Lozi society was changing comparatively slowly. King Mulambwa (9th king), for whose reign in about 1780–1830 there is more than legendary evidence, is famed as the lawgiver (*Mutomi wamilao*), but the laws ascribed to him are relatively peripheral.[1] Nowadays kuta and king are fairly often confronted with new situations which demand legislative or judicial actions. In my experience these judicial situations are not complex, and the judges can usually determine fairly easily what legal and moral principles they will apply ; we have seen how they do so in the Cases of ' the Barren Widow ' (p. 174) and ' the Headman's Fishdams ' (p. 178).

Lozi, and Barotse, laws and customs differ in very many respects from those of the Romans and ancient Greeks, and from those of Western civilization, but they share many of the ethical and legal principles of those civilizations (see pp. 205, 261). They approve the same social virtues and reprobate the same social vices. They apply similar principles of equitableness, good morals, and public policy. The application of these principles goes on in a society organized in a particular form and with a specific economic basis. These are accompanied by a set of assumptions and social ideas. Thus while all tribes in the Barotse nation are equal, people certainly are not equal. This has emerged in previous discussions of Lozi conceptions of the personalities involved in litigation. All Barotse are equal in that they have a right to be protected by the king's courts.

CASE 53 : THE CASE OF THE ABUSED BEGGAR (1942)

A notorious mendicant mental deficient once complained to SOLAMI's kuta that boys in the capital teased him and threw things at him. He said fiercely : ' I am a person, not a fool.' With heightened gentleness SOLAMI assured him : ' You are indeed a person, and we will

---

[1] These laws were recorded by missionaries towards the end of the nineteenth century : see Jalla, *Litaba za Sicaba sa Malozi*, Chap. XVI. Some of Mulambwa's laws have been cited above, pp. 100, 106, and will be discussed again below, p. 248.

protect you.' He summoned all the adults and children in the capital and warned them that anyone who laughed at the man would have to pay damages ; and sent the man to be fed at his own house.

This right to the kuta's protection extended in the past to serfs, and it was one of a number of rights incidental in Lozi citizenship. But outside of these general rights, it is clear that Lozi law is dominated by status, not equality of personality. People tend to be considered and judged by virtue of their social positions : and natural justice aims to maintain the established system of social positions and the ideas that justify that system.

This is exhibited in two judgments on suits arising out of prostitution.

CASE 54 : THE CASE OF THE OVERPAID PROSTITUTE
(from a text)

A man had told me that the kuta had upheld his suit to recover part of his payment to a woman because she had not allowed him a commensurate number of acts of intercourse. The kuta confirmed to me that it had given this judgment, but it told me that it would not uphold a prostitute's suit for her fees, since this would be against decency—though they doubted if any woman would have the courage and shamelessness to bring such a suit.

The court ruled out protection for the prostitute because her suit would arise from an immoral transaction, but did not hold it against the man who went to the prostitute. As shown in ' The Case of the Schoolboy Adulterer ' (p. 134), Lozi men commonly blame sexual immorality on the licentiousness and avarice of women, who seduce men. The modern phenomenon of prostitution is a vice of women, not a product of new social conditions. Therefore prostitutes do not in any way merit the protection of the law, but their clients are protected against exploitation by a kind of *laesio enormis* doctrine.

Lozi men similarly blame the increasing rate of divorce and adultery, and premarital conception, on women, whom they contrast most unfavourably with their ' mothers '. I have frequently heard men and women arguing this proposition : indeed I was once at Lialui requested by women to support them. Following Baudelaire, I said that men can steal, commit arson, and murder without an accomplice, but I had never heard of a woman who could commit adultery without a man to help her.

The women were delighted with my answer, the men (and the kuta to whom they reported my judgment) laughed and said I was wise, but that like all Whites I spoilt women.

This attitude of men about women, and the possibility that thay may apply it in court judgments and frame equity and morality within its assumptions, obviously is related to the *legal* (I insist on *legal*) subjection of wives.   A husband may divorce his wife at will : a woman must establish a case for divorce in the kuta.   Wives come under the control of the husband and his ancestral spirits.   Wives should follow the domicile of their husbands.   Men can marry several wives, and fornicate reasonably with unmarried women : a woman must be faithful to the one husband she may be married to at any particular time.   I believe that Lozi ideas of women's licentiousness arise from this polygamous system which produces many psychical and social strains.[1]   In practice wives often dominate their husbands and exercise considerable power and equality.   Women as mothers, sisters, aunts, and daughters, by customary rules, occupy power-ful positions.   But at all times women are theoretically in legal tutelage.   The usual formula for divorcing a woman is : ' You are your father's child.'   Notice how NAMUNDA-KATANEWKA refused to allow a man to keep his wife in the hope that someone would entice her to elope or to commit adultery : ' No-one shall place *the child of a person* [my emphasis] in slavery, to make her a trap, in order to get cattle from people.'

Accompanying this system of relations are customs by which men and women tend to work and eat separately.   If a man spends too much time with his wife, or is intensely jealous about her movements, it is proof she has seduced his reason with magic. There is a presumption that no man has platonic relations of friendship with an unrelated woman, or, as in ' The Case of Cross-Cousin Adultery ', with a relative he can marry under his tribal law.   Indeed, a man should not even be familiar with a tabooed female relative, or they will be suspected of incestuous relations (see ' The Case of the Incestuous Action ', p. 154).

Many presumptions arise from this system which determine the shape of Lozi morals and principles of natural justice.   In the courts, where there are no women though there are female

---

[1] These will be discussed in my *The Rôle of Courts in Barotse Social Life.*

rulers, these presumptions influence judicial reasoning, which thus applies and even develops existent morality in defence of the structure of male-female relations.

However, as stated above in another context (p. 121), these assumptions do not underlie the Lozi law which makes an adulterous woman pay a fine, or go to prison, and thus be guilty by our standards of a ' crime ' ; while the adulterer pays higher ' civil ' damages to her husband and is thus in our eyes guilty of a ' delict '. The Lozi do not thus rigidly classify crimes and civil offences. Indeed, the man pays more than the woman. The adulterer is punished by being made to pay cattle to the husband for his trespass on the latter's rights. The woman too should be punished. To levy damages on her in her husband's favour might encourage collusion between spouses to obtain wealth from the wife's peccadilloes : note how a wife who had committed three proved adulteries was declared to be ' a wife of the country ' (see ' The Case of the Schoolboy Adulterer '). Hence, the kuta has made it a punishable offence for a husband to pay his wife's fine for adultery. The woman therefore can only be punished by being fined by the kuta or imprisoned.

The application of Lozi law, even when it is argued in equitable terms or stated in terms of natural justice, defends not only the legal superiority of men, but also the existing hierarchy : the kingship and its officers, village headmen's rights, the power of elders, and so on. Even the equitable solution of the judicial impasse in ' The Case of the Headman's Fishdams ' involved a defence of existing relations of seniority and property : the dams remained vested in the title Mahalihali. Correspondingly, Lozi general ideas of law and morality are also riddled with ideas of respect for kingship and seniority, and for the defence of property. The youngsters in ' The Case of the Biassed Father ' had these lessons driven home to them. But on the whole, because of the comparatively undeveloped state of Lozi society, judgments secure justice for underlings. This is apparent in both the cases immediately cited. In ' The Case of the Hippo Hunter ', the king was prevented from exercising his re-established claim to half of all hippo hides on a hippo shot before the edict : the hunter had taken the risks, said the kuta, before the edict, though he had not sold the hide, and it would be inequitable (*hakulikani*) not to allow him the full profit he had anticipated. Property

is still used and authority exercised in the interests of the people
(see ' The Case of the Unused Land ', p. 71). The judges may
apply equity against rulers, seniors, and property-holders. I
never heard, or recorded for the past, an inequitable decision in
favour of the powerful by the whole kuta.

Lozi ideas of morality did not make them into Arcadian
shepherds. They still do not consider their harrying raids on
the persons and property of surrounding tribes to have been
immoral, though missionaries' moral arguments helped to induce
the Lozi to abandon those raids. These raids were carried out
with slaughter and destruction. Captives brought to Loziland
became serfs, though very few were sold to West Coast slavers.
These serfs have largely now been absorbed into the nation but
many returned home after Lewanika's edict of freedom in 1906.
After civil wars kings killed their powerful adversaries : but
Lewanika refused to punish the ordinary supporters of these
adversaries. Lozi kings and councillors have been arbitrary
tyrants : these always provoked rebellions in defence of justice
and traditional custom.   Sorcery trials, carried out by due process
which for the Lozi established guilt, used to punish people whom
we consider innocent, as did ordeals for strongly suspected thieves :
here there was no judicial process (see above, p. 97 f.). Punishments were previously far harsher. British overlordship has
restrained arbitrary actions and powers. As I emphasized in the
Introduction, many suits arising out of social inequalities in relations
with Whites go to British and not to Lozi courts. There is no
doubt that these circumstances help to explain the kindly account
I must give of the practice of Lozi trials : the present circumstances do not deny the validity of my analysis of the Lozi judicial
process, in either the present or, *mutatis mutandis*, the past.[1]   Nor
do these circumstances deny that the concept of laws of humankind—natural law—is indigenous. These laws, and the equitable
considerations which guide judges, appear to have been influenced
by Christianity and other Western influences, and the judges
occasionally quote from the Bible (see ' The Case of the Quarrelsome Teacher ', pp. 74-5). But the last six Commandments,

---

[1] I shall examine the problems of the *practice* of authority, and of the relation
of judicial activity to other forms of political activity, in *The Rôle of Courts
in Barotse Social Life*. They are not directly relevant to the judicial process
itself, as a process of reasoning.

and the principles of the Sermon on the Mount, coincide with basic premisses of Lozi ethics.

X

Lozi kutas draw on these socially influenced ideas of equity and justice, as well as on the established laws, to give judgment on any issue, however unprecedented. Indeed, the kuta must give a judgment in a dispute. If the issue is covered by an accepted legal rule, the kuta tries to apply the rule as fairly as possible. If the issue is not thus covered, the kuta and the king draw on natural justice and morality for a solution. The Lozi thus hold that the kuta should follow precedent, but that if precedent is inadequate the kuta can create law in conformity with the laws and customs of the nation and with equity and natural justice. Where equity and natural justice are held to conflict with the established law, they state that the law cannot be changed without a debate and an enactment of the king—i.e. by legislative action not affecting the case under trial.

CASE 55: THE CASE OF THE WIFE IMPREGNATED IN ADULTERY

A husband who was divorcing his wife, who had been impregnated in adultery, complained to the Mongu-Lialui District Kuta in 1947 that he should get damages additional to those levied on adultery alone, and similar to those recently imposed on infecting a woman with venereal disease in adultery. He argued that because she was bearing a child by another man, she would be taboo to him for over two years and he was thus compelled to divorce her, wasting all the money he had spent on her and her kin. He could not raise another's adulterine child. The councillors agreed with his argument, but said they could not apply it in his case. They would ask the NGAMBELA (R1) to enact it for the future. (See also 'The Case of the Exorbitant Fishmonger', p. 70.)

It is held that similar considerations—equit,, natural justice and morality, the general interests of the nation, and regard for tradition and precedent—should guide the kuta in its deliberations as a legislative body. These considerations may conflict, but the Lozi consider that the kuta, though occasionally mistaken, usually comes to the just decision. The councillors who deliberate thus on legislation are also the judges, so that no conflict arises between action in legislature and action in law.

XI

Lozi public opinion still considers only few of the laws themselves to be unjust, and the kuta has generally to enforce what is thought by the people to be right. The constitution has been criticized, not for its laws, but for its practice, by both the emerging group of educated Lozi and by the subject tribes, who have been pressing for more power in the kutas.[1] I have heard few other laws criticized.

King Lewanika had forbidden his councillors to drink beer for he said that drunkenness had led to a revolt against him. In 1921 the ascetic King Yeta III persuaded the kuta to make all beer-brewing illegal. The people beat up the police searching for beer in their homes, and the law was amended to read : ' The brewing of beer is illegal but it shall not be searched for.' The kuta applied this law by levying a fine of £2 on anyone who was present at a beerdrink where fighting broke out, or other offence was committed. For twenty-five years the law was enforced under King Yeta, though it provoked much resentment and produced sentences which the people considered unjust.

CASE 56 : THE CASE OF THE BEER-DRINKING FINES
(from a text)

Thus, for example, four Katongo women were each fined £2 after they had been persuaded to drink a cup of beer at a village through which they were passing, because much later a fight broke out in the village. At the trial of the fighters it emerged that the women had partaken of the beer and they were fined. Katongo people laughed as they described to me how MBASIWANA (R46) Mutondo [like a vicarious Hampden] insisted that the women go to prison rather than paythe unjust fines : but their husbands hurried to release them.

When King Imwiko succeeded to the throne he discussed abolishing the law, and enacting that beer-drinking leading to fighting should be an offence for the fighter alone. He died before passing the law.

I also heard various Lozi at times complain of other of their Government's orders, such as those compelling people to clean

---

[1] See my ' The Lozi of Barotseland in North-Western Rhodesia ', *Seven Tribes of British Central Africa*, pp. 17 ff. and 56 ff.

the environs of their village, to wash their mortars and poles for stamping grain, to wash their dishes immediately after meals, to clean their drainage channels. Most Lozi approved of these hygienic and agricultural rules, but very many protested against laws requiring people, without payment, to keep clean roads and paths between villages and along routes for Government officers, and to build and maintain schools. They argued that missionaries and Government, having made them free their serfs because unpaid slavery was immoral, now made them work without payment. There was more widespread dissatisfaction with the edicts of the British Government and other ' White ' laws.

Existing marriage laws were also criticized by some. As inflation during the war pushed up prices, and the demands of fathers for marriage-payment, the kuta refused to order the return of what was given above the statutory amount on the divorce of a sterile woman originally taken as a virgin. Some Lozi young men argued that their greedy elders were thus protected in exploiting them, though many elders refused to ask for more than the set amount.

Most Lozi maintained that it should be an offence to impregnate any unmarried woman, and not only a virgin. Others wanted to make a lover responsible for damages and cost of treatment if he infected a woman with venereal disease, and not to allow him to be excused on the principle that ' if you are invited to a meal you cannot sue if a fishbone sticks in your throat '. Both these rules were enacted in 1946. 1946–7 saw a general raising of the damages and fines attached to adultery, seduction, and abduction of married women ; and these were again raised in 1949–50. I have already cited how the kuta in 1947 agreed to consider a complaint that an adulterer who impregnated his mistress should pay higher damages : this was demanded too by the new Katengo Council (see p. 14) at its first meeting in 1947. Some women felt that the divorce and inheritance laws were unfair to them.

One common complaint of men against the kuta was that while it insisted on its own dues it was not sufficiently concerned with enforcing its judgments on behalf of litigants. The kuta imprisoned an adulteress till her fine was paid, but allowed the adulterer to leave and abscond to White country without paying the damages due to his cuckold. These men held that the adulterer should also be imprisoned till he had paid his dues. At

Nalolo in 1947 (in ' The Case of the Eloping Wife ', p. 119) the
kuta ordered an abductor of a married woman to proceed, handcuffed, with a policeman round his kin trying to raise the £5
damages.   I gathered this had become the common practice at
Nalolo, but omitted to ask if it was followed in other Districts.
If it was, this complaint had been met.   British District Officers
constantly exerted pressure to make kutas enforce their judgments more diligently.

Economic changes within Loziland also provoked demands for
new legislation.   Some wanted to control rising prices (see ' The
Case of the Exorbitant Fishmonger ', p. 69).   Because trade and
employment of services had become much more important, the
kuta in 1946 decided to protect executory contracts.   Land near
White stations had increased in value, and some Lozi asked for
unused land to be re-distributed, though it was generally plentiful.

On many of these points Lozi public opinion is united.
Indigenous standards of ethics are being threatened, and the
demand is for the law to be amended to protect these standards
against the effects of labour migration and other changes in social
life.   For the basic laws defining social positions and the relationships between them, and the moral way of fulfilling the obligations contained in those laws, are still commonly approved.

However, there is now some general uncertainty and difference
of opinion about the morality of various institutions, and a
number of different interest groups are emerging.   I found that
Christians' and pagans' opinions differed on important matters
like polygamy, but generally that their judgments on the morality
of familial and political situations coincided.   The Watchtower
sect, who are opposed both to the other churches and to chiefs
and magistrates, and who are considered by other Lozi to be
wild animals, worshipping in the bush and holding their women
in common, formed the only strongly dissenting religious group.
Women were beginning to compare their lot with what they
believe to be the idyllic life of white women.   Finally, the
' intelligentsia ' of clerks, teachers, and storemen, to some extent
constituted a separate group with different ethical judgments.

It is difficult to tell to what degree this divergence between
sectional or general ethics, and the law, is a new phenomenon.
The Lozi, and White observers, retail instances of legislation in
the past, some of which were opposed by part of the nation.

Lewanika's (16th king : d. 1916) decision in 1883, after two kings
had ruled by Kololo customs, to re-establish Lozi customs, and
his edict that Lozi should plant gardens and not live on the tribute
of subject tribes as the Kololo did, provoked some indunas to
rebel against him. Many Lozi blame the reputed increase of
disease and death, and shortage of food, on the banning of
sorcery trials, though they ascribe the ban to the British Government rather than to their king Lewanika ; and it is likely that
some opposed the original edict. Coillard and others recorded
that the subject tribes were dissatisfied with their status, though
one would not judge this from their present statements. It
seems probable that, especially after Arab, White, and half-caste
slavers and traders reached Barotseland, there have been within
the nation different ethical judgments on some laws and legislation. But I am prepared to affirm that most Barotse—serfs and
subject tribes as well as Lozi—were contented with the law,
however much they were as individuals disturbed by particular
acts of king or kuta which they considered tyrannical.

It seems safer, even in the absence of secure historical evidence,
to say that the divergence between general and sectional ethics
and the established law has increased since the British protectorate,
and that this divergence is likely to grow. Work for Europeans ;
evangelization, and this in different sects ; employment of, and
more frequent trade with, strangers ; the introduction of goods
which allow higher standards of living ; the possibility of flight
from Loziland to evade obligations—all these break up the homogeneity of Lozi society. In *The Rôle of Courts in Barotse Social
Life* I shall show that the presence of White authorities allows
legal action in two competing political systems. Nevertheless,
overall, Lozi society is still largely homogeneous and only
beginning to differentiate from a subsistence peasantry. Therefore at all levels of political structure Lozi kutas aim to achieve
conformity with publicly approved modes of conduct.

R

CHAPTER V

JUDICIAL LOGIC AND THE SOURCES OF LAW

I

I HAVE presented a selection of cases from my notebooks to show Lozi judges at work, and hope that it is adequate to enable me to draw some general conclusions. First, I consider that many discussions of 'primitive law' have been vitiated by a failure to recognize certain basic similarities between processes of law in simple and in complex societies. This failure has produced a corresponding assumption that 'primitive law' may be intrinsically different in most respects from developed law. Attention has frequently been concentrated on analysing the differences, and the similarities have tended to be neglected.

These similarities are marked in 'law in action'—the process of adjudication by which the judges in a particular dispute apply law as a body of rules. The late Sir Paul Vinogradoff[1] and Sir Carleton Kemp Allen,[2] among others, have indicated the importance of the fact that wherever courts of law have emerged as organs of a governmental organization, to try cases in public, they summon and examine parties and witnesses. It appears to follow that they must have an idea of relevance of evidence, even if it be wide when they strive for reconciliation ; that they must weigh evidence by credibility and cogency ; and that they must distinguish between direct, circumstantial, and hearsay evidence. I have suggested also that they will work always with that norm of the reasonable man which is basic in all branches of jurisprudence. Indeed, these juristic processes are indicated in the very existence of vernacular terms which can be precisely translated as courts, judges, litigants, witnesses, evidence, cross-examination, arguments, judgments, etc.[3] Furthermore, arguments are couched in vernacular terms which again can be trans-

---

[1] *Common-sense in Law*, London : Thornton Butterworth ; Home University Library (1913, 10th impression, 1933), Chap. IV.

[2] *Law in the Making*, op. cit., passim.

[3] In Lozi, respectively : *kuta, baatuli, bazeki, lipaki, bupaki, kubuza, libaka* or *kanana, likatulo*.

lated as law itself, custom, right and duty, wrong and injury, liability and responsibility, guilt and innocence, care and negligence, fair and equal, owner, agreement, etc.[1]

Lozi courts apply this last set of legal concepts, which are the nuclei of laws, to the raw material of disputes, which are the *litaba*, the facts (or things). These facts are established by evidence, by judicial knowledge (*zibo yabaatuli*) and presumptions (*lisupo*), and by judicial inference (*kuatula*). That is, in Loziland, as in any society where there are courts, the judicial process recognizes, at least implicitly, a fundamental distinction between facts and law from which certain incidents inevitably flow. Furthermore, this distinction and its incidents seem to inhere not only in the judicial process of societies with instituted courts, but also in the arbitrational process which occurs in societies that have not courts. Only in relationships where parties can merely assert that they are in the right and stand on their own contentions, supporting themselves by their own might, are there lacking the ascertainment of facts and their assessment against norms ; and even in these the parties are likely to justify themselves by stating that on the facts they have acted by norms of right conduct. Arbitrators, whether chance or instituted, must work as judges do. Even the use of institutional self-help implies a similar process.[2] For all societies have rules which state what ought to be done in generally formulated circumstances, and people are supposed to try to act by these rules in the varying situations of life. If a dispute arises from these situations the adjudicators have

---

[1] In Lozi, respectively : *mulao, mukwa, swanelo* or *tukelo, poso* and *sinyeho, mulatu, kufosa* and *kusafosi, tokomelo* and *buswafa, kulikana, mung'a, tumelano* or *kulumelana*.

[2] See, e.g., Barton, R. F., *Ifugao Law*, University of California Publications in American Archaeology and Ethnology, XV (1919), pp. 1–127 passim ; idem., *The Kalingas*, Chicago : University of Chicago Press (1949), passim ; Colson, Elizabeth, ' Social Control and Vengeance in Plateau Tonga Society ', *Africa*, xxiii. 3 (July, 1953) ; Evans-Pritchard, E. E., *The Nuer*, op. cit., pp. 163 ff. ; Fortes, M., *The Dynamics of Clanship among the Tallensi*, London : Oxford University Press (1945), p. 236 ; Hoebel, E. A., *The Political Organization and Law-ways of the Comanche Indians*, Memoirs of the American Anthropological Association, No. 54 (1940), passim ; Llewellyn and Hoebel, *The Cheyenne Way*, op. cit., passim. On the general point see Radcliffe-Brown, ' Primitive Law ', in *Structure and Function in Primitive Society*, at p. 217.

first to consider the situation—'the facts'; and then to assess these against the rules—'the law'.[1]

I want to avoid becoming entangled in the disputation that has accumulated around the word 'law'.[2] Much of this disputation has concerned the definition of 'law', and the relation between law as the body of enacted or customary rules recognized by a community as binding,[3] and law as a series of decisions by judges in particular cases. The 'realistic' or 'sceptical 'American schools of lawyers (Jerome Frank, Karl Llewellyn, and others) seem to maintain that law exists only in this latter sense,[4] as what Cardozo has called 'isolated dooms'.[5]

The word 'law' in English clearly has no one intrinsic meaning. The *Concise Oxford Dictionary* gives at least thirteen distinctive referents for 'law'. We have seen that the equivalent Lozi word, *mulao*, is similarly a multiple concept covering all kinds of ordered regularity and authoritative action. It is therefore obviously fruitless to dispute that the word applies more properly to one type of referent than to another, whether it be institution or process or rule. For each definition put forward as the true meaning of 'law' can be countered by an antagonist with another definition. We must in the first place examine the multiple character of the concept and how it functions in the social and judicial process. This might entail using conventional symbols, such as Law-A, Law-B, Law-C, etc., for each of the referents of law (*mulao*) in order to keep them distinct. To write thus would be awkward. I shall specialize from here on my use of 'law' itself for one referent—the body of rules, the *corpus juris*, on which judges draw to give a decision. I do so because the other meanings of *law* or *mulao* derive their significance from the idea of order and regularity which ought to exist

---

[1] Llewellyn and Hoebel's *The Cheyenne Way*, op. cit., is one of the few monographs on the law of a simple society which makes this the starting-point of analysis (p. 20).

[2] For a masterly critical summary of this disputation see Sir C. K. Allen's 'Introduction : Law and its Sources' in his *Law in the Making*.

[3] *Concise Oxford English Dictionary*, p. 671.

[4] Allen, op. cit., pp. 42 ff. And see below, pp. 348–51, and 355, where this school is referred to in more detail.

[5] Cardozo, B. J., *Nature of the Judicial Process*, New Haven : Yale University Press (1928) ; and also his *Growth of Law*, New Haven : Yale University Press (1927).

in nature and in society. To the other referents of 'law' (*mulao*) I shall apply other terms, such as adjudication, legal rule, statute, legal process, legal procedure. This is a conventional treatment for purposes of analysis. I do not assert that it is illegitimate or wrong to use 'law', or any of the other terms, with a different meaning. If anyone objects to my conventions, I can only reply that I have tried to be consistent in using them, and beg him to confine himself to factual and analytical criticisms, and not to involve us in barren terminological dispute. 'Law' is not a box containing one quality : indeed, it has too often been a Pandora's box whose many qualities, when released, have played havoc with men's reason. Therefore if anyone objects to the conventional words I use, I trust that he will substitute Law-A, Law-B, and so forth, throughout my argument.

For the time being I am concerned with law's existence in two senses : as a *corpus juris*, a body of rules, and as *adjudication*, a process by which cases are tried and judgments or *legal rulings* are given on them. Empirically, my data emphasize this distinction in the Lozi system. In disputes and on charges of wrongdoing Lozi courts give judgments (*likatulo*, singular *katulo*). A particular judgment may be spoken of as *mulao wakuta* (the law of the kuta).

CASE 55*a*: THE CASE OF THE UNWITTING 'INCESTUOUS ADULTERY'

H's wife ran away from him to her home. H's elder brother, B, a policeman of the Barotse Native Government, came on duty to her village with his carrier and was given a hut in which to sleep. It rained in the night and the hut leaked. The headman moved B and his carrier to a hut where H's wife (B's sister-in-law) was sleeping with two women. B did not know she was there. When H learnt of this, he sued his brother and the carrier, and was awarded £4 damages by the sub-district induna MWANAGUMUNE. B appealed to Lialui where the kuta held that he had done no wrong ('had no fault'—*mulatu*) because there were five people sleeping in the hut. SOLAMI (R3) said : 'If Nalukui (the husband) wishes to get damages, he will get them from his brother, and not from his brother's boy. But he will get damages only by the love of his brother, not by the decision of the kuta—'*kamulao* (law = decision) *wa kuta*'.

Thus the Lozi clearly recognize that a judgment in a case is 'the law' (*mulao*) for that case. They argue with a dissatisfied litigant that he must accept this judgment or appeal against it (see 'The Case of the Schoolboy Adulterer', at p. 133). When the final court of appeal has given its decision, that decision is the law (*mulao*) for that case and should be for future similar cases (see 'The Case of the Barren Widow', at p. 175). A man's friends will advise him thus even when they agree that the decision is not a good one according to the laws (*milao*—plural) of Loziland. The clear conception of *res judicata* (*taba iatuzwi*) emphasizes this recognition that the kuta's verdict is binding 'law'. I recorded several cases in which the kuta held that it could not again enquire into a matter on which it had given judgment. In 'The Case of the Prudish Wife', SIKOTA-MUTUMWA (L5) obtained from the Lialui kuta a clear affirmation that it had refused a divorce to his 'daughter' only on the grounds that her husband had failed to treat her reasonably, and not on the ground that her husband had married her classificatory 'mother': therefore he could bring the latter issue before a subordinate court (p. 147). However, in 'The Case of the Migrant Husband' (p. 141) the kuta reversed a decision to grant divorce on the grounds that it had not known the husband was on his way home, when the wife's father claimed a new marriage-payment on the grounds of its decision. But here I would raise the query whether it would not have insisted on its previous decision, if the wife had refused to return to her husband.

The Lozi constantly assess the judgments of their kutas against law as a body of rules. They thus dispose of the problem of 'the unjust judge', be he merely foolish or ignorant, or even partial or corrupt. There are bad and good judgments which will be recognized as such by most Lozi.

The texts of cases cited show that judges in court, and people in their everyday relations, are working with a code which they speak of as 'the law': 'kio mulao', 'that is the law'. Thus though *mulao* means a specific rule of king or kuta or of tradition, it also can be used as *law* can with us, to refer generally to the collective body of such rules and the processes by which they are enforced. Thus IMANDI affirmed in 'The Case of the Head-man's Fishdams': 'We cannot change the law against Mahalihali' (p. 185). In 'The Case of the Foreign Thief' (p. 203) the accused complained that he stood alone against the whole Lozi nation. Judges replied that 'the law is impartial' (*mulao ha'uketi* = the law does not choose), and KALONGA (R15) said that any of the councillors, if he did wrong, was 'a slave of the law' (*mutanga wamulao*). In ' The Case of the Eloping Wife' (p. 116) at Nalolo, the abductor subjected himself to the kuta : 'You tell me, you are the owners of the law' (' *mwanibulela, mina kibang'i bamulao*'). Lozi constantly discuss their rules in these terms.

I never heard a Lozi spontaneously give an elaborate definition of ' law' as a *corpus juris*, in or out of court. When I questioned them they said *mulao* in this sense was *kilinto zeswanezwa* (root—*swanela*) *kuezezwa*—' law is the things which ought to be done '. However, it is clear that they have *law* as a system of rights, duties, powers, privileges, immunities, and due processes, since, as we have seen, they have words for all these juridical conceptions. That is, the Lozi have *law* as *a set of rules accepted by all normal members of the society as defining right and reasonable ways in which persons ought to behave in relation to each other and to things, including ways of obtaining protection for one's rights*. I apply this definition to *morality* save that I substitute ' generous ways' for ' reasonable ways'. Even when their courts cannot enforce some of these rules, they are nevertheless a source on which the judges draw in various ways. Sanctions or enforcement are not essential to define law in this sense, as a *corpus juris* : all societies have it.

This is clearly a commonsense definition of *law* in one general meaning ; and I shall henceforth usually use the word with this connotation. The proviso ' *usually*' here is to protect myself against inevitable inconsistency. The word *law* has to cover so many kinds of social rules and processes of social control that it is impossible for us, as in fact it is for the Lozi, to confine it to a single meaning.

I shall call any one of these rules ' a law ', and a set of these rules ' laws . The process of giving judgment (a ' legal ruling') in court I refer to as ' adjudication '.

In the next chapter I shall consider further the social function of this ' uncertainty' of meaning of law—*mulao*—as well as of other legal concepts. Here I am attempting only to clarify the use I give to a few terms to introduce the immediate problem. In effect, I am arguing that since *law*—or *mulao*—has many definitions in social life, the student of social life has to accept this as a fact given, and not convert the word into a Procrustean bed. This view of the problem accepts the importance and partial validity of Dean Pound's definition that law is ' social control through the systematic application of the force of politically organized society '. For convenience, I have followed the distinction that law in this sense is *legal action*. That is, those rules which Lozi courts ought to enforce and the procedures, processes and sanctions of the courts, are *legal rules and institutions*. By this definition societies without courts have no legal rules, though they have rules of law ; and they lack legal institutions, procedures, sanctions, etc. *Judgments* are given in them, but not *legal rulings*. We might then adopt the suggested [1] distinction between societies which have legal rules, and those which are *alegal*, without legal institutions, but which certainly are not *lawless*. This would meet Malinowski's perhaps unnecessary objection that confining *law* to societies with courts implies that others without courts are lawless, in the sense perhaps of being uncontrolled, unbridled, and licentious. He opposed this view because ' law and order pervade the tribal usages of primitive races, they govern all the humdrum course of daily existence, as well as the leading acts of public life, whether these be quaint and sensational or important and venerable.' [2] It also emphasizes the important contrast between politically enforced law, and that maintenance of order contained in Evans-Pritchard's statement that ' in the strict sense of the word the Nuer have no law. . . . Their constitution might be called an " ordered anarchy ".' [3] The paradox is illuminating, but, if anarchy is ordered, there is law. For the Lozi *mulao* is law and order wherever it occurs. It includes regularities in rainfall and seasons, movements of the sun and moon, night and day, growth of crops, human physiology ; and it also covers all regularities in human conduct, personal, tribal, and general.

It is therefore useful and appropriate to specialize *law* to cover a body of accepted rules, and to have *legal* and *alegal* (clearly quite different from *illegal*) to define rules which are enforced in

---

[1] I have not been able to recall the source of this suggestion.

[2] Malinowski, B., *Crime and Custom in Savage Society*, London : Kegan Paul, Trench, Trubner ; New York : Harcourt Brace (1926), p. 2.

[3] ' The Nuer of the Southern Sudan ' in *African Political Systems*, op. cit., at pp. 293 and 296.

different ways in the same society, and in societies at different stages of political development. *Alegal* states that a particular fact is not concerned with or involved in ' social control through the systematic application of the force of politically organized society '. *Legal* states that a particular fact is so concerned or involved : it describes actions and rules in this process of political control. In Loziland there are legal and alegal rules of law : and there are legal and alegal institutions, processes, procedures, sanctions. It was a general rule of Lozi law that no-one should practise sorcery : the legal rule was, that if a man was accused of being a sorcerer he should be brought to the capital, be subjected to the *mwafi* ordeal, and, if convicted, be burnt to death.

In the judicial process we see the law as a body of rules applied to a set of facts which have been proved in evidence. The judges, in the above terms, state that such and such legal rules will be enforced in this dispute : by their very statement they make those rules legal. They extract these particular rules from all the rules ' accepted by all normal members of the society as defining right and reasonable ways in which persons ought to behave in relation to each other and to things ' (p. 229). In this selection they should be guided by certain criteria and rules. For the body of the law in Loziland consists of rules of varying type and origin. These are the various material ' sources of the law ' as commonly defined in Western jurisprudence. In Lozi, as in Western, jurisprudence these sources are customs, judicial precedents, legislation, equity, the laws of natural morality and of nations, and good morals and public policy. A further source, not usually listed by jurisprudents, is natural necessities—the laws or regularities operating in the environment and in human beings and criminals. Before discussing these sources separately, I must consider summarily what the judges do at a trial.

II

To achieve justice in a particular case Lozi judges draw on all these various sources of law. We would say that they do so by an artistic process, and that, in the absence of writing, the forensic science of collecting, contrasting, and applying laws is barely developed. The absence of written records so conditions the judicial process that its effects have to be reviewed at the outset. It perhaps explains the sententiousness with which Africans, like minor prophets, state and re-state obvious basic maxims, such as : ' The kuta proceeds by asking the man and woman questions' (p. 112) ; ' the kuta decides by evidence and the evidence convicts you '.

As in courts everywhere, when a dispute comes to the judges they must give a judgment on it. In senior kutas the judges have always given some decision on the dispute itself, unless nowadays they consider it beyond their jurisdiction, as in sorcery cases. Aside from these, I otherwise only heard the kutas refer to the British authorities the charge against Watchtower adherents for refusing to contribute to a war levy (see above, p. 158). I have records of judges in subordinate kutas who have declared that they could not give judgment on a case because it was too difficult, or the parties were too embittered, and that the case must go to the capital. I have also heard subordinate kutas ask the capital kuta's advice on cases they were trying, without actually referring the cases themselves to the capital. Nowadays sections 14 and 16 of the Barotse Native Courts Ordinance, which set out the powers of Barotse courts, do not distinguish between sub-district and capital kutas. However, my informants tell me that in the past any case involving the spilling of blood, an accusation of sorcery, or treason, had to be referred to the capital kutas.

The cases I have quoted and shall quote, show judges drawing on all the sources of law to try to give a decision which they regard both as just and as in conformity with the law. In cases involving kinsmen the judges often arrive at an ethical decision on the merits of the case, and then state the law to support that decision, while trying to reconcile the parties. Occasionally the whole kuta may feel compelled to support the letter of the law against their judgment of moral fitness, as in the Cases of ' the Ungenerous Husband' (p. 172) and ' the Adulterine Child' (p. 191). Some judges may do this while others ' amend' the law to meet the demands of their ethical code. This was marked in ' The Case of the Headman's Fishdams' where IMANDI, Litooma and other judges affirmed : ' We cannot change the law against Mahalihali.' But these judges all exhorted Mahalihali, as KALONGA exhorted the Ungenerous Husband, to behave generously and not to insist on the letter of his rights. Other judges seemed patently to alter the law to achieve the ethical end, though they did not make clear how their rulings would be enforced until SOLAMI threatened to discharge Mahalihali from his headmanship if he failed in generosity. This sort of issue is not so important in other cases, involving persons in transient contractual or delictual relationships, and in these the judges are more likely to enforce the recognized letter of the law (see ' The Case of the Father and his Son's Cattle ', pp. 109–10). Thus they would not before 1946 enforce equitable rights in executory promises though they disapproved of defaulters on promises.

The background for this dominance of ethical judgment in Lozi court decisions has been stated by Sir Paul Vinogradoff in general terms :

As there are few enacted laws in primitive society, and the binding tradition of case-law is not much developed on account of the difficulty of recording precedents and the lack of professional training of the lawyers, the province of discretionary justice is normally very extensive, and legal progress consists in a great measure in the substitution of fixed rules, either legislative or judge-made, for this fluctuating state of the law.[1]

Lozi legal decisions clearly fluctuate as they seek justice. This appears most markedly in the conflicts of decision between different judges in the same case even though they are applying comparatively simple rules. Lozi courts are little restrained in their attempt to obtain justice by high demands for ceremonialism or formal conformity in the transactions of everyday life, or in the procedure of the courts. The simple and untrammelled means of bringing suit prevented justice from being obstructed by writs and other procedural devices as it was in early English and Roman law. As Mr. Epstein has emphasized, there are no restrictive ' pleadings ' in the form of the preparation and sifting of the facts by professional lawyers to bring them within some form of action or some defined legal grounds. Any aggrieved person can bring a complaint to the kuta so long as he can show he has a dispute (*muzeko*) which founds a legal claim (*mubango*) (see ' The Case of the Vague Complaint ', p. 78). Each litigant

---

[1] *Common-sense in Law*, at pp. 220–1.

and each witness tells his tale without restraint so that the court
is given from the outset a view of all the circumstances of the
dispute, and often of its past history. In family disputes the kuta
is concerned to achieve a reconciliation, and it evaluates all the
facts themselves by ethical standards.

When the court comes to give its decision, the judges cannot
consult accumulated and sifted statutes or precedents, or other
records. The judges remember and cite those precedents which
seem to accord with their moral judgment, and even incidents
which never came to trial for the very reason that they exhibited
moral behaviour. Moreover, in the same way as the absence
of detailed previous precedents does not restrict the judges' moral
discretion, so this absence appears to prevent all of them feeling
that their decision on the case under trial establishes an absolute
precedent for the future. I have given my opinion that NAMAMBA
would probably not have felt bound in other cases, or in different
circumstances in the same case, to stand by his ruling that the
headman's fishdams had gone with his sister when she married
nearby.

The judges thus exercise considerable discretion in applying the
law in particular disputes, and some of them do so seemingly
without appreciating that they may be changing the law and
introducing considerable uncertainty. Nevertheless these judges
clearly believe that they are applying the law and the ethical
ende—they consider they are enforcing what they ought to
enforce and that they are not giving arbitrary decisions. Other
Lozi see that such decisions do not conform with the law, and
do not consider such judges to be good judges—impartial,
knowledgeable in law, courageous, and wise. They explicitly
say that a good judge is not influenced by morality to give a
decision that is bad in law : he must have courage (*bungangeli*)
to face the consequences when justice conflicts with law. A
judge ought to abide by the law even if its application is inequitable. Thus though there is considerable judicial discretion, this
discretion is in theory and in practice restricted by established
law (*mulao*).

This situation seems to me to help explain why there are such
marked divergences in the judgments of individual judges.
These divergences were marked in, for example, the Cases of
'the Headman's Fishdams', of 'the Schoolboy Adulterer', and

of ' the Father and his Son's Cattle '. Differences in judgment may go to the heart of the matter, as in these cases, or be confined to varying evaluation of the behaviour of the parties within a similar decision, as in ' The Case of the Biassed Father ' (pp. 41 ff.). That is, the divergences may involve chiefly the evaluation of evidence.

These divergent judgments are not co-ordinated by a majority count of separately given decisions, but the judgments of junior judges, theoretically at least and mostly in practice, are all taken into account in the judgments of their seniors until the head of the court gives the conclusive decision. This, with preceding judgments, is considered by the king, insofar as the appointed rapporteur has the skill to summarize the whole course of the case. Thus in ' The Case of the Headman's Fishdams ', ALULEYA-IFUNGA (L8), sitting as head of the royal mat, first introduced Mahalihali's uncle, the witness Sabangwa, into the case, and ordered him to rejoin his nephew's village. Almost all of the judges senior to ALULEYA took up this point, and it was stated by SOLAMI in his final judgment. Therefore the final adjudication, which states the legal rules for the dispute in question, is given by one senior judge or the king, after considering all the views of other judges. I have recorded cases in which this concluding judge differed from most of the judges, and even one in which the head of the court, who happened to be fairly junior, went against all the other judges.

This is unusual. In ' The Case of the Headman's Fishdams ' we saw how brilliantly, as the Lozi thought, SOLAMI reconciled divergent judgments. It exemplifies my impression that the final judge does generally follow the trend of the best analysis of the evidence and the application of the law to it.

This conclusion accords with Lozi opinion that with few exceptions the kuta does enforce what it ought to enforce—the law ; and that it does so by due process (*kamulao wakuta*). There is a high expectation among the general public of what the kuta will state the law to be in various circumstances. Despite some fluctuation in final decisions, and some variation in individual judges' opinions, Lozi adjudication is far from being, to quote Cardozo again, a series of ' isolated dooms '. Dooms are consistent in a system of law.

The Lozi consider that this system of law came into existence with the creation of their kingdom, and that it has had an enduring identity despite manifold changes made in it. Though they are well aware that changes have been made, and cite and date certain of these changes, they probably tend in the absence of written records to give a greater antiquity to some rules than these rightfully have. Indeed, since the form of judgment is often the bare affirmation that ' this is our law—we know it of old ', the judges can confer antiquity on comparatively recent innovations.[1] They could, indeed, enforce new usages, dating from the arrival of the British, as established custom. The law as a whole is ' received tradition ', present in the minds of the judges and drawn from living relations about them : hence it has an inherent mutability which reflects changes in social life and in the individuals who participate in that life.

Because the Lozi courts are applying an unwritten law, they cannot make a thorough survey of its various sources. Indeed, I have never seen a kuta refer to written records of Ordinances, of their own rules, or of past decisions. Statutes, including those few well-known parts of British legislation which Lozi courts enforce, are not numerous and cover limited spheres of action. Their own edicts are stated in simple sentences : they reduce British prolixity to similar simplicity. Judicial precedents tend to be regarded as illustrating the application or enforcement of custom, rather than as a separate source of law. In Loziland custom is still the main part of ' the common law '. This necessarily affects the manner of its enforcement in adjudication, where it forms a source on which the judges draw.

III

Therefore the first, and the most prolific, source of Lozi legal rulings is *custom*, defined in the everyday sense of ' usual practice ',[2] though it has too an ethical value, that it ought to be followed. Anthropologists employ the word in this sense to describe the standardized patterns of behaviour of a particular group. We have seen that the Lozi themselves speak thus of their customs (*mikwa*) and the customs of other tribes. I shall employ it in this

---

[1] Cf. Kern, F., *Kingship and Law in the Middle Ages* (tr. by S. B. Chrimes), Oxford : Blackwell (1948), p. 179.
[2] *Concise Oxford English Dictionary*, p. 295.

way, and not with its more limited modern connotation in English law—the customary right which a particular person, or a group or category of persons, has enjoyed in the past. ' Custom ' can be thus restricted in English law, because ' custom ' in the anthropological sense ceases to be a major source of legal rules in developed legal systems. As Sir C. K. Allen says of English law, ' though minor customs and usages spring up even nowadays, especially in commercial relationships, the great formative period of the more important customs belongs to the past '. He describes how custom has become hardened into the English common law of family relations, succession and inheritance, the constitution, tort and land tenure, etc.[1] In Loziland, especially as judicial precedents are not recorded, ' we must look for the basic source of . . . law in the customary usages and observances of the people '.[2]

Lozi themselves think of tribal customs as a part of law and a source of legal rulings in somewhat this fashion. Customs (*mikwa*) are by no means the same thing as laws (*milao*). Since the Lozi themselves are dominant in Barotse courts the distinction between law and custom, and the treatment of custom as a source of law, emerges most clearly in reference to the customs of subject and foreign tribes. The kuta will not enforce other tribes' customs where it considers these conflict with Lozi law. Judges state : ' The law (*mulao*) of the kuta vetoes (*uhana*) this custom (*mukwa o*).' Similarly, though less often, they say that ' the law of the kuta vetoes this custom ' in considering Lozi custom. Moreover, they recognize explicitly that ' the law of the kuta ' enforces observance of some customs, but not of all.[3] I have never myself heard a Lozi individual or judge use the combination 'laws and customs' of the Lozi nation (*milao ni mikwa yasicaba sa Malozi*), which occurs in the Barotse Native Courts Ordinance (12), and is commonly used by Europeans in similar contexts. The Lozi speak of ' laws ' and ' customs ' separately, though they may use the words interchangeably. But as we saw in the previous chapter, every rule that is forcefully

---

[1] *Law in the Making*, pp. 124–5 and 65 ff.
[2] I quote Professor Schapera's words for Tswana law in *A Handbook of Tswana Law and Custom*, pp. 34 ff., at p. 36.
[3] So too Schapera on the Tswana, loc. cit.

238 The Judicial Process Among the Barotse

sanctioned is in that sense a *mulao*—a legal rule. This is made clear in a number of Lozi phrases : *kutoma mulao* is ' to make a law ' ; *kubuluka mulao* is to observe (literally, preserve) the law ; and *kuloba* (to break) or *kutula* (to jump over) *mulao* are to ' break the law ' ; *sesilumelwa kimulao* is ' lawful ' (lit., ' is allowed by the law ') ; and *kuta ibulela mulao* is ' the kuta expounds the law '. *Mukwa*, custom, cannot be substituted for *mulao* in any of these phrases.

I have in preceding chapters cited examples of the kuta's enforcement of specific customs as legal rules—better, of the kuta's recognition of certain customs as legally enforceable. For example, in ' The Case of the Wife's Granary ' (p. 140) for the first time within memory the kuta had to consider a woman's suit for divorce on the grounds that her husband had committed a breach of the custom forbidding a man to take food from his wife's granary where he had, on her own admission, done so in her interests. The kuta granted the divorce : i.e. it held that a breach of this custom should be enforced absolutely and should entitle the wife to a divorce.

A more complex situation was presented in ' The Case of the Urinating Husband ' (p. 140). The astonished laughter from the men who heard Muyongo retail the story of the drunken man who left the bed of one wife and urinated on his other wife, supported their contention that they had never heard of such a case before. The customary or legal rule which the kuta had to apply was, in its widest terms, that a man must not take his contact or affairs with one wife to another : for example, if he talks about one wife to another the former can claim divorce. In the Urinating Husband's case, the kuta extended the rule to grant divorce to both wives, since the man had urinated on one after intercourse with the other, thus bringing them into genital contact with one another.

Lozi courts constantly enforce customs of various kinds by attaching to their breaches a variety of sanctions : the payment of damages to the offending parties, fining, the granting of divorce to a wife, and so forth.

The Lozi themselves are a comparatively homogeneous people, and the judges are drawn from and related by kinship throughout the populace, which is not cut by class divisions. Hence judges do not call for evidence on what Lozi custom is. At least I never heard of this, and when I suggested it as a possible need they laughed at me. Judges know what Lozi custom is. There is no fiction of judicial ignorance, and judicial notice is unrestricted : it embraces every aspect of life. This applies also to customary rights of individuals and groups : the judges in the Cases of ' the Prince's Gardens ' (pp. 57 ff.) and ' the Expropri- ating Stewards ' (p. 103) recited their own knowledge of the history of the disputed gardens. Judges also usually assume that they know what are the customs of the more important foreign tribes within the nation : a simple illustration of this occurred in ' The Case of Cross-Cousin Adultery ' (p. 134). However, where judges, as a court or as individuals, are not sure of a particular tribe's customs they may ask for a description of these. This may be supplied by the litigants themselves, as I heard in a case between Lubale. Or one member of the court who has had special experience with the tribe may be called on by his fellows to explain the customs involved and conduct the main cross-examination. I once heard SOLAMI (R3) send to the NGAMBELA's (R1) kuta for Prince Muimui Namabanda (F3) to help thus in a case between Nyengo, since he had once been a British Government messenger working in Nyengo country.

The judges do not ask for proof on Lozi custom because they themselves participate freely in the life of a largely homogeneous people, and constantly observe customs embedded in living relationships. Hence when they state that such-and-such is the custom, they frequently themselves bear witness to it by con- trasting a litigant's or defendant's conduct with their own conduct, and that of others, where adherence to custom and moral rule has been exhibited in practice.

Once the judges assume, or have had explained to them, the relevant customs of a particular tribal group within the nation, they decide first whether they will enforce these in the case involved, and then how they will do so. In taking these decisions they implicitly subject customs to a series of tests, though these are not formulated as a set of guiding rules. First, they have to decide whether the customs in question apply to the parties in the particular dispute. This problem arises in a sharp form only where members of different tribes are involved. Otherwise I have not struck a case which raises the question of whether custom as such is applicable. Though in practice the judges are

S

usually concerned with the customs of particular tribal groups, they regard themselves as protecting the total set of customs of the nation, which embraces all these tribes.   Therefore insofar as custom is a source of judicial decision it need not be, as in English law, a local variation, limited in its application, or an ' *exception* from the ordinary rules of the land '.[1]   Custom is the rule, and not the exception, even if it be the custom of a limited group within ' the laws of nations '.

However, custom must be the accepted practice of a group—tribal, occupational, or status—for the courts to apply it.   I have not seen this point come up for decision, but Lozi tell me that no-one could get approval of the court for some act or claim against another because it was ' his custom ' (*mukwa wakhe* : *mukwa* here is better translated as ' habit ' or ' idiosyncrasy '—p. 166, above).

Custom should not be applied if it conflicts with any statute. Thus in ' The Case of Freedom of Residence ' (p. 171) the kuta refused to compel a woman to go to her maternal kin by Lubale custom, as British Government rules and the 1906 statute of King Lewanika require that people should be allowed to reside where they please, so long as it be in a recognized village.   Some Lozi claimed during the war that marriage-payments had increased until the custom was that they exceeded the amounts laid down in the 1917 Marriage Laws ; but the kuta refused either to order husbands to pay this excess to the wife's guardian, or to order the wife's guardian to return this excess on divorce if she was married as a virgin and did not conceive.   The kuta held that this would defeat the purpose of the statute.   In ' The Case of the Allegedly Pregnant Wife ' (p. 122), the Lubale plaintiff sued also for the excess he had given as marriage-payment above the statutory £2.   He said he had paid £4 15s. according to Lubale custom : the kuta replied that he was not entitled to this under the statute.   £2 had obtained his virgin wife : the rest was ' his wealth '.

The judgments I have quoted show that in expounding their arguments the judges tend to stress that the customs they are enforcing are all well known, certain, and definite, and are

<hr>

[1] Allen, *Law in the Making*, pp. 124 ff.   I consider that this part of my analysis is best presented in comparison with the tests for the legal validity of custom as set out in his book.

(*a*) A transport barge on the Zambezi between Livingstone and Mongu (see 'The Case of the Disrespectful Induna').

(*b*) The school is part of the community. Boys clear a blocked garden drainage channel (contrast 'The Case of the Quarrelsome Teacher').

PLATE VII

(*a*) Crossing the Njoko River, where ' The Case of the Quarrelsome Teacher ' was tried.

(*b*) On the road between Livingstone and Mongu (see ' The Case of the Migrant Husband ').

PLATE VIII

LABOUR MIGRANTS

obligatory on all upright men or women in particular social positions. Where they are dealing with Lozi custom alone they tend to assume that customary rules are consistent with one another, and do not contradict each other. In ' The Case of the Man who helped his Mothers-in-Law Cross a Ford ' (p. 148) the judges pointed out to the husband that the prohibition on a man's being familiar with his senior female in-laws was essential because of its consistency with his relations with his wife : ' No-one marries a girl and then her mother. . . . You, girl, when you look at this man he is your father.' However, the problem of consistency of established custom as a whole is never raised, because in the absence of writing no-one is at any moment in a position to survey all customs together. Only the customs involved in a particular set of relationships come before the judges at one time. But problems of consistency of customs may arise in inter-tribal relationships, when the courts follow Lozi customs, or ' what is right ' (p. 207).

The judgments also show that judges state that important customs have continued from immemorial antiquity where they derived from God. Many of the customs are, in fact, moral rules : ' respect your old people : they come from long, long ago '. Where judges make these statements their claims of antiquity are primarily intended to hallow the custom or moral rule, and they themselves do not always take the primaeval antiquity literally. For in the absence of writing to record their past the Lozi can hallow almost any usage thus, and they can treat fairly recent innovations as ancient customs. The Lozi have a keen historical sense and considerable knowledge of their own history which includes the dating of technical and ritual practices, of conventions, of statutory and moral rules, and of specific rights, by the reigns of their kings. In particular they ascribe certain of their own customs to other tribes in an historical scheme of their relations with these tribes. There is probably a tendency to thrust older established customs further back into the past than is justified. Thus in ' The Case of the Man Who Helped his Mothers-in-Law Cross a Ford ' (p. 149) some judges ascribed the origin of the prohibition forbidding a man to watch a woman crossing water to a statute of King Lewanika (d. 1916) : others stated it to be immemorial custom of ' long, long ago '.

In these circumstances innovations may be hallowed, or established by judicial practice, as customary. Dr. J. A. Barnes has reported this from the Fort Jameson Ngoni of Northern Rhodesia :

The courts are required by the Administration to follow tribal custom and people know that the courts are bound in this way. In fact, however, the courts have continually to deal with new situations and to make decisions which are unprecedented. This is done under the guise of drawing attention to some good Ngoni custom which has been neglected. . . . Even without Administration stimulus, deliberate acts of legislation are not unknown among the Ngoni, but they require considerable discussion and probably a tribal meeting. It is easier . . . to appeal to the unwritten corpus of tribal custom when introducing a new rule. . . . Ngoni do not quote specific precedents in court, and in this undocumented environment new decisions, if they are not soon challenged, become part of what has always been custom since time immemorial.' [1]

Dr. Barnes cites the levying of damages against a husband who divorces his wife as an example of this practice.[2] Here, apparently, the Ngoni court was establishing a quite new legal principle —the infliction of punitive damages on a spouse soliciting divorce —under the guise of enforcing customary judicial practice.

I have not recorded a clear example of Lozi courts enforcing a quite new legal principle or usage as one of immemorial antiquity. The problems which are usually presented to the courts are of the form : how is a customary principle or relationship to be enforced in these new circumstances ? We have seen the court doing this in its decision in ' The Case of the Prudish Wife ' (p. 145), where it held that if a man had given his wife several blankets, a new form of wealth, he could take some for himself and even use them with a new wife, without being guilty of mixing his relations with the two wives. But I note here the possibility that the Lozi could thus easily enforce new rules. I think that they are more likely to do so by legislation than are

---

[1] ' History in a Changing Society ', *Rhodes-Livingstone Journal*, XI (June, 1951), at pp. 5–6.

[2] A. L. Epstein has found the same innovation among Kazembe's people on the Luapula River, Northern Rhodesia : ' Divorce Law and Stability of Marriage among the Lunda of Kazembe ', *Rhodes-Livingstone Journal*, XIV (December, 1952).

the Ngoni according to Dr. Barnes's analysis : certainly the Lozi
have constantly amended their marriage-law by statute and not
by enforcement of new usages as old custom. They say so.

On the other hand, I have recorded cases in which the courts
have deliberately held that old customary law has become
obsolete because it conflicts with modern conditions. In ' The
Case of the Father and his Son's Cattle ' (p. 109) the court held
that a father no longer has property rights which he can dispose
of to a third party, in cattle bought by his son, so that he cannot
therefore vary the customarily established reward to a herder of
these cattle without consulting his son. He may still use the
cattle for himself. Again, on a case stated by a sub-district
induna the kuta ruled that a dead man's kin are no longer responsible for his debts, and that they cannot therefore be held liable
for a judgment of damages against him if he dies (below, p. 287).
In both these decisions the kuta seemed to be altering customary
law partly to accord with changed economic and social facts in
Loziland, and partly in deference to what it believed to be the
rulings of the British Government that people should retain their
own earnings and should personally be held liable only for their
own faults. Similarly the court held for the ' Disrespectful
Induna ' that present-day needs to earn money alter the manner
in which men fulfil their duties to overlords. But women do
not yet customarily work for wages or earn money by trade,
save of illegal beer : hence a woman's guardian is still liable
for her debts, damages, and fines.

The kuta in its arguments that a father no longer has full
property rights in his son's earnings, and that a man's kin are
no longer liable for his debts, also quite clearly stated that these
customary rules were unreasonable in the circumstances of
modern life. Some judges even implied that these rules were
inconsistent with, and contradicted, modern ways of life—of
earning and disposing of property. To some extent then, the
kuta does apply the standard of reasonableness to custom, and
in this it includes the ideas that customs should not be contrary
to modern ideas of morality and public policy. Again, I have
not many clear cases to validate this statement, but it arises from
my whole perspective of the kuta's judicial work and of discussions of Lozi jurisprudence. Normally a Lozi court would not
subject Lozi customs themselves to this test, but it does so submit

the customs of other tribes. I have cited above statements of Lozi authorities that they would not allow suits arising out of the Wiko custom which entitles circumcision-mates to have access to each other's wives, or out of the saturnalia of the circumcision-ceremonies (p. 207). Similarly they would not admit suits arising from Lubale [1] or Ila customary agreements to give access to a wife in return for a similar, or another, service.

I have heard a Lozi kuta refuse, on similar grounds, to uphold a Lubale man's suit (*Case 57 : The Case of the Infant Betrothal*) for return of gifts given to the parents of a girl betrothed in her infancy to him, when the girl refused to marry him. The kuta held that infant betrothal was immoral, and it was un-reasonable to expect a girl to marry a man selected thus for her. But this custom is also directly contrary to Lozi law as established by King Lewanika (d. 1916), though I am uncertain whether he barred infant betrothal by statute or by judicial decision.

The recognition of the customs of other tribes was discussed above (pp. 206 ff.), when I described Lozi ideas which correspond to some extent with the *jus gentium.*

On the whole, therefore, allowing for the fact that Lozi law is so largely based on unrecorded custom, the courts implicitly apply to custom many of the standard tests we know, before they accept a custom as legal. Custom must be certain and definite and established, it must attach to a group or category of persons, it must not be contrary to statute or established principle of law, it must be reasonable and moral ; and preferably it should be graced with antiquity. In practice if it is not so graced, the courts may confer grace upon it.

I have listed the above conditions under which Lozi courts will recognize customary rules as legal rules, without referring to the provision in Section 12 (*a*) of the Barotse Native Courts Ordinance that :

a native court shall administer the native law and custom prevailing in the area of the jurisdiction of the court, so far as it is not repugnant

---

[1] In Epstein's *Study of The Administration of Justice and the Urban African,* op. cit., p. 49, he cites an Urban Court's refusal to entertain such a case on grounds of good morals, and he indicates that Lubale courts would no longer do so. Below I cite a report by Jalla that a Lozi king who ruled over a century ago enacted that an adulterer's wife must have intercourse with his cuckold : modern Lozi deny knowledge of this.

to justice or morality or inconsistent with the provisions of any Order of the King in Council or with any other law in force in the Territory.

I have done so to emphasize that I believe the evidence, though it is uncertain, indicates that the processes I have described above were at work in the past. The safeguard in the Ordinance's provision is theoretically a further test to which customary rules should be subjected before they are enforced as legal rules : in practice, I have never heard the provision explicitly referred to. But Lozi courts constantly support their decisions by saying that the Whites agree with what they rule, and they also in other cases state that the Whites disapprove of and do not allow certain things. Most Lozi councillors have a rather haphazard knowledge of the provisions of Orders of the King in Council and other laws in force in the Territory, and they have only been able to glean vague ideas of what is repugnant to the justice and morality of the Whites, save for a few well-known principles and prejudices. The latter point is illustrated by INYUNDWANA's rebuke of the Violent Councillor SAYWA : ' Nowadays with the White people here a whip is never taken for adults, only for children ' (p. 90). This is in fact true of English law.

Obviously the safeguard in this provision of the Ordinance is likely principally to operate when cases are reviewed by District Officers or Provincial Commissioner, or come on appeal to the Provincial Commissioner or the High Court. Nevertheless, despite ignorance of details, the kuta does have general knowledge of the more important relevant statutes deriving from British overlordship, and of the main repugnances of British officers. Most strikingly the kuta knows and enforces British disbelief in sorcery charges, though it does not always prosecute magicians and diviners.

I have not heard of the Provincial Commissioner or High Court rejecting on appeal any decision of a Lozi kuta, on the grounds that it contravened the safeguard of repugnancy to natural justice or morality, though kuta decisions have been upset for exceeding the powers of the Barotse Authorities under the 1936 Ordinances (see ' The Case of the Watchtower Pacifists ', p. 158).

I have a record of one British administrative refusal to support a legal claim by the kuta. In a proclamation in 1906 Lewanika gave effect to an agreement with the Government to set free all 'slaves' (serfs) held by the Lozi, but each such person was to pay £2 to his or her former master.[1]   The Government rejected a request from the Lozi authorities to help them seize, and compel payment of the £2 due by, escaped 'slaves', on the grounds that slavery was repugnant to British ideas of justice, and nothing would be done to connive at slavery.

It is only fair to note that if the Lozi authorities are not as fully acquainted with the requirements of the Territory's statutory law as this provision demands, little is done beyond sending them copies of Ordinances to see that they are so informed.   Ordinances are not promulgated in African languages.   Moreover, Lozi ignorance here could probably be more than matched by the ignorance of British judicial officers of the African laws and customs they are required to enforce.[2]

In the preceding paragraphs I have been discussing principally those important customs which constitute the main framework of Lozi 'common law'.   Customary usages in the wider sense of all the habitual practices and standardized ideas of the community, are also a source of law, even though the judges do not state these as rules of laws.   I refer here, for example, to the way in which these practices and ideas control the definition of reasonable behaviour in particular circumstances.   We have seen that this definition may be the very essence of a dispute.   In this sense 'custom' or 'usage' remains a major source of law even in highly developed legal systems; but I can discuss this problem more adequately when I examine the judicial process itself.

IV

The second source of Lozi legal rules is the statutes of the British Government and of their own kings.   In the past the legal rules for bringing a case to trial, conducting it, and enforcing judgment upon it, were drawn from custom.   Nowadays this branch of legal rules is set out in the Barotse Native Courts Ordinance and orders under it ; and though the kuta still hears

---

[1] The Proclamation is quoted in full in my *Essays on Lozi Land and Royal Property*, at pp. 82–4.
[2] See ' The Case of the Barren Widow ' (p. 174).

evidence and cross-examines by customary procedures, on the whole it abides by the Ordinance's regulations and keeps within the limits of jurisdiction, powers of punishment, methods of committal and enforcement, laid down in these regulations. The kuta also enforces or helps enforce a number of other Government statutory rules, such as those imposing tax or requiring residence in a village. The Barotse Native Authorities Ordinance is technically now the source of the kuta's power, and on the whole it follows the requirements of that Ordinance for the proper promulgation of these rules.

The kuta also enforces statutes of Lozi kings which were promulgated before 1936. I have already quoted as an example the way in which some judges referred the ban on watching a woman crossing water to a statute of Lewanika (p. 148). We have seen how the issue of an offence against Yeta III's *muliu* statute of 1928 may be raised in a land-suit (p. 57). In 'The Case of the Barren Widow' (p. 175) we saw how reference is made to Yeta III's set of marriage laws of 1917.

Theoretically a statute of a king overrides and changes custom, and continues to be law until repealed. However, judges do not sit in kuta with a compendium of statutes to which they can refer. They carry the statutes in their heads, and statutes are thus part of 'received tradition'. The judges themselves are legislators, and some of the older ones were members of the kuta, or attendants on the king, as far back as the first decade of the century, so that in judgment they cite not only what the statute says, but also the circumstances in which it was enacted and the purpose it was intended to achieve. Thus both MUKULWAKASHIKO (R4) and INGANGWANA (L1) in ' The Case of the Prince's Garden ' (pp. 59–60) described the enactment of the *muliu* law in 1928, and they and suu (R17) stressed that it was not intended to prevent the lending and subsequent reclamation of gardens, since these transactions are essential for the well-being of the nation. This personal range of memory of the kuta, while I sat in it, reached over the years of British overlordship when legislation must have become increasingly frequent. The death of many older members of the kuta, and the weeding out of others by the 1946 reforms (p. 14), will presumably raise new problems in this reference to legislation.

It is certain that knowledge of statutes must become less precise with the passage of time. Some judges had forgotten that Lewanika, who reigned from 1884 to 1916, ruled that men should hide if they met women crossing water. Judges may forget what was the law which was altered by the statute. Thus as far as I could gather, in ' The Case of the Barren Widow ' Prince Mboo Lewanika thought it was a law that a marriage dissolved by death was covered by the rules affecting marriages dissolved by divorce. Other statutes are disregarded by the passage of time. The late M. Adolphe Jalla came to Loziland in the 1880's and he has recorded that King Mulambwa (9th king : 1780 ?–1830 ?) was believed to have ruled (see p. 106, above) that

> A thief is a brave man and must not therefore be put to death but must be brought to the king who will give him a village or cattle or make him his tribute collector. People will then see if he will thieve again or become a good citizen.

I do not doubt that Jalla recorded the edict correctly. I was told in the 1940's that Mulambwa said a thief stole because he was poor, and he should be made rich to see if thieving was in his nature. Modern Lozi laughed at this naïveté and said the law could not be applied now or everyone would steal to get rich. They say the edict was reasonable in the days before the Whites brought wealth and when the king had wealth to distribute : it is unreasonable today.

Jalla also recorded that Mulambwa ruled :

> Anyone accused of adultery must not be immediately condemned but the charges against him must first be carefully gone into. If he is guilty, then his wife must sleep with the injured party. If a man be found to have been falsely accused his accuser must be severely punished.

My informants denied knowledge of this law, and always said that until 1920 cuckolded husbands claimed damages by a show of force against the adulterer, but were punished by the king if their demonstration led to the spilling of blood. Archives indicate that in practice these cases were tried by councillors in their courtyards but were barred from the full kuta. Informants also deny knowledge of another of Mulambwa's laws recorded by Jalla, under which a person condemned to death was entitled to fight his executioner, and be pardoned if victorious (above, p. 100).

I do not question that informants in the 1890's described these laws to Jalla, or suggest that they were wrong and my own informants in the 1940's were right. Obviously the probability is the other way. I illustrate here how knowledge of statutes, where memory is relied on, must be fallible, so that the statutes are changed or forgotten, and ultimately only those parts of them are likely to survive which become embedded in custom and are acceptable to current morality. Older statutes must tend to become customary law. This process has been halted to some extent, for the Administration in 1947 asked the Lozi to codify their statutes. I am inclined to doubt whether the judges I knew would consult such a codification.

Nevertheless the judges give priority to a few well-known statutes in deciding cases. Thus they invoke the *muliu* law to bar claims to land, which are based on ancestral title of holding prior to the day when the statute was passed. They enforce the damages and fines for adultery which have been raised through successive edicts. They have granted divorces to the wives of absentee husbands according to the period of allowed absence, which has been steadily reduced in a succession of edicts. They will not protect parties who agree to marriage-payments in excess of the statutory amounts. They have rigidly enforced the £2 fine on beer-drinking (see p. 220).

Lozi statutes are masterpieces of simple and general drafting. The *muliu* law is contained in one sentence : ' He who does not reclaim his land when the sun stands overhead in the morning [of the appointed day], if he claims it after midday will be liable to a fine of 5 beasts or £5.' The Marriage Laws of 1917 are a series of similar statements. This simplicity of legislative language therefore allows the judges to exercise considerable discretion, if they wish to, in applying the statute.[1] They rarely do so in applying statutes which lay down offences (such as beer-drinking, the failure of children to attend school, failure to cleanse villages). They do exercise this discretion in deciding whether a claim to land is *muliu* (see the Cases of ' the Prince's Gardens ',

---

[1] Cf. Allen, C. K., *Law in the Making*, at p. 365, on how English mediaeval judges applied statutory law.

p. 57, and 'the Returning Garden-Claimant', p. 53). For here they look at the purposes of statutes which many of them participated in passing. The simple language of the edict against beer-drinking was intended to enforce absolute temperance, though popular resistance prevented the search for and destruction of brews. Therefore, if during another case the kuta heard officially that any person had drunk beer, it immediately fined him or her the maximum of £2. Similarly the kuta wished all Lozi children to go to school : therefore any breach of the attendance rules was rigorously fined. But the aim of the *muliu* law was to prevent continual upsetting of existing land distribution between villages : and therefore the kuta used its discretion and did not fine relatives who sued one another, or persons involved in misunderstandings.

The Cases of 'the Prince's Gardens' (p. 57) and 'The Expropriating Stewards' (p. 103) and the case of the young man who returned to his father's mother's brother's village and tried to seize his father's old gardens by force ('The Returning Garden-Claimant', p. 53), show that in applying the *muliu* statute the judges concern themselves with trying to define whether certain claims constitute *muliu* in terms of the statute. In 'The Case of the Migrant Husband' (p. 141) the kuta in effect interpreted the rule that if a man is away from Loziland for more than three years his wife should be granted a divorce, to mean that he must begin his journey home before the three years have passed. These are the only situations in which I have seen judges really involved in problems of interpreting the words and meaning of a statute in the sense in which interpretation is usually used in Western law. In view of the paucity and brevity of statutes, and the fact that there is no written corpus of judicial precedents and customary law, one would expect this. No problems of narrow definition of words in statutes and general rules of law in relation to one another arise. However, in the wider sense the application of Lozi statutes does call for interpretation by the judges : the process is only obscured by the very general terms in which statutes are cast. Litigation arising out of the marriage laws edict requires the interpretation of concepts like 'consent of the woman and her guardian', 'a virgin' (*mwalyanjo*) as against a 'non-virgin' (*namakuka*), the physiological conception of a child, divorce, adultery, etc., in their application to a specific set of facts. That is, the court must for example declare that certain conduct amounts obviously or constructively to 'adultery' for the purposes of the statute. Similarly, the kuta has in effect interpreted beer-drinking in the relevant statute to mean the drinking of even a single cup of beer in passing, despite popular protest (see 'The Case of the Beer-drinking Fines', p. 220). For the interpretation of legal concepts is a process of giving them referents in actual life in terms of its extrinsic circumstances —specifying them—and not merely a process of extracting the intrinsic meaning of the concepts. The wide generality and flexibility of Lozi statutory concepts is akin to the wide generality and flexibility of the concepts of their laws as a whole, and therefore the problem of how they are interpreted is best held over for a while.

Here we must note further that because statutes are stated in very wide terms, they seem to leave few of the notorious gaps which raise such problems of judicial interpretation in English law. At least I have recorded only two problems which have arisen in this way. The first arose in 'The Case of the Barren Widow' since the 1917 Marriage Laws made no explicit provision about the fate of the marriage-payment if either spouse died in a marriage to which the bride came as a virgin and in which she did not conceive (pp. 175–6). We have seen how the kuta met this contingency. The second arose from the provision that if the marriage in these circumstances was broken by divorce, one beast of the two beasts or £1 of the £2, paid by the groom on marriage, was returned to him. The kuta informed me that though the statute did not specifically say which beast had to be returned, they have held that it must be the second paid. The first paid is equivalent to the one beast paid on marrying a non-virgin, which does not return on divorce : it is 'the beast of shame' which gives rights of sexual intercourse. The second is 'the beast of the child'. Hence the kuta told me that on divorce of a virgin who had not conceived :

(a) if one beast and then £1 had been paid, the £1 had to be refunded ; but if the order of payment was £1 and then one beast, the beast had to be returned ;

(b) if a sterile beast was paid before a fertile beast, the fertile beast and its offspring had to be refunded ; but if the sterile beast was handed over second it returned and the fertile beast and its offspring remained with the woman's guardians ;

(c) if two fertile beasts were handed over, the second and its off-spring were due to be returned.

The kuta has on the whole so far confined its legislation to—

(i) establishing a number of what we would call 'technical offences' (beer-drinking, breaches of school attendance, using fishing nets of too small mesh, cutting certain trees, etc.) ;

(ii) restating the king's privileges ; and

(iii) regulating marriage and the relation of spouses.

With its decisions in 1942 to enforce price-control, and in 1946 to enforce promises to sell, to manufacture, and to render services, it has entered on the control of contracts. Here Lozi law was not well-developed, and it is likely that the judges will find that their simple legislation is less able to cover variable situations.[1]

Finally, it seems to be accepted as a rule of Lozi courts that they do not apply legislation retrospectively. They do not consider legislating to make past conduct of which they have disapproved an offence. They refused to apply the raised damages and fines levied on adultery and on abduction of a married woman, and on seduction of a virgin, or the new damages levied on seduction of a non-virgin if it leads to impregnation and those levied on infecting a woman with venereal disease,[2] to offences committed before the passing of the edicts. They refused to punish a man for not rendering the king half of a hippo hide under the edict re-establishing this right of the king, when he had shot the hippo before the passing of the edict (p. 70n. : see also 'The Case of the Exorbitant Fishmonger', p. 69). I know of no instance contrary to these examples. Similarly, in passing the *muliu* law they allowed a period of grace for actions which would be barred by it.

---

[1] To be discussed under 'The Law of Contracts' in *The Ideas of Barotse Jurisprudence*.

[2] Damages were denied for these actions in the past under the maxim that ' if you are invited to a meal and a fishbone sticks in your throat you cannot sue your host.'

V

Lozi state spontaneously as well as in reply to questions that their kutas should follow previous decisions, and that subordinate kutas are bound by decisions of higher kutas. They maintain that this was the position in the past, and are supported in this contention by contemporary records. Today they also recognize that their judgments should be bound by decisions of the High Court and the Provincial Commissioner's Court on appeal, as we have seen in ' The Case of the Barren Widow ' (p. 175). Therefore we may say that previous decisions of various courts are part of Lozi law and form one source of Lozi legal rulings.

Legal rulings theoretically bind all subordinate courts, but I never heard one ruler's kuta quote the decision of another ruler's kuta. Thus Nalolo had never heard of the decisions of the Lialui kutas in 1920 and 1946, and of the High Court in 1946, on the Cases of ' the Barren Widows ' (pp. 174-5). There is no formal procedure for informing other kutas of particular decisions even where these involve important restatements of the law. The already quoted Lozi Provincial Appeal Court's decision (pp. 175-7) that a father has not transmissible property rights in his son's earnings was on an appeal from Nalolo : Nalolo would become aware of it on return of the appeal. But no steps were taken to see that other District kutas (save for that of Lialui where the two kutas refer judgments to each other) should be notified of the ruling, nor that subordinate sub-district kutas should be informed. Again, when the Saa-Katengo Kuta at Lialui in 1942 ruled on a case stated by a sub-district induna (see above, p. 243 and below, pp. 287 f.) that a man's kin are not liable for his debts, this was not notified even to the Sikalo Kuta across the way. I never heard a District kuta state that its subordinate kutas in general, other than the sub-district kuta from which the case had come, should have important judgments reported to them. Where a subordinate kuta hears of a decision, it cites this as binding.

This situation is obviously mainly a product of the fact that there is no adequate system of recording judgments and disseminating them through the country. But this alone is insufficient to account for a kuta's seeming unawareness of this problem when it makes an important new ruling. The examples in the preceding paragraph contrast markedly with SOLAMI's (R3) verdict in ' The Case of the Exorbitant Fishmonger ' (at p. 70) : ' If the kuta wishes to inform the whole country of Barotseland of the price for fish set by the kuta . . . the NGAMBELA (R1) is not here. . . . If the [NGAMBELA] agrees in this affair . . . it is easy for me to gather the country and tell the people the prices set.' SOLAMI's ruling exhibits the care which the kuta as a legislative body tries to take to inform all authorities and people of its orders. I have to conclude that in giving judgments which contain new rulings on the law, as in the above examples, and even more in ' The Case of the Headman's Fishdams ', the kuta is not fully aware that it is making new legal rules, even though judges say ' nowadays the customs have changed and therefore . . .' In effect the judges have to give a decision on a dispute, however uncertain the law be or however they feel they must change the law to meet justice, and they therefore take the view that they are stating existing law. Indeed, they are stating existing law insofar as this consists of very generally stated rules, which embrace wide moral principles, such as that ' the heir must administer the property [reasonably] in the interests of his kin '. These propositions remain constant, even when the situations in which they are exhibited have altered radically, and the applicable sanctions change. The judges are able to insist that they are applying established law, and seemingly to accept by implication the fiction that they do not legislate for new situations. The tradition of the kuta is one of legislation and adjudication in a stationary society and this tradition has persisted into modern times when new issues and unprecedented suits arise. Theoretically existing law is able to cope with these issues and suits—the judges state the law and the legal rules as self-evident. That they believe they do not make new law in judgment is suggested by their clear awareness as legislators that they should announce their new edicts to the nation. Indeed, para-doxically, because the judges are also legislators, they seem to make a complete dichotomy between legislation and adjudication.

The background to this attitude is a failure, because of the very endurance of moral principles, to appreciate the full implica-tions of the new political situation in which they are working. They seem to have failed to grasp that the capital is no longer the main centre of Barotse life. In the past more Barotse visited and participated in the kuta's deliberations, and more came to the kuta each year. For example, early travellers describe strings of tribute-carriers moving between the capital and their homes. Men were not abroad at work or so occupied in the earning of money at home. The structure of the past situation supports Lozi contentions that in the past everyone was better informed of any new edicts or decisions. The kutas assume that this situation still exists.

The rule by which representatives of District kutas since 1946 have sat in the Provincial Appeal Court (p. 149), as they have always come to legislative debates, may spread some knowledge of its decisions to the provinces.

Furthermore, the Lozi view of a precedent differs from the clear conception of a precedent held in English law. Lozi do say in effect that the kuta in a judgment is stating that some rule of statute or custom or morality will be enforced in a particular way in these circumstances and in all analogous circumstances. This was exhibited in the way they cited decisions of the kuta to me when I was questioning them about law : most of my texts were collected thus. I have also frequently heard Lozi cite precedents to each other in debates on law and morality. Notably, the kuta defended its decision in 'The Case of the Barren Widow' against the High Court's statement of the law by reference to a twenty-six-year-old precedent—which it had not quoted in its recorded judgment. In contrast, it is striking that the kuta very rarely cites its previous decisions during judgment itself. The only instance recorded in the cases I have quoted in previous chapters was in 'The Case of the Expropriating Stewards' (p. 104), and even then precedents were cited not in the course of the trial, but during the judges' general discussion of the matter : ' [The plaintiffs] were told to sit on one side till 2 p.m. [when the defendants would appear], but the kuta continued to talk about the gardens . . . The kuta cited decisions in similar cases, all to the effect that people could not be turned off the soil of their forefathers.' [1] In 'The Case of the Violent Councilor' (pp. 88–9) the kuta did not cite its previous decisions

---

[1] I have in my notebooks a few examples of the citing of precedents in a case under trial.

T

punishing violent councillors, though—illustrating my point above—my own people in discussing the probable course of the trial cited these precedents to me.

I have already suggested (p. 192) that because precedents are not recorded, judges cannot consider a series of decisions in giving judgment and even in discussing what the law is. Instead they cite, in terms of the ethical merits of the case under trial, the moral principles which have guided selected previous decisions on similar cases, without referring at all to the precise set of circumstances in which these moral principles, and the law, were applied. If judges cite precedents they cite those which they consider accord with their moralistic view of the case under trial. Precedents illustrate customary law and moral principle, rather than constitute a separate source of legal rulings.

From this view of precedent, flows the habit of judges to cite not judgments of the kuta against litigants in analogous circumstances, but instances where, in their personal experience, people have behaved morally in analogous circumstances. They thus erect the standard of the upright incumbent of the relevant social position. Many examples of this habit appear in the judgments cited.

Thus SIFUWE pointed out to the Quarrelsome Teacher that when men's cattle smashed the kuta he did not tell them to leave the country ; the clerk told the teacher that he could be discharged if he failed to work harmoniously with the people, as a foreman at the Saw Mills was discharged ; and the teacher was advised to look at the peace and full attendance of a neighbouring school (p. 74–5). SOLAMI contrasted his way of handling affairs coming to him at night, with what the Violent Councillor did (p. 87). The Schoolboy Adulterer was convicted for not producing to her kin, or husband, the woman's letter tempting him, in contrast with a man who had given a woman's seductive letter to her husband (p. 132). IMANDI contrasted the behaviour of the heir in his family village with Mahalihali's over the fishdams (p. 185).

The Lozi have a special noun, *sishupiso*, to describe one who can thus be held as a model before a troublesome person ; and this noun, significantly, is the causative [1] form of one of many nouns

---

[1] In Bantu, 'causative' suffixes change the meaning from 'to do something', into 'to cause to do something'.

describing a troublesome person (*sishupi*). *Sishupiso* thus implies someone who shows a wrongdoer how troublesome he is.

This process of ethical selection of relevant precedents, and of moral exemplification, is only partially explained by the absence of adequate records, and by the failure of the kuta to refer to the bare records it keeps under the Barotse Native Courts Ordinance.[1] Clearly the kuta has no tradition of referring to records, and its illiterate members could not do so. There is one record only and no distribution of copies to other kutas. Furthermore, there are no scholars (with the transient and exotic exception of myself) concerned with culling and analysing in writing the total body of precedents to produce convenient digests for judges.[2] When Lozi councillors and people discuss law they do not do so in terms of a series of decisions, nor are there yet *responsa jurisprudentium* or jurisprudential analyses to be a source of law or help the judges. Nor, indeed, until after 1947 (when I last visited Loziland) have judgments of the High Court on ' native cases ' been published, and I doubt if they are now circulated to the African courts concerned.

Despite the important influence of the comparative illiteracy of the Lozi, I consider that the mainspring of their ethical citation of precedent lies in the nature of their important litigation itself : it is litigation between persons involved in multiplex relationships who have to be reconciled. Procedure emphasizes this fact. The litigants present their own pleadings in terms of their views of a general body of law and a general ethical code, and are not aided by lawyers who are themselves aware of the whole corpus of precedents : and inevitably the form of pleadings shapes the whole course of trial. Litigants in these cases are deeply concerned with moral issues as well as legal rights. I cite again the way in which the plaintiff nephew in ' The Case of the Biassed Father ' pleaded : ' I cannot see how a person without a fault can lose his land . . .' (p. 38). This tends to force the kuta's attention to moral issues. Thus AWAMI reproved the

---

[1] Government Notice No. 136 of 1937 : Section 39 of Chapter 160 of *The Laws of Northern Rhodesia*.

[2] It is worth reporting as a possibility for the future that an Ashanti chief quoted R. S. Rattray's *Ashanti Law and Constitution* to Professor Fortes (personal communication). Note (p. 174, above) how the Lozi adopted the term ' bride-wealth ' from my writings.

headman Mahalihali's attempt to assert his legal claim to the
fishdams: ' If they had [done wrong], there would be a case . . .'
(p. 183). The judges are also given by the pleadings a perspective
of the whole history of the litigants' relations. In the same case,
IMANDI silenced the daughter who had been accused of sorcery :
' This you cannot tell. If you had come to us, or gone to the
District Commissioner at Mongu, to say your father accused you
of sorcery, we could have enquired. Now we cannot enter this
affair. Speak of the dams.' [1] But he continued immediately :
' Will you go back to your father's people ? ', and he and
other judges referred to this accusation in their judgments.

Thus from the beginning of a hearing in this type of case the
kuta is concerned with moral judgments, in order to achieve
reconciliation, and moral judgments have to take account of
individual circumstances. Hence the kuta makes an arbitrary
selection of the precedents it will follow, if it follows a precedent
at all. Further, moral exhortation of the parties is best achieved
by citing moral examples, and not judicial precedents.

Yet though the kuta thus considers individual circumstances,
it is giving judgment in terms of an established and well-known
legal code. Justice is by no means arbitrary in terms of untrammelled ideas of equity and morality. Therefore on occasion, the
kuta, or some of its judges, cite a rule of law or a precedent as
compelling them to give a judgment against the moral merits
of the case. They enforce the law without amending it to meet
the demands of morality particularly in disputes arising out of
temporary single-interest relationships (see ' The Case of the
Father and his Son's Cattle ', p. 109).[2]

VI

This discussion of how Lozi kutas make use of precedent
indicates that ' morality ' is a source of Lozi law, a statement
validated at length in the previous chapter. I here group together
under the single head ' morality ' a series of related sources, since
the Lozi do not always explicitly distinguish these, though they
are aware of, and have terms to indicate, the distinctions. These

---

[1] This is the nearest example to ' prescription of action ' which I obtained.
[2] This will be further exemplified in cases cited under ' The Law of Contract ', in *The Ideas of Barotse Jurisprudence*.

sources are equity (*kulikana*), natural justice (*milao yabutu*), or justice (*tukelo*—from *kuluka* = to be right) or truth (*niti*), decency or good morals (*sishemo, likute, bunde*), the laws of God (*milao yaNyambe* or *yaMulimu*), the laws of nations (*milao yamacaba kaufela*), and public policy (*bupilo bwasicaba*). I have already cited examples exhibiting the application of these several principles and expounded how the judges work with them. Here only a summary statement is required to conclude our survey of the social sources of Lozi law.

' Morality ' serves as a source of Lozi judicial decision first in that it bridges the all-important gap between the law and evidence of the facts. This gap can only be partially crossed by formal logic : morality selects from the evidence those premisses of fact which provide the foundations on which the bridge of judgment unites facts to law. The parties' pleadings, in which they state both their cases and their view of what is the applicable law begins the process, because every rule of law is a value-judgment.[1] I know of no concept of Lozi law which has not a high ethical implication. Furthermore, as stated above (p. 196), the very description of the facts is similarly impregnated with judgments of approval and disapproval. Even false evidence tries to make action appear reasonable in terms of common values. Therefore to apply law in any way at all to facts involves a process of moral selection from the evidence which is likely to condition the whole judicial process. Secondly, as we have just seen, moral considerations guide the selection of appropriate rules of laws and precedents for application. Thus morality operates in almost all disputes between kin, and between lords and underlings, as general equity, ' a liberal and humane interpretation of law in general, so far as that is possible without actual antagonism to the law itself ' (Allen, quoted above at p. 204).

Thirdly, exhortations of morality are used to awaken the consciences of litigants to accept judgments, which are sermons on parental, filial, and brotherly love. It is important in this process that the litigants themselves have the same norms as judges, and indeed even lie in terms of those norms.

---

[1] See Williams, Glanville L., ' Language and the Law ', *The Law Quarterly Review*, lxi (1945) and lxii (1946), at lxii, pp. 395 ff., for a penetrating discussion of this point.

The manner in which these rules of morality control the selection of legal rules and precedent and their application to the dispute is better considered in later sections which deal with the process of judicial reasoning and with judicial interpretation of the flexible concepts of Lozi law. Contrasting examples will suffice here to state summarily the essence of this complicated process. In the Cases of 'the Biassed Father' and 'the Headman's Fishdams' rules defining rights to land in terms of membership of a village and a kinship grouping were weighted differently, to accord with different moral evaluations of the litigants' behaviour.

The exhortations to the husband in the case of the women crossing a ford—that shame of nakedness is a natural feeling and that respect for senior female in-laws derives from God and is known to all nations—must similarly suffice to show that morality is believed generally to support the law.

The application of a rule of public policy is best exemplified in NAMUNDA-KATANEKWA's statement that the kuta would divorce a woman whose husband attempted to keep her in a marriage when he no longer fulfilled his obligations : 'This cannot be done. No-one shall place the child of a person in slavery, to make her a trap, in order to get cattle from people' (p. 142). For similar reasons SOLAMI declared the persistent adulteress in 'The Case of the Schoolboy Adulterer' to be 'a wife of the country' (p. 133) : here he established or enforced as legal a rule that after three adulteries of a wife, a husband should no longer profit from suits against her lovers.

This decision also shows how morality becomes a particular, as as well as being a general, source of law. The process is further illustrated by SOLAMI's solution in 'The Case of the Headman's Fishdams'. Similarly he drew on equity when he held that a man's kin are no longer liable for his debts (above, p. 243), as did the Provincial Appeal Court when it ruled that a father's rights in his son's property had altered, since nowadays men earn by their own labour for Whites (p. 110).

Unprecedented suits bring out the particular application of morality or equity most clearly. This is shown in the kuta's decisions in 'The Case of the Barren Widow', and in the cases arising out of prostitution. These decisions are not always stated in terms of the explicit application of specific moral or equitable doctrines, but are introduced with general homilies on morals and policy. I have compared some of the implicit moral doctrines contained in Lozi decisions with similar doctrines in Roman Law, such as *ex turpi causa non oritur actio*, and *in pari delicto potior est conditio defendentis*. The Lozi have maxims of this type, such as 'if you are invited to a meal and a fishbone sticks in your throat, you cannot sue your host' (*volenti non fit injuria*). This, however, is the only moral maxim that I heard cited in a case. Thus moral maxims are not entrenched as specific legal rules.

In discussing custom as a source of legal rulings, I cited examples of how Lozi customs will be declared obsolete on grounds of present moral ideas, and of how Lozi judges submit the customs of other tribes to moral and reasonable tests before they agree to enforce these customs. A different, but related, problem is presented by what may be called the 'social amnesia' which operates in an unrecorded system of law so that unpalatable legal rules or edicts are forgotten. It seems likely to me that the Lozi who retailed Mulambwa's laws to me, and denied knowledge of certain of his laws which Lozi in the 1890's had recounted to Jalla (above, pp. 100 and 248), had been influenced by moral ideas of State power and of the position of women derived from contact with British. Morality changes with social conditions, and hence its influence as a source of law on judicial decisions is as likely to be radical as conservative. Nevertheless, even through these changes the ethical code may seem to be stable, for it is stated in wide general terms capable of varying application to extrinsic circumstances. This problem will be the concern of the last section of the next chapter.

VII

I suggested in introducing this chapter, that certain false problems had crept into the analysis of primitive law because of a tendency to regard it as something quite different from developed law. One of these false problems is the attempt to find a distinction between law and custom, as if they are in some sense antithetical concepts. Law can only be posed in antithesis to non-law. Custom has the regularity of law but is a different kind of social fact. As we have seen, the judges may use even the least important of customs as a check on the varied flow of social life. Therefore the jurisprudential conception of custom as one source of law, in the sense of judicial decision, and also as a part of the whole *corpus juris*, can be applied without distortion to the Lozi data. Lozi judges draw on custom to give their verdicts. They state this explicitly. In doing so they also clearly speak of customs as forming, with statutes and other rules, part of the whole body of law of their nation (*mulao wasicaba*)—the Lozi *corpus juris*. This is likely to be true of all simple societies which have courts.

I cannot here produce the evidence, but I consider that similar conclusions apply to the process of social control in societies which have not developed specialized judicial tribunals, and which therefore do not have law in the sense of judicial decisions. But according to modern anthropological accounts, in these societies there is law as a *corpus juris*, a body of interconnected rights and duties, which includes the observance of customary practices. Professor Schapera stresses this for Bushmen and Hottentots.[1] Law also seems to exist as a series of acceptable judgments of rightdoing and wrongdoing in particular cases, though these judgments are not given by special officers. A short passage in Professor Evans-Pritchard's analysis of what he has called the 'ordered anarchy' of the Nuer brings this out clearly :

The Nuer has a keen sense of personal dignity and rights. The notion of right, *cuong*, is strong. It is recognized that a man ought to obtain redress for certain wrongs. This is not a contradiction of the statement that threat of violence is the main sanction for payment of compensation, but is in accord with it, for a man's kinsmen will only support him if he is right. It is doubtless true that if a man is weak it is unlikely that his being in the right will enable him to obtain satisfaction, but if he is in the right he will have the support of his kin and his opponent will not, and to resort to violence or to meet it the support of one's kin and the approval of one's community are necessary. One may say that if a man has right on his side and, in virtue of that, the support of his kinsmen and they are prepared to use force, he stands a good chance of obtaining what is due to him, so long as the parties to the dispute live near one another. When we speak of a man being in the right we do not suggest

---

[1] Schapera, I, *The Khoisan Peoples of South Africa*, London : Routledge (1930), pp. 151, 337.

that disputes are mostly a clear issue between right and wrong. Indeed, it would be correct to say that, usually, both parties are to some extent right and that the only question which arises is, who has the greater right? To state the matter in a different way : A Nuer dispute is usually a balance of wrongs, for a man does not, except in sexual matters, wantonly commit an act of aggression. He does not steal a man's cow, club him, or withhold his bride-cattle in divorce, unless he has some score to settle. Consequently it is very rare for a man to deny the damage he has caused. He seeks to justify it, so that a settlement is an adjustment between rival claims. I have been told by an officer with wide experience of Africans that Nuer defendants are remarkable in that they very seldom lie in cases brought before Government tribunals. They have no need to, since they are only anxious to justify the damage they have caused by showing that it is retaliation for damage the plaintiff has inflicted earlier.[1]

This passage shows that even in a society where ' self-help ' is the enforcing sanction, people judge situations of dispute in terms of rights and duties, and wrongs. Alleged wrongdoers justify their actions as reasonable and just in terms of common norms. Outsiders clearly give judgments and they do so in terms of a *corpus juris* of rules for rightdoing. Part of this body of rights and duties is clearly, from the text of the book, customs.

We have also seen that ' morality ', as a body of general ethical principles, is part of the Lozi *corpus juris* and a source for Lozi judgments. Presumably this is also true of the Nuer. Nuer morality seems to be a set of general rules such as, respect your father, help your kin, observe your obligations, obey Nuer custom. These moral rules must inform the way in which people abide by custom. Therefore it seems fair to say that among the Nuer, though they have no courts, there is a process of judgment by mediators and ordinary people in which custom and morality as part of the *corpus juris* constitute ' sources of law ' for particular decisions. I do not suggest that the rules are not inconsistent even to contradiction.

The application of this well-established juristic argument to the relations of custom and law, and morality and law, seems to me the soundest framework in which to tackle these problems of primitive law. Other approaches to the relation between

---

[1] Evans-Pritchard, *The Nuer*, at pp. 117–18.

custom, morality, and law, in any meaningful sense of the word 'law', have ended either in confusion or in mystique.[1]

The relation of religion with law can be clarified similarly, by treating religious beliefs and rules and practices as part of the *corpus juris* of a society and as one of the sources on which people draw for a lawful judgment in a particular situation. For the Lozi, law is, in its one widest sense, a body of rules defining the appropriate behaviour of persons in relation to one another. This behaviour should respect those rules which come from God. Appropriate actions include common offerings to the ancestors ; and, as we saw in ' The Case of the Biassed Father ', the omission of such a sacrifice may be material evidence to convict a person of wrongdoing. Similarly the omission of a wedding-ceremony before cohabitation in ' The Case of the Eloping Wife ' determined who was the guilty party. But law itself is for the Lozi, and I make bold to affirm for even simpler societies, a different kind of social phenomenon from religion. Maine stated that ' there is no system of recorded law, literally from China to Peru, which, when it first emerges to notice, is not seen to be entangled with religious ritual and observance '.[2] The examples he cites show only that when some parts of the law were codified in various societies, the codes included religious prescriptions. But, with all respect, the critics of these statements by Maine do not seem to me to clarify the problem, when they factually deny this association in the form he gave it.[3] They rightly criticize Maine's contention, in *Ancient Law*, that ' the severance of law from morality, and of religion from law, [belong] very distinctly to the later stages of mental progress '. In the swing of criticism they tend to deny all association between these social phenomena, and I consider that their arguments become confused. Clarity can be achieved by regarding ' religion ' as one of the sources of law in both its meanings, as a *corpus juris* and as a series of judgments on disputes.

---

[1] See, e.g., Seagle, *The Quest for Law*, pp. 11 ff., on this problem, and the critical discussion in Chapter I of Allen's *Law in the Making*, op. cit., of theories of jurisprudence in this field.

[2] *Early Law and Custom*, London : Murray (1883), pp. 5 ff. See also *Ancient Law*, pp. 14 ff.

[3] See, e.g., Diamond, A. S., *Primitive Law*, London : Watts (1935, 2nd ed., 1950), Chap. XVI, and Seagle, *The Quest for Law*, Chap. X. But both these authorities take ' law ' to mean only rules enforced by courts.

Indeed, though law and religion are different kinds of social fact, I consider that Maine was correct when he affirmed that they are closely associated in early law. This must surely accompany the general lack of differentiation in simple society, and disappear as social life becomes secularized. I have described how a dispute between Lozi kinsmen may provoke ancestral-spirits to inflict punishment : the essence of sacrificing to the same spirits is that one must be in amity with one's fellows. This is true of a modern church congregation, but there is no belief that this amity is liable to be protected by direct misfortune. As society differentiates, so the different departments of social life fall into the hands of special officers. The headman of a Lozi village sits as judge over his followers' quarrels and he makes offerings to God and his ancestors on their behalf : to some extent this is true of the head of a religious family in England, or even the pastor of a modern self-contained community, but it is not true of the vast area of English society. The Lozi kuta is an ecclesiastical chapter as well as a court, cabinet, civil service, and parliament : to some extent this was true of the mediaeval English parliament. But the Lozi have specialized priests and judicial bodies ; and it is to be expected that in societies which have not evolved these officers and councils, law, both as a distinct body of rules and as judgments, will be less clearly separated from general morality, from custom, and from religion. Nevertheless, law as such will be distinguishable by observers, and distinguished by the people, from other types of social fact. The existence of vernacular words for them all offers one crucial test.

The attempt to isolate ' law ' from the rest of the social process is only one of a series of similar problems to which the same general rule can be applied : as society becomes increasingly differentiated, so different social processes will become increasingly distinguished. Let us take for example the long-standing controversy over the distinction between religion and magic. In the totemic ceremonies of the comparatively undifferentiated Australian tribes, there are elements which by commonsense application of our words we may call ' magical ' and ' religious '. Yet the ceremonies as a whole have to be considered magico-religious. But in as politically developed societies as those of most South and Central African Bantu (such as the Lozi), there are priests of the ancestral-cult and there are other persons who attempt to achieve specific ends by means of medicinal substances whose operation cannot be observed. We cannot help but call these ' magicians '.[1] The priests occupy their offices by virtue of their positions in kinship groups ; they perform prescribed actions and utter certain formulae, at set times and places, with certain material objects. The magicians may be hereditary specialists but they work outside their kinship groups ; they perform other actions and utter other formulae, at other times and places, with other material objects. Priests and magicians act largely in different ranges of social relations. Here magic and religion are institutionally distinct, though both may be used and intermingled in certain ceremonies. Their elements, which we detect clearly at this stage, can be traced in less differentiated societies, and it is possible to analyse their relations with one another. So it is with law. In a society as politically advanced as that of the Lozi, we find law clearly exhibited as a body of rules and a set of judgments, and we can examine how custom, morality, and religion form sources of law in both these senses. It is reasonable to assume that a similar analysis can be applied to less developed societies. Clearly these have ' law ' both as a body of rules defining the appropriate behaviour between persons, and as judgments, acceptable to normal members of the society, in which these rules are applied to situations of dispute. The question of sanctions—of how these judgments are enforced —is a different problem, one in the field of what we call politics, rather than in the field of jurisprudence. Law as a *corpus juris* exists without enforcement. No Lozi describing to me the period of political change when Lozi kutas were lax in enforcing their judgments, spoke as if he considered it a period of ' no law '.

I have spoken of morality as constituting a part of Lozi law as a *corpus juris* and as a source of legal rulings in adjudication. I must make clear that I do not therefore mean to assert that law is more comprehensive than morality, and morality a fraction only of law. In this book my universe of discourse is the judicial process : hence my field of analysis is law and I examine how morality enters into it. Had I been writing a book on

---

[1] Junod, H. A., *The Life of a South African Tribe*, London : Macmillan (2nd ed., 1927), ii, pp. 302 and 451-2, who was a missionary and an anthropologist, made this point precisely.

Lozi ethics my universe of discourse would have been morality and I should have examined how law and adjudication entered that field of analysis. Then morality would have been treated as more comprehensive than law, and law as a fraction only of morality. In short, I argue that law is impregnated with morality, as morality is with law : neither can be discussed without reference to the other. But they are distinguishable. In *The Rôle of Courts in Barotse Social Life* I shall discuss this problem again : here one example may make the difference clear.

CASE 57*a* : THE CASE OF THE FORGIVING KINSMAN
(*from a text*)

A man committed adultery with the wife of Mutondo, his classificatory elder brother and head of their kinship grouping. Mutondo was so horrified at the heinous offence that he felt he had to bring suit at the kuta. He divorced his wife who had to pay the fine of one beast to the kuta. The kuta ordered the adulterer to pay four beasts as damages to Mutondo instead of the usual two beasts. Mutondo said he would not profit from his kinsman's wrongdoing, so he gave a beast to each of the two other senior men in the group and had the third beast killed to feast the group in reconciliation. He himself attended the feast but refused to eat of the meat to emphasize that he would not rejoice in his legal victory. He returned the fourth beast to the wrongdoer to show that he forgave him and wished to remain in amity. All these actions of Mutondo's, including his bringing suit, were highly praised to me by local people, including the wrongdoer.

This example may here clarify the relations of law and morality. Moral considerations may impel a man to bring suit and the court to uphold his suit and award him damages on moral as well as legal grounds. Other moral considerations may motivate him to abandon his legal claim or its fruits. Similar principles were canvassed by the judges in ' The Case of the Headman's Fishdams '. Law defines right and reasonable ways of acting : the ways of morality are right and generous.

VIII

I have dealt in previous sections with those constituents of Lozi law (which are therefore sources of legal rulings in adjudication), that are commonly handled in jurisprudence. ' Scientific law ', the regularities of the environment and human behaviour, is less frequently thus regarded. For example, it is not listed among the ' sources of law ' in Sir C. K. Allen's *Law in the Making*. Yet clearly the system of a society's law can only exist within the system of regularities in nature, and the judges take note of these regularities as part of law and draw on them in making legal decisions. Indeed, though I consider these regularities last, they ought perhaps to be considered before social regularities. In Loziland judges have knowledge of these regularities : in England they may have to be proved by evidence, but still, I consider, form a part of law.

Like ourselves, the Lozi describe these environmental and behavioural regularities by the same word, *mulao*, which they use for the social order. They are *milao yaNyambe*, laws of God. The Lozi use these regularities to check evidence and to come to judgment upon it. Thus they may use the regularities of the season, the growth of crops, or the movements of sun and moon to check the passage of time. These may be related to the physiology of human or animal reproduction, as we saw in ' The Case of the Allegedly Pregnant Bride ' (p. 122). Any regularity in the environment may thus become the source of a legal ruling.

Environmental regularities may be referred to human capabilities. For example, I have heard disputes about the distance which a [reasonable] man could cover in a set time, the amount of fish a particular trap could catch, the amount of woodland that should be cleared in a particular period.

These regularities are built into many rules of law. Thus, as stated in ' The Case of the Prince's Gardens ' (pp. 56, 64), a man has normally to reclaim a loaned garden at harvest in order to allow the borrower time to find another garden. This right to claim is estopped in two sets of circumstances. One, if the borrower has fertilized the soil by staking his cattle to drop manure on it, the claim can only be exerted after two more seasons, since it is recognized that the enrichment of manure lasts for this period. Secondly, if the borrower has planted cassava cuttings, he must be allowed time for the roots to grow, usually three seasons. Again, a man should allot gardens and cows to each of his wives to provide her and her children with food. But he would be foolish to allot fish-traps, since while cows and gardens yield with some certainty, fish are ' wild things ' and the catches of different traps vary from day to day. Hence he should take his fish-catch as a whole and divide it among his dependants.

The Lozi also have a science of psychology which they apply in juristic reasoning. This application has been elaborated in the discussion of ' the reasonable man '. For example, it was held against the Violent Councillor that he did not appeal against his first conviction, as would an innocent man. Similarly, when the husband in ' The Case of the Man who Helped His Mothers-in-Law Cross a Ford ' admitted that he had previously paid a pot to his father-in-law to make redress for wronging his wife, one judge said : ' You knew you were wrong and it is shown by the payment of the pot. No-one just pays—it shows you had a fault ' (p. 149). On the other issue for which he had been convicted at Libonda, a judge ruled : ' You slept with your wife's maternal uncle's wife, or you would have appealed ' (p. 149).

I have already analysed how behavioural laws, like those cited above, or the manner of intervening in a fight (' The Case of the Violent Councillor '), apply to people generally. Other laws of this type apply to specific persons—e.g. women as wives or as mistresses and men as husbands or as lovers. Fathers have specific reactions. One judge considered that the Violent Councillor acted as he did because he was enraged when his *crippled* son became involved in the fight, for parents are additionally careful of their weak children. In ' The Case of the Eloping Wife ' all the judges considered that it was impossible that a father would accept the marriage-payment from a man who came to him from a ' marriage-bed ' shared with his daughter. Insight into the paternal psyche showed in SAMBI's aside to me when he had the Eloping Wife handcuffed : ' Wait till he sees his child handcuffed and hears her weeping. Then he will find the money [for her fine]. A father's heart forgives his child anything.' Five years before Sikwela Mwangombe had told me he would disown his daughter Mushiko who, he alleged, had insulted him. I asked him what he would do if she were fined for adultery. He replied : ' I will not pay her fine ; if she cries out as they drag her to prison, I will cover my ears.' He knew he could not resist her cries if he heard them.

Thus the regularities of the Lozi environment and of human

nature, both general and specific, are laws that form a source for legal rulings by the judges.

IX

I have summarily examined the sources of Lozi law and can now consider how judges draw on these sources to give a decision in particular disputes. The Lozi judicial process involves argument which is largely conscious and explicit, for it proceeds in public by an acknowledged logic, even if the judges are influenced by subconscious cultural and personal factors. It is to this conscious and explicit process of analytic argument (*kupihana, kukanana*) that the judges refer when they tell litigants : ' The kuta proceeds by asking the man and woman questions ' . . . ' We follow *lisupo* (indications or probabilities) ' . . . ' We decide by evidence (*bupaki*) and reasons (*libaka*) '.

Clearly in many cases, after the hearing has proceeded a while, the judges come to a decision on the law or the merits of the case, and then try to arrange their arguments to defend this decision. This tendency is patent in the Lozi judicial process because the main part of cross-examination is conducted by the judges and not by counsel for each of the litigants. Each litigant states his own case, and in doing so presents his view of how the law justifies him, or he tries to present his actions so that they appear reasonable and legally valid. When the judges cross-examine they generally do so impartially, measuring the behaviour of all the parties against reasonable and upright standards. Therefore their questioning soon indicates the lines on which they are formulating the merits of the case, and may indeed give the false impression that they consider a man guilty till he proves that he is innocent. Often even at this stage the arguments by which they will justify their decisions are implicitly present. The absence of lawyers to represent the litigants and to prepare their cases leads to overt interweaving of three distinct stages of the judicial process : the investigatory analysis of the evidence presented, the taking of a decision on the evidence, and the exposition of the law to defend that decision.

The Lozi themselves explicitly recognize these three stages of adjudication, as enquiry (*kubuza*), decision (*katulo*), and exposition (*kubulela mulao*—to speak the law). They estimate the skill of different judges in one or more of these judicial tasks and consider that the really great judge excels in all three. He is *muatuli yabutali kasibili*—a judge who is truly wise. Lozi have words and syntactical devices to enable them to pursue lines of investigation and produce connected arguments, and a fairly elaborate vocabulary to define and evaluate processes of analysis at each stage. Admittedly none of the three stages of analysis is entirely logical, in the sense that it can be broken up into a series of connected syllogisms. Judges have to fit particular circumstances into legal propositions, and they do so by a largely intuitive process. Nevertheless there is a definite logic which controls the whole process of trial.

The logic that is present in Lozi judgments should be apparent from the judgments I have quoted. I shall here make this logic explicit, because it is unfortunately still necessary to demonstrate that Africans and other non-European peoples use processes of inductive and deductive reasoning which are in essence similar to those of the West, even if the premisses be different.[1]

The first stage of the process occurs after the parties have stated their case (*kubilaela, kubulela litaba*) and explained (*kutaluseza*) their actions. Witnesses give evidence (*kupaka*). The judges begin to sort the medley of evidence, which in different cases covers a great variety of social relations and fickleness of motivation, to arrive at the truth and to fit events into legal principles which contain value-judgments. To make this attack they question on the basis of a series of presumptions about the feelings and actions of upright men and malefactors. Using these presumptions they query the evidence : ' What (*king'i*) did you do ? ' . . . ' Why (*kalabakalang'i*) did you do that ? ' ' If (*haiba*) this were true, then (*cwelahe*) . . .' and so on. It may seem unnecessary for me to indicate that the Lozi have these

---

[1] This misconception prevails for obvious social reasons, and in intellectual circles Lévy-Bruhl's brilliant analysis of primitive mentality has been misinterpreted to support it. The view that African judicial and political argument is not logical was stated by Mr. R. T. Paget, K.C., M.P., in a letter to *The Observer* (8th July, 1951) in which he said of the Tswana *kgotla* : ' Thought in tribal society is governed not by logic but by fetish. To the Tribe, trial by fetish is just and trial by reason is unjust. . . . It is futile to seek a reason in tribal justice, as it is not rational.' This is contradicted by the whole of Schapera's *Handbook of Tswana Law and Custom*.

U

simple words : I have stated above why I set them out. By thus testing the evidence the judges establish what they call *lisupo*, a noun from the verb *kusupa*—' to point '—hence ' indications ' or ' probabilities '. They test these by the credibility of unrelated and related witnesses who corroborate or dispute the parties' versions, and they weigh (*kulikanyisa*) the evidence by cogency. Here explicit logic is not in full control, for the presumptions which dominate the process are not always stated.

Since the cross-examination is carried out by the judges, this very process involves preliminary statements of the legal rules that will be applied. The process takes a particular form in disputes between kinsmen, because the judges have patiently to disentangle the complexities of their relations over many years before peace can be established among them. The Lozi words for reconciling, *tatulo*, and being reconciled, *tatuluhelo*, are nouns explicitly derived from the verb *kutatuluha*, which means ' to get untwisted ' and ' to regain control of one's temper '. These words thus describe not only how the judges disentangle what people overtly did, but also how the judges probe into their motives and measure these against the motives of upright people. The judges begin to state norms which are legal rules, into which extrinsic circumstances have to be fitted. Indeed, it is because almost all litigants themselves work with these norms that the judges are able to push their questions and demonstrate to the litigants that they fail on their own evidence. Judges and litigants share the same presumptions about what is upright behaviour for a particular social position. This enables them to meet in argument.

The situation is simpler in cases of offences between strangers, though here too shared presumptions operate to control investigation. A simple example is the way convictions for adultery rest on the presumption that no man can have platonic relations of acquaintanceship, let alone friendship, with an unrelated woman. This presumption is so strong that ' adultery ' in Lozi law almost amounts constructively to behaving familiarly with an unrelated woman. Men have been convicted for talking with others' wives. Once when I was walking from Mongu to Lialui, a man asked if he could walk with me, since there was a strange woman on the path and he feared to be accused of adultery with her. When I told this to my people, Musole said : ' If you see a woman on your path, hide and let her get ahead, then you are safe from a charge of adultery.' 'The Case of the Schoolboy Adulterer' (p. 130) shows how if a man behaves thus, some judges induce the probability that he has also had sexual relations with her ; and the case where a man sat in a hut with his sister (p. 154), like 'The Case of the Man who Helped his Mothers-in-Law Cross a Ford' (p. 148), shows that a similar presumption guides convictions for 'incest' (*sindoye*). But these presumptions are rebuttable. Some judges acquitted the School-boy Adulterer because 'the evidence [was] not strong'. One judge explicitly rejected the evidence of the schoolboy's repre-hensible behaviour in visiting the woman because he produced a contrary presumption that a girl is taught, if she is trapped in adultery with an unknown man, to protect her lover by making false charges against another. This presumption that any familiar behaviour with a woman indicates that a man is her lover is fed by cases, of which I recorded several examples, where men solicited women on first meeting, and these agreed to adultery.

Metaphors indicate graphically how the Lozi conceive of this investigatory stage of the judicial process, in which they analyse and weigh evidence by credibility, verification, corroboration, and cogency. They have the same metaphor as we have to describe the complex process of analysing evidence to arrive at conclusions of this kind—the sifting of evidence. *Kuseseta* is to sift or winnow grain, and also to find the truth in a complicated matter. *Kuzuma*, to hunt, also describes this process. They weigh (*kulikanyisa*) particular pieces of evidence against each other. Again—as with ourselves—the process of apprehending the crux of a case is to seize, or catch, *kuswala*, which is used for arresting a person, seizing something in the hands, or catching something in a trap. *Kuteya*, to trap, itself describes the way in which judges entangle witnesses and get the truth from them (see p. 112). Cross-examination is also implicitly compared with making a journey through the windings of a river, so that *kufweka*, to land, is to press a line of questions to its conclusion. Thus when KALONGA (R15) rebuked INYUNDWANA for changing his attack in cross-examination of the parties in 'The Case of the Biassed Father', he said : 'Hausikafweka', 'You have not landed', though I translated this as 'you have not finished'.

If the conclusion is reached with crushing definiteness, as where the Violent Councillor was crushed by the question why no-one heard him shout if he did shout as he came with a whip, it is *kuwiseza taba falikamba*, ' to throw the affair down at the landing-place '. The series of questions which led to this damning conclusion are *kukalanga*, which describes the digging out of roots to make fishing-nets, and also clever investigation to find out the truth in a roundabout way.

These metaphors, which exist in English or are at least intelligible in English, denote that the Lozi have a very clear conception of logic in the examination of evidence. They are intended to demonstrate this only, and it must not be thought that the Lozi describe this logic only in these material terms. There are also specific, and therefore abstract, terms to cover the process. Some of these terms, like the metaphors, contain judgments on skill, and judgments of skill are added to others by the use of adverbs or applied forms of the verbs. *Kupaka*, to give evidence, in the form *kupakisisa* means to give strong evidence. Similarly *kubuza*, to ask or enquire, as *kubuzisisa*, is to press questions skilfully or to enquire carefully. *Kuutwa*, to hear or understand, as *kuutwisisa* is to understand very well or to be very sharp and as *kuutwahala* is to be reasonable or obvious. Another word to describe the process of enquiry is *kunuhela*, from the root *kunuha*, which means to smell and is one of the two common words for ' to divine by magical means '. *Kunuhela* means the preliminary beginnings of enquiry, when judges are seeking to penetrate the evidence, while *kunuha* also means to guess. These varied meanings of the word indicate the common Lozi assumption that the evidence of divination is more suspect than the judges' assessment of objective evidence.

The second stage of the judicial process, coming to a decision, is also metaphorically described. The Lozi, following the idea of hunting or fishing with a spear, say a good judge is one who can *nepa*, ' shoot straight ' (cf. our ' hit home ') by seeing the truth (*niti*) and right (*tukelo*) of an affair, as against a bad judge, who will *shuta*, ' miss the target '. The judge who hits home does so according to law and justice, and owing to the wide generality of Lozi legal principles he can usually manage to meet both demands in cases arising from multiplex relationships. In cases of contract this is not always possible (see ' The Case of the Father and his Son's Cattle', p. 109). Lozi recognize that in this process there is an element of inspiration, expressed in their comparison of the king or judge with 'a sharp knife' (*tipa yebuhali*) 'which cuts the matter' (*kukaula*). I have described judges thus coming suddenly to the crux of the matter. In 'The Case of the Biassed Father' AWAMI (L7) asked the father : 'Do you want your sons (= nephews) back?' In 'The Case of the Headman's Fishdams' the inspiration came on SOLAMI (R3) when Mahalihali, the headman, protested that he wanted the dams and would not accept the kuta's admonishments. Unfortunately I missed this part of SOLAMI's judgment, but it is possible that Mahalihali's intransigence against SOLAMI spurred him to the threat to discharge Mahalihali from the headmanship. More often, of course, the right decision on the merits of the case is obvious, and this kind of brilliant inspiration is not evoked.

Again, the Lozi have specific words to describe this process of coming to a decision. *Kusinganyeka* is to ponder over a matter in seeking to find a solution while *kuatula*, to judge, is to come to the decision. Metaphorically *kukwenuha*, to change one's course of action or turn back in a path, is to change one's opinion in the light of the evidence or previous judgments ; while *kusokela* (from *kusoka*, to stir porridge) is the active process of trying to change the course of a lawsuit.

The judges thus move to the final stage of adjudication—the exposition of their verdict and the reasons for it. Here the whole judicial process is sharper and surer ; litigants who interrupt are silenced : 'Be silent : your lord is judging.' The facts have been determined and the law is being stated. This is how the Lozi consider that judges work. They describe judges as carefully surveying the evidence which has been led, sifting (*kuseseta*) and weighing (*kulikanyisa*) it, and then stating how the law covers it. Obviously only certain judicial decisions take this form : and even when the actual judgment is thus presented, it may alter the order of judicial ratiocination. And even a judgment of this kind includes the application of presumptions and probabilities which evade logical determination. This is clear from SOLAMI's (R3) conviction of the Foreign Thief (p. 109). SOLAMI recited four separate suspicious circumstances—a process of argument the Lozi call *kutatamanisa*, to put matters in right succession, or *kunjonjaula*, to explain a matter point by point—which together constituted an unanswerable case. Nevertheless these remained probabilities, and he specifically said that they lacked only an eye-witness.

A second form of judgment consists in first stating the law, and then seeing how it applies to the facts. This is necessary in cases where the relevant laws are uncertain, or where there is a gap in the law, as in ' The Case of the Barren Widow ' (p. 174). Judges also follow this procedure where they have to give judgments by the letter of the law, against equity. All the judgments in favour of the headman in ' The Case of the Headman's Fishdams ' took this form. The dams were the headman's : *but* let him exercise his rights generously.

Most judgments, especially in cases between kinsmen, seem to show that a judge decides on the merits of the case and then works out a legal argument to defend his decision. This procedure emerges from all the judgments against the headman in ' The Case of the Headman's Fishdams ', since here the merits of the case lay against the letter of the law. The judges emphasized that the headman was in the wrong, his sisters and nephews in the right, hence the law would not support his attempt to expel them from the dams.

In whichever of these forms, or whatever combination of these forms, a judge may expound his judgment, he endeavours to cast it in the form of a reasoned logical argument. This is the technical craft of the judge. There are important syntactical devices to achieve this, including grammatical means for denoting differences of time and place, etc. There is a range of prepositions. The various derived forms of simple verbs, which are so marked a feature of Bantu, are important here. These express direction to, from, and in ; action in the interest of ; causation ; augmentation and diminution and intensification ; etc. This is not the place to summarize Lozi grammar : clearly it contributes to logical reasoning. I can perhaps make my point most simply by citing some of the appropriate conjunctions which judges have to connect their propositions :

and (*ni*) ; but (*kono*) ; as, like (*sina*) ; therefore (*kalabakaleyo*) ; because (*kakuli*) ; instead of (*sibakeng'i*) ; on account of (*nta*) ; while (*kanti*) ; whereas (*inteng'i*) ; if (*haiba*) ; then (*cwelahe*).

There are in Lozi many words to describe different modes of

expounding arguments, judicial and other. Many of them imply approval or disapproval of skill. Some of the approving terms are :

kutalungusha—to be able to classify affairs ;
kunyanyama—to be clever and of prompt decision ;
sishongololi—a judge who relates matters lengthily and correctly ;
muswanikisi—a judge who has good reasoning power and is able to ask searching questions.

Other words scorn poor reasoning :

kuyungula—to speak on matters without coming to the point ;
kunjongoloka—to wander away from the subject when speaking ;
kubulela siweko—to talk without understanding ;
muyauluki—a judge who speaks without touching on the important points at issue ;
siswasiwa—a person who gets entangled in words ;
siyambutuki—a talker at random.

There are many other words of this kind, as well as common words for wisdom and stupidity, for sage and fool, and so on. The Lozi constantly use these to evaluate the skill of judges in investigating facts and in composing logical judgments. I have heard these evaluations applied to various judgments and judges : they witness that the logic of the judicial process is publicly recognized and striven for.

X

Thus in cross-examination on the evidence, in extraction of the points in dispute, and in decision on the legal issues, the judges move by logic within a system of customary usage and social presumptions. The process is simply illustrated in ' The Case of the Cross-Cousin Adultery ' from which I extract the implicit presumptions and logical steps in NAWALA's (R42) judgment (p. 135) :

Accused asserts plaintiff's wife is his cross-cousin to whom he made gifts because of this kinship, and says she is ' his sister ' with whom he could not have intercourse. But he gave the gifts to her privately and not in public. Reasonable and upright men should give even their kinswomen gifts in public lest they be suspected of sexual designs, and if the woman is married should do so in the presence of her husband, or inform the husband. Hence it is probable that he gave her the gifts in private to seduce her or because he was her lover. Furthermore, though she is 'his sister' by Lozi reckoning, he is a Mbunda ; and Mbunda marry cross-cousins and indeed favour cross-cousin marriage. Mbunda have joking relations with cross-cousins. If she is potentially his wife he can fornicate with her. The defence that he made presents to her because she was his kinswoman would have been valid had he made the gifts in her husband's presence. Indeed, in view of their potential sexual relationship a reasonable man would have taken especial care to do so. He did not, and therefore he surely regarded her as a mistress.

NAWALA did not quote precedents in giving this decision ; but it was in subsequent discussion with the accused and me that he cited the case I have recorded as the ' The Case of the Incestuous Action ' (p. 154), in which a man was fined by his kin for sitting with his sister in a closed hut.

I have tried to make explicit, in the form of a full logical statement, the process of reasoning from premises of evidence and social presumptions which clearly were compressed in NAWALA's brief statement (p. 135) :

' For were you a Lozi, she would be your sister indeed, though even a Lozi makes gifts to his sister in public. But we know you Mbunda do not call the daughter of your mother's brother ' my sister ', and you can marry her. If you can marry her, you can commit adultery with her. If you were making presents to her because she is your relative, you should have given the things through her husband. Then he would have thanked you, for you would have been giving them to him. But you gave them on the side : you gave to her as your mistress.'

Similarly, SOLAMI (R3) did not explain explicitly to the Foreign Thief (p. 109) that a reasonable man with money would have paid his carriers immediately he arrived at his destination and not later, and would have bought relish there and not elsewhere. The accused had not done so and hence must have got his money in the interim. An honest man in these circumstances again would have been able to produce evidence of where he got this money, especially as it was newly minted.

A judgment in this type of case is often highly compressed, and the steps by which evidence is accepted, formulated in legal concepts, and used in judgment, are not always logically expounded. Here judgments are assessing behaviour as right-doing and wrongdoing, and the judges particularly do not always expound the processes by which they make the assessment against the standards of how the reasonable man (*mutu yangana*) and upright man (*mutu yalukile*) would have behaved. There are a variety of social presumptions about customary usages implicit in these standards, which attach to specific positions ; and since the presumptions are well known the judges tend to take them for granted. The contrasts are made most strongly when the judges quote the exemplary behaviour of themselves or others in analogous situations.

Logic enters into judgment in a different manner when the judges determine on which set of legal rules they will draw to settle the dispute under trial. Here they progress by a series of steps which may be summed up as follows. First, they fix the social positions of the litigants : whether it be a case between kinsmen, or between injured and wrongdoer in delict, or between say buyer and seller in contract. Thus the judges in ' The Case of the Headman's Fishdams ' (p. 179) were first concerned to settle the history of the title Mahalihali, and the positions of the incumbent's two sisters—the one living in marriage with her sons, the other and her son with her mother's people. This enabled them to consider the rights and duties which inhere in these social positions ; that is, the legal rules which applied to the dispute. Against these rules, covering both rights to land and the privileges and obligatory actions residing in the positions, they assessed the good and ill deeds of the parties. Here they entered into motivations, defined by reasonable and upright standards, of guilt and innocence, respectfulness and generosity, etc. The determining of the rights and duties involved a process of selection, in this case, of applicable laws which to some extent were in conflict, and the final determination was guided by considerations of equity. This case illustrates that in Lozi law the judges have some choice in selecting the rules they will apply to a particular dispute. These rules are not always dependent upon one another even when they are consistent. The judges' choice is guided by different kinds of consideration.

Complicated logical arguments are rarely made in this selection. The society is uncomplicated and its materials are simple, so that the relevant legal principles are also simple and of wide generality or flexibility.   The absence of written records eases the forensic task.   Juristic logic is mainly concerned to define how extrinsic circumstance fits into particular legal concepts—to specify the concepts—as in the debate whether either party in ' The Case of the Prince's Gardens' had committed *muliu* (pp. 57 f.).   I recorded few cases in which the judges argued about what the law was. Nevertheless even the simplest decision involves the relation of actual circumstance to the rights and obligations inherent in particular social positions, and therefore the logical selection of relevant laws.   This is exhibited in the rules that give statutes priority over customary law, and firm customary law priority over equity.

XI

The types of argument employed emerge more clearly where legal principles conflict, as in ' The Case of the Headman's Fishdams' (p. 178), or are uncertain, as in ' The Case of the Barren Widow' (p. 174).   Judicial logic shows most sharply in unprecedented suits.   Here the Lozi say that their judges should produce a decision (*katulo*) which fits in (*yelikana*) with the law (*mulao*).

Unfortunately I myself recorded very few cases in which judges were confronted with this type of problem.   Frequently they had to apply established law in new circumstances, but really unprecedented grounds of action were rare.   The most striking example of a case falling in a gap in the law was that of the Barren Widow.   The claim was for return of the second beast given for a virgin whose husband had died, and it was not covered by Yeta's 1917 Marriage Laws (see above, p. 210).   Most of the judges argued by analogy.[1]   Some supported the plaintiff's argument that the dissolution of marriage by death of a spouse was analogous with dissolution of marriage by divorce, provided for in the 1917 laws, and should have the same legal consequences.   Others argued that the situation created was analogous with that in which King Lewanika ruled that his courts should no longer enforce claims for payment by the kin of a deceased spouse against the survivor.   I may note here for

[1] Cf. Cardozo's analysis of the development of law by judges ' along the line of logical progression . . . the rule of analogy or the method of philosophy '—*Nature of the Judicial Process*, pp. 30 ff.

later reference that King Yeta and yet other judges started from a quite different principle of public morality. In 'The Case of the Headman's Fishdams', also defined as unprecedented, NAMAMBA (at p. 182) argued that one sister's fishdam was like a cow driven with her to her marriage to provide food.

The Lozi explicitly recognize reasoning by analogy as one important judicial method, both in cases which are common and in unprecedented suits. They argue : ' *taba ye iswana ni isili* ' ('this case resembles another'). They call this method the telling of *liswaniso* or *lipapanyo* (comparisons, analogies, parables). *Liswaniso* is a noun derived from the causative form of the verb *kuswana* : hence it means ' things which are made to be alike '. They use it to describe photographs. Their conception of ' analogies ' emerges more clearly from the use of *lipapanyo*. This noun is derived from the verbal root *kufapana*, to quarrel, to be at variance, or to differ in opinion. Hence *papanyo* (singular) also means ' causing discord '. *Fapano*, from the same verbal root, means ' a dispute ' and a ' division ' or ' distinction '. These several meanings exhibit the Lozi's clear appreciation that argument by analogy proceeds by similarity despite distinction, and that there is false analogy (*papanyo yesasikaluka*).

Analogical argument is also used to expound existent law. For example, when the Prudish Wife (pp. 145-7) complained that her husband took from her blankets and sheets and then used them with a new wife, the husband protested, with political and blood-kinship analogies, that ' the senior wife is a man's chief, she is his mother, from whom he can beg things '. One judge took up the political analogy : ' The senior wife is the NGAMBELA [the chief councillor who is the general assistant of the king in all affairs], and the junior wife is a *sikombwa* [a steward who looks after some of the king's personal affairs]. A husband can get blankets from his senior wife, since he must keep his *solume* [the husband's undistributed possessions] with her.'

Lozi judges also to some extent develop logically the implications of a legal rule to see how it covers various situations. ' The Case of the Prince's Gardens ' illustrates how they examine ' the intrinsic meaning ' of the *muliu* law to hold that it does not prevent the reclamation of borrowed gardens ; and in a case at Nalolo (and, *quaere*, ' The Case of the Returning Garden-Claimant' at Lialui, pp. 53-4) it has been held that *muliu* does not bar suits for land between members of the same kinship group who claim under the same ancestral title. However this example of forensic logic illustrates more aptly the specification of a legal concept in reference to extrinsic circumstances, and not the development of a legal rule's implications to cover a new situation. I cannot find in my records any clear example of this type of argument. Obviously the absence of written precedents and of textbooks of law, with the absence of professional lawyers using writing as a tool, limits judicial logic in this respect. If precedents are not recorded and they are not surveyed in a particular case, their rulings cannot develop to accumulate along a certain line until the legal rule is changed. Changes occur by abrupter reinterpretations of principle.

I have discussed above the manner in which this illiterate situation operates to exclude problems of distinguishing precedents. Hence the law may remain certain and consistent despite aberrant judgments, and judges need not exercise logical skill to evade these. Selective memory concentrates on the principles, the *rationes decidendi*, with their moral implications. Principles do not become loaded with a burden of refining precedents, and they require application only in terms of current social presumptions. No-one compares and contrasts a series of decisions on one point to see if they are consistent in deciding it, or a series of decisions to see if the principles involved on different points are consistent with one another.

Indeed, in cases involving kinsmen there seems to be considerable inconsistency. The decisions of all judges in 'The Case of the Biassed Father' (p. 41), and of most judges in 'The Case of the Headman's Fishdams' (p. 180), seem in radical conflict. In 'The Case of the Headman's Fishdams' judges distinguished between the two sisters on various adventitious grounds. IMANDI (with a few others) insisted : 'I do not separate the two women. I cannot see how you divide the cases, I fail to.' But this inconsistency in judgments in individual disputes, where there is concentration on the moral issues, does not alter the substantive body of law and legal principles. Their application varies : they remain unchanged. The Lozi therefore believe that their law is consistent within itself, and that judges should maintain this consistency. For example, they insist that no woman can be placed in a position where she must regard a kinswoman as a co-wife : the rules applying to these relations are in consistent divergence (see the Cases of ' the Man who Helped his Mothers-in-Law Cross a Ford ', p. 148, and ' the Prudish Wife ', p. 145). In political debate they refer to consistency as an ideal ; and the use of analogy in judicial argument demonstrates this wish.

In practice there are major consistencies and only minor contradictions in the various parts of Lozi law, and there is a fair degree of consistency between these parts. I shall try to show this in my book on *The Ideas of Barotse Jurisprudence*. However, Lozi law is not exceptional in exhibiting lack of logical consistence in all its parts. Lord Halsbury said of English law : ' A case is only an authority for what it actually decides. I entirely deny that it can be quoted for a proposition that may seem logically to follow from it. Such a mode of reasoning assumes that the law is necessarily a logical code, whereas every lawyer must acknowledge that the law is not logical at all '.[1] Inevitably this applies more strongly to Lozi law, which is never surveyed as a whole, though it does not control such varied actions as modern law. Its rules are discussed and applied separately with reference to distinct social relations, which have their own incidents and rules. A large part of the flexibility of Lozi law, and the judges' consequent ability to achieve justice, are thus accounted for. The law as a whole embraces many independent rules. In different cases different rules can be selected for enforcement (cf. the Cases of ' the Biassed Father ' and of ' the Headman's Fishdams '). Certain general principles only are manifested in all.

XII

Judicial logic is exercised on disputes arising out of particular patterns of relationship, which have their established rights and duties. The judges' arguments therefore proceed in a social framework. Every case involves some statement of patterns which have their historical validation, and their set of customary usages. Judges in deciding cases in new situations

---

[1] Quinn *v.* Leathem, 1901, A.C. 495, 506, as quoted by Cardozo, *Nature of the Judicial Process*, op. cit., p. 32.

may maintain or develop the law in accordance with these patterns.[1]

Though the history and traditions of Lozi law are not adequately recorded, they are firmly embedded in living relationships. The Lozi themselves consider that they can justify many of their institutions and customs by standards of natural justice. But they always explain the nature of their society by its history. They define and defend almost every institution and legal rule with myths and legends. Some tales explain how the royal family came into existence from God Nyambe and His daughter Mbuyamwambwa, and how Lozi chieftainship was created when a neighbouring tribe offered part of a fish catch to the eldest son of Mbuyamwambwa. Other myths and legends explain for them the division of their kingdom under northern and southern capitals, how they acquired symbols of kingship, how the seating and titles of their councils were built up, how the royal family distributed land among the people. Yet other myths and legends expound how kinship relationships developed. I have elsewhere[2] outlined the extent to which 'history' of all kinds is a social charter for Lozi society. In this book I have described how Lozi judges argue that they are working with an historically established system of law contained in just and proper institutions. Thus they accept the whole organization of government, the existence of villages, the kinship system—and British overlordship under their Treaty. Therefore they cite historical arguments to support their statements of what the law is (e.g. the prohibition on a man's watching a woman crossing a ford, p. 184), and to justify the existence of particular rights (e.g. in 'The Case of the Prince's Gardens', p. 58–9). When they legislate to meet new problems they may attempt to revive old customs, or they may reassert old privileges (e.g. reclaiming the king's rights to half of all hippo hides).

Lozi judges employ history in their judgments mainly in two

---

[1] Cf. Cardozo's analysis of judges' developing the law to fill its gaps along 'the line of historical development . . . the method of evolution'; and 'the line of the customs of the community . . . the method of tradition': *Nature of the Judicial Process*, pp. 30–1 and 127 ff.

[2] In 'The Lozi of Barotseland in North-Western Rhodesia', *Seven Tribes of British Central Africa*, passim; and see Jalla, *Litaba za Sicaba sa Malozi*, passim.

spheres. First, they use it to expound the power and the rights of kingship, and the authority vested in its officers. Thus in 'The Case of the Prince's Gardens', MUKULWAKASHIKO (R4, at p. 59) emphasized the impartial and enduring authority of the *kuta*. He spoke not as an individual, for he had not been born in his *kuta* title though it had been held by his father : 'It belongs to Loziland, it originated long long ago. It must give good living to the country.' Statements of this kind are recited whenever Lozi governmental institutions and powers are being emphasized, let alone questioned. Similar arguments are advanced in disputes involving the king's or the royal family's or the *kuta*'s rights.

Secondly, as was markedly exhibited in the same case, history is called upon to validate the distribution and holding of land. MUKULWAKASHIKO (and other judges) described how and why they passed the *muliu* law. He stated : 'The land is divided by law (*kamulao*). The *muliu* law says, who cultivated the land ?' For the present distribution of land, and the laws which control holdings of land, can only be understood in historical terms, going back theoretically to allotments of land by the first kings, and then passing to subsequent alterations in those allotments. Each village's land, again theoretically, has been part of the village since its first establishment. This is clear in Prince Mboo Sipopa's judgment in ' The Case of the Prince's Gardens ' :

Mutome [defendant], the soil is [the prince] Mubukwanu's, not this Mubukwanu, but the old Mubukwanu of long ago. Liwalela was given land because of his hunting ; and this was in the time of King Ngalama [4th king]. It was land of Ngeela village. As for *muliu*, there is no fault, because you borrowed the garden from these princes. So I do not see that there is *muliu*. The garden falls to them, not to Liwalela's name. But I do not see *muliu* because all people borrow gardens. It is we, the royal family, who loan gardens. The borrower then claims the garden, and that is not *muliu*. I asked one witness how many gardens Liwalela had, and all heard the answer. The garden belongs to Ngeela village, and the big depression is the boundary, since I do not believe a small depression would be the boundary between two villages' gardens. That of Mubukwanu is Ngeela village, of yours is Kabende village. You merely dispute later rights, you do not claim ancestral land, so I do not see *muliu*. If you had said the garden had always belonged to the name Liwalela it would have been *muliu*. Tomorrow the gardens of Kabende village will be seen to be those of a prince.

This judgment incidentally shows clearly how a judge 'interprets' a statutory concept, *muliu*, by specifying it in reference to particular extrinsic circumstances. My present interest in the judgment is its exposition of historical developments in legal relations. This history is packed with implication. King Ngalama's gift of land to Liwalela is one example of regal gifts which produced an overall distribution of land from the king to princes and princesses and queens who gave further gifts and loans to commoners, and from the king directly to village headmen. Land-holding has been fixed in relation to headmen's titles : I repeat that even the equitable judgments in ' The Case of the Headman's Fishdams ' left the rights of the title Mahalihali untouched (p. 189).

In another context (p. 212) I quoted a different kind of historical association between social position and land. Different tribes have lived in different habitats and have developed different skills. Lozi formerly cultivated only in the Plain and residence in the Plain is still one of the principal marks of their tribal identity. Hence, I was told, King Lewanika (1884–1916) was sceptical of a Lozi's suit for land on the margin of the Plain.

Any land dispute may provoke this entry into historical affiliations. In ' The Case of the Headman's Fishdams ' (p. 189), the disputing headman's uncle Sabangwa, whom the kuta had allowed to build outside the village to prevent bloodshed because of old Mahalihali's violent temper, was reminded that by rights he should live in the village. The kuta used its power over settlement on the land to order his return. The temporary emergency which forced the councillors to split the village had passed and they could reassert the rule that villages and their land should not be divided.

This case also exhibits the development of the historically validated laws of land-holding to meet an unprecedented suit, though the judgments were couched in terms of equity. The basic laws state that the land is the king's but he must distribute it to all his subjects. Every subject has the right to some land. Developments in Loziland have emphasized this right and the

kuta would not allow Mahalihali to act contrary to these developments. At the time it made this judicial decision, the kuta was
debating legislation to allow the king to expropriate unused and
resting land, and land whose drainage channels had been neglected,
for distribution to those short of land.

In my analysis of Lozi substantive law [1] I shall suggest that
the historical validation of the laws of kingship and of land-
holding, and the judicial insistence on maintaining these laws,
are related to the rôle of these institutions in serving as an enduring
structural framework through all the developments of Lozi
society. Here the judges are markedly conservative in maintaining established law.

Decisions in other spheres of law, and legislation, show that
this conservatism is not a general attribute of Lozi judges. I
have cited above instances of judges almost casually departing
from important rules (liability of kin for each other's debts, the
nature of a father's rights in his son's own property). The
judgments were partially inspired by current moral ideas : but
they were also influenced by historical factors quoted explicitly
by the judges. These are factors produced by British overlordship and the absorption of Loziland in world polity and economy.
In modern conditions men have begun by their own efforts,
independently of their fathers' material help, to acquire property.
Hence a father's rights in his son's property change. Similarly
a man can be expected to pay his own debts and not to rely on
his kin's help, so that his kin become absolved of responsibility
for these debts. Judicial interpretation of historical developments
may guide decisions and create new law.

It is to some extent irrelevant that when history is thus employed by the judges they are working with an unwritten
tradition which may well be wrong or inadequate ; and that
the judges could give false historical support to the enforcement
of quite new rules. It is also irrelevant that the process of social
amnesia may be rapid. In ' The Case of the Prince's Gardens '
the judges described their enactment of the *muliu* law as if they
of their own accord had concluded that suits for land under
century-old ancestral titles, dating to before the Kololo invasion
in 1836, were disturbing the whole land-holding pattern.

---

[1] Chapter on ' Land-Tenure ' in *The Ideas of Barotse Jurisprudence*.

No-one mentioned then—nor did any councillor when I discussed the matter with the kuta—that the British Government had stimulated the passing of the statute. Archival material [1] shows that a land-case in which a man reclaimed his ancestral land under King Lewanika's *kuliulula* (redemption) statute of the 1880's, came to the notice of Government. Government requested King Yeta to repeal the statute since its enforcement so many years after its promulgation must inevitably lead to injustice. The Lozi went further and attached a penalty to any claim based on a title before 1928. This example illustrates that there must be a falsification of history, partly because of selective shortness of memory, and partly because of current reinterpretation of what is remembered. Nevertheless the judges must be correct in arguing that the course of history has produced the present alignments of Lozi society, though they themselves largely extract that history from these alignments. Both as legislators and as judges they tend to take decisions in accordance with the alignments. Statutory and judicial law develop along the lines of current relationships and customs.

For example, Lozi marriage has always been marked by a high degree of jural instability. Men and women used to divorce freely. In 1917 the kuta assumed power to grant women divorces, and allowed men to retain the power to divorce of their own will. The kuta was then faced with the problem of deciding whether a woman was entitled to a divorce if her husband had been away in White country for several years. It ruled that she was so entitled after seven years, and it has steadily reduced that period, first to five years, then to three years, and then to two years. This legislation was partly intended to put pressure on men to return home ; but it also embodied Lozi laws which can compel a man to render his wife conjugal rights and other services under pain of divorce. I have cited a judicial decision that even where the husband had regularly sent goods to his wife, the woman should be divorced because ' she did not marry a blanket' (p. 141). The Lozi approach to this problem contrasts with that of the Southern Bantu among whom divorce was rare and difficult, since marriage was legally directed to provide

---

[1] Information given me by Mr. J. Gordon Read, formerly Provincial Commissioner of Barotse Province.

children for the husband's group.[1] For example, among the
Tswana the law stands thus :

> . . . the wife's adultery is in certain circumstances considered justi-
> fiable, even if her husband objects. If, e.g., he unreasonably refuses
> to cohabit with her, or is impotent, she is free to bear a child by any
> man she pleases. Should her husband then take action, the court
> will often fail to give him satisfaction. More recently, too, adultery
> on the part of the women seems to have considerably increased owing
> to the prolonged absences of their husbands at work in the towns.
> Many a man has come back to find that his wife has during his absence
> given birth to one or more children of whom he is not the father.
> Legally the children are his, and often he may take no action in the
> matter, recognizing that he is to blame for having stayed away so
> long : while in the few cases where he has brought a charge of
> adultery against his wife and her paramour, the court has generally
> upheld them and blamed him. It is held that the wife's procreative
> power should not be allowed to remain dormant, and if her husband
> stays away too long to enable her to bear children as regularly as she
> should, she is justified in cohabiting with other men for this purpose.[2]

The Tswana thus consider these circumstances—refusal to cohabit,
impotence and prolonged absence of the husband—as justifica-
tions for adultery by the wife. The Lozi in all these circumstances allow the wife to claim a divorce.

Judicial logic thus operates within a social and cultural milieu,
and to a large extent applies and develops the law along historical
and customary lines. But since custom is not consulted in
written records, many customs are those, if not of today, at most
of yesterday. Therefore customs still have creative energy for
Lozi law. They possess this energy in two ways. Cardozo
concluded of Anglo-American law that

> undoubtedly the creative energy of custom in the development of
> common law is less today than it was in bygone times . . . It is,
> however, not so much in the making of new rules as in the application
> of old ones that the creative energy of custom most often manifests
> itself today. General standards of right and duty are established.

---

[1] For a full analysis of these contrasting marriage complexes see my ' Kinship
and Marriage among the Lozi of Northern Rhodesia and the Zulu of Natal ',
African Systems of Kinship and Marriage.
[2] Schapera, *Handbook of Tswana Law and Custom,* p. 157.

Custom must determine whether there has been adherence or departure.[1]

Custom in the first sense still produces new rulings of the Lozi kuta, as on rights of kinsmen to each other's help and property. Custom in the second manner is at work in every case in present-day situations, determining how the judges will define and specify, and apply, basic concepts by customary and reasonable standards —law itself, right and duty, liability, the motivations of upright incumbents of all social positions.   As Cardozo said, this application of customary usage and standards by the criteria of what a reasonable person would do, leads to consideration of what he has called ' the method of sociology in the judicial process '. This raises a new and fundamental problem : the nature and operational value of legal concepts themselves.

---

[1] *Nature of the Judicial Process*, pp. 59 and 62.

CHAPTER VI

THE PARADOX OF THE 'UNCERTAINTY' OF LEGAL CONCEPTS AND THE 'CERTAINTY' OF LAW

I

WHEN Cardozo considered how philosophical, evolution-
ary and traditional modes of argument are used by judges,
he showed that these modes may offer a number of choices to
solve a judicial problem. He suggested that the decision to
adopt one or other was settled by 'the method of sociology'
which works along the lines of justice, social welfare, good
morals, and public policy. This method

is always in reserve. It is the arbiter between other methods, determining in the last analysis the choice of each, weighing their competing
claims, setting bounds to their pretensions, balancing and moderating
and harmonizing them all. Few rules in our times are so well established that they may not be called upon any day to justify their
existence as means adapted to an end.[1]

Cardozo considered this method as the arbiter between other
methods in developing the law to fill its gaps. Manifestly it
has a dominant rôle in the Lozi judicial process in every case,
since trial is comparatively untrammelled by procedural devices,
and decision by recorded statutes and precedents. In addition,
as Mr. Justice Jerome Frank has pointed out, Cardozo's analysis
of judicial methods was coloured by his own experience as an
appellate judge working on 'facts-in-law' established before a
trial judge. Hence he did not deal with the extent to which
'the sociological method' is at work in controlling the process,
in every case, whereby the raw data of evidence become facts-
in-law.

The application of this method shows most clearly in cases
where the judges explicitly decide in terms of equity. But it
lies at the heart of the judicial process whenever reasonable and
upright customary standards of right, duty or behaviour are
assessed. Hence 'the method of sociology' involves the basic

---

[1] loc. cit., at p. 98, and pp. 133 ff.

problem of what it is that Lozi judges do in a dispute. They consider that they ' speak ' (*bulela*) or ' expound ' (*taluseza*) the law, and that by the law (*kamulao*) they right (*lukisa*) a particular dispute (*muzeko*). Clearly they occasionally, unconsciously as well as consciously, develop the law to create new legal rules and sanctions in order to meet situations which they define as unprecedented. Thus AWAMI (L7) asked Mahalihali of the fishdams : ' [Though your sister's sons live with their father] do they not eat over here ? I wonder at this—I see it for the first time in the kuta.' [1] A dispute may fall in what jurists call ' gaps in the law ', whether customary or statutory law, as in ' The Case of the Barren Widow '.

This creation of new rules should be made within the framework of Lozi law. Thus in a criminal charge a man should not be convicted unless he has committed an established offence. The Exorbitant Fishmonger (p. 70) was acquitted because it was then not a ' criminal ' offence in Lozi law to overcharge, though Lozi law allowed the purchaser to claim rescission of the contract on the grounds of overcharging (cf. *laesio enormis*). The Lozi consider it sound to acquit a man charged with an offence because it was no offence ; but in litigation between two disputants some judgment on their rights must be given. This point is so important that it bears repeating. To give such a decision may involve developing the law by the philosophical methods of analogy and consistency, or it may entail extending and combining rules which already exist in statutes, customary law, morality. We have seen how Lozi judges do this. But in these circumstances—indeed in all cases—they are employing a further process which is implicit in all judicial reasoning. This process is present in the simplest application of the law to the facts. It is the essence of judicial interpretation. Dominantly it involves the specification of flexible legal concepts to cover a particular set of circumstances.

In Chapter III (at p. 160) I suggested that

the law lives and develops because its key concepts, ' reasonable ' and ' customary ', define general standards which are applicable to social

---

[1] Obviously, since cases are not adequately recorded and the records are not checked, the case may not have been unprecedented. But I have heard a father affirm that he could not prevent his married daughter, whom he wanted to disown, from using a garden on his land.

positions and actions which are themselves definable only in similarly general terms. The concepts are, in the usual jurisprudential term, flexible : more specifically, they are elastic, in that they can be stretched to cover new types of behaviour, new institutions, new customs, new ranges of leeway. . . . This attribute allows the judges to take cognisance of changes in mode of life, changes in morals, and changes in social structure. In the process of applying ' reasonable ' and ' customary ' norms (*mikwa yelukile* = rightful customs) as standards to actual occurrences, the judges work these changes into the flexible concepts, while the forms of most legal rules remain unchanged.

I further suggested that this is a characteristic of a number of other important key concepts in the Lozi legal system. The Lozi share many of these concepts with other legal systems. It is probably true of all legal concepts—indeed, of all concepts of law and ethics—that they tend to have the following characteristics :

(i) They may be *general* in that they rarely refer to a particular person, thing, occurrence, or action ; [1]

(ii) They are *unspecific* in that they usually denote a type of person, thing, occurrence, or action ; and they require to be given specific referents—to be specified—in particular circumstances. The judicial process in practice operates in both directions : for particular circumstances may be ' fitted into ' one or other legal concept ;

(iii) They are *flexible*, in that they can be stretched (*elastic* concepts) to cover various or new circumstances, and/or they can be given various referents or new types of referent (*multiple* concepts). I emphasize that by saying these are *multiple* concepts I mean that they have both many different types of definition (that is, they are multi-definitional),[2] and that they also have several referents. *Law* is clearly such a concept ;

(iv) They are ' *permeable* ', in that circumstances which are extrinsic to the concepts themselves can pervade them,

---

[1] ' King ' and 'NGAMBELA' are examples of concepts which do thus have single referents.

[2] Richards, I. A., *Mencius on the Mind : Experiments in Multiple Definition*, London : Kegan Paul, Trench, Trubner (1932), pp. 93 ff.

diffuse into them, be channelled into them—I hope the metaphors make plain this characteristic. As already indicated, moreover, they are permeated with ethical implications, which rouse strong feelings in both litigants and judges, and they do not coldly describe mere facts ; and

(v) They are *absorbent* in that they absorb into certain categories the raw facts of evidence (see further definition below, pp. 316–17).

I shall use the single term, '*flexible*', to sum up these characteristics, and the separate terms where I emphasize a special characteristic.[1]

Thus legal concepts may be precise concepts in that they are definable either in other words or by reference. Some, like right and duty, are *sui generis*, and their meaning, as Hohfeld wrote, has to be exhibited by their correlatives and opposites (above, p. 166). That is, they can be defined only in relation to each other within a system of law, in contextual situations.[2] These legal concepts are all somewhat ambiguous. Some have several referents, others define measures in a continuous series, or prescribe indefinite classes and uncertain identities, and so on.[3]

I repeat that these concepts have accepted meanings, often several meanings of different kinds. But their meanings are so wide and multiple that they are flexible enough to cover a vast variety of different circumstances. Hence despite the precision of the concepts they are also imprecise. They are both 'certain' and 'uncertain'. In this chapter I hope to resolve this paradox by showing how it lies at the root of the Lozi judicial process, so that the 'uncertainty' of legal concepts has social value in

---

[1] There is a complex technical literature on the characteristics of different types of words : see, e.g., *Logic and Language* (edited by A. Flew), Oxford : Blackwell (1951). I could not find precisely the terminology I required for my analysis and it has seemed best to me to avoid becoming involved in complex technicalities. I have used, as far as I could, everyday words to discuss my problems, but have tried to respect the accepted terms of both semantics and jurisprudence.

[2] Hart, *Definition and Theory in Jurisprudence*, op. cit.

[3] Besides Hohfeld, op. cit., on these characteristics of 'right' and 'duty', see Williams, G., 'Language and the Law', *Law Quarterly Review*, xli (1945) and xlii (1946), passim, and other books and articles cited therein.

maintaining the ' certainty ' of law.   I hope also to show that this resolution disposes of a number of perennial controversies in jurisprudence.

II

The flexible generality of Lozi legal concepts is an essential part of their functional value in judicial argument, which contains two distinct processes.   The first is the statement of some intrinsic meaning of a concept.   This may be made by reference, or it may be circular, as that ' *buswafa kikutokwa tokomelo yeswanelwa ni tokomelo kikusaeza kabuswafa* ' (negligence is lack of due care, and care is not to do negligently).   In 'The Case of the Prince's Gardens ' (pp. 56–61) judges defined what the meaning of *muliu* is, and referred to the motives which led them to enact the *muliu* law : it did not aim to prevent the lending and recovery of gardens.   The second process is the reference of this intrinsic meaning to extrinsic circumstances : the statement of whether either party's actions constituted *muliu*.   It is this second process that is most important in Lozi judicial analysis.

Lozi legal concepts are not all of equivalent value in this process of analysis.   Some concepts can be arranged in a series of hierarchies, which interlock partially, according to their position in the structure of the legal system.   Other concepts *pervade* the hierarchies, for they attach to almost all concepts. The hierarchies tend to incorporate a scale of decreasing lack of precision and the type of imprecision changes.   The words which are most fundamental and important in that they occur throughout the legal system tend to be least precise, to have multiple referents, and to be defined by those referents or circularly by contraries.

' Government ' (*mubuso*) for the Lozi lies behind all law (*mulao*) for it establishes the kuta's authority which finally states the law.   Lozi define ' government ' as ' ruling people '.   ' Law ' (*mulao*) itself is an imprecise master weapon in the kuta's arsenal, and *law* is ' things which are right ' (*linto zelukile*).   I have cited how the Lozi use this word to refer to all forms of regularity, ranging from the natural order to the persistent habits of an individual.   The kuta has to state, ' This is the law,' for situations which occur in every activity in every relationship within the orbit of its jurisdiction.   *Law* has to cover potentially all facts which are subsumed in the total process of social control. This control defines right and reasonable ways in which persons ought to behave in relation to each other and to things in many different situations, including ways of obtaining redress, and it operates by many direct and indirect means. All these rules, both substantive and procedural, are *law* in the widest sense. In the judicial process on a particular dispute the appropriate law in this wide sense has to be selected by the judges from the sources of custom, statutes, precedents, and morality, and natural regularities. The judges use *law* in order to assess the rights and wrongs of a particular dispute, on which they must give a verdict, so as to enforce conformity with certain rules and ideals, or to penalize failure to conform. Necessarily, therefore, *law* has a very general connotation and many referents. The judges have to interpret into it—to channel through the word itself— all the ideals, including certainty of law, which are extant in the society, or that social section they represent. During a period of rapid social change they may also attempt to introduce changes of mores and values. Lozi have brought under this embracing rubric of 'law' British overlordship and all that it entails. That is, in the logical structure of judgment the judges primarily decide whether there is a dispute (*muzeko*—a word also of very flexible meaning) which is covered by legal rules (*milao*—plural).

Law occupies this position at the apex of the legal hierarchy because it contains all the kuta's authority and judgments, and all the rules the kuta will enforce. But as described above, *law* does not enter first into the logical development of judgments. These usually proceed by fixing social positions, then determining rights and duties, and then entering into motivation. All disputes take place between people each of whom occupies several social positions, and the judges determine first in what rôles the litigants are disputing. The kuta fixes the litigants as headman and villager, as father and son, as husband and wife, in kinship disputes. In contracts it has first to determine if they are seller and buyer, borrower and lender, or owner of cattle and herder. After delicts it defines them as assaulted and assailant, husband and adulterer, or slandered and slanderer. All action either involves incumbents of social positions which are already related by social ties, or the action of itself establishes ties between

PLATE IX

FISH STABBING

'If you are invited to a meal and a fish bone sticks in your throat, you cannot sue your host': no suit lies if a man is injured at a fishing battue.

(*a*) Hoeing. An industrious wife in her garden.

(*b*) A granary. A husband is forbidden to go to his wife's granary
(see ' The Case of the Wife's Granary ').

PLATE X

persons thus thrust into social positions, as in contract and delict. Hence law operates in a framework of social positions, and in the judicial process these must first be settled. They set the limits within which a particular judgment has to be given : hence, they tend to have a high degree of precise definition. However, the conception of a series of social positions, in ordered and in disturbed relations, implies the overriding concept of *law*.

Social positions are precise in a dispute even where the particular legal rules covering their relations appear to involve general concepts, as, for example, the rules defining *jura in rem* (rights against the world). Lozi law states that every man should be protected in his land-holdings against all other men— the world as we put it. ' The world ' here is an imprecise concept ; but in dispute it becomes ' a particular alleged intruder or trespasser '.[1] The kuta enquires into the trespass. Should the trespasser plead that he has rights to the land, the social positions to be considered change. Thus in ' The Case of the Returning Garden-Claimant ' (above, p. 53) a man returned to his father's natal village and tried to take over his father's old gardens from the person working them : the issue became one between possessor and alleged rightful owner, if we neglect the fact that the trespasser was also under trial as one who had taken the law into his own hands. Similarly in disputes arising out of adultery, or assault, or between neighbours, the issue of social position is narrowed to fix on the relations of particular litigants. But it is clear that there is a varying degree of flexibility in the conception of different social positions : and here the judges may have to determine, in the light of extrinsic circumstance, whether a litigant does or does not occupy a particular social position. Some judges gave the two sisters in the Fishdams case different social positions in terms of their obligations as villagers or possible villagers.

Law is thus a very flexible term linking and controlling the relations between social positions, which themselves are more or less precise. Further, law in this general sense is associated

---

[1] Cf. Hohfeld, op. cit., pp. 91 ff. : ' A single claim (*jus in rem*) correlates with a duty resting on one person alone ' (p. 92). He argues that a violation of the primary right, the *jus in rem*, creates a secondary right, a paucital claim, which creates an obligation *ex delicto* (p. 101).

with justice (*tukelo*) and truth (*niti*), which also are flexible concepts of almost the same degree of uncertainty. *Law* ranks higher in the judicial process than *justice*, which is one of its sources, since a judgment may be given against the dictates of justice to maintain law (see pp. 189–91). On the Lozi ethical scale, as against their legal scale, justice would rank higher than law, though they say a legal decision in a hard case is justice for all, even if it is hard (*kitata*) on a particular litigant.

The judges draw for *legal rulings of law* on various sources. Besides *justice*, there are also statutes (*milao yetomilwe*), customs (*mikwa*), precedents (*likatulo zakale*), equity (*kulikana*), morality (*sishemo*), and public policy (*bupilo bwasicaba*). These concepts come second in the hierarchy as a whole. Only the concepts of *statute* and of *precedent* are fairly precise, and the process by which all the sources are drawn on in applying each to extrinsic circumstance renders even them flexible. Here I have given a single English equivalent for a series of Lozi words. But Lozi, like English, has several words to denote some of the concepts, and each word may have several distinct meanings. These variations in meaning of each word, and the use of ostensible synonyms, enable judges to apply them to the variety of life with some flexibility.

The judges select from these sources, contained under *law* as a whole, those rules they deem appropriate to achieve what they consider to be justice in a particular set of circumstances. If the case is between kinsmen this involves reconciliation (*tatuluhelo*) and the ' moulding ' of peace (*kozo*) among them, two very flexible concepts. In cases between strangers this is not necessary, and the judicial process as a whole is far more precise.

However, all disputes, including those between kinsmen, involve the statement of rights and duties, and conceptions of rightdoing and wrongdoing, judged both morally and legally. Hence these concepts enter high into the master hierarchy which controls all litigation, and they cover a wide range of meanings. The Lozi word *swanelo* means both right and duty or obligation : it and its derivatives are also used in contexts where we would translate them as fitness, worthiness, decorum, well-assorted. The verbal form, *kuswanela*, means ' it ought ', ' it behoves '. The other general synonym, *litukelo*, is from *kuluka*, to be right, to be upright, to be straight. Most importantly, the rights and duties covered by *liswanelo* and *litukelo* are extremely varied in type and range : there are claims on *some* land in virtue of citizenship, and on *certain* parcels of land in virtue of narrower social positions, etc. As quoted with reference to Hohfeld's analysis of the fundamental juridical conceptions of our law, the same word means claim, no-claim, privilege, power, duty, disability, immunity, and liability, though there are other words to specify some of the conceptions more precisely. Hence, as I argued on ' The Case of the Headman's Fishdams ' (p. 195), the judges may step from saying a person has done what he ought (or what is right) to saying he ought to have (or has a right in) a particular piece of land. And since *liswanelo* and *litukelo* cover duties of different types as well as rights (e.g. duties to observe general care and to show generosity to particular persons), the judges can manipulate them with great flexibility. If a man fails in his duty (*swanelo*), then he has lost his right (*swanelo*), as the headman lost some right in the fishdams.

Mulatu and *poso*, wrong crime and fault, are similarly flexible. The verbal infinitive form of *poso*, *kufosa*, particularly lends itself to judicial manipulation, since judges can step from describing actions as ' doing wrong ', to categorizing them as ' wrongs ', to opposing them to ' rights ', as in ' The Case of the Headman's Fishdams '.

The same observations apply to *sinyeho* or *sinyehelo*, injury or damage. These words also describe waste, spoiling, devastation. There are synonyms of varying degree of equivalence for all these concepts. Many express degrees of rightdoing and wrongdoing, and of injury or damage. The flexible generality of these concepts enables the judges to bring almost any action under the rubric of right or duty, or to define anything done against the interests of another as a wrong or injury. It enables the concepts to be expanded to contain all the customs and values, both historic and emergent, of Lozi law. Therefore however varied or new the circumstances of a case, the judges can apply the concepts *injury* and *damage* to maintain the law and to achieve justice.

At this stage the hierarchy splits into two distinctive sets of concepts. Substantive rights and duties attach either to things (*lika*) or to persons (*batu*). The Lozi describe the rights as inhering in *bung'a*, ownership or property, which is of very general meaning. Thus a headman has *bung'a* over his clothes, over his village land over which the king has superior *bung'a*, over his own gardens in that land, over his wife, over his kinsmen, over his children. Quite different kinds of rights and duties (the parcel containing Hohfeld's eight fundamental conceptions) are involved in each separate ' ownership ' (*bung'a*).

Bung'a of things or of one's own person in turn is reduced to, respectively, narrow concepts of use (*kusebeza*) and disposal (*kufana*), and to reputation (*libizo*), safety (*kupila*), freedom (*tukuluho*). These are rights owned by a person over a variety of personal or material objects against the world—*in rem.* Other more narrowly defined rights exist in these objects in so far as they are significant in particular relationships. Here we begin to come to concepts which are more particular to the Lozi system, and are not present in as many other legal systems as are the concepts which stand higher in the hierarchy. There are, however, few special words in Lozi to define these lower level rights, since they use *bung'a*, ownership, to describe almost all rights over and against persons and things. In Lozi, precision is introduced not by qualifying *bung'a* itself, but by specifying different kinds of persons (wife, child, brother, subject, etc.) and different kinds of things (*solume*, the husband's own property ; *sionda*, marriage-payment, which consists of *komu yamatapa*, ' the beast of shame ', and *komu yamwana*, ' the beast of the child ', or *komu yakulisa*, ' the beast of herding ', as against *komu yasicabuhobe*, ' the beast that eats porridge ', which is consumed at the wedding).

CASE 58 : THE INCIDENT OF THE CONFUSED
MARRIAGE-CATTLE
(*from a text*)

Shortly after a marriage the bride's father, to show his friendship, sent a present of a beast to the bridegroom's father. The latter sent it back, and told me : ' He is foolish. We split " the beast that eats porridge ", that was the wedding. If he gives me another beast, that is returning " the beast of herding " and dissolves the marriage. If he wants to show friendship, he must send other things, or kill a beast and give me half, another " beast that eats porridge ".'

The Lozi also have terms to define trespass on these narrower,

lower level, rights.   For example, the Lozi use general words
like ' equal share ' (*kabelo yelikana*) and ' her night ' (*busihu
bwahae*) to define the right of a polygamist's wives to equal
treatment, but *mulinda* specifically defines the offence of neglecting one of them.

Parallel with the narrowing of meaning of concepts defining
rights and duties, there is a hierarchy derived from wrongs
and injuries which covers trespass on or observance of these
rights, and hence wrongdoing as against rightdoing.   The kuta
here enters into questions of motivation, since the law assumes
that behind actions lie thought and feeling which should be
controlled by reason and ethics.   On this basis their key concept
is responsibility (*swanelo yakulukisa*—obligation to make right)
which fixes liability (the same term in Lozi), and thus may create
new rights and duties between the parties.   Primarily responsibility involves guilt and doing wrong (*kufosa*) as against innocence (*kusafosa, hakusina mulatu, kuluka*).[1]   This division is
significant even when the law fixes responsibility absolutely,
since this means that the law holds that the wrongdoer is guilty
even if he did not intend his action.   Various degrees of guilt
are defined by lower level concepts such as *mens rea*, guilty
intention or malice aforethought (*kabomu*), as against uninten-
tional wrongdoing (*kubongisa*) ; or of negligence (*buswafa*) as
against care (*tokomelo*).   Concepts like provocation (*lishemaeta*),
fraudulence (*kupuma*), reprehensibility (*kunyazeha*), constraint
(*kuhapeleza*), oppression (*kunyandisa*), further limit the range of
guilty behaviour.   Positive concepts, fewer in number, correspondingly emphasize and restrict the range of innocence : to
do right (*kueza hande*), to be trustworthy (*kusepehala*), to care
for well (*kubabalela*), to be respectful (*kutompeha*).

I am trying here to group together into a single hierarchy
a series of concepts which are all heavily impregnated with
ethical content, and which assess the behaviour and motives
of persons linked in legal relations or brought into legal relations
by specific actions.   These words are all of a wide generality,

---

[1] On reading the proofs Prof. Schapera has pointed out to me that the Lozi
use negatives of guilt for innocence, rather than a positive term, and he asks
if I see any significance in this.   I suggest it is the same form as in our courts,
where the plea is ' Not guilty ', and not ' Innocent '.

as is indicated by the fact that they are defined tautologically or circularly by their opposites, and not by referents. Like our own dictionaries the Lozi define *guilt* as 'having committed an offence' and negligence as 'want of proper care'. This hierarchy is one of concepts which can be applied to a variety of actions, ranging from crimes and delicts to breaches of status or personal obligations.

The 'uncertainty' of these concepts tends to be of the indefinite and continuous series type. Hence I have called them *elastic* as against the *multiplicity* of referents for a concept like *law*. They set up two poles of actions, of the type of guilt and innocence, negligence and care, to establish a range along which actual behaviour can be assessed. They form the constituent elements of rights and duties as practised by people who are linked by legal rules : in litigation the judges decide whether extrinsic circumstances constitute referents for one or other of a pair of them.

These pervasive moral concepts are applied to assess and right a variety of alleged wrongdoings which I therefore place lower in the hierarchy, since each defines a particular breach of others' rights. Correspondingly these latter are narrower in their scope than the pervasive concepts. Lozi have words—often several words—to describe offences which are common to most legal systems : stealing, assaulting, bribing, seducing, fornicating, abducting a wife, slandering, laying a false accusation, bearing false witness, committing arson, killing, murdering. Many words define the offence of being partial, either to one's own kin or generally (*sobozi* ; *sishongwa*—to be bribed ; *sishweka* ; *sialututi* ; *saluluti* ; *ng'atuluti*). I have emphasized this example out of the others because we have seen in cases quoted how the judges try to determine whether or not a litigant has been guilty of bias. Another pair of such concepts is 'deserts' or 'leaves' (*kuzwa*) as against 'being driven out' (*kulelekiswa*) : did the nephews in 'The Case of the Biassed Father' 'leave' the village or were they 'driven out' ? This pair of concepts, 'leaving' and 'being driven out', figures in many divorce cases. The examples illustrate how even apparently definite terms to describe actions are still flexible and elastic, and have to be given extrinsic referents in particular circumstances. This applies also to a number of wrongs which are particular to certain Lozi relationships, and are found also only in societies with similar organization. I cite examples from cases quoted :

In 'The Case of the Contemptuous Husband' the husband was adjudged to have committed *mulinda*, the neglect of one wife by a polygamist (a form of lack of care—*kusababalela*).

In 'The Case of the Prince's Gardens' it was held that neither party had committed *muliu*, the claiming of land by ancestral title prior to a set day (the Lozi consider this to be a form of false accusation, *kutanta*).

In the same case it was held that the defendant was not guilty of *muluta*, leaving one's own village to fight another in his home (a form of assault, *kulwanisa*, which need not lead to an actual physical assault).

The application of these terms to the varied actions which occur in social life theoretically, for the Lozi, does not depend wholly on the whim of judges, but on the objective standards of the reasonable man (*mutu yangana*) and beyond him of the upright man (*mutu yalukile*). Reason and uprightness are defined by Lozi custom (*kamukwa wasilozi*). However, we have seen that these words are extraordinarily flexible in assessing actual behaviour against customs and values, and cover social developments and changes. Indeed, they are almost as generally flexible in their connotation as the word *law* : they enter as pervasively as it does into every judgment. They pervade the word *law* itself, and judges may submit particular laws themselves to the tests of reasonableness and uprightness. Since every legal concept, like law itself, is by implication an 'ought' value-judgment, reason and justice, by current social standards, inhere in it. Judges attempt to amend the law by altering its extrinsic application to meet these demands. Hence *reasonableness* and *uprightness* do not have a special place in the hierarchy, but have to be bracketed with every concept in it.

I have sketched these hierarchies of concepts in part of the substantive law—later I shall discuss the separate hierarchy of trial law—tentatively because its significance has only come home to me as I was analysing my material. I did not test it in the field, and as I stated above (p. 168) my recording of judgments was not as full as it should have been. I am aware that there are some very general terms which refer to comparatively small offences, and therefore come low in the hierarchy and by my hypothesis should be of narrower definition. Examples are breach of the peace (*kuzusa ndwa*), committing a nuisance (*kukataza*), improper behaviour (*bumaswe*), vagrancy (*buhwaba*). These are important in our own law, which sometimes finds these offences politically useful. In Lozi law a similar example is 'lack of respect' for a superior. But I believe the main outlines of the hierarchy stand and I shall try to show shortly that its formulation disposes of a number of jurisprudential problems. Here I note that where Professor Williams applies semantic analysis to legal concepts, he comments that lawyers 'have been at pains to construct and preserve a moderately precise technical language. Oddly enough, it is least precise in its most fundamental parts '.[1] My hierarchies have at least the merit that they explain the 'oddly enough' to be quite reasonable, since the most fundamental legal concepts have to serve most functions and cover the widest ranges of activity both in social life and the judicial process. They also refer to the most common conditions of social life throughout the world and hence are found in all societies, though the meanings imported into them, and which *permeate* them, vary with economic and political conditions.

I have suggested further that words at different levels of the hierarchy have different kinds of flexibility and ambiguity. The flexibility or ambiguity of the most important words,—such as law, custom, right, duty, crime, things, persons, and property,— consists in that they have both many definitions and also many distinct referents. These referents are of varied kinds : e.g. law can be referred to any regularity, to substantive rules, to process of trial, to judgments, and to remedies ; property refers to rights to hold land, to clothes, and to varied claims on particular persons. This seems to be their dominant characteristic, though they also have the uncertainty of 'fringe-meaning' in an indefinite series—as whether a particular claim is legal or moral only. The 'indefinite series' uncertainty becomes more important as we descend the hierarchy, in concepts like guilt, negligence, and provocation. While the concepts may have

---

[1] 'Language and the Law', at lxi, p. 179.

more than one referent, they rarely have several.   Here concepts are increasingly defined circularly, and hardly at all by reference to outside events.   Indeed, the ' wrongful ' among these concepts are usually posed antithetically to ' rightful ' concepts which serve to define them :   as in guilt and innocence, negligence and care.   Hence they set up a line along which action is measured to determine whether it falls to one pole or the other, and judgment may be influenced by concepts of provocation, justifiability, etc.   Offences below these, and rightdoing, are defined again by referential methods.   In the parallel hierarchy—of person and thing—the characteristic uncertainty is ambiguity of identity, which also affects social position.

The accompanying chart may clarify, at this point, my argument.

III

Most Western jurists have treated the ambiguities and uncertainties of the words with which litigants, lawyers, and judges work as producing difficulties and chanciness, even though they admit that these uncertainties give flexibility and scope for development to the legal system.[1]

I do not question that unnecessary and perhaps unjust complications are thus introduced into Western judgments :   this is well authenticated.   But it is important to analyse the social and juristic functions of these ambiguities in legal concepts.   To understand the judicial process we must examine how the different kinds of uncertainty of various concepts allow the judges to manipulate the concepts themselves in order to give decisions in accordance with their ideas of the law and of justice.   This manipulation emerges clearly in a series of Lozi decisions on land-

---

[1] I shall discuss their conclusions in the next chapter, but here cite :   Williams, ' Language and the Law ', op. cit. ;   Jerome Frank, *Law and the Modern Mind*, London :   Stevens & Sons, 1949—first published in the U.S.A. in 1930 ; Z. Chafee, ' The Disorderly Conduct of Words ', *Columbia Law Review*, xli (1941), pp. 381 ff., and *Canadian Bar Review*, xx (1942), pp. 725 ff.   A typical semanticist discussion occurs in Stuart Chase, *The Tyranny of Words*, London : Methuen, 1938, pp. 214 ff.   A recent philosophical treatment is H. L. A. Hart's ' The Ascription of Responsibility and Rights ' in *Logic and Language*, Even Hohfeld complained that ' chameleon-hued words are a peril ', op. cit., p. 35.

cases, in approximately analogous circumstances : ' The Case of the Biassed Father ', ' The Case of the Headman's [Mahalihali II] Fishdams ', ' The Case of the Earlier Mahalihali and his Brother Sabangwa ', and ' The Case of the Disrespectful Induna '.

In all these cases the judges began by fixing the identity of the litigants, to set the frame for enquiry and judgment. Here problems of reference to extrinsic circumstance arise, but are not difficult. About these identities in general terms, there cluster rights and duties. These are not equivalent, but are of quite different kind. This is particularly marked in relations between kinsmen. A few of the rights and duties in these cases were :

> (a) (i) The headman has an obligation to give his villagers land which they retain unless they leave the village ;
>   (ii) if they leave the village they lose rights in its land ;
> (b) kin resident elsewhere may ask to use the land if there is sufficient ;
> (c) villagers must respect and help their headman ;
> (d) the headman must be impartial in caring for and in settling disputes among his villagers ;
> (e) the headman must rule his village to the satisfaction of the kuta.

Here is a series of different kinds of rights and duties, all termed by the Lozi *liswanelo* or *litukelo*. Thus these terms are multi-referential—as I call them, *multiple*. All rights are rights of *bung'a*, ownership. But even if we classify the different rights under our more elaborate, or even the Hohfeldian, terminology,[1] the multiple character remains.

In ' The Case of the Biassed Father ', the settlement of (a) appears to be plain : the law states that if a man ' leaves ' the village he loses his land. But ' leaves ' requires definition and application : it comes low in the hierarchy, and has to be applied to a series of actions ranging from clear voluntary departure to another pole—being ' driven out '. (In many divorce cases wives claim that their husbands drove them out of the village—the court works on similar actions from a different pole : see ' The Case of the Contemptuous Husband ', pp. 142-3.) Issues

---

[1] Distinguishing : claims, no-claims, privileges, duties, powers, disabilities, immunities, liabilities.

(c) to (e) similarly require the fitting of actual behaviour into the series sufficient–insufficient land, respect–disrespect, help–fail to help, impartial–partial, care–fail to care, settle–fail to settle, rule–fail to rule, satisfaction–dissatisfaction of kuta.   In this type of case the first task of the judges is to ascribe guilt or innocence to the parties in assessing their behaviour against many of these scales.   On each scale the judges make a judgment that one or other (or both) has done wrong (*ufosize, haasikaswanela*) and therefore has ' no-right' (*ha'ana swanelo*) ; or has done right (*ulukile, uswanezi*) and therefore has a ' right' (*unani tukelo, unani swanelo*). Here I am using ' right' with different meanings as Lozi judges use ' *swanelo* ' or ' *tukelo* '.   Balancing the rightdoing and wrong-doing on these actions the judges conclude that plaintiff or defendant is dominantly ' in the right' (*kiyena yaezize hande*, or *kiyena ulukile* [1]).   Therefore they try to give him the right to land if possible—and this is ' right' with quite a different kind of meaning.   Thus they manipulate the multiple concept of ' rights' and ' duties ', which are more abstract, to meet decisions on ' guilt' and ' innocence ', about actions assessed along lines between ' fulfilment of' and ' failure to fulfil' other kinds of ' rights' and ' duties'.   They may hold, however, that ' the law' prevents them following ' the right', as in ' The Case of the Ungenerous Husband' and in some judgments in ' The Case of the Headman's Fishdams '.

In ' The Case of the Biassed Father' the kuta found the evidence inconclusive and called for witnesses.   It was clear that the head-man's son had wronged his cousin and the headman had shown bias against his nephews ; hence, the headman and his son ' had tended to drive them out'.   On the other hand, the nephews had shown some lack of 'helpfulness' to their 'father,' even if under ' provocation ', had made illegal accusations of sorcery, and had ' tended to leave the village '.   I cannot say what the kuta would have done if the parties had refused to re-unite in the village : as they did agree the kuta was able variously to upbraid their wrongdoings and applaud their rightdoings, and then state its arguments to reunite in the decision that the nephews must return or lose their gardens.   The kuta em-phasized one of the rights in the complex to achieve its aim of

---

[1] Literally, ' it is he who has done well ', or, ' it is he who is upright '.

reconciliation because of its judgments on quite different kinds of rights. Almost the same rights were involved in the old decision that Sabangwa build apart from his quarrelsome elder brother Mahalihali I (the dead headman in 'The Case of the Headman's Fishdams'). But here, since Sabangwa was innocent of ' disrespect' and the headman guilty of 'fighting', the kuta held that Sabangwa did not 'leave the village' but was 'driven out'—hence he retained his land-rights. This was a temporary expedient to avoid bloodshed. In the present 'Case of the Headman's Fishdams', Sabangwa's rights inadvertently came before the kuta in relation to the new heir with whom he was on good terms. Now Sabangwa was in the wrong, for he had advised the heir badly in supporting instead of opposing the suit against kin resident elsewhere. Hence as ALULEYA put it :

' But why is not your uncle Sabangwa with the defendants ? He has built on his own—why do you not ask him to come back ? He works his gardens yet is not the village.'

AWAMI followed :

' Sabangwa, I blame you for not advising Mahalihali well. He is the successor but he is younger than you are.'

NAMUNDA-KATANEKWA put the conclusion strongly :

' Sabangwa, I know your affair. . . . When you had a quarrel with your elder brother Mahalihali, the Malozi split your village— they refused to let you go elsewhere. When your elder brother's son was taken to be Mahalihali you should have gone back. You were prevented from doing so because you did not like to lose the village title, Sabangwa. I say with the Malozi, go back to your elder brother's son and build with him. He is a young man, you are old. The land is all yours. The name of Mahalihali is very big —make it big : let the name of Sabangwa on the bank of the canal die. You have only two sons—go to your child and build together. Have a strong village.'

In the first Mahalihali case the kuta ' refused to let Sabangwa go elsewhere'. Splitting the village had been a temporary expedient : now Sabangwa's obligations arising from his land-rights can be used to force him into the village, as the nephews in ' The Case of the Biassed Father' were forced.

Again, similar rights were involved when Mahalihali II demanded that his nephews come to his village or abandon their use of its land.   All the judges held that he was wrong in making the demand at all ; and nearly all held that he had been wrong in not supporting his one sister when their father accused her of sorcery.   But a few held that the basic rule of land-holding must be enforced, though they exhorted him in moral terms not to insist on it.   Most judgments were reluctant to enforce the basic rule against the sister and her sons living with her husband, though they used the rule to force the widowed sister and her son to return.   SOLAMI reconciled the judgments by bringing in quite a different ' right '—the ' right ' of the kuta to discharge a headman who ' fails in ruling '.   Here ' fails in ruling ' covers lack of generosity to kin resident elsewhere, while in ' The Case of the Biassed Father ' and ' The Case of the Violent Councillor ' ' fails in ruling ' covered quite different kinds of actions.

I have from a text another case which illustrates how the kuta enforces these rights in land in terms of its decision on other rights and wrongs.   It contrasts precisely with ' The Case of the Headman's Fishdams '.

CASE 59: THE CASE OF THE VAIN GARDEN-HOLDER

Wendo left the village of his dead father's elder brother, Mutondo, and said that he was going to be appointed heir in the village of his mother, in the forest at MULOBELA'S.   Someone else was appointed heir.   Wendo returned home and was covered with shame.   He wanted to build nearby at Liuma's village, collateral relatives of his mother ; but his uncle Mutondo said he would not let Wendo work his gardens if he lived at Liuma's.   Wendo complained to the kuta, which approved of Mutondo's action, and therefore Wendo settled again at Mutondo's.

Here the kuta upheld a headman's threat to control a vain young man's desertion of his home village, in the young man's interests.

The standards of guilt or innocence in fulfilment of lower level obligations or rights are reasonable and customary, and their application enables the judges to adapt the law to cover both varying cases and also new ranges of behaviour and usage, new moral standards ideals and necessities, and new technological and other developments.   This is clearly illustrated in ' The Case of the Disrespectful Induna' (p. 152) which involved rights similar to those involved in the cases just analysed. Princess Mbuywana wanted to discharge and expropriate the induna because he did not work for her. The judges rejected this suit because nowadays men earn their living working for Whites, and not for their Lozi lords : hence he was justified in his plea that he was fully occupied in his employment. But the princess resided in Mongu, indeed near the headquarters of the transport company for which he worked, so he could reasonably be expected to greet her on his return from a journey and bid her farewell before departing again. His failure to do these things showed that he did not ' respect ' (*kupateka*) her, and he should forfeit his position (*kutulukiwa*) under her, with its increments. In another similar suit by the princess the kuta held that she was moved by personal dislike of the man, and he had done no wrong : hence she could not discharge him.

In all these cases the judges manipulated the concepts of rights and duties, involved in land-holding, which are stated in abstract terms where ' right ' and ' duty ' refer to different kinds of legal ties. They did so after determining good and ill against other concepts by reasonable and customary standards. This manipulation is possible because of the generality of all the concepts, including ' law ', ' justice ', ' certainty of law ', ' guilt ', ' innocence ', ' leave the village ', etc., and because the flexibility of the different concepts varies in kind (multiplicity or elasticity), as well as degree. The manipulation enables the judges generally to achieve their task as set by the cultural values of their society : peace and unity among kindred and in villages ; the approval of generosity ; the maintenance of rights where no wrong has been done ; the penalization of those who do act ungenerously, or wrongfully in other ways ; the avoidance of bloodshed ; and the persistence of villages and the endurance of the land-holding system within the nation. These constitute the Lozi moral order and the reign of law and justice. In a series of analogous cases different rights and obligations were emphasized, on the basis of investigation which allotted guilt and innocence of different kinds. By this manipulation the judges achieve justice stated in terms of well-known principles, and the certainty of the law (*mulao hauketi*—the law does not choose) is maintained through what is clearly chanciness in litigation. Moreover, the certainty of the law persists in these principles, composed of flexible concepts, through great social changes—' respectful behaviour' to the princess nowadays is held not necessarily to include work for her.

IV

In the preceding paragraph I have listed a number of Lozi values which the judges seek to serve in their decisions : the support of the upright against the wrongdoer, certainty of law, unity of villages, the established system of land-holding. These values themselves are principles of different kinds, made up of concepts of varying kind and degree of generality. They may conflict, as where certainty of law excludes support of the upright (' The Case of the Ungenerous Husband ', p. 172, some judgments in ' The Case of the Headman's Fishdams '). Some of the value-principles are common to most societies : others are more particular to the Lozi. The latter are related to their history and their present and preceding stages of economic and political development. They tend to be expounded in the customary and historical modes of judicial argument. Therefore the interpretation of even those principles that are found in societies at all stages of development—such as that a wrongdoer should make redress or suffer for his wrongdoing—is influenced by more particular principles. Through all land-disputes runs the determination of the judges to maintain the political structure which is based on the allocation of land from the king to headmen's titles, stated in the basic rule always emphasized by my informants : ' If you leave the village, you lose your rights in its land.' This rule was in fact asserted in all the cases : Sabangwa's departure from Mahalihali village was regarded as temporary, Mahalihali II's kin were to use the dams by his permission, and finally the dams would remain vested in Mahalihali's title but a more generous Mahalihali would be installed. I have not space here to show the significance of this rule in Lozi social structure : it must be left over for my analysis of *The Ideas of Barotse Jurisprudence*.

The historic, economic, and political load of Lozi legal concepts exercises its dominant pressure through the concepts of social position which I have so far barely touched on. I have stated that the judges first determine these positions, because they are the framework for all litigation and for the concepts of rights and duties which are *the law* itself. In these social positions are contained the particular economic and political conditions of Lozi society—king, headman, villager, in land-holding ; king, princess, induna in the political hierarchy ; and so on. The rights and obligations that lie between these social positions are influenced by prevailing technological, religious, and other cultural conditions, even though they are embodied in concepts of rightdoing and wrongdoing that are widespread in many societies. The flexibility and permeability of certain legal principles inhere in social life in all its forms : this permeability enables the principles to be applicable to social life in widely varied conditions. The incidents of being buyer and seller, promissor and promisee, husband and wife, landowner and subsidiary holder, may be brought under common legal principles, but vary considerably in detail.

I speak thus of the *permeability* of legal concepts to describe the way in which their extrinsic application is determined by the particular social circumstances in which they operate. This permeability, as well as accepted varieties of meanings, determines the actual nature of concepts in a particular legal system and in pieces of litigation and adjudication within it. I concentrate in my present analysis on the function of the concepts' generality for the certainty of law and for the judicial process : I do not intend to imply that their use is not controlled by a variety of specific social conditions.

Social positions, as a set of interlinked rôles united by purposive activities in a particular politico-economic system, thus lie at the heart of the legal system. In the legal system these positions are defined in terms of reciprocal actions, and expectations of action, which are ethically evaluated.[1] The complex manipulation of flexible concepts of different status, meaning, and kind of ambiguity or uncertainty, has to be extracted from apparently simple judicial decisions stated as : what should an upright and reasonable lord, underling, headman, villager, father, son, husband, wife, etc., have done in these circumstances, as against what the parties did ? In effect, therefore, the judges define

---

[1] Parsons and Shils, op. cit., passim.

what a lord, underling, headman, villager, father, son, husband, or wife, *should be* in terms both of historic tradition and of changing conditions and mores.   Lozi cases in these relationships are highly individualized, and the litigants come before the court not as mere right-and-duty bearing units but as whole social personalities.   Nevertheless in the apparent fluidity of judgment which this process may appear to manifest, there is certainty in the implicit erection of upright fulfilment of the duties of social positions.   The process is complicated because in kinship cases one person occupies several relevant social positions.   The fulfilment is tested by answering such questions as :   Did the Violent Councillor show bias, commit assault, and not act as an induna ?   Did the Contemptuous Husband commit *mulinda*, neglect of one wife by a polygamist ?   And so forth.   Thus the primary determination of legal fulfilment of obligations inhering in social position, is broken down into lower level legal concepts of guilt or innocence in particular actions.   When these problems have been settled, the judges determine what rights they will enforce and what obligations or punishment they will impose, and by what means.   At every stage flexible concepts require particular specification, and the skilful judge achieves justice through manipulating them.   Lower level concepts are manipulated in their *elasticity* by being stretched or contracted to cover action as rightdoing or wrongdoing—guilt or innocence—in the interests of justice ; and the *multiple* higher level concepts are manipulated in the application of unspecific general terms like law, right, duty, wrong, injury, to accommodate these lower level decisions.

Similar problems involved in the nature of legal concepts have been considered by Professor Hart in an article on ' The Ascription of Responsibility and Rights '.[1]   He suggests with some hesitation that they be described by the legal word *defeasible*, ' used of a legal interest in property which is subject to termination or " *defeat* " in a number of different contingencies but remains intact if no such contingencies mature.'   He takes as his example *contract*, since its ascription can be negatived by six types of defence, which we may sum up as misrepresentation or fraud,

---

[1] In *Essays on Logic and Language*, first published in *Proceedings of the Aristotelian Society*, lxix (1948-9).

duress, incapacity, public evil, frustration, and prescription. I draw attention to this suggestion, because it seems to me that many higher level concepts like contract and ownership, law and right and duty, responsibility and guilt, may be viewed in these terms as *defeasible*, but not lower level concepts. I venture to suggest that my analysis extracts an implicit hierarchy from Professor Hart's use of *defeasible*.

V

I have presented my analysis on land-cases between kin since these provide the most complex situations that confront Lozi judges. Rights to land and obligations to act uprightly in many ways are interwoven, since rights to land inhere in multiplex relations. Similar situations confront the judges in suits between kin over chattels, or where one charges another with assault or sorcery or slander or adultery. The relations of lords and underlings linked by multiplex ties are also adjudged thus (' The Case of the Violent Councillor '). The complexity here is largely created by the dominant value that the relationship should be maintained if possible.

Since this value does not dominate in marital disputes, judgment is more straightforward. The kuta is chiefly concerned to determine whether a husband's conduct amounted to ' driving away ' his wife, or failing to fulfil his various conjugal duties. Nevertheless in complex cases, there may be difficulty in weighing both husband's and wife's conduct to achieve a final decision, and this may entail some manipulation of the concepts of rights and obligations.

Delicts and crimes between neighbours also involve simpler issues of definition, though the court may broaden its enquiry into other aspects of their relations, as in ' The Case of the Quarrelsome Teacher '. Here the court is dealing with the hierarchy of ' guilt-innocence ' responsibility concepts, which we have considered in land-suits between kin since their relations are weighed ethically for wrongdoing. In delicts and crimes committed by a man on a stranger (as in adultery or theft cases), once the social positions of complainant and accused are fixed, the manipulation of concepts at the top level is seldom necessary, and decision in terms of the higher concepts is given in terms of the fitting of actual behaviour into the lower level concepts. I shall discuss these concepts more fully when I consider the law of wrongs.[1]

I similarly postpone a full discussion of the concepts which are considered in adjudicating on contracts between strangers. The few cases in contract cited above show that in Lozi law contracts rarely present difficult legal problems. Their dominant characteristic is that they are viewed as the transfer of property rights, and not as arising from agreement, though agreement is considered. Speaking generally, if property is transferred by a person who has the right to make such a transfer, the contract is valid. The question of whether he has a valid right is simple unless it be property of a kinsman, when complicated and disputing arguments may be advanced, as in ' The Case of the Father and his Son's Cattle ' (pp. 109–10). Since executory contracts and consequent or indirect damages were not enforced while I was in Loziland, no problems of offer and acceptance, of promise, etc., arose. This meant that the courts were not concerned with contractual motivation, or with problems of weighing damages beyond immediate loss.

Briefly, then, in contract cases the court begins by defining the social positions of the litigants : buyer and seller, lender and borrower, employer and servant, cattle-owner and herder, owner and share-cropper in fishing, partners. These positions are linked by agreement (*tumelano*), in sale (*muleko*) or barter (*musintana*), loan (*kukalimela*), employment (*kusebezisa*), herding (*kufisa*), share-fishing (*munonelo*), or partnership (*kopanyo*). Fulfilment (*kueza*) contrasts with failure to perform (*kusaeza, kupalelwa*) if one party transfers or creates any property under the agreement : then the other party is bound. But fulfilment is vitiated by fraud or misrepresentation (*kupuma*), latent defect (*kusaluka*), negligence (*buswafa*), or *laesio enormis* (*kutulisa*). Here the court, as in delicts and crimes, makes a decision by measuring reasonable and customary fulfilment in the light of these possible defences and enforces return or compensation.

VI

I pass now to consider the concepts of trial and judgment. Cardozo elaborated his judicial ' method of sociology ' in

---

[1] In *The Ideas of Barotse Jurisprudence*.

analysing how judges fill gaps in the law. The method is even more significant during trial, because it is in the process of fitting evidence into general legal concepts, and then manipulating the rights and wrongs which result, that the judges introduce both traditional and new standards of reasonableness and customariness. We have seen that as they function in the substantive law they are *permeable* in that they are saturated with the whole culture of the society. They are, in addition, *absorbent*, in that they can take into their generality a great variety of actual circumstances.

I glanced at this process in discussing both judicial logic and how 'morality' serves as a source of Lozi law, when judges hear, cross-examine on, and draw conclusions from the evidence. Here, to quote Cardozo again, custom always ' manifests creative energy '. For current mores control the application and specification of old rules by determining whether there has been adherence to or departure from accepted standards of right and obligation. This process of application depends on the flexible character of the concepts involved in trial and judgment. These concepts bring the hierarchies of substantive law into relation with actual life.

The key concept here, equivalent to *law* in which it is embraced, is trial by due process of law (*tatubo kamulao*). The process is based on hearing evidence (*bupaki*) which establishes proof (also *bupaki*) on the facts (*litaba* = also things). Evidence itself is reduced by concepts of relevance (*bupaki bobuswanela*, appropriate or right evidence ; *bupaki bobukena*, evidence which enters) ; of cogency (*bupaki bobutiile*, strong evidence) ; of credibility (*bupaki bobusepehala*) ; and of corroboration (*bupaki bobuyemela*). These types of evidence are tested as direct, circumstantial, or hearsay. The concepts of evidence have a marked double flexibility, as contrasted with those of the substantive law. First, they are multiple in their referents : they cover evidence given in court about actions committed, the judges' knowledge of the social and physical world (judicial presumptions : *linto zelwaziba*, things we know), and the judges' inferences from the evidence (*lisupo*, indications, probabilities). Secondly, these concepts are elastic, and can be stretched to cover many different facts, and to contrast the facts accepted by the judges as against irrelevant, weak, dubious, and uncorroborated evidence—I need not give the Lozi negatives. This twofold flexibility of the concepts of trial law makes it possible for the judges to manipulate the raw facts presented in court, to provide ' facts-in-law ' on which to give judgment, even more easily than they can manipulate the concepts of substantive law. On the basis of quite different evaluations of evidence judges can give the same judgment (see the Cases of ' the Biassed Father ', p. 41, ' The Headman's Fishdams ', p. 180, and ' The Schoolboy Adulterer ', p. 131), and give different judgments on the basis of the same evaluation of the evidence (see the same cases). It further enables the judges to take cognizance of, and be influenced by, many things which they themselves consider to fall outside the law itself. Current usage is continually *absorbed* into the law by the reasoning of the judges, at every step of the process of trial, which involves the preliminary specification of general legal concepts, while facts are being sifted from the evidence to become ' facts-in-law '. Parties themselves are working with these concepts in giving their evidence. This process is of crucial importance in Lozi law even though there are not pleadings and rules excluding certain evidence, as in English law, to reduce occurrences to the ' mere skeleton . . . of the event itself, from which all irrelevant circumstances have been removed '.[1] The Lozi have a conception of ' relevant evidence ' even if on occasion it be a very wide one. Thus in ' The Case of the Headman's Fishdams ' the one sister was told that the kuta could no longer enter into her father's charge of sorcery against her, though this was considered in judgment and the reaction of the present headman to that charge was relevant to the issue under trial (see also ALULEYA on the evidence of the defendant's friends in ' The Case of the Schoolboy Adulterer '). *Relevance* is very wide in cases between kinsmen, and the kuta adjudicates on a variety of circumstances besides the legal claim itself : yet there is a steady pruning of the facts to fit into them legal rules.

The judges manipulate these flexible evidential concepts, within the frame of due process of law by trial, and then give arguments on the evidence which are often rationalizations to defend conclusions on the merits of the case. They frame their judgments (*likatulo*) to produce ' reasonable proof ' (*bupaki bobulikanya*) which is built on *lisupo* (indications and probabilities)

---

[1] Vinogradoff, *Common-sense in Law*, pp. 87 ff.

and *libaka* (reasons, causes). 'Probabilities' breaks down into a series of legal concepts and presumptions about reasonable customary behaviour, which we have already examined, and 'presumptions', whose influence is surveyed below. 'Reasons' —argument—also is composed of subordinate concepts. There are analogy (*kuswanisa*) and distinction (*kufapanisa*), even if implicit, of cases. These are linked to the probabilities by variable syntactical devices, and by conjunctions whose very apparent simplicity—'therefore', 'and', 'because', etc.—not only allows them to be patently misused, but also allows the judges great play in argument. Here is another set of flexible concepts—though by no means so hierarchial a set as that of substantive law—which allows considerable manipulation.

The judges' manipulation of these concepts is implicit in their assessment of the evidence of the parties against the standard of 'the reasonable and upright man'. This standard, composed of many usages, modes of behaviour, and customary practices, is used by the parties in describing their own behaviour. Hence wherever a man's evidence shows that he has not conformed to these ways of life, the judges may decide his whole story is false. Thus the Violent Councillor was convicted because he did not 'seat the plaintiff and summon the men of the village' (pp. 89–90). The Mbunda adulterer was convicted because he did not make presents to his female cross-cousin in public (p. 135). In this way many customs and ways of life are enforced indirectly by the court, even when they are not explicitly the enforceable subjects of legal rules. These customs and ways of life specify especially elastic concepts of 'guilt'—the ethical category of motivation including 'negligence', 'provocation', etc. The Biassed Father was shown to be favouring his own son because after the latter's seduction of his nephew's wife, he did not offer a meal of reconciliation (p. 43). In deciding that this omission indicated the guilt of the father in being partial, the judge did not make the offering of a meal of reconciliation a legal rule that would be enforced,[1] though my informants said that in

---

[1] As it is in many simple societies, notably in Indonesian *adat* law. See for a summary statement Ter Haar, B., *Adat Law in Indonesia* (edited with an introduction by E. A. Hoebel and A. A. Schiller), New York : Institute of Pacific Relations, 1948, at pp. 216–17. See also Llewellyn and Hoebel, *The Cheyenne Way*, passim.

the past this might have been a legal ruling. Similarly, in the examples given above the judges did not state that they would punish a headman who failed to seat a complainant and to summon the villagers, or the Mbunda who gave his female cross-cousin gifts in private. The judgments imply that these derelictions from customary practices would help to convict of other offences, and thus become enforceable indirectly, but would not be made specific enforceable ' legal rules '.

Thus in Lozi law the judicial process begins from the moment pleadings begin, and throughout the process of listening to, cross-examining on, and giving judgment upon, evidence, the judges are fitting facts into absorbent legal concepts, and are manipulating those concepts. In doing this they work constantly with the whole of their social and personal experience which has produced in them a series of presumptions. One man had heard that girls at initiation are taught to protect their real lovers by false accusations against innocent men : therefore he acquitted the Schoolboy Adulterer. Another had been betrayed by his mistress in almost identical circumstances : therefore he acted on the contrary presumption. Other judges stated explicitly that they had mistresses and therefore knew how lovers behave to one another (see ' The Case of the Schoolboy Adulterer ', pp. 130, 136). There is the wider presumption that men do not have platonic friendships with unrelated women. Through these presumptions the judges, unrestrained by the fiction of judicial ignorance, feed into the judicial process both standardized and personal knowledge and beliefs about certain types of relationships between people.

These presumptions are present whatever be the issue before the court. Lozi men like to become village headmen : therefore the eldest nephew in ' The Case of the Biassed Father ' was seducing his brothers to leave their uncle's village and he would not let the quarrel die ; and Sabangwa had not offered to rejoin Mahalihali village. In ' The Case of the Prince's Gardens ', Prince Mboo Sipopa stated : ' I do not believe a small depression would be the boundary between two villages' gardens ' ; and INGANGWANA (LI) did not believe that the plaintiff would attempt to steal the defendant's gardens, since the plaintiff had shown the defendant his land when he succeeded to his headmanship. This would be unreasonable (*hakukolwahali*), and hence was

z

unbelievable (also *hakukolwahali*).   I need not multiply examples :
those given indicate that the establishment of the minor premiss
of fact to be fitted to the major premiss of law, involves the
skilful and socially controlled use of evidential and argumentative
concepts of varying status and kinds of uncertainty.

The presumptions enter into the treatment of the demeanour
of parties and witnesses.   Wrongdoers become angry in court
to cover their wrongs, like the Quarrelsome Teacher, or the
defendant in ' The Case of the Prince's Gardens '.   However
righteously indignant a man may be at a trespass on his rights,
he should be calm in court, confident that the judges will see
that justice is done.   From the beginning the judges approved
the plaintiffs in ' The Case of the Expropriating Stewards ', for
stating that they did not get carried away by anger, but had,
a week afterwards, brought their complaint to the Malozi (p. 140).

Thus already in the assessing of evidence, we see that law as
a general body of rules is brought into action on a particular
dispute by the temporary specification of general and flexible
concepts.   This is done in terms of the judges' acquaintance not
only with the law itself, but also with the whole body of the
values, the ways of life, and the public opinion of society as a
whole, and also in terms of the judges' personal presumptions
arising from experience in society.   This situation helps to explain why judges may vary in their decisions even though they
apply comparatively simple legal rules.

The procedure of trial also affects the whole question of where
burden of proof lies, and thus the manner in which the Lozi
apply the maxim ' a man is innocent until he is proved guilty '.
I have already argued that the impression which may be given
that in African law a man is guilty till he proves his innocence,
is wrong.   The importance of this correction warrants repetition.   In practice, since the judges conduct the main cross-
examination they automatically, in order to get at the truth,
throw all parties on to the defensive by attacking everyone's
evidence.   In short, they act in ' civil ' cases as counsel for each
party to assail the other, and in ' criminal ' trials they similarly
both prosecute and defend the accused.   To carry out their
cross-examination they have to act as if they believed the parties
or accused are lying—i.e. as if the accused were guilty.   Hence
the assumption of guilt is present in cross-examination, but not

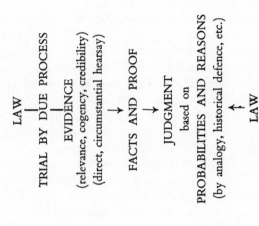

FLEXIBILITY OF BOTH MULTIPLICITY AND ELASTICITY

LAW

TRIAL BY DUE PROCESS

EVIDENCE
(relevance, cogency, credibility)
(direct, circumstantial hearsay)

→ FACTS AND PROOF

→ JUDGMENT
based on

PROBABILITIES AND REASONS
(by analogy, historical defence, etc.)

← LAW

REASONABLE AND CUSTOMARY

CHART OF THE HIERARCHY OF LOZI CONCEPTS
IN THE PROCESS OF TRIAL AND JUDGMENT

in judgment, and many accused and defendants are acquitted for lack of good evidence. In practice, the burden of proof constantly shifts from party to party since different judges follow different lines of cross-examination.

VII

I tried and failed to relate a series of judgments by particular judges to their personal histories, characters, circumstances, and social positions. I found that I had not sufficiently detailed information about their personal histories, characters and circumstances ; and I also lacked an appropriate variety of cases. A survey of the opinions of judges in cases I did record showed no particular consistency : it was difficult however to subject this material to quantitative analysis. I was left with certain general impressions. One judge who has had much trouble with his own children tended to be severe on youths who had come into conflict with their elders, and to place disaproportionate blame on them as against other judges. Another junior judge who is notorious for his unusual jealousy of his wife—an attitude attributed by the Lozi to the wife's magic—tended to convict of adultery more often than his fellows.

Lozi judges are drawn widely from the tribe as a whole and are related by kinship throughout the Barotse nation. This applies to princes as well as commoners. The judges include young and old, Christians and pagans, educated and illiterate, rich and poor. I do not believe that anyone could tell from particular judgments whether judges were Christian or pagan, educated or illiterate. The pagan SOLAMI (R3) tended most often to bring God into his exhortations. The judges do not deal with the important conflicts between Whites and Blacks. In cases over land, which are economically the most important cases they try, princes, title-holders, and headmen did not unwarrantably support superior land-holders against their inferiors. This is manifest in ' The Case of the Headman's Fishdams ', as it is, in another context, in ' The Case of the Violent Councillor '. Indeed, my impression is that the royal family, which ultimately owns the land through the king, is as ready to enforce the rights of ordinary people in land as are commoner councillors. All judges seem to vary in their judgments according to their ability, rather than their personal or group prejudices and self-interest. The Lozi themselves—and indeed all Barotse—ascribe differences in judicial decision to differences in individual knowledge, wisdom, and courage, and not to differences in social status or acquirement.

The main presumptions which influence Lozi judges are, aside from a few personal prejudices, general social presumptions. This accords with the persisting comparative homogeneity of their society.

These social presumptions are drawn from the existing system of relations in the society, with a certain nostalgia for the good old days. The rising intelligentsia castigate the kuta for being conservative. But this charge has to be evaluated in political terms. The members of this intelligentsia are themselves anxious to obtain power in the kuta, and complaints about judgments are a handy weapon. I have very rarely heard one of them differ from the appointed judges in his judgment on a specific dispute.[1]

VIII

The process of judicial interpretation which I have been analysing contains implicitly a maintenance of general legal and moral principles, composed of general concepts which can expand to meet, and which can absorb, new conditions. We have already seen (pp. 217 ff.) that the judges are not rigidly conservative, though their judgments are cast to defend the structure of the political constitution, the system of land-distribution, and the major premisses of the kinship system. These embody complex patterns of rights and duties, and the judges often combine their elements to achieve equitable solutions in terms of modern conditions, as in 'The Case of the Headman's Fishdams'. But the simplest application of a law, since it involves always the extrinsic reference of a flexible ethical concept, raises problems of similar kind.

In short, the essence of the Lozi judicial process, both during trial and in judgment, is to specify the behaviour of the parties, in terms of a series of flexible concepts, of varying kinds and degrees of uncertainty, permeability, and absorptive capacity.

---

[1] This problem will be discussed in *The Rôle of Courts in Barotse Social Life*.

The judges do this by several methods of logical argument. The concepts are already united in a variety of established relations, and the judges combine these relations in varied patterns to try to achieve law and justice. From a whole body of independent rules they extract, if they can, those which support justice. Above all, they bring the legal rules to bear on the facts of the dispute through the 'flexibility' of the concepts themselves, since this flexibility enables the judges to relate general norms to the great and changing variety of social life. The concepts are given external referents in accordance with social presumptions which include values, ideals, knowledge, mores, and usages, though these social presumptions are to some extent influenced by the personal presumptions or prejudices of various judges.

Though the concepts are flexible, they are not vague. They do have accepted definition or definitions. Over a series of disputes, and in the course of social life unmarred by dispute, their connotation is determined within limits, and judges are expected to abide by this determination. Since case-law is not recorded, the application of these flexible concepts to particular alignments of circumstance is not circumscribed by precedents which define them with increasing exactitude. Judicial discretion is unfettered in its redefinitions, and the judges do not rely on fictions to develop or amend the law in the interests of justice.

This process primarily enables Lozi judges to operate what Cardozo called 'the method of sociology' (see p. 291), by which they introduce into the law conceptions of social welfare, and changes in mores and public opinion. It further enables Lozi judges to give just decisions on disputes arising out of new circumstances. Moreover, these decisions on the whole are accepted, and expected, by the public, since they conform with a well-known body of rules. The public works with the same presumptions as the judges.

Since the judges relate existing practice with flexible concepts stating ideals which persist through social changes, they rarely appear to be revolutionary in their decisions. But I have given several examples to show that Lozi judges do manage in adjudication to cope, within the limits of their jurisdiction, with the very great changes in ways of life and in social relationships which have occurred in Loziland. Judges have contributed to the attempt Lozi are making to adjust to modern conditions, albeit within a persisting framework of political structure and land-holding. They have re-defined their basic concepts to accommodate new facts of life. They have indeed, within the definitions of the terms which stand high in the hierarchy of concepts, restated the ambit of law to include the British Protectorate, and restated the respective rights of king and subject, lord and underling, father and son, husband and wife. Though the councillors are usually conservative, they are a force, both as judges and as legislators, in developing Lozi law to cope with new disputes arising from new relationships and activities.

IX

Lozi law thus exists both as a body of rules to which people ought to conform and which the courts ought to enforce, and as a series of specific judgments on particular disputes, which are the law for those disputes. These are law in general (*corpus juris*) and law in action (*adjudication*). The two not only may diverge, as obviously where a judge gives a partial or other bad decision ; but they cannot coincide because they are quite different kinds of social phenomena. Lozi law in general is partly a body of very general principles relating general and flexible concepts (e.g. ' you cannot sue your host if a fishbone sticks in your throat '—*volenti non fit injuria*), and partly a body of general statements about the relationships of social positions (e.g. if you leave the village you lose rights in its land ; a son must respect and care for his father). These are general relations between general concepts which are applicable to many different situations. They are contained in a variety of sources : statutes, precedents, customary practice, usage, good morals, equity—I need not repeat the full list. Law in action applies the law in general to diverse actual situations, and draws on all these sources, but does so usually by emphasizing the moral decision. The judges also draw on presumptions about standardized usages, both of conduct and misconduct, in evaluating the evidence. In these processes they manipulate the general principles and the particular rules and usages of law in an attempt to achieve justice. Sometimes they cannot do so because statutory or customary rules apply too precisely. But since their main task is to specify a series of flexible concepts (ranging from ' law ' itself to ' leaves the village '), for the particular dispute, they introduce through these concepts and their interconnections equitable argument to assess reasonable performance of duties and reasonable exercise of rights.   The varied flexibility of the key concepts of Lozi law and ethics is one of their attributes as instruments of argument.   It enables the law to cover various situations and to develop so that it can accommodate social change.   In this way the law in general is channelled through law in action to cover the infinite variety of situations in social life.   Each legal ruling is unique to its situation of dispute : it is stated in terms of fixed principles.

The Lozi judicial process is thus centrally the specification of general concepts, with moral implications, in order to apply them to specific circumstances so as to defend established and emergent values of rightdoing.   These concepts can be arranged in a hierarchy in which the most important—law itself, right, duty, and wrong—are widest in their generality, and have multiple referents.   Other more limited elastic concepts refer to human motivations and these operate in the context of similarly more limited concepts of social positions.   General and flexible standards of reasonableness, rightness, and customariness pervade the hierarchy.   This series of concepts operates in actual life through other concepts of twofold flexibility, which define the process of trial and judgment on evidence.   This is the logical process by which Lozi law is made the final enforcing agency to relate ideals to the actualities of social life.   The ' certainty ' of law resides in the ' uncertainty ' of its basic concepts.   I hope my flexible use of ' certainty ' here does not negate entirely the value, or the resolution, of this paradox.

CHAPTER VII

SOME COMPARATIVE IMPLICATIONS OF THE LOZI JUDICIAL PROCESS

I

I HAVE concluded my analysis of the judicial process among the Lozi, but venture finally to comment on some wider implications. To a social anthropologist, a trial is but one of many social situations which he has to study in order to understand the life of ' his ' people. Therefore I began my analysis of the Lozi judicial process in the field and worked out the main outlines of this book in Northern Rhodesia. Such academic legal training as I had was in orthodox jurisprudence, and I did not then know of the numerous studies which have been made of the Western judicial process, particularly in the United States—notably by Holmes, Cardozo, Gray, Frank, Llewellyn, Pound, and others. I confess my ignorance not merely to claim a little belated originality, but because it shows that I was not directly influenced to detect the same elements in the Lozi judicial process, that these jurists have found in the West. My present contention that the judicial process in Lozi courts is basically similar to that of Western judges is thereby strengthened, even though I have latterly read some of these Western studies and used them to improve my analysis.

My primary duty as a field-ethnographer was to try to report my observations as intelligently as I could. I am delighted in every way that this report bears witness to some similarities of social life everywhere, and to the basic similarity of all human beings in very varied conditions. Beyond these modest hopes, as my analysis proceeded I ventured to think that my Lozi data on the social function and value of flexible legal concepts, might resolve certain problems that have produced jurisprudential controversy. I make this submission with all respect and humility, which are doubled by my inability, in the working life of an anthropologist, to consult more than a fraction of the relevant literature. The central problem which I hope has been solved is that the flexible generality of Lozi concepts enables the certainty of law as a body of rules to exist through the considerable uncertainty of judicial decision.

Lozi judgments vary markedly as the judges exercise their discretion : yet for the Lozi, and for me as an observer, these judgments were not whimsical but were given within a system of law. This statement itself requires that we have two—or several—definitions of law. And indeed the Lozi themselves use *mulao* (law) with many connotations. A priori, one would expect that any attempt to reduce to one definition as complex a set of phenomena as those we designate *law*, would fail in the face of alternative definitions referring to other of their attributes. Certainly, any attempt to explain the behaviour of Lozi judges and public when they act in reference to what they call *the law* (*mulao*) and *courts* (*likuta*) fails unless one regards *law* as a multi-referential complex of institutions. It has no one essential attribute.

I have produced evidence to show that the Lozi think *and act* as if there were a single embracing and certain *Law*, and a series of well-known rights and duties, which control their social life. It is not that judges alone rationalize particular decisions in terms of these concepts as subjective.[1] As we have seen, the litigants themselves in describing their behaviour are influenced by these conceptions. Moreover—and in a book of this kind necessarily so—I have not quoted descriptions of people fulfilling their obligations and pursuing their activities with assurance that their rights will be observed by others.[2] Cases like that of the Good Son-in-Law, and the judges' citations of exemplary behaviour, must here stand for the extent to which the Lozi conform with the law in overwhelmingly most transactions.

The Lozi associate this reign of law and order in which they live and which they consider that their kutas maintain, with the king (and his representative chiefs of the royal family). Hence at Lialui all judicial verdicts are referred to the king. Hence the king's palace, bandsmen, royal relative NATAMOYO

---

[1] I shall discuss below (p.351–2) Professor K. Olivecrona's attack on the notion of rights and duties as 'metaphysical conceptions . . . [which] emerge as pure imagination without correspondence in objective reality' : *Law as Fact*, London : Oxford University Press (1939), p. 77.

[2] This will be considered in *The Rôle of Courts in Barotse Social Life*.

(R2, a prince in the kuta), storehouses, and his queens' and the queen-mother's courtyards, and the royal cenotaphs—almost all things royal—are sanctuaries from the kuta.[1] The king symbolizes justice. As the apex of the governmental machine, he is vested with ritual as well as secular power, to secure fertility, strength, and prosperity for the nation. These good things can be obtained in the rule of law and order which enables men to own property and to co-operate with others in security.[2]

The king with his very real secular power, and his halo of ritual power, stands for the certainty of Lozi law. This was so frequently emphasized to me by the Lozi, and was so apparent in their everyday actions, that it must be taken as a ' real ' existent social fact. Yet Lozi admit that litigation is chancy : you cannot always tell in advance what judges will do. IMENDA concluded his judgment in ' The Case of the Man Who Helped his Mothers-in-Law Cross a Ford ', by stressing this uncertainty in adjudication: ' I agree with the others, but I do not know what will happen at the finish, because our law does not go straight like cattle to water, but here and there to the finisher.'

CASE 60 : THE CASE OF THE ADULTERER'S STOCKINGS
(my own observations)

A committed adultery with H's wife. H seized A's stockings to keep as proof. H reported the admitted adultery to the kuta and his wife paid the kuta's fine of £1. A delayed paying H the £2 damages due, and H retained the stockings. When A came to pay the £2 and reclaim the stockings he found that these had been eaten by white ants. H disclaimed responsibility. A held H was responsible, but when his friends advised him to sue for their value in the kuta, he refused : ' The kuta is a fearsome thing. You cannot tell where it will strike.'

Despite this chanciness in litigation, the Lozi maintain that the kuta applies certain law (*mulao ozibiwa*). They find the certainty of law in the general principles which can be applied variously to particular circumstances, and they use social devices, such as their terminology for bad and even corrupt reasoning, to dispose

---

[1] This too will be discussed in *The Rôle of Courts in Barotse Social Life*.
[2] See Fortes and Evans-Pritchard's *Introduction* to *African Political Systems*, pp. 16 ff., for an analysis of this ritual value of the political order, and my *Rituals of Rebellion in South-East Africa*, Manchester University Press (1954).

of patently unjust decisions and of poor judges. The belief in
the certainty of law persists since some of its failures in litigation
are referred to human fallibility. Beyond this, as has often been
stated, we can find the certainty of general principle in the
comparative uncertainty of judicial decision. In all decisions—
even in ' unjust ' decisions save where the law is patently mis-
applied—these certain general principles are so constructed that
they can cover varied contingencies in various ways. Their
constituent concepts are flexibly uncertain. This is necessary
to relate *The Law* to litigation and adjudication in judges' legal
rulings. The very wide generality of the simple legal rules of
the Lozi, and the illiterate situation in which they allow sweeping
judicial discretion, have forced my attention to the social value
of these flexible concepts. I have been led to accept their
flexible uncertainty as essential to legal certainty ; to examine
the nature of this uncertainty in different kinds of concepts not
as creating difficulties, but as solving juristic problems in the
relation of norms to actual life ; and to try to arrange the concepts in an ordered hierarchy in terms of this uncertainty. The
dangers which lie in the higher, more abstract words of this
widely recognized hierarchy produce difficulties and slips of
meaning,[1] but the difficulties and slips of meaning may be an
essential part of the judicial technique. At least the juristic
sociologist—and the sociological jurist—cannot merely castigate
semantic weaknesses in forensic argument : he must examine
the rôle of these obscurities in the social process. They may
be generally—as often they are patently, politically—useful. It
may be that the very nature of the judicial process prevented
judges from adopting wholesale Hohfeld's attempt to clarify
the conception of rights and duties,[2] though this would not
deny its value for jurisprudential analysis.

The points I have been making have all been separately made
by various jurists, but I know of no work in which they are
woven into a consistent theory. I admit that my reading in
jurisprudence is comparatively limited. However, it is striking
that a number of learned authorities who have recently considered

---

[1] Chafee, ' The Disorderly Conduct of Words ', op. cit., pp. 760–1 et
passim.

[2] Above pp. 166 ff. : Williams, op. cit., ii, pp. 179 ff., complains of this
failure.

these problems, have failed to appreciate the inter-related significance of a series of facts they observed separately. These facts are common to Western and to Lozi law : the structure of Lozi law has forced on me their inter-related significance.

I now proceed to validate my presumption by citing some of these authorities. My citations are fuller than they need have been had I been hoping only for an audience of lawyers ; but I must make known the background of established jurisprudential knowledge and controversy to social anthropologists. I begin by considering juristic appreciation and denigration of the 'ambiguity' of legal concepts, and various comments of fairly orthodox jurists on the judicial process. Finally I consider some of the theories of those who are sceptical of law's certainty.

II

The traditional approach to the judicial process recognizes clearly that it involves two main distinct processes of ratiocination : (1) the definition of the 'intrinsic meaning or meanings' of concepts ; and (2) the giving of 'extrinsic referents' to those concepts in a particular dispute. Many jurists have stated this.[1] However, even great jurists have failed to grasp all its implications. Thus Sir Paul Vinogradoff stated generally :

'It would be wrong . . . to suppose that statutes, however carefully formulated, reduce the application of the law to a mere mechanical process of bringing a given case under a given section. It is plain that however explicit the words of a statute may be, a Court must determine the exact meaning of the phraseology before it can apply the law. Attempts have sometimes been made to get rid of this necessity of judicial interpretation : for example, the introduction to the Prussian Code of 1794 went so far as to forbid all interpretation as distinct from direct application, and ordered that tribunals should lay all cases of doubtful verbal meaning before a special committee of jurists and statesmen. This device, however, proved entirely unsuccessful, for it was found impossible to draw a precise line between application and interpretation, and to reduce a Court to the functions of a mere sorting-machine. Statute law or codified law [or, indeed, common law in judicial precedents, and customary law] necessarily consists of sentences, the words of which may be differently understood by different people ; and the first duty of a Court is therefore

---

[1] See, e.g., Allen, *Law in the Making*, p. 108.

one of *literal interpretation*. The law-reports abound with examples of this necessity, which is perpetually imposed upon tribunals, and which often gives rise to difficult problems.' Sir Paul illustrates with a problem of the definition of ' accident in the course of employment' for purposes of the Workmen's Compensation Act, 1906, in which the murder of a clerk for money in his charge was held to be such an accident.[1]

With all respect, I submit that, as Judge Frank and others have shown, the concepts and relations contained in sentences are not only ' words . . . which may be differently understood by different people '. Of their very nature they are general and flexible terms, which are to some extent of uncertain connotation and require, as Sir Paul's example shows, not literal interpretation but specification in certain circumstances.

The main uncertainty—and value—of some of the most important concepts resides in the fact that they are loaded with presumptions which arise from social life itself, complicated by the presumptions of interests, cultural values, and traditions of a particular society. I hope that my study of Lozi law, like other studies of the law of simple peoples, has shown that certain of these basic concepts are probably common to most legal systems. Their definition and rigour vary with social conditions, but they are present. It is therefore surprising to find in Sir Carleton Allen's masterly *Law in the Making* (at pp. 70–1) the following passage, which I cite since it evidences this seeming lack of full awareness by many jurists of the character of their concepts :

It is a constant source of wonder to foreigners that our law is built up to so great an extent on *assumptions* : that in the most fundamental matters (Austin notwithstanding) there are so few direct commands and prohibitions. Where shall we find any formulated rule which expressly defines and forbids assault, or libel, or false imprisonment, or negligence ? Not only the Judges, but Parliament itself, in regulating such matters of civil liability, constantly assume an hypothesis of existing law : for example, an inquirer will search in vain the important statutes relating to libel for a definition of that very common tort. It would never occur to the House of Commons to lay down what constitutes actionable negligence in law ; the conception of

---

[1] *Common-sense at Law*, op. cit., pp. 121 ff. Williams, op. cit., lxi, p. 180, curiously criticizes this decision that ' murder' can be ' an accident', as absurd.

duty which underlies it is rooted far deeper than any English statute seeks to go. In Criminal Law, it is true, a wider field has been covered by legislation. Indeed, so much of our Criminal Law has now been embodied in statute, that there seems to be no very cogent argument against the codification of the whole of it. In some cases, statute has filled up gaps in the Common Law by 'new' crimes, like embezzlement, false pretences, publication of false balance sheets, and the like. But the foundations of criminal liability are still firmly embedded in the Common Law, and to this day our statute-book contains no definition of the highest crime but one known to the law, and the most heinous known to humanity—wilful murder. The definition of this crime which is to be found in Coke, and in any treatise on Criminal Law, is a mosaic of principles put together through ages of practice and interpretation. In all branches, the assumptions on which our law is built up are so many and so vital that it is tempting to regard them all as spontaneous outcrops of the national genius. This . . . is not entirely true ; but it is more nearly true than the conception of them as commands, direct or indirect.

With all respect, these assumptions are not ' spontaneous out-crops of the [English] national genius' alone. Some of them crop up spontaneously also in Lozi law, and I believe they must exist in all systems of law. It appears to me that Sir Carleton has confounded different kinds of general legal concepts and assumptions in discussing together actionable negligence in law, libel, assault, false imprisonment, publication of false balance sheets, murder, and the like. Some principles, of crime or civil liability, can be more or less narrowly defined in a statute—e.g. the publication of false balance sheets. Others, like guilt or negligence, cannot be restricted in a set formula, unless it be a formula containing equally general concepts like ' due care ' or ' to the injury of others'. The civil codes of the Continent may lay down rules about these principles, but they will be as pregnant with unformulated assumptions as are the rules of English law. Dr. Seagle shows that legal developments in all countries have been basically similar in similar social conditions. He states that ' it is . . . fortunate that the rules of the [French] code themselves were couched in such broad terms as to be not more than vague general principles. Thus it has been possible without altering the text of the Civil Code to adapt the law of liability for wrongs to the conditions of the machine age.'[1]

---

[1] *The Quest for Law*, passim, and at p. 288.

These assumptions thus serve in any society, and at different stages of its history, to import into the application of the law traditional and current social values, interests, technology, etc.— and also, of course, personal values.   In Cardozo's words, already quoted, ' general standards of right and duty are established. Custom must determine whether there has been adherence or departure.'   But Cardozo did not relate this all-important judicial fact to the flexible character of legal terms, though he deals with that flexible character in several contexts.

Cardozo's study of the *Nature of the Judicial Process* was based on his own experience and this was mainly in appellate and not in trial courts.   Judge Frank has attributed to this Cardozo's ' relatively placid picture of the judicial process '.[1]   I therefore consider first his view as the simplest exposition of realized uncertainty of legal rules in the judicial process.   It lays aside for the moment the main part of that uncertainty—but not all— by which evidence is converted into facts-in-law.   However, the result is that Cardozo states the problem of flexible uncertainty and then slides away from its implications in trial procedure, to concentrate on how judges cope ' with gaps in the law '.   For example, he quotes [2] with approval the words of an English judge, Sir James Parke :

> Our common law system consists in applying to new combinations of circumstances those rules of law which we derive from legal principles and judicial precedents, and for the sake of attaining uniformity, consistency and certainty, we must apply those rules when they are not plainly unreasonable and inconvenient to all cases which arise ; and we are not at liberty to reject them in those in which they have not been judicially applied, because we think that the rules are not as convenient and reasonable as we ourselves could have devised.

Cardozo proceeds :

> This does not mean that there are not gaps, yet unfilled, within which judgment moves untrammelled.   Mr. Justice Holmes has summed it up in one of his flashing epigrams : ' I recognize without hesitation that judges must and do legislate, but they do so only interstitially ; they are confined from molar to molecular motions.' . . .

---

[1] *Law and the Modern Mind*, ' Preface to Sixth Printing ', pp. xxv–xxvi.

[2] *Nature of the Judicial Process*, at pp. 68–70.   It is true that he is particularly concerned with these gaps in legal rules ; but every case, on my argument, is in a gap—the void of concepts themselves.

This conception of the legislative power of a judge as operating between spaces is akin to the theory of 'gaps in the law' familiar to foreign jurists.

Since Cardozo is concerned with gaps in law, the theme of his analysis is that 'for every tendency, one sees a counter-tendency; for every rule its antinomy. Nothing is stable. Nothing absolute. All is fluid and changeable. There is an endless "becoming". We are back with Heraclitus' (loc. cit., pp. 27–8). This presumably means that various legal rules are in conflict, or not thoroughly consistent, and that judges may develop rules differently. Cardozo fails, in my opinion, to bring out the relation between this 'rule-uncertainty' and that large part of his analysis in which he deals with the work of the American Supreme Court on cases arising from the Constitution. He explains conflicting decisions in these cases by stating that 'the great generalities of the Constitution have a content and a significance that vary from age to age. The method of free decision sees through the transitory particulars and reaches what is permanent behind them' (loc. cit., p. 17). Thus (pp. 76–7) the concept of liberty in the Constitutional doctrine that 'noone shall be robbed of liberty without due process of law' is 'a concept of the greatest generality. Yet it is put before the courts *en bloc*. Liberty is not defined. Its limits are not mapped and charted. How shall they be known? Does liberty mean the same thing for successive generations? May restraints that were arbitrary yesterday be useful and rational and therefore lawful today?' Clearly 'without due process of law' is equally 'a concept of the greatest generality'. Again, he states that 'the same fluid and dynamic conception . . . must also underlie the cognate notion of equality'. He draws attention to successive redefinitions of public use, property rights, restraints of trade, and other terms (at pp. 82 ff.).

Cardozo thus saw clearly that 'a constitution states or ought to state not rules for the passing hour, but principles for an expanding future. In so far as it deviates from that standard, and descends into details and particulars, it loses its flexibility, the scope of interpretation contracts, the meaning hardens. While it is true to its function, it maintains its power of adaptation, its suppleness, its play.' To solve these problems, and to overcome the political prejudices of individual judges, he considers

2A

that evidence from ' students of the social sciences ' should help the judges define these concepts in modern situations.

Cardozo's poetic language obscures three distinct processes : firstly, altering the intrinsic meaning of concepts ; secondly, giving them extrinsic referents in new situations ; and, thirdly, altering the weighting of various rules. I have quoted above his conclusion that ' the method of free interpretation sees through the transitory particulars and reaches what is permanent behind them '. This is not consistent with a conclusion elsewhere : ' The common law does not work from pre-established truths of universal and inflexible validity to conclusions derived from them deductively. Its method is inductive, and it draws its generalizations from particulars.' The inconsistency appears to me to arise from the fact that Cardozo is in effect not distinguishing clearly two distinct tasks laid on the judge : the maintenance of *Law*, and the giving of a just and lawful judgment on a particular dispute. Each statement refers to these separate tasks, which have to be combined in the judicial process as a whole. Sound analysis should explain these inconsistencies by one theory : and Cardozo fails to do this. I am suggesting, in all humility, that my analysis attempts this, for under its principles ' logical ' slips and jumps, and even inconsistency, may be an essential part of the judge's apparatus of argument.

In fact, on many occasions judges do work from ' pre-established truths of universal and inflexible validity . . . deductively '. Roman legal maxims have been applied through two millennia. Judges also draw their generalizations from particulars : this is the root of precedent. These contradictory tendencies supply the poles of rigid certainty and flexibility which have bothered judges for centuries, and which led Dean Pound to emphasize that the first must be an attribute of property and commercial law, and the second an attribute of law involving human conduct.[1] The contradiction shows in the distinction between the *ratio decidendi* of a case and its particular circumstances. The problem is well summarized by Sir C. K. Allen in his *Law in the Making*. He says that several judges have warned ' against the shallow notion that there is any magic in *mere* citations [of precedents], without regard to their true significance as embodi-

---

[1] Judge Frank expounds and criticizes this dichotomy in *Law and the Modern Mind*, pp. 204 ff.

ments of principle'.[1] He further quotes several warnings of Lord Mansfield's on this point, presumably because Lord Mansfield did so much to establish the doctrine of 'judicial consistency and authority'. I cite two of these warnings :

The law of England would be a strange science if indeed it were decided upon precedents only. Precedents serve to illustrate principles and to give them a fixed certainty. But the law of England, which is exclusive of positive law, enacted by statute, depends upon principles, and these principles run through all the cases according as the particular circumstances of each have been found to fall within one or the other of them' (in Jones *v.* Randall, 1774, Cowp. 37),

and

'Perhaps there is no case exactly parallel to this in all circumstances. . . . But the law does not consist in particular cases, but in general principles, which run through the cases and govern the decision in them' (in Rust *v.* Cooper, 1783, 3 Doug. 327).

Other great judges have stressed the importance of returning to these basic principles after they have become overburdened with defining precedents. This would restore to them their former flexible generality. This is a reaction to the process by which in the Anglo-American legal system—and indeed in the system of civil law countries—the application of the flexible concepts to new situations becomes restricted by precedents and jurisprudential commentaries which try to refine definitions of negligence, duty, reasonable, etc. To achieve equity the courts may employ fictions, as courts did in archaic and mediaeval law, a device which Lozi judges find unnecessary since they are not burdened with written laws or ceremonial demands.

Cardozo's inconsistent analytic statements on the judicial process thus undoubtedly reflect contradictions in the material he is examining. They are phrased in the confusing, and as it happens metaphorical, language which beclouds the mastery of judicial logic, as Judge Frank and others have pointed out. Phrases like 'embodiments of principle' . . . 'principles which run through precedents' . . . themselves are metaphors which cover the complex process by which concepts of varied uncertainty, and varying status in a number of hierarchies, are given extrinsic referents and manipulated. I suggest that the source of this

---

[1] *Law in the Making*, pp. 206 ff.

confusion in Cardozo's analysis is contained in his approving quotation [1] from François Gény :

' Assuredly, there should be no question of banishing ratiocination and logical methods from the science of positive law.' Even general principles may sometimes be followed rigorously in the deduction of their consequences. ' The abuse . . . consists, if I do not mistake, in envisaging ideal conceptions, provisional and purely subjective in their nature, as endowed with a permanent objective reality. And this false point of view, which, to my thinking, is a vestige of the absolute realism of the middle ages, ends in confining the entire system of law, *a priori*, within a limited number of logical categories, which are predetermined in essence, immovable in basis, governed by inflexible dogmas, and thus incapable of adapting themselves to the ever varied and changing exigencies of life.'

Judges and litigants (or their counsel) work with dogmas, ideal conceptions, etc.—the social scientist must therefore grant them effective existence in social life. These dogmas and ideal conceptions have to be applied in trial to actual circumstances— i.e. the circumstances have to be fitted into the generality of the dogmas and conceptions—and in result the parties gain or lose materially. Hence judges clearly legislate not only in the cases which fall in gaps in the law, but also in cases where, according to Cardozo (loc. cit., pp. 163–4),

the controversy turns not upon the rule of law, but upon its application to the facts. These cases, after all, make up the bulk of the business of the courts. They are important for the litigants concerned in them. They call for intelligence and patience and reasonable discernment on the part of the judges who must decide them. As applied to such cases, the judicial process . . . is a process of search and comparison, and little else.

This is gross oversimplification. Professor Glanville Williams surveyed the problems of ' Language and the Law ' [2] in the light of modern semantics, and discussed the ' chameleon ' character of legal terms which are ' uncertain ' in several ways. On the above point he concluded :

the theory destroys the illusion that the function of a judge is simply to administer the law. If marginal cases must occur, the function

---

[1] *Nature of the Judicial Process*, pp. 46–7.
[2] *The Law Quarterly Review*, lvi (1945) and lvii (1946).

of the judge adjudicating upon them must be legislative. The distinction between the mechanical administration of fixed rules and free judicial discretion is thus a matter of degree, not the sharp distinction that it is sometimes assumed to be. This is not to say the judges have an unlimited legislative power. A judge has a discretion to include a flying-boat within a rule as to ships or vessels : he has no discretion to include a motor car within such a rule.[1]

Appreciation of the uncertainty of legal concepts has grown increasingly in recent jurisprudential studies. Jurists have always been aware of these problems in that they arose in the vexed field of ' interpretation '. Sir C. K. Allen has summarized some of these problems in his *Law and the Making* (loc. cit., pp. 417 et passim) in a fairly orthodox manner, and says that ' " the plain and unambiguous meaning of words ", by which the Courts so often believe themselves to be governed (frequently with inconvenient consequences) is really a delusion, since no words are so plain and unambiguous that they do not need interpretation in relation to a context of language or circumstances '. This is a comment following a quotation where Professor H. A. Smith, in contrasting *Interpretation in English and Continental Law*, points out that :

Words are only one form of conduct, and the intention which they convey is necessarily conditioned by the context and circumstances in which they are written and spoken. No word has an absolute meaning, for no word can be defined *in vacuo* or without reference to some context. . . . The practical work of the Courts is very largely a matter of ascertaining the meaning of words, and their function therefore becomes the study of contexts. Since the number and variety of contexts is only limited by the possibilities of human experience, it follows that no rules of interpretation can be regarded as absolute.[2]

---

[1] But contrast Sir Alan Herbert's misleading case of Rumpelheimer *v.* Haddock in *Uncommon Law*, op. cit., p. 237, where it was held that when the Thames flooded a highway adjacent to the river, a motor-car proceeding on that highway became subject to the rules controlling vessels passing one another. The defendant in a canoe forced the plaintiff's car to go port to port and to be damaged by the water. The judges held that the car, as a motor vessel, should have given way to the man-propelled canoe. I suggest that justice could have been achieved by enforcing the final rule of all, that no vessel may force another, under any rule, into peril.

[2] *Journal of Comparative Legislation*, ix (1927) at pp. 153–4.

From this starting-point, Professor Smith pleads for greater judicial discretion in taking evidence of context, both for the meaning of wills and other documents and for the meaning of statutes.

Professor Williams' article on 'Language and the Law'[1] is but one of many formidable arraignments of legal terminology. He applied the tools of modern semantics both to legal terminology and to the words on which lawyers have to work in cases. I have not space to summarize Professor Williams' penetrating survey of legal language, or his demonstration that 'even "univocal" words prove without exception to be extremely fractious when one comes to apply them to facts of experience'. He shows that some words are ambiguous ; others have several meanings ; others describe 'continuous' series and therefore have an 'area of uncertainty' ; others are class names or define identities and their application is difficult in marginal cases ; and even concepts of number and time are uncertain. He criticizes the assumption that words have a 'proper' or 'intrinsic' meaning, and considers various kinds of meanings and implication. Finally he passes to difficulties raised by what he calls ' the emotive ' function of words. Throughout this analysis he cites how jurisprudents have waged false controversies and become bogged in difficulties and contradictions because of their unawareness of how words function in relation to referents. On the other hand he also describes how, through evidence, sometimes falsely evaluated and based, the judges give extrinsic referents to words.

It is not my task—indeed I am far from competent—to appreciate or criticize the juristic significance of this involved argument. What strikes me as a sociologist, is that Professor Williams seems to miss what this uncertainty signifies in terms of the social function of law. At the outset (loc. cit., lxi, pp. 71–3) he states that he is concerned to discuss the lessons which semantics contain for jurisprudence, and to intersperse his discussion of semantics ' with remarks on its relation to law and jurisprudence. These remarks are, I fear, on very diverse topics : for semantics touches law and jurisprudence at many points, and I

---

[1] *Law Quarterly Review,* lxi and lxii, op. cit. See also e.g. Frank, *Law and the Modern Mind;* Chase, *The Tyranny of Words;* Chafee, ' The Disorderly Conduct of Words ', op. cit.

am anxious to show the range of its importance even at the risk of making my paper seem disjointed and rambling.' Professor Williams therefore produces a paper which is organized by reference to semantic headings, and not to jurisprudential ones. This seems to me to explain why he misses certain important jurisprudential facts. For example, he writes (lxi, p. 179) :

Philosophy stands out as the striking example of the flatulencies that may gather round the unacknowledged puns of language. On the whole, lawyers have appreciated the danger, and have been at pains to construct and preserve a moderately precise technical language. *Oddly enough, it is least precise in its most fundamental parts* [my italics —M. G.]. We use the word ' right' in some half-dozen different senses and often pass insensibly from one to the other, of course with disastrous results upon our reasoning. We use the phrase ' *in rem* '—' *in personam* ' in four different meanings. It was through confusing two of them that Langdell and Maitland came to compose a famous fallacy, which has been exposed by Hohfeld. ' Ownership' has two distinct senses, called by Salmond ' corporeal' and ' incorporeal '—i.e. ownership of things and ownership of rights ; and the word ' estate ' should be similarly differentiated, for it bears a different meaning when we speak of an estate in land from its meaning when we speak of an estate in a right. This last ambiguity makes havoc of section 1 of the Law of Property Act, 1925. ' Property' has at least seven different meanings, ' acceptance ' four, ' special damage ' three, and ' specific ', ' condition ', ' warranty ' and ' implied contract ' at least two each.

I have italicized the sentence, ' oddly enough [this technical language] is least precise in its most fundamental parts ', for I suggest again that this is not at all odd, but obviously flows from the social function of law as a whole. The most important legal concepts have to cover the widest range of rules and processes of social control : hence they are widest in meaning and have many referents. I venture to suggest that the semantic study of legal terminology should therefore order its argument by arranging legal concepts in an hierarchical order, ranging from law down to details in particular relationships. Terms should be distinguished by classification according to their pervasiveness, their psychological import and their ethical implication. Concepts of procedure and evidence should be considered separately. I have drafted an outline of such a classification and hierarchy for Lozi law.

This hierarchy, in rather different perspective, has been emphasized by Chafee [1] to ' stress the dangers that we run as we get up on the heights. The more abstract the word, the greater the risk that any proposition in which it is used will not be true of all the persons and things within the class denoted by that word, and the more liable we are to forget that at bottom we are talking about persons and things.' He cites political examples like ' democracy ', ' un-American ', and ' New Deal '. ' Property ' is given as a legal example. Chafee continues by pointing out that in the higher ranges of the hierarchy these abstractions must be used cautiously because they are dangerous, but that nevertheless they are as essential as dangerous ' things like high buildings and high voltages '. ' Modern life would be hampered without [them] : and every department of intellectual activity including law would be slowed down almost to a standstill if we did not employ shorthand expressions to denote great masses of related facts.'

Williams, on the other hand, appears to shun the implications of the hierarchy : ' All things considered, it seems that the best we can hope for in this part of the law [dealing with remoteness of damage] is a number of detailed rules regulating as precisely as possible the situations that occur in practice. It seems evident that the effort to bring all cases under a very few broad principles is doomed to failure, or at best can result in nothing but the palest of generalities ' (loc. cit., lxi, p. 193). This statement contrasts with Williams' previous affirmation (p. 189) that ' the difficulty caused by continuous variation in nature is [met by] . . . a continuous variation in legal results '.

Mr. Justice Frank also observes [2] the hierarchy, but he too disapproves of it as ' that scholastic faith in the superiority of abstract terms, that tendency to establish " a hierarchy of ideas in which what is most void in content is placed highest ", which we lawyers, it is said, have inherited '. The highest ideas are not void of content if they are seen in relation to the lower level concepts. In ' The Case of the Headman's Fishdams ', the judges were down to earth in investigating and deciding on rightdoing and wrongdoing under lower level concepts : they manipulate the higher level concepts, up to ' law ' itself, to try

---

[1] 'The Disorderly Conduct of Words', *Canadian Bar Review*, xx, pp. 761–2.
[2] *Law and the Modern Mind*, p. 64.

to achieve justice—if they consider it is possible—in terms of judgments on moral and immoral actions.

None of these conclusions seem to me to attempt to cope with how various abstractions function in the structure of legal systems, or in bringing those systems into action in judicial decision.

This appears to follow from the fact that Williams and Chafee, and before them Cardozo, see in this uncertainty of concept and principles difficulties in the application of the law. Their attitude is influenced by their situation as lawyers. Williams aims largely to show that semantic analysis can clarify and simplify the law and reduce unnecessary litigation, though he gives warning (at lxi, p. 301) that :

(1) The difficulties of words of ' fringe-meaning ' ' cannot be cured by definitions, unless of course, the definition makes express provision for the particular difficulty that has arisen ' ;

and

(2) ' In the second place, such difficulties cannot be cured by the adoption of a technical language. A technical language is useful to prevent equivocation : but it cannot cause " univocal " words to become clear of application to the facts of experience.'

He criticizes Dr. Cohen, and others by implication, for seeming to argue that the adoption of a pruned technical language would get rid of these difficulties. This is patent if one considers legal terms as a semanticist only. But legal concepts are not the logical instruments of ' pure reason ' : they are operated in a society of a particular type, and they have to cope with obstructions in a particular kind of social process. Significantly Williams records (loc. cit., lxi, p. 184) in his discussion of the difficulties inherent in legal concepts, that

judges refuse to be frightened by the difficulties. They are not intimidated from saying that the case is on one side or the other of the line because they consider that the line is difficult to draw.

This statement occurs in his discussion of words with fringes of uncertain meaning. He quotes Lord Coleridge C. J. in the strain of other judges :

The Attorney-General has asked where we are to draw the line. The answer is that it is not necessary to draw it at any precise point.

It is enough for us to say that the present case is on the right side of any reasonable line that could be drawn.

Professor Williams continues :

So also, judges are not always deterred in framing new legal rules by the consideration that they may be hard to apply. In the words of Bowen L. J. : ' It is not a valid objection to a legal doctrine that it will not be always easy to know whether the doctrine is to be applied in a particular case. The law has to face such embarrassments.'

Professor Williams criticizes this judicial courage :

Despite these brave words, it is to the interest of legal certainty that, other things being equal, the rules of laws should be as clear of application as possible. Some words have a wider fringe of uncertainty than others, and for legal purposes those with the narrowest fringe are generally the best. Rules relating to ' dangerous things ', ' extra-hazardous acts ' and ' excessive excess ', are *prima facie* objectionable, because they require so many cases to be litigated.[1]

I do not comment on these particular terms : but in the light of the whole structure and history of law the judges are probably justified in their bravery. In practice, of course, Professor Williams is here considering Western legal process in the courts alone, without including the advice which lawyers give to their clients, or decisions which are taken by police and public prosecutors in their offices, though these are an essential part of the legal process. They complicate the uncertainty.[2]

Again, I suggest, sociological analysis must attempt to comprehend these difficulties. Williams (loc. cit., lxi, p. 301) writes that ' it will be noticed that the difficulties discussed above under the heading of " fringe meaning " are very different from the difficulties caused by words of multiple meaning '. Here again I have tried to relate these different kinds of uncertainties—rather than difficulties—to the logic of the judicial process as a whole.

---

[1] *Language and the Law*, lxi, pp. 184–5.

[2] For a general criticism of this limitation of jurisprudence see Seagle's *The Quest for Law*, op. cit., p. 247 et passim, and Frank's *Law and the Modern Mind*, passim.

III

Appreciation of the flexible generality of legal concepts disposes of many of the verbal controversies which have filled jurisprudential and anthropological literature. Professor Williams says (loc. cit., lxi, p. 386) :

> Realization of the fact that words have no inherently proper meanings has great importance for the student of jurisprudence, because it enables him to write off almost the whole of the vast and futile controversy concerning the proper meaning of the word ' law ', as well as many others of less magnitude.

This statement emphasizes that since in any society the word ' law ' is used with multiple referents, contained in its common uses to cover many types of order, and of rule and social control, the student must accept its complexity and not seek for any simple essential element of law—such as force, its obligatory nature, or its moral basis. Jurists have brought under its definition emergent or inadequately enforced rules such as those of private, and even public, international law, and such phenomena as the great development of administrative law. Malinowski, Llewellyn, Hoebel, and other anthropologists have insisted that law must be allowed to cover some methods of social control in societies without courts ; and after starting with jurists like Pound, Frank, Seagle, and Olivecrona, and anthropologists like Radcliffe-Brown, in favour of limiting ' law ' to social control through politically instituted force, I have come to agree with the others. For I have seen in the field that the concept of ' law ' operates in controlling human action by its wide and expanding, multiple and differentiating, generality. The Lozi have had to enfold an alien overlordship and a social revolution in their word ' *mulao* ' (law). It now enfolds all ideals, rules, procedures, penalties, and modes of enforcement, which the public considers ought to control the relations between persons, and which are not subject to individual whim—hence, all instituted regularity. The Lozi hold (as our courts do) that human law operates in the regularity of nature : the test of a herder's honesty in rendering toll of calves is what cows may be expected to bear in a given time. The test of when a woman became pregnant and who impregnated her is the range of normal gestation.

For scholars surveying comparatively the varieties and evolution of social control, 'Law' is to be grasped not by a single definition, but by being placed in relation to other forms of control by contrast, by refinement of vocabulary (as in the contrast of 'legality' and 'alegality' within 'law'), and by examining its actual rôle at the head of a hierarchy of constituent concepts. But I repeat that I accept that 'law' has many meanings, and I am prepared to admit that I suit my own ideas by limiting it thus to the body of rules of rightdoing.   Others may legitimately use it for other phenomena which I label with different terms.

A similar controversy which has failed to take account of the social function of legal concepts is that surrounding the distinction between 'crimes' and 'civil offences'.   Professor Radcliffe-Brown tried to clear the confusion, in its application to primitive law, 'by making instead the distinction between the law of public delicts and the law of private delicts'.[1] This distinction is based upon the different reactions which an offence evokes.   Professor Kenny showed that serious objections can be raised against this sort of distinction.[2] Kenny's whole authoritative discussion of 'The Nature of a Crime' emphasizes that it is one of those concepts which must stand high in the hierarchy to cover a wide range of offences affecting in various ways public and private interests, tried by different procedures before various tribunals, and sanctioned in many degrees by various kinds of punishment and moral reprobation. Kenny concludes (loc. cit., pp. 15–16) that 'crimes are wrongs whose sanction is punitive and is in no way remissible by any private person, but is remissible by the Crown alone, *if remissible at all*'.   This definition, made specifically for the purposes of English law in which the distinction has important practical consequences, covers many different attributes.   In any society *crime* or the equivalent concept stands high in the hierarchy and therefore must be multi-definitional (multiple).   It is no wonder that, in Seagle's words, 'nobody has been able to devise a definition of crime containing universally valid criteria'.[3] I have des-

---

[1] 'Primitive Law' in *Structure and Function in Primitive Society*, p. 212.
[2] *Outlines of Criminal Law*, Cambridge : University Press (1929, 13th ed.), Chap. 1.
[3] *The Quest for Law*, p. 228.

cribed above (p. 302) the flexibility of Lozi concepts for ' wrong-doings' and will discuss them in more detail in my book on *The Ideas of Barotse Jurisprudence*. I suggest that it is obvious that, for the comparative study of law, we must develop a hierarchy of terms to cover this problem.

In this connection Professor Goodhart has stressed the universal flexible character of '*crime*' and of various offences in a review of Lord Maugham's *U.N.O. and War Crimes*.[1] He protests against Lord Maugham's and Lord Hankey's (in the *Introduction*) definition of ' crimes against humanity' as *ersatz* crimes made *ex post facto* and therefore contrary to human rights :

> It seems odd to speak of the murder of 500,000 people as an *ersatz* crime. I believe that Lord Hankey is mistaken in assuming that the principle relating to retrospective punishment is an absolute one with no possible exceptions. The principle is based on the sound view that it is wrong to punish someone afterwards for doing that which he believed was lawful when he did it : but can the murderers of Belsen be allowed to say : ' We thought that we were allowed to kill and torture our victims ' ? If Lord Hankey is right, then any men who can conceive of a crime which is so horrible that no one has ever thought of it before, will be entitled to go scot-free in the sacred name of human rights.
>
> Finally, the main thesis of Lord Maugham's book is that the charge relating to crimes against peace should never have been brought. He begins by saying that the term ' wars of aggression ' cannot be precisely defined. This is a criticism which can be levelled against most legal terms because such words as ' treason ', ' sedition ', or ' larceny ' can never be defined with complete accuracy, but no one has ever suggested that these crimes should therefore be abolished. I do not think that anyone would find difficulty in describing the German attack on Poland in 1939 as an aggressive war.

Professor Goodhart is arguing here that the word ' crime ', and presumably those lower level wrongs like ' murder ', ' treason ', ' assault ', ' torture ', must be capable of expansion to cover un-foreseen wrongs, and he states this as an acceptable atribute of legal concepts defining wrongs.

---

[1] London : Murray, 1951, reviewed in *The Listener*, xlvii, No. 1207 (17th April, 1952), at p. 625.

IV

Dr. Williams considers (loc. cit., lxi, p. 302) that the theory advanced in his article ' destroys completely and for ever the illusion that the law can ever be completely certain. Since the law has to be expressed in words, and words have a penumbra of uncertainty, marginal cases are bound to occur. Certainty in law is thus seen to be a matter of degree.'

American jurists have pushed this degree of uncertainty further. Mr. Justice Frank has stated the case most strongly, so I concentrate summarily on his analysis.[1] He calls himself a ' fact-sceptic ' as against the ' rule-sceptics ' led by Professor Llewellyn. The ' rule-sceptics ', he says, believe that behind court decisions lie ' real rules ' describing regularities in actual judicial behaviour, an understanding of which will enable lawyers to predict judicial decision. He criticizes the ' rule-sceptics ' because, without admitting it, they concentrate on upper-court decisions. The ' fact-sceptics ' primary interest is in trial courts, where all sorts of imponderabilia affect the trial judges', and even more the juries', conversion of the raw material of evidence into facts-in-law. These imponderabilia range from economic interest, religious values, social prejudices, and so forth, to the judge's or a juryman's digestive state and idiosyncratic dislike of witnesses' idiosyncrasies, or their susceptibility to counsel's arguments. Hence few decisions are predictable, and law is altogether uncertain. Unfortunately—though for obvious reasons —he does not analyse a single judgment, let alone a series of judgments, to illustrate his thesis. He concludes that the certainty of law is a myth or illusion which blinds nearly all judges as well as the public, both of whom find in judges, with their robes and rituals, substitutes for the omniscient omnipotent father-figure of early childhood, who proved in the end an illusion. The established language of legal judgment, with its phrases of authority, such as ' reasonable ', ' beyond doubt ', preserves the myth. This psychological explanation is advanced as a partial explanation : he emphasizes this constantly and lists fourteen other partial explanations in an appendix.

---

[1] *Law and the Modern Mind.* The argument of this book is so interconnected that I summarize it without page references.

The learned judge supports this thesis with a wealth of material. He shows how the simple dichotomy of determination of facts, and determination of what rules apply to the facts, frequently form an undifferentiated composite which precludes any analysis, and examines the social and mental processes, operating out of conscious control, which go into this composite. He cites the way American decisions conflict, and how narrowly a majority may overrule a minority—when a few months before different judges may have gone the other way. He criticizes the way most judges cover up this variability. And so forth. It would be impertinent for me to try to pay tribute to the stimulus and brilliance of this analysis.

Yet Judge Frank gave away his whole case in his definition of law (at p. 47) :

We may now venture a rough definition of law from the point of view of the average man : For any particular lay person the law, with respect to any particular set of facts, is a decision of a court with respect to those facts so far as that decision affects that particular person. Until a court has passed on those facts no law on that subject is yet in existence. Prior to such a decision, the only law available is the opinion of lawyers as to the law relating to that person and to those facts. Such opinion is not actually law but only a guess as to what a court will decide.

It may be doubted whether the average man does conceive of law thus, though many lawyers are likely to agree that this is a definition of judicial decisions. But Mr. Justice Frank was not even content with this limited definition. In the second paragraph of his preface to the sixth printing of *Law and the Modern Mind* he reflects :

I confess, however, that I would not today write that book precisely as I wrote it eighteen years ago . . . for one thing, I seriously blundered when I offered my own definition of the word Law. Since that word drips with ambiguity, there were already at least a dozen defeasible definitions. To add one more was vanity. Worse, I found myself promptly assailed by other Law-definers who, in turn, differed with one another. A more futile time-consuming contest is scarcely imaginable. Accordingly, I promptly backed out of that silly word battle. In 1931, I published an article in which I said that, in any future writing on the subject matter of this book, I would, when possible, shun the use of the word Law : instead I would state directly—without an intervening definition of that term—what I was writing about, namely (1) specific court decisions, (2) how little they are predictable and uniform, (3) the process by which they are made, and (4) how far, in the interest of justice to citizens, that process can and should be improved. I wish I had followed that procedure in this book. I trust that the reader, whenever he comes upon ' Law ' will understand that (as I said on pages 46 and 47) I meant merely to talk of actual decisions, or guesses about future decisions, of specific law suits.

The contest he abjures was not necessarily so futile. Since he was writing *only* about specific court decisions, his analysis was of specific court decisions, and they may well be very uncertain in a heterogeneous society with a mixed bag of courts. But the definition excludes law and its constituent rules as conceived of by the members of the society, and the judges, and as it enables the majority of men to go about their business with others without dispute—which he does not consider. He himself, however, repudiates in the same preface the accusation that he denied the existence of these rules :

> Because, in common with other fact skeptics, I stressed the effects of many non-rule ingredients in the making of court decisions, several critics complained that I cynically sneered at legal rules, considered them unreal or useless. That criticism, I submit, is absurd. If a man says there is hydrogen as well as oxygen in water, discussing both, surely he cannot be charged with denigrating the oxygen or with saying that it is unreal or useless. I have always heartily endorsed the aim of those, who, following Holmes, point out that the rules (whether made by legislatures or judge-made) are embodiments of social policies, values, ideals, and who urge that for that reason, the rules should be recurrently and informedly re-examined. I may add that since, for the past seven years, I have sat on an upper court which concerns itself primarily with the rules and which has little to do with fact-finding, it should be plain that I regard the rules as significant.
> But rules, statutory or judge-made, are not self-operative. They are frustrated, inoperative, whenever, due to faulty fact-finding in trial courts, they are applied to non-existent facts. . . .

This amounts to saying not that there is no certainty in ' law ', but that there is no certainty in court decisions. Similarly, Professor Williams' statement above (p. 338–9), should read : Certainty in legal rulings, and not in law, is thus seen to be a matter of degree. On this analysis, since Mr. Justice Frank admits that the rules are not only significant, but are not ' unreal ', the ' law ' in a commonsense conception, apart from court decisions, may remain certain. The ' unjust judge ' is a general social phenomenon.

Can Mr. Justice Frank's myth of certainty of law be restated as the myth of certainty of court decisions ? If so, only those without any acquaintance with the work of courts can believe in it, or those with this acquaintance who delude themselves. It is on the latter that the judge, with admitted exaggeration, launches his attack. Nevertheless, the conception of law in the sense of a body of normative rules may be considered to be a myth without objective referents. Professor Williams' semantic analysis led him to write an introduction which implies this conclusion though he does not sustain it in his analysis. He writes : ' " law " is a collection of symbols capable of evoking ideas and emotions, together with the ideas and emotions so evoked '. This is set in ' the denial of the independent reality of universals ' as propounded by Professor Olivecrona in his *Law as Fact* :

We are dimly conscious of a permanent existence of the rules of law. We talk of them as if they were always there as real entities. But this is not exact. It is impossible to ascribe a permanent existence to a rule of law or to any other rule. A rule exists only as the content of a notion in a human being. No notion of this kind is permanently present in the mind of anyone. The imperative appears in the mind only intermittently. Of course the position is not changed by the fact that the imperative words are put down in writing. The written text—in itself only figures on paper—has the function of calling up certain notions in the mind of the reader. That is all.

In reality, the law of a country consists of an immense mass of ideas concerning human behaviour, accumulated during centuries through the contributions of innumerable collaborators. . . . The ideas are again and again revived in human minds accompanied by the imperative expression : ' This line of conduct *shall* be taken ' or something else to the same effect.[1]

Professor Olivecrona argues that the idea of a right is a mystical, metaphysical notion which has no objective existence, but is to be understood in terms of a magical origin, and

---

[1] Williams, op. cit., pp. 85–6. Olivecrona, op. cit., pp. 47–8.

2B

the idea of a duty is clearly subjective. When the binding force of the law is an illusion there can be no legal duties in an objective sense. Duty has no place in the actual world of men, but only in the imagination of men. What really exists is certain feelings of duty with which the idea of an imaginary bond is connected (loc. cit., p. 75 ff.).

His conclusion (p. 134) is that ' law—the body of rules summed up as law—consists chiefly of rules *about* force, rules which contain patterns of conduct for the exercise of force '. This force, acting according to the rules through instituted officers by instituted procedures, establishes rights and duties of particular persons in reference to other particular persons.

These propositions raise fundamental epistemological problems of how rules exist, in which I do not need, as an anthropologist, to become involved. I consider that it is sufficient for me to state that empirically *law*, both in its most general sense as a *corpus juris* and also as particular *legal rules*, influences the behaviour of both Lozi judges and public. The rules of law are spoken in everyday relationships and in judgments, and some exist as widely known maxims. They form a large part of my field data. Indeed, it is a fact of everyday commonsense experience that there is law in the general sense as a body of rights and duties. As Durkheim said of religion in a similar context, ' a human institution cannot rest upon an error and a lie '. Further, it is also empirically observable that all societies believe that law has been *certain* save when they are undergoing revolutionary change. Then sections of the society have rejected the established law : they have not rejected its certainty. Indeed, it is against the certainty of law, as enforcing rejected norms, or accepted norms in rejected manner, that they have revolted.

The certainty of law in a stable society is a fact accepted by almost all members of the society. This conception is manifest in the constant use of the phrase *The Law* : thus SOLAMI said ' If it is right [the law], I will condemn my sister. . . .' The conception states a number of legal and moral norms of which some are taken to be axiomatic in that they should be beyond question. Other norms inhere in particular institutional arrangements, validated by history and therefore hallowed. The judges should protect the norms : ultimately they speak *ex cathedra* in that their decisions will be enforced even if they are considered wrong. Ritual surrounds them, and thus sanctifies the law. Mine is a sociological statement : Mr. Justice Frank's statement of the psychological values of the belief may also be sound.

I have been examining legal concepts in order to see how the judicial process functions : but I repeat that I do not consider them to be ideal constructions which exist independently. They function in societies at varied stages of economic and political development. Many concepts, and combinations of concepts, are found in many different types of societies. Presumably they arise from the basic conditions of social life. Others are particular to certain stages, and influence interpretation of those in the first category. For always social conditions, presumptions, prejudices, and interests permeate concepts of law to influence their use and interpretation. Cardozo has shown this in describing how the courts' interpretation of ' liberty ' and ' equality ' in the American Constitution has altered through time. The very ' disastrous results upon . . . reasoning ' (Williams) caused by failure to appreciate that ' right ' has many meanings and by the resultant insensible passage from one meaning to the other, may be controlled by social factors, and not be mere flaws of ratiocination. Dr. Seagle's *The Quest for Law* as a whole demonstrates how the implications of legal concepts have been altered to express the dominant interest of a society : he points out (at p. 182) that ' all legal rules tend to be formulated in general universal terms, whether legal or equitable'. He does not draw from this the general conclusion that this enables law to be certain and traditional while it serves the interests of different masters and social drives, though this is the main theme of his study. This conclusion emerges in a few passages, as where he states (at p. 247) that ' such vague crimes as " disorderly conduct ", " crimes against public morals ", and the like are the prosecutor's blunderbusses . . . against the enemies of the state who are comprised in the classifications of " radicals ", " troublemakers " and " labour agitators " '. However, he shows that as law has developed first *person*, then *property*, and then *contract*, have come to dominate the law. This, despite Seagle's criticism, was the path that Maine trod. And it is striking in this connection that the most effective citation in Cardozo's analysis of the judicial process, for this perspective of the problem, is from a statesman, President Theodore Roosevelt, in a message to Congress in 1908 :

The chief lawmakers in our country may be, and often are, the judges, because they are the final seat of authority. Every time they interpret contract, property, vested rights, liberty, they necessarily enact into law parts of a system of social philosophy ; and as such interpretation is fundamental, they give direction to all law-making. The decisions of the courts on economic and social questions depend upon their economic and social philosophy ; and for the peaceful progress of our people during the twentieth century we shall owe most to those judges who hold to a twentieth century economic and social philosophy, and not to a long outworn philosophy, which was itself the product of primitive economic conditions.[1]

I submit that Williams and other jurists who have tackled these problems have not followed the full implications of their demand for flexibility of law. Had they done so, they would have criticized particular judicial distortions of words, without emphasizing only the difficulties that arise from verbal ' generality '. This uncertainty is an attribute of their value as *judicial* instruments of argument and in it resides an important social function. Thus Williams concludes that when the court defines certain of these words, its decisions ' are often unpredictable, because the court is not determining facts but is simply deciding upon the attitude that it wishes to adopt towards facts ' (loc. cit., lxi, p. 299). But in Cardozo's words (loc. cit., p. 89), ' their standard must be an objective one '. This objective standard is that of ' resonableness ', and as we have seen for Lozi law, this objective standard is socially influenced through the collection of evidence and in other ways. When the court determines ' its attitude to facts ', it does so judicially by fitting facts into flexible concepts with high ethical implication.

Hence I believe the controversy can be resolved by accepting, for present purposes, at least two definitions of law : First, it is a body of rules which theoretically are certain and have socially permeated ' intrinsic ' meanings. Secondly, the law also exists in court decisions in which concepts are specified for extrinsic referents in a particular dispute. Commonsense empirical observation shows that the law as adjudication is not only a body of

---

[1] *Nature of the Judicial Process*, p. 171.

isolated dooms as envisaged by the American 'rule-sceptic' jurists, nor is it a body of ideals. It exists in both ways : for judges give decisions, not all of which can be predicted, on disputes, and these decisions are stated in terms of principles. These principles are 'logical categories, which [*to some extent*— M. G.] are predetermined in essence, immovable in basis, governed by inflexible dogmas', despite Gény's protest, but they are not, as he suggested, 'thus incapable of adapting themselves to the ever varied and changing exigencies of life'. For the principles —which have objective existence in words of maxims and now in books, and in actual behaviour—are composed of flexible general concepts which can absorb, and be permeated by, 'the ever varied and changing exigencies of life'.

Jurists of both schools—those who contend that judges do not 'legislate' but merely apply a body of unchanging principles, and those sceptics who see law only in action in adjudication— have apparently both been led away by the 'myth of the certainty of law'. The first have defended it absolutely, the second have revolted too strongly against it in the light of the obvious uncertainty of litigation and adjudication. For it is obvious that potentially every piece of litigation is uncertain, as the American sceptical lawyers have argued, partly because of the 'penumbra of uncertainty' of words. Some of the uncertainty resides in the relation of these words to extrinsic circumstance : this process covers the way judges or juries read the facts, the flaws in which are emphasized by Mr. Justice Frank. Genuine uncertainty of law itself occurs only in 'the gaps of the law', as in 'The Case of the Barren Widow'. On the other hand, the basic concepts of law are axiomatic. And if these legal (and ethical) concepts are to serve their function of relating law, as a body of rules, to life, and thus to give some stability and certainty in the infinite variety of experience through changes of social conditions, paradoxically they must be 'uncertain' in their definition.

This is how the certainty of legal rule and ethical principle control varying circumstance in an ordered community. Through the 'uncertain' flexibility of legal concepts both public opinion and judges' arguments bring the certainty of law in general into action to settle a particular dispute. The intrinsic meaning attributed to concepts may alter as social change occurs, for their intrinsic meaning is always associated with their extrinsic referents in the circumstances of life they are supposed to control. However, changes in meaning are slow. The concepts are not only flexible, but they are also absorbent and can be specified in reference to quite new kinds of social experience. Furthermore they are permeable, so that at any one time they contain the presumptions of their social milieu. These several characteristics of concepts of law, and their varying hierarchical value, allow them to be manipulated in judicial argument to serve law and give justice, which in turn may serve varied social values and interests.

CHAPTER VIII

THE SOCIAL CONTEXT OF THE JUDICIAL PROCESS

WE may glance summarily at the main points which have emerged from this analysis of the Lozi judicial process. On the whole, it is true to say that the Lozi judicial process corresponds with, more than it differs from, the judicial process in Western society. Lozi judges draw on the same sources of law as Western judges—the regularities of the environment, of the animal kingdom, of human beings ; and custom, legislation, precedent, equity, the laws of nature and of nations, public policy, morality. They assess evidence in the same way. They manipulate the different types of legal rule which can be applied to a particular situation, and the ambiguity of the concepts which make up the legal rules, in a similar attempt to achieve justice according to their lights. Nevertheless their work is affected at every point by the general level of technology, and the economic and social structure, of Lozi society. The dominant factors which produce important differences are the comparatively egalitarian and undifferentiated nature of social relations, the absence of pleadings and counsel and complex procedure, and the unwritten state of the law.

Analyses of African adjudication have stressed that the judges try to effect reconciliation of the parties—' to restore the social equilibrium '. In Loziland this process applies where the parties are kinsmen or lord and underling, in a permanent multiplex relationship which the judges are trying to preserve. Then— though the judges will only enquire into a breach of a legal right—the concept of relevance is wide and the judges broaden their examination to investigate everything that the parties and other related persons may have done. They are not restricted by a doctrine of judicial ignorance or concepts of irrelevant, incompetent, etc., evidence. This tendency is less marked in cases between spouses, since the marital relationship is easily broken, and it is barely present in cases between strangers involved in delictual or contractual relationship. But it may reassert itself at any moment where the judges consider that a public or other interest is involved : they will enquire into this issue, and give judgment on it. What we would call a criminal or administrative trial may thus emerge from a civil suit. Lozi judges are also administrators and legislators, and, as they are accustomed to reason in these capacities, they may take administrative decisions ; for though they have several rôles, they distinguish these clearly.

Even when the judges are striving to reconcile disputants who are kinsmen, they will not do so at the cost of glossing over wrongdoing. Those who have erred are always reprimanded. It is a basic axiom of Lozi law that wrongdoers should be scolded and punished : hence if it is impossible or inappropriate to secure this end by making them pay recompense to those they have harmed, the judges inflict a fine or other punishment. Again, a criminal trial may emerge from a civil suit. This is the reasoning at the basis of legislation which levies damages on an adulterer in favour of the cuckolded husband, and a fine on the erring wife. The requirements of good morals and public policy prevent her paying her husband : she can only pay the state. This may well be one spring of differentiated criminal law.

The standards of right behaviour against which the behaviour of the parties is assessed to see if they have acted rightly or wrongly, are those of ' the reasonable and customary man '. This exists as a distinct concept in the Lozi language, though it is not always explicitly stated by the judges. There is both a generally reasonable man, acting sensibly and conforming to custom, and a particular reasonable and customary incumbent of any social position—father, son, husband, wife, son-in-law, lord, underling. The chief standards of good behaviour and the customary usages of these various social positions are widely known to all Lozi. It is expected that everyone should conform to these standards and usages. Hence wherever it emerges in evidence that a person has departed from them, his actions and motives become suspect, and the judges attack him in cross-examination, demanding that he explain his deviation. This deviation may convict him. Therefore the standard of the reasonable man may be said to provide the main check on evidence and to be the main weapon in judicial cross-examination. The judges thus use custom as a yardstick for controlling the variety of social life. Custom has a social certainty akin to the physical ecological and physiological certainties of diurnal and seasonal time, vegetation growth, gestation, etc., which are also checks on evidence.

Custom can operate in this manner because it is widespread and generally known, and because every relationship tends to have its distinctive usages. These usages and customs are known to and accepted by litigants and witnesses as well as judges. Even when a person lies in court, he tries to cast his story so that he appears to have conformed to custom, and to standards of upright behaviour. This enables judges to cross-examine on the story by the standards of reasonable and customary behaviour and to expose lies. Further it enables them to give judgments which are intelligible to the litigants even if these reject the judicial conclusions. It is only rarely that litigants are operating with quite different values, though situations of this kind are probably increasing in number. In effect, in this process the judges hold that a person intends the reasonable or natural consequences of his actions. In practice, in the judicial process the argument is transposed, to say that a person has those motives which can be reasonably deduced from his witnessed actions. The courts therefore punish for wrongful actions, but judgments lay stress on the motives associated with those actions. ' The reasonable man ' therefore imports psychology into the judicial process, and it is an ethical psychology.

Judges work not only with standards of reasonable behaviour for upright incumbents of particular social positions, but also with standards of behaviour which are reasonably interpreted as those of particular kinds of wrongdoers. There are social stereotypes of how thieves, adulterers, and other malefactors act. If the witnessed actions of a defendant assemble into one of these stereotypes, he is found guilty, though the judges prefer direct evidence to convict. It is a pertinent, and on my part not properly investigated, problem, to ask whether these sterotypes in fact influence the behaviour of wrongdoers.

In this summary of how Lozi judges assess evidence, as in the text, I have started by emphasizing the importance of the reasonable man, because this point is often overlooked. It entails recognition of the fact that any departure from normal behaviour, reported by a litigant himself or by other witness, contributes to judicial conviction. Its importance is heightened for Lozi judges because, to establish guilt or innocence, they have not the support of detectives or of a technology of expertise on finger-printing, handwriting, blood-tests, etc. But departures from custom must be established by good evidence, and Lozi judges distinguish various kinds of evidence as good and bad. No decision should be given before both sides are heard (this is due process of law), and all available evidence should be ascertained. There are direct and circumstantial evidence, direct and hearsay evidence, corroborative, impartial, and cogent evidence. All these kinds of evidence, and the evidence of reasonable and customary behaviour, are tested by judicial cross-examination. The Lozi quite explicitly affirm that it is by cross-examination that they arrive at the truth. Only in sorcery cases, and some charges of theft, were oracles used in the past.

Lozi judges expect cross-examination to establish the truth of an accusation or a plaintiff's suit. They will dismiss a case if the evidence is not conclusive enough. They do not convict on a past bad record. Since the judges, and not counsel for the parties, cross-examine, it may appear as if they consider a person guilty until he proves he is innocent, but this is a fallacious appearance. A person is innocent until he is proved guilty. The apparent assumption of guilt flows from the fact that it is only possible to cross-examine, if the cross-examiner frames his questions as if he believes the examinee is lying—hence, guilty. Where judges conduct the cross-examination, this makes an onlooker assume they believe in the guilt of defendant or accused. Again, Lozi judges are well-aware of the implications of their technique ; and I stress that there is no assumption of guilt in Lozi law.

The standard of reasonable and customary behaviour has importance as a technique for arriving at the truth. In addition, it often forms the crux of a law-suit. A wife sues for divorce on the grounds that her husband has not been a reasonable and customary husband to her ; or a headman claims that he is justified in expelling a man from gardens because the man has not been a reasonable villager ; or a lord claims the right to dismiss an underling from position and lands because of unreasonable behaviour. In all these situations, the standards of ' reasonable ' and ' customary ' vary with the social positions involved. They also vary with outside circumstances and with the changing conditions of life in Loziland. ' Reasonable ' and ' customary ', like other legal concepts, are highly flexible, and they become permeated with changing social presumptions, values, and conditions of life, and can absorb a variety of actual situations. Their flexibility has enabled Lozi judges to adjust rules of law to cope with Christianity, schools, work for money in Loziland and at distant towns, and so forth.

The Lozi have a developed vocabulary to define different kinds (legal, moral, decent, natural) of rules, rights, duties, wrongs, injuries, taboos. As in other languages, some of these words have many referents and several definitions, and others are elastic to cover a series of events or things. This leads to some confusion, but they have a clear idea that there are certain approved rules which their courts will enforce, while other approved rules they can only recommend as worthy of decent observance. They recognize that hard cases may make good law. This gives them a distinctive body of legal rules, as against other rules which are only morally binding. But where strict adherence to the letter of the law leads to an unjust decision, the judges strive to interpret the law so as to avoid this unpalatable conclusion. In all cases they apply ' general equity ' in their reasoning, and they seek for a ' particular equity ' to achieve justice in special hard cases. In doing so they may ' create ' new law, albeit within the established body of law which Lozi believe derives from antiquity and which binds king and judges. They achieve these particular equities chiefly in two ways. First, they may specify—give temporary definition to —a particular legal concept to meet special circumstances. Secondly, a variety of different *kinds* of legal rules apply in varying ways to some situations, and the judges have considerable latitude in the way they apply these rules. They may achieve justice in one relationship, by enforcing a sanction in another. Here their power as administrators, acting as supreme controllers of land and village settlement and in other ways, is important.

Equity—justice—morality : these are therefore sources on which the judges draw in adjudicating on disputes. Formally, they recognize these sources under several terms, of which we may here note chiefly ' the laws of God ' and ' the laws of humankind '. Their principles are axiomatic and patent to all reasonable men. These constitute at least an embryonic *jus naturale*. This *jus naturale* is applied by the Lozi in deciding which of the laws of their subject tribes they will protect. Here they also recognize ' the laws of nations ' (*jus gentium*), being those rules and institutions which are common to all African tribes of the region, and many of which are also accepted by Whites. Since the economy of the region, insofar as it is controlled by Lozi courts, is largely based on status and not on contract, their *jus gentium* covers chiefly the law of persons and constitutional law : marriage, succession, citizenship, overlordship, etc.

It emerges from this analysis that certain problems, such as the distinction between law and custom or the relation of law and religion, which have concerned students of ' primitive law ', are resolved if we see that ' law ' in the sense of judicial decision— *legal rulings*—has the same material sources everywhere. When Lozi judges have to give a decision on a dispute, they draw, both during trial and in adjudication, on custom, legislation, judicial precedent, equity, the laws of nature and of nations, and good morals and public policy. They do so in a very complicated process, but it is a process which is controlled by publicly known logic. The whole process is conditioned by the absence of writing, which prevents the development of a forensic science. Its chief effect is that the judges are able to come to a moral decision on the dispute and then select those statutes, precedents, etc., for attention which support this decision. However, they cannot go against certain well-known statutes or ' common law ' rules. Statutes overrule customary law. Custom must pertain to a group, be well-known and reasonable : the last proviso enables some customs to become obsolete while new ones are recognized. This latter process of development is assisted by the absence of historical records : new usages and standards can be graced with antiquity, and old standards and usages which are in conflict with new values are forgotten. Morality and equity control the weighing of laws, besides being a particular source of judicial rulings. Precedents are not surveyed, since they are barely recorded, and are quoted haphazardly. Indeed, the judges less often cite a precedent in the form of a previous judicial decision, than they cite moral exemplifications of rightdoing from their own actions or experience with others. The course of Lozi life, where it runs smoothly and without dispute—customary life—thus is a prime source of judicial decision, under the guise of precedent.

In drawing on these sources of law, and applying them to the facts of a particular dispute, the Lozi act by a logic which is akin to our own. It was necessary to make this point in view of frequent statements that African courts operate by oracles, or fetishes, and to cite in support their syntactical devices and conjunctions which enable them to build up coherent, reasoned arguments. Indeed, they have a vocabulary to describe ' arguments ', and the ' reasons ' and ' presumptions ', ' probabilities ' and ' indications ', which go into them. Moreover, they have a developed vocabulary to evaluate the skill of good judges, and the stupidity or cowardice or corruption of bad judges. ' The unjust judge ' is an accepted figure to explain away bad judgments.

Judicial logic operates in three stages, recognized as such by the Lozi : the hearing of and cross-examination on evidence, the taking of a decision on evidence, and the exposition of the law in support of the decision. Each stage has its own techniques, but the stages are not always kept apart. This is particularly so among the Lozi since the judges carry out examination and cross-examination. They may begin to arrive at a decision, and even to state the law for the case under trial, while hearing evidence. However, they have words to distinguish each stage and think little of judges who come to decision before all the evidence has been heard.

This is how judicial logic works in all cases. Some cases may fall in ' gaps in the law ', and then different kinds of logic are employed by the judges. I have cited examples to show that here Lozi judges have been effective in aiding their people to cope with changes in social life due to British overlordship and all it entails. They have developed the law by employing all the methods isolated by Cardozo for Anglo-American adjudication : the method of philosophy by the rule of analogy ; the method of evolution along the lines of historical development ; and the method of tradition along the line of the customs of the community. Finally, they use Cardozo's method of sociology, which works along the lines of justice, social welfare, good morals, and public policy.

Consideration of this last method led to an attempt to resolve the paradox of the ' uncertainty ' of legal concepts and the ' certainty ' of law. I defined legal concepts as being *general* and *unspecific* in that they rarely referred to a particular person, thing, occurrence, or action ; *flexible* in that they are *elastic*, capable of being stretched to cover various circumstances, and/or in that they are *multiple* in having several referents or definitions ; *permeable* in that they can be pervaded by mores, values, and social and individual presumptions ; and *absorbent* in that they can absorb the raw facts of evidence into their categories. In trial, the judges have to *specify*—give extrinsic referents to— these categories. In this process of specification the judges are able to operate the method of sociology, since general morality can control the adaptation of the flexible concepts to new circumstances. The judges manipulate the flexibility of the concepts—what is often denigrated as their ' ambiguity '—as they do the multiplicity of laws, to achieve justice.

This judicial manipulation is aided by the fact that, as I suggest, the concepts can be arranged in a number of hierarchies. In one hierarchy, that of the laws of persons and property, ' law ' itself occurs at the top, rooted in government, in regularity of the natural and social order, based on the laws of God, nature, and nations, on customs, statutes, precedents. Law in this sense exists in a structure of social positions. This is law as *corpus juris*, a set of rules accepted by all normal members of the society as defining right and reasonable ways in which persons ought to behave in relation to each other and things. It includes right and reasonable ways of seeking protection for one's rights— adjectival as well as substantive law. The *corpus juris* consists of rights and duties as against wrongs and injuries. Rights and duties rest in ownership over things and persons. Wrongs and injuries give rise to responsibility which creates a liability giving rise to other rights and duties. Wrongs and injuries are assessed by guilt and innocence as judged on particular actions—particular rightdoings and wrongdoings. The standards of ' reasonableness and customariness ' pervade the hierarchy as a whole. It is characteristic of this hierarchy, that the higher level concepts are the most general in meaning and their ambiguity consists chiefly in that they are *multiple*. Lower level concepts are chiefly *elastic*, measuring guilt or innocence, care or negligence, along a scale between two poles. A similar hierarchy is suggested for the law of contracts ; and a distinctive one for the law of trial and evidence. In the latter, concepts are both elastic and multiple, which increases their flexibility.

I examined a series of apparently conflicting decisions on land cases to show that what the judges do in practice is to decide that one party has done *right* and the other done *wrong* in particular actions. From these decisions, they jump to decide that the party who has done *right* has *the right* to the land : in Lozi, as in English, the same word is used for these quite different meanings of ' right'. This is a typical example, which must suffice in this summary, to illustrate how the judges manipulate the flexibility of the concepts, in their hierarchical value, to achieve justice. My conclusion is that the law as a *corpus juris* remains certain, through some uncertainty of judicial decision, because of the flexible uncertainty of legal concepts. This is particularly marked among the Lozi since their *corpus juris*, what I call law in general, consists of general statements linking social positions—in custom, in statute, and in morality. Since they lack writing, these statements are not circumscribed by refining precedents or constricting terminology.

I do not suggest that these concepts, many of which are shared with other systems of law, exist *in vacuo*. I argue that they carry the historic, political, and economic load of their social milieu : they are permeated with a specific set of social presumptions, interests, values, etc.

Empirically it is clear that the Lozi believe there exists ' the law '—a *corpus juris* which binds king and court. It is well known to judges and litigants and they reason with it. It operates in social life unmarred by dispute. ' Law ' in this sense is certain. Empirically also ' law ' consists of a series of decisions by judges not all of which are certain in that they can be predicted in advance. This apparent contradiction can be resolved by examining the nature of Lozi legal concepts in all their flexibility, and seeing how judges manipulate them. But the Lozi share most of these concepts with Western law. I was therefore emboldened to apply my analysis, in all humility, to some recent studies of the Western judicial process and to suggest that it offered some solution to a number of controversies in jurisprudence. Western jurists on the whole have treated the ' ambiguity ' of legal concepts as a weakness, without examining in general how the judges operate the ambiguities. I think this statement is justified, despite praise of particular flexibilities. I suggest that we must accept that words like law, right, property, have several meanings, and examine how these varied meanings function in the judicial process, in legal practice, and in social life. If we do this we avoid the sterile disputes which have raged over the many offered definitions of law, of criminal and civil law, and so on. For against every definition another can be offered, or an instance cited of what is by commonsense 'law' or 'crime' but is not covered by the proffered definition. More particularly, we dispose of the dispute between what I may call the orthodox jurists who consider 'law' to be on the whole certain, and the American sceptical jurists who argue that it is not. The case is made clear by Judge Jerome Frank's attack on the 'myth of certainty of law'. He examines litigation and probable litigation, calls them 'law', and concludes that they are uncertain : which they are. But he concedes that there are rules of law, which are more or less certain, and which control judges—and, one might add, control social life. If he talked about 'litigation and adjudication' instead of about 'law', there would be at least only factual discussion, and not sterile terminological disputation about his analysis. I go further, and suggest that a theory based on an analysis of actual judicial logic, and the nature of concepts of law, can resolve the paradox of certainty in the *corpus juris* and uncertainty in adjudication or legal rulings.

Similarly, by recognizing that the word 'law' has many meanings, sterile argument can be avoided over administrative law, public international law, and law that is not sanctioned. In at least one sense of 'law'—the sense of *corpus juris*—all societies have 'law', whether or not they have courts to enforce rights and punish wrongs under that law. Normal members of these societies recognize and are influenced by this *corpus juris*. Sanctions of enforcement are not necessary for 'law' in this sense ; they are only necessary if we say 'law is what the court will enforce *and nothing else*'. But these societies are certainly not without law—*lawless*. I have suggested that we call them *alegal*, without legal sanctions, institutions, procedures, etc. They have *judgments* but not *adjudication*—this is proposed as a conventional use of words and does not inhere in the words themselves.

I suggest to both jurists and anthropologists that in this field, and perhaps in others, a first step in analysis is to accept the ambiguity of the words which are in common use, whether it be the ambiguity of multiple referents and definitions, or of elasticity in an uncertain series. A main part of our task is to examine the function of this ambiguity—how it is manipulated in the legal or other system within the social system as a whole. Critical problems are raised in this way, and barren terminological dispute avoided. Nevertheless it is clear that we need specialized, specific, univocal terms for analysis. This end is not to be achieved either by giving specific meanings to words like *law*, or by broadening their meaning till they mean everything. We should specialize series of words so that it is clear to which of many forms and processes we are referring : the *corpus juris*, litigation, adjudication, legal and alegal rules, etc. For our present problem I suggest that this specialization should be made in terms of a series of hierarchies such as I have drawn. It emphasizes the patent truth that concepts of ' law ' can only be defined in relation to each other, by context, in a system of ' law '. Since many of these concepts have many referents in social life, there is no one legitimate referent. We can only specialize them by conventional agreement. It is a pleasanter, though doubtless more difficult, alternative than to write about Law-A, Law-B, Law-C, etc., and the like.

CHAPTER IX

REAPPRAISAL (1966)[1]

THIS book first appeared at about the same time as J. N. D. Anderson's *Islamic Law in Africa* (1954), A. L. Epstein's *Juridical Techniques and The Judicial Process: A Study in African Customary Law* (1954), and P. P. Howell's *A Manual of Nuer Law* (1954). A couple of years later P. J. Bohannan published his book on *Justice and Judgment among the Tiv* (1957) of Northern Nigeria. My book on its own was the subject (to my knowledge) of six review articles (one very long indeed),[2] and of a fair number of longish reviews considering its own arguments and its significance in the development of the sociology of law.[3] In addition, in company with one or more of the other books cited, it was considered at length in six other essays.[4] This is aside from discussion of its arguments and suggestions in books and articles, and its appearance in summary form in Schubert's *Reader* on judicial behaviour, with March's review and the review by Ayoub of Bohannan's and my book (to be cited shortly). In this new chapter I discuss mainly criticisms and do not cite the appreciation, both of which I value highly. Since I do not cite appreciative remarks but only enter into dispute, this

---

[1] In giving references to books and articles in the next two chapters, I cite now author's name, (short) title, and date, since these are the essential information a reader requires. Details of publisher and place of publication of books, and of the journals in which articles appeared, are given at the end of the essay. References to review articles and reviews of this book, and of it in company with other books on African law, are given in an appendix to this chapter on pp. 417–18, because of difficulties in setting lengthy footnotes near to one another. There I discuss some comments not included in the text.

[2] By Douglas (1956); March (1956); Marshall (1955); Seguin (1956); Stumpf (1956); Schiller (1957): see Appendix to this chapter, paragraph (a), p. 417.

[3] By Allott (1956); Krige (1956); Anderson (1955); Kilgour (1955); Southall (1956): see Appendix to this chapter, paragraph (b), p. 417.

[4] By Nadel (1956); Kerr (1956); Ayoub (1961); Hoebel (1962); Schubert (1964); Nader (1965): see Appendix to this chapter, paragraph (c), pp. 417–18.

makes me appear ungracious, particularly to Ayoub, Hoebel, March, Nadel, Nader and Schubert. I first put my analysis into perspective against my other work on the Barotse.

I had already published a general account of the Barotse, as well as specialized studies on their ecological relations, general economy, land use, political and administrative organization, and marriage and kinship institutions, when I began work on an analysis of Barotse law. An anthropologist writing about the law of a particular tribe is in a difficult position when compared with a student of law in modern Europe or America. The latter often merely refers, without explanation or details, to an institution, official, statute, or leading case. Even an historical jurist may assume knowledge of the era he is considering. To follow Maine's *Ancient Law* properly one requires considerable knowledge of Roman history as well as law. Maine assumes every reader has this knowledge. The anthropologist cannot similarly assume that his readers have any background knowledge and hence in every book has to provide some of it. In this book on the one hand I have compressed data and analysis published elsewhere to what I thought was essential and relevant to comprehend the central analysis in order to restrict the size of the book. On the other hand I have recapitulated summaries of Barotse institutions to save readers who were unaccustomed to studying these types of society from constantly checking back. This has led to some repetition which some reviewers have found unnecessary. It was deliberate and intended to be helpful. On the other hand, others have complained that I did not give data which in fact I had documented as published already ; and one cannot put all the data on an elaborate organization and culture into every book.[1]

---

[1] My background publications and the relevant writings of others are referred to in footnotes where appropriate, and listed in the bibliography on pp. 449–50. As an example of a reader who paid no attention to the references, I cite Albert, in a review in the *American Anthropologist*, where she complained that I did not give information on the social background though she did not specify what further information she required, or where it would have been relevant in this book itself. It is true that I have published more fully on Barotse political organization than on their domestic life. Latterly, a review of *The Ideas in Barotse Jurisprudence* (1965), signed 'J. P. M.' in *African Affairs* (1966), complains that I did not then deal with topics which I showed I had covered in this book on the judicial process!

From an early period of my initial research in Barotseland I became deeply interested in their handling of disputes, and in related problems ; and as soon as I had published my background analyses, I began work, as described in Chapter I, on a single volume in three parts, each part of which grew. The outlines of the other parts were written in brief when I found that to treat the judicial process alone had taken a book. In the following years our Department of Anthropology and Sociology expanded very rapidly, both in the numbers of its staff and students, and in the research fields it covered ; and I was not able to concentrate on completing the other two books. I have now published the second part as *The Ideas in Barotse Jurisprudence* (1965).

A quite different type of difficulty is now delaying the last part of the trilogy, on *The Role of Courts in Barotse Life*. I have come to realize that to treat this subject adequately, I need to do further research in Barotseland. From 1953 until the independence of Zambia (formerly Northern Rhodesia), I was not able to do this, because I was informed by a senior Minister of the Federation of the Rhodesias and Nyasaland that the Immigration Department would not allow me to enter the Federation, presumably because of my public opposition to the creation of the Federation. I would like to do this further research not only because there are gaps in my projected study, such as all anthropologists find when they analyse problems that were not fully worked out when they did their field research, but also because of certain developments in the study of social interaction. The anthropologists of my generation, faced with a great variety of tribal systems, illustrated an analysis of the interrelation of the parts of a social system, and how it functioned as a whole, with examples culled from the experience of different persons and groups. We selected these examples by the method I have termed ' apt illustration '.[1] Examples to illustrate various social

---

[1] In my ' The Use of Ethnographic Data in British Social Anthropology' (1961), and ' Foreword' to Turner, *Schism and Continuity in an African Society* (1957). The ' extended-case ' method of using ethnographic data on tribal societies, in my opinion first appeared in Mitchell's *The Yao Village* (1956), was developed by Turner in the book cited, and carried further—some reviewers say too far—in Van Velsen's *The Politics of Kinship* (1964). Uberoi has shown how illuminating the method can be by bringing together data scattered through Malinowski's books, about the same people (*Politics of the*

principles were not connected with one another. Some younger anthropologists have ceased to use occurrences and actions thus to illustrate general principles of social organization, and instead have begun to analyse occurrences and actions themselves so as to extract dynamic social processes set in a socio-cultural framework. This involves tracing these processes through a whole series of events in the life of particular sets of people.

As stated above (pp. 25-8) in the early 1950's I had drafted chapters examining ' the circumstances in which a family quarrel flares up, and the pressures which are exerted to bring about a reconciliation between the parties '. I had related the pressures of the courts to economic penalties, and the influence of beliefs in ancestral spirits and in sorcery or witchcraft. I discussed why political authorities constantly took the initiative to intervene in family disputes ; and I gave four reasons which I believed explained why Barotse frequently went to court (above, pp. 25-6). I had intended to proceed to consider the powers of courts, and the difference between state courts and village moots, as well as the relation of judicial to legislative and administrative action ; public reaction to the Barotse courts and to British courts ; and so forth. But I was already becoming dissatisfied with my material on some of these subjects in view of the developments which, as outlined above, my younger colleagues and I were working out at the Rhodes–Livingstone Institute and later in England. It was in the light of these developments that I noted at the end of key-cases in this book (such as the Cases of the Biassed Father and the Violent Councillor, both heard in 1942, and the Headman's Fishdams, heard in 1947) that I had failed to trace adequately the origins of these disputes before they

---

Kula Ring, 1962). Outside of these Rhodes–Livingstone Institute and Manchester University scholars, the method is admirably used by Middleton in Chapter IV of *Lugbara Religion* (1960), where he examines a whole series of divinations of ancestral wrath in a single lineage. For recent theoretical discussions see Mitchell's ' Foreword ' to Van Velsen's book above, and essays by Epstein on ' The Case Method ' and Van Velsen on ' Situational Analysis ' in Epstein (editor), *The Craft of Social Anthropology* (in press, due 1966) and my own ' Introduction ' to this book, as well as my *Politics, Law and Ritual in Tribal Society* (1965), pp. 235 f. This particular line of development in social anthropology is in accord with the increasing use of ' case-studies ' in other social sciences.

came into the courts.   I was at that time concerned to study the
courts themselves and this blocked my mind from investigating
how these disputes between people closely involved with one
another had developed.   Furthermore when after hearing cases
in 1940 and 1942 I returned to Barotseland in 1947 for a visit of
three months, I went to study changes in the courts and to collect
more judicial hearings ; and I did not go to the people involved
in the cases I had recorded in the earlier years to see how the
judicial decisions had, or had not, influenced social relationships.
This information is clearly of the greatest importance in assessing
The Role of Courts in Barotse Social Life.

I believe that this deficiency in my fieldwork was not merely
personal, but also arose from the then state of our discipline.
No reviewer drew attention to this deficiency, though I had
myself clearly stated it in this book.   I have discussed similar
omissions in the work of other anthropologists of my generation
in my ' Introduction ' to Epstein's *The Craft of Social Anthropology*
(1966).   For example, in editing Barton's *The Kalingas* (1949)
Hoebel did not insert cross-references between the various cases
cited by Barton where these referred to the same persons and/or
groups.   Nor did he and Llewellyn connect up their various
cases in their brilliant *The Cheyenne Way* (1941), and Pospisil has
not done so adequately in his *Kapauka Papuans and Their Law*
(1958).   In my *Politics, Law and Ritual* (1965, pp. 191–5) I analyse
in detail how Bohannan also did not investigate the full context
of what he calls 'drumming the scandal' among the Tiv (his
pp. 142 f.) to bring out the different ways in which various
mechanisms of social control operate.   I am deeply conscious of
this weakness in my own field research and analysis.   I believe it
affects my planned study of the rôle of courts, so that I could
not now adequately deal with a problem raised by Douglas
(at her p. 373), ' l'efficacité des peines que les tribunaux lozi sont
en mesure de prononcer '.   But I do not believe that this type of
data is relevant to my analyses of *The Judicial Process* or *The
Ideas in Barotse Jurisprudence*, though there are also gaps in the
data I collected so far as these are concerned.

My colleagues Dr. J. Van Velsen and Mr. R. Werbner have
told me that they consider one part of the date I reserved for the
book on the rôle of courts to be relevant to my study of the
judicial process.   Forty-one out of sixty of the cases or incidents

cited I heard tried in a court at a capital, or had described to me as having been tried in a capital. There is some overlap since cases in texts given me report the original familial or local court verdict before appeal. (Courts at capitals, save for the provincial appeal court, were also courts of the first instance for the surrounding local district.) Van Velsen and Werbner, if I understand them correctly, therefore consider that my analysis is of judicial action and reasoning in appeal courts, and that action and reasoning may differ in local district courts and village moots.

Factually I have on the whole presented mainly detailed trials in appeal courts. I have cited in fairly full detail only one case in a gazetted local district subordinate court (The Case of the Quarrelsome Teacher, pp. 71-6) and the reasoning of the judges in a local court which was not gazetted in two cases (The Cases of the Immigrant Land-Borrower, pp. 62-4, and Cross-Cousin Adultery, pp. 134-5). I did not cite more cases from local courts because they did not raise special issues in the judicial process. Clearly complex cases, arising from many local districts, are more likely to be found in the capital ; and each of the widely separated gazetted local district courts sat only one or two days a week. So even when I was not at the capital, I recorded fewer local cases. But I consider that those cases reported above from local district courts, and particularly the Case of the Quarrelsome Teacher, show that the judicial process is the same in these subordinate courts as in the appeal courts at the capitals. Moreover, as my records above show, appeal courts hear all cases anew, with full pleas and evidence.

Village moots do not operate dissimilarly in respect of taking evidence and reasoning. I noted frequently how, when a dispute flared up, the men of a village, or a group of kin and affines, or a neighbourhood, would quickly dispose themselves as in a Barotse state court, with the most senior at the centre and the others to right and left in order of rank, so that they could enquire into the quarrel. (This happened in my own entourage, if there was a dispute among my attendants and servants and their wives, or between myself and one of them.) The Cases of the Biassed Father (pp. 37-45) and the Violent Councillor (pp. 83-90) show that a village headman may not always summon a moot to sit on a dispute. That he should act thus, judicially, is exhibited in the appeal court's rebukes to the Biassed Father and the Violent

Councillor. And many disputes of course provoke violent verbal altercations and may end in blows. But when the moot formed in my presence, the participants cross-examined and judged as did judges in the capitals. I reserved my treatment of village moots and disputes for the later book.

Werbner also raised with me a further important point. He asked me whether there was a change in the way litigants presented their cases and evidence or in the kinds of witnesses who became involved as a dispute proceeded from a village to a local district court and then on appeal—with possibly a second appeal to the Barotse provincial court, before going to a British court. He has noted this among the Kalanga ; and he considers that in terms of my own analysis changes should occur. I was able to follow only two divorce cases, from my own neighbourhood, through the Barotse hierarchy, and I did not note any major changes. The capacity of the Barotse to reiterate the facts of a dispute and how rightly they had acted is considerable, if not unique. The hearings I have reported from the court in the capital suggest that litigants and witnesses press their evidence and views in somewhat the same way, though decorum is maintained at all state courts, and accusations of sorcery or witchcraft are not shouted as they may be in village moots. Some cases show that the appeal courts may criticize judges in subordinate courts for failing to summon the appropriate witnesses. I noted in discussing the Case of the Barren Widow (pp. 174–5) that some litigants considered it a good move in appealing to British courts from Barotse courts to allege that the Barotse judges were corrupt.

Nevertheless I see that here are problems I studied in the field, as well as reported, inadequately, on a par with the weakness in following up and tracing back the disputes I heard tried.

With the break-up of the Federation of the Rhodesias and Nyasaland and the granting of independence to Zambia, it became possible for me to return to Barotseland. In January 1966 I went to Ethiopia to participate in a seminar organized by the International African Institute on ' Ideas and Procedures in Traditional African Legal Systems ', and I obtained leave to go to Zambia for a short visit, which enabled me to be in Barotseland for sixteen days. It was difficult to travel far out into the plain as the flood had begun to rise, so that travel either on foot or by dugout was very slow. I could not in the time I had reach all villages involved in the major cases cited in this book. Where I could not do so, I collected information from reliable persons ; and I report what has happened in all these villages in Chapter X, and discuss briefly the implications of these developments for the new method of analysis. I shall also summarize in that chapter certain major changes in Barotse life and law over the past eighteen years, for in many respects the situation described above has altered radically. I turn now to comments on my study of the Barotse judicial process.[1]

March, Marshall, Douglas and Ayoub are doubtful about my statement (at p. 357 above) that 'on the whole, it is true to say that the Lozi judicial process corresponds with, more than it differs from, the judicial process in Western society'.[2] They all rightly lay stress on the importance of the differences between the two judicial processes. I realize now that it would have been better had I merely stated the similarities and the differences, without coming to the overall assessment that similarities outweighed differences. Douglas points out in her review, correctly, that this overall assessment has to be judged in an historical context within the study of tribal law. So much emphasis had been placed by many authors (jurisprudents, anthropologists and others) on the differences between modern and tribal law, that I was to some extent carried away by my demonstration of the similarities in the judicial process. (*Note*: not in the whole of law.) Ayoub (op. cit., p. 248) goes further than March. He argues that I was influenced throughout by the fact that, as he puts it, I saw 'Lozi law from the point of view of Western jurisprudence by and large'. I shall have to approach this major criticism after looking at the problem of terminology.

Ayoub contrasts my alleged approach with that of Bohannan,

---

[1] In his collection for a *Reader in Theory and Research on Judicial Behaviour* (1964), Schubert includes summaries of Bohannan's and my books, and of March's treatment of my book and Ayoub's essay on my book and Bohannan's, thus establishing the independent value of these essays. He does not include my reply to March and March's response in a later issue of the *Stanford Law Review* (see bibliography under March). He also discusses Bohannan's and my books at length in an editorial introduction.

[2] They nevertheless find the comparison stimulating, as have Stumpf, Kilgour, Hoebel, Schiller, and others.

who saw ' Tiv conceptions and our concepts as quite distinct '. Bohannan argues that each society's system of law is a 'folk-system' and that no one folk-system (such as the Western) can be raised to the status of an analytical system and applied to the study of another folk-system.   I am not clear exactly what this implies ; but it seems to mean that one should not use concepts and terms of say, English law, to analyse Tiv law.   On the other hand, I considered I could use some English words to trans-late Barotse words (as *bupaki* by ' evidence '), to name Barotse officials (as *muatuli* by ' judge '), and to summarize Barotse processes of action (as *kubuza*, more commonly by ' to ask ', but also by ' to cross-examine ') and processes of thought (as *kusefa*, used metaphorically, by ' to sift evidence ').

At the outset I must emphasize what the differences between Bohannan's approach and mine are, if I am to reappraise my own analysis in the light of criticisms and of his book and others' later work.   In particular, the publication shortly after my book of Bohannan's book, with its apparent insistence that to use English words was automatically to make an analysis in terms of English law and thus convert the English ' folk-system ' into an ' analytical system ', seems to have created a myth about my work among some anthropologists studying law.   (I at once exclude that doyen of juristic anthropologists, E. A. Hoebel. Nor has any lawyer, as far as I know, adopted this view.)   The myth is that I forced the concepts and processes of Barotse law into a [Procrustean] mould of English terminology and, as some apparently hold, of Roman-Dutch law.

Take the following, from Nader's introductory ' The Anthro-pological Study of Law ' to a recent symposium she edited on *The Ethnography of Law* (1965, p. 11) : Bohannan

implicitly charges Gluckman with having converted the Western legal folk system into an analytical system and having forced the Lozi folk concepts into a Western model. . . . Nadel (1956) and Ayoub (1961) discuss the perplexing questions inherent in Gluckman's assumptions [see below], as does the whole body in ethnoscience. . . . Gluckman's work has been characterized as analogous to that of a linguist who attempts comparison by jamming Barotse grammar into Roman Dutch [*sic*] categories [source not cited].

It is not clear how far Nader accepts this kind of statement : in her full text, she believes the answer to lie ' solely neither with

Gluckman nor with Bohannan '. But whoever made the last
statement, about Roman-Dutch categories, has accepted the
myth implicit in Bohannan, and clearly knows nothing about
Roman-Dutch law.   There is not a single instance in this book
where I have used a Roman-Dutch category and jammed into
it Barotse grammar—or law.   I have very occasionally, when
discussing a trial and after showing a principle of Barotse law in
that trial, stated that the principle can be compared with one in
Roman (and hence Roman-Dutch, and here English) law.
Thus the Barotse maxim that ' if you are invited to a meal and a
fish-bone sticks in your throat, you cannot sue your host ',
clearly invites comparison with *volenti non fit injuria* (which is
important in Roman, Roman-Dutch and English law) (pp. 206,
325).   But the whole of my analysis is concerned to show that,
even if the principles of law be similar in the different systems,
they are ' permeated ' by quite different economic and social
conditions.   This being so, it is nevertheless important to state
that there are similar principles.   Similarly, I refer to Roman
principles such as, *ex nuda pacta non oritur actio*, or *in pari delicto
potior est conditio defendentis*.   After I demonstrate that there are
such principles, in *Barotse* law, out of my discussion of *Barotse*
cases, I exhibit in detail the specific conditions in which *Barotse*
apply these principles of law.   And it is part of my argument—
I claim no originality for I follow many who preceded me—
that the Roman principles of law I cite covered disputes from
ancient into modern times.   Hence my analysis of how Barotse
judges meet new contingencies by respecifying their own general
concepts and principles, applies in a new milieu an analysis
frequently made in comparative jurisprudence and the sociology
of law.

This is all so clear in my text, that I can only conclude that the
perpetrator of this particular statement about ' jamming . . .
into Roman-Dutch categories ' did not get beyond the second
paragraph of my Preface.   I stated there that my own studies
' were in Roman-Dutch and Roman Law ; and English lawyers
will find that my implicit comparative background for Lozi law
is South African law '.   I did so to excuse my failure to draw
attention, where another might have, to parallels in English law.
I must conclude that when the anonymous authority cited by
Nader read my prefatory excuse, he shuddered, as Hamlet did

at his father's ghost's recital of his murder : ' O, horrible ! O, horrible ! most horrible ! ' ' This murderer has killed Lozi law with
cursed juice of Roman Dutch categories '—and he promptly cast
away the book to hell ' with all [its] imperfections on [its] head .'

Nevertheless, clearly if ' the whole body of literature in
ethnoscience ', as Nader alleges, is puzzled by my assumptions,
I may have failed to clarify the building up of my argument
sufficiently.   I consider that a more open-minded appraisal of my
book would have shown that whenever I discussed any important
word used in Barotse trials, I examined its connotations carefully before translating it by an English word.   I refer here, for
example, to my discussion, with parallel citations from Schapera's
study of Tswana law (see Chapter IV above), of the multivocal
Barotse words *mulao* and *mukwa*, before I used for them our
equally multivocal ' law ' and ' custom ' respectively.   Other
Barotse concepts, particularly those involved in evidence, are
carefully discussed in the context of a trial or series of trials.
These discussions should bring out that I was fully aware, like
' the whole body of ethnoscience ', of the difficulties and dangers
involved in any kind of translating of a word from one language
into another language, of comparing an idea or custom in one
culture with those in another, and of equating an official in one
society with an official in another.   I was aware too that each
word in English carries with it certain general connotations, and
words used in jurisprudence carry also technical connotations. I
made my awareness clear in the very first sentence of my Preface :
' In analysing legal problems in an African society one has to use
terms and concepts which have been employed by jurists through
two millennia, and therefore one ought to be well aware of what
these jurists have written. . . .'   And on the next page I went
on to say that

. . . to maintain the clarity of my own analysis I have on the whole
eschewed any references to their writings.   I have not become involved in complex discussions of the meanings of [English] terms,
nor considered whether my definitions for this particular analysis will
cover the facts of law in other systems.   I have tried to use terms with
due regard for their instituted use in comparative jurisprudence ;
but in general analysis I have found it best to use the most common
terms (law, right, duty, etc.) with the connotations given in the *Concise
Oxford Dictionary* . . . (pp. xix–xx).

As already stated, I tried as best I could in the light of my research, while writing in English, to expound the structure of Barotse courts, the rôles of judges and other officials, the course of trials, the background of social relations and institutions in which the trials were set, local concepts and legal maxims, the logic of judges' reasoning, etc. At every point I made clear, from my case-material, how the Barotse conceive of, and operate with, such ideas as evidence—*bupaki* (whether direct, circumstantial, or hearsay), and proof—also *bupaki*, or *niti* = truth.

I judge that I did not do so as comprehensively or as subtly as Bohannan analysed many Tiv ideas. On other types of ideas, I was I believe clearer. But I set about my task in the same way as he did. The difference is that, as he admits, at the time when he wrote his book he did not take the further step and make any comparison.[1] I made the further step to essay a comparison, as Epstein did. We compared the Barotse judicial process and their use of principles and concepts of their law with, e.g., Cardozo's analysis of the Anglo-American judicial process. I believe I showed similarities as well as differences in the cases I cited : of course, I may have missed other similarities and other differences, in these cases ; and perhaps cases I did not cite—or did not hear !—may exhibit yet others. My use of, e.g., C. K. Allen's discussion of custom, particularly, and precedent, equity, natural law, statute, public policy, laws of nature, good morals, as sources of judicial law in Anglo-American law also, I believe, is validated by the evidence I produce and illuminates my Barotse data, in similitude and difference. Again, when I take up the problem of certainty and uncertainty of law, in the light of what Western jurists have written on this theme, I do so with my Barotse data, given in detail ; and this light illuminates the Barotse data. Hoebel's discussion of 'Fundamental Cultural Postulates and Judicial Lawmaking in Pakistan' (1965, at p. 53) similarly shows that it is now held that the opinion of a *mufti*, or religious interpreter of the law, ' is binding only so long as it " correctly " relates Quranic precepts to the social environment of the day '. This is in Nader's *Ethnography of Law.* Yet she fails to see its general implications, or those in an article by Kay

---

[1] See his ' The Differing Realms of Law ' in Nader (editor), *The Ethnography of Law* (1965), p. 42.

on how Californian courts are re-defining the family and kinship system in considering the rights of illegitimate children, in the same volume. It may be that more could be made of my data. But I reject sweeping statements that this kind of comparison distorts the Barotse facts, unless the critic gives an example of such a distortion—or even cites data from another tribal society to show that there is potentially distortion. Or unless he shows specifically that my analysis could be improved throughout, because in making these particular comparisons I went wrong, or the analysis could be improved in some particulars, or that the comparison has inevitably led to a neglect of important areas. It is easy to take an isolated sentence, such as that I studied Roman-Dutch law, and build it into a myth which is then condemned. A complex argument merits an examination in its totality and its parts. It has to be examined in the light of the data it presents ; how it handles those data explicitly and where, in detail, any implicit assumptions lead to distortion or sterility ; and how far its argument advances or retards our understanding.

It is with this approach, and expecting this amount of courtesy from my colleagues—which I extend to them—that I reappraise my work in the light of criticisms and my own awareness of its deficiencies. I do so in terms of the problem of using English at all for analytic concepts, the problem of comparison, and the problem arising from specific obscurities created by my failure to use clearly the concepts I define.

I used English words because I was writing in English, and I have always felt that it is unfair to readers to ask them to carry in their heads a large number of vernacular terms. I remember always Mark Twain's scathing comments on his agent's report on an expedition in *A Tramp Abroad*, where words from many languages were used. Bohannan uses many Tiv terms. And when he does translate, he sometimes avoids obvious English parallels : e.g. ' Anongo *calls* Iyorkyaha . . .' avoids ' summons ', with its many implications of complicated processes, though the ' calls ' is apparently authoritative to come before a court, since there is presumably a penalty if the defendant fails to attend. Ayoub considers (at his p. 248) that Bohannan's method makes

---

[1] Pocock (*Social Anthropology*, 1961, pp. 106 f.) discusses Vico's concern with the same problem.

for greater conceptual clarity than my use of English terms. But in fact Bohannan, since he writes in English, can only avoid the use of a certain number of English jurisprudential terms, such as tort, contract, crime, court, judges. He in fact makes considerable use of English words which have many technical jurisprudential connotations, such as right, duty, obligation, and in the end crime. He explicitly avoids contract and tort because Tiv categorize actions akin to these as ' debt '. But ' debt ' itself is a very complex conception : and I have argued in the final chapter of my *The Ideas in Barotse Jurisprudence* (1965) that we can only understand what this Tiv category of ' debt ' means if we examine this particular type of categorizing as it occurred in early English law, and a variety of other tribal and early legal systems. I cite this example to show here firstly, that however determined one may be to present a folk-system in its purity, one cannot escape from the use of one's own language. Secondly, it emphasizes that for deeper understanding the presentation solely, allegedly, of the ideas of a folk-system, restricts one's analysis severely. In sociological jurisprudence, comparison puts problems in a more illuminating perspective.[1]

I feel therefore that everyone will agree with Bohannan that the first task in reporting a legal system is clearly to describe its ' folk-concepts '. I consider that very many of these concepts can, without distortion after careful and perhaps lengthy description and discussion, be given English equivalents, at least out of courtesy to one's readers. But some such step is essential at the next stage, when one essays comparative work, unless, as Ayoub seems to favour, one invents neologisms. Unfortunately he does not himself suggest any ; nor do I know of anyone who has done so in this field. However, Ayoub's discussion of the problems involved is clear and stimulating.

Failing the use of neologisms, a research worker writing in his own language is, in my opinion, entitled to try to specialize by stipulation the riches in the vocabulary of that language ; and it

---

[1] Bohannan informs me that he will be discussing how he will do comparative work with his approach in an additional chapter to the second edition of his book (in press). Nader (' Anthropological Study of Law,' 1965, pp. 11-12) supports my plea in my *African Jurisprudence* (1962) for this step to comparison.

seems to me that the refinements of English, and in general European, jurisprudence provide us with a more suitable vocabulary, despite its connotations, than do the languages of tribal law.

In this book I tried to stipulate that I would thus specialize words like adjudication, legal, litigation, custom, while using 'law' in all its inherent multivocality. I found this pragmatically useful. A glance at the dictionary, a reading of any book on law, shows how many referents 'law' has, like all socially important words. I consider it impossible to analyse social control without using 'law' in its many senses. In addition, there has been so much argument about 'What is Law?', as if the word could be only one thing, I wished to avoid sterile controversy. In a recent *Introduction to Social Anthropology* (1965, pp. 132–3), Mair, unlike many others, has seen that this is what I attempted, in distinguishing 'law' from 'the legal', and she concludes that this is 'the most satisfactory way to get out of [the] rather absurd situation' created by too narrow a definition of 'law'.[1] But I would here emphasize that I merely stipulate that : I shall use 'law' thus, . . . and I shall use 'legal' thus . . . I do not say 'law' is this, . . . and 'legal' is this. I shall return to my specific suggestions below.

I feel that even if in this book I did not state this position explicitly enough, I was clear about what I was doing. Hence I do not accept Ayoub's assumption that I was over-influenced by my starting-point, where I used established English terms and concepts, including those used by jurists. He argues that I therefore obscured and misconstrued the Barotse judicial process more than Bohannan did justice and judgment among the Tiv. On careful reflection, I consider that it is the events I recorded in Barotse courts that have directed my analysis. Theoretically it can be argued that my preconceptions dominated my records in the field, my abbreviations of my records, and my selections from my records. In practice, I have reported some cases virtually

---

[1] Nader ('Anthropological Study of Law', 1965, pp. 12, 18, 23, 24 f.) approves of my proposal in my *African Jurisprudence* (1961, p. 6) that by distinguishing between the 'champion-at-law, the intermediary, the negotiator, the conciliator, and the arbitrator, we could clarify our problems by focusing attention on the ranges of social pressures which back their actions'. Inconsistently, she is somewhat scornful of my proposal to specialize a range of words to deal with law, legal, the judicial process, etc.

verbatim and summaries of other cases are from equally detailed records.[1] My analysis of Barotse judicial reasoning is woven out of these cases, and if anyone feels that I have allowed my framework to be dominated by my comparative approach, the cases are there for re-analysis by anyone with a different approach.[2] In my opinion my observations drove me to adopt the viewpoint I did ; and, indeed, it was only after I had made preliminary analyses of these observations in lectures at Oxford in 1947-9, that I began to read the studies by Holmes, Cardozo and other jurists of the American and British judicial process, and was stimulated by them to greater insight.

I can immediately clear up some of the problems involved in weighing my stress on similarity against the obvious differences to which my reviewers (and this book above) draw attention. March lists my statements on similarities as follows : Barotse judges utilize the same sources of law as those appealed to by Western judges ; they rely on statute, legal precedent, social customs, natural laws, equity ; they have some of the same rules of court procedure, distinguishing evidence similarly, on a hearing of both sides ; and they operate with some of the criteria of judgment and with presumptions which are well known to Western law. I have also described further similarities in the logic of applying and developing law. March then lists differences : Barotse law is largely unwritten ; they have little statutory interpretation in the Western sense ; cases are heard without benefit of counsel and without formal pleadings : there is no fiction of judicial ignorance ; the rules of relevancy pertaining to evidence are substantially different from the rules of Western courts.

March therefore questions whether the comparison is valid, or indeed has any meaning. I cannot here—since my publishers have granted me limited space—set out his argument in full. But examination of the procedure which I followed in this book shows that when I had stated the similarities and had referred

---

[1] For publishing reasons, I could not give verbatim records on all the cases I cited. But others have reported cases in similar strain from Africa : this is some independent check on my records.

[2] As I have tried to re-analyse the case material on other writers on African law in a later article on ' Reasonableness and Responsibility in the Law of Segmentary Societies ' (1966).

them to widespread constancies in both social life and the judicial process, I turned to the differences and tried to relate one set of differences, to certain other differences. That is, I did not consider all the differences—or indeed similarities—to be variables of the same type ; but I tried to show that certain material differences, such as the absence of counsel, and lack of writing and records, and above all the dominance of relationships of status in Barotse life, operated to explain why criteria of relevancy varied in different types of dispute, why there was no fiction of judicial ignorance, and why, in Barotse (and indeed French) courts, Anglo-Saxon lawyers might think the defendant is assumed to be guilty. Some of what March lists as differences on a par with differences in judicial hearing and analysis, were for me controlling variables. And I feel that, operating in this way, I was able to illuminate both Barotse judicial reasoning and its social context, as I could not have done without the comparison. Clearly, comparison is for certain purposes and problems : looked at in terms of reproduction, blood circulation, respiration, etc., whales can be said to be like mammals ; in terms of feeding and propulsion, they are like fish ; for students of turbulence, they are like submarines or even aeroplanes. By failing to adopt a relative point of view, March fails to see that I try to explain similarities and differences between the Barotse and Western judicial processes by reference to similarities and differences in the social context of litigation.

I now interpolate here that it may be necessary to go below the surface of events to arrive at functional similarities. Both Epstein (in his *Juridical Techniques and the Judicial Process*, 1954) and I felt that a key difference in African courts and modern courts was the absence of counsel to prepare pleadings setting out the issues and the relevant evidence. Mr. Justice Nii Ollennu, of the Ghana Supreme Court, during the course of the International African Institute's seminar on 'The Ideas and Procedures of Traditional African Legal Systems' (1966 : to be published shortly) stressed that the very informality of proceedings in traditional courts achieved similar forensic ends to those achieved for developed courts by counsel and counsel's preparation of pleadings. This informality of procedure obtains in the mode in which litigants present their cases, in the manner of obtaining evidence, and in the rôle played by the court. Procedure may vary from court to court, and in one court for different cases. But it is usual to hear evidence from both litigants before requiring witnesses for the plaintiff to substantiate, if they can, his case. Ollennu points out that both parties are heard by traditional courts before witnesses are called in order to clarify and settle the issues and to determine on whom the onus lies, and hence who should first call witnesses in evidence of his claim. This procedure therefore serves one of the purposes which pleadings, prepared by professional counsel, serve in developed courts. Furthermore, since the plaintiff, lacking trained counsel's advice, may not be seized of the law, but perhaps merely feel that he has been badly treated, justice cannot be achieved unless he is allowed to speak about many things, which at first are apparently irrelevant, but which may later turn out to be crucial. The same observation applies to the other party's initial statement. In the absence of advance preparation and examination in court by counsel, litigants may not be able to present their grievances in coherent, logical and relevant form. Here, as in cross-examination, traditional judges play the rôle of counsel—as an English judge may on behalf of a litigant who appears without benefit of counsel. And—again similarly to such an English judge in this situation—when traditional judges enter on judgment, they eliminate the irrelevant and their arguments are couched in an accumulating logic leading to a verdict on the balance of probabilities in the light of the law. We must remember too that, as demonstrated above, parties are responsible themselves for deciding what witnesses they require, while they lack experts to collect and evaluate evidence.

I am most grateful to Ollennu for allowing me to quote him here, because his analysis makes sense of matters I had overlooked, including both the order in which judges cross-examined the parties and witnesses, and the order in which they investigated different points. Ollennu has gone beneath striking superficial differences in procedure in traditional courts and in what he called developed courts, to extricate what may be called 'functional similarities'. If we define a judicial procedure, at minimum, as the hearing of both parties to a dispute and their witnesses by theoretically impartial persons who find for one or other party on the balance of facts in evidence with reference to certain accepted rules of rightful and wrongful action, Ollennu emphasizes that certain processes must be secured. First, there must be a dispute of which the judges can take cognisance (see the Case of the Vague Complaint, above, p. 78). The issues in dispute have to be clarified out of the rambling grievances of excited people either in counsel's chambers or in the police station, or in the court itself. The man who feels he is a plaintiff may in both situations turn out to be defendant. Thus the onus may shift. With us, counsel may advise his client that he has no case, or is himself in the wrong. So too traditional African judges may say there is no case, or shift the onus. Of course, in seeing the similarities we must not lose sight of the differences, which also have to be analysed.

Douglas (at her p. 372) raises the problem of other kinds of differences between Barotse and modern European law : differences in approaches to property where, as Maine put it, the Law of Persons and the Law of Things are barely separated ; where goods are only involved to a relatively small extent in freely established commercial contracts but are mainly significant in political and kinship status relationships ; and so forth. These are the kinds of problems which I have tried to handle in my *The Ideas in Barotse Jurisprudence* (1965) ; and I hope that Douglas and others will feel I have made some advance in thinking on these problems. I may perhaps note here for clarification of this new book, that I followed Maine in separating transactions involved in status relationships, despite their 'contractual' elements, from the law of 'contract'. I then tried to examine the effect of the dominant elements in status relationships on the law of 'contract'. Discussion on this theme with others has led me to see that there can be a fruitless disputation here. To avoid this, I would in future distinguish international treaties[1] and contracts of status from *commercial* contracts : and I hope that readers of my second book, who may see this Preface, will bear in mind the verbal amendment I here belatedly realize is necessary. I am pleased to see that in his recent essay on ' Funda-

---

[1] I insert these because in an article on Somali pacts to share in paying and receiving blood-money, Lewis (1959) concludes that their existence invalidates Maine's generalization about the movement from Status to [commercial] Contracts. I consider these pacts to be equivalent to international treaties which clearly Maine knew to exist in earliest classical times.

mental Cultural Postulates and Judicial Lawmaking in Pakistan'
(1965, at p. 52), Hoebel states clearly that in Maine's aphorism
about the movement from familial status to contract, '" Contract" means individual obligations arising from the free agreement of individuals', as Maine himself wrote.

Several critics have objected to my analysis of Barotse cases in
terms of 'the reasonable man', and then to my making 'the
reasonable man a central emphasis' of Barotse law. These
criticisms vary in kind. Anderson, in his review in *The Modern
Law Review*, says of my argument that here there is a parallel
with Western law : ' Surely it amounts, in fact, to no more than
a regard for what an ordinary man, or an average headman,
father, son, or husband . . . would normally do in given
circumstances—and, as such, represents a canon of judgment
which is basic to human thinking, however inarticulate it may
be ? ' If the canon is ' basic to human thinking ', it surely
merits analysis ; and there is a wealth of litigation, both among
ourselves and the Barotse, contained in Anderson's ' it amounts,
in fact, to no more than a regard. . . .' I cite below a somewhat similar statement by Nadel, cited approvingly by Nader.

I here repeat that I believe my cases demonstrate that something like this idea is fundamental in Barotse thought, both of
judges and of litigants. I have elsewhere recorded, in published
broadcasts,[1] how this vision of the reasonable man in Barotse
law suddenly burst on me during the hearing of the Case against
the Violent Councillor (above, pp. 83–90). This vision illumi-
nated all my other cases. The whole concept had been overlooked in the records in tribal law known to me. I examined
the rôle of the reasonable man in cross-examination and judicial
reasoning. Epstein also showed that other tribes in the region
argued similarly, in his *Juridical Techniques and the Judicial Process*
(1954). Following on my work, Howell (who acknowledges
my work before publication) reported the conception among the
Nuer and Meggitt found it among the Walbiri of Australia.[2]
Bohannan described clearly how the Tiv have this conception

---

[1] ' The Reasonable Man in Barotse Law ' (1963), p. 179.

[2] Detailed references to these other works are given in my ' Reasonableness
and Responsibility in the Law of Segmentary Societies' (1966). There also
are references to Bohannan and Gulliver, cited below. On Bohannan's
cases, see also Epstein's review of Bohannan in *Man* (1959), No. 33.

(at his pp. 33–4), but stated that it is not employed by judges in courts. Here Epstein and I agree with him that it may not be used explicitly, but that an analysis of Bohannan's cases shows that these cannot be understood unless one sees that the conception is constantly, if implicitly, in the judges' minds.[1] Gulliver has similarly stated in a study of the Arusha of Tanganyika that he did not find it

empirically or analytically valid to adopt Gluckman's hypothesis of ' the reasonable man '. In so far as this concept ' corresponds closely with the concept of " the *rôle* of a particular *status* [in Gluckman's words] " ' Arusha, like other peoples, have some idea of it which they more or less explicitly put into words, and which can be readily inferred from their behaviour, at relevant times. . . .[2]

Gulliver proceeds to state that disputes are argued, 'not altogether as a conscious technique . . . by reference to reasonable expectations'. However, Gulliver's central concern is with the political pressures which among the Arusha, who had no courts, produced settlements. This is an entirely different problem. Yet re-analysis of his longest case, the only one of which anything like a full record is given, shows that at every point protagonists argue as reasonable men about what reasonable incumbents of social positions should do in the light of demands on their resources.[3]

   This implicit use of the conception of a reasonable man by Tiv in court judgments has been conceded by Bohannan,[4] but he considers that since the conception is not explicitly formulated, it is not a Tiv ' folk-concept '. But clearly then some such analytic concept should be used to make sense of Tiv judgments. More generally, Bohannan states that Tiv elders and judges do not give a public explanation of the logic by which they have come to a conclusion and state their verdict. Gulliver says the Arusha also do not publicly expound the logic of their arguments ;

---

[1] See preceding footnote.
[2] *Social Control in an African Society* (1963), p. 300.
[3] I have not space to present a full re-analysis here, but I have done so sufficiently in my ' Reasonableness and Responsibility in the Law of Segmentary Societies ' (1966).
[4] In discussion of a paper I read in 1963 to the Law School of Northwestern University, cited in Gluckman, ' Reasonableness and Responsibility ' (1966).

and he suggests that explicit analysis by judges of cases may occur where there are courts with power to summons, hear and cross-examine parties and witnesses. This suggested association that clear and explicit argument emerges only in courts needs careful checking : it is not supported by a number of records on societies such as Ifugao, Kalinga, Yurok, Nuer, and Walbiri who do not have courts.

As far as the use of the conception of ' the reasonable man ' is concerned, I consider we have to keep two things clear. First, I insist that primarily I report a Barotse conception which is akin to what we call 'a reasonable man '—their phrase is *mutu yangana*. Epstein has reported the same conception from other Zambian tribes. This being so, it is impossible to analyse the way judges cross-examine and give decisions in these courts without dealing with ' the reasonable man ' and what Epstein calls ' reasonable expectations '. Allott, a lawyer specializing on African law, lends his support to the utility of the conception :

The court, by setting custom as its standard, makes what is otherwise normal, normative ; that which is done, ought to be done. But custom *alone* [Gluckman's italics] will not always yield a rule of decision, and in such cases another standard is required. This standard is that of the reasonable man : what would an ordinary, prudent or reasonable man have done in the circumstances of the case ? The conduct of the reasonable man since he steps into the shoes of the defendant, must vary according to the circumstances posited. In societies without written law the two standards, the customary and the reasonable, often overlap ; for, as that percipient Gold Coast judge, Sir W. Brandford Griffith, C.J., remarked: 'Native custom generally consists of the performance of the reasonable in the special circumstances of the case ' (Yerenchi *v.* Akuffo (1905), Renner's Reports, 362, 367).

Allott then discusses my use of the concept in explicating how Lozi judges use reasonable standards to incorporate prevailing ideas of morality and justice, changing standards, etc., but he does not approve of the extent to which I argue that the judges may be seen as ' interpreting ' ideas in the law. This doubt I discuss below. He also draws attention to what he considers to be my too ' flexible ' use of ' reasonable behaviour ' (a point I also discuss below).

None of those who have criticized my use of the conception of the reasonable man on general grounds have attempted to re-analyse the cases I reported without using the conception or some similar conception.   It is easy for March (at his p. 733) to say, in the abstract, that I include so much under the single rubric of the reasonable man that it becomes virtually meaningless, and that the confusing use of this concept, with its extensive connotations in Western law, is ' simply rhetoric related to [an] unfortunate attempt to strengthen [a] claim of similarity between Lozi and Western law '.   But I would like a demonstration that the cases can be better analysed otherwise.   March in fact goes on to extract from my book itself three forms in which social norms enter into judicial reasoning (see below).   But I still persist in considering that the social conception which pulls these together is the assemblage of norms, with defined leeways, into 'the reasonable man '.

Having established that ' the reasonable man ' is a Barotse concept, perhaps I would have been wiser to use the Barotse term when reporting, and confined my use of the English phrase, or invented a neologism, for analytical purposes.   I did not do so because I wished to suggest that the central position of the conception in the Barotse judicial process encouraged me to believe that a more meticulous examination of how, in Britain, litigants or accused in a large number of cases presented their evidence, and how this evidence was cross-examined by counsel and adjudicated on by judges and juries, would reveal that a series of reasonable men of somewhat different types exist in English social life and therefore in English courts.   That is, I suggested that research in Western courts of trial in these terms would reveal what are the shared and the divergent norms which various types of persons attached to different rôles. Some of my reviewers, such as the lawyers Stumpf, Kilgour and Schiller, and also March, have seen value in this suggestion. But above all, I used the established phrase to state my hypothesis that ' the reasonable man ' appears to dominate the Barotse judicial process, and possibly the judicial process in similar societies, because most disputes involve persons in related status positions, so that courts are dominantly concerned with the rôles of such positions and with much of a litigant's total social personality.   In a more differentiated society, contractual relations and injuries by one stranger on another are what primarily come to courts. Hence what would ' the reasonable man ' have done in certain circumstances appears only to be a judicial device to assess reasonable duty, care, support, etc., in specialized branches of the law. But law becomes divided into specialized branches only as the society of which it is a part becomes more differentiated. My text above shows how little this specialization had developed in Barotseland. That is, my hypothesis is that in the relatively undifferentiated law of Barotseland ' the reasonable man ' emerges as a more clearly defined social cluster of rights and duties around a specific status than he does in the developed law of Britain. If this is seen, it is, I believe, quite clear when I am reporting Barotse use of ' the reasonable man ', and when I use the conception for objective analysis. March did not see that I used the device to emphasize divergence as well as similarity between Barotse and Western law. I repeat here, from the text of the book (p. 129), that I also saw ' the reasonable man ' as representing the forensic aspect of rôles, and hence a means of linking analysis of the judicial process to this central concept in sociology and anthropology (cf. Epstein's ' reasonable expectations ').

To sum up, Barotse law is concerned with status: hence definition of the reasonable incumbent of a status lies at the heart of the judicial process. The law of economically more developed societies is concerned with specialized rights and duties : hence the reasonable man is a judicial fiction to assess whether, where and how duties lie in relation to others' rights.

Hoebel[1] has criticized my use of the phrase on a different basis. He too considers that ' the reasonable man ' is not an effective tool for the job to be done. The job calls, he argues, for the identification of clusters of behavioral norms (rôles) linked to specific social statuses, with determination of how much leeway in deviations is permitted without the invocation of legal restraint. (These are what Epstein defined as 'reasonable expectations'.) Hoebel continues to argue that ' much more particularistic concepts are required than such a loose and general one as " the reasonable man ", which is not by pedigree an analytical concept at all, but a highly specialized folk concept out of

---

[1] Hoebel, ' Three Studies in African Law ' (1961), pp. 436 f.

Anglo-American legal practice '—and he cites Bohannan's warning against raising one folk-system to the status of an analytical
system.   Hoebel (who should be read in full) stresses that the
concept of the reasonable man in Anglo-American law ' is a
very special concept devised to establish some sort of workable
norms in areas of negligence wherein particular facts may be
highly variable and specific to particular situations '.   Hence
he considers that it will not be useful in formulating hypotheses
and building theories.   It fails by those tests to justify use for
analytical purposes, though he agrees it may fit the Barotse data.

I differ from Hoebel on a number of points.   First, as I suggest
in my text and have stated above, I consider that our process of
trial makes more use of the conception than Hoebel allows.
It is not used only to determine negligence.   Furthermore, I
suggest that an analysis of cross-examination of parties and
witnesses, of judicial analysis, and of jury deliberations[1] will
show that the reasonable man is often present in our courts, as
Sir Alan Herbert satirized in his *Uncommon Law* (see p. 83
above).

Second, I feel I have used the conception to pose problems
and work out a theory of the judicial process.   But I agree here
with Hoebel that it may not itself be a sufficiently ' particularistic
concept ' for the job which lies before us.   A concept may be
useful at a certain stage in doing the job then seen : and this was
the state of the material on tribal law when I wrote my book.
But each concept becomes a block to further analysis, and more
refined concepts have to be developed.[2]   I agree that I used
'the reasonable man ', for example, to analyse how he is used by
Barotse judges both in cross-examination on evidence and in
judgment, without always distinguishing these processes—as
Douglas (at her p. 370), Nadel (at his p. 165), Allott, and others
point out.   I did so because the Barotse judges themselves do not
make this distinction, and other distinctions, in their application

---

[1] See, e.g., Devons, ' Serving as a Juryman in Britain' (1965), for a discussion
of how middle-class jurymen conjecture about reasonableness in specific
groups, as well as an account of how their own interests, prejudices and
principles influence their decisions.
[2] See Gluckman and Eggan, ' Introduction' to *New Approaches in Social
Anthropology* (1964–66).

of the conception. Now I would distinguish several distinct processes covered by the conception for tribal law :

1. The measurement of standards of fulfilment of specific obligations ;
2. The combination of several such standards (degree of performance, observance of etiquette or custom, adherence to rule) to assess whether a party has fulfilled the demands of his or her rôle, as the crux and main issue of the case. Here it is of key importance that the court has to assess how far an individual can meet a particular obligation to a particular other person in the light of his specific wealth and his obligations to all other persons. That is, the court assesses by reasonable standards each individual's administration of his private economy ;
3. The use of this model as a technique of cross-examination to destroy an ostensibly reasonable story ;
4. The establishment of proof through demonstration of unreasonable deviation from custom or failure in degree of performance of obligation ;
5. The relation of proof to questions of whether responsibility and liability are strict and absolute in the specific relationship involved, with problems of onus of proof and possibilities of rebutting presumptions about intention ;
6. The whole question of judicial views on intention in terms of ethics and law, as against actual motivation.[1]

But it is a key point in my whole analysis of the judicial process that the most crucial concepts of law are elastic or of multiple meaning, and that they can absorb a variety of different facts and be permeated by various social and/or individual presumptions. Above all, I stressed that this applied to specification of the meaning of ' reasonable ' in variable situations. Hence these multiple facets of ' the reasonable man ', and the way judges examine them together and apart, are central to the judicial process. This is emphasized by the large number of judicial procedures, just cited, which are involved in it.

---

[1] These six—there may well be more—elements are validated in my ' Reasonableness and Responsibility in the Law of Segmentary Societies ' (1966).

March (at pp. 526 f.) draws three sets of propositions partly out of my data, partly out of his general view of the law :

1. ' The determination of punishable wrongs on the basis of ' norms ' relative to specific rôles. These norms have to be plotted on ' a graph ' against group approval, to show the extent of allowed deviation for transgression, and the heightened approval gained by over-fulfilment. March phrases thus my discussion of the relation between the reasonable man—what courts will make a man do— and the upright man—what morality expects of a man.

2. The way in which ' social norms enter into the evaluation of testimony '. This involves a set of presumptions on the court's part.

3. The ' norms of society are used generally for purposes of inference in much the same way as they are used for purposes of validating evidence '. March here adds that this draws attention to ' the sometimes forgotten similar dependence in Western law ' on ' the extent to which the structure of circumstantial evidence is based on elaborate sets of expectations concerning human behaviour that comprise a substantial part of the norm structure '. I I stress this point, since I consider that decisions on guilt or innocence which are based on circumstantial evidence are likely to be most revealing of people's presumptions and values. I cite here too Krige's (1956, p. 96) perspicacious comment in a review : ' Moral standards are applied to assess behaviour for evidential purposes, but the standard of the reasonable man is used to decide whether a man has complied with legal requirements.'

These are the kinds of principles into which the way the Barotse judges operate their view of the reasonable man can be broken. I appreciate that after showing how Barotse judges operate with constellations of reasonable standards, a more refined breakdown would have allowed me to make a more meticulous analysis of judicial reasoning. It is tools of this kind which I feel should be designed, though we may still have to start with ' the reasonable man ' as a folk-concept found in widely different societies and cultures, and in some form as an analytical concept which can pull together many judicial presumptions.

My third disagreement with Hoebel is therefore with his already cited statement that 'the job calls for the identification of clusters of behavioral norms (rôles) linked to specific statuses, with determination of how much leeway in deviations is permitted without invocation of legal restraint'. This is a job : but it is a job in the delineation of substantive rules of law in a fuller than formal sense, not a job in the analysis of judicial reasoning. Here something like the reasonable man is a key feature, even if it be advisable to drop that culture-bound term and coin some other English phrase (for writing in English) which can be applied to judicial processes in several or many societies.

This brings me to Hoebel's fourth comment. He concludes (his pp. 438 f.) that, rather than the conception of the reasonable man, 'more appropriate as a model for characterization of the Lozi law could be the concept of parental law developed by Llewellyn with reference to the American Pueblo Indians [in unpublished but mimeographed lectures] and applied to the analysis of Soviet law' by Berman in his *Justice in Russia* (1950). The contrast in the latter, Hoebel says, is between a Western view of a central figure 'who is not the reasonable man of the law of negligence but rational man in the full possession of matured sensibilities', and a Soviet view which regards a man in Berman's own words, 'as a dependent member of the collective group, a youth, whom the law must not only protect against the consequences of his own ignorance but must also guide and train and discipline'. Soviet 'criminal procedure deals with " the whole man ", but it deals with him in a particular way, as a teacher or parent deals with a child'. In civil suits, the court may consider 'not merely the issues litigated but any issue arising from the situation may be adjudicated'. The situation, says Berman, is similar in Soviet intercorporate litigation : '. . . the judicial contest is waged against the background of a more intimate relationship among the participants, a relationship more akin to that of a family than to that of an impersonal " civil " society.'

Hoebel points out how similar this is to the Barotse stress, exhibited in this book, on maintaining certain key relationships in being. Barotse judgments are homilies on the theme of love and mutual helpfulness. Therefore their courts broaden the issues involved, and strive to effect a rapprochement. Hoebel adds that here American commercial arbitration and juvenile courts and courts of domestic-relations 'reveal Lozi-like qualities of broad tolerance in the scope of relevance'. Hoebel concludes of these relations, that

the common quality that is found in these disparate legal systems stems not from like systems of social structure but rather from general similarity of basic values—values which place the maintenance of group solidarity first and transactional rights and duties second. Whether the social structure is based on lineages or is bilateral, whether it is monarchic, communistic or democratic, appears to be relatively irrelevant but not absolutely so. The reasonable-man concept enjoys a closer fit with individual-centred systems of action than it does with collective. It is for this reason that the concept of 'parental' law could possibly be more apposite to the Lozi than is that of the reasonable man.

This is fascinating and heady stuff. Hoebel (at his p. 433) wrote, before coming to this discussion of my own efforts at broad comparison, that 'the boundary at which Bohannan halts is but the taking-off point for Gluckman, who obviously finds it exhilarating to take intellectual risks for the sake of intellectual gain'. I myself, in the text of this book, indicated that industrial conciliation and marriage guidance counselling were two methods of attempting to adjust relationships involving not limited, and possibly ephemeral, interests, but multiple interests, and hence here courts could not lay down decisions to maintain the relationships in effective functioning. Broader enquiry was called for.[1] I think the gains he indicates are great. The concept of 'parental law' systems, bringing together such diverse types of relations, is more grandiose than my comparison of two judicial processes.

I do not consider that this argument disposes of the reasonable man : rather, as I have already indicated, it emphasizes that the reasonable man is differently delineated in what Hoebel calls parental and individual-centred systems.

---

[1] Douglas (1956, p. 373) draws attention to my statement and cites studies of industrial conciliation to support it ; but she notes that the comparison requires to be supported by evidence on the effectiveness of penalties imposed by Barotse courts, a problem I have referred to above.

I have discussed March and Hoebel at some length, and come now to Nadel's ' Reason and Unreason in African Law ' (1956). It is difficult to compress his full argument, since he has written into a review of three books, a compressed discussion of reasonableness in African law.   He considers that there is ' great merit ' in my having formulated this basic fiction (as he calls it) of ' the reasonable man ' in the Barotse system, and 'thus to have made explicit a principle which other students of tribal law might overlook or take for granted ' (at his p. 166).   But he argues, like the others, that I have made too much of it, since it is ' a principle so basic that indeed it may be taken for granted '.[1]   It must operate, he says.   But he is more concerned with my failure to underline instances where reasonableness may prove a very inadequate, if not meaningless, standard, when he believes the Lozi would abandon it for ' the sharper dichotomy of things simply lawful and unlawful, permitted and forbidden '.[2]   In his study of *Ifugao Law* (1919) Barton stated that certain things are ' rather *arbitrarily* forbidden ', and he gave examples of such rules.   He then went on to state ' a small part of Ifugao law consists even yet of taboos that are arbitrary and, except in essence, unreasonable.   But the greater part has advanced far beyond this stage and is on a firm and reasonable basis of justice.'   He does not make clear whether he is speaking of this by Ifugao or his own standards.   In the main text, I cited cases involving such rules ; and I showed that though breach of some carries a strict liability, the Barotse judges nevertheless argue that this is because they are observed by all reasonable men.   Hence I think that Nadel here raises a problem in the substantive law, which is more complicated when applied in the judicial process.   Indeed, Nadel seems to agree with me that the concept of the reasonable man is of crucial importance even here when the judges reason with guilty parties.   They try to persuade the guilty to acknowledge ' their " unreasonable behaviour " ' where the ' overall aim is always to achieve consensus '.   Reason in law, he considers, is

---

[1] I have commented above on this proposition, as made by Anderson. Nader (' Anthropological Study of Law ', 1965, p. 7) uncritically cites this remark of Nadel's.

[2] I have discussed this problem in my ' Reasonableness and Responsibility ' (1966). Nadel's statement is again taken over without consideration by Nader (1965), pp. 7–8.

'closely linked with conceptions of equity and justice', and therefore is reduced in importance where the rules of law are strict. I would rather put it that, where the rules are strict, every reasonable man conforms with them. No leeway is allowed, so no problem of a reasonable standard of deviation arises.

Nadel raises a quite new point when he suggests that rules may be more strictly enforced, and therefore the conception of a [variably—M.G.] reasonable man may be less significant, if the political machinery is weak. This is the position in the newly established Nuer courts (described by Howell), where parties' political groups are represented by some of the judges, and also among the Nuba, as reported by Nadel (1947). Recourse to arbitrary and invariable penalties may be the easiest solution for a dilemma posed by the demands that judges administer justice and that they support their own party. Like the other articles I am considering, Nadel's essay stands independently, setting out ranges of problems for research.

I note one last point on this concept of the reasonable man. At p. 135 of this book I said that 'it is a false paradox, but perhaps illuminating', to say 'the [Barotse court] has a view of the "reasonable and customary" adulterer or adultress'. March, Krige and others have used this little jest to illustrate my alleged tendency to take the reasonable man too far. I stated it was a false paradox—Barotse never speak thus. But I used the phrasing to stress through actual cases how wrongdoers give themselves away by conforming with certain social stereotypes of how adulterers and thieves and the like behave, and observe certain modes of behaviour which Barotse believe to characterize particular types of wrongdoers. I specifically stressed that I made the statement because I felt I had not investigated this problem adequately, and I wanted graphically to draw the attention of other anthropologists to it. I pointed out that what was entailed was that judges interpreted the accused's actions as only reasonably explicable in terms of unlawful relations and motives.

The third major criticism of my work has been that I have not succeeded in using my concepts clearly and consistently. This is a main point of Ayoub's article (1961), but Nadel, March, Hoebel, Krige and others draw attention to it. Ayoub poses the difficulties clearly (at his pp. 247–8) : ' This possibility of confusion is, it seems to me, prevalent in Western jurisprudence, because the concepts used in " the law " (i.e. American, British, French, etc.) are often used in "the study of the law", as well.' Concepts used in ' the law ' itself may have ambiguity as a strength. The ambiguity of these concepts becomes a weakness if the same words are used as part of ' an analytic system ', when ' the reduction of ambiguity and the increase of conceptual clarity and consistency are always goals for which to aim '. Hence Ayoub favours that we devise neologisms. The problem therefore has to be examined at two levels. The first is whether a researcher, writing an analysis in English, can employ standard English terms which are used in ' the law ' also in ' the study of the law ' (even of England) without inevitably creating misconceptions and causing some confusion. Here I can only plead that judgment at any stage must be on results. While Ayoub and Hoebel both state that Bohannan, in restricting himself to setting out Tiv folk-concepts, has greater 'conceptual clarity ', his study has less ' heuristic value ' than mine (Ayoub), and my method poses greater ranges of comparative problems than his (Hoebel). I cite these statements not in vanity, but because, as I have argued elsewhere, I believe that if we do not essay comparative work, but remain in individual folk-systems, we lose sight of many problems, and actually may misinterpret forms of thought within a particular folk-system.[1] Douglas (at her p. 369) states that several critics felt that I had imposed foreign forms of thought on indigenous categories and distinctions, but ' c'est précisément dans cette interposition de formes de pensées étrangères que reside l'acte d'interprétation '.

I have discussed how I tried to stipulate that I would use English terms in certain ways. The only stipulation to which specific objection has been taken is my attempt to confine the word ' legal ' to rules enforced, and actions in, courts : so a society without courts would be ' alegal ' (cf. ' amoral '), but not without law, and in one society there would be 'legal ' rules, sanctioned by courts, and ' alegal ' rules, otherwise sanctioned. All my reviewers have approved my aim—save that Ayoub seems to favour neologisms though he does not propose any.

---

[1] ' African Jurisprudence ' (1961), *The Ideas in Barotse Jurisprudence* (1965), passim, and *Politics, Law and Ritual in Tribal Society* (1965), Chapter V.

2E

They have indicated the difficulties involved in reaching agreement among scholars on such stipulations. Two have specifically pointed out that many writers have already used ' legal ' in a different sense, and more would in the future do so.[1] In my later writings[2] I have therefore proposed ' forensic ' as a possible term to cover what is done in courts, because I agree with many scholars that the development of courts, and the rôle of courts when established, must be crucially distinguished in sociological/ jurisprudential analysis of social control. Until someone proposes a new vocabulary (and I wish someone would do so), I hope we can agree that some such procedure by which we stipulate the meanings of a series of words, related to one another, will enable us to avoid sterile controversy over the allegedly intrinsic and single meaning of words and instead to concentrate on real problems of analysis.[3]

The second level of this problem is whether one is then consistent. Unhappily, I arrived at the importance of this procedure during the course of writing this book ; and hence, as my critics demonstrate, I did not faithfully abide by my own stipulations. And in the course of failing to do so, I fell, as Ayoub (at his pp. 244 f.) points out, into unwarranted and obscuring ambiguities. He rightly pleads for conceptual clarity and consistency. It is, he, Krige and others say, perhaps clear to me what I am doing, but it is not always possible for an outsider to see when I am reporting Barotse thought and when I am analysing that thought, since I use the same set of concepts for both reports and analysis. I realize now that, when I had finished the book, I should have re-written it again from the beginning—perhaps I would still be writing it

---

[1] Among others I may mention Radcliffe-Brown in several well-known essays ; Llewellyn and Hoebel in *The Cheyenne Way* (1940) ; and Hoebel in his *The Law of Primitive Man* (1954 : published when my book was well on its way through the press). And see Bohannan's ' The Differing Realms of Law ' (1965, p. 35), where he defines a ' legal institution ' in his own way, but by using the phrasing ' a legal institution is . . . ' obscures that this is the way he chooses to use the word ' legal '. I do not feel that I need comment on his statement (at p. 42) that ' we may, like Gluckman's first book, cut our insights short by defining "legal" too rigidly before we start to write '. It is not validated in any way, and it overlooks that I use words in a series of related stipulations. I used ' law ' without rigid definition.

[2] See my arguments in works referred to in second preceding footnote.

[3] A procedure argued for by many jurists such as Stone and Hart.

yet again.   For the obscurity that exists, I now can only apologize to Ayoub (and other readers), and thank him for struggling through this obscurity to find stimulus in my analysis (as I hope they also have).

Ayoub (at his p. 245) therefore considers that if he has understood my argument about concepts of law it is ' more the result of the . . . repetition of the argument than the result of conceptual clarity in stating it at any one time ', and Nadel (at his p. 161) and others complain too of repetitiveness.   Here I enter a second special plea on repetitiveness.   A book of this kind, one hopes, will be used by students as well as by mature scholars ; and I have recapitulated the argument as it developed to help students, a procedure unnecessary for their senior fellows.   In this I followed the procedure of Evans-Pritchard's *Witchcraft, Oracles and Magic among the Azande* (1937), without, alas ! attaining his elegance.   In the course of repetition, for this good end, I have sometimes slipped into careless ambiguity.

But in fact I believe that part of my ambiguity resides in the complexity of the problems I tried to solve, a complexity which my reviewers stress and of which the reader who has pursued his way through the book will become aware.   Much of my argument is concerned with trying to explain how the Barotse, living through a period of great change, can consider that their *mulao*—their law—remains certain (' well-known ', ' of old ') when their life is changing radically and when, like American realist lawyers, they believe adjudication on a particular dispute is not always predictable.   I will not essay to reproduce my analysis here : but it has involved a discussion of their use of their word which can be translated as ' law ', at several different levels.   I have cited that I stipulated that I would use ' legal ' to refer to actions in court.   Ayoub asks, do societies without courts have legal concepts, like rights and duties ?   In my use above of this term, they do not ; they do have rights and duties in law.   But this particular query would fall away if my new proposal that we use ' forensic ' for courts works better.   Then in courts we are dealing with the selection of forensic rights and duties which the courts can enforce from out of a more general body of (legal) rights and duties in law.

Other problems in these fields are cited by the reviewers, and each of these raises new problems for research.   In particular,

I draw attention to Nadel's discussion of the difference, and the relation, between law and custom. The difficulty here seems to arise from the fact that I used ' custom ' in what I took to be the standard anthropological sense of ' standardized and approved behaviour ' (summarized by the dictionary in one meaning as ' usual practice ').   I then argued that ' custom ' in this sense is best treated in tribal society, like statutes or moral rules, as one of the sources of law in its meaning of a *corpus juris*, in the way that jurisprudence treats customs in, say, England (cf. another definition of custom in the dictionary, ' (Law) established usage having the force of law ').   This entailed that I had to say that some customs were ' legally enforceable '—I would now phrase it, ' forensically enforceable ', or ' enforceable in court ', while other customs were not directly enforced though failure to observe them might be accepted as evidence of wrongdoing. Nadel himself, in his study of *The Nuba* (1947, pp. 499 f.) saw custom as approved actions which lack forceful sanction, law as those customs which are sanctioned by socially approved force even if not in a court.   This is a perfectly legitimate way of using the terms, and the difference between Nadel and me indicates the difficulties in specializing these multivocal words.   But the theoretical idea of custom as a source of law is clear enough in Western jurisprudence, and I do not see why it should not be helpful in the analysis of tribal law.   Nadel finds obscuring my statement that the Lozi will not enforce ' other tribes' customs . . . if they conflict with their own law ' (p. 237).   I meant by this, that Lozi will not enforce other tribes' customs (usual, approved practices) if these conflicted with Lozi statute, moral rule, public policy, or custom (any rule among the sources of law).   As I noted above, the Lozi do not consider enforced matrilineal succession in conflict with their system of selecting heirs from any line : they do so consider wife-lending between persons circumcised in the same lodge.

An essay by Bohannan on ' the Differing Realms of Law ' in Nader's *The Ethnography of Law* (1965) emphasizes for me that too little thought has been given to the problem of how far using Western jurisprudential approaches distorts other systems of law. For some, it is become a shibboleth that this is misleading.   Let us look at how Bohannan relates what he calls ' custom ' to what he calls ' legal ' and see if there is a fundamental logical difference between his procedure and my procedure (following Western jurists) whereby I call ' custom ' a source of what I call ' law ' and hence of what I call ' forensic ' (formerly legal) rulings. Bohannan states (pp. 34 f.) that :

A norm is a rule, more or less overt, which expresses ' ought ' aspects of relationships between human beings. Custom is a body of such norms—including regular deviations and compromises with norms—that is actually followed in practice much of the time. . . . A legal institution is one by means of which the people of a society settle disputes that arise between one another and counteract any gross and flagrant abuses of the rules . . . of at least some of the other institutions of society. Every on-going society has legal institutions in this sense, as well as a wide variety of nonlegal institutions.

(Note he does not say, ' I will use the words " norms," " customs " and " legal " in this way,' but ' norms are,' ' custom is,' and ' a legal institution is . . .')

. . . Seen in this light, a fairly simple distinction can be made between law and custom. Customs are norms or rules (more or less strict, and with greater or less support of moral, ethical or even physical coercion) about the ways in which people must behave if social institutions are to perform their tasks and society is to endure. All institutions (including legal institutions) develop customs. Some customs, in some societies, are *re*institutionalized at another level ; they are restated for the more precise purposes of legal institutions. When this happens, therefore, law may be regarded [the first time he stipulates] as a custom that has been restated in order to make it amenable to the activities of the legal institutions. In this sense, it is one of the most characteristic attributes of legal institutions that some of these ' laws ' are about the legal institutions themselves, although most are about the other institutions of society—the familial, economic, political, ritual, or whatever.

We might rephrase this as : the customs of all institutions of a society are liable to be involved in a dispute, and may be settled by a legal institution. In such circumstances, the legal institution restates [certain ?] customs in the institution involved, i.e. it reinstitutionalizes these. These customs can be called ' law '. Customs are therefore the source of law in legal institutions. We are then back with the standard jurisprudential approach— but with a difference.

The difference is that Bohannan sees the reinstitutionalization into legal institutions of custom as occurring out of 'familial, economic, political and ritual, or whatever' institutions (domains of life Fortes calls them), and out of the legal institutions themselves. He does not discriminate between types of what he calls 'custom'. The Western jurisprudential approach, which I have followed to analyse the Barotse judicial process, not only discriminates between the domains of social relations, but it also discriminates between the types of rules and regularities which are restated as 'law', or as 'legal' or 'forensic rulings', in the judicial process. I have described these, for the Barotse, as statutes, precedents, moral exemplifications, public policy, good morals, equity, natural law (called laws of Gods) and laws of nature (also called laws of God),[1] reasonableness, and custom. Bohannan might say that these are in fact Barotse ideas on public policy, ideas about good morals, ideas about the laws of nature ; and hence they can all be called 'customs' in his definition of the word. To do so would in my opinion obscure the complicated balancing of these different types of rule, practice, principle, etc., which is involved in a judicial process or a process of settlement, mediation, negotiation, and so forth. I therefore believe that the standard jurisprudential approach to this process is, *for certain problems*, more refined and fruitful than Bohannan's here. His approach may be more refined and fruitful if we shift our interest to examine problems involved in the maintenance of norms within specific domains of social relationships. But my major point is that there is no difference between using the language of Western social anthropology and using the language of Western jurisprudence in tackling these sorts of problems. Theoretically, both are equally distorting even while they may be illuminating. It is mere prejudice for social anthropologists to consider that the scheme which jurisprudents have used successfully for the analysis of Western law, cannot be applied to clarify the law of another 'folk-system'. It is particularly prejudice, if in fact their own systems of analysis can be reduced to almost exactly the same logical procedures.

Schiller, an American scholar on Roman and on tribal law, also is concerned about the relation between customary practice and

---

[1] Calling all these 'the laws of God' indicates Barotse identification of morality and normal natural conditions.

the manner in which a court gives a judgment on observance or non-observance of such a practice in terms of demands for reasonable conformity. I have in the text argued that this is the crux of the judges' problem—which is indeed difficult. Schiller's concern here leads him to question the whole utility, or so I understand, of trying to analyse judicial action from the use of concepts. He writes :

[Gluckman] believes that the flexible generality of Lozi concepts brings about certainty of law as a body of rules through the acknowledged uncertainty of judicial decision. This principle has broad implications for the nature of law generally, and goes far beyond the confines of Lozi law or, indeed, of primitive law. It may serve as a corrective to much of the discussion about law in Western legal thinking. The chapter on the comparative implications of the Lozi judicial process will undoubtedly stimulate further discussion. The reviewer has a certain hesitancy in ascribing so much weight to conceptual ideas in the anlysis of any legal system. Just how far do Lozi courts, or any courts, employ abstract concepts in arriving at decisions ? In comment on a primitive legal system it does not lead to clarity, I submit, to employ a term like ' custom ' in a non-technical connotation. Possibly the view of Llewellyn and Hoebel is a wise one, that broad concepts like custom or mores should not be used ; to paraphrase these authors, they are ambiguous, they diffuse their reference indiscriminately, they lend a passing solidity to supposed lines of behaviour and a seeming uniformity to deviating phenomena, they take away attention from the fact that the firmest and clearest practice or standard operates only upon and through the minds and activities of persons (*The Cheyenne Way*, pp. 275 f. ; cf. E. A. Hoebel, *The Law of Primitive Man*, 1954, pp. 21 f., 276). What, for example, is the meaning of ' reasonable and customary behaviour ' ? What about the behaviour that is reasonable but not customary, or customary but not reasonable ? And certainly the phrase ' customary law ' should be discarded in spite of its common employment in works on indigenous African law.

With all respect, I believe Schiller is here over-influenced by Llewellyn, as perhaps Hoebel was. I cannot here consider *The Cheyenne Way* in detail, but I feel there is too little relation of disputes to Cheyenne social structure and its established standards in it. Social life, always and not only in a period of great changes, is marked by (to use Schiller's words) ambiguity, diffuseness, deviating phenomena. When disputes arise out of these shifting and variable situations in social life, litigants use words and concepts to summarize their version of their activities and motivations, and, as I show in my text, in doing so the Barotse at least employ both words and concepts which put a moral/legal gloss on what they report.   As judges cross-examine and adjudicate on evidence, they too do so in words and concepts which simultaneously handle facts and evaluate those facts ethically.   On the basis of judges' verdicts, action is taken.   It is true that the judicial process is a set of standards operating on evidence (to quote Schiller) ' through the minds and activities of persons ', but minds think in words, and activities include speaking words.   Frank (as quoted above, p. 350), who stressed the potential uncertainty of judicial rulings, recognized the importance of rules and their conceptual parts.   To repeat Durkheim's starting-point in his definition of sociology,[1] words, and the rules of law which consist of words and which influence behaviour, are greater than any individual and constrain his actions.   Hence to study the interaction of language and rules, which are greater than the judge and constrain him, and also a judge's reasoning, in the judicial process, inevitably involves looking at concepts.   And that type of analysis alone enables us to examine one important problem : if a judge is moved by his biasses, how does he formulate his judgments so that they fit into the judicial pattern of applying law ?[2]

I have already discussed the problem involved in using broad concepts like ' custom ' and ' mores ' : even if they are useful at one stage of analysis, it may be necessary to break them down later into more refined concepts.   And doubtless I have failed with custom, as with other words, always to make clear when I report how Barotse judges refer to ' custom ' as they see it, and when I use ' custom ' for objective analysis.

Allott has made more specific Schiller's doubt (above) ' just how far do Lozi courts, or any courts, employ abstract concepts in arriving at decisions ? '   For Allott concentrates on the Lozi, whom he sees to act, as judges, differently from English judges. He quotes a writer from the former Belgian Congo who main-

---

[1] *Les Règles de la méthode sociologique* (9th edition, 1938), Chapter I.
[2] The verdicts of judges on the definition of ' sedition ' in present-day South Africa, and their rejection of prosecutions for it, emphasize this fact.

tained that (as Allott puts it) '. . . an African court does not normally use abstract terms or concepts in arriving at its decision : the law is implicit rather than explicit'. Hence Allott asserts that ' analysis of African legal terminology may therefore be not merely unfruitful, but misleading '. He then points out that I (at p. 193 above) say when a Lozi court specifies the significance of a conception like *bung'a* (which I translate as ownership), the court does not always work with the concept, but more often ascribes rights by the use of possessive formatives. In my words, which here commented on a specific case, ' the judges take the definition of " ownership " (*bung'a*) for granted throughout '. Allott therefore concludes : ' There is surely a fundamental difference between a Lozi court's deciding what rights are inherent in a headman's ownership of fish dams (without actually mentioning " ownership ") and an English court's interpreting, say, the word " property " in a statute.'

There is indeed a difference ; and this difference needs examination, which I have essayed as far as my material allowed, and the stage which my analysis had reached when I wrote this book. I hinted at one solution then when I stated (as also quoted by Allott), that ' the judgments do not proceed by defining *ownership* and seeing how it covers the respective rights of the parties. They have indeed to work with one word, *bung'a*, though it covers a range of quite different rights which depend on one another.' I stressed that the first problem of the judges, in this society dominated by status relations, is to determine the respective social positions of the parties vis-à-vis one another. This clarifies the rights and obligations (all covered by *bung'a*) due between them. From this point the judges examine the facts about the piece of land under dispute : and hence they can use possessive formatives to state who in this dispute has the stronger claim, or describe one man, as against the other, as owner (*mung'a* : the personal form of the abstract *bung'a*). The main interpretation is of status.

Yet Allott is right. I did lay mistaken emphasis here, even though the conception of clusters of rights, of *bung'a*, is held and often discussed by judges and laymen : like other conceptions it may be only implicit in judicial cross-examination and argument, but these cannot be understood without taking the conception—as with the reasonable man—into account. But the modes of interpretation are different. This appears when other conceptions of law, like *muliu* (the offence of claiming land on ancient ancestral title), theft, violence, guilt, incest, marriage, as well as *bung'a* itself, are more explicitly construed in some of the other cases. In a chapter on 'Ownership and The Technical Vocabulary of Barotse Jurisprudence' in my *The Ideas in Barotse Jurisprudence* (1965) I have reported judicial argument around the conception of *bung'a* and I have clarified and developed my analysis.

Despite these doubts, most of my reviewers (as the citation from Schiller shows) feel that my attempt to examine the nature of concepts of law, and how they are used, has its merits. But I would like to state here that I would have been immensely helped had the late Charles P. Curtis published his *It's Your Law* (1954) two years earlier. Much of my discussion is concerned with the flexibility and yet the certainty of these concepts : Curtis summed up the pith of the argument in seven words which head one of his sections : these concepts have 'A Precise Degree of Imprecision'.

I pass now to lesser problems. One important problem has been raised by Hoebel, and as it involves an important issue of fact, I cite him in full :

In Lozi [Barotse] law there is no strong doctrine of stare decisis. Gluckman suggests that this is a consequence of absence of written records and lack of communication between courts of different districts. At this point, however, a lack in his research of materials on judicial review by the Lozi king takes on critical importance. If it is true that in fact no judgment of a court of first instance is effective until affirmed by the king, it would be imperative to know what occurs in the review process. It may be predicted that royal holdings on the law would set standards of precedence sufficiently consistent and well-publicized to have an effect of stare decisis throughout the system. If this is true, then the linchpin of the Lozi system has not been examined.

I have answered Hoebel's point at some length in the *Stanford Law Review* of December 1961. Here I comment more briefly. First, I can only ascribe my failure to pull together various references in the book to the rôle of the king's review in the judicial process, to one of those blockages in the mind which occur when one is engaged on a major task. I was blocked on this point largely because I do not consider that the king has any important differential effect on 'the judicial process', and in my general discussion I therefore treated him as the final judge, and examined royal decisions together with those of councillors, with two important exceptions. In Barotse theory, the king (or the royal ruler at other capitals) alone should excuse a man who has broken the law, while the council should not. That is, the prerogative of mercy rests in the royal rulers : and this agrees with the general Barotse belief that in royalty resides justice and mercy. As described in the text, everything that pertains to the king, and a special prince sitting in the council, are sanctuaries.[1] This practice exists for trials at law, though it must be noted that in the past kings were accustomed to execute their enemies without trial.

Second, though the king does not appear as a party in court, he may be indirectly involved in a suit where one of the parties is a councillor or servant. In such cases, the king may accept a verdict in his favour, but he may then relieve the commoner, who is the other party, of obligation to make payment.[2]

Normally, the king, who does not sit in court, confirms the verdict of the senior judge who gives the penultimate judgment in a trial in the capital. (If the case is heard outside the capital, it is held that the losing party accepts the decision unless he gives notice of appeal. Failing such notice, the winning party gives the royal salute to the local court, as if to the king, to acknowledge his success.) In all the cases I recorded or heard discussed, the king only arrived at a decision contrary to that of the head of the court in one—the Case of the Barren Widow (discussed at pp. 175 f. above). From what I was able to learn about kings from my own observations and tales told me, in the past as well as the present, and about rulers at the southern capital, these rulers act like final councillors, save for the prerogative of mercy. No effort was made to see that decisions by the king were made known throughout the land, though knowledge of them did spread informally. As the record of the Case of the Barren Widow shows, the king's judgment, reversing the court's on a new type of suit, was not reported to the southern capital.

---

[1] See Chapter II of my *The Ideas in Barotse Jurisprudence* (1965).
[2] See ibid., 178 f., for a case where commoners believed the king would have acted thus, had he not been paralysed by a stroke.

However, my whole discussions of the manner in which precedents are referred to in Barotseland, suggests that the doctrine of *stare decisis* is not applicable there. As I explain in the text, the judges state that they should follow earlier decisions ; but they rarely quote such decisions, and they never when I was there looked up the brief records of cases they kept for the British officers. More often, the judges cite not past decisions of courts, but instances of upright behaviour, to show how people ought to behave, in reputed contrast with the alleged actions of one of the parties (see especially the Cases of the Violent Councillor, pp. 83–90, and of the Headman's Fishdams, pp. 178–87). Moral exemplification is thus the commoner practice than citation of precedent.[1] How this operates is fully discussed in the text.

Perhaps therefore I should not have used the term 'precedent' in this situation. But most books on the enforcement of law in African states emphasize that precedents are followed. I therefore used this term, while trying to describe clearly (I believe for the first time in a study of African law), exactly how judges cite and use both precedents and examples of moral action. I venture to affirm that this is the common situation in African tribes. I observed it among the Zulu of Natal. Note the conclusion to a recent article by Professor I. Schapera :[2]

(3) Since, in every individual case, the judge's decision is shaped at least partly by the opinions of the people present, it is unlikely that judicial precedents can be as significant as is sometimes asserted of similar systems. Whether or not a precedent exists depends in fact merely upon whether someone present has seen or heard of a similar case before.

(4) In the circumstances, and considering the inevitable limitations of personal experience, the tendency will be for judgments to be based more upon recognized general principles than upon specific decisions of the past.

(5) This in turn means that the law is not rigid but flexible, and can be readily adapted to meet new situations or, if need be, to reject customary norms that are now considered obsolete.

(6) What effect the introduction of written records in Tswana

---

[1] This point answers problems raised by Marshall in his article.

[2] 'The Sources of Law in Tswana Tribal Courts : Legislation and Precedent' (1957), pp. 161–2.

courts will have upon the development of Tswana law is still uncertain. I should imagine, however, that unless and until professional
lawyers become part of the legal system the courts will continue, as in
the past, to rely upon personal experience and opinion, and not feel
bound to adhere in all instances to previous decisions.

Schapera here comes to the conclusion that I did.

March makes a number of specific points I feel I may profit-
ably emphasize. First, he rightly points out that I do not give
sufficient information to enable one to determine the factors
which influence Barotse when they discriminate 'just' from
'unjust' decisions. I do not have that information, possibly
because I was living with Barotse and thinking too much like
them, so that I saw the discrimination of good and bad decisions
as obvious. He cites the Case of the Headman's Fishdams to
show that judges may suggest alternatives that had not been
perceived, and therefore not evaluated ; and he concludes here
that 'the whole phenomenon of rationalization through the
perception of justice after the fact is one that entirely escapes'
my attention. I commend it to future fieldworkers, together
with March's suggestions of how this problem, and judicial
inspiration, may be studied.

March's preliminary statement is due to misreading of what
I wrote. I stated that I could not in many cases myself decide
how to judge on the evidence. I did not know enough of
Barotse custom to test the evidence. When the judges expounded their reasons, I found these were sound. March interprets this as an ex post facto judgment on my part, and hence
that it depended on the judges' rulings. But this did not apply
to Barotse. My difficulty lay in my lack of easy familiarity with
both Barotse customary behaviour and reasonable standards of
conformity ; and the manner in which reconciliation could be
achieved. I cited (p. 95) how Professor J. D. Krige, a barrister
as well as an anthropologist, confessed to similar difficulties when
he sat in Lovhedu courts.

The main new field of research delineated by March lies in a
closer study of interpersonal relations and personalities, both
inside and outside the courts, than I was able to make. In the
Case of the Headman's Fishdams (at p. 195 above), I state that it
did not occur to me until I was writing the book, and saw the
point in my notes, that a decision in a particular direction might

mean that fish-traps from which the king drew a share might not be fished and the king not get fish from them. I wrote that :
' As . . . the significance of this did not come to my mind, I feel it was not present in the minds of either judges or litigants. The sisters and their sons did not plead this as a reason that they be allowed to fish the dams : and I therefore consider that we may conclude it was not significant in influencing the judges' decisions.' I may add now that none of my Barotse followers mentioned this in discussing the case with me. I recorded this to show a gap in my enquiries, and March comments on it :
' Taken at its face value, this is an incredible statement unless one is willing to reject out of hand everything that is known about human motivation' (at his p. 505). At p. 154 of this book, I report my recognition that though Barotse ' are well aware of the complexities, and in a sense of the unconscious pressures, in human motivation', they work in judicial decision with a straightforward psychology in which action is directly related to motive. Since I reported this of the Barotse, I knew it myself. In this particular case, the judges split so severely, that for an analysis of the judicial process it might be regarded as irrelevant that some judges were moved by a desire to safeguard the king's fish supplies. What is important in March's comment, is that it might have been this desire that spurred the head of the court to find an inspired new solution of the judicial dilemma, a solution which maintained substantive rules yet saw justice done to those who were being unfairly penalized, and incidentally (see below) spared the king the problem of finding other people to fish his dams at a time when many men were working out-side Barotseland. I do not know how an anthropologist who is not a psycho-analyst could study a problem such as this, but clearly I could have asked the judge if he understood his own process of inspiration.

When I visited Barotseland in 1965 I found that this great judge, Solami Inete, had died so I could not question him. The courts were not in session as their clerks had gone to a course in Lusaka. I put the problem to the Barotse Paramount Chief and some of his councillors in the Palace, to the Chief at Man-koya and his council, and to a number of good informants. All affirmed that as far as the Paramount Chief and the judges were concerned the case was a dispute within a family and could be treated as such, because if the family ceased to be able to fish the dams, the Paramount Chief would be entitled to point this out to them ; and he could then fairly exercise his controlling rights and expel the family from the dams in order to appoint others able to fish these. It was therefore a sanction that the headman, and not the judges, had to worry about—though, as noted above, workers were not in plentiful supply at the time. The headman's one set of nephews thereafter have continued to fish the dams, to the present day. Further information on what happened in later years in the village is given in the next chapter.

March raises a whole series of problems of this type which need study. Again, I reported that I had tried to relate differences in the attitudes and judgments of particular judges on specific issues, but could do little since I lacked an appropriate variety of cases. In a case reported in *The Ideas in Barotse Jurisprudence* (pp. 178–81), but not in this book, a judge, who unusually happened to be senior that day, reversed the opinions of his junior judges to give a decision indirectly favourable to the king, whose senior queen was his sister. I am not sure that this influenced his decision. I noted above that a judge who had troublesome children tended to favour elders in similar situations, and an unusually jealous judge seemed readier than others to convict on charges of adultery (p. 322). I discussed where judges were most conservative and where radical (pp. 323–5). But I worked this out from their reasoning in words, not from judgments in a whole series of cases, since I did not have enough of these. March pleads for more of this kind of analysis, and a more detailed examination of how succeeding judgments were influenced by preceding judgments.[1] He sees it as part of a general study of decision-taking and indicates possible solutions.

Schubert (in his editorial comments on articles and summaries of books republished in his symposium on *Judicial Behaviour*) has argued, as March does not, that only the detailed analysis of how the implicit presumptions and values held by different

---

[1] I have since found in my notebooks a statement by Barotse which I overlooked when I wrote this book. When a senior judge follows on (*kutatamana:* the word also used to describe one child who is born immediately after another) junior judges, it is poor judgemanship if he repeats the arguments he agrees with. He should state his agreement, and go on to develop new points.

judges influence their decisions, and the strategies they follow, gives a hard-core scientific analysis of judicial behaviour. His justification for this conclusion is studies made of how judges have varied in their decisions on crucial social issues in the United States Supreme Court, in the Michigan State Supreme Court when Democratic judges replaced Republicans, and so forth. These studies of judicial behaviour in court without reference to the reasoning and social situation of judges take a lot for granted, including the existence of verbatim court records and commentaries upon them, written biographies of judges, studies of American history and American political parties, and, indeed the whole structure of American society, with its social problems and the varied reactions of different sections of the society to these problems. My situation in studying Barotse judges was very different. There were no adequate case records or commentaries or text books on the law, no good full history of the whole society or parts of it—merely a few short records, and a number of books by missionaries and administrators. The only scientific analyses were of forests, grasses, crops, and agricultural systems, with one short account of political structure. I had to analyse a whole society, provide the case records, and demonstrate the logic used by Barotse judges. Schubert (and to some extent March) has overlooked this difference in our research situations. On top of that, they appear not to have noticed clear statement that I had tried to make the kind of analysis for which they ask and did not have enough variety of cases to do it, while I elaborately drew attention in a number of cases to the way in which personal (as well as social) presumptions and experience clearly influenced judges' decisions. They over-look also my insistence on the homogeneity, in terms of standards of living and outlook, of judges and litigants, while cases arising out of inequality between Africans and Whites did not come to Barotse courts, but were tried by British magistrates.

Furthermore it is here perhaps worth noting that of 33 articles listed by Schubert in his collection as showing the new (and in his judgment the only satisfactory) line of research, 26 were published after my book went to press. That is, studies of this type are possible after adequate research has been done on a series of problems which are greater than the extent to which judges' personal principles and prejudices guide their decisions.

I feel I have dealt, so far as I could and as much as was relevant, with the major problems raised in the other articles selected by Schubert for republication.

In short, I cannot agree with Schubert in the restricting of ' hard-core ' scientific analysis *only* to a study of how judges are influenced by their social relations and individual histories to make certain types of decisions on controversial issues, and of how judges design their strategies so as to try to secure that their views may prevail in a multi-judge court. I do not accept that the kind of study which Holmes, Cardozo, Llewellyn, and other jurists, and anthropologists like Hoebel and myself, have made of the reasoning involved in the process of adjudication, set in a social context, is not scientific. Nor can I accept that what Nader in ' The Anthropological Study of Law ' (1965, p. 22) calls ' Gluckman's conceptual model [is] . . . much too general for comparative usefulness '. I am honoured to be given credit that should go to the great jurists cited above. What Epstein and I did was to take their work as a model for our analyses. We were able to illuminate the processes of trial which we studied in some ways, I dare affirm, more than Bohannan and Gulliver could without this model. Hence the model clearly is useful for comparative purposes.

I have discussed a similar point in considering Schiller's doubt whether it is worth while to start a study of the judicial process from concepts. These must, of course, for *sociological* analysis be examined in their interdependence with social relations. If one followed the narrow social-psychological line of Schubert, one would have to say that the only hard-core scientific study of Christianity is an analysis of the interrelations within a single congregation, in terms of the individual histories of its members. This would palpably leave much that is important unexamined. A study of political movements would also concentrate, presumably, on relationships within small groups, and this too might well be inadequate for sensible understanding.

Given all this, I accept that I should have studied the problem emphasized by Schubert and March more carefully. Now I shall not be able to do so on old-style Barotse kutas since, as I shall describe in the next chapter, the structure of courts in Barotseland has been radically altered.

I have gone at some length into some of the criticisms of this book, partly to develop and clarify problems, in the hope that in this way we could advance our joint endeavour. I wanted also to draw attention to a series of articles which, in discussion of others' books as well as my own, pose problems for investigation by those who may follow us into the field. I have learnt much by working through these articles whose full implications I have not been able to explore here. These articles leave me feeling that it is worth republishing my book as it stands, with weaknesses that may stimulate new leads through criticism, as well as strengths that set models. I have also tried to show how, in the 1950's, some of us opened new fields in the study of African law, as Llewellyn and Hoebel in the 1940's did for American Indian law. We have, I feel, helped them bring tribal law into a better perspective in the total purview of comparative sociological jurisprudence.[1]

---

[1] See, e.g., the references to my own book in Frankfurter, ' John Marshall and the Judicial Function ' (1955), pp. 236–7 ; Hart, *The Concept of Law* (1961), passim ; Powell, ' The Unreasonableness of the Reasonable Man ' (1957) ; Devlin, *The Enforcement of Morals*, p. 20 ; Allen, *Law in the Making* (6th edition, 1958), pp. 66, 156 ; as well as reviews by Stumpf, Kilgour, and others not directly concerned with tribal law.

APPENDIX TO CHAPTER IX

Details of reviews of the book

(*a*) *Review articles :*

Douglas, 'L'Homme primitif et la loi' (1956) ; March, 'Sociological Jurisprudence Revisited, A Review (More or Less) of Max Gluckman' (1956), with Gluckman and March, 'In Reply' (1956) ; Marshall, 'Gluckman on the Judicial Process of the Barotse' (1955) ; Seguin, Review in *The International Review of Missions* (1956) ; Stumpf, Review of *The Judicial Process among the Barotse* in *The Harvard Law Review* (1956). Stumpf makes a generous assessment of my book, so I do not discuss these parts of his review : I refer only to his following this up by arguing (as Schiller, another American lawyer, also does in a review (*Rhodes–Livingstone Journal*, xxi, 1957)), that it raises problems for the study of Western Law. Unsigned reviews (seemingly by English lawyers) in *The Economist* (3/9/1955) and *The Listener* (16/6/1955) also made this point. Seguin, a missionary with long experience in Barotseland, contends that before the beginning of his mission's work and of the British protectorate, the Lozi had no morality, no lawfulness, and no reasonableness, and that they still do not decide cases by evidence. In fairness I draw attention to his statements, but there is little point to my discussing them. My book gives adequate reply.

(*b*) *Reviews :*

Other reviews referred to in this preface are : Allott, *Law Quarterly Review*, lxii (January, 1956) ; Krige, J. D., *Man*, lvi (July, 1956) ; Anderson, *The Modern Law Review*, xviii (1955) ; Kilgour, *The Canadian Bar Review*, xxiii (May, 1955) ; Southall, *The Sociological Review*, iv, 1 (July, 1956).

(*c*) *Reviews of this book together with other books :*

Nadel, 'Reason and Unreason in African Law' (1956), on Anderson, Gluckman and Howell ; Kerr, 'Some Recent Studies of African Law' (1956) on Epstein, Gluckman, and Howell ;

Ayoub, ' Review : The Judicial Process in Two African Societies '
(1961), on Bohannan and Gluckman ; Hoebel, ' Three Studies
in African Law ' (1961), on Bohannan, Gluckman and Howell.
The analysis of African judicial reasoning in its social context in
Epstein's *Juridical Techniques and the Judicial Process* (1954) apparently escaped the attention (of authors other than Kerr and
Schiller) which it merited as much as the others because it was
published in the series of Rhodes–Livingstone Papers, and not
as a separate book. I have not discussed Kerr's review in this
preface, because his only points that are not made by others are
protests against the failure of Barotse and African Urban courts
always to observe the letter of the Northern Rhodesian Ordinances under which they operated, or their converting civil into
criminal trials, or a judge giving a verdict in a case on which he
had not sat. He cites a number of South African (European)
court judgments to show how wrong such practices are.
Finally, my book and Bohannan's are summarized and published
with March's and Ayoub's articles in Schubert's *Judicial Behavior*
(1964). Schubert discusses all our arguments in his editorial
introduction. Nader does so also in an editorial introduction
to *The Ethnography of Law* (1965).

CHAPTER X

BAROTSELAND IN 1965-66

IN December 1965 I was able to go to Barotseland for sixteen days, of which I spent fourteen in Mongu District and two at Naliele, the Lozi capital in Mankoya District, with the Lozi Chief Mwendawelie Lewanika who had formerly been my Research Assistant. A large part of my time was taken up in social visits to old friends, but I was able briefly to follow up what had happened to the persons involved in most of the important cases cited in this book, and to check on certain changes in the law. I shall give this specific information after outlining some of the major changes that have occurred in Barotseland between 1947 and 1965. I deal with economic relations and the value of land, and with relations between elders and juniors, since these seem to have altered and with them the social perspective on kinship relationships and village unity which were so important in cases discussed above. Amendments to the political organization have radically altered the setting of the judicial process.

When I first visited the Barotse flood-plain in 1940 it appeared to be a land of milk and honey, to quote David Livingstone, who in 1854 compared it with Canaan. There was in 1940 an abundance of grain, tubers, fish, milk, meat, chickens and eggs, wildfowl, vegetables and fruits. During my next visit in 1942 shortages had begun to appear and meal was being imported from the North ; and by my third short visit in 1947 other shortages were becoming apparent. I have described this process and its effects on the law both in this book and in *The Ideas of Barotse Jurisprudence* (1965 : pp. 190 f.). In general, I saw this fall in production as probably being due to the effects of an increasing labour migration rate, for I argued that the withdrawal of more and more workers would affect deleteriously a complex economy in which several scattered productive activities had to be performed simultaneously, much more than it would affect a simple economy where absentees could be compensated for by harder work on the part of those left behind.[1]   Thus in 1965 gardens were overgrown with weeds and neglected as they had not been in the 1940's.

In 1965 I found the Barotse Plain area to be notorious even beyond its borders as almost a permanent famine area, importing large quantities of meal from districts to the east.   This meal was brought by lorries on the much-improved roads.   Fish, allowing for the period of the year (December),[2] seemed[3] plentiful, but some Whites and Africans in Mongu complained of shortages of milk, eggs, vegetables and fruit.   Where previously a local butcher had supplied meat once a week, where eggs had been brought in quantities to the doors of houses by Lozi, and where milk had been so plentiful that all European householders bought enough to make their own cream and butter, now these commodities were brought in by refrigerated lorry from Lusaka to meet the much increased consumers' demands in Mongu.   (The lorry was said to be about to cease running, as uneconomic.)

Some Mongu residents in 1965 could hardly believe that my account of the plenty in the *Economy of the Central Barotse Plain* (1941) was accurate, while a former District Officer from the 1940's, Mr. F. J. Passmore, could not believe my report on the present conditions.   In that book (pp. 18 f.) I stated that the types of food which would be in plentiful supply in the months of any year would depend on the depth and date of the flood, so that an early deep flood would lead to large-scale loss of crops, but should, later in the year, produce many fish.   It may be that I did not weight this variation in flood sufficiently;[4] and probably in 1940 the flood was about perfect for the balance of all types of production, so I then saw things at their best.   1942 was also, from this point of view, by chance a good year ; in 1947 the

---

[1] See my ' Introduction' (with W. Allan) to Peters, *Land Usage in Barotseland* (1960).

[2] See my *Economy of the Central Barotse Plain* (1941), pp. 64–5, for an account of the fishing activities at this time. In a year of good rain, fish supplies are low in December. In 1965 the rains were late, and the flood had not set in fully, so fishermen were still fishing with gill-nets in open waters.

[3] I say ' seemed ', because it must be borne in mind that this visit was very brief, and my observations were very limited as to area and time.

[4] I tried in 1940 from figures of the flood kept at Senanga and Livingstone to work out the incidence of variations in the flood, but the figures were unsatisfactory.

flood came early, but not disastrously so. Yet overall, in the light of my own and other evidence, bad years were not so bad before ; and it seems definite that there has been a steady and increasing decline in productivity.

My 1940 judgment on the fertility and productivity of the soils of the area, despite their relative scarcity, was partly based on the report of an ecologist and agriculturist.[1] To my un-trained eye, agreeing with the Lozi's judgment, it seemed in 1965 that the fertility of the soils where I saw them near Mongu had dropped considerably, particularly in the drained gardens along the margin of the plain which the ecologist in 1937 had considered to be perpetually fertile. The soils seemed worked out and acid ; and drainage channels, dug by machine, were con-sidered by Lozi as well as me to be too efficient and to have drained the underground water on which crops planted there before the rains had relied. The slopes above the plain are even more worked out than before. In an area I knew well, plots of land which had formerly carried exotic fruits and vegetables for sale to Europeans, now carried staple food crops. The population of the whole of Mongu District had risen from some 75,000 to 110,000 (though I do not know how it is distributed between woodland and plain). I judged that the population now ex-ceeded what Allan has called the plain's critical density of popu-lation,[2] and radical land deterioration of the soil on plains gardens had been accelerated by a succession of deep floods in the 1960's which had carried away the manure dropped by cattle staked in these gardens, but I cannot say whether this is correct or, if so, why such floods should deplete the soils more than in the past. Maybe they had not had time to recover. The succession of early and high floods were succeeded by a series of very dry years. What these floods and dry years do definitely seem to have done, is to dishearten many people and make them feel it was hardly worth cultivating in the plain. Lozi had begun to move to the good agricultural lands to the eastward in Mankoya District. Incidentally some Lozi complained to others in my hearing that the Paramount Chief had ceased to send sacrifices to the royal

---

[1] Trapnell and Clothier, *The Soils, Vegetation and Agricultural Systems of North Western Rhodesia* (1937).
[2] Allan, *The African Husbandman* (1965), passim.

graves, and it was no wonder that their activities were un-
productive.

With the increase in population, on the other hand, logically
it should have been easier to cope with cultivation, pasturing
cattle, and fishing. Fishing was being carried out on a larger
scale than I had noted, at that season, in earlier years. But cattle
owners near Mongu complained that as all the young men were
away in employment at distant centres or working in Mongu
itself, and boys were at school, they had to herd and milk themselves, and hence could not deliver milk for sale in Mongu.

In this situation, many of the older men and women had
become desperately dependent on sons and nephews working
outside Barotseland for money to purchase their staple food, and
the younger members of the family were indeed sending this
money. Researches in South Africa and Central Africa have
demonstrated that in systems of labour migration the temporary
migrants send this money to their elders who in turn keep for
them holdings in the land, against their periodical sojourns at
home, and against their permanent return from the insecurities of
industrial employment or for ultimate retirement. Hence the
migrants had a more than sentimental interest in sending this
money home ; but clearly once the land has deteriorated badly,
only sentiment remains.[1]

This situation has exacerbated relations between elders and
their younger relatives, for there seems to be a definite shift in
their respective access to successful productive work and resources.
I overheard a number of middle-aged men discussing the problem and one said to the others something that I cannot imagine
being said in the 1940's : ' Which of you now, whose wife did
not become pregnant, would go searching in the woodland to
get medicines to make her conceive ? Why have children ?' On
another occasion, an elder quoted the proverb, *Kwashema ukoto*,
kono amatina : ' to give birth is easy, but the names . . . .'
That is, to have children is easy, but then troubles come in rearing
and dealing with them.

Differences between those roughly over thirty-five years old

---

[1] I discuss the application of this situation generally and cite many studies on
the point in ' Tribalism in Modern British Central Africa ' (1960 : reprinted
1965).

and younger people—how generally I cannot say—had also arisen over political problems. The Paramount Chief and his principal councillors had at one period supported the Federal Government of Rhodesia and Nyasaland against the Zambian nationalists who wished to break up the Federation. Even after it had become clear that Zambia would become independent, he resisted the entry of the United National Independent Party (UNIP), led by the first President Dr. Kenneth Kaunda, into his Barotseland ; and then he strove for the status of continuing as an independent protectorate, and then as a special protectorate in Zambia. Many young and older people became increasingly hostile to the Paramount : in the elections UNIP virtually eliminated the Paramount's Tribal Party. There was a strong movement for the abolition of the whole traditional political structure, how widespread I cannot say. Many Whites and educated Lozi told me that particularly the young intellectuals were against the traditional authorities, but several young educated Lozi, holding important positions in the national system, expressed doubts about what the movement for abolition would lead to. The protagonists for this abolition were at the crucial period of diverse ages, and they had apparently to be restrained by the Zambian and UNIP leaders. The fears of elderly cultivators, used to the security of their traditional system under British protection, about what they saw as an uncertain future, were clearly expressed by one who asked me : ' Do you think we [the Africans of Zambia] can rule ourselves ? ' And I heard him repeat the question to a group of older men, who were discussing the waywardness of the young. It was during this conversation that I heard another man ask who would seek now for medicines to enable his wife to conceive.

The general change in relations between younger and older people has clearly affected the latter's forebodings about the situation created by Zambian independence and the loss of the Barotse's specially protected status. Friction between young and old, as well as general fears, were also aggravated by an outbreak of witchcraft accusations in 1957-8.[1] In Kalabo District

---

[1] See Reynolds, *Magic, Divination and Witchcraft among the Barotse* (1963) for an account of what happened, based on District Officers' Reports and court records, as well as an examination of charms, substances, etc. sent to the Museum

in 1956, a woman was shot by a witch-finder, on allegations of being a witch. When the murder was discovered, the District Commissioner at Kalabo decided that many more crimes of this pattern were occurring, and he apparently persuaded his fellow-officers to agree to invite denunciations of similar, murderous witch-finders. The result was that a very large number of anonymous letters, making denunciations of people as witches in addition to denunciations of alleged witch-finders, flooded into the District Commissioners' Officers. The old fears that no man advances save by using witchcraft to kill his close kin (reported above, p. 98), on which fears actions had been restrained by Barotse as well as British Authorities since the 1890's, burst out. I had several accounts from Lozi of how, on the basis of denunciations, alleged witches were arrested by District Commissioners' staff, or the court police of minor (not capital) Barotse courts, were starved of food and water, and were flogged or otherwise maltreated, many for some days, until they produced a charm as evidence of their witchcraft or sorcery. They were, it is said, then fined or imprisoned by British officers. These accounts were given me by men who watched the flogging and by one who was flogged for four days (confirmed by others). Chiefs and missionaries also confirmed that there had been a virtual breakdown of civil administration, and one missionary and one Chief, as well as several councillors and teachers, told me they had protested to District Commissioners. Reynolds' *Magic, Divination and Witchcraft among the Barotse of Northern Rhodesia* (1963), which if anything is biassed in favour of the actions taken, reports that of twenty-six suicides and one attempted suicide all but three

are known to have acted through fear of being accused of, or arrested for witchcraft practices. The rest probably feared such arrest but,

---

at Livingstone. The book in my opinion does not eliminate all the confusion, probably arising from the documents used, between witch-finding and allegations of witchcraft. I must note the following about Reynolds' use of my own work. In this book on the judicial process I wrote (at p. 98) ' I have been told . . . that since witches only kill members of their own family, members of a suspicious family may test a suspected witch by putting *mwati* oracle-poison in his beer, to see if he vomits it to prove innocence or is killed by it to prove guilt.' Reynolds cites this without the introductory ' I have been told that . . .', as if it were a definite fact I had observed, and not completely and clearly hearsay as far as I was concerned.

while available information points to this fact, the magistrate was not sufficiently sure to record it as the actual case. That the desire for escape from what must have appeared an impossible situation was very strong, is shown by the fact that seven of the intending suicides escaped from custody in order to kill themselves (p. 158).

It is not clear how far Reynolds, who saw the District files and court records but was not allowed to visit Barotseland, accepts the accusations as valid. I see a certain acceptance in the following:

In Mankoya, which the main spate of investigations had left almost untouched, there was a surprising recrudescence late in 1958 when the rest of the Protectorate was returning to normal. Some fifty to sixty cases of necrophagy, brought by irate villagers against their neighbours, suddenly flooded the subordinate courts. The strength of the feelings aroused could be gauged by the amount of manhandling that occurred before each miscreant arrived at the boma (District Commissioner's Office).

The phrasing, miscreants, is used though Reynolds records elsewhere that people confessed to eating corpses which when exhumed were found to be intact (p. 146). Maybe the accused were confessing to a 'mystical' eating (p. 23). He says also that the evidence was mainly hearsay (p. 25).

Reynolds does not refer to 'manhandling' of alleged witches in other Districts, but this statement on Mankoya—where the Chief's Council told me at least one suspect was suspended by his ankles in one subordinate court—seems to confirm the stories of maltreatment I heard from Lozi and missionaries in Mongu District, where indeed I noted references to these floggings of suspected witches coming casually into conversation. Unfortunately, the District Secretary at Mongu could not find the relevant files in the office there, and they were not in the Archives at Lusaka when I reached there. I am endeavouring to trace them before I write a fuller account of this episode.

Reynolds could not trace social relationships between accusers and accused from the data available to him. I collected a list of twelve denounced persons (eleven men and one woman) who were arrested in the neighbourhood I knew best. All were over forty-five years of age. My former servant said he did not know who had denounced him and the others, but in fact he spoke of his related ' *babanyinyani* '—the young ; and other older people seemed convinced it must have been these. In another part of Zambia I met a skilled Lozi whom I had known before, who was about thirty-five years old when the episode occurred. In 1957 in one letter he denounced twelve elderly relatives as witches. None was arrested : presumably twelve at a blow were too many. His evidence was the occurrence of a death in a situation where the older man might envy a younger man's possession of new skills as a threat to his position.

It seems more general in Central Africa for younger people to accuse older people, than the reverse ; but in the 1940's when I collected stories of witchcraft accusations, about one-third of the suspected were young people who, it was alleged, had taken the life of some relative in order to acquire success.[1]

I have described this episode because of its importance as a possible sign of radical change and crisis in Barotseland since I last was there in 1947, and particularly because there are indications that it was influenced by a worsening of the relations between persons of different age. It has left the country very disturbed and insecure : while a few people openly wished for a new ' hunt for witches ' as they saw what had happened, and a few considered the hunt had been a disaster, most were highly ambivalent. They wanted the witches they believed to exist to be hunted down : they feared a repetition of the maltreatment. My impression was that the inability of Barotse, and British, officials to control the situation had affected attitudes to political authorities deeply.

All this entails that courts in Barotseland will no longer be

---

[1] Reynolds, *Magic . . . Witchcraft in Barotseland* (1963), p. 157, gives age distribution at the trials of those tried for having needles inserted under the skin (alleged to be a sign of guilt). All these presumably had been arrested after denunciation. Unfortunately the ages of 59 out of 198 were not known, and without data on the age distribution of the total population the figures cannot be assessed. On other tribes, the only figures are given by Marwick in *Sorcery in its Social Setting* (1965), p. 104. He gives his figures with reservations : in a small minority of cases (9 in 99) the alleged sorcerer was younger than his victim. The sorcerer was believed to be either in the same age category as his victim in 49 out of 99 cases or older in 41 out of 99 cases. But when generation, and not age, differences are examined for alleged sorcerers and victims related to them, sorcery was believed to be directed to those of junior generation in 42 out of 89 cases, within the generation in 34 out of 89 cases, and to those of senior generation in 13 out of 89 cases.

operating in the situation so strongly emphasized in cases in the 1940's. Then land was valuable in itself and as a means of holding and attracting dependants (The Cases of the Biased Father, the Headman's Fishdams, et al.) ; seniority was not only backed by the courts but also supported by this control (the same cases) ; relations between kinsmen depended on this land ; the younger accepted that a meed of respect was due to their elders ; most Lozi operated with a common assemblage of values.

More specifically, the situation was so disturbed and tense that I judged it to be inadvisable to study villages in detail by carrying out census and genealogical investigations, and by enquiring into past quarrels, lest these awaken fears that I was hunting for deaths and witches responsible for these deaths. This handicapped my direct enquiries into the villages whose disputes I had heard on earlier visits ; and inevitably a lot of time I had intended to devote to those enquiries, and into changes in the law, was spent on tracing what had happened during the witchfinder-hunting episode.

In this background of increasing impoverishment and social malaise, as well as national change and independence, the position of the kingship in the estimation of many of the people had altered. More importantly, the Zambian Government had by direct action altered the powers both of the Paramount Chief and of his kutas, whose complicated organization I described in Chapter I. In effect, these kutas have been abolished, though councillors, in reduced numbers, are left to attend on the chiefs. In the 1950's already, each District capital court had been reduced to five paid judges. Now control of all courts in Barotse Province, as elsewhere in Zambia, is to be vested in the Ministry of Justice : it is planned that as soon as they are trained, magistrates will be sent to sit with local assessors on all trials, except possibly those involving disputes over land. The police, directed from Zambian headquarters, instead of the Barotse councils and their local representatives, are to be immediately and solely responsible for public order. Shares of taxation for, and control of, development work are to come under local District Councils, popularly elected, working under the Ministry of Local Government, instead of the Barotse councils. What is reserved for the Paramount Chief, and his representatives in Districts within the Province, is control over the distribution of

land and possibly of disputes arising from that control : but
with increasing denudation of the land this may well turn out
to be a burden rather than a privilege in the Lozi plain itself.
The Paramount Chief and his family are to be subsidized generously from national funds, instead of from the Barotse National
Treasury, which is abolished. Hence the Chief and his councils
have lost most of their powers, which have been dispersed among
specialized Departments and officers of the national government.
The Barotse Provincial Council has been altogether abolished.
The multi-judge courts I studied will soon cease to exist, and the
personnel of the new courts will be quite different. It will
therefore in practice be impossible for me, or another, to follow
up some of the leads which critics of my study have suggested ;
but the field is open for study of new developments in legal and
judicial administration, for which this book may provide some
help.

DEVELOPMENTS IN MAJOR CASES CITED

I now outline what has happened to some of the protagonists
involved in major cases in this book :

The Case of the Biassed Father (pp. 37–45) : This case I heard
at the capital, on appeal, in 1942, but I had not known the litigants.
I had noted then that the people were related to Chief Mwenekandala, in charge of Mongu township. The present Chief had
succeeded his father, whom I had known. We became friendly
and he agreed to visit the village with me. It took about three
hours to drive to the village by Land-Rover on a bushtrack into
the woodlands. (I had never been to this village, but in 1940
and 1942 it took two days to cover the same distance whit
carriers. Land-Rovers and roads have altered economic and
administrative relations substantially.) The headman remembered seeing me at the trial, and welcomed both the Chief and
myself. The Chief was his father's mother's brother's son.
The old 'biassed father' had died. The present headman,
Muteto, succeeding to the headman's title Mulyachi, was the
man called ' B ' in the record above : one of the group of sons of
the younger brother of the ' biassed father '. He was the person
in the case who was most praised by various judges in 1942 for his
uprightness and his attempts to settle quarrels, and also by his
uncle, biassed as he was. One judge put this view succinctly ;

'. . . You, Muteto, I see you really are a man . . .' (p. 43)—
implying an 'upright man'. And everything he did during our
visit, everything he said, his discussions with his dependants,
emphasized how the qualities which the judges had noted in
him had developed : his commonsense, wisdom, generosity,
courtliness, and industriousness. He told us that when they
reached home after the case, his uncle had killed a beast for a
family feast and they had settled down well. The cousin who
had committed adultery with the wife of one of the group of
brothers had died shortly afterwards. The present headman's
elder brother, who had been reproved by the court for trying to
lead his brothers out of the village, had gone to work in ' White
Country', and contact with him had been lost. Muteto inherited the headmanship when his uncle died. Most of the
men of the village were away working in ' White Country',
leaving in his care most of their wives and children (who were
there in numbers). He was otherwise alone, with his brother's
son, a teacher elsewhere, and his own adolescent schoolboy son
(both home during the school holidays). He had been involved
in a number of cases, one of which over a dog eaten by a hyaena
is recorded below (p. 443). While we were there his father's
sister arrived. He explained to us that he, as ' parent', had just
been awarded £8 (where £3 was awarded in 1947) against a
seducer who had impregnated one of his brother's daughters,
a blind girl. He had called in his aunt, as she was entitled to
some of the money, to suggest that they agree to give all the
money to the blind girl, since ' she was a cripple'. The woman
agreed. He also told the Chief, in reply to a question about it,
that he had not yet settled a dispute with a distantly related
woman whom he had allowed to build apart from the village
and to cultivate its land, on condition she did not settle other
people on the land, which she had done. But he had won a
case against another village over where the boundary between
their lands lay. Even the most equable Lozi seem to be involved constantly in lawsuits—a phenomenon I plan to discuss
in *The Rôle of Courts in Barotse Life*. He told us that the soil
was not sufficiently productive for good maize ; and he proposed
to beg land from the Paramount Chief in the next stream valley,
Namitome, which King Lewanika (1884–1916) had drained.
At present they were borrowing land at Namitome where they

grew maize, and his male kin sent money to feed their families. But he said that where they lived there was no need to be in want : ' A wise man can always earn well '. There were plenty of rushes from which mats could be made, good wood to be carved into stools and utensils, and so on. (Indeed we gave a lift to a man with a load of mats to sell in Mongu.)

The Case of the Immigrant Land-Borrower : I visited him in the plain at his gardens and village : and it was he who first told me of the alleged flogging of denounced witches. Most of the villages near the margin around Mongu have moved to the margin which is now much more densely settled. He had refused to do so, he said, because there was too much quarelling and drinking in the line of villagers there. Others gave me this as his reason. When the flood comes in and he has to leave his village in the plain, he does not move to a settlement on the margin, but right up the slope across the new road to Sefula Mission, where the village stands deserted in the dry season by the road along which many people pass and might damage it. He said this was to avoid quarrels : in fact he does not own land along the margin to which he could move. However, he stressed that it was fear of quarrels which made him stay apart from others : ' Why, even though I am out in the plain, X came all the way from the margin to accuse me of bewitching him. What kind of sense is it to go all that way to accuse a man of being a witch ? ' He protested thus, even though he had approved of the denunciation and beating of witches, and said it should be done again, for the witches had regained courage. (I noted too, as bearing on the use of ' my owner ' as a respectful term of address among the Lozi, which I discuss in Chapter V (pp. 163–5) of my *The Ideas in Barotse Jurisprudence* (1965), that when he and X were talking at my camp, they used ' my owner ' in addressing each other much more than most men do.) He had effectively prevented his sons, including one married son, from leaving the village for advanced schooling or to work for wages. When an unmarried son escorted me from my camp to their village, and then the married son from the village to the garden where his father was ploughing, each replied to my question : ' What work do you do ? ', with, ' None.' Cultivation is not work in their opinion. He is still short of land. He told me he had begun to plough some very poor mound gardens near his village, belonging to people living far out in the plain, but they had sued him in court and he had been stopped.

The Case of the Prince's Gardens (pp. 56–61), heard in the Barotse Provincial Appeal Court (the Sikalo) in 1942, involved a dispute between a prince and a commoner from a neighbouring village over ownership of a garden. The parties at the time were extremely excited and there were references to their not getting on well together. It was held that the prince had lent the garden to the commoner and was entitled to reclaim it. Some judges warned the commoner that his sons were also cultivating gardens lent them by the prince's family who might now reclaim their gardens : they implied this should not be done. Because of the state of the flood I could not reach the villages, but I saw the prince when I visited the Paramount Chief in his palace. I asked the prince how he and the other litigant were getting on, and he laughed and said : ' It is all over. He is now my best friend ' (in English). The Paramount Chief and other councillors there, as well as the prince's two brothers at Mankoya, confirmed that they were now on good terms. The sons were not expropriated.

The Case of the Barren Widow (pp. 174–5), in 1946–7 caused considerable discussion in Mongu District. Here the kin of a dead husband sued the family of his widow, whom he had married as a virgin and who had not conceived during the marriage, for the ' beast of the child ' (i.e. for the second payment for virgin fertility : see below under change in marriage law). The Provincial Appeal Court held it was not returnable, in terms of a decision of the then-king, in about 1920, that in these circumstances it was wrong to sue. The judgment was reversed by the High Court of Northern Rhodesia on the advice of two Lozi assessors about Lozi law. The Barotse courts told me they were bound by this High Court decision, but that they would amend the law it established by legislation. They have not done so. In view of the change in marriage law reported below the old law is no longer relevant.

The Case of the Violent Councillor (pp. 83–90), heard in 1942, involved an incident when the headman of the then-king's designated burial village, who was also a senior councillor of the court, was held to have joined his children in assaulting an unrelated villager. The councillor died in 1963, and has not yet been replaced. This village also could not be reached in the state of the flood when I was in Mongu District in 1965. I was informed by the Paramount Chief and his councillors, and by two reliable independent informants, that there had been no further trouble in the village. In 1947 the village as a whole had been shocked when the new king, succeeding his sick brother, had taken some of its gardens to give to a councillor who had come with him to the central capital from the provincial capital where he had previously ruled. The opposition was unsuccessful.

The Case of the Headman's Fishdams (pp. 178–87) : The village had no-one in it on the day when I drove into its neighbourhood. As stated above, in this case, heard in 1947, a headman sued to expropriate some sisters' sons from fishdams allocated to their mothers by his father, unless they returned to the village. In the main text, I recorded how the senior judge held that the fishdams belonged to the title of the headman, but if the headman was not generous enough to allow kin who were not resident in the village to fish them, the court would dismiss him from the title and appoint a more generous headman. Reliable informants told me there had continued to be frequent deaths in the village. After I left Barotseland in 1965, Mr. Francis L. Suu kindly went to the village to investigate what had happened and has reported to me by letter. The one group of nephews, sons of one sister, are still fishing dams. The other nephew, who had been advised or ordered by the court to go into the village, did not do so ; and about three years ago the headman brought another suit over the dam which resulted in a fight before the hearing. The headman was killed by his nephew who was jailed. During the course of the hearing in 1947, the first headman's younger brother, who had been allowed to move out of the village after a bitter quarrel, and who had built some 50 yards away, was reprimanded by the court for supporting his nephew in the ill-advised suit. He was instructed to return to the original village. He had not moved his huts, but he and his dependents had had their names entered in the tax-registers under the title of the original village.[1]

---

[1] I discuss the decisions in this case at length in *The Ideas in Barotse Jurisprudence* (1965), Chapter IV, for the understanding it gives of the difference in Barotse law between the holding of land and the holding of chattels.

The Case of the Expropriating Stewards (pp. 103–4) I heard as a complaint brought to the Mongu District court in 1942. Here some people complained that six of their gardens were being taken away from them by the two senior stewards, as gardens of the senior steward's title, Ingangwana, to be given to the king to grant to a prince who had moved near Mongu from the distant north. As recorded in this book, the steward Ingangwana said he knew nothing of the gardens save that when he was installed they were pointed out to him as belonging to the title he was receiving. Several members of the court knew the gardens, which they said the fathers of the present cultivators had also cultivated. The case was adjourned for witnesses, but the sympathies of most of the judges were clearly with the complainants, though the head of the court (Solami) instructed them not to discuss the matter lest the litigants feel that it had been prejudged. When I left the field in 1942 the case had not come up again, and I was told the complainants were confirmed in their holdings. I did not find a note of it arising in the court records in the years between then and 1947, and I therefore took this to be correct. But on the last day of my visit in 1965 Mr. Francis L. Suu, formerly Administrative Secretary, told me he thought the case did come up again more than a year later, at the end of 1943. Suu said that witnesses were called, who gave evidence that the complainants' forefathers had entered on the gardens without permission. The evidence was definite that the gardens were attached to the title Ingangwana. It was therefore held that the people had to vacate the gardens, because one of the written laws of the nation was that 'no-one ploughs unless he has granted land and has given the royal salute for it'. The law states, *minya mupu nangombe*— the king is owner of the land and cattle (*minya* being the Luyana form of the modern Lozi *mung'a*). The gardens had therefore been restored to the title Ingangwana whose incumbent had given them to the Paramount Chief to grant to the prince. The prince had moved back to the north, but his people still reside and cultivate in the area. Ingangwana has confirmed this by letter.

Consideration of the cases : These brief notes show how unsatisfactory it is, for certain problems, not to trace back the origins of a dispute before the court into the past, and to follow it into the future. Quarrels in groups such as Barotse family-villages can rarely be finally settled. Increase in numbers leads to dispute over resources : failure to conceive children or deaths can leave resources plentiful, but, largely through fears of witchcraft, produce quarrels of another kind. An attempt by the court to give a ruling which hopes to produce harmony cannot in fact eradicate the likelihood that either the old quarrel will be renewed, or new quarrels will arise. And luck and chance always are important.[1]

We have here only a very few cases ; but it is worth noting the leads they suggest. The villages of the biassed father and of the headman's fishdams show opposite developments. In the former, the sacrifice of a beast, as ordered by the court, apparently brought temporary relief. Then the death of the headman's own son, a major troublemaker, removed the genealogically strongest competitor for the headmanship, a man as it happens who was unlikely to remain on good terms with his cousins. The disappearance in ' White Country ' of the eldest cousin, who was judged to have kept the quarrel going, removed the other troublemaker. It left the way clear for the man with the most suitable character to assume charge of the village without strong opposition. His brothers and younger cousins seem content to leave him in charge of the village and their families, which, judging from their numbers (remember I could not enquire too closely), are doing well. Increase of numbers has in fact left them short of good land, and they maintain themselves by borrowing land and by the money sent by men out at work. The headman implied that he earned money by using the products of the woodland. Younger men in the family have been, and are being, educated to take new skilled posts. By virtue of his character, the headman seemingly remains on good terms with his kin. He has been involved in at least three cases, but all are with outsiders. Unlike many other Barotse I knew, he discussed these cases calmly : he did not even speak bitterly of a man who had deceived him by selling him a dog claimed to be good at hunting when in fact it was not (below, pp. 443–4).

On the other hand, the difficulties of the village involved in the dispute over the fishdams have worsened. It is one of four villages of related Ndebele who immigrated into Barotseland

---

[1] See my *The Ideas in Barotse Jurisprudence* (1966), pp. 8–9.

many decades ago. Two of them moved some distance to the north : they then moved back, because they could not ' get on ' with their Lozi and Mbunda neighbours, and decided they must remain with their fellow-Ndebele. I could not study all these villages. They are said always to have remained isolated, despite intermarrying with others. The quarrels caused by the first headman of the village which was involved in the case, have seemingly not abated ; and ill-health and death have continued to prevent it recouping its population. The one nephew did not obey the court's not very clearly stated order to move into the village : a later attempt by the new headman to force him to do so culminated in a fight and his own death. This nephew, as the full record at pp. 178–87 shows, was very embittered over his uncle's failure to support his mother when she was accused of witchcraft and driven out of the village. He asserted that he himself did not get a good reception from the heir (p. 179) and his mother would never live well in the village (p. 180). Seemingly this quarrel could never be redressed, and the attempt by the court to overlook this accumulated bitterness and to consider the accusation of witchcraft past and done with, led to disaster. Sabangwa, the heir's uncle, did not move his huts, as ordered by the courts, into the old village : he moved only titularly. This case, looked at over a longer period of time, shows that the courts did not always try to enforce their decisions. It also shows that the attempt to enforce harmony and observance of the value of unity by judicial reprimands is fraught with danger, when quarrels between closely related persons are very bitter. I wonder what would have happened if the biassed father's son, who committed adultery with his cousin's wife, had not died shortly afterwards. This case appears to me to show why these closely involved groups so often have to go through a crisis involving accusations of sorcery or witchcraft, or other mystical causes of misfortune, before they can settle down in cooler relations at a greater geographical distance in a separate village.[1]

---

[1] This is a central theme in Mitchell's *The Yao Village* (1956), Turner's *Schism and Continuity* (1958) and Marwick's *Sorcery in its Social Setting* (1965), to cite only studies of Central African tribes. I consider the general problem in my *Custom and Conflict in Africa* (1955), Chapter IV, and *Politics, Law and Ritual* (1965), Chapter VI.

The quarrels in the case of the Violent Councillor had also been very acrimonious, but as it was between unrelated persons, assembled together in a royal village, they may have settled down there again in bearable, if aloof, relationships, more easily than closely related persons can. This is a point I shall try to follow up during my next visit to Barotseland. But it is again striking that despite the surface bitterness of the dispute, and the evident excitement of the parties, in the Case of the Prince's Gardens, the prince could claim the contestant as 'my best friend' in public before the Paramount Chief, and laugh over the memory of the case. One has to assume that the contestant has enough land : foolishly, I did not ask if the prince had lent him another garden.

The Immigrant Land-Borrower continues to suffer from lack of land : he tried to take over the neglected resources of others. He refuses, or is unable for lack of land, to move his village into the line of villages where almost all of his neighbours now live. When he described the denunciation of witches to me, he mentioned with, it seemed to me, special pleasure, the flogging of members of the group owning most of the land on the margin opposite his village, and the flogging of the younger brother of the now deceased man who had taken back the garden loaned to him (pp. 62–4). More than most, he favoured another witch-hunt, though he himself had recently been accused of witchcraft by another. He is withdrawn from neighbourhood life and has kept his sons out of the schools and migration to work in which most young Lozi participate.

The Case of the Expropriating Stewards exhibits the slow pace at which some disputes are fought out. Second, we must note that the expropriated commoners and their forefathers had clearly worked the gardens of the title Ingangwana for very many years to the knowledge of powerful councillors. Yet the court decided that they were not entitled to do so. How this occurred, is explained in a letter from the senior steward, Ingang-wana, which I have received as I correct proofs. According to him, from the time when he was appointed to that title in 1919, he had no need of the gardens-of-the-title. Nor had the people of the village attached to the title, which had one site at Mukusi on the margin and a site at Nawike in the plain, where the gardens were. These people remained throughout the year at the margin village and did not move into the plain after the flood. The complainants used the gardens without Ingangwana's permission ; and at the final trial, when the witnesses supported his title to the gardens, the complainants admitted this and were ordered to leave them. The prince was given these gardens which were moved from Ingangwana's title, and the complainants continue to work their own gardens in the neighbourhood. Solami was right to warn his fellows not to prejudge the issue (above, pp. 103–4). To judge without ' judicial ignorance ' is dangerous.

The later histories of events in these few cases bear out my remarks, in the previous chapter, that to analyse *The Rôle of Courts in Barotse Life* I need to do further research in the field, and quite a different kind of research. Only by tracing a series of disputes, handled in various ways, through the lives of the same people and sets of people, could I assess the effectiveness of judicial action. I was able to gather on a very brief visit, at a time when people were disturbed at the thought of detailed investigation, enough data to emphasize that, in the type of relationships under examination, a case in court is a climax to one series of events, and sets in train other events. Major problems remained after I had analysed judicial reprimands and judgments on a case as a theoretically closed situation. This is brought out vividly in the Case of the Headman's Fishdams. Here I thought Solami's judgment the most brilliant judgment, looked at from a lawyer's point of view,[1] that I heard. It was brilliant in maintaining the existing law yet doing justice to those who had done no wrong. Yet the outcome in the lives of two of the people involved seems to have been disastrous. This judge had not sat in court and therefore had not heard the bitterness of the nephew's attack on his uncle. But other judges, who also advised the nephew to join his uncle, had done so ; and they overlooked this in the interests of unity. The judgments in the Case of the Biassed Father, involving similar issues, entailed no judicial brilliance : their outcome was successful. It is the chances of sickness and life and death, and of emigration, which seem to have made in the end the crucial difference.

---

[1] Several lawyers have told me they consider it a brilliant judgment.

CHANGES IN THE LAW

Here I discuss only a few points, into which I particularly enquired, or which came to my notice.

Procedure : As the court clerks were on a course in Lusaka, there were no trials in Mongu District during my visit. I heard one trial at Naliele Court, Mankoya, where I had not worked before so I had not seen this court as a full old-style Barotse court. It now consists of five judges, two Lozi, two Nkoya, and one Luchaze (there are many immigrants of the Luchaze and kindred tribes in the District). The litigants were all Luchaze, and the cross-examination was in Nkoya, Luchaze and Lozi (one Nkoya judge deliberately cross-examined in Lozi for my benefit). Four men were suing a fifth for assaulting them with a stick at a beer-drink. All five gave statements to the clerk. The first plaintiff alleged that he approached the defendant at a beer-drink and asked him to pay a debt. He said the defendant got angry and complained this was not the time to ask for payment ; the defendant then seized a stick, and attacked him. The defendant broke his arm (which was in plaster). The other three plaintiffs all said they were beaten by the defendant with a stick, two of them saying they had tried to intervene in the fight, the other that he had done nothing. The defendant admitted he angrily refused to pay his debt, but denied that he attacked anyone. The judges attacked the plaintiffs in cross-examination, concentrating on what kind of stick it was, where the defendant picked up the stick, and why they had not brought the stick to court. Through this phase of the trial the defendant, and his relatives from the side of the court, kept clapping their hands in approval. The stress all the time was that the court needed witnesses to give evidence, since they decided cases on evidence (cf. the missionary Seguin in a review of my book, in which he says the Barotse had no idea of morality or reasonableness, wrote that ' most cases are not substantiated by evidence '.[1] This is a palpably incorrect statement in the light of this case and those presented in the main text). Eventually that plaintiff who said he had not intervened in the fight but had just been attacked from behind, was told he had no suit since he had not seen, and

---

[1] See Appendix to Chapter IX, p. 412.

had not a witnesss to prove, who had hit him. Three judges, in Lozi and Nkoya and Luchaze, emphasized : ' If you do not know, how can the court ? '

An adulterer then came to plead to the court for grace of time to pay the £1 fine due to the court on his adultery, but he had brought the husband's compensation of £5 (in 1947 it was £2). The Lozi judge said they could not accept the £5 : two months had gone by and he should also have raised the other £1. Let him produce the other £1 or go to jail : he could sell some of his clothes or blankets. When he pleaded again for grace, the judge said : ' It is not us, but the law (*mulao*), which binds you.' If he did wrong, he must pay for it : he should have thought of this at the time of his wrong. Like other Barotse judges, in the end they gave him grace—a month to get the £1. (I cite this case also to emphasize, as I do in the text, how the Barotse speak in this personified way of ' the law '.)

A man who was being sued in a case where he had herded cattle under agistment, said he could not come since his white employer would not release him, but he had sent his younger brother. The younger brother was told his elder would be jailed for contempt of court unless he came himself, and he was given too a note requesting the release of the defendant by his employer. (I was then called by the Chief to visit the District Secretary.)

These three examples indicate that, despite the reduction in size of the court, the Mankoya court operated in the same way as the Lozi courts described in the main text. In short, judges of other tribes in Barotseland do not seem to differ from Lozi judges, though I must note that one of the Nkoya judges had in fact in 1947 served a period as Nkoya tribal representative on the Barotse Provincial Appeal Court at the Paramount Chief's capital.

Executory Contracts :[1] In a study published in 1943 I had noted that the Barotse courts did not enforce executory contracts, and I pointed out some of the difficulties which resulted when a person who had undertaken to cut a garden, or do other work for another, but had not been paid, did not carry out the undertaking. In 1947 the councillors at Lialui told me they had passed a law to enforce such promises. Since the court clerks were

---

[1] See my *The Ideas in Barotse Jurisprudence* (1965), pp. 176 f., 180–1.

away, I could not consult court records on this and other points in 1965.   But I was told that the courts were not in fact holding bare promises to be binding.   Here is what the Lozi Chief at Mankoya told me, first in reply to a question : ' If a man sends money for his wife to arrange for a garden to be cut and she arranges for a man to do it but pays him nothing, and he then does not do the work, the court will not punish him, but can only reprimand him severely for not fulfilling his promise and causing people to fall into want.   In the case of a fisherman who orders a net to be made by a netmaker, the court cannot punish or order compensation from the netmaker to the fisherman whether or not he was paid.   But the fisherman is entitled to any net made by the netmaker if he has paid the money.'   (The Chief remembered a case involving these issues which he and I heard in Lialui, the central capital, in 1942 ; and his councillors had heard of it.   The case was also remembered clearly at Lialui.)[1] The Chief then spontaneously volunteered the following case : ' A man had assembled all the material for building a hut, and the builder after starting work, dropped it.   The builder had not been paid anything.   The court could do nothing but scold him for not carrying out his promise, as with the cutting of gardens.' To my question, he replied that if the builder had been paid for the work, the court would order him to build the house ; and it could commit him for contempt of court if he refused.

The failure to enforce executory contracts after the national council had reputedly taken a decision to do so, seems to me to go deeper than a weakness in the courts.   It arises from certain inherent limitations in Barotse ideas about ' contracts ' (*litu-melano* = to agree with each other for mutual benefit).   When I asked the Barotse why they had passed the law, they told me that they had read in my study of Lozi land tenure (1943) that this was a gap in their law, and they saw that it produced consider-able hardship for innocent people.   Before I returned to Barotse-land, I discussed in my *The Ideas in Barotse Jurisprudence* (1965, pp. 181 f.) how they were likely to set about enforcement, in the light of their basic approach to commercial agreements and hire of services :

With the increasing importance of free contractual relations in

---

[1] See ibid., pp. 178 f.

Barotseland under modern conditions, the need for enforcement of executory contracts is aggravated : yet the bias of the law against this enforcement is shown by the fact that the Barotse decided to pass this law only after an outsider had drawn attention to resulting difficulties. I heard no cases under this law, so I cannot say how the courts would punish breaches. The judges told me that defaulters on promises were like thieves and should be punished. They said they would order specific performance or levy damages. I asked how damages would be assessed. Would they be fixed, or would the court make a de-faulter pay the other party for losses from inability to fish or to plant a garden ? The judges said they had not thought about this and would decide when cases came up. Barotse law up to that time had allowed no claims for damages flowing from failure of another person to carry out an obligation.

This failure, I argued, was inherent in their whole conception of what a transaction is and hence of the remedies they provided for breach of a transaction. They did not divide transaction into undertakings by each party to do a particular thing for the other. They looked at transactions instead in terms of rights in property and the transfer of such rights. In short, they thought in terms of Maine's summary view of archaic legal thought, where he says in *Ancient Law* (1861, pp. 324 f.) : '. . . conveyances and contracts were practically confounded' and ' a *Contract* was long regarded as an *incomplete Conveyance*'. Following Maine's phrasing, I concluded that ' Barotse sales are reciprocal convey-ances, rather than contracts creating obligations . . . Barotse law arms with its sanctions . . . the yielding of property, which in some situations should be set in a ceremonial context'. This was clear in barter and sale, and in hiring of services even payment in advance did not give the employer enforceable claims.

For this and other reasons, I argued throughout my book on Barotse jurisprudential ideas that the model relationship for Barotse judges was a relationship of status, and primarily one between closely related kinsfolk. This affected the Barotse approach to both agreements and injuries. And since I (follow-ing others) had shown how rights in property and transfers of property were critical in fixing obligations in relationships between kinsfolk and affines, I suggested that similar elements were emphasized in commercial contracts.

Since the judges in 1947, like English judges, said they would decide when cases arose, I myself felt and wrote in my notes that they would probably enforce contracts by treating defaulters, in their own words, as thieves; and they would try to secure some kind of restitution by ordering payment of double the value of either the goods ordered (say a fishing-net) or double the money which it had been arranged would be paid for service. They seem in fact to have baulked at actually calling such a defaulter a thief. What is clear is that adequate enforcement of executory contracts (and indeed of executed contracts) involves the development of a set of radical ideas about damages, and not only the idea of restitution. There has to develop the conception of consequential damages—as for a fisherman whose ordered net is not made and therefore loses his catch, or for a woman whose garden is not cut or ploughed and therefore loses her crop. The concentration of the Barotse on the material elements involved in contract, which I discuss in Chapter VI of *The Ideas in Barotse Jurisprudence* (1965), leads them to think of all contracts as involving debts (ibid., Chapter VIII), and of their main remedy in terms of restitution. In the hypothetical case of the paid for, and partly built, hut, cited above, Chief Mwendawelie said the court would order performance, and commit for contempt if it was disobeyed. He had no view of damages. The Lozi, not surprisingly in view of the slow development of contractual ideas and remedies in Europe, are restricted by their original ideas. I leave this matter here, since I begin to follow leads advanced by Mr. Y. P. Ghai at the International Institute's 1966 seminar on African law; and it would be unfair of me to anticipate publication of his work, presented at a seminar of which I was chairman.

On the other hand I found that there had been a radical change in the Barotse law of implied warranties in sale.

Warranty in sales : In my study of Barotse law of commercial contracts in *The Ideas in Barotse Jurisprudence*[1] I cited cases, actual and hypothetical, to show that there was a strong implied warranty in such contracts, which were of the utmost good faith. I showed that the Barotse enforced a rule that the seller had to take care to supply sound goods to which he had a good title, lest he be punished for fraud ('theft'). It was not demanded

---

[1] See ibid., pp. 201–3.

of the buyer that he check the goods. I argued that this was consistent with the whole Barotse view of contracts which they saw as involving the highest good faith, like transactions between kinsmen. I quoted evidence from other studies of tribal law, and from the development of English and other law, to suggest that this view of commercial contracts was widespread in tribal and early law. This view of the Barotse law of commercial contracts was confirmed by informants in 1965 as true of the past, but some ten years before the courts had begun to decide that the buyer must check the goods at the time of sale. They began to hold that the buyer had made an agreement (*tumelelano*) and it was up to him to be sensible and check what he was getting.

The following incident illustrates the change in approach. When Chief Mwenekandala and I were at the village involved in The Case of the Biassed Father (see above, pp. 37-45, and p. 428), the headman consulted us on his rights in a dispute over a dog. He had bought a dog from a man in a neighbouring village who said that the dog was a good hunter. He had paid ten shillings for it. He found that it was useless for hunting. He had gone with the dog to complain to the seller, who kept the dog through a night during which it was tied up in the village. A hyaena ate the dog. The headman asked us whether he was entitled to his ten shillings, because the dog had been destroyed while in the care of the seller. To my question, he and the others present agreed that the court would not uphold a suit for return of his money because he had been deceived about the dog's skill at hunting. He should have tested it before completing the transaction. They said that in the past the court would have ruled that the seller had deceived him and the court would have ordered return of the purchase price, perhaps doubled as punishment for the deception. As a Western jurist would say, if the headman's story were true there was a misrepresentation on the seller's part, not merely ignorance of a defect. It may be that this charge is associated with increasing use for 'agreement' of *tumelelano* (by root and suffixes, agreement with each other for mutual advantage) in place of *tumelano* (agreement with each other).[1] Chief Mwenekandala said he had not heard of a suit similar to the proposed action over the eating of the dog in these

---

[1] See ibid., pp. 182, 194.

circumstances, and he could not therefore say what the court was likely to decide.   As this was my second last day in Mongu District, I could not make enquiries there.   At Mankoya, the council was also uncertain what the decision would be.   I can only assume that this radical change in the law is due to the increasing number and importance of commercial transactions, and is influenced by a desire to secure a freer commerce.

Warranty has changed only in regard to the quality of goods supplied.   The seller still guarantees that he owns and can transfer rights : an owner can still pursue his property and regain it from others who have acquired it in good faith.

Clearly the abandonment of the implied warranty of quality, and a shift of responsibility for testing the goods, should make commercial transactions freer.   This change does not raise the difficulties, discussed above, inherent in the view that transactions involve fundamentally rights in, and transfers of, property. Indeed, the doctrine *caveat emptor* only requires that the buyer test the property he is getting, before accepting it, and that once he has paid the price that price is more firmly the seller's.   And it avoids, I think, the problems of considering whether the seller is responsible for damages flowing from his delivery of unsound goods.   But it involves a shift in the emphasis I found in Barotse law that all transactions were of the utmost good faith.   In *The Ideas in Barotse Jurisprudence* (1965) I argued that this emphasis also emerged from the fact that Barotse took as their model relationship one between closely related kinsfolk.   I cannot evaluate the further implications of this example (so far the only one I know, though there may be others) of a shift in Barotse law away from the insistence on good faith.

Marriage laws :[1]   There are many references in the main text to marriage laws under which a man gave two beasts or £2 for a virgin in marriage.   One payment was for the marriage, the other for the bride's untouched virginity and fertility. Therefore one beast or £1 was returnable to him if they divorced and she had not conceived.   Only one beast or £1 was given to pay for marriage to a bride who was not a virgin. Extra payments on the demand of the bride's kin were not returnable.   I also recorded efforts of the Barotse authorities

---

[1] See ibid., pp. 159 f., and above, pp. 122-3, 174 f.

to restrain a rise in marriage payments. They have finally failed to control this rise, and now payments vary, I was told, from £30 to £40, and occasionally are even higher. Since there is no longer the equivalence of one payment for the marriage, and one for a virgin's untouched fertility, on divorce there is no longer a suit for the latter payment. Chief Mwenekandala and others told me that if there was a divorce within two years, a man might get back £10 or £15, but after two years all was lost. I did not have the opportunity to enquire closely into these changes. The increase in face value of the marriage-payment is clearly partly a result of the general fall in value of money. There may be substantial shifts in the Lozi views of the function of marriage-payments and in the rights and duties of spouses. It would be fascinating to know if the increase has affected the high rate of divorce.[1]

Lozi Terminology : I noted that *bung'i* had increasingly ousted *bung'a* as the word I translate as ' ownership ', a concept whose use I discuss in detail in Chapter V of *The Ideas in Barotse Jurisprudence* (1965).

---

[1] Gluckman, ' Kinship and Marriage among the Lozi of Northern Rhodesia and the Zulu of Natal ' (1950).

ACKNOWLEDGMENTS

I AM grateful to the following publishers and editors, and authors, for permission to quote passages verbatim from books and articles in the bibliography below :

Messrs. B. H. Blackwell and Professor H. L. A. Hart, ' The Ascription of Responsibility and Rights ' in *Logic and Language* ;

The Editor of the *Journal of Comparative Legislation and International Law*, and Professor H. A. Smith, ' Interpretation in English and Continental Law ' ;

The Editor of the *Columbia Law Review* and Mr. Z. Chafee, Jun., ' The Disorderly Conduct of Words ' ;

Mr. Geoffrey Cumberlege of the Clarendon Press and Sir Carleton Kemp Allen, *Law in the Making* ;

Mr. Geoffrey Cumberlege of the Clarendon Press and Professor E. E. Evans-Pritchard, *The Nuer* ;

Mr. Geoffrey Cumberlege of the Oxford University Press, and Professor K. Olivecrona, *Law as Fact* ;

Mr. Geoffrey Cumberlege of the Oxford University Press, The Director of the International African Institute, and Professor I. Schapera, *A Handbook of Tswana Law and Custom* ;

Messrs. Alfred Knopf and Dr. W. Seagle, *The Quest for Law* ;

Messrs. John Lane, for the late Major A. St. Hill Gibbons, *Africa from South to North through Marotseland* ;

The Editor of the *Law Quarterly Review* and Professor Glanville Williams, ' Language and the Law ', lxi (1945) and lxii (1946) ;

The Editor of *The Listener* and Professor A. L. Goodhart, ' The United Nations and War Crimes ', xlvii, No. 1207 (17th April, 1952) ;

The Paris Evangelical Mission, Barotseland, and Miss Graziella Jalla for the late M. Adolphe Jalla, *Litaba za Sicaba Sa Malozi* ;

The Trustees and Director of the Rhodes-Livingstone Institute and Dr. J. A. Barnes, ' History in a Changing Society ', *Rhodes-Livingstone Journal : Human Problems in British Central Africa*, No. 11 ;

Messrs. Coward-McCann Inc. and Messrs. Stevens & Sons, and Mr. Justice Jerome Frank, *Law and the Modern Mind* ;

Messrs. Thornton Butterworth & Co. for the late Sir Paul Vinogradoff, *Common-sense in Law* ;

The University of Oklahoma Press and Professors K. Llewellyn and E. A. Hoebel, *The Cheyenne Way* ;

The Yale University Press, from the late Mr. Justice B. Cardozo, *Growth of the Law*, and *Nature of the Judicial Process*

BIBLIOGRAPHY

ALBERT, E.   Review of *The Judicial Process among the Barotse*, in *American Anthropologist*, vol. 61 (1959), pp. 318–19.

ALLAN, W.   *The African Husbandman*, Edinburgh : Oliver and Boyd (1965).

ALLEN, SIR CARLETON KEMP.   *Law in the Making*, Oxford : Clarendon Press (1946 ; 6th edition, 1958).

ALLOTT, A. N.   Review of *The Judicial Process among the Barotse*, in *The Law Quarterly Review*, lxxii (January, 1956), pp. 144–7.

ANDERSON, J. N. D.   *Islamic Law in Africa*, London : H.M.S.O. (1954).

—— Review of *The Judicial Process among the Barotse*, in *The Modern Law Review*, xviii (December, 1955), pp. 643–4.

ANDREZJEWSKI, S.   *Military Organisation and Society*, London : Routledge and Kegan Paul (1953).

ARNOT, F. S.   *Garenganze : or Seven Years' Pioneer Mission Work in Central Africa*, London : Hawkins (? 1889).

AYOUB, V.   'Review : The Judicial Process in Two African Societies,' in M. Janowitz (editor), *Community Political Systems*, Volume 1, *International Yearbook of Political Research Behaviour*, Glencoe, Illinois : Free Press (1961), pp. 237–50.   (Reprinted in Schubert, *Judicial Behaviour*, 1964, below.)

BARNES, J. A.   'History in a Changing Society,' *Rhodes–Livingstone Journal*, XI (June, 1951) ; and *Human Relations*, iv. 3 (1951).

BARTON, R. F.   *Ifugao Law*, University of California Publications in American Archeology and Ethnology, xv (1919).

—— *The Kalingas*, Chicago : University of Chicago Press (1949).

BOHANNAN, P. J.   *Justice and Judgment among the Tiv*, London : Oxford University Press for the International African Institute (1957).

—— 'The Differing Realms of Law ' in L. Nader (editor), *The Ethnography of Law* (1965), pp. 33–42.

CARDOZO, B. J.   *Growth of the Law*, New Haven : Yale University Press (1927).

—— *Nature of the Judicial Process*, New Haven : Yale University Press (1928).

CHAFEE, Jun., Z.   'The Disorderly Conduct of Words ', *Columbia Law Review*, xli (1941), and (here quoted) *Canadian Bar Review*, xx (1942).

CHASE, STUART.   *The Tyranny of Words*, London : Methuen (1938).

COLSON, E.   'Social Control and Vengeance in Plateau Tonga Society', *Africa*, xxiii, 3 (July, 1953).

CURTIS, C. P.   *It's Your Law*, Cambridge, Mass. : Harvard University Press (1954).

DEVONS, E.   'Serving as a Juryman in Britain', *The Modern Law Review*, xxviii (September, 1965), pp. 561–70.

DIAMOND, A. S.   *Primitive Law*, London : Watts (1935, 2nd ed., 1950).

DOUGLAS, M. 'L'homme primitif et la loi', *Zaire* (April, 1956), no. 4, pp. 367–74.

DRIBERG, J. H. 'The African Conception of Law', *The Journal of Comparative Legislation and International Law*, xv (November, 1934).

DURKHEIM, E. *Les règles de la sociologique*, Paris : Librairie Felix Alcan (1938).

EMPSON, W. *The Structure of Complex Words*, London : Chatto & Windus (1951).

EPSTEIN, A. L. Review of Bohannan, *Justice and Judgment among the Tiv*, in *Man*, Vol. 59 (February, 1959), No. 33.

—— 'Some Aspects of the Conflict of Law and Urban Courts in Northern Rhodesia', *Rhodes–Livingstone Journal*, XII (December, 1951).

—— 'The Rôle of African Courts in Urban Communities of the Northern Rhodesian Copperbelt', *Rhodes–Livingstone Journal*, XIII (July, 1952).

—— 'Divorce Law and Stability of Marriage among the Lunda of Kazembe', *Rhodes–Livingstone Journal*, XIV (December, 1952).

—— *Juridical Techniques and the Judicial Process : A Study in African Customary Law. Rhodes–Livingstone Paper No. 23*, Manchester University Press (1954).

—— *The Administration of Justice and the Urban African : A Study of Urban Native Courts in Northern Rhodesia*, London : H.M.S.O. (1953).

EPSTEIN, A. L. (editor). *The Craft of Social Anthropology*, London : Tavistock (1966).

EVANS-PRITCHARD, E. E. *The Nuer*, Oxford : Clarendon Press (1940).

—— 'The Nuer of the Southern Sudan', in *African Political Systems*, London : Oxford University Press (1940).

FLEW, A. (editor). *Logic and Language*, Oxford : Blackwell (1951–3).

FORTES, M. *The Dynamics of Clanship among the Tallensi*, London : Oxford University Press (1945).

FORTES, M. and EVANS-PRITCHARD, E. E. (editors) *African Political Systems*, London : Oxford University Press (1940).

FRANK, JEROME. *Law and the Modern Mind*, New York : Coward-McCann (1930) ; London : Stevens & Sons (1949).

FRANKFURTER, F. 'John Marshall and the Judicial Function', *Harvard Law Review*, vol. 69, no. 2 (December, 1959), pp. 217–38.

GIBBONS, MAJOR ST. J. *Africa from South to North through Barotseland*, London and New York : John Lane, The Bodley Head (1904).

GIBBS, Jun., J. L. 'Poro Values and Courtroom Procedures in a Kpelle Chiefdom', *Southwestern Journal of Anthropology*, 18.4 (1962), pp. 341–50.

—— 'The Kpelle Moot : A Therapeutic Model for the Informal Settlement of Disputes', *Africa*, xxxiii, 1 (January, 1963), pp. 1–11.

GLUCKMAN, M. 'Analysis of a Social Situation in Modern Zululand', *Bantu Studies*, xiv (March and June, 1940), reprinted *Rhodes–Livingstone Paper No. 28* (1958).

—— *Economy of the Central Barotse Plain*, Livingstone : *Rhodes–Livingstone Paper No. 7* (1941).

—— *Administrative Organization of the Barotse Native Authorities*, Livingstone : *Rhodes–Livingstone Institute Communications No. 1* (1943).

GLUCKMAN, M.   Essays on Lozi Land and Royal Property, Livingstone: Rhodes-Livingstone Paper No. 10 (1943).
——— 'A Lozi Price-Control Debate', South African Journal of Economics, xi, 3 (September, 1943), summarized in Colonial Review (March, 1944).
——— 'African Land Tenure', The Rhodes-Livingstone Journal, III (June, 1945).
——— 'Kinship and Marriage among the Lozi of Northern Rhodesia and the Zulu of Natal', in A. R. Radcliffe-Brown and C. D. Forde (editors), African Systems of Kinship and Marriage, London : Oxford University Press (1950).
——— 'The Lozi of Barotseland in North-Western Rhodesia', in Seven Tribes of British Central Africa, edited by E. Colson and M. Gluckman, London : Oxford University Press (1951) ; Manchester : Manchester University Press (1959).
——— 'Political Institutions', in E. E. Evans-Pritchard (editor), The Institutions of Primitive Society, Oxford : Blackwell (1954).
——— Rituals of Rebellion in South-East Africa, Manchester University Press (1954), republished in Order and Rebellion in Tribal Africa, London : Cohen and West (1962).
——— Custom and Conflict in Africa, Oxford : Blackwell (1955, 1961).
——— 'Tribalism in Modern British Central Africa', Cahiers d'Etudes Africaines, I, i (January, 1960), reprinted in P. Van den Berghe, P. (editor), Africa : Social Problems of Change and Conflict, San Francisco : Chandler (1965), and in I. Wallerstein (editor), Social Change in the Colonial Situation, New York : Wiley (1966).
——— 'Ethnographic Data in British Social Anthropology', The Sociological Review, N.S. vol. 9, no. 1 (1961).
——— 'African Jurisprudence', The Advancement of Science, No. 74 (November, 1961).
——— 'The Reasonable Man in Barotse Law', reprinted from The Journal of African Administration, 1955-6, in Gluckman, Order and Rebellion in Tribal Africa, London : Cohen and West (1962).
——— The Ideas in Barotse Jurisprudence, New Haven: Yale University Press (1965) ; Manchester University Press for Institute for African Studies, University of Zambia (1972).
——— Politics, Law and Ritual in a Tribal Society, Oxford: Blackwell; Chicago: Aldine; New York: Mentor Books (1965).
——— 'Reasonableness and Responsibility in the Law of Segmentary Societies', in L. and H. Kuper (editors), African Law: Adaptation and Development, Los Angeles: University of California (1966).
GLUCKMAN, M. and COLSON, E.   Seven Tribes of British Central Africa, Manchester University Press (1959, 1961), reprinted for Institute for Social Research, University of Zambia, as Seven Tribes of Central Africa (1968).
GLUCKMAN, M. and EGGAN, F.   'Introduction' to New Approaches in Social Anthropology, vols. I-IV, London : Tavistock (1964-6).
GOODHART, A. L.   'The United Nations and War Crimes', The Listener, xlvii, No. 1207 (17th April, 1952).

GULLIVER, P. H.   *Social Control in an African Society : A Study of the Arusha*, London : Routledge and Kegan Paul (1963).

HAILEY, LORD, *An African Survey*, London : Oxford University Press (1946).

—— *Native Administration in the British African Territories*, London : H.M.S.O. Part II (1951).

HART, H. L. A.   ' The Ascription of Responsibility and Rights ', in A. Flew (editor), *Logic and Language*, Oxford : Blackwell (1951–3).

—— ' Definition and Theory in Jurisprudence : An Inaugural Lecture delivered before the University of Oxford ', Oxford : Clarendon Press (1953).

—— *The Concept of Law*, Oxford : Clarendon Press (1961).

HERBERT, SIR ALAN, *Uncommon Law*, London : Methuen (1935).

HOEBEL, E. A.   *The Political Organization and Law-ways of the Comanche Indians*, Memoirs of the American Anthropological Association, No. 54, (1940).

—— ' Fundamental Legal Concepts as Applied in the Study of Primitive Law ', *Yale Law Journal*, li (1942).

—— *The Law of Primitive Man*, Cambridge, Mass. : Harvard University Press (1954).

—— ' Three Studies in African Law ', *Stanford Law Review*, xiii, 2 (March, 1961), pp. 418–42 ; with Gluckman, ' Comment : The Rôle of the King in the Barotse Judicial Process ', *Stanford Law Review*, xiv, i (December, 1961), pp. 110–19.

—— ' Fundamental Cultural Postulates and Judicial Lawmaking in Pakistan ', in L. Nader (editor), *The Ethnography of Law* (1965), pp. 43–56.

HOHFELD, W. N.   *Fundamental Legal Conceptions as Applied in Judicial Reasoning, and Other Legal Essays* (edited by W. W. Cook), New Haven : Yale University Press (1923) (reprinted from the *Yale Law Journal*, xxiii and xxvi, 1917).

HOMANS, G. C.   *The Human Group*, London : Routledge & Kegan Paul ; New York : Harcourt Brace (1951).

HOWELL, P. P.   *A Manual of Nuer Law*, London : Oxford University Press (1954).

J. P. M.   Review of Gluckman, *The Ideas in Barotse Jurisprudence* (1965), in *African Affairs*, vol. 65, No. 258 (January, 1966), pp. 108–9.

JALLA, ADOLPHE.   *Litaba za Sicaba sa Malozi* (History of the Lozi Nation), Sefula, Barotseland : The Book Depot of the Paris Missionary Society (4th ed., 1939).

—— *Dictionary of the Lozi Language*, London : The United Society for Christian Literature (n.d.).

JUNOD, H. A.   *The Life of a South African Tribe*, London : Macmillan (1927, 2nd ed.).

KAY, H. H.   ' The Family and Kinship System of Illegitimate Children in California Law ', in L. Nader (editor), *The Ethnography of Law* (1965), pp. 57–81.

KENNY, C. S.   *Outlines of Criminal Law*, Cambridge : University Press (1929, 13th ed.)

KERN, F.   *Kingship and Law in the Middle Ages* (tr. by S. B. Chrimes), Oxford : Blackwell (1948).

KERR, A. J.   'Some Recent Studies in African Law', *African Studies*, xv, 3 (September, 1956), pp. 139–44.

KILGOUR, D. G.   Review of *The Judicial Process among the Barotse*, in *Canadian Bar Review*, xxiii (May, 1955), pp. 623–4.

KRIGE, E. J. and J. D.   *The Realm of a Rain-Queen* (Lovhedu), London : Oxford University Press (1943).

KRIGE, J. D.   'Some Aspects of Lovhedu Judicial Arrangements', *Bantu Studies*, xiii, 2 (June, 1939). .

—— Review of *The Judicial Process among the Barotse*, in *Man*, lvi (July, 1956), No. 98.

KUPER, H.   'Kinship among the Swazi', in A. R. Radcliffe-Brown and C. D. Forde (editors), *African Systems of Kinship and Marriage*, London : Oxford University Press (1950).

LEWIS, I. M.   'Clanship and Contract in Northern Somaliland', *Africa*, xxix, 3 (July, 1959), pp. 274–93.

LINTON, R.   *The Study of Man*, New York and London : Appleton-Century (1936).

LIVINGSTONE, D.   *Missionary Travels and Researches in South Africa*, London : John Murray (1857).

LLEWELLYN, K. and HOEBEL, E. A., *The Cheyenne Way : Conflict and Case Law in Primitive Jurisprudence*, Norman : University of Oklahoma Press (1941).

MAINE, SIR HENRY.   *Ancient Law*, London : John Murray (1909, 10th ed.).

—— *Early Law and Custom*, London : John Murray (1883).

MAIR, L.   *An Introduction to Social Anthropology*, London : Oxford University Press (1965).

MALINOWSKI, B.   *Crime and Custom in Savage Society*, London : Kegan Paul, Trench, Trubner ; New York : Harcourt Brace (1926).

MARCH, J. G.   'Sociological Jurisprudence Revisited, A Review (More or Less) of Max Gluckman', *Stanford Law Review*, vol. 8, no. 3 (May, 1956), pp. 499–534, with a reply by Gluckman and response by March, same journal, 8, 3 (July, 1956), pp. 767–73.   (March's essay reprinted in Schubert, *Judicial Behavior*, 1963—below.)

MARSHALL, T. H.   'Gluckman on the Judicial Process of the Barotse', *The British Journal of Sociology*, vi, 4 (December, 1955), pp. 369–73.

MARWICK, M. G.   *Sorcery in its Social Setting : A Study of the Northern Rhodesian Ceŵa*, Manchester : Manchester University Press (1965).

MEGGITT, M. J.   *Desert People, A Study of the Walbiri Aborigines of Central Australia*, London and Sydney : Angus and Robertson (1962).

MIDDLETON, J.   *Lugbara Religion*, London : Oxford University Press (1960).

MITCHELL, J. C.   *The Yao Village*, Manchester: Manchester University Press (1956, 1966) and for Institute for African Studies (1971).

NADEL, S. F.   'Reason and Unreason in African Law', *Africa*, xxvi, 2 (April, 1956), pp. 160–73.

—— *The Nuba*, London: Oxford University Press (1947).

NADER, L. 'The Anthropological study of Law', in Nader (editor), *The Ethnography of Law* (1965), pp. 3–32.

NADER, L. (editor). *The Ethnography of Law*, Special Publication, *American Anthropologist*, vol. 67, no. 6, part 2 (December, 1965).

OLIVECRONA, K. *Law as Fact*, London: Oxford University Press (1939).

PARSONS, T. *and* SHILS, E. (editors). *Towards a General Theory of Action*, Cambridge: Harvard University Press (1951).

PETERS, D. U. *Land Usage in Barotseland*, edited by N. W. Smyth, *Rhodes–Livingstone Institute Communication No. 19* (1960).

PIM, SIR ALAN *and* MILLIGAN, S. *Financial and Economic Conditions in Northern Rhodesia, 1938*, London: H.M.S.O. (1938).

POCOCK, D. F. *Social Anthropology*, London and New York: Sheed and Ward (1961).

POSPISIL, L. *Kapauku Papuans and Their Law*, Yale University Publications in Anthropology, No. 54 (1959).

POWELL, R. 'The Unreasonableness of The Reasonable Man', *Current Legal Problems* (1957), pp. 104–26.

RADCLIFFE-BROWN, A. R. 'Preface', in M. Fortes and E. E. Evans-Pritchard (editors), *African Political Systems*, London: Oxford University Press (1940).

—— 'Primitive Law', in *Structure and Function in Primitive Society*, London: Cohen and West (1952).

REYNOLDS, B. *Magic, Divination and Witchcraft among the Barotse of Northern Rhodesia*, London: Chatto and Windus (1963).

RICHARDS, A. I. 'A Modern Movement of Witch-finders', *Africa*, viii, 4 (October, 1935), pp. 448–61.

RICHARDS, I. A. *Mencius on the Mind: Experiments in Multiple Definition*, London: Kegan Paul, Trench, Trubner & Co. (1932).

SCHAPERA, I. *A Handbook of Tswana Law and Custom*, London: Oxford University Press (1938), (2nd edition, 1955).

—— *Married Life in an African Tribe* (Tswana), London: Faber and Faber (1940).

—— *The Khoisan Peoples of South Africa*, London: Routledge (1930).

—— 'The Sources of Law in Tswana Tribal Courts', *Journal of African Law*, (1957), pp. 150–62.

SCHILLER, A. A. Review of *The Judicial Process among the Barotse*, in *The Rhodes–Livingstone Journal*, xxi (March, 1957), pp. 75–9.

SCHUBERT, G. *Judicial Behaviour: A Reader in Theory and Research*, Chicago: Rand McNally (1964).

SEAGLE, W. *The Quest for Law*, New York: Knopf (1941).

SEGUIN, S. Review of *The Judicial Process among the Barotse*, in *International Review of Missions*, (April, 1956), pp. 238–42.

SMITH, H. A. 'Interpretation in English and Continental Law', *Journal of Comparative Legislation and International Law*, ix (1927).

SOUTHALL, A. W. Review of *The Judicial Process among the Barotse*, in *Sociological Review*, N.S. iv (1956), pp. 110–13.

STUMPF, S. K. Review of *The Judicial Process among the Barotse*, in *Harvard Law Review*, vol. 69, no. 4 (February, 1956), pp. 780–7.

TER HAAR, B.   *Adat Law in Indonesia* (edited with an introduction by E. A. Hoebel and A. A. Schiller), New York : Institute of Pacific Relations (1948).

TRAPNELL, C. G. and CLOTHIER, J. N.   *The Soils, Vegetation and Agricultural Systems of North-Western Rhodesia*, Lusaka : Government Printer (1937).

TURNER, V. W.   *Schism and Continuity in an African Society*, Manchester : Manchester University Press (1957, 1964, 1968) and for Institute for African Studies (1971).

UBEROI, J. P. S.   *Politics of the Kula Ring*, Manchester : Manchester University Press (1962).

VAN VELSEN, J.   *The Politics of Kinship: A Study in Social Manipulation among the Lakeside Tonga of Nyasaland*, Manchester : Manchester University Press (1964) and for Institute for African Studies (1971).

VINOGRADOFF, SIR PAUL.   *Common-Sense in Law*, London : Thornton Butterworth ; The Home University Library (1913 ; 10th impression 1933).

WILLIAMS, GLANVILLE L.   ' Language and the Law ', *The Law Quarterly Review*, lxi (1945) and lxii (1946).

WORTLEY, B. A.   ' On Re-reading Dean Wigmore's Panorama of the World's Legal Systems ', *Problèmes Contemporains de Droit Comparé*, Université Chao, Tokyo, ii (1962), 537–49.

INDEX

abduction of wife (v. *elopement*)

abolition of Barotse Provincial Council, 428

absorbent concepts, 294, **316–17**

accident, 206

adjudication: defined, 227, 229 ; Frank on, 349 f. ; frequent need of, 26; uncertainty of, 349 f.

administrative action : by court, 21, 51, 77 ; distinguished from judgment, 70 ; effects of new roads and Land-Rovers, 428 ; judicial procedure contrary to Northern Rhodesian ordinances, 418 ; taken in case, 71 f. ; treatment of witchcraft accusations, 424

administrative system, 13–14

adulterer : reasonable, 135

adultery : endangers pregnancy, 66 ; evidence of, 106, 154, 272–3 ; judicial bias on, 413 ; *mufubalume*, 59 ; not divined, 99 ; norms of, 134 ; old statute on, 248 ; punishment, of, 37, 65, 131 n., 217 ; punishment is test of marriage, 118

agistment, 439

Albert, E., review by, 369 n. 1

alegal, 230–1, 346

Allen, C. K., on : assumptions of English law, 332–3 ; custom, 237 f. ; equity, 204 ; judicial interpretation, 339 ; mediaeval statutory law, 249 n. ; precedents, 336–7 ; on sources of judicial law, 379, 416

Allott, A. N. : on African judicial reasoning, 406 ; on ' reasonable ' and 'customary' man, 389

ambiguity : Allen on, 339 ; function of complexity, 401 ; judicial value of, 170, 305 ; scholars must accept, 229–30 ; of ' right ', 195, 405

American judicial behaviour, 414

analogy, 24, 280 f. ; cow and fishdam, 182, 183–4, 192 ; divorce and death spouse, 176 ; mourning and marriage beasts, 176

' analytical system ' : and comparative jurisprudence, 376

ancestral titles to land, 54

Anderson, J. N. D. : on ' reasonable man ', 387

Anglo-American law : concept of ' reasonable man ' in, 392

anthropology : field-work and development of theory, 370 ; and tribal law, 369

appeal courts and judicial process, 372–3

appeals : allegations bias on, 28 ; to British courts, 3 ; evidence heard anew, 105 ; indigenous system of, 13 ; modern system of, 13–14, 174 ; political basis of, 27 ; as proof of innocence, 87, 91, 94, 149 ; unity of Lozi system of, 114

argument, judicial (v.q. *analogy, interpretation, logic, reasoning*), 270 f. ; decision, 274–5 ; exemplified, 227 f. ; explicit, 389 f. ; exposition, 275 ; flexible concepts for, 317–21 ; investigation, 271 f. ; logic of, 276–7 ; use logical slips, 336 ; justice through flaws in, 353 ; value of uncertainty of words in, 354–6

Arusha : ' reasonable man ' among, 388

assault : *muluta* offence, 58

authorities : rôle of, 125–6 ; attitudes to—and crisis, 426

Ayoub, V. : on influence of English legal terminology, 382 ; on neologisms, 381 ; on ' reasonable man,' 398–9 ; review by, 368–9, 375–6

Balovale independence, 7 n., 204

Barotse : defined, 1 ; National Treasury, 428

barter, 17

Barton, R. F. : and case method, 372

beer-drinking, 220–1 ; king breaks pots, 88

bias, judicial (v.q. *reasonable man, rôles, trial by jury*) : in Fishdam's

2·1

curses : in 'Biassed Father', 40 ; smiting ground, 63

custom : antiquity of, 241 f. ; adulterers', 135–6 ; Barnes on Ngoni, 242 ; breaches of, convict, 94 ; and common law, **236** f. ; consistency of, 241 ; creative energy of, 289–90 ; deviation from, unreasonable, 124 ; dictionary definition of, xx ; everyday — absorbed, 317 ; foreign tribes', 204, 234, 244 f. ; imported through legal assumptions, 334 ; and law, 237 f., 261 f. ; Lozi term for, 165–6 ; modern, 289 ; and morality, 241 ; multivocality of Barotse term, 378 ; multivocality in notion of, 405 ; reasonableness of, 243 f. ; and reasonable man, 138 f., 389 ; relation to law, 402 ; repugnant to British, 245 ; respect of each tribe's, 210–11 ; sanctioning of, 94 ; Schapera on flexibility of, 410 ; significance of, **155** f. ; tests of, **239** f. ; test of evidence, 156 ; wrongdoers', **137** f. ; in cross-examination and judgment, 392–3

damages : for adultery, 37, 65, 131 n., 217 ; assessment of, 75–6, 440 ; and executory contracts, 442 ; for crops, 75–6 ; only direct — recognized, 315 ; voluntary, 156

debt : **438** ; Tiv categories of, 381

decisions, judicial : bind lower courts, 175, 253

default : judgment by, 143

demeanour in court : evidentially significant, 75, 320

development of law, 24, **324–5** ; abrupt reinterpretations, 282 ; accommodation of new actions, 309–10 ; Cardozo on generality of concepts, 335 ; and Civil Codes, 333 ; and equity, 204 ; and flexibility of concepts, 160 ; guiding principles for, 219 ; in 'Headman's Fishdams', 190 ; of injury, 299 ; by judicial decisions, 254 f. ; of marriage, 288–9 ; of property, 110 ; of responsibility

for debts, etc., 243 ; Roosevelt on, 354

Devons, E. : on jurymen, 392

discretion, judicial, 202 ; and simple statutes, 249–50 ; Vinogradoff on, 223

disease : payment for cure, 159 ; treatment of, 145

disputes : must be clear, 79 ; nature of, 20–2, 25–6, 139, 196 ; produce ethical citation, 257–8

districts, **13–14**

Districts, Magisterial, **8–9**, 13–14

Districts, Offices : associated with Barotse capitals, 8–9

divination : of disease, 145 ; evidence of, is suspect, 274 ; not used in civil suits, 99

divorce : and breaches of custom, 140 ; constructive, 144, 147, 204 ; division of property on, **123**, 144, 172 ; frequent, 67 ; grounds for, 141 f., 150 f., 237 ; how obtained, **65,** 142, 199 ; husband's letter of, 112, 114 ; and marriage-payments, **123,** 174 f. ; for neglect of in-laws, 79 ; cases, 374

Douglas, M. : 386, 375, 396 n. 2, 399

'driving out' : of villager, 38–9, 42, 183–4, 194, 302, 306 ; of wife, 142

due process, 235, **316** ; hear both sides, 102, 103

'duty' : hierarchical place of, 298 ; Lozi terms for, 166 f. ; stressed by Lozi, 29–30

educated men : form an interest-group, 210, 220, 222, 323

elastic concepts, 293 ; defined, 160 ; of guilt, 302

elopement, **113** f., 147 ; punishment of, 117

enforcement of judgments : British officers urge, 2, 222 ; evading by flight, 119, 142, 221–2 ; and 'law', 163, 230–1, 262 f., 266, 345 ; and Lozi polity, 163 ; public disatisfaction over, 221–2

enrichment, unjust, 141

Epstein, A. L. : 371 n. 4, 368, 379, 387, 389–91, 415

equality, legal, 75, 117 f., 143, 208–10, 211, 214–15